N. GREGORY MANKIW

BRIEF PRINCIPLES OF
MACRO
ECONOMICS

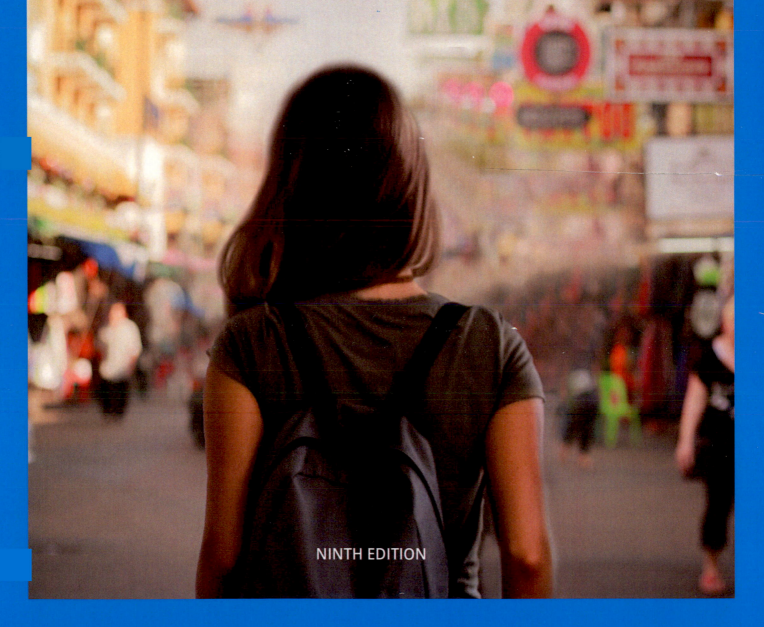

NINTH EDITION

Brief Principles of Macroeconomics: a Guided Tour

BRIEF PRINCIPLES OF
MACRO ECONOMICS

NINTH EDITION

N. GREGORY MANKIW
HARVARD UNIVERSITY

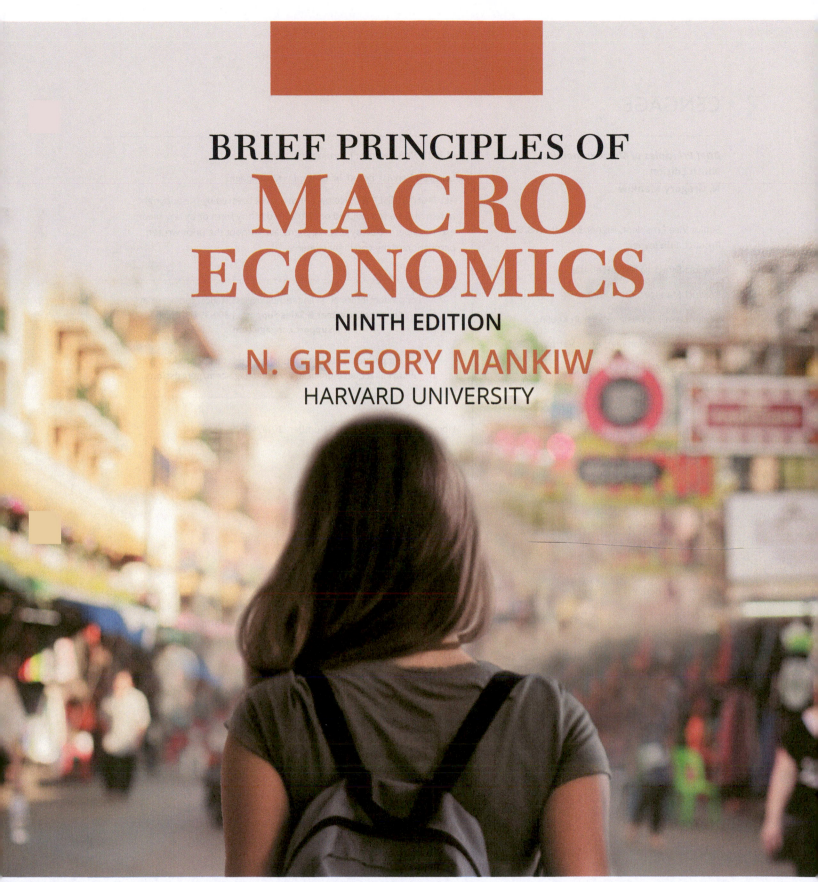

CENGAGE

Australia • Brazil • Canada • Mexico • Singapore • United Kingdom • United States

Brief Principles of Macroeconomics,
Ninth Edition
N. Gregory Mankiw

Senior Vice President, Higher Education & Skills Product: Erin Joyner

Product Director: Jason Fremder

Product Manager: Chris Rader

Senior Learning Designer: Sarah Keeling

Senior Content Manager: Anita Verma

In House Subject Matter Experts:
Eugenia Belova, Kasie Jean, Shannon Aucoin

Product Assistant: Matt Schiesl

Digital Delivery Lead: Timothy Christy

Marketing Manager: John Carey

Intellectual Property Analysts: Ashley M. Maynard, Reba Frederics

Intellectual Property Project Managers:
Betsy Hathaway, Erika Mugavin

Production Service: SPi Global US

Art Director: Bethany Bourgeois

Text Designer: Harasymczuk Design/Bethany Bourgeois

Design Images: iStock.com/lolostock; iStock.com/eurobanks; iStock.com/peeterv; George Rudy/Shutterstock.com; iStock.com/4x6

Cover Image: iStock.com/lolostock; George Rudy/Shutterstock.com

Library of Congress Control Number: 2019941006

ISBN: 978-0-357-13350-7

Loose-leaf Edition:
ISBN: 978-0-357-13373-6

Cengage
200 Pier 4 Boulevard
Boston, MA 02210
USA

Cengage is a leading provider of customized learning solutions with employees residing in nearly 40 different countries and sales in more than 125 countries around the world. Find your local representative at **www.cengage.com.**

To learn more about Cengage platforms and services, register or access your online learning solution, or purchase materials for your course, visit **www.cengage.com.**

Printed at CLDPC, USA, 01-22

To Catherine, Nicholas, and Peter,
my other contributions to the next generation

About the Author

N. Gregory Mankiw is the Robert M. Beren Professor of Economics at Harvard University. As a student, he studied economics at Princeton University and MIT. As a teacher, he has taught macroeconomics, microeconomics, statistics, and principles of economics. He even spent one summer long ago as a sailing instructor on Long Beach Island.

Professor Mankiw is a prolific writer and a regular participant in academic and policy debates. His work has been published in scholarly journals, such as the *American Economic Review, Journal of Political Economy,* and *Quarterly Journal of Economics*, and in more popular forums, such as the *New York Times* and *The Wall Street Journal*. He is also author of the best-selling intermediate-level textbook *Macroeconomics* (Worth Publishers).

In addition to his teaching, research, and writing, Professor Mankiw has been a research associate of the National Bureau of Economic Research, an adviser to the Congressional Budget Office and the Federal Reserve Banks of Boston and New York, a trustee of the Urban Institute, and a member of the ETS test development committee for the Advanced Placement exam in economics. From 2003 to 2005, he served as chairman of the President's Council of Economic Advisers.

Preface: To the Instructor

During my 20-year career as a student, the course that excited me most was the two-semester sequence on the principles of economics that I took during my freshman year in college. It is no exaggeration to say that it changed my life.

I had grown up in a family that often discussed politics over the dinner table. The pros and cons of various solutions to society's problems generated fervent debate. But in school, I had been drawn to the sciences. Whereas politics seemed vague, rambling, and subjective, science was analytic, systematic, and objective. While political debate continued without end, science made progress.

My freshman course on the principles of economics opened my eyes to a new way of thinking. Economics combines the virtues of politics and science. It is, truly, a social science. Its subject matter is society—how people choose to lead their lives and how they interact with one another—but it approaches the subject with the dispassion of a science. By bringing the methods of science to the questions of politics, economics tries to make progress on the challenges that all societies face.

I was drawn to write this book in the hope that I could convey some of the excitement about economics that I felt as a student in my first economics course. Economics is a subject in which a little knowledge goes a long way. (The same cannot be said, for instance, of the study of physics or the Chinese language.) Economists have a unique way of viewing the world, much of which can be taught in one or two semesters. My goal in this book is to transmit this way of thinking to the widest possible audience and to convince readers that it illuminates much about the world around them.

I believe that everyone should study the fundamental ideas that economics has to offer. One purpose of general education is to inform people about the world and thereby make them better citizens. The study of economics, as much as any discipline, serves this goal. Writing an economics textbook is, therefore, a great honor and a great responsibility. It is one way that economists can help promote better government and a more prosperous future. As the great economist Paul Samuelson put it, "I don't care who writes a nation's laws, or crafts its advanced treaties, if I can write its economics textbooks."

What's New in the Ninth Edition?

Economics is fundamentally about understanding the world in which we live. Most chapters of this book include Case Studies illustrating how the principles of economics can be applied. In addition, In the News boxes offer excerpts from newspapers, magazines, and online news sources showing how economic ideas shed light on current issues facing society. After students finish their first course in economics, they should think about news stories from a new perspective and with greater insight. To keep the study of economics fresh and relevant for each new cohort of students, I update each edition of this text to keep pace with the ever-changing world.

The new applications in this ninth edition are too numerous to list in their entirety, but here is a sample of the topics covered (and the chapters in which they appear):

- Technology companies are increasingly using economists to better run their businesses. (Chapter 2)
- The theory of economic growth can help explain why so many of the world's poorest nations are in sub-Saharan Africa. (Chapter 7)
- Economist Martin Feldstein explains why the United States is so prosperous. (Chapter 7)
- Cryptocurrencies may be the money of the future, or they may be a passing fad. (Chapter 11)
- Living during a hyperinflation, such as the recent situation in Venezuela, is a surreal experience. (Chapter 12)
- Recent discussion of trade deficits has included a lot of misinformation. (Chapter 14)
- The Federal Reserve has started to reassess what it means to target an inflation rate of 2 percent. (Chapter 18)

In addition to updating the book, I have refined its coverage and pedagogy with input from many users of the previous edition. There are numerous changes, large and small, aimed at making the book clearer and more student-friendly.

All the changes that I made, and the many others that I considered, were evaluated in light of the benefits of brevity. Like most things that we study in economics, a student's time is a scarce resource. I always keep in mind a dictum from the great novelist Robertson Davies: "One of the most important things about writing is to boil it down and not bore the hell out of everybody."

How Is This Book Organized?

The organization of this book was designed to make economics as student-friendly as possible. What follows is a whirlwind tour of this text. The tour will, I hope, give instructors some sense of how the pieces fit together.

Introductory Material

Chapter 1, "Ten Principles of Economics," introduces students to the economist's view of the world. It previews some of the big ideas that recur throughout economics, such as opportunity cost, marginal decision making, the role of incentives, the gains from trade, and the efficiency of market allocations. Throughout the book, I refer regularly to the *Ten Principles of Economics* introduced in Chapter 1 to remind students that these ideas are the foundation for all economics.

Chapter 2, "Thinking Like an Economist," examines how economists approach their field of study. It discusses the role of assumptions in developing a theory and introduces the concept of an economic model. It also explores the role of economists in making policy. This chapter's appendix offers a brief refresher course on how graphs are used, as well as how they can be abused.

Chapter 3, "Interdependence and the Gains from Trade," presents the theory of comparative advantage. This theory explains why individuals trade with their neighbors, as well as why nations trade with other nations. Much of economics is about how market forces coordinate many individual production and consumption decisions. As a starting point for this analysis, students see in this chapter why specialization, interdependence, and trade can benefit everyone.

I next introduce the basic tools of supply and demand. Chapter 4, "The Market Forces of Supply and Demand," develops the supply curve, the demand curve, and the notion of market equilibrium. This microeconomic model is the starting point for much of macroeconomic theory.

Macroeconomics

My overall approach to teaching macroeconomics is to examine the economy in the long run (when prices are flexible) before examining the economy in the short run (when prices are sticky). I believe that this organization simplifies learning macroeconomics for several reasons. First, the classical assumption of price flexibility is more closely linked to the basic lessons of supply and demand, which students have already mastered. Second, the classical dichotomy allows the study of the long run to be broken up into several easily digested pieces. Third, because the business cycle represents a transitory deviation from the economy's long-run growth path, studying the transitory deviations is more natural after the long-run equilibrium is understood. Fourth, the macroeconomic theory of the long run is less controversial among economists than is the macroeconomic theory of the short run. For these reasons, most upper-level courses in macroeconomics now follow this long-run-before-short-run approach; my goal is to offer introductory students the same advantage.

I start the coverage of macroeconomics with issues of measurement. Chapter 5, "Measuring a Nation's Income," discusses the meaning of gross domestic product and related statistics from the national income accounts. Chapter 6, "Measuring the Cost of Living," examines the measurement and use of the consumer price index.

The next four chapters describe the behavior of the real economy in the long run. Chapter 7, "Production and Growth," examines the determinants of the large variation in living standards over time and across countries. Chapter 8, "Saving, Investment, and the Financial System," discusses the types of financial institutions in our economy and examines their role in allocating resources. Chapter 9, "The Basic Tools of Finance," introduces present value, risk management, and asset pricing. Chapter 10, "Unemployment," considers the long-run determinants of the unemployment rate, including job search, minimum-wage laws, the market power of unions, and efficiency wages.

Having described the long-run behavior of the real economy, the book then turns to the long-run behavior of money and prices. Chapter 11, "The Monetary System," introduces the economist's concept of money and the role of the central bank in controlling the quantity of money. Chapter 12, "Money Growth and Inflation," develops the classical theory of inflation and discusses the costs that inflation imposes on a society.

The next two chapters present the macroeconomics of open economies, maintaining the long-run assumptions of price flexibility and full employment. Chapter 13, "Open-Economy Macroeconomics: Basic Concepts," explains the relationship among saving, investment, and the trade balance, the distinction between the nominal and real exchange rate, and the theory of purchasing-power parity. Chapter 14, "A Macroeconomic Theory of the Open Economy," presents a classical model of the international flow of goods and capital. The model sheds light on various issues, including the link between budget deficits and trade deficits and the macroeconomic effects of trade policies. Because instructors differ in their emphasis on this material, these chapters are written so they can be used in different ways. Some may choose to cover Chapter 13 but not Chapter 14; others may skip both chapters; and still others may choose to defer the analysis of open-economy macroeconomics until the end of their courses.

After developing the long-run theory of the economy in Chapters 7 through 14, the book turns to explaining short-run fluctuations around the long-run trend. Chapter 15, "Aggregate Demand and Aggregate Supply," begins with some facts about the business cycle and then introduces the model of aggregate demand and aggregate supply. Chapter 16, "The Influence of Monetary and Fiscal Policy on Aggregate Demand," explains how policymakers can use the tools at their disposal to shift the aggregate-demand curve. Chapter 17, "The Short-Run Trade-Off between Inflation and Unemployment," explains why policymakers who control aggregate demand face a trade-off between inflation and unemployment. It examines why this trade-off exists in the short run, why it shifts over time, and why it does not exist in the long run.

The book concludes with Chapter 18, "Six Debates over Macroeconomic Policy." This capstone chapter considers six controversial issues facing policymakers: the proper degree of policy activism in response to the business cycle, the relative efficacy of government spending hikes and tax cuts to fight recessions, the choice between rules and discretion in the conduct of monetary policy, the desirability of reaching zero inflation, the importance of balancing the government's budget, and the need for tax reform to encourage saving. For each issue, the chapter presents both sides of the debate and encourages students to make their own judgments.

Learning Tools

The purpose of this book is to help students learn the fundamental lessons of economics and to show how they can apply these lessons to their lives and the world in which they live. Toward that end, I have used various learning tools that recur throughout the book.

Case Studies

Economic theory is useful and interesting only if it can be applied to understanding actual events and policies. This book, therefore, contains numerous case studies that apply the theory that has just been developed.

In the News Boxes

One benefit that students gain from studying economics is a new perspective and greater understanding about news from around the world. To highlight this benefit, I have included excerpts from many newspaper and magazine articles, some of which are opinion columns written by prominent economists. These articles, together with my brief introductions, show how basic economic theory can be applied. Most of these boxes are new to this edition. And for the first time in this edition, each news article ends with "Questions to Discuss," which can be used to start a dialogue in the classroom.

FYI Boxes

These boxes provide additional material "for your information." Some of them offer a glimpse into the history of economic thought. Others clarify technical issues. Still others discuss supplementary topics that instructors might choose either to discuss or skip in their lectures.

Ask the Experts Boxes

This feature summarizes results from the IGM Economics Experts Panel, an ongoing survey of several dozen prominent economists. Every few weeks, these experts are offered a statement and then asked whether they agree with it, disagree with it, or are uncertain about it. The survey results appear in the chapters near the coverage of the relevant topic. They give students a sense of when economists are united, when they are divided, and when they just don't know what to think.

Definitions of Key Concepts

When key concepts are introduced in the chapter, they are presented in **bold** typeface. In addition, their definitions are placed in the margins. This treatment should aid students in learning and reviewing the material.

Quick Quizzes

After each major section in a chapter, students are offered a brief multiple-choice Quick Quiz to check their comprehension of what they have just learned. If students cannot readily answer these quizzes, they should stop and review material before continuing. The answers to all Quick Quizzes are available at the end of each chapter.

Chapter in a Nutshell

Each chapter concludes with a brief summary that reminds students of the most important lessons that they have learned. Later in their study, it offers an efficient way to review for exams.

List of Key Concepts

A list of key concepts at the end of each chapter offers students a way to test their understanding of the new terms that have been introduced. Page references are included so that students can review the terms they do not understand.

Questions for Review

Located at the end of each chapter, questions for review cover the chapter's primary lessons. Students can use these questions to check their comprehension and prepare for exams.

Problems and Applications

Each chapter also contains a variety of problems and applications asking students to apply the material that they have learned. Some instructors may use these questions for homework assignments. Others may use them as a starting point for classroom discussions.

Alternative Versions of the Book

The book you are now holding is one of five versions of this text that are available for introducing students to economics. Cengage and I offer this menu of books because instructors differ in how much time they have and what topics they choose to cover. Here is a brief description of each:

- *Principles of Economics*. This complete version of the book contains all 36 chapters. It is designed for two-semester introductory courses that cover both microeconomics and macroeconomics.
- *Principles of Microeconomics*. This version contains 22 chapters and is designed for one-semester courses in introductory microeconomics.
- *Principles of Macroeconomics*. This version contains 23 chapters and is designed for one-semester courses in introductory macroeconomics. It contains a full development of the theory of supply and demand.
- *Brief Principles of Macroeconomics*. This shortened macro version of 18 chapters contains only one chapter on the basics of supply and demand. It is designed for instructors who want to jump to the core topics of macroeconomics more quickly.
- *Essentials of Economics*. This version of the book contains 24 chapters. It is designed for one-semester survey courses that cover the basics of both microeconomics and macroeconomics.

The accompanying table shows precisely which chapters are included in each book. Instructors who want more information about these alternative versions should contact their local Cengage representative.

TABLE 1

The Five Versions of This Book

Principles of Economics	Principles of Microeconomics	Principles of Macroeconomics	Brief Principles of Macroeconomics	Essentials of Economics
1 Ten Principles of Economics	X	X	X	X
2 Thinking Like an Economist	X	X	X	X
3 Interdependence and the Gains from Trade	X	X	X	X
4 The Market Forces of Supply and Demand	X	X	X	X
5 Elasticity and Its Application	X	X		X
6 Supply, Demand, and Government Policies	X	X		X
7 Consumers, Producers, and the Efficiency of Markets	X	X		X
8 Application: The Costs of Taxation	X	X		X
9 Application: International Trade	X	X		X
10 Externalities	X			X
11 Public Goods and Common Resources	X			X
12 The Design of the Tax System	X			
13 The Costs of Production	X			X
14 Firms in Competitive Markets	X			X
15 Monopoly	X			X
16 Monopolistic Competition	X			
17 Oligopoly	X			
18 The Markets for the Factors of Production	X			
19 Earnings and Discrimination	X			
20 Income Inequality and Poverty	X			
21 The Theory of Consumer Choice	X			
22 Frontiers of Microeconomics	X			
23 Measuring a Nation's Income		X	X	X
24 Measuring the Cost of Living		X	X	X
25 Production and Growth		X	X	X
26 Saving, Investment, and the Financial System		X	X	X
27 The Basic Tools of Finance		X	X	X
28 Unemployment		X	X	X
29 The Monetary System		X	X	X
30 Money Growth and Inflation		X	X	X
31 Open-Economy Macroeconomics: Basic Concepts		X	X	
32 A Macroeconomic Theory of the Open Economy		X	X	
33 Aggregate Demand and Aggregate Supply		X	X	X
34 The Influence of Monetary and Fiscal Policy on Aggregate Demand		X	X	X
35 The Short-Run Trade-Off between Inflation and Unemployment		X	X	
36 Six Debates over Macroeconomic Policy		X	X	

Supplements

Cengage offers various supplements for instructors and students who use this book. These resources make teaching the principles of economics easy for the instructor and learning them easy for the student. David R. Hakes of the University of Northern Iowa, a dedicated teacher and economist, supervised the development of the supplements for this edition. A complete list of available supplements follows this Preface.

Modules

I have written four modules, or mini-chapters, with optional material that instructors can include in their courses. For instructors using the digital version of the book, these modules can be added with a few mouse clicks. As of now, there are modules on The Economics of Healthcare, The European Union, The Keynesian Cross, and How Economists Use Data. I expect to add more modules to the library available to instructors in the years to come.

Translations and Adaptations

I am delighted that versions of this book are (or will soon be) available in many of the world's languages. Currently scheduled translations include Azeri, Chinese (in both standard and simplified characters), Croatian, Czech, Dutch, French, Georgian, German, Greek, Indonesian, Italian, Japanese, Korean, Macedonian, Montenegrin, Portuguese, Romanian, Russian, Serbian, and Spanish. In addition, adaptations of the book for Australian, Canadian, European, and New Zealand students are also available. Instructors who would like more information about these books should contact Cengage.

Acknowledgments

In writing this book, I benefited from the input of many talented people. Indeed, the list of people who have contributed to this project is so long, and their contributions so valuable, that it seems an injustice that only a single name appears on the cover.

Let me begin with my colleagues in the economics profession. The many editions of this text and its supplemental materials have benefited enormously from their input. In reviews and surveys, they have offered suggestions, identified challenges, and shared ideas from their own classroom experience. I am indebted to them for the perspectives they have brought to the text. Unfortunately, the list has become too long to thank those who contributed to previous editions, even though students reading the current edition are still benefiting from their insights.

Most important in this process has been David Hakes (University of Northern Iowa). David has served as a reliable sounding board for ideas and a hardworking partner with me in putting together the superb package of supplements. I am also grateful to Stephanie Thomas (Cornell University), who helped in the planning process for this new edition.

The following reviewers of the eighth edition provided suggestions for refining the content, organization, and approach in the ninth.

Anil Aba, *University of Utah*

Mark Abajian, *San Diego Mesa College*

Dorian Abreu, *Hunter College*

Goncalo Alves Pina, *Santa Clara University*

Bob Barnes, *Loyola University Chicago*

James Bathgate, *Western Nevada College*

Nicole Bissessar, *Southern New Hampshire University*

Joseph Brignone, *Brigham Young University*

William Byrd, *Troy University*

Samantha Cakir, *Macalester College*

John Carter, *Modesto Junior College*

Avik Chakrabarti, *University of Wisconsin–Milwaukee*

Yong Chao, *University of Louisville*

David Chaplin, *Northwest Nazarene University*

Mitch Charkiewicz, *Central Connecticut State University*

LaPorchia Collins, *Tulane University*

Andrew Crawley, *University of Maine*

Maria DaCosta, *University of Wisconsin–Eau Claire*

Dennis Debrecht, *Carroll University*

Amrita Dhar, *University of Mary Washington*

Lynne Elkes, *Loyola University Maryland*

Elena Ermolenko, *Oakton Community College*

Sarah Estelle, *Hope College*

John Flanders, *Central Methodist University*

Gary Gray, *Umpqua Community College*

Jessica Hennessey, *Furman University*

Alexander Hill, *Arizona State University*

Miren Ivankovic, *Anderson University*

Justin Jarvis, *Truman State University*

Aaron Johnson, *Albany State University*

Bonnie Johnson, *Wayne State University*

Rutherford Johnson, *University of Minnesota Crookston*

Venoo Kakar, *San Francisco State University*

Jennifer Klein, *University of Colorado Boulder*

Audrey Kline, *University of Louisville*

Fred Kolb, *University of Wisconsin–Eau Claire*

Janet Koscianski, *Shippensburg University*

Mikhail Kouliavtsev, *Stephen F. Austin State University*

Nakul Kumar, *Bloomsburg University*

Jim Leggette, *Belhaven University*

David Lewis, *Oregon State University*

Hank Lewis, *Houston Community College*

Yan Li, *University of Wisconsin–Eau Claire*

Zhen Li, *Albion College*

Dan Marburger, *Arizona State University*

Jim McGibany, *Marquette University*

Steven McMullen, *Hope College*

Meghan Mihal, *St. Thomas Aquinas College*

Martin Milkman, *Murray State University*

Soonhong Min, *University at Albany*

Phillip Mixon, *Troy University*

Chau Nguyen, *Mesa Community College*

Scott Niederjohn, *Lakeland University*

Carla Nietfeld, *Francis Marion University*

John Nyhoff, *Oakton Community College*

Andrew Paizis, *New York University*

Jason Patalinghug, *Southern Connecticut State University*

Jodi Pelkowski, *Wichita State University*

Sougata Poddar, *Chapman University*

Lana Podolak, *Community College of Beaver County*

Gyan Pradhan, *Eastern Kentucky University*

Elena Prado, *San Diego State University*

John Reardon, *Hamline University*

Ty Robbins, *Manchester University*

Jason Rudbeck, *University of Georgia*

Anthony Scardino, *Felician University*

Helen Schneider, *University of Texas at Austin*

Alex Shiu, *McLennan Community College*

Harmeet Singh, *Texas A&M University–Kingsville*

Catherine Skura, *Sandhills Community College*

Gordon Smith, *Anderson University*

Nathan Smith, *University of Hartford*

Mario Solis-Garcia, *Macalester College*

Arjun Sondhi, *Wayne State University*

Derek Stimel, *University of California, Davis*

Paul Stock, *University of Mary Hardin Baylor*

Yang Su, *University of Washington*

Anna Terzyan, *Loyola Marymount University*

Elsy Thomas, *Bowling Green State University*

Kathryn Thwaites, *Sandhills Community College*

Phillip Tussing, *Houston Community College*

William Walsh, *University of Alabama*

Beth Wheaton, *Southern Methodist University*

Oxana Wieland, *University of Minnesota Crookston*

Christopher Wimer, *Heidelberg University*

Jim Wollscheid, *University of Arkansas–Fort Smith*

Doyoun Won, *University of Utah*

Kelvin Wong, *Arizona State University*

Fan Yang, *University of Washington*

Ying Yang, *University of Rhode Island*

The team of editors who worked on this book improved it tremendously. Jane Tufts, developmental editor, provided truly spectacular editing—as she always does. Jason Fremder, economics Product Director, and Christopher Rader, Product Manager, did a splendid job of overseeing the many people involved in such a large project. Sarah Keeling, Senior Learning Designer, was crucial in assembling an extensive and thoughtful group of reviewers to give me feedback on the previous edition and shape up the new edition. Anita Verma, Senior Content Manager, was crucial in putting together an excellent team to revise the supplements and with Beth Asselin and Phil Scott, project managers at SPi Global, had the patience and dedication necessary to turn my manuscript into this book. Bethany Bourgeois, Senior Designer, gave this book its clean, friendly look. Irwin Zucker, copyeditor, refined my prose, and Val Colligo, indexer, prepared a careful and thorough index. John Carey, Executive Marketing Manager, worked long hours getting the word out to potential users of this book. The rest of the Cengage team has, as always, been consistently professional, enthusiastic, and dedicated.

We have a top team of veterans who have worked across multiple editions producing the supplements that accompany this book. Working with those at Cengage, the following have been relentless in making sure that the suite of ancillary materials is unmatched in both quantity and quality. No other text comes close.

PowerPoint: Andreea Chiritescu (Eastern Illinois University)

Test Bank: Shannon Aucoin, Eugenia Belova, Ethan Crist, Kasie Jean, and Brian Rodriguez (in-house Subject Matter Experts)

Instructor manual: David Hakes (University of Northern Iowa)

I am grateful also to Rohan Shah and Rohit Goyal, two star undergraduates at Harvard and Yale, respectively, who helped me refine the manuscript and check the page proofs for this edition.

As always, I must thank my "in-house" editor Deborah Mankiw. As the first reader of most things I write, she continued to offer just the right mix of criticism and encouragement.

Finally, I should mention my three children Catherine, Nicholas, and Peter. Their contribution to this book was putting up with a father spending too many hours in his study. The four of us have much in common—not least of which is our love of ice cream (which becomes apparent in Chapter 4).

N. Gregory Mankiw
May 2019

Brief Contents

Contents

PART II How Markets Work 61

CHAPTER 4

The Market Forces of Supply and Demand 61

PART III The Data of Macroeconomics 87

CHAPTER 5

Measuring a Nation's Income 87

CHAPTER 6

Measuring the Cost of Living 107

PART V   Money and Prices in the Long Run   209

CHAPTER 11

The Monetary System   209

CHAPTER 12

Money Growth and Inflation   233

PART VI   The Macroeconomics of Open Economies   259

CHAPTER 13

Open-Economy Macroeconomics: Basic Concepts   259

PART VII   Short-Run Economic Fluctuations 303

CHAPTER 15

Aggregate Demand and Aggregate Supply 303

PART VIII   Final Thoughts   389

CHAPTER 18

Six Debates over Macroeconomic Policy   389

Preface: To the Student

"Economics is a study of mankind in the ordinary business of life." So wrote Alfred Marshall, the great 19th-century economist, in his textbook, *Principles of Economics*. We have learned much about the economy since Marshall's time, but this definition of economics is as true today as it was in 1890, when the first edition of his text was published.

Why should you, as a student in the 21st century, embark on the study of economics? There are three reasons.

The first reason to study economics is that it will help you understand the world in which you live. There are many questions about the economy that might spark your curiosity. Why are apartments so hard to find in New York City? Why do airlines charge less for a round-trip ticket if the traveler stays over a Saturday night? Why is Emma Stone paid so much to star in movies? Why are living standards so meager in many African countries? Why do some countries have high rates of inflation while others have stable prices? Why are jobs easy to find in some years and hard to find in others? These are just a few of the questions that a course in economics will help you answer.

The second reason to study economics is that it will make you a more astute participant in the economy. As you go about your life, you make many economic decisions. While you are a student, you decide how many years to stay in school. Once you take a job, you decide how much of your income to spend, how much to save, and how to invest your savings. Someday you may find yourself running a small business or a large corporation, and you will decide what prices to charge for your products. The insights developed in the coming chapters will give you a new perspective on how best to make these decisions. Studying economics will not by itself make you rich, but it will give you some tools that may help in that endeavor.

The third reason to study economics is that it will give you a better understanding of both the potential and the limits of economic policy. Economic questions are always on the minds of policymakers in mayors' offices, governors' mansions, and the White House. What are the burdens associated with alternative forms of taxation? What are the effects of free trade with other countries? What is the best way to protect the environment? How does a government budget deficit affect the economy? As a voter, you help choose the policies that guide the allocation of society's resources. An understanding of economics will help you carry out that responsibility. And who knows: Perhaps someday you will end up as one of those policymakers yourself.

Thus, the principles of economics can be applied in many of life's situations. Whether the future finds you following the news, running a business, or sitting in the Oval Office, you will be glad that you studied economics.

N. Gregory Mankiw
May 2019

Ten Principles of Economics

The word *economy* comes from the Greek word *oikonomos*, which means "one who manages a household." At first, this origin might seem peculiar. But in fact, households and economies have much in common.

A household faces many decisions. It must decide which household members do which tasks and what each member receives in return: Who cooks dinner? Who does the laundry? Who gets the extra dessert at dinner? Who gets to drive the car? In short, a household must allocate its scarce resources (time, dessert, car mileage) among its various members, taking into account each member's abilities, efforts, and desires.

Like a household, a society faces many decisions. It must find some way to decide what jobs will be done and who will do them. It needs some people to grow food, other people to make clothing, and still others to design computer software. Once society has allocated people (as well as land, buildings, and machines) to various jobs, it must also allocate the goods and services they produce. It must decide who will eat caviar and who will eat potatoes. It must decide who will drive a Ferrari and who will take the bus.

ISTOCK.COM/LOLLOSTOCK

scarcity
the limited nature of society's resources

economics
the study of how society manages its scarce resources

The management of society's resources is important because resources are scarce. **Scarcity** means that society has limited resources and therefore cannot produce all the goods and services people wish to have. Just as each member of a household cannot get everything she wants, each individual in a society cannot attain the highest standard of living to which she might aspire.

Economics is the study of how society manages its scarce resources. In most societies, resources are allocated not by an all-powerful dictator but through the combined choices of millions of households and firms. Economists therefore study how people make decisions: how much they work, what they buy, how much they save, and how they invest their savings. Economists also study how people interact with one another. For instance, they examine how the many buyers and sellers of a good together determine the price at which the good is sold and the quantity that is sold. Finally, economists analyze the forces and trends that affect the economy as a whole, including the growth in average income, the fraction of the population that cannot find work, and the rate at which prices are rising.

The study of economics has many facets, but it is unified by several central ideas. In this chapter, we look at *Ten Principles of Economics*. Don't worry if you don't understand them all at first or if you aren't completely convinced. We explore these ideas more fully in later chapters. The ten principles are introduced here to give you a sense of what economics is all about. Consider this chapter a "preview of coming attractions."

1-1 How People Make Decisions

There is no mystery to what an economy is. Whether we are talking about the economy of Los Angeles, the United States, or the whole world, an economy is just a group of people dealing with one another as they go about their lives. Because the behavior of an economy reflects the behavior of the individuals who make up the economy, our first four principles concern individual decision making.

1-1a Principle 1: People Face Trade-Offs

You may have heard the old saying, "There ain't no such thing as a free lunch." Grammar aside, there is much truth to this adage. To get something that we like, we usually have to give up something else that we also like. Making decisions requires trading off one goal against another.

Consider a student who must decide how to allocate her most valuable resource—her time. She can spend all of her time studying economics, spend all of it studying psychology, or divide it between the two fields. For every hour she studies one subject, she gives up an hour she could have used studying the other. And for every hour she spends studying, she gives up an hour she could have spent napping, bike riding, playing video games, or working at her part-time job for some extra spending money.

Consider parents deciding how to spend their family income. They can buy food, clothing, or a family vacation. Or they can save some of their income for retirement or their children's college education. When they choose to spend an extra dollar on one of these goods, they have one less dollar to spend on some other good.

When people are grouped into societies, they face different kinds of trade-offs. One classic trade-off is between "guns and butter." The more a society spends on national defense (guns) to protect itself from foreign aggressors, the less it can spend on consumer goods (butter) to raise its standard of living. Also important in modern society is the trade-off between a clean environment and a high level of income. Laws that require firms to reduce pollution raise the cost of producing goods and services. Because of these higher costs, the firms end up earning smaller profits, paying lower wages, charging higher prices, or doing some combination of these three. Thus, while pollution regulations yield a cleaner environment and the improved health that comes with it, this benefit comes at the cost of reducing the well-being of the regulated firms' owners, workers, and customers.

Another trade-off society faces is between efficiency and equality. **Efficiency** means that society is getting the maximum benefits from its scarce resources. **Equality** means that those benefits are distributed uniformly among society's members. In other words, efficiency refers to the size of the economic pie, and equality refers to how the pie is divided into individual slices.

When government policies are designed, these two goals often conflict. Consider, for instance, policies aimed at equalizing the distribution of economic well-being. Some of these policies, such as the welfare system or unemployment insurance, try to help the members of society who are most in need. Others, such as the individual income tax, ask the financially successful to contribute more than others to support the government. Though these policies achieve greater equality, they reduce efficiency. When the government redistributes income from the rich to the poor, it reduces the reward for working hard; as a result, people work less and produce fewer goods and services. In other words, when the government tries to cut the economic pie into more equal slices, the pie shrinks.

Recognizing that people face trade-offs does not by itself tell us what decisions they will or should make. A student should not abandon the study of psychology just because doing so would increase the time available for the study of economics. Society should not stop protecting the environment just because environmental regulations would reduce our material standard of living. The government should not ignore the poor just because helping them would distort work incentives. Nonetheless, people are likely to make good decisions only if they understand the options available to them. Our study of economics, therefore, starts by acknowledging life's trade-offs.

efficiency
the property of society getting the most it can from its scarce resources

equality
the property of distributing economic prosperity uniformly among the members of society

1-1b Principle 2: The Cost of Something Is What You Give Up to Get It

Because people face trade-offs, making decisions requires comparing the costs and benefits of alternative courses of action. In many cases, however, the cost of an action is not as obvious as it might first appear.

Consider the decision to go to college. The main benefits are intellectual enrichment and a lifetime of better job opportunities. But what are the costs? To answer this question, you might be tempted to add up the money you spend on tuition, books, room, and board. Yet this total does not truly represent what you give up to spend a year in college.

This calculation has two problems. First, it includes some things that are not really costs of going to college. Even if you quit school, you need a place to sleep and food to eat. Room and board are costs of going to college only to the extent that they exceed the cost of living and eating at home or in your own apartment. Second, this calculation ignores the largest cost of going to college—your time. When you spend a year listening to lectures, reading textbooks, and writing papers, you cannot spend that time working at a job and earning money. For most students, the earnings they give up to attend school are the largest cost of their education.

opportunity cost
whatever must be given up to obtain some item

The **opportunity cost** of an item is what you give up to get that item. When making any decision, decision makers should take into account the opportunity costs of each possible action. In fact, they usually do. College athletes who can earn millions dropping out of school and playing professional sports are well aware that their opportunity cost of attending college is very high. Not surprisingly, they often decide that the benefit of a college education is not worth the cost.

1-1c Principle 3: Rational People Think at the Margin

rational people
people who systematically and purposefully do the best they can to achieve their objectives

Economists normally assume that people are rational. **Rational people** systematically and purposefully do the best they can to achieve their objectives, given the available opportunities. As you study economics, you will encounter firms that decide how many workers to hire and how much product to make and sell to maximize profits. You will also encounter individuals who decide how much time to spend working and what goods and services to buy with the resulting income to achieve the highest possible level of satisfaction.

Rational people know that decisions in life are rarely black and white but often involve shades of gray. At dinnertime, you don't ask yourself "Should I fast or eat like a pig?" More likely, the question you face is "Should I take that extra spoonful of mashed potatoes?" When exams roll around, your decision is not between blowing them off and studying 24 hours a day but whether to spend an extra hour reviewing your notes instead of playing video games. Economists use the term **marginal change** to describe a small incremental adjustment to an existing plan of action. Keep in mind that *margin* means "edge," so marginal changes are adjustments around the edges of what you are doing. Rational people make decisions by comparing *marginal benefits* and *marginal costs*.

marginal change
a small incremental adjustment to a plan of action

For example, suppose you are considering watching a movie tonight. You pay $40 a month for a movie streaming service that gives you unlimited access to its film library, and you typically watch 8 movies a month. What cost should you take into account when deciding whether to stream another movie? You might at first think the answer is $40/8, or $5, which is the *average* cost of a movie. More relevant for your decision, however, is the *marginal* cost—the extra cost that you would incur by streaming another film. Here, the marginal cost is zero because you pay the same $40 for the service regardless of how many movies you stream. In other words, at the margin, streaming a movie is free. The only cost of watching a movie tonight is the time it takes away from other activities, such as working at a job or (better yet) reading this textbook.

Thinking at the margin also works for business decisions. Consider an airline deciding how much to charge passengers who fly standby. Suppose that flying a 200-seat plane across the United States costs the airline $100,000. The average cost of each seat is $500 ($100,000/200). One might be tempted to conclude that the airline should never sell a ticket for less than $500. But imagine that a plane is about to take off with 10 empty seats and a standby passenger waiting at the gate is willing to pay $300 for a seat. Should the airline sell the ticket? Of course it should. If the plane has empty seats, the cost of adding one more passenger is tiny. The *average* cost of flying a passenger is $500, but the *marginal* cost is merely the cost of the can of soda that the extra passenger will consume and the small bit of jet fuel needed to carry the extra passenger's weight. As long as the standby passenger pays more than the marginal cost, selling the ticket is profitable. Thus, a rational airline can increase profits by thinking at the margin.

Marginal decision making can explain some otherwise puzzling phenomena. Here is a classic question: Why is water so cheap, while diamonds are so expensive? Humans need water to survive, while diamonds are unnecessary. Yet people are willing to pay much more for a diamond than for a cup of water. The reason is that a person's willingness to pay for a good is based on the marginal benefit that an extra unit of the good would yield. The marginal benefit, in turn, depends on how many units a person already has. Water is essential, but the marginal benefit of an extra cup is small because water is plentiful. By contrast, no one needs diamonds to survive, but because diamonds are so rare, the marginal benefit of an extra diamond is large.

Many movie streaming services set the marginal cost of a movie equal to zero.

A rational decision maker takes an action if and only if the action's marginal benefit exceeds its marginal cost. This principle explains why people use their movie streaming services as much as they do, why airlines are willing to sell tickets below average cost, and why people pay more for diamonds than for water. It can take some time to get used to the logic of marginal thinking, but the study of economics will give you ample opportunity to practice.

1-1d Principle 4: People Respond to Incentives

An **incentive** is something that induces a person to act, such as the prospect of a punishment or reward. Because rational people make decisions by comparing costs and benefits, they respond to incentives. You will see that incentives play a central role in the study of economics. One economist went so far as to suggest that the entire field could be summarized as simply "People respond to incentives. The rest is commentary."

incentive
something that induces a person to act

Incentives are key to analyzing how markets work. For example, when the price of apples rises, people decide to eat fewer apples. At the same time, apple orchards decide to hire more workers and harvest more apples. In other words, a higher price in a market provides an incentive for buyers to consume less and an incentive for sellers to produce more. As we will see, the influence of prices on the behavior of consumers and producers is crucial to how a market economy allocates scarce resources.

Public policymakers should never forget about incentives: Many policies change the costs or benefits that people face and, as a result, alter their behavior. A tax on gasoline, for instance, encourages people to drive smaller, more fuel-efficient cars. That is one reason people drive smaller cars in Europe, where gasoline taxes are high, than in the United States, where gasoline taxes are low. A higher gasoline tax also encourages people to carpool, take public transportation, live closer to where they work, or switch to hybrid or electric cars.

When policymakers fail to consider how their policies affect incentives, they often face unintended consequences. For example, consider public policy regarding auto safety. Today, all cars have seat belts, but this was not true 60 years ago. In 1965, Ralph Nader's book *Unsafe at Any Speed* generated much public concern over auto safety. Congress responded with laws requiring seat belts as standard equipment on new cars.

How does a seat belt law affect auto safety? The direct effect is obvious: When a person wears a seat belt, the likelihood of surviving an auto accident rises. But that's not the end of the story. The law also affects behavior by altering incentives. The relevant behavior here is the speed and care with which drivers operate their cars. Driving slowly and carefully is costly because it uses the driver's time and energy. When deciding how safely to drive, rational people compare, perhaps unconsciously, the marginal benefit from safer driving to the marginal cost. As a result, they drive more slowly and carefully when the benefit of increased safety is high. For example, when road conditions are icy, people drive more attentively and at lower speeds than they do when road conditions are clear.

Consider how a seat belt law alters a driver's cost–benefit calculation. Seat belts make accidents less costly by reducing the risk of injury or death. In other words, seat belts reduce the benefits of slow and careful driving. People respond to seat belts as they would to an improvement in road conditions—by driving faster and less carefully. The result of a seat belt law, therefore, is a larger number of accidents. The decline in safe driving has a clear, adverse impact on pedestrians, who are more likely to find themselves in an accident but (unlike the drivers) don't have the benefit of added protection.

At first, this discussion of incentives and seat belts might seem like idle speculation. Yet in a classic 1975 study, economist Sam Peltzman argued that auto-safety laws have had many of these effects. According to Peltzman's evidence, these laws give rise not only to fewer deaths per accident but also to more accidents. He concluded that the net result is little change in the number of driver deaths and an increase in the number of pedestrian deaths.

Peltzman's analysis of auto safety is an offbeat and controversial example of the general principle that people respond to incentives. When analyzing any policy, we must consider not only the direct effects but also the less obvious indirect effects that work through incentives. If the policy changes incentives, it will cause people to alter their behavior.

Quick**Quiz**

1. Economics is best defined as the study of
   a. how society manages its scarce resources.
   b. how to run a business most profitably.
   c. how to predict inflation, unemployment, and stock prices.
   d. how the government can stop the harm from unchecked self-interest.

2. Your opportunity cost of going to a movie is
   a. the price of the ticket.
   b. the price of the ticket plus the cost of any soda and popcorn you buy at the theater.
   c. the total cash expenditure needed to go to the movie plus the value of your time.
   d. zero, as long as you enjoy the movie and consider it a worthwhile use of time and money.

3. A marginal change is one that
   a. is not important for public policy.
   b. incrementally alters an existing plan.
   c. makes an outcome inefficient.
   d. does not influence incentives.

4. Because people respond to incentives,
   a. policymakers can alter outcomes by changing punishments or rewards.
   b. policies can have unintended consequences.
   c. society faces a trade-off between efficiency and equality.
   d. All of the above.

Answers at end of chapter.

1-2 How People Interact

The first four principles discussed how individuals make decisions. As we go about our lives, many of our decisions affect not only ourselves but other people as well. The next three principles concern how people interact with one another.

1-2a Principle 5: Trade Can Make Everyone Better Off

You may have heard on the news that the Chinese are our competitors in the world economy. In some ways, this is true because American firms and Chinese firms produce many of the same goods. Companies in the United States and China compete for the same customers in the markets for clothing, toys, solar panels, automobile tires, and many other items.

Yet it is easy to be misled when thinking about competition among countries. Trade between the United States and China is not like a sports contest in which one side wins and the other side loses. The opposite is true: Trade between two countries can make each country better off.

To see why, consider how trade affects your family. When a member of your family looks for a job, she competes against members of other families who are looking for jobs. Families also compete against one another when they go shopping because each family wants to buy the best goods at the lowest prices. In a sense, each family in an economy competes with all other families.

Despite this competition, your family would not be better off isolating itself from all other families. If it did, your family would need to grow its own food, sew its own clothes, and build its own home. Clearly, your family gains much from being able to trade with others. Trade allows each person to specialize in the activities she does best, whether it is farming, sewing, or home building. By trading with others, people can buy a greater variety of goods and services at lower cost.

Like families, countries also benefit from being able to trade with one another. Trade allows countries to specialize in what they do best and to enjoy a greater variety of goods and services. The Chinese, as well as the French, Egyptians, and Brazilians, are as much our partners in the world economy as they are our competitors.

THE WALL STREET JOURNAL

ENGLEMAN.

FROM THE WALL STREET JOURNAL - PERMISSION, CARTOON FEATURES SYNDICATE

"For $5 a week you can watch baseball without being nagged to cut the grass!"

1-2b Principle 6: Markets Are Usually a Good Way to Organize Economic Activity

The collapse of communism in the Soviet Union and Eastern Europe in the late 1980s and early 1990s was one of the last century's most transformative events. Communist countries operated on the premise that government officials were in the best position to allocate the economy's scarce resources. These central planners decided what goods and services were produced, how much was produced, and who produced and consumed these goods and services. The theory behind central planning was that only the government could organize economic activity in a way that promoted well-being for the country as a whole.

Most countries that once had centrally planned economies have abandoned the system and instead have adopted market economies. In a **market economy**, the decisions of a central planner are replaced by the decisions of millions of firms and households. Firms decide whom to hire and what to make. Households decide which firms to work for and what to buy with their incomes. These firms and households interact in the marketplace, where prices and self-interest guide their decisions.

At first glance, the success of market economies is puzzling. In a market economy, no one is looking out for the well-being of society as a whole. Free markets contain many buyers and sellers of numerous goods and services, and all of them are interested primarily in their own well-being. Yet despite decentralized decision making and self-interested decision makers, market economies have proven remarkably successful in organizing economic activity to promote overall prosperity.

In his 1776 book *An Inquiry into the Nature and Causes of the Wealth of Nations,* economist Adam Smith made the most famous observation in all of economics:

market economy

an economy that allocates resources through the decentralized decisions of many firms and households as they interact in markets for goods and services

Households and firms interacting in markets act as if they are guided by an "invisible hand" that leads them to desirable market outcomes. One of our goals in this book is to understand how this invisible hand works its magic.

As you study economics, you will learn that prices are the instrument with which the invisible hand directs economic activity. In any market, buyers look at the price when deciding how much to demand, and sellers look at the price when deciding how much to supply. As a result of these decisions, market prices reflect both the value of a good to society and the cost to society of making the good. Smith's great insight was that prices adjust to guide buyers and sellers to reach outcomes that, in many cases, maximize the well-being of society as a whole.

Smith's insight has an important corollary: When a government prevents prices from adjusting naturally to supply and demand, it impedes the invisible hand's ability to coordinate the decisions of the households and firms that make up an economy. This corollary explains why taxes adversely affect the allocation of resources: They distort prices and thus the decisions of households and firms. It also explains the problems caused by policies that control prices, such as rent control. And it explains the failure of communism. In communist countries, prices were not determined in the marketplace but were dictated by central planners. These planners lacked the necessary information about consumers' tastes and producers' costs, which in a market economy is reflected in prices. Central planners failed because they tried to run the economy with one hand tied behind their backs—the invisible hand of the marketplace.

FYI — Adam Smith and the Invisible Hand

It may be only a coincidence that Adam Smith's great book *The Wealth of Nations* was published in 1776, the exact year in which American revolutionaries signed the Declaration of Independence. But the two documents share a point of view that was prevalent at the time: Individuals are usually best left to their own devices, without the heavy hand of government directing their actions. This political philosophy provides the intellectual foundation for the market economy and for a free society more generally.

Why do decentralized market economies work well? Is it because people can be counted on to treat one another with love and kindness? Not at all. Here is Adam Smith's description of how people interact in a market economy:

Man has almost constant occasion for the help of his brethren, and it is in vain for him to expect it from their benevolence only. He will be more likely to prevail if he can interest their self-love in his favour, and show them that it is for their own advantage to do for him what he requires of them. . . . Give me that which I want, and you shall have this which you want, is

Adam Smith.

the meaning of every such offer; and it is in this manner that we obtain from one another the far greater part of those good offices which we stand in need of.

It is not from the benevolence of the butcher, the brewer, or the baker that we expect our dinner, but from their regard to their own interest. We address ourselves, not to their humanity but to their self-love, and never talk to them of our own necessities but of their advantages. Nobody but a beggar chooses to depend chiefly upon the benevolence of his fellow-citizens. . . .

Every individual . . . neither intends to promote the public interest, nor knows how much he is promoting it. . . . He intends only his own gain, and he is in this, as in many other cases, led by an invisible hand to promote an end which was no part of his intention. Nor is it always the worse for the society that it was no part of it. By pursuing his own interest he frequently promotes that of the society more effectually than when he really intends to promote it.

Smith is saying that participants in the economy are motivated by self-interest and that the "invisible hand" of the marketplace guides this self-interest into promoting general economic well-being.

Many of Smith's insights remain at the center of modern economics. Our analysis in the coming chapters will allow us to express Smith's conclusions more precisely and to analyze more fully the strengths and weaknesses of the market's invisible hand. ■

ADAM SMITH WOULD HAVE LOVED UBER

CASE STUDY

You have probably never lived in a centrally planned economy, but if you have ever tried to hail a cab in a major city, you have likely experienced a highly regulated market. In many cities, the local government imposes strict controls in the market for taxis. The rules usually go well beyond regulation of insurance and safety. For example, the government may limit entry into the market by approving only a certain number of taxi medallions or permits. It may determine the prices that taxis are allowed to charge. The government uses its police powers—that is, the threat of fines or jail time—to keep unauthorized drivers off the streets and prevent drivers from charging unauthorized prices.

In 2009, however, this highly controlled market was invaded by a disruptive force: Uber, a company that provides a smartphone app to connect passengers and drivers. Because Uber cars do not roam the streets looking for taxi-hailing pedestrians, they are technically not taxis and so are not subject to the same regulations. But they offer much the same service. Indeed, rides from Uber cars are often more convenient. On a cold and rainy day, who wants to stand on the side of the road waiting for an empty cab to drive by? It is more pleasant to remain inside, use your smartphone to arrange a ride, and stay warm and dry until the car arrives.

Uber cars often charge less than taxis, but not always. Uber's prices rise significantly when there is a surge in demand, such as during a sudden rainstorm or late on New Year's Eve, when numerous tipsy partiers are looking for a safe way to get home. By contrast, regulated taxis are typically prevented from surge pricing.

Not everyone is fond of Uber. Drivers of traditional taxis complain that this new competition cuts into their source of income. This is hardly a surprise: Suppliers of goods and services often dislike new competitors. But vigorous competition among producers makes a market work well for consumers.

That is why economists love Uber. A 2014 survey of several dozen prominent economists asked whether car services such as Uber increased consumer well-being. Every single economist said "Yes." The economists were also asked whether surge pricing increased consumer well-being. "Yes," said 85 percent of them. Surge pricing makes consumers pay more at times, but because Uber drivers respond to incentives, it also increases the quantity of car services supplied when they are most needed. Surge pricing also helps allocate the services to those consumers who value them most highly and reduces the costs of searching and waiting for a car.

If Adam Smith were alive today, he would surely have the Uber app on his phone. ●

Technology can improve this market.

1-2c Principle 7: Governments Can Sometimes Improve Market Outcomes

If the invisible hand of the market is so great, why do we need government? One purpose of studying economics is to refine your view about the proper role and scope of government policy.

One reason we need government is that the invisible hand can work its magic only if the government enforces the rules and maintains the institutions that are key to a market economy. Most important, market economies need institutions to enforce **property rights** so individuals can own and control scarce resources. A farmer won't grow food if she expects her crop to be stolen; a restaurant won't serve meals unless it is assured that customers will pay before they leave; and a film company won't produce movies if too many potential customers avoid paying by making illegal copies. We all rely on government-provided police and courts to enforce our rights over the things we produce—and the invisible hand counts on our ability to enforce those rights.

Another reason we need government is that, although the invisible hand is powerful, it is not omnipotent. There are two broad rationales for a government to

property rights
the ability of an individual to own and exercise control over scarce resources

intervene in the economy and change the allocation of resources that people would choose on their own: to promote efficiency or to promote equality. That is, most policies aim either to enlarge the economic pie or to change how the pie is divided.

Consider first the goal of efficiency. Although the invisible hand usually leads markets to allocate resources to maximize the size of the economic pie, this is not always the case. Economists use the term **market failure** to refer to a situation in which the market on its own fails to produce an efficient allocation of resources. As we will see, one possible cause of market failure is an **externality**, which is the impact of one person's actions on the well-being of a bystander. The classic example of an externality is pollution. When the production of a good pollutes the air and creates health problems for those who live near the factories, the market on its own may fail to take this cost into account. Another possible cause of market failure is **market power**, which refers to the ability of a single person or firm (or a small group of them) to unduly influence market prices. For example, if everyone in town needs water but there is only one well, the owner of the well does not face the rigorous competition with which the invisible hand normally keeps self-interest in check; she may take advantage of this opportunity by restricting the output of water so she can charge a higher price. In the presence of externalities or market power, well-designed public policy can enhance economic efficiency.

Now consider the goal of equality. Even when the invisible hand yields efficient outcomes, it can nonetheless leave sizable disparities in economic well-being. A market economy rewards people according to their ability to produce things that other people are willing to pay for. The world's best basketball player earns more than the world's best chess player simply because people are willing to pay more to watch basketball than chess. The invisible hand does not ensure that everyone has sufficient food, decent clothing, and adequate healthcare. This inequality may, depending on one's political philosophy, call for government intervention. In practice, many public policies, such as the income tax and the welfare system, aim to achieve a more equal distribution of economic well-being.

To say that the government *can* improve market outcomes does not mean that it always *will*. Public policy is made not by angels but by a political process that is far from perfect. Sometimes policies are designed to reward the politically powerful. Sometimes they are made by well-intentioned leaders who are not fully informed. As you study economics, you will become a better judge of when a government policy is justifiable because it promotes efficiency or equality and when it is not.

market failure
a situation in which a market left on its own fails to allocate resources efficiently

externality
the impact of one person's actions on the well-being of a bystander

market power
the ability of a single economic actor (or small group of actors) to have a substantial influence on market prices

---

Quick**Quiz**

5. International trade benefits a nation when
   a. its revenue from selling abroad exceeds its outlays from buying abroad.
   b. its trading partners experience reduced economic well-being.
   c. all nations are specializing in producing what they do best.
   d. no domestic jobs are lost because of trade.

6. Adam Smith's "invisible hand" refers to
   a. the subtle and often hidden methods that businesses use to profit at consumers' expense.
   b. the ability of free markets to reach desirable outcomes, despite the self-interest of market participants.

   c. the ability of government regulation to benefit consumers even if the consumers are unaware of the regulations.
   d. the way in which producers or consumers in unregulated markets impose costs on innocent bystanders.

7. Governments may intervene in a market economy in order to
   a. protect property rights.
   b. correct a market failure due to externalities.
   c. achieve a more equal distribution of income.
   d. All of the above.

Answers at end of chapter.

1-3 How the Economy as a Whole Works

We started by discussing how individuals make decisions and then looked at how people interact with one another. All these decisions and interactions together make up "the economy." The last three principles concern the workings of the economy as a whole.

1-3a Principle 8: A Country's Standard of Living Depends on Its Ability to Produce Goods and Services

The differences in living standards around the world are staggering. In 2017, the average American earned about $60,000. In the same year, the average German earned about $51,000, the average Chinese about $17,000, and the average Nigerian only $6,000. Not surprisingly, this large variation in average income is reflected in various measures of quality of life. Citizens of high-income countries have more computers, more cars, better nutrition, better healthcare, and a longer life expectancy than do citizens of low-income countries.

Changes in living standards over time are also large. In the United States, incomes have historically grown about 2 percent per year (after adjusting for changes in the cost of living). At this rate, average income doubles every 35 years. Over the past century, average U.S. income has risen about eightfold.

What explains these large differences in living standards among countries and over time? The answer is surprisingly simple. Almost all variation in living standards is attributable to differences in countries' **productivity**—that is, the amount of goods and services produced by each unit of labor input. In nations where workers can produce a large quantity of goods and services per hour, most people enjoy a high standard of living; in nations where workers are less productive, most people endure a more meager existence. Similarly, the growth rate of a nation's productivity determines the growth rate of its average income.

The relationship between productivity and living standards is simple, but its implications are far-reaching. If productivity is the primary determinant of living standards, other explanations must be less important. For example, it might be tempting to credit labor unions or minimum-wage laws for the rise in living standards of American workers over the past century. Yet the real hero of American workers is their rising productivity. As another example, some commentators have claimed that increased competition from Japan and other countries explained the slow growth in U.S. incomes during the 1970s and 1980s. Yet the real villain was flagging productivity growth in the United States.

The relationship between productivity and living standards also has profound implications for public policy. When thinking about how any policy will affect living standards, the key question is how it will affect our ability to produce goods and services. To boost living standards, policymakers need to raise productivity by ensuring that workers are well educated, have the tools they need to produce goods and services, and have access to the best available technology.

productivity
the quantity of goods and services produced from each unit of labor input

1-3b Principle 9: Prices Rise When the Government Prints Too Much Money

In January 1921, a daily newspaper in Germany cost 0.30 marks. Less than 2 years later, in November 1922, the same newspaper cost 70,000,000 marks. All other prices in the economy rose by similar amounts. This episode is one of history's most spectacular examples of **inflation**, an increase in the overall level of prices in the economy.

inflation
an increase in the overall level of prices in the economy

"Well it may have been 68 cents when you got in line, but it's 74 cents now!"

Although the United States has never experienced inflation even close to that of Germany in the 1920s, inflation has at times been a problem. During the 1970s, the overall level of prices more than doubled, and President Gerald Ford called inflation "public enemy number one." By contrast, inflation in the two decades of the 21st century has run about 2 percent per year; at this rate, it takes 35 years for prices to double. Because high inflation imposes various costs on society, keeping inflation at a reasonable rate is a goal of economic policymakers around the world.

What causes inflation? In almost all cases of large or persistent inflation, the culprit is growth in the quantity of money. When a government creates large quantities of the nation's money, the value of the money falls. In Germany in the early 1920s, when prices were on average tripling every month, the quantity of money was also tripling every month. Although less dramatic, the economic history of the United States points to a similar conclusion: The high inflation of the 1970s was associated with rapid growth in the quantity of money, and the return of low inflation in the 1980s was associated with slower growth in the quantity of money.

1-3c Principle 10: Society Faces a Short-Run Trade-Off between Inflation and Unemployment

While an increase in the quantity of money primarily raises prices in the long run, the short-run story is more complex. Most economists describe the short-run effects of money growth as follows:

- Increasing the amount of money in the economy stimulates the overall level of spending and thus the demand for goods and services.
- Higher demand may over time cause firms to raise their prices, but in the meantime, it also encourages them to hire more workers and produce a larger quantity of goods and services.
- More hiring means lower unemployment.

This line of reasoning leads to one final economy-wide trade-off: a short-run trade-off between inflation and unemployment.

Although some economists still question these ideas, most accept that society faces a short-run trade-off between inflation and unemployment. This simply means that, over a period of a year or two, many economic policies push inflation and unemployment in opposite directions. Policymakers face this trade-off regardless of whether inflation and unemployment both start out at high levels (as they did in the early 1980s), at low levels (as they did in the late 1990s), or someplace in between. This short-run trade-off plays a key role in the analysis of the **business cycle**—the irregular and largely unpredictable fluctuations in economic activity, as measured by the production of goods and services or the number of people employed.

Policymakers can exploit the short-run trade-off between inflation and unemployment using various policy instruments. By changing the amount that the government spends, the amount it taxes, and the amount of money it prints, policymakers can influence the overall demand for goods and services. Changes in demand in turn influence the combination of inflation and unemployment that the economy experiences in the short run. Because these instruments of economic policy are so powerful, how policymakers should use them to control the economy, if at all, is a subject of continuing debate.

business cycle
fluctuations in economic activity, such as employment and production

8. The main reason that some nations have higher average living standards than others is that
   a. the richer nations have exploited the poorer ones.
   b. the central banks of some nations have created more money.
   c. some nations have stronger laws protecting worker rights.
   d. some nations have higher levels of productivity.

9. If a nation has high and persistent inflation, the most likely explanation is
   a. the central bank creating excessive amounts of money.
   b. unions bargaining for excessively high wages.

   c. the government imposing excessive levels of taxation.
   d. firms using their market power to enforce excessive price hikes.

10. If a central bank uses the tools of monetary policy to reduce the demand for goods and services, the likely result is _____ inflation and _____ unemployment in the short run.
    a. lower; lower
    b. lower; higher
    c. higher; higher
    d. higher; lower

Answers at end of chapter.

1-4 Conclusion

You now have a taste of what economics is all about. In the coming chapters, we develop many specific insights about people, markets, and economies. Mastering these insights will take some effort, but the task is not overwhelming. The field of economics is based on a few big ideas that can be applied in many different situations.

Throughout this book, we will refer back to the *Ten Principles of Economics* introduced in this chapter and summarized in Table 1. Keep these building blocks in mind. Even the most sophisticated economic analysis is founded on these ten principles.

TABLE 1

Ten Principles of Economics

How People Make Decisions
 1. People face trade-offs.
 2. The cost of something is what you give up to get it.
 3. Rational people think at the margin.
 4. People respond to incentives.

How People Interact
 5. Trade can make everyone better off.
 6. Markets are usually a good way to organize economic activity.
 7. Governments can sometimes improve market outcomes.

How the Economy as a Whole Works
 8. A country's standard of living depends on its ability to produce goods and services.
 9. Prices rise when the government prints too much money.
 10. Society faces a short-run trade-off between inflation and unemployment.

CHAPTER IN A NUTSHELL

- The fundamental lessons about individual decision making are that people face trade-offs among alternative goals, that the cost of any action is measured in terms of forgone opportunities, that rational people make decisions by comparing marginal costs and marginal benefits, and that people change their behavior in response to the incentives they face.
- The fundamental lessons about interactions among people are that trade and interdependence can be mutually beneficial, that markets are usually a good way of coordinating economic activity among people, and that governments can potentially improve market outcomes by remedying a market failure or by promoting greater economic equality.
- The fundamental lessons about the economy as a whole are that productivity is the ultimate source of living standards, that growth in the quantity of money is the ultimate source of inflation, and that society faces a short-run trade-off between inflation and unemployment.

KEY CONCEPTS

scarcity, *p. 2*
economics, *p. 2*
efficiency, *p. 3*
equality, *p. 3*
opportunity cost, *p. 4*
rational people, *p. 4*

marginal change, *p. 4*
incentive, *p. 5*
market economy, *p. 7*
property rights, *p. 9*
market failure, *p. 10*

externality, *p. 10*
market power, *p. 10*
productivity, *p. 11*
inflation, *p. 11*
business cycle, *p. 12*

QUESTIONS FOR REVIEW

1. Give three examples of important trade-offs that you face in your life.

2. What items would you include to figure out the opportunity cost of a vacation to Disney World?

3. Water is necessary for life. Is the marginal benefit of a glass of water large or small?

4. Why should policymakers think about incentives?

5. Why isn't trade between two countries like a game in which one country wins and the other loses?

6. What does the "invisible hand" of the marketplace do?

7. What are the two main causes of market failure? Give an example of each.

8. Why is productivity important?

9. What is inflation and what causes it?

10. How are inflation and unemployment related in the short run?

PROBLEMS AND APPLICATIONS

1. Describe some of the trade-offs faced by each of the following:
   a. a family deciding whether to buy a new car
   b. a member of Congress deciding how much to spend on national parks
   c. a company president deciding whether to open a new factory
   d. a professor deciding how much to prepare for class
   e. a recent college graduate deciding whether to go to graduate school

2. You are trying to decide whether to take a vacation. Most of the costs of the vacation (airfare, hotel, and forgone wages) are measured in dollars, but the benefits of the vacation are psychological. How can you compare the benefits to the costs?

3. You were planning to spend Saturday working at your part-time job, but a friend asks you to go skiing. What is the true cost of going skiing? Now suppose you had been planning to spend the day studying at the library. What is the cost of going skiing in this case? Explain.

4. You win $100 in a basketball pool. You have a choice between spending the money now and putting it away for a year in a bank account that pays 5 percent interest. What is the opportunity cost of spending the $100 now?

5. The company that you manage has invested $5 million in developing a new product, but the development is not quite finished. At a recent meeting, your salespeople report that the introduction of competing products has reduced the expected sales of your new product to $3 million. If it would cost $1 million to finish development and make the product, should you go ahead and do so? What is the most that you should pay to complete development?

6. A 1996 bill reforming the federal government's antipoverty programs limited many welfare recipients to only 2 years of benefits.
   a. How does this change affect the incentives for working?
   b. How might this change represent a trade-off between equality and efficiency?

7. Explain whether each of the following government activities is motivated by a concern about equality or a concern about efficiency. In the case of efficiency, discuss the type of market failure involved.
   a. regulating cable TV prices
   b. providing some poor people with vouchers that can be used to buy food
   c. prohibiting smoking in public places
   d. breaking up Standard Oil (which once owned 90 percent of all U.S. oil refineries) into several smaller companies
   e. imposing higher personal income tax rates on people with higher incomes
   f. enacting laws against driving while intoxicated

8. Discuss each of the following statements from the standpoints of equality and efficiency.
   a. "Everyone in society should be guaranteed the best healthcare possible."
   b. "When workers are laid off, they should be able to collect unemployment benefits until they find a new job."

9. In what ways is your standard of living different from that of your parents or grandparents when they were your age? Why have these changes occurred?

10. Suppose Americans decide to save more of their incomes. If banks lend this extra saving to businesses that use the funds to build new factories, how might this lead to faster growth in productivity? Who do you suppose benefits from the higher productivity? Is society getting a free lunch?

11. During the Revolutionary War, the American colonies could not raise enough tax revenue to fully fund the war effort. To make up the difference, the colonies decided to print more money. Printing money to cover expenditures is sometimes referred to as an "inflation tax." Who do you think is being "taxed" when more money is printed? Why?

Quick**Quiz Answers**

1. a 2. c 3. b 4. d 5. c 6. b 7. d 8. d 9. a 10. b

E very field of study has its own language and way of thinking. Mathematicians talk about axioms, integrals, and vector spaces. Psychologists talk about ego, id, and cognitive dissonance. Lawyers talk about venue, torts, and promissory estoppel.

Economics is no different. Supply, demand, elasticity, comparative advantage, consumer surplus, deadweight loss—these terms are part of the economist's language. In the coming chapters, you will encounter many new terms and some familiar words that economists use in specialized ways. At first, this new language may seem needlessly arcane. But as you will see, its value lies in its ability to provide you with a new and useful way of thinking about the world in which you live.

The purpose of this book is to help you learn the economist's way of thinking. Just as you cannot become a mathematician, psychologist, or lawyer overnight, learning to think like an economist will take some time. Yet with a combination of theory, case studies, and examples of economics in the news, this book will give you ample opportunity to develop and practice this skill.

Before delving into the substance and details of economics, it is helpful to have an overview of how economists approach the world. This chapter discusses the field's methodology. What is distinctive about how economists confront a question? What does it mean to think like an economist?

Thinking Like an Economist

2-1   The Economist as Scientist

"I'm a social scientist, Michael. That means I can't explain electricity or anything like that, but if you ever want to know about people, I'm your man."

Economists try to address their subject with a scientist's objectivity. They approach the study of the economy in much the same way a physicist approaches the study of matter and a biologist approaches the study of life: They devise theories, collect data, and then analyze these data to verify or refute their theories.

To beginners, the claim that economics is a science can seem odd. After all, economists do not work with test tubes or telescopes. The essence of science, however, is the *scientific method*—the dispassionate development and testing of theories about how the world works. This method of inquiry is as applicable to studying a nation's economy as it is to studying the earth's gravity or a species' evolution. As Albert Einstein once put it, "The whole of science is nothing more than the refinement of everyday thinking."

Although Einstein's comment is as true for social sciences such as economics as it is for natural sciences such as physics, most people are not accustomed to looking at society through a scientific lens. Let's discuss some of the ways economists apply the logic of science to examine how an economy works.

2-1a   The Scientific Method: Observation, Theory, and More Observation

Isaac Newton, the famous 17th-century scientist and mathematician, allegedly became intrigued one day when he saw an apple fall from a tree. This observation motivated Newton to develop a theory of gravity that applies not only to an apple falling to the earth but to any two objects in the universe. Subsequent testing of Newton's theory has shown that it works well in many circumstances (but not all, as Einstein would later show). Because Newton's theory has been so successful at explaining what we observe around us, it is still taught in undergraduate physics courses around the world.

This interplay between theory and observation also occurs in economics. An economist might live in a country experiencing rapidly increasing prices and be moved by this observation to develop a theory of inflation. The theory might assert that high inflation arises when the government prints too much money. To test this theory, the economist could collect and analyze data on prices and money from many different countries. If growth in the quantity of money were unrelated to the rate of price increase, the economist would start to doubt the validity of this theory of inflation. If money growth and inflation were correlated in international data, as in fact they are, the economist would become more confident in the theory.

Although economists use theory and observation like other scientists, they face an obstacle that makes their task especially challenging: In economics, conducting experiments is often impractical. Physicists studying gravity can drop objects in their laboratories to generate data to test their theories. By contrast, economists studying inflation are not allowed to manipulate a nation's monetary policy simply to generate useful data. Economists, like astronomers and evolutionary biologists, usually have to make do with whatever data the world gives them.

To find a substitute for laboratory experiments, economists pay close attention to the natural experiments offered by history. When a war in the Middle East interrupts the supply of crude oil, for instance, oil prices skyrocket around the world. For consumers of oil and oil products, such an event depresses living standards. For economic policymakers, it poses a difficult choice about how best to respond. But for economic scientists, the event provides an opportunity to study the effects of a key natural resource on the world's economies. Throughout this book, we consider many historical episodes. Studying these episodes is valuable because they give us insight into the economy of the past and allow us to illustrate and evaluate economic theories of the present.

2-1b The Role of Assumptions

If you ask a physicist how long it would take a marble to fall from the top of a ten-story building, he will likely answer the question by assuming that the marble falls in a vacuum. Of course, this assumption is false. In fact, the building is surrounded by air, which exerts friction on the falling marble and slows it down. Yet the physicist will point out that the friction on the marble is so small that its effect is negligible. Assuming the marble falls in a vacuum simplifies the problem without substantially affecting the answer.

Economists make assumptions for the same reason: Assumptions can simplify the complex world and make it easier to understand. To study the effects of international trade, for example, we might assume that the world consists of only two countries and that each country produces only two goods. In reality, there are many countries, each of which produces thousands of different types of goods. But by considering a world with only two countries and two goods, we can focus our thinking on the essence of the problem. Once we understand international trade in this simplified imaginary world, we are in a better position to understand international trade in the more complex world in which we live.

The art in scientific thinking—whether in physics, biology, or economics—is deciding which assumptions to make. Suppose, for instance, that instead of dropping a marble from the top of the building, we were dropping a beach ball of the same weight. Our physicist would realize that the assumption of no friction is less accurate in this case: Friction exerts a greater force on the beach ball because it is much larger than a marble. The assumption that gravity works in a vacuum is reasonable when studying a falling marble but not when studying a falling beach ball.

Similarly, economists use different assumptions to answer different questions. Suppose that we want to study what happens to the economy when the government changes the number of dollars in circulation. An important piece of this analysis, it turns out, is how prices respond. Many prices in the economy change infrequently: The newsstand prices of magazines, for instance, change only once every few years. Knowing this fact may lead us to make different assumptions when studying the effects of the policy change over different time horizons. For studying the short-run effects of the policy, we may assume that prices do not change much. We may even make the extreme assumption that all prices are completely fixed. For studying the long-run effects of the policy, however, we may assume that all prices are completely flexible. Just as a physicist uses different assumptions when studying falling marbles and falling beach balls, economists use different assumptions when studying the short-run and long-run effects of a change in the quantity of money.

2-1c Economic Models

High school biology teachers teach basic anatomy with plastic replicas of the human body. These models have all the major organs—the heart, liver, kidneys, and so on—and allow teachers to show their students very simply how the important parts of the body fit together. Because these plastic models are stylized and omit many details, no one would mistake one of them for a real person. Despite this lack of realism—indeed, because of this lack of realism—studying these models is useful for learning how the human body works.

Economists also use models to learn about the world, but unlike plastic manikins, their models mostly consist of diagrams and equations. Like a biology teacher's plastic model, economic models omit many details to allow us to see what is truly important. Just as the biology teacher's model does not include all the body's muscles and blood vessels, an economist's model does not include every feature of the economy.

As we use models to examine various economic issues throughout this book, you will see that all the models are built with assumptions. Just as a physicist begins the analysis of a falling marble by assuming away the existence of friction, economists assume away many details of the economy that are irrelevant to the question at hand. All models—in physics, biology, and economics—simplify reality to improve our understanding of it.

2-1d Our First Model: The Circular-Flow Diagram

The economy consists of millions of people engaged in many activities—buying, selling, working, hiring, manufacturing, and so on. To understand how the economy works, we must find some way to simplify our thinking about all these activities. In other words, we need a model that explains, in general terms, how the economy is organized and how participants in the economy interact with one another.

circular-flow diagram
a visual model of the economy that shows how dollars flow through markets among households and firms

Figure 1 presents a visual model of the economy called the **circular-flow diagram**. In this model, the economy is simplified to include only two types of decision makers—firms and households. Firms produce goods and services using inputs, such as labor, land, and capital (buildings and machines). These inputs are called the *factors of production*. Households own the factors of production and consume all the goods and services that the firms produce.

FIGURE 1

The Circular Flow
This diagram is a schematic representation of the organization of the economy. Decisions are made by households and firms. Households and firms interact in the markets for goods and services (where households are buyers and firms are sellers) and in the markets for the factors of production (where firms are buyers and households are sellers). The outer set of arrows shows the flow of dollars, and the inner set of arrows shows the corresponding flow of inputs and outputs.

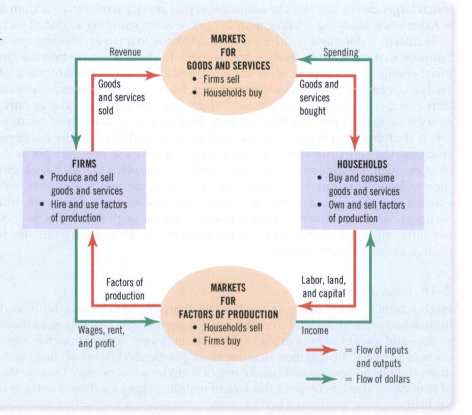

Households and firms interact in two types of markets. In the *markets for goods and services*, households are buyers, and firms are sellers. In particular, households buy the output of goods and services that firms produce. In the *markets for the factors of production*, households are sellers, and firms are buyers. In these markets, households provide the inputs that firms use to produce goods and services. The circular-flow diagram offers a simple way of organizing all the transactions that occur between households and firms in an economy.

The two loops of the circular-flow diagram are distinct but related. The inner loop represents the flows of inputs and outputs. Households sell the use of their labor, land, and capital to firms in the markets for the factors of production. Firms then use these factors to produce goods and services, which in turn are sold to households in the markets for goods and services. The outer loop of the diagram represents the corresponding flow of dollars. Households spend money to buy goods and services from firms. The firms use some of the revenue from these sales for payments to the factors of production, such as workers' wages. What's left is the profit for the firm owners, who are themselves members of households.

Let's take a tour of the circular flow by following a dollar bill as it makes its way from person to person through the economy. Imagine that the dollar begins at a household—say, in your wallet. If you want a cup of coffee, you take the dollar (along with a few of its brothers and sisters) to the market for coffee, which is one of the many markets for goods and services. When you buy your favorite drink at your local Starbucks, the dollar moves into the shop's cash register, becoming revenue for the firm. The dollar doesn't stay at Starbucks for long, however, because the firm spends it on inputs in the markets for the factors of production. Starbucks might use the dollar to pay rent to its landlord for the space it occupies or to pay the wages of its workers. In either case, the dollar enters the income of some household and, once again, is back in someone's wallet. At that point, the story of the economy's circular flow starts once again.

The circular-flow diagram in Figure 1 is a simple model of the economy. A more complex and realistic circular-flow model would include, for instance, the roles of government and international trade. (A portion of that dollar you gave to Starbucks might be used to pay taxes or to buy coffee beans from a farmer in Brazil.) Yet these details are not crucial for a basic understanding of how the economy is organized. Because of its simplicity, this circular-flow diagram is useful to keep in mind when thinking about how the pieces of the economy fit together.

2-1e Our Second Model: The Production Possibilities Frontier

Most economic models, unlike the circular-flow diagram, are built using the tools of mathematics. Here we use one of the simplest such models, called the production possibilities frontier, to illustrate some basic economic ideas.

Although real economies produce thousands of goods and services, let's consider an economy that produces only two goods—cars and computers. Together, the car industry and the computer industry use all of the economy's factors of production. The **production possibilities frontier** is a graph that shows the various combinations of output—in this case, cars and computers—that the economy can possibly produce given the available factors of production and the available production technology that firms use to turn these factors into output.

Figure 2 shows this economy's production possibilities frontier. If the economy uses all its resources in the car industry, it produces 1,000 cars and no computers. If it uses all its resources in the computer industry, it produces 3,000 computers and no cars. The two endpoints of the production possibilities frontier represent these extreme possibilities.

production possibilities frontier
a graph that shows the combinations of output that the economy can possibly produce given the available factors of production and the available production technology

FIGURE 2

The Production Possibilities Frontier
The production possibilities frontier shows the combinations of output—in this case, cars and computers—that the economy can possibly produce. The economy can produce any combination on or inside the frontier. Points outside the frontier are not feasible given the economy's resources. The slope of the production possibilities frontier measures the opportunity cost of a car in terms of computers. This opportunity cost varies, depending on how much of the two goods the economy is producing.

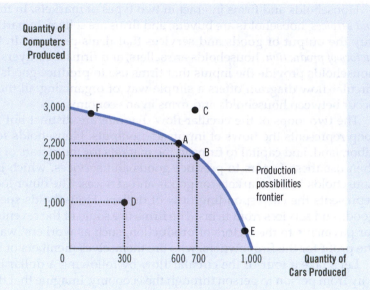

More likely, the economy divides its resources between the two industries, producing some cars and some computers. For example, it can produce 600 cars and 2,200 computers, shown in the figure by point A. Or, by moving some of the factors of production to the car industry from the computer industry, the economy can produce 700 cars and 2,000 computers, represented by point B.

Because resources are scarce, not every conceivable outcome is feasible. For example, no matter how resources are allocated between the two industries, the economy cannot produce the amount of cars and computers represented by point C. Given the technology available for making cars and computers, the economy does not have enough of the factors of production to support that level of output. With the resources it has, the economy can produce at any point on or inside the production possibilities frontier, but it cannot produce at points outside the frontier.

An outcome is said to be *efficient* if the economy is getting all it can from the scarce resources it has available. Points on (rather than inside) the production possibilities frontier represent efficient levels of production. When the economy is producing at such a point, say point A, there is no way to produce more of one good without producing less of the other. Point D represents an *inefficient* outcome. For some reason, perhaps widespread unemployment, the economy is producing less than it could from the resources it has available: It is producing only 300 cars and 1,000 computers. If the source of the inefficiency is eliminated, the economy can increase its production of both goods. For example, if the economy moves from point D to point A, its production of cars increases from 300 to 600, and its production of computers increases from 1,000 to 2,200.

One of the *Ten Principles of Economics* in Chapter 1 is that people face trade-offs. The production possibilities frontier shows one trade-off that society faces. Once we have reached an efficient point on the frontier, the only way of producing more of one good is to produce less of the other. When the economy moves from point A to point B, for instance, society produces 100 more cars at the expense of producing 200 fewer computers.

This trade-off helps us understand another of the *Ten Principles of Economics*: The cost of something is what you give up to get it. This is called the *opportunity cost*. The production possibilities frontier shows the opportunity cost of one good as measured in terms of the other good. When society moves from point A to point B, it gives up 200 computers to get 100 additional cars. That is, at point A, the opportunity cost of 100 cars is 200 computers. Put another way, the opportunity cost of each car is two computers. Notice that the opportunity cost of a car equals the slope of the production possibilities frontier. (Slope is discussed in the graphing appendix to this chapter.)

The opportunity cost of a car in terms of the number of computers is not constant in this economy but depends on how many cars and computers the economy is producing. This is reflected in the shape of the production possibilities frontier. Because the production possibilities frontier in Figure 2 is bowed outward, the opportunity cost of a car is highest when the economy is producing many cars and few computers, such as at point E, where the frontier is steep. When the economy is producing few cars and many computers, such as at point F, the frontier is flatter, and the opportunity cost of a car is lower.

Economists believe that production possibilities frontiers often have this bowed-out shape. When the economy is using most of its resources to make computers, the resources best suited to car production, such as skilled autoworkers, are being used in the computer industry. Because these workers probably aren't very good at making computers, increasing car production by one unit will cause only a slight reduction in the number of computers produced. Thus, at point F, the opportunity cost of a car in terms of computers is small, and the frontier is relatively flat. By contrast, when the economy is using most of its resources to make cars, such as at point E, the resources best suited to making cars are already at work in the car industry. Producing an additional car now requires moving some of the best computer technicians out of the computer industry and turning them into autoworkers. As a result, producing an additional car requires a substantial loss of computer output. The opportunity cost of a car is high, and the frontier is steep.

The production possibilities frontier shows the trade-off between the outputs of different goods at a given time, but the trade-off can change over time. For example, suppose a technological advance in the computer industry raises the number of computers that a worker can produce per week. This advance expands society's set of opportunities. For any given number of cars, the economy can now make more computers. If the economy does not produce any computers, it can still produce 1,000 cars, so one endpoint of the frontier stays the same. But if the economy devotes some of its resources to the computer industry, it will produce more computers from those resources. As a result, the production possibilities frontier shifts outward, as in Figure 3.

This figure shows what happens when an economy grows. Society can move production from a point on the old frontier to a point on the new frontier. Which point it chooses depends on its preferences for the two goods. In this example, society moves from point A to point G, enjoying more computers (2,300 instead of 2,200) and more cars (650 instead of 600).

FIGURE 3

A Shift in the Production Possibilities Frontier
A technological advance in the computer industry enables the economy to produce more computers for any given number of cars. As a result, the production possibilities frontier shifts outward. If the economy moves from point A to point G, then the production of both cars and computers increases.

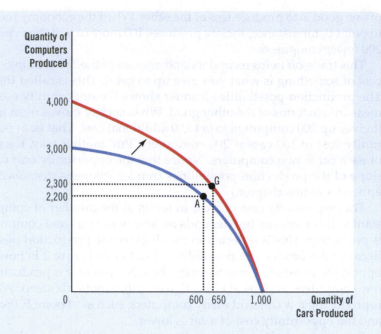

The production possibilities frontier simplifies a complex economy to highlight some basic but powerful ideas: scarcity, efficiency, trade-offs, opportunity cost, and economic growth. As you study economics, these ideas will recur in various forms. The production possibilities frontier offers one simple way of thinking about them.

2-1f Microeconomics and Macroeconomics

Many subjects are studied on various levels. Consider biology, for example. Molecular biologists study the chemical compounds that make up living things. Cellular biologists study cells, which are made up of many chemical compounds and, at the same time, are themselves the building blocks of living organisms. Evolutionary biologists study the many varieties of animals and plants and how species gradually change over the centuries.

Economics is also studied on various levels. We can study the decisions of individual households and firms. We can study the interaction of households and firms in markets for specific goods and services. Or we can study the operation of the economy as a whole, which is the sum of the activities of all these decision makers in all these markets.

The field of economics is traditionally divided into two broad subfields. **Microeconomics** is the study of how households and firms make decisions and how they interact in specific markets. **Macroeconomics** is the study of economy-wide phenomena. A microeconomist might study the effects of rent control on housing in New York City, the impact of foreign competition on the U.S. auto industry, or the effects of education on workers' earnings. A macroeconomist might study the effects of borrowing by the federal government, the changes over time in the economy's unemployment rate, or alternative policies to promote growth in national living standards.

microeconomics
the study of how households and firms make decisions and how they interact in markets

macroeconomics
the study of economy-wide phenomena, including inflation, unemployment, and economic growth

Microeconomics and macroeconomics are closely intertwined. Because changes in the overall economy arise from the decisions of millions of individuals, it is impossible to understand macroeconomic developments without considering the underlying microeconomic decisions. For example, a macroeconomist might study the effect of a federal income tax cut on the overall production of goods and services. But to analyze this issue, he must consider how the tax cut affects households' decisions about how much to spend on goods and services.

Despite the inherent link between microeconomics and macroeconomics, the two fields are distinct. Because they address different questions, each field has its own set of models, which are often taught in separate courses.

QuickQuiz

1. An economic model is
   a. a mechanical machine that replicates the functioning of the economy.
   b. a fully detailed, realistic description of the economy.
   c. a simplified representation of some aspect of the economy.
   d. a computer program that predicts the future of the economy.

2. The circular-flow diagram illustrates that, in markets for the factors of production,
   a. households are sellers, and firms are buyers.
   b. households are buyers, and firms are sellers.
   c. households and firms are both buyers.
   d. households and firms are both sellers.

3. A point inside the production possibilities frontier is
   a. efficient but not feasible.
   b. feasible but not efficient.
   c. both efficient and feasible.
   d. neither efficient nor feasible.

4. All of the following topics fall within the study of microeconomics EXCEPT
   a. the impact of cigarette taxes on the smoking behavior of teenagers.
   b. the role of Microsoft's market power in the pricing of software.
   c. the effectiveness of antipoverty programs in reducing homelessness.
   d. the influence of the government budget deficit on economic growth.

Answers at end of chapter.

2-2 The Economist as Policy Adviser

Often, economists are asked to explain the causes of economic events. Why, for example, is unemployment higher for teenagers than for older workers? Sometimes, economists are asked to recommend policies to improve economic outcomes. What, for instance, should the government do to improve the well-being of teenagers? When economists are trying to explain the world, they are scientists. When they are helping improve it, they are policy advisers.

2-2a Positive versus Normative Analysis

To clarify the two roles that economists play, let's examine the use of language. Because scientists and policy advisers have different goals, they use language in different ways.

For example, suppose that two people are discussing minimum-wage laws. Here are two statements you might hear:

PRISHA: Minimum-wage laws cause unemployment.
NOAH: The government should raise the minimum wage.

IN THE NEWS

Why Tech Companies Hire Economists

Many high-tech companies find expertise in economics a useful input into their decision making.

Goodbye, Ivory Tower. Hello, Silicon Valley Candy Store

By Steve Lohr

For eight years, Jack Coles had an economist's dream job at Harvard Business School.

His research focused on the design of efficient markets, an important and growing field that has influenced such things as Treasury bill auctions and decisions on who receives organ transplants. He even got to work with Alvin E. Roth, who won a Nobel in economic science in 2012.

But prestige was not enough to keep Mr. Coles at Harvard. In 2013, he moved to the San Francisco Bay Area. He now works at Airbnb, the online lodging marketplace, one of a number of tech companies luring economists with the promise of big sets of data and big salaries.

Silicon Valley is turning to the dismal science in its never-ending quest to squeeze more money out of old markets and build new ones. In turn, the economists say they are eager to explore the digital world for fresh insights into timeless economic questions of pricing, incentives and behavior.

"It's an absolute candy store for economists," Mr. Coles said. . . .

Businesses have been hiring economists for years. Usually, they are asked to study macroeconomic trends—topics like recessions and currency exchange rates—and help their employers deal with them.

But what the tech economists are doing is different: Instead of thinking about national or global trends, they are studying the data trails of consumer behavior to help digital companies make smart decisions that strengthen their online marketplaces in areas like advertising, movies, music, travel and lodging.

Tech outfits including giants like Amazon, Facebook, Google and Microsoft and up-and-comers like Airbnb and Uber hope that sort of improved efficiency means more profit.

At Netflix, Randall Lewis, an economic research scientist, is finely measuring the effectiveness of advertising. His work also gets at the correlation-or-causation conundrum in economic behavior: What consumer actions occur coincidentally after people see ads, and what actions are most likely caused by the ads?

At Airbnb, Mr. Coles is researching the company's marketplace of hosts and guests

---

Ignoring for now whether you agree with these statements, notice that Prisha and Noah differ in what they are trying to do. Prisha is speaking like a scientist: She is making a claim about how the world works. Noah is speaking like a policy adviser: He is making a claim about how he would like to change the world.

In general, statements about the world come in two types. One type, such as Prisha's, is positive. **Positive statements** are descriptive. They make a claim about how the world *is*. A second type of statement, such as Noah's, is normative. **Normative statements** are prescriptive. They make a claim about how the world *ought to be*.

A key difference between positive and normative statements is how we judge their validity. We can, in principle, confirm or refute positive statements by examining evidence. An economist might evaluate Prisha's statement by analyzing data on changes in minimum wages and changes in unemployment over time. By contrast, evaluating normative statements involves values as well as facts. Noah's statement cannot be judged using data alone. Deciding what is good or bad policy is not just a matter of science. It also involves our views on ethics, religion, and political philosophy.

Positive and normative statements are fundamentally different, but within a person's set of beliefs, they are often intertwined. In particular, positive views about how the world works affect normative views about what policies are desirable.

positive statements
claims that attempt to describe the world as it is

normative statements
claims that attempt to prescribe how the world should be

for insights, both to help build the business and to understand behavior. One study focuses on procrastination—a subject of great interest to behavioral economists—by looking at bookings. Are they last-minute? Made weeks or months in advance? Do booking habits change by age, gender or country of origin?

"They are microeconomic experts, heavy on data and computing tools like machine learning and writing algorithms," said Tom Beers, executive director of the National Association for Business Economics.

Understanding how digital markets work is getting a lot of attention now, said Hal Varian, Google's chief economist. But, he said, "I thought it was fascinating years ago."

Mr. Varian, 69, is the godfather of the tech industry's in-house economists. Once a well-known professor at the University of California, Berkeley, Mr. Varian showed up at Google in 2002, part time at first, but soon became an employee. He helped refine Google's AdWords

Source: *New York Times*, September 4, 2016.

marketplace, where advertisers bid to have their ads shown on search pages. . . .

For the moment, Amazon seems to be the most aggressive recruiter of economists. It even has an Amazon Economists website for soliciting résumés. In a video on the site, Patrick Bajari, the company's chief economist, says the economics team has contributed to decisions that have had "multibillion-dollar impacts" for the company. . . .

A current market-design challenge for Amazon and Microsoft is their big cloud computing services. These digital services, for example, face a peak-load problem, much as electric utilities do.

How do you sell service at times when there is a risk some customers may be bumped off? Run an auction for what customers are willing to pay for interruptible service? Or offer set discounts for different levels of risk? Both Amazon and Microsoft are working on that now.

To answer such questions, economists work in teams with computer scientists and people in business. In tech companies, market design involves not only economics but also engineering and marketing. How hard is a certain approach technically? How easy is it to explain to customers?

"Economics influences rather than determines decisions," said Preston McAfee, Microsoft's chief economist, who previously worked at Google and Yahoo. ■

Questions to Discuss

1. Think of some firms that you often interact with. How might the input of economists improve their businesses?

2. After studying economics in college, what kind of businesses would be most fun to work for?

Prisha's claim that the minimum wage causes unemployment, if true, might lead her to reject Noah's conclusion that the government should raise the minimum wage. Yet normative conclusions cannot come from positive analysis alone; they involve value judgments as well.

As you study economics, keep in mind the distinction between positive and normative statements because it will help you stay focused on the task at hand. Much of economics is positive: It just tries to explain how the economy works. Yet those who use economics often have normative goals: They want to learn how to improve the economy. When you hear economists making normative statements, you know they are speaking not as scientists but as policy advisers.

2-2b Economists in Washington

President Harry Truman once said that he wanted to find a one-armed economist. When he asked his economists for advice, they always answered, "On the one hand, ... On the other hand, ..."

Truman was right that economists' advice is not always straightforward. This tendency is rooted in one of the *Ten Principles of Economics*: People face trade-offs. Economists are aware that trade-offs are involved in most policy decisions. A policy might increase efficiency at the cost of equality. It might help future generations but hurt the current generation. An economist who says that all policy decisions are easy is an economist not to be trusted.

"Let's switch. I'll make the policy, you implement it, and he'll explain it."

Truman was not the only president who relied on economists' advice. Since 1946, the president of the United States has received guidance from the Council of Economic Advisers, which consists of three members and a staff of a few dozen economists. The council, whose offices are just a few steps from the White House, has no duty other than to advise the president and to write the annual *Economic Report of the President*, which discusses recent developments in the economy and presents the council's analysis of current policy issues.

The president also receives input from economists in many administrative departments. Economists at the Office of Management and Budget help formulate spending plans and regulatory policies. Economists at the Department of the Treasury help design tax policy. Economists at the Department of Labor analyze data on workers and those looking for work to help formulate labor-market policies. Economists at the Department of Justice help enforce the nation's antitrust laws.

Economists are also found outside the executive branch of government. To obtain independent evaluations of policy proposals, Congress relies on the advice of the Congressional Budget Office, which is staffed by economists. The Federal Reserve, the institution that sets the nation's monetary policy, employs hundreds of economists to analyze developments in the United States and throughout the world.

The influence of economists on policy goes beyond their role as advisers: Their research and writings can affect policy indirectly. Economist John Maynard Keynes offered this observation:

> The ideas of economists and political philosophers, both when they are right and when they are wrong, are more powerful than is commonly understood. Indeed, the world is ruled by little else. Practical men, who believe themselves to be quite exempt from intellectual influences, are usually the slaves of some defunct economist. Madmen in authority, who hear voices in the air, are distilling their frenzy from some academic scribbler of a few years back.

These words were written in 1935, but they remain true today. Indeed, the "academic scribbler" now influencing public policy is often Keynes himself.

2-2c Why Economists' Advice Is Not Always Followed

Economists who advise presidents and other elected leaders know that their recommendations are not always heeded. Frustrating as this can be, it is easy to understand. The process by which economic policy is actually made differs in many ways from the idealized policy process assumed in economics textbooks.

Throughout this text, whenever we discuss policy, we often focus on one question: What is the best policy for the government to pursue? We act as if policy were set by a benevolent king. Once the king figures out the right policy, he has no trouble putting his ideas into action.

In the real world, figuring out the right policy is only part of a leader's job, sometimes the easiest part. After a president hears from his economic advisers what policy they deem best, he turns to other advisers for related input. His communications advisers will tell him how best to explain the proposed policy to the public, and they will try to anticipate any misunderstandings that might make the challenge more difficult. His press advisers will tell him how the news media will report on his proposal and what opinions will likely be expressed on the nation's editorial pages. His legislative affairs advisers will tell him how Congress will view the proposal, what amendments members of Congress will suggest, and the likelihood that Congress will pass some version of the president's proposal into law. His political advisers will tell him which groups will organize to support or oppose the proposed policy, how this proposal will affect his standing among different groups in the electorate, and whether it will change support for any of the president's other policy initiatives. After weighing all this advice, the president then decides how to proceed.

Making economic policy in a representative democracy is a messy affair, and there are often good reasons why presidents (and other politicians) do not advance the policies that economists advocate. Economists offer crucial input to the policy process, but their advice is only one ingredient of a complex recipe.

Quick**Quiz**

5. Which of the following is a positive, rather than a normative, statement?
   a. Law X will reduce national income.
   b. Law X is a good piece of legislation.
   c. Congress ought to pass law X.
   d. The president should veto law X.

6. The following parts of government regularly rely on the advice of economists:
   a. Department of Treasury.
   b. Office of Management and Budget.
   c. Department of Justice.
   d. All of the above.

Answers at end of chapter.

2-3 Why Economists Disagree

"If all the economists were laid end to end, they would not reach a conclusion." This quip from George Bernard Shaw is revealing. Economists as a group are often criticized for giving conflicting advice to policymakers. President Ronald Reagan once joked that if the game Trivial Pursuit were designed for economists, it would have 100 questions and 3,000 answers.

Why do economists so often appear to give conflicting advice to policymakers? There are two basic reasons:

- Economists may disagree about the validity of alternative positive theories of how the world works.
- Economists may have different values and therefore different normative views about what government policy should aim to accomplish.

Let's discuss each of these reasons.

2-3a Differences in Scientific Judgments

Several centuries ago, astronomers debated whether the earth or the sun was at the center of the solar system. More recently, climatologists have debated whether the earth is experiencing global warming and, if so, why. Science is an ongoing search to understand the world around us. It is not surprising that as the search continues, scientists sometimes disagree about the direction in which truth lies.

Economists often disagree for the same reason. Although the field of economics sheds light on much about the world (as you will see throughout this book), there is still much to be learned. Sometimes economists disagree because they have different hunches about the validity of alternative theories. Sometimes they disagree because of different judgments about the size of the parameters that measure how economic variables are related.

For example, economists debate whether the government should tax a household's income or its consumption (spending). Advocates of a switch from the current income tax to a consumption tax believe that the change would encourage households to save more because income that is saved would not be taxed. Higher saving, in turn, would free resources for capital accumulation, leading to more rapid growth in productivity and living standards. Advocates of the current income tax system believe that household saving would not respond much to a change in the tax laws. These two groups of economists hold different normative views about the tax system because they have different positive views about saving's responsiveness to tax incentives.

2-3b Differences in Values

Suppose that Jack and Jill both take the same amount of water from the town well. To pay for maintaining the well, the town taxes its residents. Jill has income of $150,000 and is taxed $15,000, or 10 percent of her income. Jack has income of $40,000 and is taxed $6,000, or 15 percent of his income.

Is this policy fair? If not, who pays too much and who pays too little? Does it matter whether Jack's low income is due to a medical disability or to his decision to pursue an acting career? Does it matter whether Jill's high income is due to a large inheritance or to her willingness to work long hours at a dreary job?

These are difficult questions about which people are likely to disagree. If the town hired two experts to study how it should tax its residents to pay for the well, it would not be surprising if they offered conflicting advice.

This simple example shows why economists sometimes disagree about public policy. As we know from our discussion of normative and positive analysis, policies cannot be judged on scientific grounds alone. Sometimes, economists give conflicting advice because they have different values or political philosophies. Perfecting the science of economics will not tell us whether Jack or Jill pays too much.

2-3c Perception versus Reality

Because of differences in scientific judgments and differences in values, some disagreement among economists is inevitable. Yet one should not overstate the amount of disagreement. Economists agree with one another more often than is sometimes understood.

Table 1 contains twenty propositions about economic policy. In surveys of professional economists, these propositions were endorsed by an overwhelming majority of respondents. Most of these propositions would fail to command a similar consensus among the public.

The first proposition in the table is about rent control, a policy that sets a legal maximum on the amount landlords can charge for their apartments. Almost all economists believe that rent control adversely affects the availability and quality of housing and is a costly way of helping the neediest members of society. Nonetheless, many city governments ignore the advice of economists and place ceilings on the rents that landlords may charge their tenants.

The second proposition in the table concerns policies that restrict trade among nations: tariffs (taxes on imports) and import quotas (limits on how much of a good can be purchased from abroad). For reasons we discuss more fully in later chapters,

TABLE 1

Propositions about Which Most Economists Agree

Proposition (and percentage of economists who agree)

1. A ceiling on rents reduces the quantity and quality of housing available. (93%)
2. Tariffs and import quotas usually reduce general economic welfare. (93%)
3. Flexible and floating exchange rates offer an effective international monetary arrangement. (90%)
4. Fiscal policy (e.g., tax cut and/or government expenditure increase) has a significant stimulative impact on a less than fully employed economy. (90%)
5. The United States should not restrict employers from outsourcing work to foreign countries. (90%)
6. Economic growth in developed countries like the United States leads to greater levels of well-being. (88%)
7. The United States should eliminate agricultural subsidies. (85%)
8. An appropriately designed fiscal policy can increase the long-run rate of capital formation. (85%)
9. Local and state governments should eliminate subsidies to professional sports franchises. (85%)
10. If the federal budget is to be balanced, it should be done over the business cycle rather than yearly. (85%)
11. The gap between Social Security funds and expenditures will become unsustainably large within the next 50 years if current policies remain unchanged. (85%)
12. Cash payments increase the welfare of recipients to a greater degree than do transfers-in-kind of equal cash value. (84%)
13. A large federal budget deficit has an adverse effect on the economy. (83%)
14. The redistribution of income in the United States is a legitimate role for the government. (83%)
15. Inflation is caused primarily by too much growth in the money supply. (83%)
16. The United States should not ban genetically modified crops. (82%)
17. A minimum wage increases unemployment among young and unskilled workers. (79%)
18. The government should restructure the welfare system along the lines of a "negative income tax." (79%)
19. Effluent taxes and marketable pollution permits represent a better approach to pollution control than the imposition of pollution ceilings. (78%)
20. Government subsidies on ethanol in the United States should be reduced or eliminated. (78%)

Source: Richard M. Alston, J. R. Kearl, and Michael B. Vaughn, "Is There Consensus among Economists in the 1990s?" *American Economic Review* (May 1992): 203–209; Dan Fuller and Doris Geide-Stevenson, "Consensus among Economists Revisited," *Journal of Economics Education* (Fall 2003): 369–387; Robert Whaples, "Do Economists Agree on Anything? Yes!" *Economists' Voice* (November 2006): 1–6; Robert Whaples, "The Policy Views of American Economic Association Members: The Results of a New Survey," *Econ Journal Watch* (September 2009): 337–348.

almost all economists oppose such barriers to free trade. Nonetheless, over the years, presidents and Congress have often chosen to restrict the import of certain goods. The policies of the Trump administration are a vivid example.

Why do policies such as rent control and trade barriers persist if the experts are united in their opposition? It may be that the realities of the political process stand

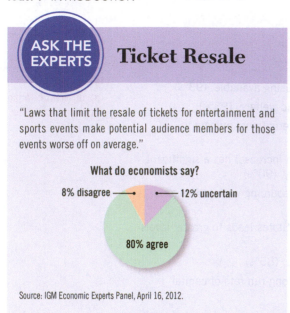

ASK THE EXPERTS

Ticket Resale

"Laws that limit the resale of tickets for entertainment and sports events make potential audience members for those events worse off on average."

What do economists say?

8% disagree — 12% uncertain

80% agree

Source: IGM Economic Experts Panel, April 16, 2012.

as immovable obstacles. But it also may be that economists have not yet convinced enough of the public that these policies are undesirable. One purpose of this book is to help you understand the economist's view on these and other subjects and, perhaps, to persuade you that it is the right one.

As you read the book, you will occasionally see small boxes called "Ask the Experts." These are based on the IGM Economics Experts Panel, an ongoing survey of several dozen prominent economists. Every few weeks, these experts are offered a proposition and then asked whether they agree with it, disagree with it, or are uncertain. The results in these boxes will give you a sense of when economists are united, when they are divided, and when they just don't know what to think.

You can see an example here regarding the resale of tickets to entertainment and sporting events. Lawmakers sometimes try to prohibit reselling tickets, or "scalping" as it is sometimes called. The survey results show that many economists side with the scalpers rather than the lawmakers.

QuickQuiz

7. Economists may disagree because they have different
   a. hunches about the validity of alternative theories.
   b. judgments about the size of key parameters.
   c. political philosophies about the goals of public policy.
   d. All of the above.

8. Most economists believe that tariffs are
   a. a good way to promote domestic economic growth.
   b. a poor way to raise general economic well-being.
   c. an often necessary response to foreign competition.
   d. an efficient way for the government to raise revenue.

Answers at end of chapter.

2-4 Let's Get Going

The first two chapters of this book have introduced you to the ideas and methods of economics. We are now ready to get to work. In the next chapter, we start learning in more detail the principles of economic behavior and economic policy.

As you proceed through this book, you will be asked to draw on many intellectual skills. You might find it helpful to keep in mind some advice from the great economist John Maynard Keynes:

The study of economics does not seem to require any specialized gifts of an unusually high order. Is it not . . . a very easy subject compared with the higher branches of philosophy or pure science? An easy subject, at which very few excel! The paradox finds its explanation, perhaps, in that the master-economist must possess a rare *combination* of gifts. He must be mathematician, historian, statesman, philosopher—in some degree. He must understand symbols and speak in words. He must contemplate the particular in terms of the general, and touch abstract and concrete in the same flight of thought. He must study the present in the light of the past for the purposes of the future. No part of man's nature or his institutions must lie entirely outside his regard. He must be purposeful and disinterested in a simultaneous mood; as aloof and incorruptible as an artist, yet sometimes as near the earth as a politician.

This is a tall order. But with practice, you will become more and more accustomed to thinking like an economist.

CHAPTER IN A NUTSHELL

- Economists try to address their subject with a scientist's objectivity. Like all scientists, they make appropriate assumptions and build simplified models to understand the world around them. Two simple economic models are the circular-flow diagram and the production possibilities frontier. The circular-flow diagram shows how households and firms interact in markets for goods and services and in markets for the factors of production. The production possibilities frontier shows how society faces a trade-off between producing different goods.

- The field of economics is divided into two subfields: microeconomics and macroeconomics. Microeconomists study decision making by households and firms and the interactions among households and firms in the marketplace. Macroeconomists study the forces and trends that affect the economy as a whole.

- A positive statement is an assertion about how the world *is*. A normative statement is an assertion about how the world *ought to be*. While positive statements can be judged based on facts and the scientific method, normative statements entail value judgments as well. When economists make normative statements, they are acting more as policy advisers than as scientists.

- Economists who advise policymakers sometimes offer conflicting advice either because of differences in scientific judgments or because of differences in values. At other times, economists are united in the advice they offer, but policymakers may choose to ignore the advice because of the many forces and constraints imposed on them by the political process.

KEY CONCEPTS

circular-flow diagram, *p. 20*
production possibilities frontier, *p. 21*

microeconomics, *p. 24*
macroeconomics, *p. 24*

positive statements, *p. 26*
normative statements, *p. 26*

QUESTIONS FOR REVIEW

1. In what ways is economics a science?

2. Why do economists make assumptions?

3. Should an economic model describe reality exactly?

4. Name a way that your family interacts in the markets for the factors of production and a way that it interacts in the markets for goods and services.

5. Name one economic interaction that isn't covered by the simplified circular-flow diagram.

6. Draw and explain a production possibilities frontier for an economy that produces milk and cookies.

What happens to this frontier if a disease kills half of the economy's cows?

7. Use a production possibilities frontier to describe the idea of *efficiency*.

8. What are the two subfields of economics? Explain what each subfield studies.

9. What is the difference between a positive and a normative statement? Give an example of each.

10. Why do economists sometimes offer conflicting advice to policymakers?

PROBLEMS AND APPLICATIONS

1. Draw a circular-flow diagram. Identify the parts of the model that correspond to the flow of goods and services and the flow of dollars for each of the following activities.
   a. Selena pays a storekeeper $1 for a quart of milk.
   b. Stuart earns $8 per hour working at a fast-food restaurant.
   c. Shanna spends $40 to get a haircut.
   d. Salma earns $20,000 from her 10 percent ownership of Acme Industrial.

2. Imagine a society that produces military goods and consumer goods, which we'll call "guns" and "butter."
   a. Draw a production possibilities frontier for guns and butter. Using the concept of opportunity cost, explain why it most likely has a bowed-out shape.
   b. Show a point on the graph that is impossible for the economy to achieve. Show a point on the graph that is feasible but inefficient.
   c. Imagine that the society has two political parties, called the Hawks (who want a strong military) and the Doves (who want a smaller military). Show a point on your production possibilities frontier that the Hawks might choose and a point that the Doves might choose.
   d. Imagine that an aggressive neighboring country reduces the size of its military. As a result, both the Hawks and the Doves reduce their desired production of guns by the same amount. Which party would get the bigger "peace dividend," measured by the increase in butter production? Explain.

3. The first principle of economics in Chapter 1 is that people face trade-offs. Use a production possibilities frontier to illustrate society's trade-off between two "goods"—a clean environment and the quantity of industrial output. What do you suppose determines the shape and position of the frontier? Show what happens to the frontier if engineers develop a new way of producing electricity that emits fewer pollutants.

4. An economy consists of three workers: Larry, Moe, and Curly. Each works 10 hours a day and can produce two services: mowing lawns and washing cars. In an hour, Larry can either mow one lawn or wash one car; Moe can either mow one lawn or wash two cars; and Curly can either mow two lawns or wash one car.
   a. Calculate how much of each service is produced in the following scenarios, which we label A, B, C, and D:
      • All three spend all their time mowing lawns. (A)
      • All three spend all their time washing cars. (B)
      • All three spend half their time on each activity. (C)
      • Larry spends half his time on each activity, while Moe only washes cars and Curly only mows lawns. (D)
   b. Graph the production possibilities frontier for this economy. Using your answers to part *a*, identify points A, B, C, and D on your graph.
   c. Explain why the production possibilities frontier has the shape it does.
   d. Are any of the allocations calculated in part *a* inefficient? Explain.

5. Classify each of the following topics as relating to microeconomics or macroeconomics.
   a. a family's decision about how much income to save
   b. the effect of government regulations on auto emissions
   c. the impact of higher national saving on economic growth
   d. a firm's decision about how many workers to hire
   e. the relationship between the inflation rate and changes in the quantity of money

6. Classify each of the following statements as positive or normative. Explain.
   a. Society faces a short-run trade-off between inflation and unemployment.
   b. A reduction in the growth rate of the money supply will reduce the rate of inflation.
   c. The Federal Reserve should reduce the growth rate of the money supply.
   d. Society ought to require welfare recipients to look for jobs.
   e. Lower tax rates encourage more work and more saving.

QuickQuiz Answers

1. **c**　　2. **a**　　3. **b**　　4. **d**　　5. **a**　　6. **d**　　7. **d**　　8. **b**

Appendix

Graphing: A Brief Review

Many of the concepts that economists study can be expressed with numbers—the price of bananas, the quantity of bananas sold, the cost of growing bananas, and so on. Often, these economic variables are related to one another: When the price of bananas rises, people buy fewer bananas. One way of expressing the relationships among variables is with graphs.

Graphs serve two purposes. First, when developing theories, graphs offer a visual way to express ideas that might be less clear if described with equations or words. Second, when analyzing data, graphs provide a powerful way of finding and interpreting patterns. Whether we are working with theory or with data, graphs provide a lens through which a recognizable forest emerges from a multitude of trees.

Numerical information can be expressed graphically in many ways, just as there are many ways to express a thought in words. A good writer chooses words that will make an argument clear, a description pleasing, or a scene dramatic. An effective economist chooses the type of graph that best suits the purpose at hand.

In this appendix, we discuss how economists use graphs to study the mathematical relationships among variables. We also discuss some of the pitfalls that can arise when using graphical methods.

Graphs of a Single Variable

Three common graphs are shown in Figure A-1. The *pie chart* in panel (a) shows how total income in the United States is divided among the sources of income,

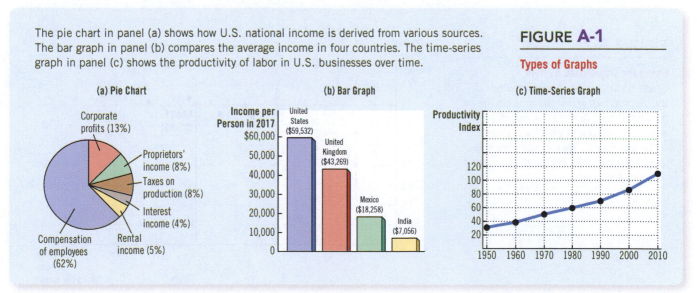

The pie chart in panel (a) shows how U.S. national income is derived from various sources. The bar graph in panel (b) compares the average income in four countries. The time-series graph in panel (c) shows the productivity of labor in U.S. businesses over time.

FIGURE **A-1**

Types of Graphs

(a) Pie Chart

Corporate profits (13%)
Proprietors' income (8%)
Taxes on production (8%)
Interest income (4%)
Rental income (5%)
Compensation of employees (62%)

(b) Bar Graph

Income per Person in 2017
United States ($59,532)
United Kingdom ($43,269)
Mexico ($18,258)
India ($7,056)

(c) Time-Series Graph

Productivity Index

including compensation of employees, corporate profits, and so on. A slice of the pie represents each source's share of the total. The *bar graph* in panel (b) compares income in four countries. The height of each bar represents the average income in each country. The *time-series graph* in panel (c) traces the rising productivity in the U.S. business sector over time. The height of the line shows output per hour in each year. You have probably seen similar graphs in newspapers and magazines.

Graphs of Two Variables: The Coordinate System

The three graphs in Figure A-1 are useful in showing how a variable changes over time or across individuals, but they are limited in how much they can tell us. These graphs display information only about a single variable. Economists are often concerned with the relationships between variables. Thus, they need to display two variables on a single graph. The *coordinate system* makes this possible.

Suppose you want to examine the relationship between study time and grade point average. For each student in your class, you could record a pair of numbers: hours per week spent studying and grade point average. These numbers could then be placed in parentheses as an *ordered pair* and appear as a single point on the graph. Albert E., for instance, is represented by the ordered pair (25 hours/week, 3.5 GPA), while his "what-me-worry?" classmate Alfred E. is represented by the ordered pair (5 hours/week, 2.0 GPA).

We can graph these ordered pairs on a two-dimensional grid. The first number in each ordered pair, called the *x-coordinate*, tells us the horizontal location of the point. The second number, called the *y-coordinate*, tells us the vertical location of the point. The point with both an *x*-coordinate and a *y*-coordinate of zero is known as the *origin*. The two coordinates in the ordered pair tell us where the point is located in relation to the origin: *x* units to the right of the origin and *y* units above it.

Figure A-2 graphs grade point average against study time for Albert E., Alfred E., and their classmates. This type of graph is called a *scatter plot* because it plots scattered points. Looking at this graph, we immediately notice that points farther to the right (indicating more study time) also tend to be higher (indicating

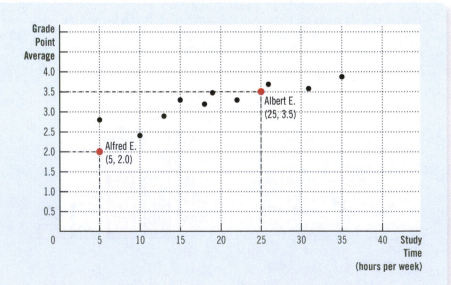

FIGURE A-2

Using the Coordinate System

Grade point average is measured on the vertical axis and study time on the horizontal axis. Albert E., Alfred E., and their classmates are represented by various points. We can see from the graph that students who study more tend to get higher grades.

a better grade point average). Because study time and grade point average typically move in the same direction, we say that these two variables have a *positive correlation*. By contrast, if we were to graph party time and grades, we would likely find that higher party time is associated with lower grades. Because these variables typically move in opposite directions, we say that they have a *negative correlation*. In either case, the coordinate system makes the correlation between two variables easy to see.

Curves in the Coordinate System

Students who study more do tend to get higher grades, but other factors also influence a student's grades. Previous preparation is an important factor, for instance, as are talent, attention from teachers, even eating a good breakfast. A scatter plot like Figure A-2 does not attempt to isolate the effect that studying has on grades from the effects of other variables. Often, however, economists prefer looking at how one variable affects another, holding everything else constant.

To see how this is done, let's consider one of the most important graphs in economics: the *demand curve*. The demand curve traces out the effect of a good's price on the quantity of the good consumers want to buy. Before showing a demand curve, however, consider Table A-1, which shows how the number of novels that Emma buys depends on her income and on the price of novels. When novels are cheap, Emma buys them in large quantities. As they become more expensive, she instead borrows books from the library or chooses to go to the movies rather than read. Similarly, at any given price, Emma buys more novels when she has a higher income. That is, when her income increases, she spends part of the additional income on novels and part on other goods.

We now have three variables—the price of novels, income, and the number of novels purchased—which is more than we can represent in two dimensions. To put the information from Table A-1 in graphical form, we need to hold one of the three variables constant and trace out the relationship between the other two. Because the demand curve represents the relationship between price and quantity demanded, we hold Emma's income constant and show how the number of novels she buys varies with the price of novels.

Suppose that Emma's income is $40,000 per year. If we place the number of novels Emma purchases on the x-axis and the price of novels on the y-axis, we

Price	For $30,000 Income:	For $40,000 Income:	For $50,000 Income:
$10	2 novels	5 novels	8 novels
9	6	9	12
8	10	13	16
7	14	17	20
6	18	21	24
5	22	25	28
	Demand curve, D_3	Demand curve, D_1	Demand curve, D_2

TABLE A-1

Novels Purchased by Emma
This table shows the number of novels Emma buys at various incomes and prices. For any given level of income, the data on price and quantity demanded can be graphed to produce Emma's demand curve for novels, as shown in Figures A-3 and A-4.

can graphically represent the middle column of Table A-1. When the points that represent these entries from the table—(5 novels, $10), (9 novels, $9), and so on—are connected, they form a line. This line, pictured in Figure A-3, is known as Emma's demand curve for novels; it tells us how many novels Emma purchases at any given price, holding income constant. The demand curve is downward-sloping, indicating that a higher price reduces the quantity of novels demanded. Because the quantity of novels demanded and the price move in opposite directions, we say that the two variables are *negatively related*. (Conversely, when two variables move in the same direction, the curve relating them is upward-sloping, and we say that the variables are *positively related*.)

Now suppose that Emma's income rises to $50,000 per year. At any given price, Emma will purchase more novels than she did at her previous level of income. Just as we earlier drew Emma's demand curve for novels using the entries from the middle column of Table A-1, we now draw a new demand curve using the entries from the right column of the table. This new demand curve (curve D_2) is pictured alongside the old one (curve D_1) in Figure A-4; the new curve is a similar line drawn farther to the right. We therefore say that Emma's demand curve for novels *shifts* to the right when her income increases. Likewise, if Emma's income were to fall to $30,000 per year, she would buy fewer novels at any given price and her demand curve would shift to the left (to curve D_3).

In economics, it is important to distinguish between *movements along a curve* and *shifts of a curve*. As we can see from Figure A-3, if Emma earns $40,000 per year and novels cost $8 apiece, she will purchase 13 novels per year. If the price of novels falls to $7, Emma will increase her purchases of novels to 17 per year. The demand curve, however, stays fixed in the same place. Emma still buys the same

FIGURE A-3

Demand Curve
The line D_1 shows how Emma's purchases of novels depend on the price of novels when her income is held constant. Because the price and the quantity demanded are negatively related, the demand curve slopes downward.

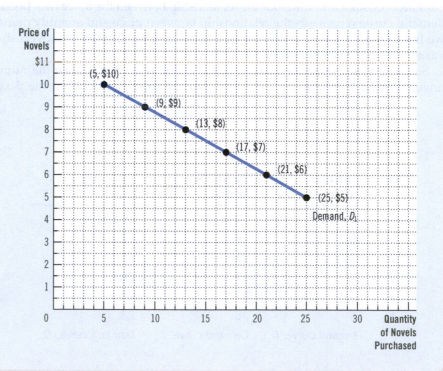

number of novels *at each price*, but as the price falls, she moves along her demand curve from left to right. By contrast, if the price of novels remains fixed at $8 but her income rises to $50,000, Emma increases her purchases of novels from 13 to 16 per year. Because Emma buys more novels *at each price*, her demand curve shifts out, as shown in Figure A-4.

There is a simple way to tell when it is necessary to shift a curve: *When a relevant variable that is not named on either axis changes, the curve shifts.* Income is on neither the *x*-axis nor the *y*-axis of the graph, so when Emma's income changes, her demand curve must shift. The same is true for any change that affects Emma's purchasing habits, with the sole exception of a change in the price of novels. If, for instance, the public library closes and Emma must buy all the books she wants to read, she will demand more novels at each price, and her demand curve will shift to the right. Or if the price of movies falls and Emma spends more time at the movies and less time reading, she will demand fewer novels at each price, and her demand curve will shift to the left. By contrast, when a variable on an axis of the graph changes, the curve does not shift. We read the change as a movement along the curve.

Slope

One question we might want to ask about Emma is how much her purchasing habits respond to changes in price. Look at the demand curve pictured in Figure A-5. If this curve is very steep, Emma purchases nearly the same number of novels regardless of whether they are cheap or expensive. If this curve is much flatter, the number of novels Emma purchases is more sensitive to changes in the price. To answer questions about how much one variable responds to changes in another variable, we can use the concept of *slope*.

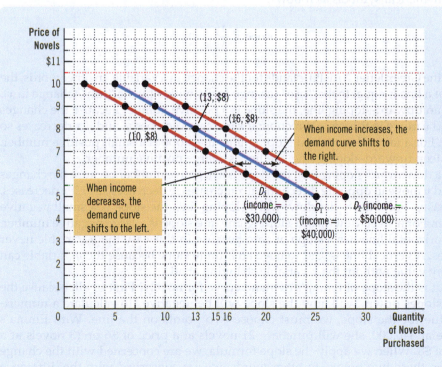

FIGURE A-4

Shifting Demand Curves
The location of Emma's demand curve for novels depends on how much income she earns. The more she earns, the more novels she will purchase at any given price, and the farther to the right her demand curve will lie. Curve D_1 represents Emma's original demand curve when her income is $40,000 per year. If her income rises to $50,000 per year, her demand curve shifts to D_2. If her income falls to $30,000 per year, her demand curve shifts to D_3.

FIGURE A-5

Calculating the Slope of a Line
To calculate the slope of the demand curve, we can look at the changes in the x- and y-coordinates as we move from the point (21 novels, $6) to the point (13 novels, $8). The slope of the line is the ratio of the change in the y-coordinate (−2) to the change in the x-coordinate (+8), which equals −¼.

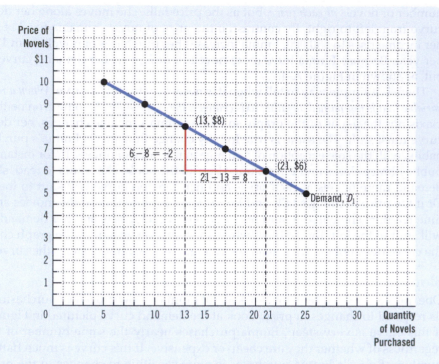

The slope of a line is the ratio of the vertical distance covered to the horizontal distance covered as we move along the line. This definition is usually written out in mathematical symbols as follows:

$$\text{slope} = \frac{\Delta y}{\Delta x},$$

where the Greek letter Δ (delta) stands for the change in a variable. In other words, the slope of a line is equal to the "rise" (change in y) divided by the "run" (change in x).

For an upward-sloping line, the slope is a positive number because the changes in x and y move in the same direction: if x increases so does y, and if x decreases so does y. For a fairly flat upward-sloping line, the slope is a small positive number. For a steep upward-sloping line, the line is a large positive number.

For a downward-sloping line, the slope is a negative number because the changes in x and y move in opposite directions: if x increases, y decreases, and if x decreases, y increases. For a fairly flat downward-sloping line, the slope is a small negative number. For a steep downward-sloping line, the slope is a large negative number.

A horizontal line has a slope of zero because in this case the y-variable never changes. A vertical line is said to have an infinite slope because the y-variable can take any value without the x-variable changing at all.

What is the slope of Emma's demand curve for novels? First of all, because the curve slopes down, we know the slope will be negative. To calculate a numerical value for the slope, we must choose two points on the line. With Emma's income at $40,000, she will purchase 21 novels at a price of $6 or 13 novels at a price of $8. When we apply the slope formula, we are concerned with the change between these two points. In other words, we are concerned with the difference between them, which lets us know that we will have to subtract one set of values from the other, as follows:

$$\text{slope} = \frac{\Delta y}{\Delta x} = \frac{\text{first } y\text{-coordinate} - \text{second } y\text{-coordinate}}{\text{first } x\text{-coordinate} - \text{second } x\text{-coordinate}} = \frac{6 - 8}{21 - 13} = \frac{-2}{8} = \frac{-1}{4}$$

Figure A-5 shows graphically how this calculation works. Try computing the slope of Emma's demand curve using two different points. You should get the same result, −¼. One of the properties of a straight line is that it has the same slope everywhere. This is not true of other types of curves, which are steeper in some places than in others.

The slope of Emma's demand curve tells us something about how responsive her purchases are to changes in the price. A small slope (a negative number close to zero) means that Emma's demand curve is relatively flat; in this case, she adjusts the number of novels she buys substantially in response to a price change. A larger slope (a negative number farther from zero) means that Emma's demand curve is relatively steep; in this case, she adjusts the number of novels she buys only slightly in response to a price change.

Cause and Effect

Economists often use graphs to advance an argument about how the economy works. In other words, they use graphs to argue about how one set of events *causes* another set of events. With a graph like the demand curve, there is no doubt about cause and effect. Because we are varying price and holding all other variables constant, we know that changes in the price of novels cause changes in the quantity Emma demands. Remember, however, that our demand curve came from a hypothetical example. When graphing data from the real world, it is often more difficult to establish how one variable affects another.

The first problem is that it is difficult to hold everything else constant when studying the relationship between two variables. If we are not able to hold other variables constant, we might decide that one variable on our graph is causing changes in the other variable when those changes are actually being caused by a third *omitted variable* not pictured on the graph. Even if we have identified the correct two variables to look at, we might run into a second problem—*reverse causality*. In other words, we might decide that A causes B when in fact B causes A. The omitted-variable and reverse-causality traps require us to proceed with caution when using graphs to draw conclusions about causes and effects.

Omitted Variables   To see how omitting a variable can lead to a deceptive graph, let's consider an example. Imagine that the government, spurred by public concern about the large number of deaths from cancer, commissions an exhaustive study from Big Brother Statistical Services, Inc. Big Brother examines many of the items found in people's homes to see which of them are associated with the risk of cancer. Big Brother reports a strong relationship between two variables: the number of cigarette lighters that a household owns and the probability that someone in the household will develop cancer. Figure A-6 shows this relationship.

What should we make of this result? Big Brother advises a quick policy response. It recommends that the government discourage the ownership of cigarette lighters by taxing their sale. It also recommends that the government require warning labels: "Big Brother has determined that this lighter is dangerous to your health."

In judging the validity of Big Brother's analysis, one question is key: Has Big Brother held constant every relevant variable except the one under consideration? If the answer is no, the results are suspect. An easy explanation for Figure A-6 is that people who own more cigarette lighters are more likely to smoke cigarettes and that cigarettes, not lighters, cause cancer. If Figure A-6 does not hold constant the amount of smoking, it does not tell us the true effect of owning a cigarette lighter.

This story illustrates an important principle: When you see a graph used to support an argument about cause and effect, it is important to ask whether the movements of an omitted variable could explain the results you see.

Reverse Causality   Economists can also make mistakes about causality by misreading its direction. To see how this is possible, suppose the Association of American Anarchists commissions a study of crime in America and arrives at Figure A-7, which plots the number of violent crimes per thousand people in major cities against the number of police officers per thousand people. The Anarchists note the curve's upward slope and argue that because police increase rather than decrease the amount of urban violence, law enforcement should be abolished.

Figure A-7, however, does not prove the Anarchists' point. The graph simply shows that more dangerous cities have more police officers. The explanation may be that more dangerous cities hire more police. In other words, rather than police causing crime, crime may cause police. We could avoid the danger of reverse

FIGURE A-6

Graph with an Omitted Variable
The upward-sloping curve shows that members of households with more cigarette lighters are more likely to develop cancer. Yet we should not conclude that ownership of lighters causes cancer because the graph does not take into account the number of cigarettes smoked.

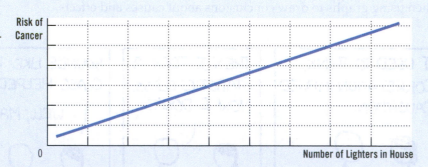

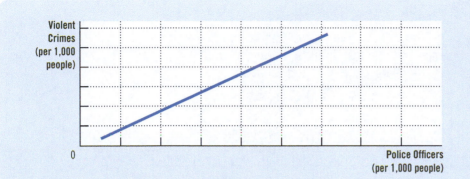

FIGURE A-7

Graph Suggesting Reverse Causality
The upward-sloping curve shows that cities with a higher concentration of police are more dangerous. Yet the graph does not tell us whether police cause crime or crime-plagued cities hire more police.

causality by running a controlled experiment. In this case, we would randomly assign different numbers of police to different cities and then examine the correlation between police and crime. Without such an experiment, establishing the direction of causality is difficult at best.

It might seem that we could determine the direction of causality by examining which variable moves first. If we see crime increase and then the police force expand, we reach one conclusion. If we see the police force expand and then crime increase, we reach the other conclusion. This approach, however, is also flawed: Often, people change their behavior not in response to a change in their present conditions but in response to a change in their *expectations* about future conditions. A city that expects a major crime wave in the future, for instance, might hire more police now. This problem is even easier to see in the case of babies and minivans. Couples often buy a minivan in anticipation of the birth of a child. The minivan comes before the baby, but we wouldn't want to conclude that the sale of minivans causes the population to grow!

There is no complete set of rules that says when it is appropriate to draw causal conclusions from graphs. Yet just keeping in mind that cigarette lighters don't cause cancer (omitted variable) and that minivans don't cause larger families (reverse causality) will keep you from falling for many faulty economic arguments.

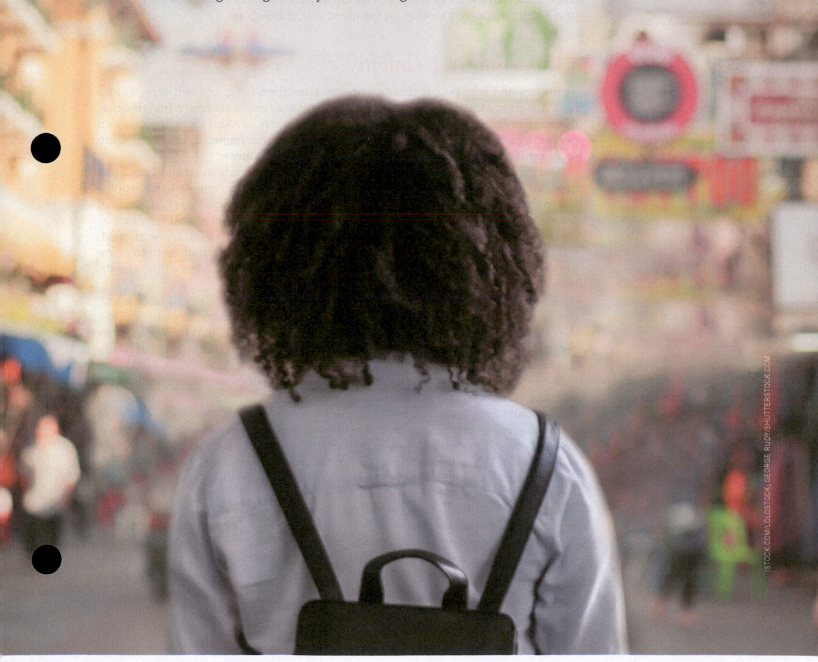

onsider your typical day. You wake up in the morning and pour yourself juice from oranges grown in Florida and coffee from beans grown in Brazil. Over breakfast, you read a newspaper written in New York on a tablet made in China. You get dressed in clothes made of cotton grown in Georgia and sewn in factories in Thailand. You drive to class in a car made of parts manufactured in more than a dozen countries around the world. Then you open up your economics textbook written by an author living in Massachusetts, published by a company located in Ohio, and printed on paper made from trees grown in Oregon.

Every day, you rely on many people, most of whom you have never met, to provide you with the goods and services that you enjoy. Such interdependence is possible because people trade with one another. Those people providing you with goods and services are not acting out of generosity. Nor is some government

Interdependence and the Gains from Trade

agency directing them to satisfy your desires. Instead, people provide you and other consumers with the goods and services they produce because they get something in return.

In subsequent chapters, we examine how an economy coordinates the activities of millions of people with varying tastes and abilities. As a starting point for this analysis, this chapter considers the reasons for economic interdependence. One of the *Ten Principles of Economics* in Chapter 1 is that trade can make everyone better off. We now examine this principle more closely. What exactly do people gain when they trade with one another? Why do people choose to become interdependent?

The answers to these questions are key to understanding the modern global economy. Most countries today import from abroad many of the goods and services they consume, and they export to foreign customers many of the goods and services they produce. The analysis in this chapter explains interdependence not only among individuals but also among nations. As we will see, the gains from trade are much the same whether you are buying a haircut from your local barber or a T-shirt made by a worker on the other side of the globe.

3-1   A Parable for the Modern Economy

To understand why people choose to depend on others for goods and services and how this choice improves their lives, let's examine a simple economy. Imagine that there are only two goods in the world: meat and potatoes. And there are only two people: a cattle rancher named Ruby and a potato farmer named Frank. Both Ruby and Frank would like to eat a diet of both meat and potatoes.

The gains from trade are clearest if Ruby can produce only meat and Frank can produce only potatoes. In one scenario, Frank and Ruby could choose to have nothing to do with each other. But after several months of eating beef roasted, broiled, seared, and grilled, Ruby might decide that self-sufficiency is not all it's cracked up to be. Frank, who has been eating potatoes mashed, fried, baked, and scalloped, would likely agree. It is easy to see that trade would allow both of them to enjoy greater variety: Each could then have a steak with a baked potato or a burger with fries.

Although this scene shows most simply how everyone can benefit from trade, the gains would be similar if Frank and Ruby were each capable of producing the other good, but only at great cost. Suppose, for example, that Ruby can grow potatoes but her land is not very well suited for it. Similarly, suppose that Frank can raise cattle and produce meat but is not very good at it. In this case, Frank and Ruby each benefit by specializing in what he or she does best and then trading with the other person.

The gains from trade are less obvious, however, when one person is better at producing *every* good. For example, suppose that Ruby is better at raising cattle *and* better at growing potatoes than Frank. In this case, should Ruby remain self-sufficient? Or is there still reason for her to trade with Frank? To answer this question, let's look more closely at the factors that affect such a decision.

3-1a   Production Possibilities

Suppose that Frank and Ruby each work 8 hours per day and can devote this time to growing potatoes, raising cattle, or a combination of the two. The table in Figure 1 shows the amount of time each person requires to produce 1 ounce of each good. Frank can produce an ounce of potatoes in 15 minutes and an ounce of meat in 60 minutes. Ruby, who is more productive in both activities, can produce an ounce of potatoes in 10 minutes and an ounce of meat in 20 minutes. The last two columns in the table show the amounts of meat or potatoes Frank and Ruby can produce if they devote all 8 hours to producing only that good.

Panel (b) of Figure 1 illustrates the amounts of meat and potatoes that Frank can produce. If he spends all 8 hours of his time growing potatoes, Frank produces 32 ounces of potatoes (measured on the horizontal axis) and no meat. If he spends all of his time raising cattle, he produces 8 ounces of meat (measured on the vertical axis) and no potatoes. If Frank divides his time equally between the two activities, spending 4 hours on each, he produces 16 ounces of potatoes and 4 ounces of meat. The figure shows these three possible outcomes and all others in between.

This graph is Frank's production possibilities frontier. As we discussed in Chapter 2, a production possibilities frontier shows the various mixes of output that an economy can produce. It illustrates one of the *Ten Principles of Economics* in

---

Panel (a) shows the production opportunities available to Frank the farmer and Ruby the rancher. Panel (b) shows the combinations of meat and potatoes that Frank can produce. Panel (c) shows the combinations of meat and potatoes that Ruby can produce. Both production possibilities frontiers are derived assuming that Frank and Ruby each work 8 hours per day. If there is no trade, each person's production possibilities frontier is also his or her consumption possibilities frontier.

FIGURE 1

The Production Possibilities Frontier

(a) Production Opportunities

	Minutes Needed to Make 1 Ounce of:		Amount Produced in 8 Hours	
	Meat	Potatoes	Meat	Potatoes
Frank the farmer	60 min/oz	15 min/oz	8 oz	32 oz
Ruby the rancher	20 min/oz	10 min/oz	24 oz	48 oz

(b) Frank's Production Possibilities Frontier

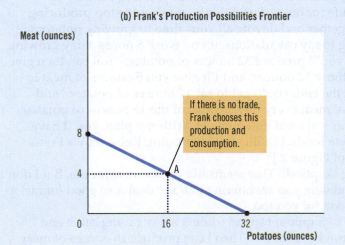

(c) Ruby's Production Possibilities Frontier

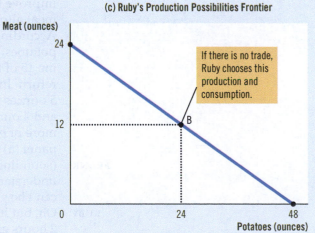

Chapter 1: People face trade-offs. Here Frank faces a trade-off between producing meat and producing potatoes.

You may recall that the production possibilities frontier in Chapter 2 was drawn bowed out. In that case, the rate at which society could trade one good for the other depended on the amounts that were being produced. Here, however, Frank's technology for producing meat and potatoes (as summarized in Figure 1) allows him to switch between the two goods at a constant rate. Whenever Frank spends 1 hour less producing meat and 1 hour more producing potatoes, he reduces his output of meat by 1 ounce and raises his output of potatoes by 4 ounces—and this is true regardless of how much he is already producing. As a result, the production possibilities frontier is a straight line.

Panel (c) of Figure 1 shows Ruby's production possibilities frontier. If she spends all 8 hours of her time growing potatoes, Ruby produces 48 ounces of potatoes and no meat. If she spends all of her time raising cattle, she produces 24 ounces of meat and no potatoes. If Ruby divides her time equally, spending 4 hours on each activity, she produces 24 ounces of potatoes and 12 ounces of meat. Once again, the production possibilities frontier shows all the possible outcomes.

If Frank and Ruby choose to be self-sufficient rather than trade with each other, then each consumes exactly what he or she produces. In this case, the production possibilities frontier is also the consumption possibilities frontier. That is, without trade, Figure 1 shows the possible combinations of meat and potatoes that Frank and Ruby can each produce and then consume.

These production possibilities frontiers are useful in showing the trade-offs that Frank and Ruby face, but they do not tell us what each will choose to do. To determine their choices, we need to know something about their tastes. Let's suppose that Frank and Ruby choose the combinations identified by points A and B in Figure 1. Based on his production opportunities and food preferences, Frank decides to produce and consume 16 ounces of potatoes and 4 ounces of meat, while Ruby decides to produce and consume 24 ounces of potatoes and 12 ounces of meat.

3-1b Specialization and Trade

After several years of eating combination B, Ruby gets an idea and visits Frank:

RUBY: Frank, my friend, have I got a deal for you! I know how to improve life for both of us. I think you should stop producing meat altogether and devote all your time to growing potatoes. According to my calculations, if you work 8 hours a day growing potatoes, you'll produce 32 ounces of potatoes. You can then give me 15 of those 32 ounces, and I'll give you 5 ounces of meat in return. In the end, you'll get to eat 17 ounces of potatoes and 5 ounces of meat every day, instead of the 16 ounces of potatoes and 4 ounces of meat you now get. With my plan, you'll have more of *both* foods. [To illustrate her point, Ruby shows Frank panel (a) of Figure 2.]

FRANK: (sounding skeptical): That seems like a good deal for me. But I don't understand why you are offering it. If the deal is so good for me, it can't be good for you too.

RUBY: Oh, but it is! Suppose I spend 6 hours a day raising cattle and 2 hours growing potatoes. Then I can produce 18 ounces of meat and 12 ounces of potatoes. After I give you 5 ounces of my meat in

The proposed trade between Frank the farmer and Ruby the rancher offers each of them a combination of meat and potatoes that would be impossible in the absence of trade. In panel (a), Frank gets to consume at point A* rather than point A. In panel (b), Ruby gets to consume at point B* rather than point B. Trade allows each to consume more meat and more potatoes.

FIGURE 2

How Trade Expands the Set of Consumption Opportunities

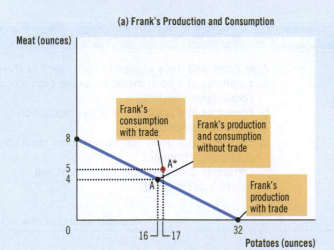

(a) Frank's Production and Consumption

Meat (ounces)

- Frank's consumption with trade
- Frank's production and consumption without trade
- Frank's production with trade

A*

A

8
5
4

0   16 ─┘ └─17   32   Potatoes (ounces)

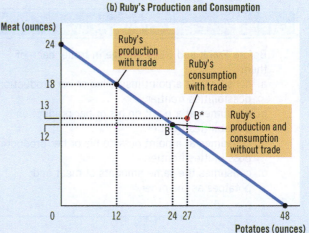

(b) Ruby's Production and Consumption

Meat (ounces)

24
18
13
12

- Ruby's production with trade
- Ruby's consumption with trade
- Ruby's production and consumption without trade

B*
B

0   12   24 27   48   Potatoes (ounces)

(c) The Gains from Trade: A Summary

	Frank		Ruby	
	Meat	**Potatoes**	**Meat**	**Potatoes**
Without Trade:				
Production and Consumption	4 oz	16 oz	12 oz	24 oz
With Trade:				
Production	0 oz	32 oz	18 oz	12 oz
Trade	Gets 5 oz	Gives 15 oz	Gives 5 oz	Gets 15 oz
Consumption	5 oz	17 oz	13 oz	27 oz
GAINS FROM TRADE:				
Increase in Consumption	+1 oz	+1 oz	+1 oz	+3 oz

> exchange for 15 ounces of your potatoes, I'll end up with 13 ounces of meat and 27 ounces of potatoes, instead of the 12 ounces of meat and 24 ounces of potatoes that I now get. So I will also consume more of both foods than I do now. [She points out panel (b) of Figure 2.]

FRANK: I don't know. . . . This sounds too good to be true.

RUBY: It's really not as complicated as it seems. Here—I've summarized my proposal for you in a simple table. [Ruby shows Frank a copy of the table at the bottom of Figure 2.]

FRANK: (after pausing to study the table): These calculations seem correct, but I am puzzled. How can this deal make us both better off?

RUBY: We can both benefit because trade allows each of us to specialize in doing what we do best. You will spend more time growing potatoes and less time raising cattle. I will spend more time raising cattle and less time growing potatoes. As a result of specialization and trade, each of us can consume more meat and more potatoes without working any more hours.

Quick**Quiz**

1. Before Frank and Ruby engage in trade, each of them
   a. consumes at a point inside his or her production possibilities frontier.
   b. consumes at a point on his or her production possibilities frontier.
   c. consumes at a point outside his or her production possibilities frontier.
   d. consumes the same amounts of meat and potatoes as the other.

2. After Frank and Ruby engage in trade, each of them
   a. consumes at a point inside his or her production possibilities frontier.
   b. consumes at a point on his or her production possibilities frontier.
   c. consumes at a point outside his or her production possibilities frontier.
   d. consumes the same amounts of meat and potatoes as the other.

Answers at end of chapter.

3-2 Comparative Advantage: The Driving Force of Specialization

Ruby's explanation of the gains from trade, though correct, poses a puzzle: If Ruby is better at both raising cattle and growing potatoes, how can Frank ever specialize in doing what he does best? Frank doesn't seem to do anything best. To solve this puzzle, we need to look at the principle of *comparative advantage*.

As a first step in developing this principle, consider the following question: In our example, who can produce potatoes at a lower cost—Frank or Ruby? There are two possible answers, and in these two answers lie the solution to our puzzle and the key to understanding the gains from trade.

3-2a Absolute Advantage

absolute advantage
the ability to produce a good using fewer inputs than another producer

One way to answer the question about the cost of producing potatoes is to compare the inputs required by the two producers. Economists use the term **absolute advantage** when comparing the productivity of one person, firm, or nation to that of another. The producer that requires a smaller quantity of inputs to produce a good is said to have an absolute advantage in producing that good.

In our example, time is the only input, so we can determine absolute advantage by looking at how much time each type of production takes. Ruby has an absolute advantage in producing both meat and potatoes because she requires less time than Frank to produce a unit of either good. Ruby needs to input only 20 minutes to produce an ounce of meat, whereas Frank needs 60 minutes. Similarly, Ruby needs only 10 minutes to produce an ounce of potatoes, whereas Frank needs 15 minutes. Thus, if we measure cost in terms of the quantity of inputs, Ruby has the lower cost of producing potatoes.

3-2b Opportunity Cost and Comparative Advantage

opportunity cost
whatever must be given up to obtain some item

There is another way to look at the cost of producing potatoes. Rather than comparing inputs required, we can compare opportunity costs. Recall from Chapter 1 that the **opportunity cost** of some item is what we give up to get that item. In our example, we assumed that Frank and Ruby each spend 8 hours a day working. Time spent producing potatoes takes away from time available for producing meat. When reallocating time between the two goods, Ruby and Frank give up units of one good to produce units of the other, thereby moving along the production possibilities frontier. The opportunity cost measures the trade-off between the two goods that each producer faces.

Let's first consider Ruby's opportunity cost. According to the table in panel (a) of Figure 1, producing 1 ounce of potatoes takes 10 minutes of work. When Ruby spends those 10 minutes producing potatoes, she spends 10 fewer minutes producing meat. Because Ruby needs 20 minutes to produce 1 ounce of meat, 10 minutes of work would yield ½ ounce of meat. Hence, Ruby's opportunity cost of producing 1 ounce of potatoes is ½ ounce of meat.

Now consider Frank's opportunity cost. Producing 1 ounce of potatoes takes him 15 minutes. Because he needs 60 minutes to produce 1 ounce of meat, 15 minutes of work would yield ¼ ounce of meat. Hence, Frank's opportunity cost of producing 1 ounce of potatoes is ¼ ounce of meat.

Table 1 shows the opportunity costs of meat and potatoes for the two producers. Notice that the opportunity cost of meat is the inverse of the opportunity cost of potatoes. Because 1 ounce of potatoes costs Ruby ½ ounce of meat, 1 ounce of meat costs her 2 ounces of potatoes. Similarly, because 1 ounce of potatoes costs Frank ¼ ounce of meat, 1 ounce of meat costs him 4 ounces of potatoes.

Economists use the term **comparative advantage** when describing the opportunity costs faced by two producers. The producer who gives up less of other goods to produce Good X has the smaller opportunity cost of producing Good X and is said to have a comparative advantage in producing it. In our example, Frank has a lower opportunity cost of producing potatoes than Ruby: An ounce of potatoes costs Frank only ¼ ounce of meat, but it costs Ruby ½ ounce of meat. Conversely, Ruby has a lower opportunity cost of producing meat than Frank: An ounce of meat costs Ruby 2 ounces of potatoes, but it costs Frank 4 ounces of potatoes. Thus, Frank has a comparative advantage in growing potatoes, and Ruby has a comparative advantage in producing meat.

Although it is possible for one person to have an absolute advantage in both goods (as Ruby does in our example), it is impossible for one person to have a comparative advantage in both goods. Because the opportunity cost of one good is the inverse of the opportunity cost of the other, if a person's opportunity cost of one good is relatively high, the opportunity cost of the other good must be relatively low. Comparative advantage reflects the relative opportunity cost. Unless two people have the same opportunity cost, one person will have a comparative advantage in one good, and the other person will have a comparative advantage in the other good.

comparative advantage
the ability to produce a good at a lower opportunity cost than another producer

	Opportunity Cost of:	
	1 oz of Meat	1 oz of Potatoes
Frank the farmer	4 oz potatoes	¼ oz meat
Ruby the rancher	2 oz potatoes	½ oz meat

TABLE 1

The Opportunity Cost of Meat and Potatoes

3-2c Comparative Advantage and Trade

The gains from specialization and trade are based not on absolute advantage but on comparative advantage. When each person specializes in producing the good in which he or she has a comparative advantage, total production in the economy rises. This increase in the size of the economic pie can be used to make everyone better off.

In our example, Frank spends more time growing potatoes, and Ruby spends more time producing meat. As a result, the total production of potatoes rises from 40 to 44 ounces, and the total production of meat rises from 16 to 18 ounces. Frank and Ruby share the benefits of this increased production.

We can also view the gains from trade in terms of the price that each party pays the other. Because Frank and Ruby have different opportunity costs, they can both get a bargain. That is, each of them benefits from trade by obtaining a good at a price that is lower than his or her opportunity cost of that good.

Consider the proposed deal from Frank's viewpoint. Frank receives 5 ounces of meat in exchange for 15 ounces of potatoes. In other words, Frank buys each ounce of meat for a price of 3 ounces of potatoes. This price of meat is lower than his opportunity cost of an ounce of meat, which is 4 ounces of potatoes. Frank benefits from the deal because he gets to buy meat at a good price.

Now consider the deal from Ruby's viewpoint. Ruby gets 15 ounces of potatoes in exchange for 5 ounces of meat. That is, the price of an ounce of potatoes is $\frac{1}{3}$ ounce of meat. This price of potatoes is lower than her opportunity cost of an ounce of potatoes, which is ½ ounce of meat. Ruby benefits because she gets to buy potatoes at a good price.

The story of Ruby the rancher and Frank the farmer has a simple moral, which should now be clear: *Trade can benefit everyone in society because it allows people to specialize in the activities in which they have a comparative advantage.*

3-2d The Price of the Trade

The principle of comparative advantage establishes that there are gains from specialization and trade, but it raises a couple of related questions: What determines the price at which trade takes place? How are the gains from trade shared between the trading parties? The precise answers to these questions are beyond the scope of this chapter, but we can state one general rule: *For both parties to gain from trade, the price at which they trade must lie between their opportunity costs.*

In our example, Frank and Ruby agreed to trade at a rate of 3 ounces of potatoes for each ounce of meat. This price is between Ruby's opportunity cost (2 ounces of potatoes per ounce of meat) and Frank's opportunity cost (4 ounces of potatoes per ounce of meat). The price need not be exactly in the middle for both parties to gain, but it must be somewhere between 2 and 4.

To see why the price has to be in this range, consider what would happen if it were not. If the price of meat were below 2 ounces of potatoes, both Frank and Ruby would want to buy meat, because the price would be below each of their opportunity costs. Similarly, if the price of meat were above 4 ounces of potatoes, both would want to sell meat, because the price would be above their opportunity costs. But this economy has only two people. They cannot both be buyers of meat, nor can they both be sellers. Someone has to take the other side of the deal.

A mutually advantageous trade can be struck at a price between 2 and 4. In this price range, Ruby wants to sell meat to buy potatoes, and Frank wants to sell potatoes to buy meat. Each party can buy a good at a price that is lower than his or her opportunity cost of that good. In the end, each person specializes in the good in which he or she has a comparative advantage and, as a result, is better off.

FYI

The Legacy of Adam Smith and David Ricardo

Economists have long understood the gains from trade. Here is how the great economist Adam Smith put the argument:

It is a maxim of every prudent master of a family, never to attempt to make at home what it will cost him more to make than to buy. The tailor does not attempt to make his own shoes, but buys them of the shoemaker. The shoemaker does not attempt to make his own clothes but employs a tailor. The farmer attempts to make neither the one nor the other, but employs those different artificers. All of them find it for their interest to employ their whole industry in a way in which they have some advantage over their neighbors, and to purchase with a part of its produce, or what is the same thing, with the price of part of it, whatever else they have occasion for.

This quotation is from Smith's 1776 book *The Wealth of Nations*, which was a landmark in the analysis of trade and economic interdependence.

David Ricardo

BETTMANN/GETTY IMAGES

Smith's book inspired David Ricardo, a millionaire stockbroker, to become an economist. In his 1817 book *On the Principles of Political Economy and Taxation*, Ricardo developed the principle of comparative advantage as we know it today. He considered an example with two goods (wine and cloth) and two countries (England and Portugal). He showed that both countries can gain by opening up trade and specializing based on comparative advantage.

Ricardo's theory is the starting point of modern international economics, but his defense of free trade was not a mere academic exercise. Ricardo put his beliefs to work as a member of the British Parliament, where he opposed the Corn Laws, which restricted grain imports.

The conclusions of Adam Smith and David Ricardo on the gains from trade have held up well over time. Although economists often disagree on questions of policy, they are united in their support of free trade. Moreover, the central argument for free trade has not changed much in the past two centuries. Even though the field of economics has broadened its scope and refined its theories since the time of Smith and Ricardo, economists' opposition to trade restrictions is still based largely on the principle of comparative advantage. ■

Quick Quiz

3. In an hour, Mateo can wash 2 cars or mow 1 lawn, and Sophia can wash 3 cars or mow 1 lawn. Who has the absolute advantage in car washing, and who has the absolute advantage in lawn mowing?
   a. Mateo in washing, Sophia in mowing
   b. Sophia in washing, Mateo in mowing
   c. Mateo in washing, neither in mowing
   d. Sophia in washing, neither in mowing

4. Between Mateo and Sophia, who has the comparative advantage in car washing, and who has the comparative advantage in lawn mowing?
   a. Mateo in washing, Sophia in mowing
   b. Sophia in washing, Mateo in mowing

   c. Mateo in washing, neither in mowing
   d. Sophia in washing, neither in mowing

5. When Mateo and Sophia produce efficiently and make a mutually beneficial trade based on comparative advantage,
   a. Mateo mows more and Sophia washes more.
   b. Mateo washes more and Sophia mows more.
   c. Mateo and Sophia both wash more.
   d. Mateo and Sophia both mow more.

Answers at end of chapter.

3-3 Applications of Comparative Advantage

The principle of comparative advantage explains interdependence and the gains from trade. Because interdependence is so prevalent in the modern world, the principle of comparative advantage has many applications. Here are two examples, one fanciful and one of great practical importance.

3-3a Should LeBron James Mow His Own Lawn?

LeBron James is a great athlete. One of the best basketball players of all time, he can jump higher and shoot better than most other people. Most likely, he is talented at other physical activities as well. For example, let's imagine that LeBron can mow his lawn faster than anyone else. But just because he *can* mow his lawn fast, does this mean he *should*?

To answer this question, we can use the concepts of opportunity cost and comparative advantage. Let's say that LeBron can mow his lawn in 2 hours. In those same 2 hours, he could film a television commercial and earn $30,000. By contrast, Kaitlyn, the girl next door, can mow LeBron's lawn in 4 hours. In those same 4 hours, Kaitlyn could work at McDonald's and earn $50.

In this example, LeBron has an absolute advantage in mowing lawns because he can do the work with a lower input of time. Yet because LeBron's opportunity cost of mowing the lawn is $30,000 and Kaitlyn's opportunity cost is only $50, Kaitlyn has a comparative advantage in mowing lawns.

The gains from trade here are tremendous. Rather than mowing his own lawn, LeBron should film the commercial and hire Kaitlyn to mow the lawn. As long as LeBron pays Kaitlyn more than $50 and less than $30,000, both of them are better off.

3-3b Should the United States Trade with Other Countries?

Just as individuals can benefit from specialization and trade with one another, so can populations of people in different countries. Many of the goods that Americans enjoy are produced abroad, and many of the goods produced in the United States are sold abroad. Goods produced abroad and sold domestically are called **imports**. Goods produced domestically and sold abroad are called **exports**.

To see how countries can benefit from trade, suppose there are two countries, the United States and Japan, and two goods, food and cars. Imagine that the two countries produce cars equally well: An American worker and a Japanese worker can each produce one car per month. By contrast, because the United States has more fertile land, it is better at producing food: A U.S. worker can produce 2 tons of food per month, whereas a Japanese worker can produce only 1 ton of food per month.

The principle of comparative advantage states that each good should be produced by the country that has the lower opportunity cost of producing that good. Because the opportunity cost of a car is 2 tons of food in the United States but only 1 ton of food in Japan, Japan has a comparative advantage in producing cars. Japan should produce more cars than it wants for its own use and export some of them to the United States. Similarly, because the opportunity cost of a ton of food is 1 car in Japan but only ½ car in the United States, the United States has a comparative advantage in producing food. The United States should produce more food than it wants to consume and export some to Japan. Through specialization and trade, both countries can enjoy more food and more cars.

To be sure, the issues involved in trade among nations are more complex than this example suggests. Most important, each country has many people, and trade may

LeBron James may be good at pushing a lawn-mower, but it's not his comparative advantage.

PATRICK SMITH/GETTY IMAGES SPORT/GETTY IMAGES

imports

goods produced abroad and sold domestically

exports

goods produced domestically and sold abroad

affect them in different ways. When the United States exports food and imports cars, the impact on an American farmer is not the same as the impact on an American autoworker. As a result, international trade can make some individuals worse off, even as it makes the country as a whole better off. Yet this example teaches an important lesson: Contrary to the opinions sometimes voiced by politicians and pundits, international trade is not like war, in which some countries win and others lose. Trade allows all countries to achieve greater prosperity.

3-4 Conclusion

You should now understand more fully the benefits of living in an interdependent economy. When Americans buy tube socks from China, when residents of Maine drink orange juice from Florida, and when a homeowner hires the kid next door to mow her lawn, the same economic forces are at work. The principle of comparative advantage shows that trade can make everyone better off.

Having seen why interdependence is desirable, you might ask how it is possible. How do free societies coordinate the diverse activities of all the people involved in their economies? What ensures that goods and services will get from those who should be producing them to those who should be consuming them? In a world with only two people, such as Ruby the rancher and Frank the farmer, the answer is simple: These two people can bargain and allocate resources between themselves. In the real world with billions of people, the answer is less obvious. We take up this issue in the next chapter, where we see that free societies allocate resources through the market forces of supply and demand.

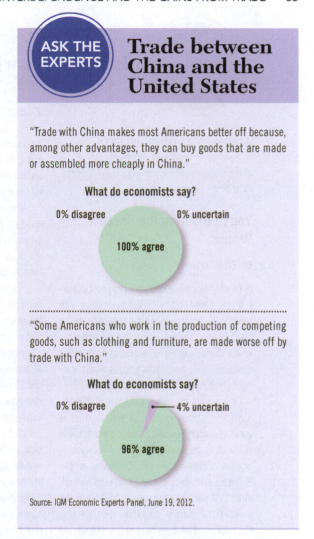

ASK THE EXPERTS

Trade between China and the United States

"Trade with China makes most Americans better off because, among other advantages, they can buy goods that are made or assembled more cheaply in China."

What do economists say?

0% disagree   0% uncertain

100% agree

"Some Americans who work in the production of competing goods, such as clothing and furniture, are made worse off by trade with China."

What do economists say?

0% disagree   4% uncertain

96% agree

Source: IGM Economic Experts Panel, June 19, 2012.

QuickQuiz

6. A nation will typically import those goods in which
   a. the nation has an absolute advantage.
   b. the nation has a comparative advantage.
   c. other nations have an absolute advantage.
   d. other nations have a comparative advantage.

7. Suppose that in the United States, producing an aircraft takes 10,000 hours of labor and producing a shirt takes 2 hours of labor. In China, producing an aircraft takes 40,000 hours of labor and producing a shirt takes 4 hours of labor. What will these nations trade?
   a. China will export aircraft, and the United States will export shirts.
   b. China will export shirts, and the United States will export aircraft.

   c. Both nations will export shirts.
   d. There are no gains from trade in this situation.

8. Kayla can cook dinner in 30 minutes and wash the laundry in 20 minutes. Her roommate takes twice as long to do each task. How should the roommates allocate the work?
   a. Kayla should do more of the cooking based on her comparative advantage.
   b. Kayla should do more of the washing based on her comparative advantage.
   c. Kayla should do more of the washing based on her absolute advantage.
   d. There are no gains from trade in this situation.

Answers at end of chapter.

Economics within a Marriage

An economist argues that you shouldn't always unload the dishwasher just because you're better at it than your partner.

You're Dividing the Chores Wrong

By Emily Oster

No one likes doing chores. In happiness surveys, housework is ranked down there with commuting as activities that people enjoy the least. Maybe that's why figuring out who does which chores usually prompts, at best, tense discussion in a household and, at worst, outright fighting.

If everyone is good at something different, assigning chores is easy. If your partner is great at grocery shopping and you are great at the laundry, you're set. But this isn't always—or even usually—the case. Often one person is better at everything. (And let's be honest, often that person is the woman.) Better at the laundry, the grocery shopping, the cleaning, the cooking. But does that mean she should have to do everything?

Before my daughter was born, I both cooked and did the dishes. It wasn't a big deal,

it didn't take too much time, and honestly I was a lot better at both than my husband. His cooking repertoire extended only to eggs and chili, and when I left him in charge of the dishwasher, I'd often find he had run it "full" with one pot and eight forks.

After we had a kid, we had more to do and less time to do it in. It seemed like it was time for some reassignments. But, of course, I was still better at doing both things. Did that mean I should do them both?

I could have appealed to the principle of fairness: We should each do half. I could have appealed to feminism—surveys show that women more often than not get the short end of the chore stick. In time-use data, women do about 44 minutes more housework than men (2 hours and 11 minutes versus 1 hour and 27 minutes). Men outwork women only in the areas of "lawn" and "exterior maintenance." I could have suggested he do more chores to rectify this imbalance, to show our daughter, in the *Free to Be You and Me* style, that Mom and Dad are equal and that housework is fun if we do it together! I could have simply smashed around the pans in the dishwasher while sighing loudly in the hopes he would notice and offer to do it himself.

But luckily for me and my husband, I'm an economist, so I have more effective tools than passive aggression. And some basic economic

principles provided the answer. We needed to divide the chores because it is simply not *efficient* for the best cook and dishwasher to do all the cooking and dishwashing. The economic principle at play here is increasing marginal cost. Basically, people get worse when they are tired. When I teach my students at the University of Chicago this principle, I explain it in the context of managing their employees. Imagine you have a good employee and a not-so-good one. Should you make the good employee do literally everything?

Usually, the answer is no. Why not? It's likely that the not-so-good employee is better at 9 a.m. after a full night of sleep than the good employee is at 2 a.m. after a 17-hour workday. So you want to give at least a few tasks to your worse guy. The same principle applies in your household. Yes, you (or your spouse) might be better at everything. But anyone doing the laundry at 4 a.m. is likely to put the red towels in with the white T-shirts. Some task splitting is a good idea. How much depends on how fast people's skills decay.

To "optimize" your family efficiency (every economist's ultimate goal—and yours, too), you want to equalize effectiveness on the final task each person is doing. Your partner does the dishes, mows the lawn, and makes the grocery list. You do the cooking, laundry, shopping,

CHAPTER IN A NUTSHELL

- Each person consumes goods and services produced by many other people both in the United States and around the world. Interdependence and trade are desirable because they allow everyone to enjoy a greater quantity and variety of goods and services.

- There are two ways to compare the abilities of two people to produce a good. The person who can produce the good with the smaller quantity of inputs is said to have an *absolute advantage* in producing the good. The person who has the lower opportunity cost

of producing the good is said to have a *comparative advantage*. The gains from trade are based on comparative advantage, not absolute advantage.

- Trade makes everyone better off because it allows people to specialize in those activities in which they have a comparative advantage.

- The principle of comparative advantage applies to countries as well as to people. Economists use the principle of comparative advantage to advocate free trade among countries.

cleaning, and paying the bills. This may seem imbalanced, but when you look at it, you see that by the time your partner gets to the grocery-list task, he is wearing thin and starting to nod off. It's all he can do to figure out how much milk you need. In fact, he is just about as good at that as you are when you get around to paying the bills, even though that's your fifth task.

If you then made your partner also do the cleaning—so it was an even four and four—the house would be a disaster, since he is already exhausted by his third chore while you are still doing fine. This system may well end up meaning one person does more, but it is unlikely to result in one person doing everything.

Once you've decided you need to divide up the chores in this way, how should you decide who does what? One option would be randomly assigning tasks; another would be having each person do some of everything. One spousal-advice website I read suggested you should divide tasks based on which ones you like the best. None of these are quite right. (In the last case, how would anyone ever end up with the job of cleaning the bathroom?)

To decide who does what, we need more economics. Specifically, the principle of comparative advantage. Economists usually talk about this in the context of trade. Imagine Finland is better than Sweden at making both reindeer hats and snowshoes. But they are much, much better at the hats and only a

little better at the snowshoes. The overall world production is maximized when Finland makes hats and Sweden makes snowshoes.

We say that Finland has an *absolute advantage* in both things but a *comparative advantage* only in hats. This principle is part of the reason economists value free trade, but that's for another column (and probably another author). But it's also a guideline for how to trade tasks in your house. You want to assign each person the tasks on which he or she has a comparative advantage. It doesn't matter that you have an absolute advantage in everything. If you are much, much better at the laundry and only a little better at cleaning the toilet, you should do the laundry and have your

ROBERT NEUBECKER

spouse get out the scrub brush. Just explain that it's efficient!

In our case, it was easy. Other than using the grill—which I freely admit is the husband domain—I'm much, much better at cooking. And I was only moderately better at the dishes. So he got the job of cleaning up after meals, even though his dishwasher loading habits had already come under scrutiny. The good news is another economic principle I hadn't even counted on was soon in play: *learning by doing*. As people do a task, they improve at it. Eighteen months into this new arrangement the dishwasher is almost a work of art: neat rows of dishes and everything carefully screened for "top-rack only" status. I, meanwhile, am forbidden from getting near the dishwasher. Apparently, there is a risk that I'll "ruin it." ∎

Questions to Discuss

1. In your family, do you think tasks are divided among family members according to comparative advantage? If so, how? If not, how might the allocation of tasks be improved?

2. Do you think being married to an economist would facilitate family harmony or just the opposite?

Ms. Oster is a professor of economics at Brown University.

Source: *Slate*, November 21, 2012.

KEY CONCEPTS

absolute advantage, *p. 50*
opportunity cost, *p. 50*

comparative advantage, *p. 51*
imports, *p. 54*

exports, *p. 54*

QUESTIONS FOR REVIEW

1. Under what conditions is the production possibilities frontier linear rather than bowed out?

2. Explain how absolute advantage and comparative advantage differ.

3. Give an example in which one person has an absolute advantage in doing something but another person has a comparative advantage.

4. Is absolute advantage or comparative advantage more important for trade? Explain your reasoning using the example in your answer to question 3.

5. If two parties trade based on comparative advantage and both gain, in what range must the price of the trade lie?

6. Why do economists oppose policies that restrict trade among nations?

PROBLEMS AND APPLICATIONS

1. Maria can read 20 pages of economics in an hour. She can also read 50 pages of sociology in an hour. She spends 5 hours per day studying.
   a. Draw Maria's production possibilities frontier for reading economics and sociology.
   b. What is Maria's opportunity cost of reading 100 pages of sociology?

2. American and Japanese workers can each produce 4 cars per year. An American worker can produce 10 tons of grain per year, whereas a Japanese worker can produce 5 tons of grain per year. To keep things simple, assume that each country has 100 million workers.
   a. For this situation, construct a table analogous to the table in Figure 1.
   b. Graph the production possibilities frontiers for the American and Japanese economies.
   c. For the United States, what is the opportunity cost of a car? Of grain? For Japan, what is the opportunity cost of a car? Of grain? Put this information in a table analogous to Table 1.
   d. Which country has an absolute advantage in producing cars? In producing grain?
   e. Which country has a comparative advantage in producing cars? In producing grain?
   f. Without trade, half of each country's workers produce cars and half produce grain. What quantities of cars and grain does each country produce?
   g. Starting from a position without trade, give an example in which trade makes each country better off.

3. Diego and Darnell are roommates. They spend most of their time studying (of course), but they leave some time for their favorite activities: making pizza and brewing root beer. Diego takes 4 hours to brew a gallon of root beer and 2 hours to make a pizza. Darnell takes 6 hours to brew a gallon of root beer and 4 hours to make a pizza.
   a. What is each roommate's opportunity cost of making a pizza? Who has the absolute advantage in making pizza? Who has the comparative advantage in making pizza?

   b. If Diego and Darnell trade foods with each other, who will trade away pizza in exchange for root beer?
   c. The price of pizza can be expressed in terms of gallons of root beer. What is the highest price at which pizza can be traded that would make both roommates better off? What is the lowest price? Explain.

4. Suppose that there are 10 million workers in Canada and that each of these workers can produce either 2 cars or 30 bushels of wheat in a year.
   a. What is the opportunity cost of producing a car in Canada? What is the opportunity cost of producing a bushel of wheat in Canada? Explain the relationship between the opportunity costs of the two goods.
   b. Draw Canada's production possibilities frontier. If Canada chooses to consume 10 million cars, how much wheat can it consume without trade? Label this point on the production possibilities frontier.
   c. Now suppose that the United States offers to buy 10 million cars from Canada in exchange for 20 bushels of wheat per car. If Canada continues to consume 10 million cars, how much wheat does this deal allow Canada to consume? Label this point on your diagram. Should Canada accept the deal?

5. England and Scotland both produce scones and sweaters. Suppose that an English worker can produce 50 scones per hour or 1 sweater per hour. Suppose that a Scottish worker can produce 40 scones per hour or 2 sweaters per hour.
   a. Which country has the absolute advantage in the production of each good? Which country has the comparative advantage?
   b. If England and Scotland decide to trade, which commodity will Scotland export to England? Explain.
   c. If a Scottish worker could produce only 1 sweater per hour, would Scotland still gain from trade? Would England still gain from trade? Explain.

6. The following table describes the production possibilities of two cities in the country of Baseballia:

	Pairs of Red Socks per Worker per Hour	Pairs of White Socks per Worker per Hour
Boston	3	3
Chicago	2	1

a. Without trade, what is the price of white socks (in terms of red socks) in Boston? What is the price in Chicago?

b. Which city has an absolute advantage in the production of each color sock? Which city has a comparative advantage in the production of each color sock?

c. If the cities trade with each other, which color sock will each export?

d. What is the range of prices at which mutually beneficial trade can occur?

7. A German worker takes 400 hours to produce a car and 2 hours to produce a case of wine. A French worker takes 600 hours to produce a car and X hours to produce a case of wine.

a. For what values of X will gains from trade be possible? Explain.

b. For what values of X will Germany export cars and import wine? Explain.

8. Suppose that in a year an American worker can produce 100 shirts or 20 computers and a Chinese worker can produce 100 shirts or 10 computers.

a. For each country, graph the production possibilities frontier. Suppose that without trade the workers in each country spend half their time producing each good. Identify this point in your graphs.

b. If these countries were open to trade, which country would export shirts? Give a specific numerical example and show it on your graphs. Which country would benefit from trade? Explain.

c. Explain at what price of computers (in terms of shirts) the two countries might trade.

d. Suppose that China catches up with American productivity so that a Chinese worker can produce 100 shirts or 20 computers in a year. What pattern of trade would you predict now? How does this advance in Chinese productivity affect the economic well-being of the two countries' citizens?

9. Are the following statements true or false? Explain in each case.

a. "Two countries can achieve gains from trade even if one of the countries has an absolute advantage in the production of all goods."

b. "Certain talented people have a comparative advantage in everything they do."

c. "If a certain trade is good for one person, it can't be good for the other one."

d. "If a certain trade is good for one person, it is always good for the other one."

e. "If trade is good for a country, it must be good for everyone in the country."

Quick**Quiz Answers**

1. **b**   2. **c**   3. **d**   4. **b**   5. **a**   6. **d**   7. **b**   8. **d**

When a cold snap hits Florida, the price of orange juice rises in supermarkets throughout the country. When the weather turns warm in New England every summer, the price of hotel rooms in the Caribbean plummets. When a war breaks out in the Middle East, the price of gasoline in the United States rises and the price of a used Cadillac falls. What do these events have in common? They all show the workings of supply and demand.

Supply and *demand* are the two words economists use most often—and for good reason. Supply and demand are the forces that make market economies work. They determine the quantity of each good produced and the price at which it is sold. If you want to know how any event or policy will affect the economy, you must think first about how it will affect supply and demand.

This chapter introduces the theory of supply and demand. It considers how buyers and sellers behave and how they interact. It shows how supply and demand determine prices in a market economy and how prices, in turn, allocate the economy's scarce resources.

The Market Forces of Supply and Demand

4-1 Markets and Competition

The terms *supply* and *demand* refer to the behavior of people as they interact with one another in competitive markets. Before discussing how buyers and sellers behave, let's first consider more fully what we mean by the terms *market* and *competition*.

4-1a What Is a Market?

market
a group of buyers and sellers of a particular good or service

A **market** is a group of buyers and sellers of a particular good or service. The buyers as a group determine the demand for the product, and the sellers as a group determine the supply of the product.

Markets take many forms. Some markets are highly organized, such as the markets for agricultural commodities like wheat and corn. In these markets, buyers and sellers meet at a specific time and place. Buyers come knowing how much they are willing to buy at various prices, and sellers come knowing how much they are willing to sell at various prices. An auctioneer facilitates the process by keeping order, arranging sales, and (most importantly) finding the price that brings the actions of buyers and sellers into balance.

More often, markets are less organized. For example, consider the market for ice cream in a particular town. Buyers of ice cream do not meet together at any one time or at any one place. The sellers of ice cream are in different locations and offer somewhat different products. There is no auctioneer calling out the price of ice cream. Each seller posts a price for an ice-cream cone, and each buyer decides how many cones to buy at each store. Nonetheless, these consumers and producers of ice cream are closely connected. The ice-cream buyers are choosing from the various ice-cream sellers to satisfy their cravings, and the ice-cream sellers are all trying to appeal to the same ice-cream buyers to make their businesses successful. Even though it is not as organized, the group of ice-cream buyers and ice-cream sellers forms a market.

4-1b What Is Competition?

The market for ice cream, like most markets in the economy, is highly competitive. Each buyer knows that there are several sellers from which to choose, and each seller is aware that his product is similar to that offered by other sellers. As a result, the price and quantity of ice cream sold are not determined by any single buyer or seller. Rather, price and quantity are determined by all buyers and sellers as they interact in the marketplace.

competitive market
a market in which there are many buyers and many sellers so that each has a negligible impact on the market price

Economists use the term **competitive market** to describe a market in which there are so many buyers and so many sellers that each has a negligible impact on the market price. Each seller of ice cream has limited control over the price because other sellers are offering similar products. A seller has little reason to charge less than the going price, and if he charges more, buyers will make their purchases elsewhere. Similarly, no single buyer of ice cream can influence the price of ice cream because each buyer purchases only a small amount.

In this chapter, we assume that markets are *perfectly competitive*. To reach this highest form of competition, a market must have two characteristics: (1) The goods offered for sale are all exactly the same, and (2) the buyers and sellers are so numerous that no single buyer or seller has any influence over the market price. Because buyers and sellers in perfectly competitive markets must accept the price the market determines, they are said to be *price takers*. At the market price, buyers can buy all they want, and sellers can sell all they want.

There are some markets in which the assumption of perfect competition applies perfectly. In the wheat market, for example, there are thousands of farmers who sell wheat and millions of consumers who use wheat and wheat products. Because no single buyer or seller can influence the price of wheat, each takes the market price as given.

Not all goods and services, however, are sold in perfectly competitive markets. Some markets have only one seller, and this seller sets the price. Such a market is called a *monopoly*. Local cable television, for instance, is a monopoly if residents of the town have only one company from which to buy cable service. Many other markets fall between the extremes of perfect competition and monopoly.

Despite the diversity of market types we find in the world, assuming perfect competition is a useful simplification and a natural place to start. Perfectly competitive markets are the easiest to analyze because everyone participating in them takes the price as given by market conditions. Moreover, because some degree of competition is present in most markets, many of the lessons that we learn by studying supply and demand under perfect competition apply to more complex markets as well.

Quick**Quiz**

1. The best definition of a market is
   a. a store that offers a variety of goods and services.
   b. a place where buyers meet and an auctioneer calls out prices.
   c. a group of buyers and sellers of a good or service.
   d. a venue where the sole supplier of a good offers its product.

2. In a perfectly competitive market,
   a. every seller tries to distinguish itself by offering a better product than its rivals.
   b. every seller takes the price of its product as set by market conditions.

   c. every seller tries to undercut the prices charged by its rivals.
   d. one seller has successfully outcompeted its rivals so no other sellers remain.

3. The market for which product best fits the definition of a perfectly competitive market?
   a. eggs
   b. tap water
   c. movies
   d. computer operating systems

Answers at end of chapter.

4-2 Demand

We begin our study of markets by examining the behavior of buyers. To focus our thinking, let's keep in mind a particular good—ice cream.

4-2a The Demand Curve: The Relationship between Price and Quantity Demanded

The **quantity demanded** of any good is the amount of the good that buyers are willing and able to purchase. As we will see, many things determine the quantity demanded of a good, but in our analysis of how markets work, one determinant plays a central role: the good's price. If the price of ice cream rose to $20 per scoop, you would buy less ice cream. You might buy frozen yogurt instead. If the price of ice cream fell to $0.50 per scoop, you would buy more. This relationship between price and quantity demanded is true for most goods in the economy and, in fact, is so pervasive that economists call it the **law of demand**: Other things being equal, when the price of a good rises, the quantity demanded of the good falls, and when the price falls, the quantity demanded rises.

quantity demanded
the amount of a good that buyers are willing and able to purchase

law of demand
the claim that, other things being equal, the quantity demanded of a good falls when the price of the good rises

FIGURE 1

Catherine's Demand Schedule and Demand Curve

The demand schedule is a table that shows the quantity demanded at each price. The demand curve, which graphs the demand schedule, illustrates how the quantity demanded of the good changes as its price varies. Because a lower price increases the quantity demanded, the demand curve slopes downward.

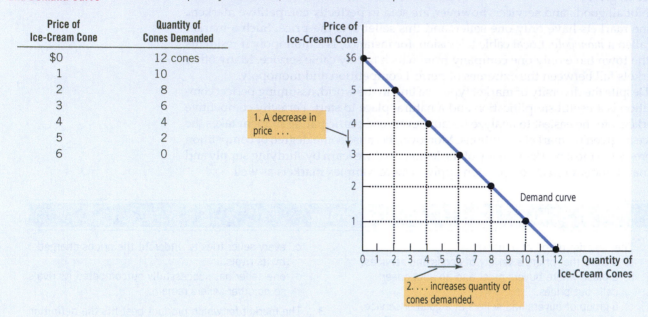

Price of Ice-Cream Cone	Quantity of Cones Demanded
$0	12 cones
1	10
2	8
3	6
4	4
5	2
6	0

1. A decrease in price . . .

2. . . . increases quantity of cones demanded.

demand schedule
a table that shows the relationship between the price of a good and the quantity demanded

demand curve
a graph of the relationship between the price of a good and the quantity demanded

The table in Figure 1 shows how many ice-cream cones Catherine would buy each month at different prices. If ice-cream cones are free, Catherine buys 12 cones per month. At $1 per cone, Catherine buys 10 cones each month. As the price rises further, she buys fewer and fewer cones. When the price reaches $6, Catherine doesn't buy any cones at all. This table is a **demand schedule**, a table that shows the relationship between the price of a good and the quantity demanded, holding constant everything else that influences how much of the good consumers want to buy.

The graph in Figure 1 uses the numbers from the table to illustrate the law of demand. By convention, the price of ice cream is on the vertical axis, and the quantity of ice cream demanded is on the horizontal axis. The line relating price and quantity demanded is called the **demand curve**. The demand curve slopes downward because, other things being equal, a lower price means a greater quantity demanded.

4-2b Market Demand versus Individual Demand

The demand curve in Figure 1 shows an individual's demand for a product. To analyze how markets work, we need to determine the *market demand*, the sum of all the individual demands for a particular good or service.

The table in Figure 2 shows the demand schedules for ice cream of the two individuals in this market—Catherine and Nicholas. At any price, Catherine's demand schedule tells us how many cones she buys, and Nicholas's demand schedule tells us how many cones he buys. The market demand at each price is the sum of the two individual demands.

The quantity demanded in a market is the sum of the quantities demanded by all the buyers at each price. Thus, the market demand curve is found by adding horizontally the individual demand curves. At a price of $4, Catherine demands 4 ice-cream cones and Nicholas demands 3 ice-cream cones. The quantity demanded in the market at this price is 7 cones.

FIGURE **2**

Market Demand as the Sum of Individual Demands

Price of Ice-Cream Cone	Catherine		Nicholas		Market
$0	12	+	7	=	19 cones
1	10		6		16
2	8		5		13
3	6		4		10
4	4		3		7
5	2		2		4
6	0		1		1

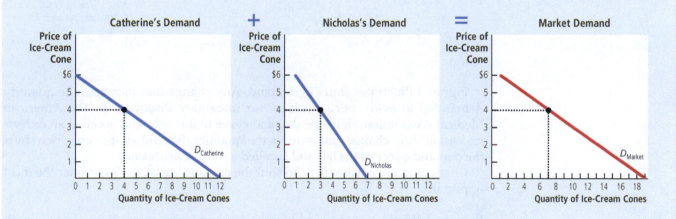

The graph in Figure 2 shows the demand curves that correspond to these demand schedules. Notice that we sum the individual demand curves *horizontally* to obtain the market demand curve. That is, to find the total quantity demanded at any price, we add the individual quantities demanded, which are found on the horizontal axis of the individual demand curves. Because we are interested in analyzing how markets function, we work most often with the market demand curve. The market demand curve shows how the total quantity demanded of a good varies as the price of the good varies, while all other factors that affect how much consumers want to buy are held constant.

4-2c Shifts in the Demand Curve

Because the market demand curve holds other things constant, it need not be stable over time. If something happens to alter the quantity demanded at any given price, the demand curve shifts. For example, suppose the American Medical Association discovers that people who regularly eat ice cream live longer, healthier lives. The discovery would raise the demand for ice cream. At any given price, buyers would now want to purchase a larger quantity of ice cream, and the demand curve for ice cream would shift.

FIGURE **3**

Shifts in the Demand Curve
Any change that raises the quantity that buyers wish to purchase at any given price shifts the demand curve to the right. Any change that lowers the quantity that buyers wish to purchase at any given price shifts the demand curve to the left.

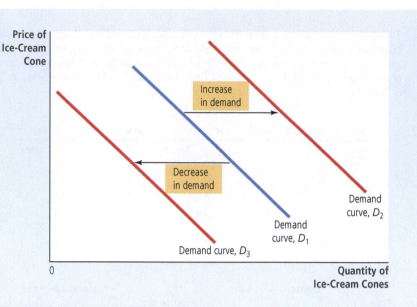

Figure 3 illustrates shifts in demand. Any change that increases the quantity demanded at every price, such as our imaginary discovery by the American Medical Association, shifts the demand curve to the right and is called an *increase in demand*. Any change that reduces the quantity demanded at every price shifts the demand curve to the left and is called a *decrease in demand*.

Changes in many variables can shift the demand curve. Let's consider the most important.

Income   What would happen to your demand for ice cream if you lost your job one summer? Most likely, your demand would fall. A lower income means that you have less to spend in total, so you would have to spend less on some—and probably most—goods. If the demand for a good falls when income falls, the good is called a **normal good**.

Normal goods are the norm, but not all goods are normal goods. If the demand for a good rises when income falls, the good is called an **inferior good**. An example of an inferior good might be bus rides. As your income falls, you are less likely to buy a car or take a cab and more likely to ride a bus.

Prices of Related Goods   Suppose that the price of frozen yogurt falls. The law of demand says that you will buy more frozen yogurt. At the same time, you will probably buy less ice cream. Because ice cream and frozen yogurt are both cold, sweet, creamy desserts, they satisfy similar desires. When a fall in the price of one good reduces the demand for another good, the two goods are called **substitutes**. Substitutes are often pairs of goods that are used in place of each other, such as hot dogs and hamburgers, sweaters and sweatshirts, and movie tickets and film streaming services.

Now suppose that the price of hot fudge falls. According to the law of demand, you will buy more hot fudge. Yet in this case, you will likely buy more ice cream as well because ice cream and hot fudge are often consumed together. When a

normal good
a good for which, other things being equal, an increase in income leads to an increase in demand

inferior good
a good for which, other things being equal, an increase in income leads to a decrease in demand

substitutes
two goods for which an increase in the price of one leads to an increase in the demand for the other

fall in the price of one good raises the demand for another good, the two goods are called **complements**. Complements are often pairs of goods that are used together, such as gasoline and automobiles, computers and software, and peanut butter and jelly.

Tastes   Perhaps the most obvious determinant of your demand for any good or service is your tastes. If you like ice cream, you buy more of it. Economists normally do not try to explain people's tastes because tastes are based on historical and psychological forces that are beyond the realm of economics. Economists do, however, examine what happens when tastes change.

Expectations   Your expectations about the future may affect your demand for a good or service today. If you expect to earn a higher income next month, you may choose to save less now and spend more of your current income on ice cream. If you expect the price of ice cream to fall tomorrow, you may be less willing to buy an ice-cream cone at today's price.

Number of Buyers   In addition to the preceding factors, which influence the behavior of individual buyers, market demand depends on the number of these buyers. If Peter were to join Catherine and Nicholas as another consumer of ice cream, the quantity demanded in the market would be higher at every price, and market demand would increase.

Summary   The demand curve shows what happens to the quantity demanded of a good as its price varies, holding constant all the other variables that influence buyers. When one of these other variables changes, the quantity demanded at each price changes, and the demand curve shifts. Table 1 lists the variables that influence how much of a good consumers choose to buy.

If you have trouble remembering whether you need to shift or move along the demand curve, it helps to recall a lesson from the appendix to Chapter 2. A curve shifts when there is a change in a relevant variable that is not measured on either axis. Because the price is on the vertical axis, a change in price represents a movement along the demand curve. By contrast, income, the prices of related goods, tastes, expectations, and the number of buyers are not measured on either axis, so a change in one of these variables shifts the demand curve.

complements
two goods for which an increase in the price of one leads to a decrease in the demand for the other

Variable	A Change in This Variable . . .
Price of the good itself	Represents a movement along the demand curve
Income	Shifts the demand curve
Prices of related goods	Shifts the demand curve
Tastes	Shifts the demand curve
Expectations	Shifts the demand curve
Number of buyers	Shifts the demand curve

TABLE 1

Variables That Influence Buyers
This table lists the variables that affect how much of any good consumers choose to buy. Notice the special role that the price of the good plays: A change in the good's price represents a movement along the demand curve, whereas a change in one of the other variables shifts the demand curve.

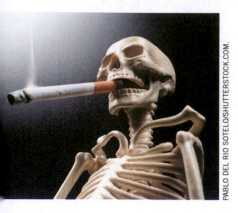

CASE STUDY

TWO WAYS TO REDUCE SMOKING

Because smoking can lead to various illnesses, policymakers often want to reduce the amount that people smoke. There are two ways that they can attempt to achieve this goal.

One way to reduce smoking is to shift the demand curve for cigarettes and other tobacco products. Public service announcements, mandatory health warnings on cigarette packages, and the prohibition of cigarette advertising on television are all policies aimed at reducing the quantity of cigarettes demanded at any given price. If successful, these policies shift the demand curve for cigarettes to the left, as in panel (a) of Figure 4.

Alternatively, policymakers can try to raise the price of cigarettes. If the government taxes the manufacture of cigarettes, for example, cigarette companies pass much of this tax on to consumers in the form of higher prices. A higher price encourages smokers to reduce the number of cigarettes they smoke. In this case, the reduced amount of smoking does not represent a shift in the demand curve. Instead, it represents a movement along the same demand curve to a point with a higher price and lower quantity, as in panel (b) of Figure 4.

How much does the amount of smoking respond to changes in the price of cigarettes? Economists have attempted to answer this question by studying what happens when the tax on cigarettes changes. They have found that a 10 percent

---

FIGURE 4

Shifts in the Demand Curve versus Movements along the Demand Curve

If warnings on cigarette packages convince smokers to smoke less, the demand curve for cigarettes shifts to the left. In panel (a), the demand curve shifts from D_1 to D_2. At a price of $4 per pack, the quantity demanded falls from 20 to 10 cigarettes per day, as reflected by the shift from point A to point B. By contrast, if a tax raises the price of cigarettes, the demand curve does not shift. Instead, we observe a movement to a different point on the demand curve. In panel (b), when the price rises from $4 to $8, the quantity demanded falls from 20 to 12 cigarettes per day, as reflected by the movement from point A to point C.

(a) A Shift in the Demand Curve

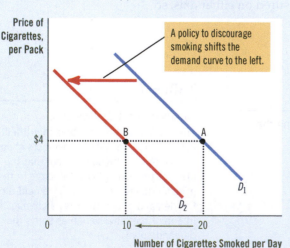

(b) A Movement along the Demand Curve

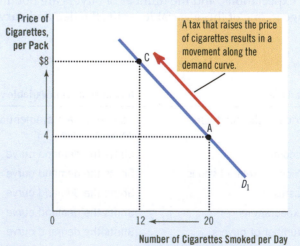

increase in the price causes a 4 percent reduction in the quantity demanded. Teenagers are especially sensitive to the price of cigarettes: A 10 percent increase in the price causes a 12 percent drop in teenage smoking.

A related question is how the price of cigarettes affects the demand for other products, such as marijuana. Opponents of cigarette taxes often argue that tobacco and marijuana are substitutes so that high cigarette prices encourage marijuana use. By contrast, many experts on substance abuse view tobacco as a "gateway drug" leading young people to experiment with other harmful substances. Most studies of the data are consistent with this latter view: They find that lower cigarette prices are associated with greater use of marijuana. In other words, tobacco and marijuana appear to be complements rather than substitutes. ●

Quick**Quiz**

4. A change in which of the following will NOT shift the demand curve for hamburgers?
    a. the price of hot dogs
    b. the price of hamburgers
    c. the price of hamburger buns
    d. the income of hamburger consumers

5. Which of the following will shift the demand curve for pizza to the right?
    a. an increase in the price of hamburgers, a substitute for pizza
    b. an increase in the price of root beer, a complement to pizza

    c. the departure of college students, as they leave for summer vacation
    d. a decrease in the price of pizza

6. If pasta is an inferior good, then the demand curve shifts to the _____ when _____ rises.
    a. right; the price of pasta
    b. right; consumers' income
    c. left; the price of pasta
    d. left; consumers' income

Answers at end of chapter.

4-3 Supply

We now turn to the other side of the market and examine the behavior of sellers. Once again, to focus our thinking, let's consider the market for ice cream.

4-3a The Supply Curve: The Relationship between Price and Quantity Supplied

The **quantity supplied** of any good or service is the amount that sellers are willing and able to sell. There are many determinants of quantity supplied, but once again, price plays a special role in our analysis. When the price of ice cream is high, selling ice cream is quite profitable, and so the quantity supplied is large. Sellers of ice cream work long hours, buy many ice-cream machines, and hire many workers. By contrast, when the price of ice cream is low, the business is less profitable, so sellers produce less ice cream. At a low price, some sellers may even shut down, reducing their quantity supplied to zero. This relationship between price and quantity supplied is called the **law of supply**: Other things being equal, when the price of a good rises, the quantity supplied of the good also rises, and when the price falls, the quantity supplied falls as well.

The table in Figure 5 shows the quantity of ice-cream cones supplied each month by Ben, an ice-cream seller, at various prices of ice cream. At a price below $2, Ben does not supply any ice cream at all. As the price rises, he supplies

quantity supplied
the amount of a good that sellers are willing and able to sell

law of supply
the claim that, other things being equal, the quantity supplied of a good rises when the price of the good rises

FIGURE 5

Ben's Supply Schedule and Supply Curve

The supply schedule is a table that shows the quantity supplied at each price. This supply curve, which graphs the supply schedule, illustrates how the quantity supplied of the good changes as its price varies. Because a higher price increases the quantity supplied, the supply curve slopes upward.

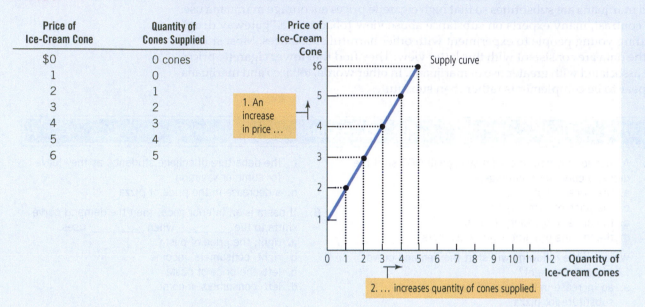

Price of Ice-Cream Cone	Quantity of Cones Supplied
$0	0 cones
1	0
2	1
3	2
4	3
5	4
6	5

1. An increase in price …

2. … increases quantity of cones supplied.

supply schedule
a table that shows the relationship between the price of a good and the quantity supplied

supply curve
a graph of the relationship between the price of a good and the quantity supplied

a greater and greater quantity. This is the **supply schedule**, a table that shows the relationship between the price of a good and the quantity supplied, holding constant everything else that influences how much of the good producers want to sell.

The graph in Figure 5 uses the numbers from the table to illustrate the law of supply. The curve relating price and quantity supplied is called the **supply curve**. The supply curve slopes upward because, other things being equal, a higher price means a greater quantity supplied.

4-3b Market Supply versus Individual Supply

Just as market demand is the sum of the demands of all buyers, market supply is the sum of the supplies of all sellers. The table in Figure 6 shows the supply schedules for the two ice-cream producers in the market—Ben and Jerry. At any price, Ben's supply schedule tells us the quantity of ice cream that Ben supplies, and Jerry's supply schedule tells us the quantity of ice cream that Jerry supplies. The market supply is the sum of the two individual supplies.

The graph in Figure 6 shows the supply curves that correspond to the supply schedules. As with demand curves, we sum the individual supply curves *horizontally* to obtain the market supply curve. That is, to find the total quantity supplied at any price, we add the individual quantities, which are found on the horizontal axis of the individual supply curves. The market supply curve shows how the total quantity supplied varies as the price of the good varies, holding constant all other factors that influence producers' decisions about how much to sell.

The quantity supplied in a market is the sum of the quantities supplied by all the sellers at each price. Thus, the market supply curve is found by adding horizontally the individual supply curves. At a price of $4, Ben supplies 3 ice-cream cones and Jerry supplies 4 ice-cream cones. The quantity supplied in the market at this price is 7 cones.

FIGURE 6

Market Supply as the Sum of Individual Supplies

Price of Ice-Cream Cone	Ben		Jerry		Market
$0	0	+	0	=	0 cones
1	0		0		0
2	1		0		1
3	2		2		4
4	3		4		7
5	4		6		10
6	5		8		13

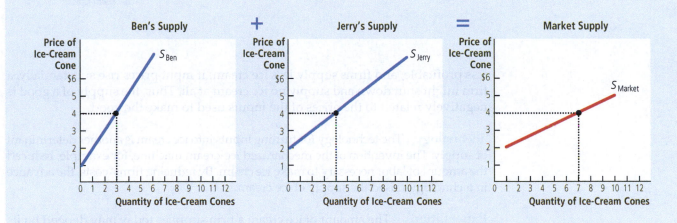

4-3c   Shifts in the Supply Curve

Because the market supply curve is drawn holding other things constant, when one of these factors changes, the supply curve shifts. For example, suppose the price of sugar falls. Sugar is an input in the production of ice cream, so the lower price of sugar makes selling ice cream more profitable. This raises the supply of ice cream: At any given price, sellers are now willing to produce a larger quantity. As a result, the supply curve for ice cream shifts to the right.

Figure 7 illustrates shifts in supply. Any change that raises quantity supplied at every price, such as a fall in the price of sugar, shifts the supply curve to the right and is called an *increase in supply*. Any change that reduces the quantity supplied at every price shifts the supply curve to the left and is called a *decrease in supply*.

There are many variables that can shift the supply curve. Let's consider the most important ones.

Input Prices   To produce their output of ice cream, sellers use various inputs: cream, sugar, flavoring, ice-cream machines, the buildings in which the ice cream is made, and the labor of workers who mix the ingredients and operate the machines. When the price of one or more of these inputs rises, producing ice cream becomes

FIGURE 7

Shifts in the Supply Curve
Any change that raises the quantity
that sellers wish to produce at any
given price shifts the supply curve to
the right. Any change that lowers the
quantity that sellers wish to produce
at any given price shifts the supply
curve to the left.

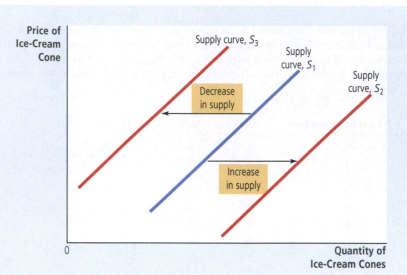

less profitable, and firms supply less ice cream. If input prices rise substantially, a
firm might shut down and supply no ice cream at all. Thus, the supply of a good is
negatively related to the prices of the inputs used to make the good.

Technology   The technology for turning inputs into ice cream is another determinant
of supply. The invention of the mechanized ice-cream machine, for example, reduced
the amount of labor necessary to make ice cream. By reducing firms' costs, the advance
in technology raised the supply of ice cream.

Expectations   The amount of ice cream a firm supplies today may depend on its
expectations about the future. For example, if a firm expects the price of ice cream
to rise in the future, it will put some of its current production into storage and supply less to the market today.

Number of Sellers   In addition to the preceding factors, which influence the
behavior of individual sellers, market supply depends on the number of these
sellers. If Ben or Jerry were to retire from the ice-cream business, the supply in the
market would fall.

Summary   The supply curve shows what happens to the quantity supplied of a
good when its price varies, holding constant all the other variables that influence
sellers. When one of these other variables changes, the quantity supplied at each
price changes, and the supply curve shifts. Table 2 lists the variables that influence
how much of a good producers choose to sell.
   Once again, to remember whether you need to shift or move along the supply curve, keep in mind that a curve shifts only when there is a change in a
relevant variable that is not named on either axis. The price is on the vertical
axis, so a change in price represents a movement along the supply curve. By
contrast, because input prices, technology, expectations, and the number of sellers are not measured on either axis, a change in one of these variables shifts the
supply curve.

Variable	A Change in This Variable . . .
Price of the good itself	Represents a movement along the supply curve
Input prices	Shifts the supply curve
Technology	Shifts the supply curve
Expectations	Shifts the supply curve
Number of sellers	Shifts the supply curve

TABLE 2

Variables That Influence Sellers
This table lists the variables that affect how much of any good producers choose to sell. Notice the special role that the price of the good plays: A change in the good's price represents a movement along the supply curve, whereas a change in one of the other variables shifts the supply curve.

Quick**Quiz**

7. Which of the following moves the pizza market up along a given supply curve?
   a. an increase in the price of pizza
   b. an increase in the price of root beer, a complement to pizza
   c. a decrease in the price of cheese, an input to pizza
   d. a kitchen fire that destroys a popular pizza joint

8. Which of the following shifts the supply curve for pizza to the right?
   a. an increase in the price of pizza
   b. an increase in the price of root beer, a complement to pizza

   c. a decrease in the price of cheese, an input to pizza
   d. a kitchen fire that destroys a popular pizza joint

9. Movie tickets and film streaming services are substitutes. If the price of film streaming increases, what happens in the market for movie tickets?
   a. The supply curve shifts to the left.
   b. The supply curve shifts to the right.
   c. The demand curve shifts to the left.
   d. The demand curve shifts to the right.

Answers at end of chapter.

4-4 Supply and Demand Together

Having analyzed supply and demand separately, we now combine them to see how they determine the price and quantity of a good sold in a market.

4-4a Equilibrium

Figure 8 shows the market supply curve and market demand curve together. Notice that there is one point at which the supply and demand curves intersect. This point is called the market's **equilibrium**. The price at this intersection is called the **equilibrium price**, and the quantity is called the **equilibrium quantity**. Here the equilibrium price is $2.00 per cone, and the equilibrium quantity is 7 ice-cream cones.

The dictionary defines the word *equilibrium* as a situation in which various forces are in balance. This definition applies to a market's equilibrium as well. *At the equilibrium price, the quantity of the good that buyers are willing and able to buy exactly balances the quantity that sellers are willing and able to sell.* The equilibrium price is sometimes called the *market-clearing price* because, at this price, everyone in the market has been satisfied: Buyers have bought all they want to buy, and sellers have sold all they want to sell.

equilibrium
a situation in which the market price has reached the level at which quantity supplied equals quantity demanded

equilibrium price
the price that balances quantity supplied and quantity demanded

equilibrium quantity
the quantity supplied and the quantity demanded at the equilibrium price

FIGURE 8

The Equilibrium of Supply and Demand

The equilibrium is found where the supply and demand curves intersect. At the equilibrium price, the quantity supplied equals the quantity demanded. Here the equilibrium price is $4: At this price, 7 ice-cream cones are supplied and 7 ice-cream cones are demanded.

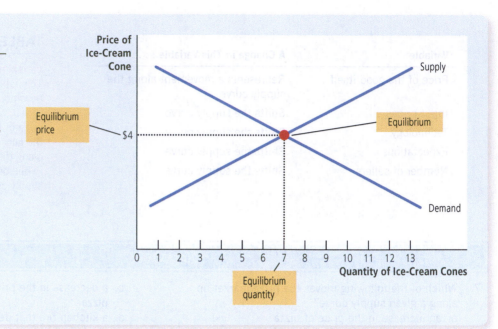

surplus

a situation in which quantity supplied is greater than quantity demanded

shortage

a situation in which quantity demanded is greater than quantity supplied

The actions of buyers and sellers naturally move markets toward the equilibrium of supply and demand. To see why, consider what happens when the market price is not equal to the equilibrium price.

Suppose first that the market price is above the equilibrium price, as in panel (a) of Figure 9. At a price of $5 per cone, the quantity of the good supplied (10 cones) exceeds the quantity demanded (4 cones). There is a **surplus** of the good: Producers are unable to sell all they want at the going price. A surplus is sometimes called a situation of *excess supply*. When there is a surplus in the ice-cream market, sellers of ice cream find their freezers increasingly full of ice cream they would like to sell but cannot. They respond to the surplus by cutting their prices. Falling prices, in turn, increase the quantity demanded and decrease the quantity supplied. These changes represent movements *along* the supply and demand curves, not shifts in the curves. Prices continue to fall until the market reaches the equilibrium.

Suppose now that the market price is below the equilibrium price, as in panel (b) of Figure 9. In this case, the price is $3 per cone, and the quantity of the good demanded exceeds the quantity supplied. There is a **shortage** of the good: Consumers are unable to buy all they want at the going price. A shortage is sometimes called a situation of *excess demand*. When a shortage occurs in the ice-cream market, buyers have to wait in long lines for a chance to buy one of the few cones available. With too many buyers chasing too few goods, sellers can respond to the shortage by raising their prices without losing sales. These price increases cause the quantity demanded to fall and the quantity supplied to rise. Once again, these changes represent movements *along* the supply and demand curves, and they move the market toward the equilibrium.

Thus, regardless of whether the price starts off too high or too low, the activities of the many buyers and sellers automatically push the market price toward the equilibrium price. Once the market reaches its equilibrium, all buyers and sellers are satisfied, and there is no upward or downward pressure on the price. How quickly equilibrium is reached varies from market to market depending on how quickly prices adjust. In most free markets, surpluses and shortages are

In panel (a), there is a surplus. Because the market price of $5 is above the equilibrium price, the quantity supplied (10 cones) exceeds the quantity demanded (4 cones). Producers try to increase sales by cutting the price of a cone, which moves the price toward its equilibrium level. In panel (b), there is a shortage. Because the market price of $3 is below the equilibrium price, the quantity demanded (10 cones) exceeds the quantity supplied (4 cones). With too many buyers chasing too few goods, producers can take advantage of the shortage by raising the price. Hence, in both cases, the price adjustment moves the market toward the equilibrium of supply and demand.

FIGURE 9

Markets Not in Equilibrium

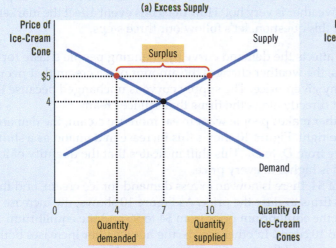

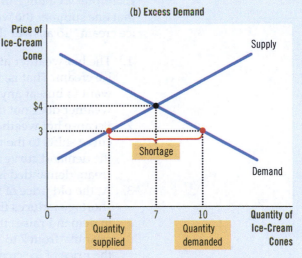

only temporary because prices eventually move toward their equilibrium levels. Indeed, this phenomenon is so pervasive that it is called the **law of supply and demand**: The price of any good adjusts to bring the quantity supplied and quantity demanded of that good into balance.

4-4b Three Steps to Analyzing Changes in Equilibrium
So far, we have seen how supply and demand together determine a market's equilibrium, which in turn determines the price and quantity of the good that buyers purchase and sellers produce. The equilibrium price and quantity depend on the positions of the supply and demand curves. When some event shifts one of these curves, the equilibrium in the market changes, resulting in a new price and a new quantity exchanged between buyers and sellers.

law of supply and demand
the claim that the price of any good adjusts to bring the quantity supplied and the quantity demanded of that good into balance

When analyzing how some event affects the equilibrium in a market, we proceed in three steps. First, we decide whether the event shifts the supply curve, the demand curve, or, in some cases, both. Second, we decide whether the curve shifts to the right or to the left. Third, we use the supply-and-demand diagram to compare the initial equilibrium with the new one, which shows how the shift affects the equilibrium price and quantity. Table 3 summarizes these three steps. To see how this recipe is used, let's consider various events that might affect the market for ice cream.

Example: A Change in Market Equilibrium Due to a Shift in Demand   Suppose that one summer the weather is very hot. How does this event affect the market for ice cream? To answer this question, let's follow our three steps.

1. The hot weather affects the demand curve by changing people's taste for ice cream. That is, the weather changes the amount of ice cream that people want to buy at any given price. The supply curve is unchanged because the weather does not directly affect the firms that sell ice cream.
2. Because hot weather makes people want to eat more ice cream, the demand curve shifts to the right. Figure 10 shows this increase in demand as a shift in the demand curve from D_1 to D_2. This shift indicates that the quantity of ice cream demanded is higher at every price.
3. At the old price of $4, there is now an excess demand for ice cream, and this shortage induces firms to raise the price. As Figure 10 shows, the increase in demand raises the equilibrium price from $4 to $5 and the equilibrium quantity from 7 to 10 cones. In other words, the hot weather increases both the price of ice cream and the quantity of ice cream sold.

Shifts in Curves versus Movements along Curves   Notice that when hot weather increases the demand for ice cream and drives up the price, the quantity of ice cream that firms supply rises, even though the supply curve remains the same. In this case, economists say there has been an increase in "quantity supplied" but no change in "supply."

Supply refers to the position of the supply curve, whereas the *quantity supplied* refers to the amount producers wish to sell. In this example, supply does not change because the weather does not alter firms' desire to sell at any given price. Instead, the hot weather alters consumers' desire to buy at any given price and thereby shifts the demand curve to the right. The increase in demand causes the equilibrium price to rise. When the price rises, the quantity supplied rises. This increase in quantity supplied is represented by the movement along the supply curve.

TABLE **3**	
Three Steps for Analyzing Changes in Equilibrium	1. Decide whether the event shifts the supply or demand curve (or perhaps both). 2. Decide in which direction the curve shifts. 3. Use the supply-and-demand diagram to see how the shift changes the equilibrium price and quantity.

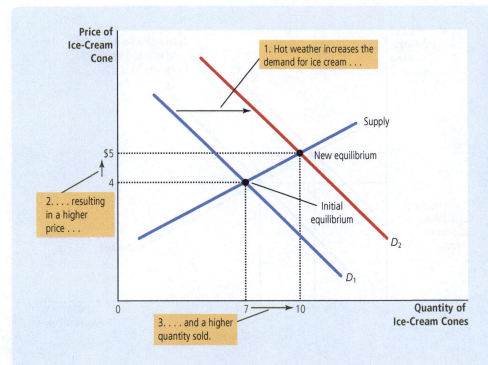

FIGURE 10

How an Increase in Demand Affects the Equilibrium
An event that raises quantity demanded at any given price shifts the demand curve to the right. The equilibrium price and the equilibrium quantity both rise. Here an abnormally hot summer causes buyers to demand more ice cream. The demand curve shifts from D_1 to D_2, which causes the equilibrium price to rise from $4 to $5 and the equilibrium quantity to rise from 7 to 10 cones.

To summarize, a shift *in* the supply curve is called a "change in supply," and a shift *in* the demand curve is called a "change in demand." A movement *along* a fixed supply curve is called a "change in the quantity supplied," and a movement *along* a fixed demand curve is called a "change in the quantity demanded."

Example: A Change in Market Equilibrium Due to a Shift in Supply Suppose that during another summer, a hurricane destroys part of the sugarcane crop and drives up the price of sugar. How does this event affect the market for ice cream? Once again, to answer this question, we follow our three steps.

1. The change in the price of sugar, an input for making ice cream, affects the supply curve. By raising the costs of production, it reduces the amount of ice cream that firms produce and sell at any given price. The demand curve does not change because the higher cost of inputs does not directly affect the amount of ice cream consumers wish to buy.
2. The supply curve shifts to the left because, at every price, the total amount that firms are willing and able to sell is reduced. Figure 11 illustrates this decrease in supply as a shift in the supply curve from S_1 to S_2.
3. At the old price of $4, there is now an excess demand for ice cream, and this shortage causes firms to raise the price. As Figure 11 shows, the shift in the supply curve raises the equilibrium price from $4 to $5 and lowers the equilibrium quantity from 7 to 4 cones. As a result of the sugar price increase, the price of ice cream rises, and the quantity of ice cream sold falls.

FIGURE 11

How a Decrease in Supply Affects the Equilibrium
An event that reduces quantity supplied at any given price shifts the supply curve to the left. The equilibrium price rises, and the equilibrium quantity falls. Here an increase in the price of sugar (an input) causes sellers to supply less ice cream. The supply curve shifts from S_1 to S_2, which causes the equilibrium price of ice cream to rise from $4 to $5 and the equilibrium quantity to fall from 7 to 4 cones.

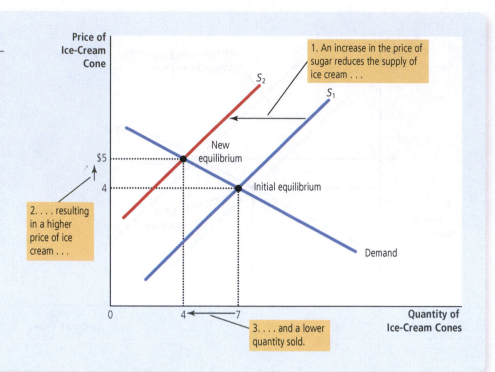

Price of Ice-Cream Cone

1. An increase in the price of sugar reduces the supply of ice cream . . .

S_2

S_1

New equilibrium

$5

2. . . . resulting in a higher price of ice cream . . .

4

Initial equilibrium

Demand

0   4   7

3. . . . and a lower quantity sold.

Quantity of Ice-Cream Cones

Example: Shifts in Both Supply and Demand   Now suppose that the heat wave and the hurricane occur during the same summer. To analyze this combination of events, we again follow our three steps.

1. We determine that both curves must shift. The hot weather affects the demand curve because it alters the amount of ice cream that consumers want to buy at any given price. At the same time, when the hurricane drives up sugar prices, it alters the supply curve for ice cream because it changes the amount of ice cream that firms want to sell at any given price.
2. The curves shift in the same directions as they did in our previous analysis: The demand curve shifts to the right, and the supply curve shifts to the left. Figure 12 illustrates these shifts.
3. As Figure 12 shows, two possible outcomes might result depending on the relative size of the demand and supply shifts. In both cases, the equilibrium price rises. In panel (a), where demand increases substantially while supply falls just a little, the equilibrium quantity also rises. By contrast, in panel (b), where supply falls substantially while demand rises just a little, the equilibrium quantity falls. Thus, these events certainly raise the price of ice cream, but their impact on the amount of ice cream sold is ambiguous (that is, it could go either way).

Here we observe a simultaneous increase in demand and decrease in supply. Two outcomes are possible. In panel (a), the equilibrium price rises from P_1 to P_2, and the equilibrium quantity rises from Q_1 to Q_2. In panel (b), the equilibrium price again rises from P_1 to P_2, but the equilibrium quantity falls from Q_1 to Q_2.

FIGURE 12

A Shift in Both Supply and Demand

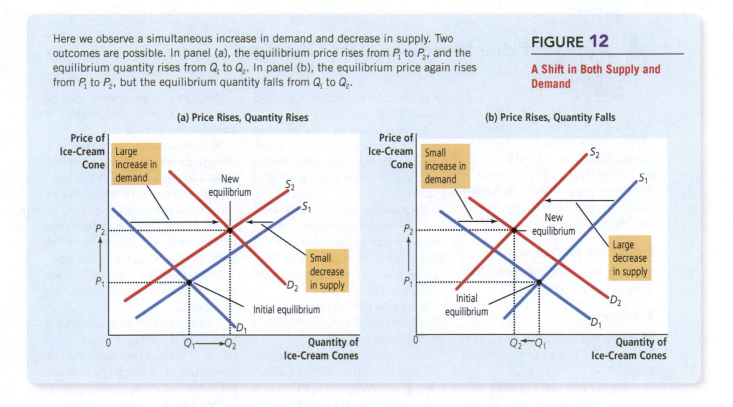

(a) Price Rises, Quantity Rises

(b) Price Rises, Quantity Falls

Summary   We have just seen three examples of how to use supply and demand curves to analyze a change in equilibrium. Whenever an event shifts the supply curve, the demand curve, or perhaps both curves, you can use these tools to predict how the event will alter the price and quantity sold in equilibrium. Table 4 shows the predicted outcome for any combination of shifts in the two curves. To make sure you understand how to use the tools of supply and demand, pick a few entries in this table and make sure you can explain to yourself why the table contains the prediction that it does.

	No Change in Supply	An Increase in Supply	A Decrease in Supply
No Change in Demand	P same Q same	P down Q up	P up Q down
An Increase in Demand	P up Q up	P ambiguous Q up	P up Q ambiguous
A Decrease in Demand	P down Q down	P down Q ambiguous	P ambiguous Q down

TABLE 4

What Happens to Price and Quantity When Supply or Demand Shifts?
As a quick quiz, make sure you can explain at least a few of the entries in this table using a supply-and-demand diagram.

IN THE NEWS

Price Increases after Disasters

When a disaster such as a hurricane strikes a region, many goods experience an increase in demand or a decrease in supply, putting upward pressure on prices. Policymakers often object to these price hikes, but some economists disagree.

Economists don't think price gouging is a problem. But what about our social values?

By Adriene Hill

Charging flood victims $30 for a case of water or $10 for a gallon of gas doesn't sit right.

And a majority of states, including Texas, have laws against price gouging. The state attorney general has threatened to prosecute people who jack up their prices in the wake of the flooding caused by Hurricane Harvey.

He said his office has received hundreds of reports of profiteering.

But most economists think those high prices can actually benefit communities during a crisis. Sky-high prices are the market at work, the basic laws of supply and demand in action.

"Price gouging laws stand in the way of the normal workings of competitive markets," explained Michael Salinger, an economics professor at Boston University and former director of the Bureau of Economics at the Federal Trade Commission.

To make his point, Salinger recounted a "Dennis the Menace" cartoon he remembers from his childhood.

Dennis asked his father what causes tides. "The moon," his father answered. Dennis offered up another explanation, that the tides were caused by a big whale in the ocean. When the whale swishes his tail one way, the tide goes in, and when he swishes his tail the other way, the tide goes out.

"You don't really believe that?" asked the father. "No," said Dennis, "but it makes a lot more sense than the moon."

Salinger said letting the markets work, allowing price hikes during disasters is the moon answer. It isn't intuitive, he said, but it's right.

There are a couple of reasons economists don't like laws against price gouging.

On the demand side, laws that keep prices artificially low can encourage overbuying. They benefit the people who get to the store first.

"If prices don't rise," explained Texas Tech economics professor Michael Giberson, "they just get plenty."

If water is cheap, I might be tempted to buy as much as I can jam in my car—just in case. If, on the other hand, prices shoot up, Giberson said, "it encourages consumers to be a little more careful in using the goods."

There's also a supply-side argument that economists make.

"When the price of vital goods go up in an area affected by an emergency, that sends a

QuickQuiz

10. The discovery of a large new reserve of crude oil will shift the _____ curve for gasoline, leading to a _____ equilibrium price.
    a. supply; higher
    b. supply; lower
    c. demand; higher
    d. demand; lower

11. If the economy goes into a recession and incomes fall, what happens in the markets for inferior goods?
    a. Prices and quantities both rise.
    b. Prices and quantities both fall.
    c. Prices rise and quantities fall.
    d. Prices fall and quantities rise.

12. Which of the following might lead to an increase in the equilibrium price of jelly and a decrease in the equilibrium quantity of jelly sold?
    a. an increase in the price of peanut butter, a complement to jelly

    b. an increase in the price of Marshmallow Fluff, a substitute for jelly
    c. an increase in the price of grapes, an input into jelly
    d. an increase in consumers' incomes, as long as jelly is a normal good

13. An increase in _____ will cause a movement along a given supply curve, which is called a change in _____.
    a. supply; demand
    b. supply; quantity demanded
    c. demand; supply
    d. demand; quantity supplied

Answers at end of chapter.

signal to areas not affected by the emergency to bring more," explained Matt Zwolinski, director of the University of San Diego's Center for Ethics, Economics, and Public Policy.

Zwolinski argues that the practice of price gouging can actually be admirable from a purely moral perspective: "It allocates goods and services in a way that best meets human needs."

But, as with so much of economics, there is disagreement.

What are economists missing when they make these arguments?

"They are misunderstanding that if you piss people off, you pay a price," said Richard Thaler, an economist at the Booth School of Business at the University of Chicago. Thaler co-wrote a well-known paper on price gouging that looked at what people think is fair.

It begins with the following scenario: A hardware store has been selling snow shovels for $15, and the morning after a blizzard, it raises the price to $20.

Thaler and his colleagues asked people if they thought that was fair.

How much would you pay for this in an emergency?

"And people hate it," he said. "They all think that's a terrible idea."

Thaler argued that any business that wants to still be in business tomorrow shouldn't raise

prices, because when it's time to rebuild, no one is going to want to buy new flooring from the guy that sold them the generator for double the normal rate.

Businesses and economists should pay more attention to our shared social values, argued Thaler. "During a time of crisis, it's a time for all of us to pitch in, it's not a time for us to grab."

We have to think beyond the laws of supply and demand, he said, beyond pure economics. ∎

Questions to Discuss

1. After a disaster, do you think you are more or less likely to find water for sale if sellers are allowed to increase prices? Why?

2. If sellers of scarce resources are not allowed to increase prices to equilibrate supply and demand after a disaster, how do you think these resources should be allocated among the population? What are the benefits of your proposal? What problems might arise with your proposal in practice?

Source: Marketplace.org, September 1, 2017.

4-5 Conclusion: How Prices Allocate Resources

This chapter has analyzed supply and demand in a single market. Our discussion has centered on the market for ice cream, but the lessons learned here apply to most other markets as well. Whenever you go to a store to buy something, you are contributing to the demand for that item. Whenever you look for a job, you are contributing to the supply of labor services. Because supply and demand are such pervasive economic phenomena, the model of supply and demand is a powerful tool for analysis. We use this model repeatedly in the following chapters.

"Two dollars" *"—and seventy-five cents."*

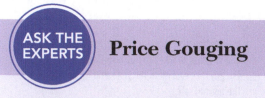

Price Gouging

"Connecticut should pass its Senate Bill 60, which states that during a 'severe weather event emergency, no person within the chain of distribution of consumer goods and services shall sell or offer to sell consumer goods or services for a price that is unconscionably excessive.'"

What do economists say?

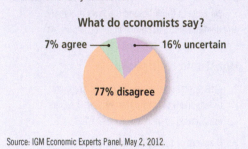

7% agree · 16% uncertain

77% disagree

Source: IGM Economic Experts Panel, May 2, 2012.

One of the *Ten Principles of Economics* in Chapter 1 is that markets are usually a good way to organize economic activity. Although it is still too early to judge whether market outcomes are good or bad, in this chapter we have begun to see how markets work. In any economic system, scarce resources have to be allocated among competing uses. Market economies harness the forces of supply and demand to serve that end. Supply and demand together determine the prices of the economy's many different goods and services; prices in turn are the signals that guide the allocation of resources.

For example, consider the allocation of beachfront land. Because the amount of this land is limited, not everyone can enjoy the luxury of living by the beach. Who gets this resource? The answer is whoever is willing and able to pay the price. The price of beachfront land adjusts until the quantity of land demanded exactly balances the quantity supplied. Thus, in market economies, prices are the mechanism for rationing scarce resources.

Similarly, prices determine who produces each good and how much is produced. For instance, consider farming. Because we need food to survive, it is crucial that some people work on farms. What determines who is a farmer and who is not? In a free society, there is no government planning agency making this decision and ensuring an adequate supply of food. Instead, the allocation of workers to farms is based on the job decisions of millions of workers. This decentralized system works well because these decisions depend on prices. The prices of food and the wages of farmworkers (the price of their labor) adjust to ensure that enough people choose to be farmers.

If a person had never seen a market economy in action, the whole idea might seem preposterous. Economies are enormous groups of people engaged in a multitude of interdependent activities. What prevents decentralized decision making from degenerating into chaos? What coordinates the actions of the millions of people with their varying abilities and desires? What ensures that what needs to be done is in fact done? The answer, in a word, is *prices*. If an invisible hand guides market economies, as Adam Smith famously suggested, the price system is the baton with which the invisible hand conducts the economic orchestra.

CHAPTER IN A NUTSHELL

- Economists use the model of supply and demand to analyze competitive markets. In a competitive market, there are many buyers and sellers, each of whom has little or no influence on the market price.
- The demand curve shows how the quantity of a good demanded depends on the price. According to the law of demand, as the price of a good falls, the quantity demanded rises. Therefore, the demand curve slopes downward.
- In addition to price, other determinants of how much consumers want to buy include income, the prices of substitutes and complements, tastes, expectations, and the number of buyers. When one of these factors changes, the quantity demanded at each price changes, and the demand curve shifts.

- The supply curve shows how the quantity of a good supplied depends on the price. According to the law of supply, as the price of a good rises, the quantity supplied rises. Therefore, the supply curve slopes upward.
- In addition to price, other determinants of how much producers want to sell include input prices, technology,

expectations, and the number of sellers. When one of these factors changes, the quantity supplied at each price changes, and the supply curve shifts.

- The intersection of the supply and demand curves represents the market equilibrium. At the equilibrium price, the quantity demanded equals the quantity supplied.

- The behavior of buyers and sellers naturally drives markets toward their equilibrium. When the market price is above the equilibrium price, there is a surplus of the good, which causes the market price to fall. When the market price is below the equilibrium price, there is a shortage, which causes the market price to rise.

- To analyze how any event influences the equilibrium price and quantity in a market, we use the supply-and-demand diagram and follow three steps. First, we decide whether the event shifts the supply curve or the demand curve (or both). Second, we decide in which direction the curve shifts. Third, we compare the new equilibrium with the initial equilibrium.

- In market economies, prices are the signals that guide decisions and allocate scarce resources. For every good in the economy, the price ensures that supply and demand are in balance. The equilibrium price then determines how much of the good buyers choose to consume and how much sellers choose to produce.

KEY CONCEPTS

market, *p. 62*
competitive market, *p. 62*
quantity demanded, *p. 63*
law of demand, *p. 63*
demand schedule, *p. 64*
demand curve, *p. 64*
normal good, *p. 66*

inferior good, *p. 66*
substitutes, *p. 66*
complements, *p. 67*
quantity supplied, *p. 69*
law of supply, *p. 69*
supply schedule, *p. 70*
supply curve, *p. 70*

equilibrium, *p. 73*
equilibrium price, *p. 73*
equilibrium quantity, *p. 73*
surplus, *p. 74*
shortage, *p. 74*
law of supply and demand, *p. 75*

QUESTIONS FOR REVIEW

1. What is a competitive market? Briefly describe a type of market that is *not* perfectly competitive.

2. What are the demand schedule and the demand curve, and how are they related? Why does the demand curve slope downward?

3. Does a change in consumers' tastes lead to a movement along the demand curve or to a shift in the demand curve? Does a change in price lead to a movement along the demand curve or to a shift in the demand curve? Explain your answers.

4. Harry's income declines, and as a result, he buys more pumpkin juice. Is pumpkin juice an inferior or a normal good? What happens to Harry's demand curve for pumpkin juice?

5. What are the supply schedule and the supply curve, and how are they related? Why does the supply curve slope upward?

6. Does a change in producers' technology lead to a movement along the supply curve or to a shift in the supply curve? Does a change in price lead to a movement along the supply curve or to a shift in the supply curve?

7. Define the equilibrium of a market. Describe the forces that move a market toward its equilibrium.

8. Beer and pizza are complements because they are often enjoyed together. When the price of beer rises, what happens to the supply, demand, quantity supplied, quantity demanded, and price in the market for pizza?

9. Describe the role of prices in market economies.

PROBLEMS AND APPLICATIONS

1. Explain each of the following statements using supply-and-demand diagrams.
   a. "When a cold snap hits Florida, the price of orange juice rises in supermarkets throughout the country."
   b. "When the weather turns warm in New England every summer, the price of hotel rooms in Caribbean resorts plummets."
   c. "When a war breaks out in the Middle East, the price of gasoline rises and the price of a used Cadillac falls."

2. "An increase in the demand for notebooks raises the quantity of notebooks demanded but not the quantity supplied." Is this statement true or false? Explain.

3. Consider the market for minivans. For each of the events listed here, identify which of the determinants of demand or supply are affected. Also indicate whether demand or supply increases or decreases. Then draw a diagram to show the effect on the price and quantity of minivans.
   a. People decide to have more children.
   b. A strike by steelworkers raises steel prices.
   c. Engineers develop new automated machinery for the production of minivans.
   d. The price of sports utility vehicles rises.
   e. A stock market crash lowers people's wealth.

4. Consider the markets for film streaming services, TV screens, and tickets at movie theaters.
   a. For each pair, identify whether they are complements or substitutes:
      • Film streaming and TV screens
      • Film streaming and movie tickets
      • TV screens and movie tickets
   b. Suppose a technological advance reduces the cost of manufacturing TV screens. Draw a diagram to show what happens in the market for TV screens.
   c. Draw two more diagrams to show how the change in the market for TV screens affects the markets for film streaming and movie tickets.

5. Over the past 40 years, technological advances have reduced the cost of computer chips. How do you think this has affected the market for computers? For computer software? For typewriters?

6. Using supply-and-demand diagrams, show the effects of the following events on the market for sweatshirts.
   a. A hurricane in South Carolina damages the cotton crop.
   b. The price of leather jackets falls.

   c. All colleges require morning exercise in appropriate attire.
   d. New knitting machines are invented.

7. Ketchup is a complement (as well as a condiment) for hot dogs. If the price of hot dogs rises, what happens in the market for ketchup? For tomatoes? For tomato juice? For orange juice?

8. The market for pizza has the following demand and supply schedules:

Price	Quantity Demanded	Quantity Supplied
$4	135 pizzas	26 pizzas
5	104	53
6	81	81
7	68	98
8	53	110
9	39	121

   a. Graph the demand and supply curves. What are the equilibrium price and quantity in this market?
   b. If the actual price in this market were *above* the equilibrium price, what would drive the market toward the equilibrium?
   c. If the actual price in this market were *below* the equilibrium price, what would drive the market toward the equilibrium?

9. Consider the following events: Scientists reveal that eating oranges decreases the risk of diabetes, and at the same time, farmers use a new fertilizer that makes orange trees produce more oranges. Illustrate and explain what effect these changes have on the equilibrium price and quantity of oranges.

10. Because bagels and cream cheese are often eaten together, they are complements.
    a. We observe that both the equilibrium price of cream cheese and the equilibrium quantity of bagels have risen. What could be responsible for this pattern: a fall in the price of flour or a fall in the price of milk? Illustrate and explain your answer.
    b. Suppose instead that the equilibrium price of cream cheese has risen but the equilibrium quantity of bagels has fallen. What could be responsible for this pattern: a rise in the price of flour or a rise in the price of milk? Illustrate and explain your answer.

11. Suppose that the price of basketball tickets at your college is determined by market forces. Currently, the demand and supply schedules are as follows:

Price	Quantity Demanded	Quantity Supplied
$4	10,000 tickets	8,000 tickets
8	8,000	8,000
12	6,000	8,000
16	4,000	8,000
20	2,000	8,000

a. Draw the demand and supply curves. What is unusual about this supply curve? Why might this be true?

b. What are the equilibrium price and quantity of tickets?

c. Your college plans to increase total enrollment next year by 5,000 students. The additional students will have the following demand schedule:

Price	Quantity Demanded
$4	4,000 tickets
8	3,000
12	2,000
16	1,000
20	0

Now add the old demand schedule and the demand schedule for the new students to calculate the new demand schedule for the entire college. What will be the new equilibrium price and quantity?

When you finish school and start looking for a full-time job, your experience will, to a large extent, be shaped by prevailing economic conditions. In some years, firms throughout the economy are expanding their production of goods and services, employment is rising, and jobs are easy to find. In other years, firms are cutting back production, employment is declining, and jobs are hard to find. Not surprisingly, any college graduate would rather enter the labor force in a year of economic expansion than in a year of economic contraction.

Because the health of the overall economy profoundly affects all of us, changes in economic conditions are widely reported by the media. Indeed, it is hard to pick up a newspaper, check an online news service, or turn on the TV without seeing some newly reported economic statistic. The statistic might measure the total income of everyone in the economy (gross domestic product), the rate at which average prices are rising or falling (inflation/deflation), the percentage of the labor force that is out of work (unemployment), total spending at stores (retail sales), or the imbalance of trade between the

Measuring a Nation's Income

United States and the rest of the world (the trade deficit). All these statistics are *macroeconomic*. Rather than telling us about a particular household, firm, or market, they tell us something about the entire economy.

As you may recall from Chapter 2, economics is divided into two branches: microeconomics and macroeconomics. **Microeconomics** is the study of how individual households and firms make decisions and how they interact with one another in markets. **Macroeconomics** is the study of the economy as a whole. The goal of macroeconomics is to explain the economic changes that affect many households, firms, and markets simultaneously. Macroeconomists address a broad variety of questions: Why is average income high in some countries and low in others? Why are prices sometimes rapidly rising and other times more stable? Why do production and employment expand in some years and contract in others? What, if anything, can the government do to promote rapid growth in incomes, low inflation, and stable employment? These questions are all macroeconomic in nature because they concern the workings of the entire economy.

Because the economy as a whole is a collection of many households and many firms interacting in many markets, microeconomics and macroeconomics are closely linked. The tools of supply and demand, for instance, are as central to macroeconomic analysis as they are to microeconomic analysis. Yet studying the economy in its entirety raises some new and intriguing challenges.

In this and the next chapter, we discuss some of the data that economists and policymakers use to monitor the performance of the overall economy. These data reflect the economic changes that macroeconomists try to explain. This chapter considers *gross domestic product* (GDP), which measures the total income of a nation. GDP is the most closely watched economic statistic because it is thought to be the single best measure of a society's economic well-being.

microeconomics
the study of how households and firms make decisions and how they interact in markets

macroeconomics
the study of economy-wide phenomena, including inflation, unemployment, and economic growth

5-1 The Economy's Income and Expenditure

If you were to judge how a person is doing economically, you might first look at her income. A person with a high income can more easily afford life's necessities and luxuries. It is no surprise that people with higher incomes enjoy higher standards of living—larger houses, better healthcare, fancier cars, more opulent vacations, and so on.

The same logic applies to a nation's overall economy. When judging whether the economy is doing well or poorly, it is natural to look at the aggregate income that everyone in the economy is earning. Gross domestic product allows us to do just that.

GDP measures two things at once: the total income of everyone in the economy and the total expenditure on the economy's output of goods and services. GDP can perform the trick of measuring both total income and total expenditure because these two things are the same. *For an economy as a whole, income must equal expenditure.*

Why is this true? An economy's income equals its expenditure because every transaction has two parties: a buyer and a seller. Every dollar of spending by some buyer is a dollar of income for some seller. Suppose, for instance, that Karen pays Doug $100 to mow her lawn. In this case, Doug is a seller of a service and Karen is a buyer. Doug earns $100 and Karen spends $100. Thus, the transaction contributes equally to the economy's income and to its expenditure. GDP, whether measured as total income or total expenditure, rises by $100.

Another way to see the equality of income and expenditure is with the circular-flow diagram in Figure 1. As you may recall from Chapter 2, this diagram describes all the transactions between households and firms in a simple economy. It simplifies matters by assuming that all goods and services are bought by households and that households spend all of their income. In this economy, when households buy goods and services from firms, these expenditures flow through the markets for goods and services. When the firms use the money they receive from sales to pay workers' wages, landowners' rent, and firm owners' profit, this income flows through the markets for the factors of production. Money continuously flows from households to firms and then back to households.

GDP measures this flow of money. We can compute it for this economy in either of two ways: by adding up the total expenditure by households or by adding up the total income (wages, rent, and profit) paid by firms. Because all expenditure in the economy ends up as someone's income, GDP is the same regardless of how we compute it.

The actual economy is, of course, more complicated than the one illustrated in Figure 1. Households do not spend all of their income; they pay some of it to the government in taxes, and they save some for use in the future. In addition, households do not buy all goods and services produced in the economy; some goods and services are bought by governments, and some are bought by firms that plan to use them in the future to produce their own output. Yet the basic lesson remains the same: Regardless of whether a household, government, or firm buys a good or service, the transaction always has a buyer and a seller. Thus, for the economy as a whole, expenditure and income are the same.

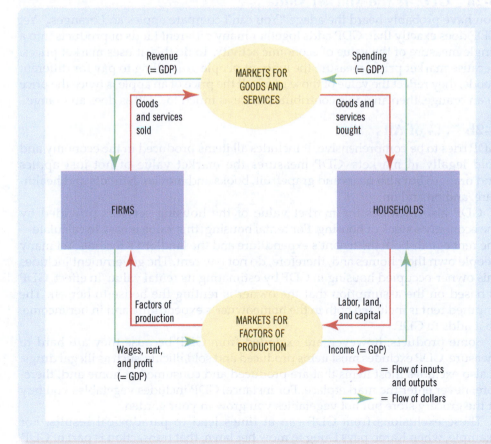

FIGURE 1

The Circular-Flow Diagram
Households buy goods and services from firms, and firms use their revenue from sales to pay wages to workers, rent to landowners, and profit to firm owners. GDP equals the total amount spent by households in the market for goods and services. It also equals the total wages, rent, and profit paid by firms in the markets for the factors of production.

5-2 The Measurement of GDP

Having discussed the meaning of gross domestic product in general terms, let's be more precise about how this statistic is measured. Here is a definition of GDP that focuses on GDP as a measure of total expenditure:

gross domestic product (GDP)

the market value of all final goods and services produced within a country in a given period of time

- **Gross domestic product (GDP)** is the market value of all final goods and services produced within a country in a given period of time.

This definition might seem simple enough. But in fact, many subtle issues arise when computing an economy's GDP. Let's therefore consider each phrase in this definition with some care.

5-2a "GDP Is the Market Value . . ."

You have probably heard the adage "You can't compare apples and oranges." Yet GDP does exactly that. GDP adds together many different kinds of products into a single measure of the value of economic activity. To do this, it uses market prices. Because market prices measure the amount people are willing to pay for different goods, they reflect the value of those goods. If the price of an apple is twice the price of an orange, then an apple contributes twice as much to GDP as does an orange.

5-2b ". . . of All . . ."

GDP tries to be comprehensive. It includes all items produced in the economy and sold legally in markets. GDP measures the market value of not just apples and oranges but also pears and grapefruit, books and movies, haircuts and health-care, and on and on.

GDP also includes the market value of the housing services provided by the economy's stock of housing. For rental housing, this value is easy to calculate—the rent equals both the tenant's expenditure and the landlord's income. Yet many people own their homes and, therefore, do not pay rent. The government includes this owner-occupied housing in GDP by estimating its rental value. In effect, GDP is based on the assumption that the owner is renting the house to herself. The imputed rent is included both in the homeowner's expenditure and in her income, so it adds to GDP.

Some products, however, are excluded from GDP because they are hard to measure. GDP excludes most items produced and sold illicitly, such as illegal drugs. It also excludes most items that are produced and consumed at home and, therefore, never enter the marketplace. For instance, GDP includes vegetables you buy at the grocery store but not vegetables you grow in your garden.

These exclusions from GDP can at times lead to paradoxical results. For example, when Karen pays Doug to mow her lawn, that transaction is part of GDP.

But suppose Doug and Karen get married. Even though Doug may continue to mow Karen's lawn, the value of the mowing is now left out of GDP because Doug's service is no longer sold in a market. Thus, their marriage reduces GDP.

5-2c "... Final ..."

When International Paper makes paper, which Hallmark then uses to make a greeting card, the paper is called an *intermediate good* and the card is called a *final good*. GDP includes only the value of final goods because the value of intermediate goods is already included in the prices of the final goods. Adding the market value of the paper to the market value of the card would be double counting. That is, it would (incorrectly) count the paper twice.

An important exception to this principle arises when an intermediate good is produced and, rather than being used, is added to a firm's inventory of goods for use or sale at a later date. In this case, the intermediate good is taken to be "final" for the moment, and its value as inventory investment is included as part of GDP. Thus, additions to inventory add to GDP, and when the goods in inventory are later used or sold, the reductions in inventory subtract from GDP.

5-2d "... Goods and Services ..."

GDP includes both tangible goods (food, clothing, cars) and intangible services (haircuts, housecleaning, doctor visits). When you buy a CD by your favorite band, you are buying a good, and the purchase price is part of GDP. When you pay to hear a concert by the same band, you are buying a service, and the ticket price is also part of GDP.

5-2e "... Produced ..."

GDP includes goods and services currently produced. It does not include transactions involving items produced in the past. When Ford produces and sells a new car, the value of the car is included in GDP. But when one person sells a used car to another person, the value of the used car is not included in GDP.

5-2f "... Within a Country ..."

GDP measures the value of production within the geographic confines of a country. When a Canadian citizen works temporarily in the United States, her production counts toward U.S. GDP. When an American citizen owns a factory in Haiti, the production at her factory does not contribute to U.S. GDP. (It contributes to Haiti's GDP.) Thus, items are included in a nation's GDP if they are produced domestically, regardless of the nationality of the producer.

5-2g "... In a Given Period of Time."

GDP measures the value of production that takes place within a specific interval of time. Usually, that interval is a year or a quarter (three months). GDP measures the economy's flow of income, as well as its flow of expenditure, during that interval.

When the government reports the GDP for a quarter, it usually presents GDP "at an annual rate." This means that the figure reported for quarterly GDP is the amount of income and expenditure during the quarter multiplied by four. The government uses this convention so that quarterly and annual figures on GDP can be compared more easily.

In addition, when the government reports quarterly GDP, it presents the data after they have been modified by a statistical procedure called *seasonal adjustment*. The unadjusted data show that the economy produces more goods and services during some times of the year than during others. (As you might guess,

December's holiday shopping season is a high point.) When monitoring the economy, economists and policymakers often want to look beyond these regular seasonal changes. Therefore, government statisticians adjust the quarterly data to take out the seasonal cycle. The GDP data reported in the news are always seasonally adjusted.

Now let's repeat the definition of GDP:

- Gross domestic product (GDP) is the market value of all final goods and services produced within a country in a given period of time.

This definition focuses on GDP as total expenditure in the economy. But recall that every dollar spent by a buyer of a good or service becomes a dollar of income to the seller of that good or service. Therefore, in addition to adding up total expenditure in the economy to calculate GDP, the government also adds up total income in the economy to arrive at *gross domestic income* (GDI). GDP and GDI give almost exactly the same number. (Why "almost"? The two measures should be precisely the same, but data sources are not perfect. The difference between GDP and GDI is called the *statistical discrepancy*.)

It should be apparent that GDP is a sophisticated measure of the value of economic activity. In advanced courses in macroeconomics, you will learn more about the nuances of its calculation. But even now you can see that each phrase in this definition is packed with meaning.

FYI   Other Measures of Income

When the U.S. Department of Commerce computes the nation's GDP, it also computes various other measures of income to get a more complete picture of what's happening in the economy. These other measures differ from GDP by excluding or including certain categories of income. What follows is a brief description of five of these income measures, ordered from largest to smallest.

- *Gross national product* (GNP) is the total income earned by a nation's permanent residents (called *nationals*). It differs from GDP in that it includes income that our citizens earn abroad and excludes income that foreigners earn here. For example, when a Canadian citizen works temporarily in the United States, her production is part of U.S. GDP, but it is not part of U.S. GNP. (It is part of Canada's GNP.) For most countries, including the United States, domestic residents are responsible for most domestic production, so GDP and GNP are quite close.
- *Net national product* (NNP) is the total income of a nation's residents (GNP) minus losses from depreciation. *Depreciation* is the wear and tear on the economy's stock of equipment and structures, such as trucks rusting and old computer models becoming obsolete. In the national income accounts prepared by the Department of Commerce, depreciation is called the "consumption of fixed capital."
- *National income* is the total income earned by a nation's residents in the production of goods and services. It is almost identical to

net national product. These two measures differ because of the *statistical discrepancy* that arises from problems in data collection.

- *Personal income* is the income that households and noncorporate businesses receive. Unlike national income, it excludes *retained earnings*, the income that corporations earn but do not pay out to their owners. It also subtracts indirect business taxes (such as sales taxes), corporate income taxes, and contributions for social insurance (mostly Social Security taxes). In addition, personal income includes the interest income that households receive from their holdings of government debt and the income that households receive from government transfer programs, such as welfare and Social Security.
- *Disposable personal income* is the income that households and noncorporate businesses have left after satisfying all their obligations to the government. It equals personal income minus personal taxes and certain nontax payments (such as traffic tickets).

Although the various measures of income differ in detail, they almost always tell the same story about economic conditions. When GDP grows rapidly, these other measures of income tend to grow rapidly. And when GDP falls, these other measures tend to fall as well. As a result, for monitoring fluctuations in the overall economy, it does not matter much which measure of income we use. ■

QuickQuiz

3. If the price of a hot dog is $2 and the price of a hamburger is $4, then 30 hot dogs contribute as much to GDP as _____ hamburgers.
   a. 5
   b. 15
   c. 30
   d. 60

4. Angus the sheep farmer sells wool to Barnaby the knitter for $20. Barnaby makes two sweaters, each of which has a market price of $40. Collette buys one of them, while the other remains on the shelf of Barnaby's store to be sold later. What is GDP here?

    a. $40
    b. $60
    c. $80
    d. $100

5. After graduation, an American college student moves to Japan to teach English. Her salary is included
   a. only in U.S. GDP.
   b. only in Japan's GDP.
   c. in both U.S. GDP and Japan's GDP.
   d. in neither U.S. GDP nor Japan's GDP.

Answers at end of chapter.

5-3 The Components of GDP

Spending in an economy takes many forms. At any moment, the Lopez family may be having lunch at Burger King; Ford may be building a car factory; the U.S. Navy may be procuring a submarine; and British Airways may be buying an airplane from Boeing. GDP includes all of these various forms of spending on domestically produced goods and services.

To understand how the economy is using its scarce resources, economists study the composition of GDP among various types of spending. To do this, GDP (which we denote as Y) is divided into four components: consumption (C), investment (I), government purchases (G), and net exports (NX):

$$Y = C + I + G + NX.$$

This equation is an *identity*—an equation that must be true because of how the variables in the equation are defined. In this case, because each dollar of expenditure included in GDP is placed into one of the four components of GDP, the total of the four components must be equal to GDP. Let's look at each of these four components more closely.

5-3a Consumption

Consumption is spending by households on goods and services, with the exception of purchases of new housing. Goods include durable goods, such as automobiles and appliances, and nondurable goods, such as food and clothing. Services include such intangible items as haircuts and medical care. Household spending on education is also included in consumption of services (although one might argue that it would fit better in the next component).

consumption
spending by households on goods and services, with the exception of purchases of new housing

5-3b Investment

Investment is the purchase of goods (called *capital goods*) that will be used in the future to produce more goods and services. Investment is the sum of purchases of business capital, residential capital, and inventories. Business capital includes business structures (such as a factory or office building), equipment (such as a

investment
spending on business capital, residential capital, and inventories

worker's computer), and intellectual property products (such as the software that runs the computer). Residential capital includes the landlord's apartment building and a homeowner's personal residence. By convention, the purchase of a new house is the one type of household spending categorized as investment rather than consumption.

As mentioned earlier, the treatment of inventory accumulation is noteworthy. When Apple produces a computer and adds it to its inventory instead of selling it, Apple is assumed to have "purchased" the computer for itself. That is, the national income accountants treat the computer as part of Apple's investment spending. (When Apple later sells the computer out of inventory, the sale will subtract from Apple's inventory investment, offsetting the positive expenditure of the buyer.) Inventories are treated this way because GDP aims to measure the value of the economy's production, and goods added to inventory are part of that period's production.

Note that GDP accounting uses the word *investment* differently from how you might hear the term in everyday conversation. When you hear the word *investment*, you might think of financial investments, such as stocks, bonds, and mutual funds—topics that we study later in this book. By contrast, because GDP measures expenditure on goods and services, here the word *investment* means purchases of goods (such as business capital, residential structures, and inventories) that will be used to produce other goods and services in the future.

5-3c Government Purchases

government purchases
spending on goods and services by local, state, and federal governments

Government purchases measure spending on goods and services by local, state, and federal governments. This component includes the salaries of government workers as well as expenditures on public works. Recently, the U.S. national income accounts have switched to the longer label *government consumption expenditure and gross investment*, but here we will use the traditional and shorter term *government purchases*.

The meaning of government purchases requires some clarification. When the government pays the salary of an Army general or a schoolteacher, that salary is included in government purchases. But when the government pays a Social Security benefit to an elderly person or an unemployment insurance benefit to a recently laid off worker, the story is very different: These are called *transfer payments* because they are not made in exchange for a currently produced good or service. Transfer payments alter household income, but they do not reflect the economy's production. (From a macroeconomic standpoint, transfer payments are like negative taxes.) Because GDP is intended to measure income from, and expenditure on, the production of goods and services, transfer payments are not counted as government purchases.

5-3d Net Exports

net exports
spending on domestically produced goods by foreigners (exports) minus spending on foreign goods by domestic residents (imports)

Net exports equal the foreign purchases of domestically produced goods (exports) minus the domestic purchases of foreign goods (imports). A domestic firm's sale to a buyer in another country, such as Boeing's sale of an airplane to British Airways, increases net exports.

The *net* in *net exports* refers to the fact that imports are subtracted from exports. This subtraction is made because other components of GDP include imports of goods and services. For example, suppose that a household buys a $50,000 car from Volvo, the Swedish carmaker. This transaction increases consumption by $50,000 because car purchases are part of consumer spending. It also reduces net exports by $50,000 because the car is an import. In other words, net exports include goods and services produced abroad (with a minus sign) because these goods and services are included in consumption, investment, and government purchases (with a plus sign). Thus, when a domestic household, firm, or government buys a good or service from abroad, the purchase does not affect GDP because it reduces net exports by the same amount that it raises consumption, investment, or government purchases.

THE COMPONENTS OF U.S. GDP

Table 1 shows the composition of U.S. GDP in 2018. In this year, the GDP of the United States was more than $20 trillion. Dividing this number by the 2018 U.S. population of 327 million yields GDP per person (sometimes called GDP per capita) and reveals that the income and expenditure of the average American in 2018 was $62,609.

Consumption made up 68 percent of GDP, or $42,609 per person. Investment was $11,154 per person. Government purchases were $10,758 per person. Net exports were –$1,911 per person. This number is negative because Americans spent more on foreign goods than foreigners spent on American goods.

These data come from the Bureau of Economic Analysis, the part of the U.S. Department of Commerce that produces the national income accounts. You can find more recent data on GDP on its website, http://www.bea.gov. ●

	Total (in billions of dollars)	Per Person (in dollars)	Percent of Total
Gross domestic product, Y	$20,501	$62,609	100%
Consumption, C	13,952	42,609	68
Investment, I	3,652	11,154	18
Government purchases, G	3,523	10,758	17
Net exports, NX	–626	–1,911	–3

Source: U.S. Department of Commerce. Parts may not sum to totals due to rounding.

TABLE 1

GDP and Its Components
This table shows total GDP for the U.S. economy in 2018 and the breakdown of GDP among its four components. When reading this table, recall the identity $Y = C + I + G + NX$.

Quick Quiz

6. Which of the following does NOT add to U.S. GDP?
   a. Boeing manufactures and sells a plane to Air France.
   b. General Motors builds a new auto factory in North Carolina.
   c. The city of New York pays a salary to a policeman.
   d. The federal government sends a Social Security check to your grandmother.

7. An American buys a pair of shoes made in Italy. How do the U.S. national income accounts treat the transaction?
   a. Net exports and GDP both rise.
   b. Net exports and GDP both fall.
   c. Net exports fall, while GDP does not change.
   d. Net exports do not change, while GDP rises.

8. Which is the largest component of GDP?
   a. consumption
   b. investment
   c. government purchases
   d. net exports

Answers at end of chapter.

5-4 Real versus Nominal GDP

As we have seen, GDP measures the total spending on goods and services in all markets in the economy. If total spending rises from one year to the next, at least one of two things must be true: (1) the economy is producing a larger output of goods and services, or (2) goods and services are being sold at higher prices. When studying changes in the economy over time, economists want to separate these two effects. In particular, they want a measure of the total quantity of goods and services the economy is producing independent of changes in the prices of those goods and services.

To do this, economists use a measure called *real GDP*. Real GDP answers a hypothetical question: What would be the value of the goods and services produced this year if valued using the prices that prevailed in some specific year in the past? By evaluating current production using prices that are fixed at past levels, real GDP shows how the economy's overall production of goods and services changes over time.

To see more precisely how real GDP is constructed, let's consider an example.

5-4a A Numerical Example

Table 2 shows some data for an economy that produces only two goods: hot dogs and hamburgers. The table shows the prices and quantities produced of the two goods in the years 2019, 2020, and 2021.

To compute total spending in this economy, we multiply the quantities of hot dogs and hamburgers by their prices. In the year 2019, 100 hot dogs are sold at a price of $1 per hot dog, so expenditure on hot dogs equals $100. In the same year, 50 hamburgers are sold for $2 per hamburger, so expenditure on hamburgers also

---

TABLE 2

Real and Nominal GDP

This table shows how to calculate real GDP, nominal GDP, and the GDP deflator for a hypothetical economy that produces only hot dogs and hamburgers.

	Prices and Quantities			
Year	Price of Hot Dogs	Quantity of Hot Dogs	Price of Hamburgers	Quantity of Hamburgers
2019	$1	100	$2	50
2020	2	150	3	100
2021	3	200	4	150

Calculating Nominal GDP

2019	($1 per hot dog × 100 hot dogs) + ($2 per hamburger × 50 hamburgers) = $200
2020	($2 per hot dog × 150 hot dogs) + ($3 per hamburger × 100 hamburgers) = $600
2021	($3 per hot dog × 200 hot dogs) + ($4 per hamburger × 150 hamburgers) = $1,200

Calculating Real GDP (base year 2019)

2019	($1 per hot dog × 100 hot dogs) + ($2 per hamburger × 50 hamburgers) = $200
2020	($1 per hot dog × 150 hot dogs) + ($2 per hamburger × 100 hamburgers) = $350
2021	($1 per hot dog × 200 hot dogs) + ($2 per hamburger × 150 hamburgers) = $500

Calculating the GDP Deflator

2019	($200/$200) × 100 = 100
2020	($600/$350) × 100 = 171
2021	($1,200/$500) × 100 = 240

equals $100. Total expenditure in the economy—the sum of expenditure on hot dogs and expenditure on hamburgers—is $200. This amount, the production of goods and services valued at current prices, is called **nominal GDP**.

The table shows the calculation of nominal GDP for these three years. Total spending rises from $200 in 2019 to $600 in 2020 and then to $1,200 in 2021. Part of this rise is attributable to the increase in the quantities of hot dogs and hamburgers, and part is attributable to the increase in the prices of hot dogs and hamburgers.

To remove the effect of price changes and obtain a measure of the amount produced, we use **real GDP**, which is the production of goods and services valued at constant prices. We calculate real GDP by first designating one year as a *base year*. We then use the prices of hot dogs and hamburgers in the base year to compute the value of goods and services in all the years. In other words, the prices in the base year provide the basis for comparing quantities in different years.

Suppose that we choose 2019 to be the base year in our example. We can then use the prices of hot dogs and hamburgers in 2019 to compute the value of goods and services produced in 2019, 2020, and 2021. Table 2 shows these calculations. To compute real GDP for 2019, we multiply the prices of hot dogs and hamburgers in 2019 (the base year) by the quantities of hot dogs and hamburgers produced in 2019. (Thus, for the base year, real GDP always equals nominal GDP.) To compute real GDP for 2020, we multiply the prices of hot dogs and hamburgers in 2019 (the base year) by the quantities of hot dogs and hamburgers produced in 2020. Similarly, to compute real GDP for 2021, we multiply the prices in 2019 by the quantities in 2021. When we find that real GDP has risen from $200 in 2019 to $350 in 2020 and then to $500 in 2021, we know that the increase is attributable to an increase in the quantities produced because the prices are being held fixed at base-year levels.

To sum up: *Nominal GDP uses current prices to value the economy's production of goods and services. Real GDP uses constant base-year prices to value the economy's production of goods and services.* Because price changes do not affect real GDP, changes in real GDP reflect only changes in the quantities produced. Thus, real GDP measures the economy's production of goods and services.

Our goal in computing GDP is to gauge how well the overall economy is performing. Because real GDP measures the economy's production of goods and services, it reflects the economy's ability to satisfy people's needs and desires. Thus, real GDP is a better gauge of economic well-being than is nominal GDP. When economists talk about the economy's GDP, they usually mean real GDP rather than nominal GDP. And when they talk about growth in the economy, they measure that growth as the percentage change in real GDP from one period to another.

5-4b The GDP Deflator

As we have just seen, nominal GDP reflects both the quantities of goods and services the economy is producing and the prices of those goods and services. By contrast, by holding prices constant at base-year levels, real GDP reflects only the quantities produced. From these two statistics, we can compute a third, called the GDP deflator, which reflects only the prices of goods and services.

The **GDP deflator** is calculated as follows:

$$\text{GDP deflator} = \frac{\text{Nominal GDP}}{\text{Real GDP}} \times 100.$$

Because nominal GDP and real GDP must be the same in the base year, the GDP deflator for the base year always equals 100. The GDP deflator for subsequent years measures the change in nominal GDP from the base year that cannot be attributable to a change in real GDP.

nominal GDP
the production of goods and services valued at current prices

real GDP
the production of goods and services valued at constant prices

GDP deflator
a measure of the price level calculated as the ratio of nominal GDP to real GDP times 100

The GDP deflator measures the current level of prices relative to the level of prices in the base year. To see why this is true, consider a couple of simple examples. First, imagine that the quantities produced in the economy rise over time but prices remain the same. In this case, both nominal and real GDP rise at the same rate, so the GDP deflator is constant. Now suppose, instead, that prices rise over time but the quantities produced stay the same. In this second case, nominal GDP rises but real GDP remains the same, so the GDP deflator rises. Notice that, in both cases, the GDP deflator reflects what's happening to prices but not to quantities.

Let's now return to our numerical example in Table 2. The GDP deflator is computed at the bottom of the table. For the year 2019, nominal GDP is $200 and real GDP is $200, so the GDP deflator is 100. (The deflator is always 100 in the base year.) For the year 2020, nominal GDP is $600 and real GDP is $350, so the GDP deflator is 171.

Economists use the term *inflation* to describe a situation in which the economy's overall price level is rising. The *inflation rate* is the percentage change in some measure of the price level from one period to the next. Using the GDP deflator, the inflation rate between two consecutive years is computed as follows:

$$\text{Inflation rate in year 2} = \frac{\text{GDP deflator in year 2} - \text{GDP deflator in year 1}}{\text{GDP deflator in year 1}} \times 100.$$

Because the GDP deflator rose in year 2020 from 100 to 171, the inflation rate is $100 \times (171 - 100)/100$, or 71 percent. In 2021, the GDP deflator rose to 240 from 171 the previous year, so the inflation rate is $100 \times (240 - 171)/171$, or 40 percent.

The GDP deflator is one measure that economists use to monitor the average level of prices in the economy and thus the rate of inflation. The GDP deflator gets its name because it can be used to take inflation out of nominal GDP—that is, to "deflate" nominal GDP for the rise that is due to increases in prices. In the next chapter, we examine another measure of the economy's price level, called the *consumer price index*, and discuss the differences between the two measures.

A HALF CENTURY OF REAL GDP

Now that we know how real GDP is defined and measured, let's look at what this macroeconomic variable tells us about the recent history of the United States. Figure 2 shows quarterly data on real GDP for the U.S. economy since 1965.

The most obvious feature of these data is that real GDP grows over time. The real GDP of the U.S. economy in 2018 was more than four times its 1965 level. Put differently, the output of goods and services produced in the United States has grown on average about 3 percent per year. Because this continued growth in real GDP exceeds the rate of population growth, it enables most Americans to enjoy greater economic prosperity than their parents and grandparents did.

A second feature of the GDP data is that growth is not steady. The upward climb of real GDP is occasionally interrupted by periods during which GDP declines, called *recessions*. Figure 2 marks recessions with shaded vertical bars. (There is no ironclad rule for when the official business cycle dating committee will declare that a recession has occurred, but an old rule of thumb is two consecutive quarters of falling real GDP.) Recessions are associated not only with lower incomes but also with other forms of economic distress: rising unemployment, falling profits, increased bankruptcies, and so on.

This figure shows quarterly data on real GDP for the U.S. economy since 1965.
Recessions—periods of falling real GDP—are marked with the shaded vertical bars.

FIGURE 2

Real GDP in the United States

Source: U.S. Department of Commerce.

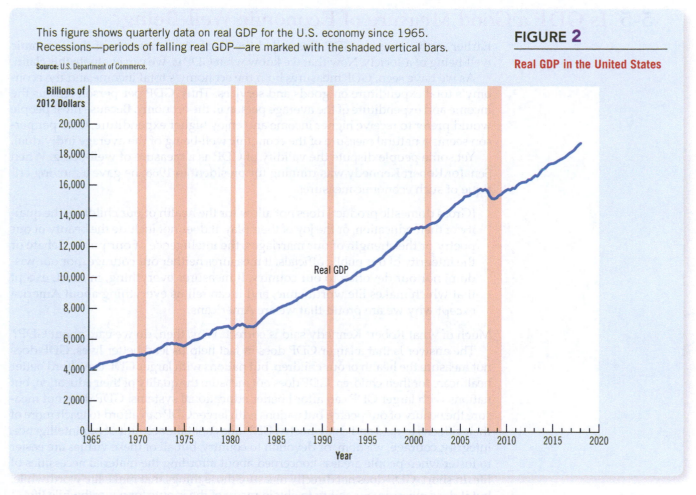

Much of macroeconomics aims to explain the long-run growth and short-run fluctuations in real GDP. As we will see in the coming chapters, we need different models for these two purposes. Because the short-run fluctuations represent deviations from the long-run trend, we first examine the behavior of key macroeconomic variables, including real GDP, in the long run. Then in later chapters, we build on this analysis to explain short-run fluctuations. ●

Quick**Quiz**

9. An economy produces 10 cookies in year 1 at a price of $2 per cookie and 12 cookies in year 2 at a price of $3 per cookie. From year 1 to year 2, real GDP increases by
   a. 20 percent.
   b. 50 percent.
   c. 70 percent.
   d. 80 percent.

10. If all quantities produced rise by 5 percent and all prices fall by 5 percent, which of the following best describes what occurs?
   a. Real GDP rises by 5 percent, while nominal GDP falls by 5 percent.
   b. Real GDP rises by 5 percent, while nominal GDP is unchanged.
   c. Real GDP is unchanged, while nominal GDP rises by 5 percent.
   d. Real GDP is unchanged, while nominal GDP falls by 5 percent.

Answers at end of chapter.

5-5   Is GDP a Good Measure of Economic Well-Being?

Earlier in this chapter, GDP was called the single best measure of the economic well-being of a society. Now that we know what GDP is, we can evaluate this claim.

As we have seen, GDP measures both the economy's total income and the economy's total expenditure on goods and services. Thus, GDP per person tells us the income and expenditure of the average person in the economy. Because most people would prefer to receive higher income and enjoy higher expenditure, GDP per person seems a natural measure of the economic well-being of the average individual.

Yet some people dispute the validity of GDP as a measure of well-being. When Senator Robert Kennedy was running for president in 1968, he gave a moving critique of such economic measures:

> [Gross domestic product] does not allow for the health of our children, the quality of their education, or the joy of their play. It does not include the beauty of our poetry or the strength of our marriages, the intelligence of our public debate or the integrity of our public officials. It measures neither our courage, nor our wisdom, nor our devotion to our country. It measures everything, in short, except that which makes life worthwhile, and it can tell us everything about America except why we are proud that we are Americans.

Much of what Robert Kennedy said is correct. Why, then, do we care about GDP?

The answer is that a larger GDP does in fact help us lead better lives. GDP does not measure the health of our children, but nations with larger GDP can afford better healthcare for their children. GDP does not measure the quality of their education, but nations with larger GDP can afford better educational systems. GDP does not measure the beauty of our poetry, but nations with larger GDP can afford to teach more of their citizens to read and enjoy poetry. GDP does not take account of our intelligence, integrity, courage, wisdom, or devotion to country, but all of these virtues are easier to foster when people are less concerned about affording the material necessities of life. In short, GDP does not directly measure those things that make life worthwhile, but it does measure our ability to obtain many of the inputs for a worthwhile life.

GDP is not, however, a perfect measure of well-being. It omits some things that contribute to a good life, such as leisure. Suppose, for instance, that everyone in the economy suddenly started working every day of the week, rather than taking weekends off. More goods and services would be produced, and GDP would rise. But despite the increase in GDP, we should not conclude that everyone would be better off. The loss from reduced leisure would offset the gain from producing and consuming a greater quantity of goods and services.

Because GDP uses market prices to value goods and services, it excludes the value of almost all activity that takes place outside markets. In particular, GDP omits the value of goods and services produced at home. When a chef prepares a delicious meal and sells it at her restaurant, the value of that meal is part of GDP. But if the chef prepares the same meal for her family, the value she has added to the raw ingredients is left out of GDP. Similarly, child care provided in day-care centers is part of GDP, whereas child care by parents at home is not. Volunteer work also contributes to the well-being of those in society, but GDP does not reflect these contributions.

Another thing that GDP excludes is the quality of the environment. Imagine that the government eliminated all environmental regulations. Firms could then produce goods and services without considering the pollution they create, and GDP might rise. Yet well-being would most likely fall. The deterioration in the quality of air and water would more than offset the gains from greater production.

GDP also says nothing about the distribution of income. Consider two societies, one in which 100 people have annual incomes of $50,000 and another in which

10 people earn $500,000 and 90 suffer with nothing at all. Both societies have GDP of $5 million and GDP per person of $50,000. Yet few people would consider the two situations equivalent. While GDP per person tells us what's happening to the average person, behind the average lies a large variety of personal experiences.

In the end, we can conclude that GDP is a good measure of economic well-being for most—but not all—purposes. It is important to keep in mind what GDP includes and what it leaves out.

CASE STUDY

INTERNATIONAL DIFFERENCES IN GDP AND THE QUALITY OF LIFE

One way to gauge the usefulness of GDP as a measure of economic well-being is to examine international data. Rich and poor countries have vastly different levels of GDP per person. If a large GDP leads to a higher standard of living, then we should observe GDP to be strongly correlated with various measures of the quality of life. And, in fact, we do.

Table 3 shows 12 large nations ranked in order of GDP per person. The table also shows life expectancy at birth, the average years of schooling among adults, and an index of life satisfaction based on asking people to gauge how they feel about their lives on a scale of 0 to 10 (with 10 being the best). These data show a clear pattern. In rich countries, such as the United States and Germany, people have life expectancy of about 80, acquire about 13 years of schooling, and rate their life satisfaction at about 7. In poor countries, such as Bangladesh and Nigeria, people typically die about 10 years earlier, have less than half as much schooling, and rate their life satisfaction about 2 points lower on the 10-point scale.

Data on other aspects of the quality of life tell a similar story. Countries with low GDP per person tend to have more infants with low birth weight, higher rates of infant mortality, higher rates of maternal mortality, and higher rates of child malnutrition. They also have lower rates of access to electricity, paved roads, and clean drinking water. In these countries, fewer school-age children are actually in school, those who are in school must learn with fewer teachers per student, and

Country	Real GDP per Person	Life Expectancy	Average Years of Schooling	Overall Life Satisfaction (0 to 10 scale)
United States	$54,941	80 years	13 years	7.0
Germany	46,136	81	14	7.1
Japan	38,986	84	13	5.9
Russia	24,233	71	12	5.6
Mexico	16,944	77	9	6.4
China	15,270	76	8	5.1
Brazil	13,755	76	8	6.3
Indonesia	10,846	69	8	5.1
India	6,353	69	6	4.0
Pakistan	5,311	67	5	5.8
Nigeria	5,231	54	6	5.3
Bangladesh	3,677	73	6	4.3

TABLE 3

GDP and the Quality of Life
The table shows GDP per person and three other measures of the quality of life for 12 major countries.

Source: *Human Development Indices and Indicators: 2018 Statistical Update,* United Nations. Real GDP is for 2017, expressed in 2011 dollars. Average years of schooling is among adults 25 years and older.

IN THE NEWS

Sex, Drugs, and GDP

Some nations are debating what to include in their national income accounts.

No Sex, Please, We're French

By Zachary Karabell

The government of France has just made what on the face of it appears to be a nonannouncement announcement: It will not include illegal drugs and prostitution in its official calculation of the country's gross domestic product.

What made the announcement odd was that it never has included such activities, nor have most countries. Nor do most governments announce what they do not plan to do. ("The U.S. government has no intention of sending a man to Venus.") Yet the French decision comes in the wake of significant pressure from neighboring countries and from the European Union to integrate these activities into national accounts and economic output. That raises a host of questions: *Should* these activities be included, and if those are, why not others? And what exactly are we measuring—and why?

Few numbers shape our world today more than GDP. It has become the alpha and omega of national success, used by politicians and pundits as the primary gauge of national strength and treated as a numerical proxy for greatness or the lack thereof.

Yet GDP is only a statistic, replete with the limitations of all statistics. Created as an outgrowth of national accounts that were themselves only devised in the 1930s, GDP was never an all-inclusive measure, even as it is treated as such. Multiple areas of economic life were left out, including volunteer work and domestic work.

Now Eurostat, the official statistical agency of the European Union, is leading the drive to include a host of illegal activities in national calculations of GDP, most notably prostitution and illicit drugs. The argument, as a United Nations commission laid out in 2008, is fairly simple: Prostitution and illicit drugs are significant economic activities, and if they're not factored into economic statistics, then we're looking at an incomplete picture—which in turn will make it that much harder to craft smart policy. Additionally, different countries have different laws: In the Netherlands, for instance, prostitution is legal, as is marijuana. Those commercial transactions (or at least those that are recorded and taxed) are already part of Dutch GDP. Not including them in Italy's or Spain's GDPs can thus make it challenging to compare national numbers.

That is why Spain, Italy, Belgium, and the U.K. have in recent months moved to include

illiteracy among adults is more common. The citizens of these nations tend to have fewer televisions, fewer telephones, and fewer opportunities to access the Internet. International data leave no doubt that a nation's GDP per person is closely associated with its population's standard of living. ●

Quick**Quiz**

11. If Mr. Keating quits his job as a teacher to home school his own children, GDP
    a. stays the same because he is engaged in the same activity.
    b. rises because he now pays lower income taxes.
    c. falls because his market income decreases.
    d. could rise or fall, depending on the value of home schooling.

12. GDP is an imperfect measure of well-being because it
    a. includes physical goods produced but not intangible services.
    b. excludes goods and services provided by the government.
    c. ignores the environmental degradation from economic activity.
    d. is not correlated with other measures of the quality of life.

Answers at end of chapter.

illegal drugs and nonlicensed sex trade in their national accounts. The U.K. Office for National Statistics in particular approached its mandate with wonkish seriousness, publishing a 20-page précis of its methodology that explained how it would, say, calculate the dollar amount of prostitution (police records help) or deal with domestically produced drugs versus imported drugs. The result, which will be formally announced in September, will be an additional 10 billion pounds added to Great Britain's GDP.

France, however, has demurred. A nation with a clichéd reputation for a certain savoir faire when it comes to sex and other nocturnal activities has decided (or at least its bureaucrats have) that in spite of an EU directive, it will not calculate the effects of illegal activities that are often nonconsensual or nonvoluntary. That is clearly the case for some prostitution—one French minister stated that "street prostitution" is largely controlled by the Mafia—and the same could be reasonably

said of the use of some hard drugs, given their addictive nature.

There is undeniably a strong moralistic component in the French decision. By averring that because they are not voluntary or consensual these exchanges should not be included in GDP, the French government is placing a moral vision of what society *should be* ahead of an economic vision of what society *is*. That in turn makes an already messy statistic far messier, and that serves no one's national interests. . . .

With all of GDP's limitations, adding a new moral dimension would only make the number that much less useful. After all, why stop at not including prostitution because it degrades women? Why not refuse to measure coal production because it degrades the environment? Why not leave out cigarette usage because it causes cancer? The list of possible exclusions on this basis is endless.

If GDP is our current best metric for national output, then at the very least it should

attempt to include all measurable output. The usually moralistic United States has actually been including legal prostitution in Nevada and now marijuana sales and consumption in Colorado, California, and Washington without any strong objections based solely on the argument that these are commercial exchanges that constitute this fuzzy entity we call "the economy." . . .

Not measuring drugs and sex won't make them go away, but it will hobble efforts to understand the messy latticework of our economic lives, all in a futile attempt to excise what we do not like. ∎

Questions to Discuss

1. Do you think illegal activities should be included in GDP? Why or why not?

2. Are there legal activities that you view as socially undesirable? If so, which ones? Do you think that GDP should include these activities? Why or why not?

Source: *Slate*, June 20, 2014.

5-6 Conclusion

In this chapter we learned how economists measure the total income of a nation. Measurement is, of course, only a starting point. Much of macroeconomics is aimed at revealing the long-run and short-run determinants of a nation's gross domestic product. Why, for example, is GDP higher in the United States and Japan than in India and Nigeria? What can the governments of the poorest countries do to promote more rapid GDP growth? Why does GDP in the United States rise rapidly in some years and fall in others? What can U.S. policymakers do to reduce the severity of these fluctuations in GDP? These are the questions we will take up shortly.

At this point, it is important to acknowledge the significance of just measuring GDP. We all get some sense of how the economy is doing as we go about our lives. But to do their jobs well, economists and policymakers need more than this vague sense: They need concrete data on which to base their judgments. Quantifying the behavior of the economy with statistics such as GDP is, therefore, the first step to developing a science of macroeconomics.

CHAPTER IN A NUTSHELL

- Because every transaction has a buyer and a seller, the total expenditure in the economy must equal the total income in the economy.
- Gross domestic product (GDP) measures an economy's total expenditure on newly produced goods and services and the total income earned from the production of these goods and services. More precisely, GDP is the market value of all final goods and services produced within a country in a given period of time.
- GDP consists of four components of expenditure: consumption, investment, government purchases, and net exports. Consumption includes spending on goods and services by households, with the exception of purchases of new housing. Investment includes spending on business capital, residential capital, and inventories. Government purchases include spending on goods and services by local, state, and federal governments. Net exports equal the value of goods and services produced domestically and sold abroad (exports) minus the value of goods and services produced abroad and sold domestically (imports).
- Nominal GDP uses current prices to value the economy's production of goods and services. Real GDP uses constant base-year prices to value the economy's production of goods and services. The GDP deflator—calculated from the ratio of nominal GDP to real GDP—measures the level of prices in the economy.
- GDP is a good measure of economic well-being because people prefer higher to lower incomes. But it is not a perfect measure of well-being. For example, GDP excludes the value of leisure and the value of a clean environment.

KEY CONCEPTS

microeconomics, *p. 88*
macroeconomics, *p. 88*
gross domestic product (GDP), *p. 90*
consumption, *p. 93*

investment, *p. 93*
government purchases, *p. 94*
net exports, *p. 94*
nominal GDP, *p. 97*

real GDP, *p. 97*
GDP deflator, *p. 97*

QUESTIONS FOR REVIEW

1. Explain why an economy's income must equal its expenditure.

2. Which contributes more to GDP—the production of an economy car or the production of a luxury car? Why?

3. A farmer sells wheat to a baker for $2. The baker uses the wheat to make bread, which is sold for $3. What is the total contribution of these transactions to GDP?

4. Many years ago, Sophie paid $500 to put together a record collection. Today, she sold her albums at a garage sale for $100. How does this sale affect current GDP?

5. List the four components of GDP. Give an example of each.

6. Why do economists use real GDP rather than nominal GDP to gauge economic well-being?

7. In the year 2020, the economy produces 100 loaves of bread that sell for $2 each. In the year 2021, the economy produces 200 loaves of bread that sell for $3 each. Calculate nominal GDP, real GDP, and the GDP deflator for each year. (Use 2020 as the base year.) By what percentage does each of these three statistics rise from one year to the next?

8. Why is it desirable for a country to have a large GDP? Give an example of something that would raise GDP and yet be undesirable.

PROBLEMS AND APPLICATIONS

1. What components of GDP (if any) would each of the following transactions affect? Explain.
   a. Uncle Fester buys a new refrigerator from a domestic manufacturer.
   b. Aunt Dolly hires a local contractor to build her a new house.
   c. The Huang family buys an old Victorian house from the Ellis family.
   d. You pay a hairdresser for a haircut.
   e. Ford sells a Mustang from its inventory to the Martinez family.

f. Ford manufactures a Focus and sells it to Avis, the car rental company.

g. California hires workers to repave Highway 66.

h. The federal government sends your grandmother a Social Security check.

i. Your parents buy a bottle of French wine.

j. Honda expands its factory in Ohio.

2. Fill in the blanks:

Year	Real GDP (in 2000 dollars)	Nominal GDP (in current dollars)	GDP deflator (base year 2000)
1970	3,000	1,200	_____
1980	5,000	_____	60
1990	_____	6,000	100
2000	_____	8,000	_____
2010	_____	15,000	200
2020	10,000	_____	300
2030	20,000	50,000	_____

3. The government purchases component of GDP does not include spending on transfer payments such as Social Security. Thinking about the definition of GDP, explain why transfer payments are excluded.

4. As the chapter states, GDP does not include the value of used goods that are resold. Why would including such transactions make GDP a less informative measure of economic well-being?

5. Below are some data from the land of milk and honey.

Year	Price of Milk	Quantity of Milk	Price of Honey	Quantity of Honey
2020	$1	100 quarts	$2	50 quarts
2021	1	200	2	100
2022	2	200	4	100

a. Compute nominal GDP, real GDP, and the GDP deflator for each year, using 2020 as the base year.

b. Compute the percentage change in nominal GDP, real GDP, and the GDP deflator in 2021 and 2022 from the preceding year. For each year, identify the variable that does not change. Explain why your answer makes sense.

c. Did economic well-being increase more in 2021 or 2022? Explain.

6. Consider an economy that produces only chocolate bars. In year 1, the quantity produced is 3 bars and the price is $4 per bar. In year 2, the quantity produced is 4 bars and the price is $5 per bar. In year 3, the quantity produced is 5 bars and the price is $6 per bar. Year 1 is the base year.

a. What is nominal GDP for each of these three years?

b. What is real GDP for each of these years?

c. What is the GDP deflator for each of these years?

d. What is the percentage growth rate of real GDP from year 2 to year 3?

e. What is the inflation rate as measured by the GDP deflator from year 2 to year 3?

f. In this one-good economy, how might you have answered parts (d) and (e) without first answering parts (b) and (c)?

7. Consider the following data on the U.S. economy:

Year	Nominal GDP (in billions of dollars)	GDP Deflator (base year 2012)
2018	20,501	110.4
1998	9,063	75.3

a. What was the growth rate of nominal GDP between 1998 and 2018? (*Hint*: The growth rate of a variable X over an N-year period is calculated as $100 \times [(X_{final} / X_{initial})^{1/N} - 1]$.)

b. What was the growth rate of the GDP deflator between 1998 and 2018?

c. What was real GDP in 1998 measured in 2012 prices?

d. What was real GDP in 2018 measured in 2012 prices?

e. What was the growth rate of real GDP between 1998 and 2018?

f. Was the growth rate of nominal GDP higher or lower than the growth rate of real GDP? Explain.

8. Revised estimates of U.S. GDP are usually released by the government near the end of each month. Find a newspaper article that reports on the most recent release, or read the news release yourself at http://www.bea.gov, the website of the U.S. Bureau of Economic Analysis. Discuss the recent changes in real and nominal GDP and in the components of GDP.

9. A farmer grows wheat, which she sells to a miller for $100. The miller turns the wheat into flour, which she sells to a baker for $150. The baker turns the wheat into bread, which she sells to consumers for $180. Consumers eat the bread.

a. What is GDP in this economy? Explain.

b. *Value added* is defined as the value of a producer's output minus the value of the intermediate goods that the producer buys to make the output. Assuming there are no intermediate goods beyond those described above, calculate the value added of each of the three producers.

c. What is total value added of the three producers in this economy? How does it compare to the economy's GDP? Does this example suggest another way of calculating GDP?

10. Goods and services that are not sold in markets, such as food produced and consumed at home, are generally not included in GDP. How might this cause the numbers in the second column of Table 3 to be misleading in a comparison of the economic well-being of the United States and India? Explain.

11. The participation of women in the U.S. labor force has risen dramatically since 1970.
    a. How do you think this rise affected GDP?
    b. Now imagine a measure of well-being that includes time spent working in the home and taking leisure. How would the change in this measure of well-being compare to the change in GDP?
    c. Can you think of other aspects of well-being that are associated with the rise in women's labor-force participation? Would it be practical to construct a measure of well-being that includes these aspects?

12. One day, Barry the Barber, Inc., collects $400 for haircuts. Over this day, his equipment depreciates in value by $50. Of the remaining $350, Barry sends $30 to the government in sales taxes, takes home $220 in wages, and retains $100 in his business to add new equipment in the future. From the $220 that Barry takes home, he pays $70 in income taxes. Based on this information, compute Barry's contribution to the following measures of income.
    a. gross domestic product
    b. net national product
    c. national income
    d. personal income
    e. disposable personal income

QuickQuiz Answers

1. **c**　2. **d**　3. **b**　4. **c**　5. **b**　6. **d**　7. **c**　8. **a**　9. **a**　10. **b**　11. **c**　12. **c**

I n 1931, as the U.S. economy was suffering through the Great Depression, the New York Yankees paid famed baseball player Babe Ruth a salary of $80,000. At the time, this pay was extraordinary, even among the stars of baseball. According to one story, a reporter asked Ruth whether he thought it was right that he made more than President Herbert Hoover, who had a salary of $75,000. Ruth replied, "I had a better year."

In 2018, the average salary earned by major league baseball players was about $4.5 million, and Los Angeles Dodgers pitcher Clayton Kershaw was paid $33 million, making him the highest paid player in the league. At first, this fact might lead you to think that baseball has become vastly more lucrative over the past nine decades. But as everyone knows, the prices of goods and services have also risen. In 1931, a nickel would buy an ice-cream cone and a quarter would buy a ticket at the local movie theater. Because prices were so much lower in Babe Ruth's day than they are today, it is not clear whether Ruth enjoyed a higher or lower standard of living than today's players.

In the preceding chapter, we looked at how economists use gross domestic product (GDP) to measure the quantity of goods and

Measuring the Cost of Living

services that the economy is producing. This chapter examines how economists measure the overall cost of living. To compare Babe Ruth's salary of $80,000 with today's salaries, we need to turn dollar figures into meaningful measures of purchasing power. That is exactly the job of a statistic called the *consumer price index*, or simply the CPI. After seeing how the CPI is constructed, we discuss how we can use such a price index to compare dollar figures from different points in time.

The CPI is used to monitor changes in the cost of living over time. When the CPI rises, the typical family has to spend more money to maintain the same standard of living. Economists use the term *inflation* to describe a situation in which the economy's overall price level is rising. The *inflation rate* is the percentage change in the price level from the previous period. The preceding chapter showed how economists can measure inflation using the GDP deflator. The inflation rate you are likely to hear on the nightly news, however, is calculated from the CPI, which better reflects the goods and services bought by consumers.

As we will see in the coming chapters, inflation is a closely watched aspect of macroeconomic performance and is a key variable guiding macroeconomic policy. This chapter provides the background for that analysis by showing how economists measure the inflation rate using the CPI and how this statistic can be used to compare dollar figures from different times.

6-1 The Consumer Price Index

consumer price index (CPI)
a measure of the overall cost of the goods and services bought by a typical consumer

The **consumer price index (CPI)** is a measure of the overall cost of the goods and services bought by a typical consumer. Every month, the Bureau of Labor Statistics (BLS), which is part of the Department of Labor, computes and reports the CPI. In this section, we discuss how the CPI is calculated and what problems arise in its measurement. We also consider how this index compares with the GDP deflator, another measure of the overall level of prices, which we examined in the preceding chapter.

6-1a How the CPI Is Calculated

When the BLS calculates the CPI and the inflation rate, it uses data on the prices of thousands of goods and services. To see exactly how these statistics are constructed, let's consider a simple economy in which consumers buy only two goods: hot dogs and hamburgers. Table 1 shows the five steps that the BLS follows.

1. *Fix the basket.* Determine which prices are most important to the typical consumer. If the typical consumer buys more hot dogs than hamburgers, then the price of hot dogs is more important than the price of hamburgers and, therefore, should be given greater weight in measuring the cost of living. The BLS sets these weights by surveying consumers to find the basket of goods and services bought by the typical consumer. In the example in the table, the typical consumer buys a basket of 4 hot dogs and 2 hamburgers.
2. *Find the prices.* Find the prices of each of the goods and services in the basket at each point in time. The table shows the prices of hot dogs and hamburgers for three different years.
3. *Compute the basket's cost.* Use the data on prices to calculate the cost of the basket of goods and services at different times. The table shows this calculation for each of the three years. Notice that only the prices in this calculation change. By keeping the basket of goods the same (4 hot dogs and 2 hamburgers), we isolate the effects of price changes from the effects of any quantity changes that might be occurring at the same time.

TABLE 1

Calculating the Consumer Price Index and the Inflation Rate: An Example
This table shows how to calculate the CPI and the inflation rate for a hypothetical economy in which consumers buy only hot dogs and hamburgers.

Step 1: Survey Consumers to Determine a Fixed Basket of Goods

Basket = 4 hot dogs, 2 hamburgers

Step 2: Find the Price of Each Good in Each Year

Year	Price of Hot Dogs	Price of Hamburgers
2019	$1	$2
2020	2	3
2021	3	4

Step 3: Compute the Cost of the Basket of Goods in Each Year

2019 ($1 per hot dog × 4 hot dogs) + ($2 per hamburger × 2 hamburgers) = $8 per basket

2020 ($2 per hot dog × 4 hot dogs) + ($3 per hamburger × 2 hamburgers) = $14 per basket

2021 ($3 per hot dog × 4 hot dogs) + ($4 per hamburger × 2 hamburgers) = $20 per basket

Step 4: Choose One Year as a Base Year (2019) and Compute the CPI in Each Year

2019	($8/$8) × 100 = 100
2020	($14/$8) × 100 = 175
2021	($20/$8) × 100 = 250

Step 5: Use the CPI to Compute the Inflation Rate from Previous Year

| 2020 | (175 − 100)/100 × 100 = 75% |
| 2021 | (250 − 175)/175 × 100 = 43% |

4. *Choose a base year and compute the index.* Designate one year as the base year, the benchmark against which other years are to be compared. (The choice of base year is arbitrary. The index is used to measure percentage changes in the cost of living, and these changes are the same regardless of the choice of base year.) Once the base year is chosen, the index is calculated as follows:

$$\text{Consumer price index} = \frac{\text{Price of basket of goods and services in current year}}{\text{Price of basket in base year}} \times 100.$$

That is, the CPI in any given year is the price of the basket of goods and services in that year divided by the price of the basket in the base year, multiplied by 100.

In the example in Table 1, 2019 is the base year. In this year, the basket of hot dogs and hamburgers costs $8. Therefore, to calculate the CPI, the price of the basket in each year is divided by $8 and multiplied by 100. The CPI is 100 in 2019. (The index is always 100 in the base year.) The CPI is 175 in 2020. This means that the price of the basket in 2020 is 175 percent of its price in the base year. Put differently, a basket of goods that costs $100 in the base year costs $175 in 2020. Similarly, the CPI is 250 in 2021, indicating that the price level in 2021 is 250 percent of the price level in the base year.

inflation rate

the percentage change in the price index from the preceding period

5. *Compute the inflation rate.* Use the CPI to calculate the **inflation rate**, which is the percentage change in the price index from the preceding period. That is, the inflation rate between two consecutive years is computed as follows:

$$\text{Inflation rate in year 2} = \frac{\text{CPI in year 2} - \text{CPI in year 1}}{\text{CPI in year 1}} \times 100.$$

As shown at the bottom of Table 1, the inflation rate in our example is 75 percent in 2020 and 43 percent in 2021.

Although this example simplifies the real world by considering a basket of only two goods, it shows how the BLS computes the CPI and the inflation rate. The BLS collects and processes data on the prices of thousands of goods and services every month and, by following the five foregoing steps, determines how quickly the cost of living for the typical consumer is rising. When the BLS makes its monthly announcement of the CPI, you can usually hear the number on the evening news or see it in your newsfeed.

core CPI

a measure of the overall cost of consumer goods and services excluding food and energy

In addition to the CPI for the overall economy, the BLS calculates several other price indexes. It reports the index for some narrow categories of goods and services, such as food, clothing, and energy. It also calculates the CPI for all goods and services excluding food and energy, a statistic called the **core CPI**. Because

---

FYI

What's in the CPI's Basket?

When constructing the consumer price index, the Bureau of Labor Statistics tries to include all the goods and services that the typical consumer buys. Moreover, it tries to weight these goods and services according to how much consumers buy of each item.

Figure 1 shows the breakdown of consumer spending into the major categories of goods and services. By far the largest category is housing, which makes up 42 percent of the typical consumer's budget. This category includes the cost of shelter (33 percent), fuel and utilities (5 percent), and household furnishings and operation (4 percent). The next largest category, at 17 percent, is transportation, which includes spending on cars, gasoline, buses, subways, and so on. The next largest category, at 14 percent, is food and beverages; this category includes food at home (7 percent), food away from home (6 percent), and alcoholic beverages (1 percent). Next are medical care at 9 percent, education and communication at 7 percent, and recreation at 6 percent. Apparel, which includes clothing, footwear, and jewelry, makes up 3 percent of the typical consumer's budget.

Also included in the figure, at 3 percent of spending, is a category for other goods and services. This category is a catchall for consumer purchases (such as cigarettes, haircuts, and funeral expenses) that do not naturally fit into the other categories. ■

FIGURE 1

The Typical Basket of Goods and Services
This figure shows how the typical consumer divides spending among various categories of goods and services. The Bureau of Labor Statistics calls each percentage the "relative importance" of the category.

Source: Bureau of Labor Statistics. Parts do not sum to 100 because of rounding.

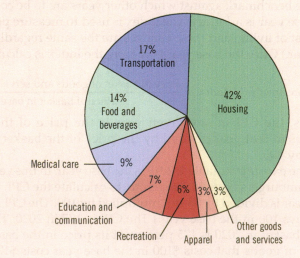

food and energy prices show substantial short-run volatility, the core CPI better reflects underlying inflation trends. Finally, the BLS also calculates the **producer price index (PPI)**, which measures the cost of a basket of goods and services bought by firms rather than consumers. Because firms eventually pass on their costs to consumers in the form of higher consumer prices, changes in the PPI are often thought to be useful for predicting changes in the CPI.

producer price index (PPI)
a measure of the cost of a basket of goods and services bought by firms

6-1b Problems in Measuring the Cost of Living

The goal of the consumer price index is to measure changes in the cost of living. In other words, the CPI tries to gauge how much incomes must rise to maintain a constant standard of living. The CPI, however, is not a perfect measure of the cost of living. Three problems with the index are widely acknowledged but difficult to solve.

The first problem is called *substitution bias*. When prices change from one year to the next, they do not all change proportionately: Some prices rise more than others. Consumers respond to these differing price changes by buying less of the goods whose prices have risen by relatively large amounts and by buying more of the goods whose prices have risen less or perhaps even have fallen. That is, consumers substitute toward goods that have become relatively less expensive. If a price index is computed assuming a fixed basket of goods, it ignores the possibility of consumer substitution and, therefore, overstates the increase in the cost of living from one year to the next.

Let's consider a simple example. Imagine that in the base year, apples are cheaper than pears, so consumers buy more apples than pears. When the BLS constructs the basket of goods, it will include more apples than pears. Suppose that next year pears are cheaper than apples. Consumers will naturally respond to the price changes by buying more pears and fewer apples. Yet when computing the CPI, the BLS uses a fixed basket, which in essence assumes that consumers continue buying the now expensive apples in the same quantities as before. For this reason, the index will measure a much larger increase in the cost of living than consumers actually experience.

A second problem with the CPI arises from the *introduction of new goods*. When a new good is introduced, consumers have more variety from which to choose, and this increased variety in turn reduces the cost of maintaining the same level of economic well-being. To see why, consider a hypothetical situation: Suppose you could choose between a $100 gift certificate at a large store that offered a wide array of goods and a $100 gift certificate at a small store with the same prices but a more limited selection. Which would you prefer? Most people would pick the store with greater variety. In essence, the increased set of possible choices makes each dollar more valuable. The same is true with the evolution of the economy over time: As new goods are introduced, consumers have more choices, and each dollar is worth more. But because the CPI is based on a fixed basket of goods and services, it does not reflect the increase in the value of the dollar that results from the introduction of new goods.

Again, let's consider an example. In 2001, Apple introduced the iPod, a small music-playing device that was a precursor to the iPhone. Devices to play music were available previously, but they were not nearly as portable and versatile. The iPod was a new option that increased consumers' opportunities. For any given number of dollars, the introduction of the iPod made people better off; conversely, achieving the same level of well-being required fewer dollars. A perfect cost-of-living index would have reflected the decrease in the cost of living from the iPod's introduction. But because the CPI uses a fixed basket, it did not decrease when this new good was introduced. Eventually, the BLS revised the basket of goods to include the iPod, and subsequently, the index reflected changes in iPod prices. But the reduction in the cost of living associated with the initial introduction of the iPod never showed up in the index.

The third problem with the CPI is *unmeasured quality change*. If the quality of a good deteriorates from one year to the next while its price remains the same, you are getting a lesser good for the same amount of money, so the value of a dollar falls. Similarly, if the quality rises from one year to the next, the value of a dollar rises. The BLS does its best to account for quality change. When the quality of a good in the basket changes—for example, when a car model has more horsepower or gets better gas mileage from one year to the next—the Bureau adjusts the price of the good to account for the quality change. In doing so, it is trying to compute the price of a basket of goods of constant quality. Despite these efforts, changes in quality remain a problem because quality is hard to measure.

There is much debate among economists about how severe these measurement problems are and what should be done about them. Studies put the upward bias in measured inflation at about 0.5 to 1.0 percent per year. The issue is important because many government programs use the CPI to adjust for changes in the overall level of prices. Recipients of Social Security, for instance, get annual increases in benefits that are tied to the CPI. Some economists have suggested modifying these programs to correct for the measurement problems by, for instance, reducing the magnitude of the automatic benefit increases.

6-1c The GDP Deflator versus the Consumer Price Index

In the preceding chapter, we examined another measure of the overall level of prices in the economy—the GDP deflator. The GDP deflator is the ratio of nominal GDP to real GDP. Because nominal GDP is current output valued at current prices and real GDP is current output valued at base-year prices, the GDP deflator reflects the current level of prices relative to the level of prices in the base year.

Economists and policymakers monitor both the GDP deflator and the CPI to gauge how quickly prices are rising. Usually, these two statistics tell a similar story. Yet two important differences can cause them to diverge.

The first difference is that the GDP deflator reflects the prices of all goods and services *produced domestically*, whereas the CPI reflects the prices of all goods and services *bought by consumers*. For example, suppose that the price of an airplane produced by Boeing and sold to the Air Force rises. Even though the plane is part of GDP, it is not part of the basket of goods and services bought by a typical consumer. Thus, the price increase shows up in the GDP deflator but not in the CPI.

As another example, suppose that Volvo raises the price of its cars. Because Volvos are made in Sweden, the car is not part of U.S. GDP. But U.S. consumers buy Volvos, so the car is part of the typical consumer's basket of goods. Hence, a price increase in an imported consumption good, such as a Volvo, shows up in the CPI but not in the GDP deflator.

This first difference between the CPI and the GDP deflator is particularly important when the price of oil changes. The United States produces some oil, but much of the oil we use is imported. As a result, oil and oil products such as gasoline and

THE WALL STREET JOURNAL

AUDIO - VIDEO

A.BACALL

"The price may seem a little high, but you have to remember that's in today's dollars."

FROM THE WALL STREET JOURNAL—PERMISSION, CARTOON FEATURES SYNDICATE.

heating oil make up a much larger share of consumer spending than of GDP. When the price of oil rises, the CPI rises by much more than does the GDP deflator.

The second and subtler difference between the GDP deflator and the CPI concerns how various prices are weighted to yield a single number for the overall level of prices. The CPI compares the price of a *fixed* basket of goods and services with the price of the basket in the base year. Only occasionally does the BLS change the basket of goods. By contrast, the GDP deflator compares the price of *currently produced* goods and services with the price of those goods and services in the base year. Thus, the group of goods and services used to compute the GDP deflator changes automatically over time. This difference is not important when all prices are changing proportionately. But if the prices of different goods and services are changing by varying amounts, the way we weight the various prices affects the calculation of the overall inflation rate.

Figure 2 shows the inflation rate as measured by both the GDP deflator and the CPI for each year since 1965. You can see that sometimes the two measures diverge. When they do, it is possible to go behind these numbers and explain the divergence with the two differences we have discussed. For example, in 1979 and 1980, CPI inflation spiked up by more than inflation as measured by the GDP deflator largely because oil prices more than doubled during these two years. Conversely, in 2009 and 2015, CPI inflation fell well below inflation as gauged by the GDP deflator because of plummeting oil prices. Yet divergence between these two measures is the exception rather than the rule. Both the GDP deflator and the CPI show high rates of inflation in the 1970s and low rates of inflation since the mid-1980s.

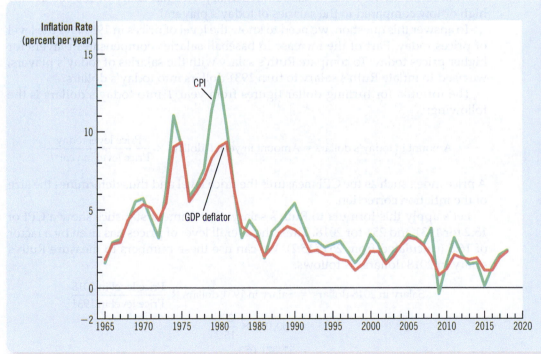

FIGURE 2

Two Measures of Inflation

This figure shows the inflation rate—the percentage change in the level of prices—as measured by the GDP deflator and the CPI using annual data since 1965. Notice that the two measures of inflation generally move together.

Source: U.S. Department of Labor; U.S. Department of Commerce.

Quick Quiz

1. The CPI measures approximately the same economic phenomenon as
   a. nominal GDP.
   b. real GDP.
   c. the GDP deflator.
   d. the unemployment rate.

2. The largest component in the basket of goods and services used to compute the CPI is
   a. food and beverages.
   b. housing.
   c. medical care.
   d. apparel.

3. If a Pennsylvania gun manufacturer raises the price of rifles it sells to the U.S. Army, its price hikes will increase
   a. both the CPI and the GDP deflator.
   b. neither the CPI nor the GDP deflator.
   c. the CPI but not the GDP deflator.
   d. the GDP deflator but not the CPI.

4. Because consumers can sometimes substitute cheaper goods for those that have risen in price,
   a. the CPI overstates inflation.
   b. the CPI understates inflation.
   c. the GDP deflator overstates inflation.
   d. the GDP deflator understates inflation.

Answers at end of chapter.

6-2 Correcting Economic Variables for the Effects of Inflation

The purpose of measuring the overall level of prices in the economy is to allow us to compare dollar figures from different times. Now that we know how price indexes are calculated, let's see how we might use such an index to compare a dollar figure from the past with a dollar figure in the present.

6-2a Dollar Figures from Different Times

We first return to the issue of Babe Ruth's salary. Was his salary of $80,000 in 1931 high or low compared to the salaries of today's players?

To answer this question, we need to know the level of prices in 1931 and the level of prices today. Part of the increase in baseball salaries compensates players for higher prices today. To compare Ruth's salary with the salaries of today's players, we need to inflate Ruth's salary to turn 1931 dollars into today's dollars.

The formula for turning dollar figures from year T into today's dollars is the following:

$$\text{Amount in today's dollars} = \text{Amount in year } T \text{ dollars} \times \frac{\text{Price level today}}{\text{Price level in year } T}.$$

A price index such as the CPI measures the price level and thus determines the size of the inflation correction.

Let's apply this formula to Ruth's salary. Government statistics show a CPI of 15.2 for 1931 and 251 for 2018. Thus, the overall level of prices has risen by a factor of 16.5 (calculated from 251/15.2). We can use these numbers to measure Ruth's salary in 2018 dollars, as follows:

$$\text{Salary in 2018 dollars} = \text{Salary in 1931 dollars} \times \frac{\text{Price level in 2018}}{\text{Price level in 1931}}$$

$$= \$80,000 \times \frac{251}{15.2}$$

$$= \$1,321,053.$$

We find that Babe Ruth's 1931 salary is equivalent to a salary today of over $1.3 million. That is a high income, but it is less than a third of the average player's salary today and only 4 percent of what star pitcher Clayton Kershaw earns. Various forces, including overall economic growth and the increasing income shares earned by superstars, have substantially raised the living standards of the best athletes.

Let's also examine President Hoover's 1931 salary of $75,000. To translate that figure into 2018 dollars, we again multiply it by the ratio of the price levels in the two years. We find that Hoover's salary is equivalent to $75,000 × (251/15.2), or $1,238,487 in 2018 dollars. This is well above President Donald Trump's salary of $400,000. It seems that President Hoover did have a pretty good year after all.

FYI · Mr. Index Goes to Hollywood

What is the most popular movie of all time? The answer might surprise you.

Movie popularity is often gauged by box office receipts. By that measure, *Star Wars: The Force Awakens* is the number-one movie of all

"May the force of inflation be with you."

LUCASFILM/PHOTO 12/ALAMY STOCK PHOTO

time with domestic receipts of $937 million, followed by *Avatar* ($761 million) and *Black Panther* ($700 million). But this ranking ignores an obvious but important fact: Prices, including those of movie tickets, have been rising over time. Inflation gives an advantage to newer films.

When we correct box office receipts for the effects of inflation, the story is very different. The number-one movie is now *Gone with the Wind* ($1,784 million), followed by the original *Star Wars* ($1,573 million) and *The Sound of Music* ($1,258 million). *Star Wars: The Force Awakens* falls to number 11.

Gone with the Wind was released in 1939, before everyone had televisions in their homes. In the 1930s, about 90 million Americans went to the cinema each week, compared with about 25 million today. But the movies from that era don't show up in conventional popularity rankings because ticket prices were only a quarter. And indeed, in the ranking based on nominal box office receipts, *Gone with the Wind* does not make the top 100 films. Scarlett and Rhett fare a lot better once we correct for the effects of inflation. ∎

CASE STUDY · REGIONAL DIFFERENCES IN THE COST OF LIVING

When you graduate from college, you may well have several job offers from which to choose. Not surprisingly, some jobs pay more than others. If the jobs are located in different places, however, be careful when comparing them. The cost of living varies not only over time but also across locations. What seems like a larger paycheck might not turn out to be so once you take into account regional differences in the prices of goods and services.

The Bureau of Economic Analysis has used the data collected for the CPI to compare prices around the United States. The resulting statistic is called *regional price parities*. Just as the CPI measures variation in the cost of living from year to year, regional price parities measure variation in the cost of living from state to state.

Figure 3 shows the regional price parities for 2016. For example, living in the state of New York costs 115.6 percent of what it costs to live in the typical place in the United States (that is, New York is 15.6 percent more expensive than average). Living in Mississippi costs 86.4 percent of what it costs to live in the typical place (that is, Mississippi is 13.6 percent less expensive than average).

What accounts for these differences? It turns out that the prices of goods, such as food and clothing, explain only a small part of these regional differences. Most goods are tradable: They can be easily transported from one state to another. Because of regional trade, large price disparities are unlikely to persist for long.

FIGURE 3

Regional Variation in the Cost of Living

This figure shows how the costs of living in the 50 U.S. states and the District of Columbia compare to the U.S. average.

Source: U.S. Department of Commerce.

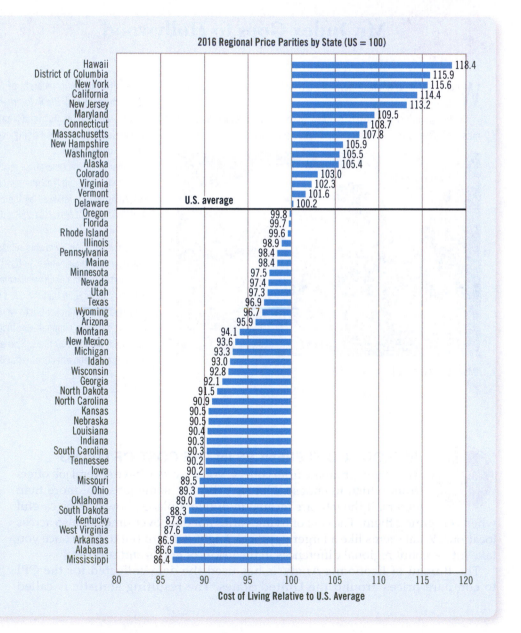

2016 Regional Price Parities by State (US = 100)

Hawaii	118.4
District of Columbia	115.9
New York	115.6
California	114.4
New Jersey	113.2
Maryland	109.5
Connecticut	108.7
Massachusetts	107.8
New Hampshire	105.9
Washington	105.5
Alaska	105.4
Colorado	103.0
Virginia	102.3
Vermont	101.6
Delaware	100.2
Oregon	99.8
Florida	99.7
Rhode Island	99.6
Illinois	98.9
Pennsylvania	98.4
Maine	98.4
Minnesota	97.5
Nevada	97.4
Utah	97.3
Texas	96.9
Wyoming	96.7
Arizona	95.9
Montana	94.1
New Mexico	93.6
Michigan	93.3
Idaho	93.0
Wisconsin	92.8
Georgia	92.1
North Dakota	91.5
North Carolina	90.9
Kansas	90.5
Nebraska	90.5
Louisiana	90.4
Indiana	90.3
South Carolina	90.3
Tennessee	90.2
Iowa	90.2
Missouri	89.5
Ohio	89.3
Oklahoma	89.0
South Dakota	88.3
Kentucky	87.8
West Virginia	87.6
Arkansas	86.9
Alabama	86.6
Mississippi	86.4

U.S. average

Cost of Living Relative to U.S. Average

Services explain a larger part of these regional differences. A haircut, for example, can cost more in one state than in another. If barbers were willing to move to places where the price of a haircut is high, or if customers were willing to fly across the country in search of cheap haircuts, then the prices of haircuts across regions might well converge. But because transporting haircuts is so costly, large price disparities can persist.

Housing services are particularly important for understanding regional differences in the cost of living. Such services represent a large share of a typical consumer's budget. Moreover, once built, a house or apartment building can't easily be moved, and the land on which it sits is completely immobile. As a result, differences in housing costs can be persistently large. For example, rents in New York are almost twice those in Mississippi.

Keep these facts in mind when it comes time to compare job offers. Look not only at the dollar salaries but also at the local prices of goods and services, especially housing. ●

6-2b Indexation

As we have just seen, price indexes are used to correct for the effects of inflation when comparing dollar figures from different times. This type of correction shows up in many places in the economy. When some dollar amount is automatically corrected for changes in the price level by law or contract, the amount is said to be **indexed** for inflation.

For example, some long-term contracts between firms and unions include partial or complete indexation of the wage to the CPI. Such a provision, called a *cost-of-living allowance* (or COLA), automatically raises the wage when the CPI rises.

Indexation is also a feature of many laws. Social Security benefits, for instance, are adjusted every year to compensate the elderly for increases in prices. The brackets of the federal income tax—the income levels at which the tax rates change—are also indexed for inflation. There are, however, many ways in which the tax system is not indexed for inflation, even when perhaps it should be. We discuss these issues more fully when we discuss the costs of inflation later in this book.

indexation
the automatic correction by law or contract of a dollar amount for the effects of inflation

6-2c Real and Nominal Interest Rates

Correcting economic variables for the effects of inflation is particularly important, and somewhat tricky, when we look at data on interest rates. The very concept of an interest rate necessarily involves comparing amounts of money at different points in time. When you deposit your savings in a bank account, you give the bank some money now, and the bank returns your deposit with interest in the future. Similarly, when you borrow from a bank, you get some money now, but you will have to repay the loan with interest in the future. In both cases, to fully understand the deal between you and the bank, it is crucial to acknowledge that future dollars could have a different value than today's dollars. In other words, you have to correct for the effects of inflation.

Let's consider an example. Suppose Sara Saver deposits $1,000 in a bank account that pays an annual interest rate of 10 percent. A year later, after Sara has accumulated $100 in interest, she withdraws her $1,100. Is Sara $100 richer than she was when she made the deposit a year earlier?

The answer depends on what we mean by "richer." Sara does have $100 more than she had before. In other words, the number of dollars in her possession has risen by 10 percent. But Sara does not care about the amount of money itself: She cares about what she can buy with it. If prices have risen while her money was in the bank, each dollar now buys less than it did a year ago. In this case, her purchasing power—the amount of goods and services she can buy—has not risen by 10 percent.

To keep things simple, let's suppose that Sara is a film buff and spends all her money on movie tickets. When Sara made her deposit, a ticket cost $10. Her deposit of $1,000 was equivalent to 100 tickets. A year later, after getting her 10 percent interest, she has $1,100. How many tickets can she buy now? The answer depends on what has happened to the price of a ticket. Here are a few scenarios:

- Zero inflation: If the price of a ticket remains at $10, the amount she can buy has risen from 100 to 110 tickets. The 10 percent increase in the number of dollars means a 10 percent increase in her purchasing power.
- Six percent inflation: If the price of a ticket rises from $10 to $10.60, then the number of tickets she can buy has risen from 100 to approximately 104. Her purchasing power has increased by about 4 percent.
- Ten percent inflation: If the price of a ticket rises from $10 to $11, she can still buy only 100 tickets. Even though Sara's dollar wealth has risen, her purchasing power is the same as it was a year earlier.
- Twelve percent inflation: If the price of a ticket increases from $10 to $11.20, the number of tickets she can buy has fallen from 100 to approximately 98. Even with her greater number of dollars, her purchasing power has decreased by about 2 percent.

And if Sara were living in an economy with deflation—negative inflation or, more simply, falling prices—another possibility could arise:

- Two percent deflation: If the price of a ticket falls from $10 to $9.80, then the number of tickets she can buy rises from 100 to approximately 112. Her purchasing power increases by about 12 percent.

These examples show that the higher the rate of inflation, the smaller the increase in Sara's purchasing power. If the rate of inflation exceeds the rate of interest, her purchasing power actually falls. And if there is deflation, her purchasing power rises by more than the rate of interest.

To understand how much a person earns in a savings account, we need to consider both the interest rate and the change in prices. The interest rate that measures the change in dollar amounts is called the **nominal interest rate**, and the interest rate corrected for inflation is called the **real interest rate**. The nominal interest rate, the real interest rate, and inflation are related approximately as follows:

$$\text{Real interest rate} = \text{Nominal interest rate} - \text{Inflation rate.}$$

nominal interest rate
the interest rate as usually reported without a correction for the effects of inflation

real interest rate
the interest rate corrected for the effects of inflation

The real interest rate is the difference between the nominal interest rate and the rate of inflation. The nominal interest rate tells you how fast the number of dollars in your bank account rises over time, while the real interest rate tells you how fast the purchasing power of your bank account rises over time.

INTEREST RATES IN THE U.S. ECONOMY

CASE STUDY

Figure 4 shows real and nominal interest rates in the U.S. economy since 1965. The nominal interest rate in this figure is the rate on three-month Treasury bills (although data on other interest rates would be similar). The real interest rate is computed by subtracting the rate of inflation from this nominal interest rate. Here the inflation rate is measured as the percentage change in the CPI.

One feature of this figure is that the nominal interest rate almost always exceeds the real interest rate. This reflects the fact that the U.S. economy has experienced rising consumer prices in almost every year during this period. By contrast, if you look at data for the U.S. economy during the late 19th century or for the Japanese economy in some recent years, you will find periods of deflation. During deflation, the real interest rate exceeds the nominal interest rate.

The figure also shows that because inflation is variable, real and nominal interest rates do not always move together. For example, in the late 1970s, nominal interest rates were high. But because inflation was very high, real interest rates were low. Indeed, during much of the 1970s, real interest rates were negative, for inflation eroded people's savings more quickly than nominal interest payments increased them. By contrast, in the late 1990s, nominal interest rates were lower than they had been two decades earlier. But because inflation was much lower, real interest rates were higher. In the coming chapters, we will examine the economic forces that determine both real and nominal interest rates. ●

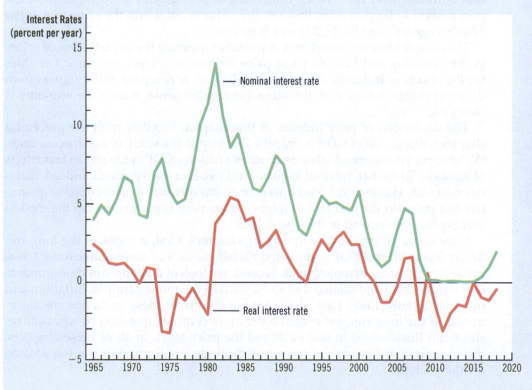

FIGURE 4

Real and Nominal Interest Rates

This figure shows nominal and real interest rates using annual data since 1965. The nominal interest rate is the rate on a three-month Treasury bill. The real interest rate is the nominal interest rate minus the inflation rate as measured by the CPI. Notice that nominal and real interest rates often do not move together.

Source: U.S. Department of Labor; U.S. Department of Treasury.

Answers at end of chapter.

Quick**Quiz**

5. If the CPI is 200 for the year 1980 and 300 today, then $600 in 1980 has the same purchasing power as _____ has today.
   a. $400
   b. $500
   c. $700
   d. $900

6. The main reason the cost of living varies across regions of the country is differences in the price of
   a. food.
   b. clothing.
   c. housing.
   d. medical care.

7. You deposit $2,000 in a savings account, and a year later you have $2,100. Meanwhile, the CPI rises from 200 to 204. In this case, the nominal interest rate is _____ percent, and the real interest rate is _____ percent.
   a. 1; 5
   b. 3; 5
   c. 5; 1
   d. 5; 3

6-3 Conclusion

"A nickel ain't worth a dime anymore," the late, great baseball player Yogi Berra once observed. Indeed, throughout recent history, the real values behind the nickel, dime, and dollar have not been stable. Persistent increases in the overall level of prices have been the norm. Such inflation reduces the purchasing power of each unit of money over time. When comparing dollar figures from different times, it is important to keep in mind that a dollar today is not worth the same as a dollar 20 years ago or, most likely, 20 years from now.

This chapter has discussed how economists measure the overall level of prices in the economy and how they use price indexes to correct economic variables for the effects of inflation. Price indexes allow us to compare dollar figures from different points in time and, therefore, get a better sense of how the economy is changing.

The discussion of price indexes in this chapter, together with the preceding chapter's discussion of GDP, is only the first step in the study of macroeconomics. We have not yet examined what determines a nation's GDP or the causes and effects of inflation. To do that, we need to go beyond issues of measurement. Indeed, that is our next task. Having explained how economists measure macroeconomic quantities and prices in the past two chapters, we are now ready to develop the models that explain movements in these variables.

Here is our strategy in the upcoming chapters. First, we look at the long-run determinants of real GDP and related variables, such as saving, investment, real interest rates, and unemployment. Second, we look at the long-run determinants of the price level and related variables, such as the money supply, inflation, and nominal interest rates. Last of all, having seen how these variables are determined in the long run, we examine the more complex question of what causes short-run fluctuations in real GDP and the price level. In all of these chapters, the measurement issues we have just discussed will provide the foundation for the analysis.

CHAPTER IN A NUTSHELL

- The consumer price index (CPI) shows the cost of a basket of goods and services relative to the cost of the same basket in the base year. The index is used to measure the overall level of prices in the economy. The percentage change in the CPI measures the inflation rate.

- The CPI is an imperfect measure of the cost of living for three reasons. First, it does not take into account consumers' ability to substitute toward goods that become relatively cheaper over time. Second, it does not take into account increases in the purchasing power of the dollar that result from the introduction of new goods. Third, it is distorted by unmeasured changes in the quality of goods and services. Because of these measurement problems, the CPI overstates true inflation.

- Like the CPI, the GDP deflator measures the overall level of prices in the economy. The two price indexes usually move together, but there are important differences. The GDP deflator differs from the CPI because it reflects the prices of goods and services produced domestically rather than of goods and services bought by consumers. As a result, imported goods affect the CPI but not the GDP deflator. In addition, while the CPI uses a fixed basket of goods, the group of goods and services reflected in the GDP deflator automatically changes over time as the composition of GDP changes.

- Dollar figures from different times do not represent a valid comparison of purchasing power. To compare a dollar figure from the past with a dollar figure today, the older figure should be inflated using a price index.

- Various laws and private contracts use price indexes to correct for the effects of inflation. Tax laws, however, are only partially indexed for inflation.

- Correcting for inflation is especially important when looking at data on interest rates. The nominal interest rate—the interest rate usually reported—is the rate at which the number of dollars in a savings account increases over time. By contrast, the real interest rate is the rate at which the purchasing power of a savings account increases over time. The real interest rate equals the nominal interest rate minus the rate of inflation.

KEY CONCEPTS

consumer price index (CPI), *p. 108*   producer price index (PPI), *p. 111*   real interest rate, *p. 118*
inflation rate, *p. 110*   indexation, *p. 117*
core CPI, *p. 110*   nominal interest rate, *p. 118*

QUESTIONS FOR REVIEW

1. Which do you think has a greater effect on the CPI: a 10 percent increase in the price of chicken or a 10 percent increase in the price of caviar? Why?

2. Describe the three problems that make the CPI an imperfect measure of the cost of living.

3. Does an increase in the price of imported French wine affect the CPI or the GDP deflator more? Why?

4. Over a long period of time, the price of a candy bar rose from $0.20 to $1.20. Over the same period, the CPI rose from 150 to 300. Adjusted for overall inflation, how much did the price of the candy bar change?

5. Explain the meanings of *nominal interest rate* and *real interest rate*. How are they related?

PROBLEMS AND APPLICATIONS

1. Suppose that the year you were born someone bought $100 of goods and services for your baby shower. How much would you guess it would cost today to buy a similar amount of goods and services? Now find data on the CPI and compute the answer based on it. (You can find the BLS's inflation calculator here: http://www.bls.gov/data/inflation_calculator.htm.)

2. The residents of Vegopia spend all of their income on cauliflower, broccoli, and carrots. In 2020, they spend a total of $200 for 100 heads of cauliflower, $75 for 50 bunches of broccoli, and $50 for 500 carrots. In 2021, they spend a total of $225 for 75 heads of cauliflower, $120 for 80 bunches of broccoli, and $100 for 500 carrots.
   a. Calculate the price of one unit of each vegetable in each year.
   b. Using 2020 as the base year, calculate the CPI for each year.
   c. What is the inflation rate in 2021?

3. Suppose that people consume only three goods, as shown in this table:

	Tennis Balls	Golf Balls	Bottles of Gatorade
2020 price	$2	$4	$1
2020 quantity	100	100	200
2021 price	$2	$6	$2
2021 quantity	100	100	200

   a. What is the percentage change in the price of each of the three goods?
   b. Using a method similar to the CPI, compute the percentage change in the overall price level.
   c. If you were to learn that a bottle of Gatorade increased in size from 2020 to 2021, should that information affect your calculation of the inflation rate? If so, how?
   d. If you were to learn that Gatorade introduced new flavors in 2021, should that information affect your calculation of the inflation rate? If so, how?

4. Go to the website of the Bureau of Labor Statistics (http://www.bls.gov) and find data on the CPI. By how much has the index including all items risen over the past year? For which categories of spending have prices risen the most? The least? Have any categories experienced price declines? Can you explain any of these facts?

5. A small nation idolizes the TV show *The Voice*. All they produce and consume are karaoke machines and CDs, in the following amounts:

	Karaoke Machines		CDs	
	Quantity	Price	Quantity	Price
2020	10	$40	30	$10
2021	12	60	50	12

   a. Using a method similar to the CPI, compute the percentage change in the overall price level. Use 2020 as the base year and fix the basket at 1 karaoke machine and 3 CDs.
   b. Using a method similar to the GDP deflator, compute the percentage change in the overall price level. Again, use 2020 as the base year.
   c. Is the inflation rate in 2021 the same using the two methods? Explain why or why not.

6. Which of the problems in the construction of the CPI might be illustrated by each of the following situations? Explain.
   a. the invention of cell phones
   b. the introduction of air bags in cars
   c. increased personal computer purchases in response to a decline in their price
   d. more scoops of raisins in each package of Raisin Bran
   e. greater use of fuel-efficient cars after gasoline prices increase

7. A dozen eggs cost $0.88 in January 1980 and $1.77 in January 2018. The average hourly wage for production and nonsupervisory workers was $6.57 in January 1980 and $22.36 in January 2018.
   a. By what percentage did the price of eggs rise?
   b. By what percentage did the wage rise?
   c. In each year, how many minutes did a worker have to work to earn enough to buy a dozen eggs?
   d. Did workers' purchasing power in terms of eggs rise or fall?

8. The chapter explains that Social Security benefits are increased each year in proportion to the increase in the CPI, even though most economists believe that the CPI overstates actual inflation.
   a. If the elderly consume the same market basket as other people, does Social Security provide the elderly with an improvement in their standard of living each year? Explain.
   b. In fact, the elderly consume more healthcare compared with younger people, and healthcare costs have risen faster than overall inflation. What would you do to determine whether the elderly are actually better off from year to year?

9. Suppose that a borrower and a lender agree on the nominal interest rate to be paid on a loan. Then inflation turns out to be higher than they both expected.

   a. Is the real interest rate on this loan higher or lower than expected?

   b. Does the lender gain or lose from this unexpectedly high inflation? Does the borrower gain or lose?

   c. Inflation during the 1970s was much higher than most people had expected when the decade began. How did this unexpectedly high inflation affect homeowners who obtained fixed-rate mortgages during the 1960s? How did it affect the banks that lent the money?

Quick**Quiz Answers**

1. **c**   2. **b**   3. **d**   4. **a**   5. **d**   6. **c**   7. **d**

When you travel around the world, you see tremendous variation in the standard of living. The average income in a rich country, such as the United States, Japan, or Germany, is about 10 times the average income in a poor country, such as India, Nigeria, or Nicaragua. These large differences in income are reflected in large differences in the quality of life. People in richer countries have better nutrition, safer housing, better healthcare, and longer life expectancy as well as more automobiles, more telephones, and more computers.

Even within a country, there are large changes in the standard of living over time. In the United States over the past century, average income as measured by real gross domestic product (GDP) per person has grown by about 2 percent per year. Although this rate of growth may seem small, it implies that average income has roughly doubled every 35 years. Because of this growth, most Americans enjoy much greater economic prosperity than did their parents, grandparents, and great-grandparents.

CHAPTER 7

Production and Growth

Growth rates vary substantially from country to country. From 1990 to 2017, GDP per person in China grew at a rate of 9 percent per year, resulting in a tenfold increase in average income. This growth has moved China from being one of the poorest countries in the world to being a middle-income country in roughly one generation. If this rapid growth continues for another generation, China will become one of richest countries in the world. By contrast, over the same span of time, income per person in Zimbabwe fell by a total of 27 percent, leaving the typical person in that nation mired in poverty.

What explains these diverse experiences? How can rich countries maintain their high standard of living? What policies can poor countries pursue to promote more rapid growth and join the developed world? These questions are among the most important in macroeconomics. As the Nobel-Prize-winning economist Robert Lucas put it, "The consequences for human welfare in questions like these are simply staggering: Once one starts to think about them, it is hard to think about anything else."

In the previous two chapters, we discussed how economists measure macroeconomic quantities and prices. We can now begin to study the forces that determine these variables. As we have seen, an economy's GDP measures both the total income earned in the economy and the total expenditure on the economy's output of goods and services. The level of real GDP is a good gauge of economic prosperity, and the growth of real GDP is a good gauge of economic progress. In this chapter we focus on the long-run determinants of the level and growth of real GDP. Later, we study the short-run fluctuations of real GDP around its long-run trend.

We proceed here in three steps. First, we examine international data on real GDP per person. These data will give you some sense of how much the level and growth of living standards vary around the world. Second, we examine the role of *productivity*—the amount of goods and services produced for each hour of work. In particular, we see that a nation's standard of living is determined by the productivity of its workers, and we consider the factors that determine a nation's productivity. Third, we consider the link between productivity and the economic policies that a nation pursues.

7-1 Economic Growth around the World

As a starting point for our study of long-run growth, let's look at the experiences of some of the world's economies. Table 1 shows data on real GDP per person for 13 countries. For each country, the data span more than a century of history. The first and second columns of the table present the countries and time periods. (The time periods differ somewhat from country to country because of differences in data availability.) The third and fourth columns show estimates of real GDP per person more than a century ago and for a recent year.

The data on real GDP per person show that living standards vary widely from country to country. Income per person in the United States, for instance, is now almost four times that in China and about eight times that in India. The poorest countries have average levels of income not seen in the developed world for many decades. The typical resident of Pakistan in 2017 had about the same real income as the typical resident of the United Kingdom in 1870. The typical Bangladeshi in 2017 had less real income than the typical American in 1870.

The last column of the table shows each country's growth rate. The growth rate measures how rapidly real income per person grew in the typical year. In the United States, for example, where real income per person was $4,443 in 1870 and

TABLE **1**

The Variety of Growth
Experiences

Country	Period	Real GDP per Person (in 2017 dollars)		Growth Rate (per year)
		At Beginning of Period	At End of Period	
China	1900–2017	$ 794	$16,807	2.64%
Japan	1890–2017	1,667	43,279	2.60
Brazil	1900–2017	863	15,484	2.50
Mexico	1900–2017	1,285	18,258	2.29
Indonesia	1900–2017	988	12,284	2.18
Germany	1870–2017	2,422	50,639	2.09
Canada	1870–2017	2,633	46,705	1.98
India	1900–2017	748	7,056	1.94
Argentina	1900–2017	2,542	20,787	1.81
United States	1870–2017	4,443	59,532	1.78
Pakistan	1900–2017	818	5,527	1.65
Bangladesh	1900–2017	691	3,869	1.48
United Kingdom	1870–2017	5,332	43,269	1.43

Source: Robert J. Barro and Xavier Sala-i-Martin, *Economic Growth* (New York: McGraw-Hill, 1995), Tables 10.2 and 10.3; *World Bank* online data; and author's calculations. To account for international price differences, data are PPP-adjusted when available.

$59,532 in 2017, the growth rate was 1.78 percent per year. This means that if real income per person, beginning at $4,443, were to increase by 1.78 percent for each of 147 years, it would end up at $59,532. Of course, income did not rise exactly 1.78 percent every year: Some years it rose by more, other years it rose by less, and in still other years it fell. The growth rate of 1.78 percent per year ignores short-run fluctuations around the long-run trend and represents an average rate of growth for real income per person over many years.

The countries in Table 1 are ordered by growth rate from the most to the least rapid. Here you can see the large variety in growth experiences. High on the list are Brazil and China, which went from being among the poorest nations in the world to being among middle-income nations. Also high on the list is Japan, which went from being a middle-income nation to being among the richest nations.

Near the bottom of the list you can find Pakistan and Bangladesh, which were among the poorest nations at the end of the nineteenth century and remain so today. At the bottom of the list is the United Kingdom. In 1870, the United Kingdom was the richest country in the world, with average income about 20 percent higher than that of the United States and about twice Canada's. Today, average income in the United Kingdom is 27 percent below that of the United States and 7 percent below Canada's.

These data show that the world's richest countries are not guaranteed to remain the richest and that the world's poorest countries are not doomed to endless poverty. But what explains these changes over time? Why do some countries zoom ahead while others lag behind? These are precisely the questions that we take up next.

FYI

Are You Richer Than the Richest American?

John D. Rockefeller

*A*merican Heritage magazine once published a list of the richest Americans of all time. The number 1 spot went to John D. Rockefeller, the oil entrepreneur who lived from 1839 to 1937. According to the magazine's calculations, after adjusting for inflation, his wealth would be the equivalent of about $250 billion today, roughly twice that of Jeff Bezos, the online retailing entrepreneur who is today's richest American.

Despite his great wealth, Rockefeller did not enjoy many of the conveniences that we now take for granted. He couldn't watch television, play video games, surf the Internet, or send e-mail. During the heat of summer, he couldn't cool his home with air-conditioning. For much of his life, he couldn't travel by car or plane, and he couldn't use a telephone to call friends or family. If he became ill, he couldn't take advantage of

many medicines, such as antibiotics, that doctors today routinely use to prolong and enhance life.

Now consider: How much money would someone have to pay you to give up for the rest of your life all the modern conveniences that Rockefeller lived without? Would you do it for $250 billion? Perhaps not. And if you wouldn't, is it fair to say that you are better off than John D. Rockefeller, allegedly the richest American ever?

As the preceding chapter discussed, standard price indexes used to compare sums of money from different times fail to fully reflect the introduction of new goods. As a result, the rate of inflation is overestimated. The flip side of this observation is that the rate of real economic growth is underestimated. Pondering Rockefeller's life shows how significant this problem might be. Because of tremendous technological advances, the average American today is arguably "richer" than the richest American a century ago, even if that fact is lost in standard economic statistics. ■

Quick Quiz

1. Over the past century, real GDP per person in the United States has grown about _____ percent per year, meaning it has roughly doubled every _____ years.
   a. 2; 14
   b. 2; 35
   c. 5; 14
   d. 5; 35

2. The world's rich countries, such as the United States and Germany, have income per person that is about _____ times the income per person in the world's poor countries, such as Pakistan and India.
   a. 2
   b. 4
   c. 10
   d. 30

3. Over the past century, _____ has experienced particularly strong growth, and _____ has experienced particularly weak growth.
   a. Japan; the United Kingdom
   b. Japan; Canada
   c. the United Kingdom; Canada
   d. Canada; Japan

Answers at end of chapter.

7-2 Productivity: Its Role and Determinants

Explaining why living standards vary so much around the world is, in one sense, very easy. The answer can be summarized in a single word—*productivity*. But in another sense, the international variation in living standards is deeply puzzling. To explain why incomes are so much higher in some countries than in others, we must look at the many factors that determine a nation's productivity.

7-2a Why Productivity Is So Important

Let's begin our study of productivity and economic growth by developing a simple model based loosely on Daniel Defoe's famous novel *Robinson Crusoe* about a sailor stranded on a desert island. Because Crusoe lives alone, he catches his own fish, grows his own vegetables, and makes his own clothes. We can think of Crusoe's activities—his production and consumption of fish, vegetables, and clothing—as a simple economy. By examining Crusoe's economy, we can learn some lessons that also apply to more complex and realistic economies.

What determines Crusoe's standard of living? In a word, **productivity**, the quantity of goods and services produced from each unit of labor input. If Crusoe is good at catching fish, growing vegetables, and making clothes, he lives well. If he is bad at doing these things, he lives poorly. Because Crusoe gets to consume only what he produces, his living standard is tied to his productivity.

In the case of Crusoe's economy, it is easy to see that productivity is the key determinant of living standards and that growth in productivity is the key determinant of growth in living standards. The more fish Crusoe can catch per hour, the more he eats at dinner. If Crusoe finds a better place to catch fish, his productivity rises. This increase in productivity makes Crusoe better off: He can eat the extra fish, or he can spend less time fishing and devote more time to making other goods he enjoys.

Productivity's key role in determining living standards is as true for nations as it is for stranded sailors. Recall that an economy's GDP measures two things at once: the total income earned by everyone in the economy and the total expenditure on the economy's output of goods and services. GDP can measure these two things simultaneously because, for the economy as a whole, they must be equal. Put simply, an economy's income is the economy's output.

Like Crusoe, a nation can enjoy a high standard of living only if it can produce a large quantity of goods and services. Americans live better than Nigerians because American workers are more productive than Nigerian workers. The Japanese have enjoyed more rapid growth in living standards than Argentineans because Japanese workers have experienced more rapid growth in productivity. Indeed, one of the *Ten Principles of Economics* in Chapter 1 is that a country's standard of living depends on its ability to produce goods and services.

Hence, to understand the large differences in living standards across countries or over time, we must focus on the production of goods and services. But seeing the link between living standards and productivity is only the first step. It leads naturally to the next question: Why are some economies so much better at producing goods and services than others?

> **productivity**
> the quantity of goods and services produced from each unit of labor input

7-2b How Productivity Is Determined

Although productivity is uniquely important in determining Robinson Crusoe's standard of living, many factors determine Crusoe's productivity. Crusoe will be better at catching fish, for instance, if he has more fishing poles, if he has been trained in the best fishing techniques, if his island has a plentiful fish supply, or if he invents a better fishing lure. Each of these determinants of Crusoe's productivity—which we can call *physical capital, human capital, natural resources,* and *technological knowledge*—has a counterpart in more complex and realistic economies. Let's consider each factor in turn.

Physical Capital per Worker Workers are more productive if they have tools with which to work. The stock of equipment and structures used to produce goods and services is called **physical capital**, or just *capital*. For example, when

> **physical capital**
> the stock of equipment and structures that are used to produce goods and services

woodworkers make furniture, they use saws, lathes, and drill presses. More tools allow the woodworkers to produce their output more quickly and more accurately: A worker with only basic hand tools can make less furniture each week than a worker with sophisticated and specialized woodworking equipment.

As you may recall, the inputs used to produce goods and services—labor, capital, and so on—are called the *factors of production*. An important feature of capital is that it is a *produced* factor of production. That is, capital is an input into the production process that in the past was an output from the production process. The woodworker uses a lathe to make the leg of a table. Earlier, the lathe itself was the output of a firm that manufactures lathes. The lathe manufacturer in turn used other equipment to make its product. Thus, capital is a factor of production used to produce all kinds of goods and services, including more capital.

human capital
the knowledge and skills that workers acquire through education, training, and experience

Human Capital per Worker   A second determinant of productivity is human capital. **Human capital** is the economist's term for the knowledge and skills that workers acquire through education, training, and experience. Human capital includes the skills accumulated in early childhood programs, grade school, high school, college, and on-the-job training for adults in the labor force.

Education, training, and experience are less tangible than lathes, bulldozers, and buildings, but human capital is similar to physical capital in many ways. Like physical capital, human capital raises a nation's ability to produce goods and services. Also like physical capital, human capital is a produced factor of production. Producing human capital requires inputs in the form of teachers, libraries, and student time. Indeed, students can be viewed as "workers" who have the important job of producing the human capital that will be used in future production.

natural resources
the inputs into the production of goods and services that are provided by nature, such as land, rivers, and mineral deposits

Natural Resources per Worker   A third determinant of productivity is **natural resources**. Natural resources are inputs into production that are provided by nature, such as land, rivers, and mineral deposits. Natural resources take two forms: renewable and nonrenewable. A forest is an example of a renewable resource. When one tree is cut down, a seedling can be planted in its place to be harvested in the future. Oil is an example of a nonrenewable resource. Because oil is produced by nature over many millions of years, there is only a limited supply. Once the supply of oil is depleted, it is impossible to create more.

Differences in natural resources are responsible for some of the differences in standards of living around the world. The historical success of the United States was driven in part by the large supply of land well suited for agriculture. Today, some countries in the Middle East, such as Kuwait and Saudi Arabia, are rich simply because they happen to be on top of some of the largest pools of oil in the world.

Although natural resources can be important, they are not necessary for an economy to be highly productive in producing goods and services. Japan, for instance, is one of the richest countries in the world, despite having few natural resources. International trade makes Japan's success possible. Japan imports many of the natural resources it needs, such as oil, and exports its manufactured goods to economies rich in natural resources.

technological knowledge
society's understanding of the best ways to produce goods and services

Technological Knowledge   A fourth determinant of productivity is **technological knowledge**—the understanding of the best ways to produce goods and services. Two hundred years ago, most Americans worked on farms because the farm technology available at the time required a high input of labor to feed the entire population. Today, thanks to advances in farm technology, a small fraction of the population can produce enough food to feed the entire country. This technological change freed up labor, which could then be used to produce other goods and services.

Technological knowledge takes many forms. Some technology is common knowledge—after one person uses it, everyone becomes aware of it. For example, once Henry Ford successfully introduced assembly-line production, other carmakers quickly followed suit. Other technology is proprietary—it is known only by the company that discovers it. Only the Coca-Cola Company, for instance, knows the secret recipe for making its famous soft drink. Still other technology is proprietary for a short time. When a pharmaceutical company discovers a new drug, the patent system gives that company a temporary right to be its exclusive manufacturer. When the patent expires, however, other companies are allowed to make the drug. All these forms of technological knowledge are important for the economy's production of goods and services.

It is worthwhile to distinguish between technological knowledge and human capital. They are closely related, but there is an important difference. Technological knowledge refers to society's understanding about how the world works. Human capital refers to the resources expended transmitting this understanding to the labor force. To use a relevant metaphor, technological knowledge is the quality of society's textbooks, whereas human capital is the amount of time that the population has spent reading them. Workers' productivity depends on both.

FYI   The Production Function

Economists often use a *production function* to describe the relationship between the quantity of inputs used in production and the quantity of output from production. For example, suppose Y denotes the quantity of output, L the quantity of labor, K the quantity of physical capital, H the quantity of human capital, and N the quantity of natural resources. Then we might write

$$Y = AF(L, K, H, N),$$

where $F(\ )$ is a function that shows how the inputs are combined to produce output. A is a variable that reflects the available production technology. As technology improves, A rises, so the economy produces more output from any given combination of inputs.

Many production functions have a property called *constant returns to scale*. If a production function has constant returns to scale, then doubling all inputs causes the amount of output to double as well. Mathematically, we write that a production function has constant returns to scale if, for any positive number x,

$$xY = AF(xL, xK, xH, xN).$$

A doubling of all inputs would be represented in this equation by $x = 2$. The right side shows the inputs doubling, and the left side shows output doubling.

Production functions with constant returns to scale have an interesting and useful implication. To see this implication, set $x = 1/L$ so that the preceding equation becomes

$$Y/L = AF(1, K/L, H/L, N/L).$$

Notice that Y/L is output per worker, which is a measure of productivity. This equation says that labor productivity depends on the amounts of physical capital per worker (K/L), human capital per worker (H/L), and natural resources per worker (N/L) and on the state of technology, as represented by the variable A. Thus, this equation provides a mathematical summary of the four determinants of productivity we have just discussed. ◼

ARE NATURAL RESOURCES A LIMIT TO GROWTH?

Today, the world's population is almost 8 billion, about four times what it was a century ago. At the same time, many people are enjoying a much higher standard of living than did their great-grandparents. A perennial debate concerns whether this growth in population and living standards can continue in the future.

Many commentators have argued that natural resources will eventually limit how much the world's economies can grow. At first, this argument might seem hard to ignore. If the world has only a fixed supply of nonrenewable natural resources, how can population, production, and living standards continue to grow over time? Eventually, won't supplies of oil and minerals start to run out? When these shortages start to occur, won't they stop economic growth and, perhaps, even force living standards to fall?

Despite the apparent appeal of such arguments, most economists are less concerned about such limits to growth than one might guess. They argue that technological progress often yields ways to avoid these limits. If we compare the economy today to the economy of the past, we see various ways in which the use of natural resources has improved. Modern cars have better gas mileage. New houses have better insulation and require less energy to heat and cool. More efficient oil rigs waste less oil in the process of extraction. Recycling allows some nonrenewable resources to be reused. The development of alternative fuels, such as ethanol instead of gasoline, allows us to substitute renewable for nonrenewable resources.

Seventy years ago, some conservationists were concerned about the excessive use of tin and copper. At the time, these were crucial commodities: Tin was used to make many food containers, and copper was used to make telephone wire. Some people advocated mandatory recycling and rationing of tin and copper so that supplies would be available for future generations. Today, however, plastic has replaced tin as a material for making many food containers, and phone calls often travel over fiber-optic cables, which are made from sand. Technological progress has made once crucial natural resources less necessary.

But are all these efforts enough to sustain economic growth? One way to answer this question is to look at the prices of natural resources. In a market economy, scarcity is reflected in market prices. If the world were running out of natural resources, then the prices of those resources would be rising over time. But in fact, the opposite is more often true. Natural resource prices exhibit substantial short-run fluctuations, but over long spans of time, the prices of most natural resources (adjusted for overall inflation) are stable or falling. It appears that our ability to conserve these resources is growing more rapidly than their supplies are dwindling. Market prices give no reason to believe that natural resources are a limit to economic growth. ●

Quick**Quiz**

4. Increases in the amount of human capital in the economy tend to _____ real incomes because they increase the _____ of labor.
   a. increase; bargaining power
   b. increase; productivity
   c. decrease; bargaining power
   d. decrease; productivity

5. Most economists are _____ that natural resources will eventually limit economic growth. As evidence, they note that the prices of most natural resources, adjusted for overall inflation, have tended to _____ over time.
   a. concerned; rise
   b. concerned; fall
   c. not concerned; rise
   d. not concerned; fall

Answers at end of chapter.

7-3 Economic Growth and Public Policy

So far, we have determined that a society's standard of living depends on its ability to produce goods and services and that its productivity in turn depends on physical capital per worker, human capital per worker, natural resources per worker, and technological knowledge. Let's now turn to the question faced by policymakers around the world: What can government policy do to raise productivity and living standards?

7-3a Saving and Investment

Because capital is a produced factor of production, a society can change the amount of capital it has. If today the economy produces a large quantity of new capital goods, then tomorrow it will have a larger stock of capital and be able to produce more goods and services. Thus, one way to raise future productivity is to devote more current resources to the production of capital.

One of the *Ten Principles of Economics* in Chapter 1 is that people face trade-offs. This principle is especially important when considering the accumulation of capital. Because resources are scarce, devoting more resources to producing capital requires devoting fewer resources to producing goods and services for current consumption. That is, for society to invest more in capital, it must consume less and save more of its current income. The growth that arises from capital accumulation is not a free lunch: It requires that society sacrifice consumption of goods and services in the present to enjoy higher consumption in the future.

The next chapter examines in more detail how an economy's financial markets coordinate saving and investment. It also examines how government policies influence the amount of saving and investment that take place. At this point, it is important to note that encouraging saving and investment is one way that a government can encourage growth and, in the long run, raise an economy's standard of living.

7-3b Diminishing Returns and the Catch-Up Effect

Suppose that a government pursues policies that raise the nation's saving rate—the percentage of GDP devoted to saving rather than consumption. What happens? With the nation saving more, fewer resources are needed to make consumption goods and more resources are available to make capital goods. As a result, the capital stock increases, leading to rising productivity and more rapid growth in GDP. But how long does this higher rate of growth last? Assuming that the saving rate remains at its new, higher level, does the growth rate of GDP stay high indefinitely or only for a period of time?

The traditional view of the production process is that capital is subject to **diminishing returns**: As the stock of capital rises, the extra output produced from an additional unit of capital falls. In other words, when workers already have a large quantity of capital to use in producing goods and services, giving them an additional unit of capital increases their productivity only slightly. This phenomenon is illustrated in Figure 1, which shows how the amount of capital per worker determines the amount of output per worker, holding constant all the other determinants of output (such as natural resources and technological knowledge). Capital's diminishing returns is sometimes called the *diminishing marginal product of capital*.

Because of diminishing returns, an increase in the saving rate leads to higher growth only for a while. As the higher saving rate allows more capital to be accumulated, the benefits from additional capital become smaller over time, and so growth slows down. *In the long run, the higher saving rate leads to a higher level of productivity and income but not to higher growth in these variables.* Reaching this long run, however, can take quite a while. According to studies of international data on

diminishing returns
the property whereby the benefit from an extra unit of an input declines as the quantity of the input increases

FIGURE 1

Illustrating the Production Function
This figure shows how the amount of capital per worker influences the amount of output per worker. Other determinants of output, including human capital, natural resources, and technology, are held constant. The curve becomes flatter as the amount of capital increases because of diminishing returns to capital.

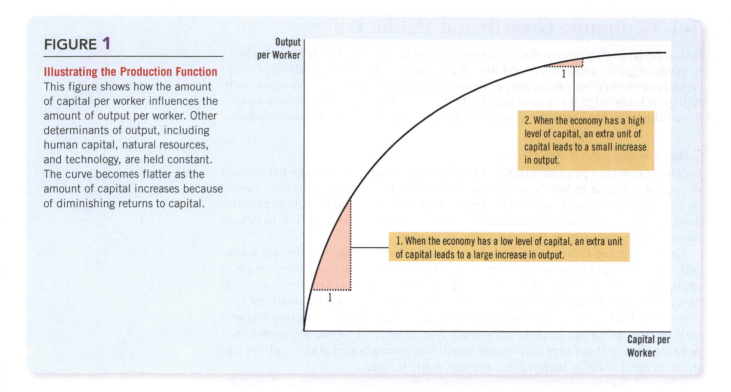

Output per Worker

2. When the economy has a high level of capital, an extra unit of capital leads to a small increase in output.

1. When the economy has a low level of capital, an extra unit of capital leads to a large increase in output.

Capital per Worker

economic growth, increasing the saving rate can lead to substantially higher growth for a period of several decades.

The property of diminishing returns to capital has another important implication: Other things being equal, it is easier for a country to grow fast if it starts out relatively poor. This effect of initial conditions on subsequent growth is sometimes called the **catch-up effect**. In poor countries, workers lack even the most rudimentary tools and, as a result, have low productivity. Thus, small amounts of capital investment can substantially raise these workers' productivity. By contrast, workers in rich countries have high productivity partly because they have large amounts of capital with which to work. When the amount of capital per worker is already so high, additional capital investment has a relatively small effect on productivity. Studies of international data on economic growth confirm this catch-up effect: Controlling for other variables, such as the percentage of GDP devoted to investment, poor countries tend to grow at faster rates than rich countries.

This catch-up effect can help explain some otherwise puzzling facts. Here's an example: From 1960 to 1990, the United States and South Korea devoted a similar share of GDP to investment. Yet over this time, the United States experienced only moderate growth of about 2 percent, while South Korea experienced spectacular growth of more than 6 percent. The explanation is the catch-up effect. In 1960, South Korea had GDP per person less than one-tenth the U.S. level, in part because previous investment had been so low. With a small initial capital stock, South Korea realized greater benefits to capital accumulation and thus had a higher subsequent growth rate.

This catch-up effect shows up in other aspects of life. When a school gives an end-of-year award to the "Most Improved" student, that student is usually one who began the year with relatively poor performance. Students who began the year not studying find improvement easier than students who always worked hard. Note that it is good to be "Most Improved," given the starting point, but it is even

catch-up effect
the property whereby countries that start off poor tend to grow more rapidly than countries that start off rich

better to be "Best Student." Similarly, economic growth between 1960 and 1990 was much more rapid in South Korea than in the United States, but GDP per person was still higher in the United States.

7-3c Investment from Abroad

So far, we have discussed how policies aimed at increasing a country's saving rate can increase investment and long-term economic growth. Yet saving by domestic residents is not the only way for a country to invest in new capital. The other way is investment by foreigners.

Investment from abroad takes several forms. Ford Motor Company might build a car factory in Mexico. A capital investment that is owned and operated by a foreign entity is called *foreign direct investment*. Alternatively, an American might buy stock in a Mexican corporation (that is, buy a share in the ownership of the corporation), and the corporation can use the proceeds from the stock sale to build a new factory. An investment financed with foreign money but operated by domestic residents is called *foreign portfolio investment*. In both cases, Americans provide the resources necessary to increase the stock of capital in Mexico. That is, American saving is being used to finance Mexican investment.

When foreigners invest in a country, they do so because they expect to earn a return on their investment. Ford's car factory increases the Mexican capital stock and, therefore, increases Mexican productivity and Mexican GDP. Yet Ford takes some of this additional income back to the United States in the form of profit. Similarly, when an American investor buys Mexican stock, the investor has a right to a portion of the profit that the Mexican corporation earns.

Investment from abroad, therefore, does not have the same effect on all measures of economic prosperity. Recall that a country's gross domestic product (GDP) is the income earned within the country by both residents and nonresidents, whereas a country's gross national product (GNP) is the income earned by residents of the country both at home and abroad. When Ford opens its car factory in Mexico, some of the income the factory generates accrues to people who do not live in Mexico. As a result, foreign investment in Mexico raises the income of Mexicans (measured by GNP) by less than it raises the production in Mexico (measured by GDP).

Nonetheless, investment from abroad is one way for a country to grow. Even though some of the benefits from this investment flow back to the foreign owners, this investment does increase the economy's stock of capital, leading to higher productivity and higher wages. Moreover, investment from abroad is one way for poor countries to learn the state-of-the-art technologies developed and used in richer countries. For these reasons, many economists who advise governments in less developed economies advocate policies that encourage investment from abroad. Often, this means removing restrictions that governments have imposed on foreign ownership of domestic capital.

An organization that tries to encourage the flow of capital to poor countries is the World Bank. This international organization obtains funds from the world's advanced countries, such as the United States, and uses these resources to make loans to less developed countries so that they can invest in roads, sewer systems, schools, and other types of capital. It also offers the countries advice about how the funds might best be used. The World Bank and its sister organization, the International Monetary Fund, were set up after World War II. One lesson from the war was that economic distress often leads to political turmoil, international tensions, and military conflict. Thus, every country has an interest in promoting economic prosperity around the world. The World Bank and the International Monetary Fund were established to achieve that common goal.

7-3d Education

Education—investment in human capital—is at least as important as investment in physical capital for a country's long-run economic success. In the United States, each year of schooling has historically raised a person's wage by an average of about 10 percent. In less developed countries, where human capital is especially scarce, the gap between the wages of educated and uneducated workers is even larger. Thus, government policy can enhance the standard of living by providing good schools and encouraging the population to take advantage of them.

Investment in human capital, like investment in physical capital, has an opportunity cost. When students are in school, they forgo the wages they could have earned as members of the labor force. In less developed countries, children often drop out of school at an early age, even though the benefit of additional schooling is very high, simply because their labor is needed to help support the family.

Some economists have argued that human capital is particularly important for economic growth because human capital confers positive externalities. An *externality* is the effect of one person's actions on the well-being of a bystander. An educated person, for instance, might generate new ideas about how best to produce goods and services. If these ideas enter society's pool of knowledge so that everyone can use them, then the ideas are an external benefit of education. In this case, the return from schooling for society is even greater than the return for the individual. This argument would justify the large subsidies to human-capital investment that we observe in the form of public education.

One problem facing some poor countries is the *brain drain*—the emigration of many of the most highly educated workers to rich countries, where these workers can enjoy a higher standard of living. If human capital does have positive externalities, then this brain drain makes those people left behind even poorer. This problem offers policymakers a dilemma. On the one hand, the United States and other rich countries have the best systems of higher education, and it would seem natural for poor countries to send their best students abroad to earn higher degrees. On the other hand, those students who have spent time abroad may choose not to return home, and this brain drain will reduce the poor nation's stock of human capital even further.

7-3e Health and Nutrition

The term *human capital* usually refers to education, but it can also be used to describe another type of investment in people: expenditures that lead to a healthier population. Other things being equal, healthier workers are more productive. The right investments in the health of the population provide one way for a nation to increase productivity and raise living standards.

According to the late economic historian Robert Fogel, improved health from better nutrition has been a significant factor in long-run economic growth. Fogel estimated that in Great Britain in 1780, about one in five people were so malnourished that they were incapable of manual labor. Among those who could work, insufficient caloric intake substantially reduced the work effort they could put forth. As nutrition improved, so did workers' productivity.

Fogel studied these historical trends in part by looking at the height of the population. Short stature can be an indicator of malnutrition, especially during gestation and the early years of life. Fogel found that as nations develop economically, people eat more and the population gets taller. From 1775 to 1975, the average caloric intake in Great Britain rose by 26 percent and the height of the average man rose by 3.6 inches. Similarly, during the spectacular economic growth in South Korea from 1962 to 1995, caloric consumption rose by 44 percent and average male height rose by 2 inches. Of course, a person's height is determined by a combination of genetics and environment. But because the genetic makeup of a population is slow to change, such increases in average height are most likely due to changes in the environment—nutrition being the obvious explanation.

Moreover, studies have found that height is an indicator of productivity. Looking at data on a large number of workers at a point in time, researchers have found that taller workers tend to earn more. Because wages reflect a worker's productivity, this finding suggests that taller workers tend to be more productive. The effect of height on wages is especially pronounced in poorer countries, where malnutrition is a bigger risk.

Fogel won the Nobel Prize in Economics in 1993 for his work in economic history, which includes not only his studies of nutrition but also his studies of American slavery and the role of railroads in the development of the American economy. In the lecture he gave when he was awarded the prize, he surveyed the evidence on health and economic growth. He concluded that "improved gross nutrition accounts for roughly 30 percent of the growth of per capita income in Britain between 1790 and 1980."

Today, malnutrition is fortunately rare in developed nations such as Great Britain and the United States. (Obesity is a more widespread problem.) But for people in developing nations, poor health and inadequate nutrition remain obstacles to higher productivity and improved living standards. The United Nations estimates that about a quarter of the population in sub-Saharan Africa is undernourished.

The causal link between health and wealth runs in both directions. Poor countries are poor in part because their populations are not healthy, and their populations are not healthy in part because they are poor and cannot afford adequate healthcare and nutrition. It is a vicious circle. But this fact opens the possibility of a virtuous circle: Policies that lead to more rapid economic growth would naturally improve health outcomes, which in turn would further promote economic growth.

7-3f Property Rights and Political Stability

Another way policymakers can foster economic growth is by protecting property rights and promoting political stability. This issue goes to the very heart of how market economies work.

Production in market economies arises from the interactions of millions of individuals and firms. When you buy a car, for instance, you are buying the output of a car dealer, a car manufacturer, a steel company, an iron ore mining company, and so on. This division of production among many firms allows the economy's factors of production to be used as effectively as possible. To achieve this outcome, the economy has to coordinate transactions among these firms, as well as between firms and consumers. Market economies achieve this coordination through market prices. That is, market prices are the instrument with which the invisible hand of the marketplace brings supply and demand into balance in each of the many thousands of markets that make up the economy.

An important prerequisite for the price system to work is an economy-wide respect for *property rights*. Property rights refer to the ability of people to exercise authority over the resources they own. A mining company will not make the effort to mine iron ore if it expects the ore to be stolen. The company mines the ore only if it is confident that it will benefit from the ore's subsequent sale. For this reason, courts serve an important role in a market economy: They enforce property rights. Through the criminal justice system, the courts discourage theft. In addition, through the civil justice system, the courts ensure that buyers and sellers live up to their contracts.

Those of us in developed countries tend to take property rights for granted, but those living in less developed countries understand that a lack of property rights can be a major problem. In many countries, the system of justice does not work well. Contracts are hard to enforce, and fraud often goes unpunished. In more extreme cases, the government not only fails to enforce property rights but actually infringes upon them. To do business in some countries, firms are expected to bribe government officials. Such corruption impedes the coordinating power of markets. It also discourages domestic saving and investment from abroad.

One threat to property rights is political instability. When revolutions and coups are common, there is doubt about whether property rights will be respected in the future. If a revolutionary government might confiscate the capital of some businesses, as was often true after communist revolutions, domestic residents have less incentive to save, invest, and start new businesses. At the same time, foreigners have less incentive to invest in the country. Even the threat of revolution can act to depress a nation's standard of living.

Thus, economic prosperity depends in part on favorable political institutions. A country with an efficient court system, honest government officials, and a stable constitution will enjoy a higher standard of living than a country with a poor court system, corrupt officials, and frequent revolutions and coups.

7-3g Free Trade

Some of the world's poorest countries have tried to achieve more rapid economic growth by pursuing *inward-oriented policies*. These policies aim to increase productivity and living standards within the country by avoiding interaction with the rest of the world. Domestic firms often advance the infant-industry argument, claiming that they need protection from foreign competition to thrive and grow. Together with a general distrust of foreigners, this argument has at times led policymakers in less developed countries to impose tariffs and other trade restrictions.

Most economists today believe that poor countries are better off pursuing *outward-oriented policies* that integrate these countries into the world economy. International trade in goods and services can improve the economic well-being of a country's citizens. Trade is, in some ways, a type of technology. When a country exports wheat and imports textiles, the country benefits as if it had invented a technology for turning wheat into textiles. A country that eliminates trade restrictions will, therefore, experience the same kind of economic growth that would occur after a major technological advance.

The adverse impact of inward orientation becomes clear when one considers the small size of many less developed economies. The total GDP of Argentina, for instance, is roughly equal to that of Ohio. Imagine what would happen if the Ohio legislature were to prohibit state residents from trading with people living in other states. Without being able to take advantage of the gains from trade, Ohio would need to produce all the goods it consumes. It would also have to produce all its own capital goods, rather than importing state-of-the-art equipment from other states. Living standards in Ohio would fall immediately, and the problem would likely only get worse over time. This is precisely what happened when Argentina pursued inward-oriented policies throughout much of the 20th century. In contrast, countries that pursued outward-oriented policies, such as South Korea, Singapore, and Taiwan, enjoyed high rates of economic growth.

The amount that a nation trades with others is determined not only by government policy but also by geography. Countries with natural seaports find trade easier than those without this resource. It is not a coincidence that many of the world's major cities, such as New York, San Francisco, and Hong Kong, are located next to oceans. Similarly, because landlocked countries find international trade more difficult, they tend to have lower levels of income than countries with easy access to the world's waterways.

7-3h Research and Development

The primary reason that living standards are higher today than they were a century ago is that technological knowledge has advanced. The telephone, the transistor, the computer, and the internal combustion engine are among the thousands of innovations that have improved the ability to produce goods and services.

Most technological advances come from private research by firms and individual inventors, but there is also a public interest in promoting these efforts. To a large extent, knowledge is a *public good*: That is, once one person discovers an idea, the idea enters society's pool of knowledge and other people can freely use it. Just as government has a role in providing a public good such as national defense, it also has a role in encouraging the research and development of new technologies.

The U.S. government has long played a role in the creation and dissemination of technological knowledge. A century ago, the government sponsored research about farming methods and advised farmers how best to use their land. More recently, the U.S. government, through the Air Force and NASA, has supported aerospace research; as a result, the United States is a leading maker of rockets and planes. The government continues to encourage advances in knowledge with research grants from the National Science Foundation and the National Institutes of Health and with tax breaks for firms engaging in research and development.

Yet another way in which government policy encourages research is through the patent system. When a person or firm creates an innovative product, such as a new drug, the inventor can apply for a patent. If the product is deemed truly original, the government awards the patent, which gives the inventor the exclusive right to make the product for a specified number of years. In essence, the patent gives the inventor a property right over her invention, turning her new idea from a public good into a private good. By allowing inventors to profit from their inventions—even if only temporarily—the patent system increases the incentive for individuals and firms to engage in research.

ASK THE EXPERTS

Innovation and Growth

"Future innovations worldwide will not be transformational enough to promote sustained per-capita economic growth rates in the United States and western Europe over the next century as high as those over the past 150 years."

What do economists say?

34% disagree
59% uncertain
7% agree

Source: IGM Economic Experts Panel, February 11, 2014.

7-3i Population Growth

Economists and other social scientists have long debated how population affects a society. The most direct effect is on the size of the labor force: A large population means there are more workers to produce goods and services. The tremendous size of the Chinese population is one reason China is such an important player in the world economy.

At the same time, however, a large population means there are more people to consume those goods and services. So while a large population means a larger total output of goods and services, it need not mean a higher standard of living for the typical citizen. Indeed, both large and small nations are found at all levels of economic development.

Beyond these obvious effects of population size, population growth interacts with the other factors of production in ways that are more subtle and open to debate.

Thomas Robert Malthus

Stretching Natural Resources Thomas Robert Malthus (1766–1834), an English minister and early economic thinker, is famous for his book called *An Essay on the Principle of Population as It Affects the Future Improvement of Society*. In it, he offered what may be history's most chilling forecast. Malthus argued that an ever-increasing population would continually strain society's ability to provide for itself. As a result, mankind was doomed to forever live in poverty.

Malthus's logic was simple. He began by noting that "food is necessary to the existence of man" and that "the passion between the sexes is necessary and will remain nearly in its present state." He concluded that "the power of population is infinitely greater than the power in the earth to produce subsistence for man." According to Malthus, the only check on population growth was "misery and vice." Attempts by charities or governments to alleviate poverty were counterproductive, he argued, because they merely allowed the poor to have more children, placing even greater strains on society's productive capabilities.

Malthus may have correctly described the world at the time when he lived, but fortunately, his dire forecast was far off the mark. World population has increased about sixfold over the past two centuries, but living standards around the world have significantly increased as well. As a result of economic growth, chronic hunger and malnutrition are less common now than they were in Malthus's day. Modern famines occur from time to time but more often result from income inequality or political instability than from inadequate food production.

Where did Malthus go wrong? As we discussed in a case study earlier in this chapter, growth in human ingenuity has offset the effects of a larger population. Pesticides, fertilizers, mechanized farm equipment, new crop varieties, and other technological advances that Malthus never imagined have allowed each farmer to feed ever greater numbers of people. Even with more mouths to feed, fewer farmers are necessary because each farmer is much more productive.

Diluting the Capital Stock Whereas Malthus worried about the effects of population on the use of natural resources, some modern theories of economic growth emphasize its effects on capital accumulation. According to these theories, high population growth reduces GDP per worker because rapid growth in the number of workers forces the capital stock to be spread more thinly. In other words, when population growth is rapid, each worker is equipped with less capital. A smaller quantity of capital per worker leads to lower productivity and lower GDP per worker.

This problem is most apparent in the case of human capital. Countries with high population growth have large numbers of school-age children. This places a larger burden on the educational system. It is not surprising, therefore, that educational attainment tends to be low in countries with high population growth.

The differences in population growth around the world are large. In developed countries, such as the United States and those in Western Europe, the population has risen only about 1 percent per year in recent decades and is expected to rise even more slowly in the future. By contrast, in many poor African countries, population grows at about 3 percent per year. At this rate, the population doubles every 23 years. This rapid population growth makes it harder to provide workers with the tools and skills they need to achieve high levels of productivity.

Rapid population growth is not the main reason that less developed countries are poor, but some analysts believe that reducing the rate of population growth would help these countries raise their standards of living. In some countries, this goal is accomplished directly with laws that regulate the number of children families may have. For example, from 1980 to 2015, China allowed only one child per family; couples who violated this rule were subject to substantial fines. In countries with greater freedom, the goal of reduced population growth is accomplished less directly by increasing awareness of birth control techniques.

Another way in which a country can influence population growth is to apply one of the *Ten Principles of Economics*: People respond to incentives. Bearing a child, like any decision, has an opportunity cost. When the cost rises, people choose to have smaller families. In particular, women with good educations and employment prospects tend to want fewer children than those with fewer opportunities outside the home. Hence, policies that foster equal treatment of women are one way for less developed economies to reduce their rates of population growth and raise their standards of living.

Promoting Technological Progress Rapid population growth may depress economic prosperity by reducing the amount of capital each worker has, but it may also have some benefits. Some economists have suggested that world population growth has been an engine of technological progress and economic prosperity. The mechanism is simple: If there are more people, then there are more scientists, inventors, and engineers to contribute to technological advance, which benefits everyone.

Economist Michael Kremer provided some support for this hypothesis in an article titled "Population Growth and Technological Change: One Million B.C. to 1990," which was published in the *Quarterly Journal of Economics* in 1993. Kremer began by noting that over the broad span of human history, world growth rates have increased with world population. For example, world growth was more rapid when the world population was 1 billion (around the year 1800) than when the population was only 100 million (around 500 B.C.). This fact is consistent with the hypothesis that a larger population induces more technological progress.

Kremer's second piece of evidence comes from comparing regions of the world. The melting of the polar icecaps at the end of the Ice Age around 10,000 B.C. flooded the land bridges and separated the world into several distinct regions that could not communicate with one another for thousands of years. If technological progress is more rapid when there are more people to discover things, then the more populous regions should have experienced more rapid growth.

According to Kremer, that is exactly what happened. The most successful region of the world in 1500 (when Columbus reestablished contact) comprised the "Old World" civilizations of the large Eurasia-Africa region. Next in technological development were the Aztec and Mayan civilizations in the Americas, followed by the hunter-gatherers of Australia, and then the primitive people of Tasmania, who lacked even fire-making and most stone and bone tools.

The smallest isolated region was Flinders Island, a tiny island between Tasmania and Australia. With the smallest population, Flinders Island had the fewest opportunities for technological advance and, indeed, seemed to regress. Around 3000 B.C., human society on Flinders Island died out completely. The larger population, Kremer concluded, the greater the potential for technological advance.

CASE STUDY

WHY IS SO MUCH OF AFRICA POOR?

Many of the poorest people on the planet live in sub-Saharan Africa. In 2017, GDP per person in this region (measured in 2011 dollars) was only $3,489, just 23 percent of the world average. It is not surprising, then, that sub-Saharan Africa has a high rate of extreme poverty: 41 percent of its population lives on less than $1.90 per day, compared with 10 percent of the population worldwide.

What explains this low level of economic development? There is no easy answer. Many interrelated forces are at work, and sometimes it is hard to distinguish the causes of poverty from the effects. But here are some of the factors that may help explain this distressing phenomenon.

Low capital investment. Because sub-Saharan Africa has low levels of income and capital per worker, one might expect the returns to capital to be high, making the region an attractive place to invest for both domestic savers and investors abroad. But, in fact, as a percentage of GDP, investment in sub-Saharan Africa is 5 percentage points lower than the world average. The low level of investment may be driven by some of the following factors.

Low educational attainment. Those living in sub-Saharan Africa have on average only 5.6 years of schooling, compared with 8.4 years of schooling worldwide. And their quality of schooling is lower as well: The student–teacher ratio in primary schools is 39 in sub-Saharan Africa, compared with a world average of 23. As a result, only 60 percent of adults in sub-Saharan Africa are literate, compared with 82 percent of adults worldwide. Less educated workers are less productive.

Poor health. Among one-year-olds in sub-Saharan Africa, 21 percent have not been immunized for DPT (diphtheria, pertussis, and tetanus), and 31 percent have not been immunized for measles—in both cases, about twice the world average. Among children under age 5, 36 percent are malnourished enough to have stunted growth, compared with 27 percent worldwide. Among adults, 4.5 percent are infected with HIV, four times the world average. These statistics not only reflect extreme personal tragedy but also help explain an economic one. Less healthy workers are less productive.

High population growth. The population in sub-Saharan Africa has recently grown about 2.8 percent per year, meaning the population doubles every 25 years. By contrast, the world population has grown at 1.2 percent per year, doubling every 58 years. Rapid population growth makes it hard to equip workers with the physical and human capital needed to achieve high productivity.

Geographic disadvantages. More than 25 percent of the people in sub-Saharan Africa live in a landlocked nation, such as Ethiopia, Uganda, Chad, Niger, and Mali, compared with 7 percent of the world population. Landlocked nations tend to be poor. Without easy access to the oceans for purposes of transport, it is difficult for them to take advantage of the gains from trade.

Restricted freedom. Social scientists have developed indexes to gauge the degree of human freedom available to a nation's citizens. These indexes measure characteristics such as the reliability of the justice system, personal security and safety, freedom of expression, the right to engage in international trade, and so on. Nations in sub-Saharan Africa tend to rank low on these measures, as do those in South Asia, Eastern Europe, and the Middle East. The freest nations tend to be those in Western Europe, Northern Europe, and North America. (Other regions of the world, such as South America, fall between these extreme cases.) These freedom indexes are positively correlated with economic prosperity: Greater freedom is associated with higher incomes, perhaps because restrictions on freedom impede the invisible hand's ability to allocate resources efficiently.

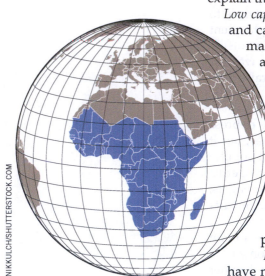

NIKKULCH/SHUTTERSTOCK.COM

Sub-Saharan Africa is the poorest region of the world.

Rampant corruption. The governments in many African nations exhibit high levels of corruption. According to Transparency International, a nonprofit organization that monitors corruption, the African nation of Somalia was the most corrupt country in the world in 2018. Of the 14 most corrupt nations, more than half were in sub-Saharan Africa. (None were in North America or Europe.) High levels of corruption discourage domestic residents from saving and investing and deter investment from abroad.

The legacy of colonization. Economists Daron Acemoglu and James Robinson attribute the low level of economic development in much of Africa to flawed institutions, which they trace back to colonization. In the 17th and 18th centuries, when Europeans were looking for places to colonize and settle, they preferred locations with moderate climates, such as the United States, Canada, and New Zealand. Because the colonizers planned to stay there, they brought *inclusive institutions* like those in Europe. Inclusive institutions spread political power widely, respect property rights and the rule of law, and thereby foster economic prosperity. In places with less appealing tropical climates, including much of Africa, the colonizers had little interest in permanent settlement. As a result, they established *extractive institutions*, such as authoritarian governments, designed to exploit the region's population and natural resources. Even after the colonizers left, the extractive institutions remained and were taken over by new ruling elites, impeding economic development.

None of these causes suggests an easy solution to Africa's problems. But neither is poverty a foregone conclusion. Through a combination of good policy and good luck, the African nation of Botswana has managed to become a middle-income country, with GDP per person about equal to the world average and a rate of extreme poverty less than half of that in the rest of sub-Saharan Africa. Botswana has the disadvantage of being landlocked, and it is plagued by widespread HIV. But compared with most of its neighbors, Botswana has higher investment, better education, lower population growth, higher vaccination rates, lower malnutrition, greater freedoms, and less corruption. It has successfully transitioned from once being a colonized country to now being Africa's oldest continuous democracy. In many ways, Botswana is a role model for what a nation can accomplish by focusing on the forces that shape economic growth. ●

Quick**Quiz**

6. Because capital is subject to diminishing returns, higher saving and investment do not lead to higher
   a. income in the long run.
   b. income in the short run.
   c. growth in the long run.
   d. growth in the short run.

7. When the Japanese car maker Toyota expands one of its car factories in the United States, what is the likely impact of this event on the gross domestic product and gross national product of the United States?
   a. GDP rises and GNP falls.
   b. GNP rises and GDP falls.
   c. GDP and GNP both rise but GDP rises by more.
   d. GDP and GNP both rise but GNP rises by more.

8. Thomas Robert Malthus believed that population growth would
   a. put stress on the economy's ability to produce food, dooming humans to remain in poverty.
   b. spread the capital stock too thinly across the labor force, lowering each worker's productivity.
   c. promote technological progress, because there would be more scientists and inventors.
   d. eventually decline to sustainable levels, as birth control improved and people had smaller families.

Answers at end of chapter.

IN THE NEWS

The Secret Sauce of American Prosperity

Among large countries, the United States has long had the highest average income. Here, an economist ponders the reasons for that success.

Why the U.S. Is Still Richer Than Every Other Large Country

By Martin Feldstein

Each year, the United States produces more per person than most other advanced economies. In 2015 real GDP per capita was $56,000 in the United States. The real GDP per capita in that same year was only $47,000 in Germany, $41,000 in France and the United Kingdom, and just $36,000 in Italy, adjusting for purchasing power.

In short, the U.S. remains richer than its peers. But why? I can think of 10 features that distinguish America from other industrial economies. . . .

An entrepreneurial culture. Individuals in the U.S. demonstrate a desire to start businesses and grow them, as well as a willingness to take risks. There is less penalty in U.S. culture for failing and starting again. Even students who have gone to college or a business school show this entrepreneurial desire, and it is self-reinforcing: Silicon Valley successes like Facebook inspire further entrepreneurship.

A financial system that supports entrepreneurship. The U.S. has a more developed system of equity finance than the countries of Europe, including angel investors willing to finance startups and a very active venture capital market that helps finance the growth of those firms. We also have a decentralized banking system, including more than 7,000 small banks, that provides loans to entrepreneurs.

World-class research universities. U.S. universities produce much of the basic research that drives high-tech entrepreneurship. Faculty members and doctoral graduates often spend time with nearby startups, and the culture of both the universities and the businesses encourage this overlap. Top research universities attract talented students from around the world, many of whom end up remaining in the United States.

Labor markets that generally link workers and jobs unimpeded by large trade unions, state-owned enterprises, or excessively restrictive labor regulations. Less than 7% of the private sector U.S. labor force is unionized, and there are virtually no state-owned enterprises. While the U.S. does regulate working conditions and hiring, the rules are much less onerous than in Europe. As a result, workers have a better chance of finding the right job, firms find it easier to innovate, and new firms find it easier to get started.

A growing population, including from immigration. America's growing population means a younger and therefore more flexible and trainable workforce. Although there are restrictions on immigration to the United States, there are also special rules that provide access to the U.S. economy and a path for citizenship (green cards), based on individual talent and industrial sponsorship. A separate "green card lottery" provides a way for eager people to come to the United States. The country's ability to attract immigrants has been an important reason for its prosperity.

7-4 Conclusion: The Importance of Long-Run Growth

In this chapter, we have discussed what determines the standard of living in a nation and how policymakers can try to raise it through policies that promote economic growth. Most of this chapter is summarized in one of the *Ten Principles of Economics*: A country's standard of living depends on its ability to produce goods and services. Policymakers who want to foster growth in living standards must aim to increase their nation's productive ability by encouraging rapid accumulation of the factors of production and ensuring that these factors are employed as effectively as possible.

Economists differ in their views on the role of government in promoting economic growth. At the very least, government can lend support to the invisible hand by maintaining property rights and political stability. More controversial is whether government should target and subsidize specific industries that might be especially important for technological progress. There is no doubt that these issues are among the most important in economics. The success of one generation's policymakers in learning and heeding the fundamental lessons about economic growth determines what kind of world the next generation will inherit.

A culture (and a tax system) that encourages hard work and long hours. The average employee in the United States works 1,800 hours per year, substantially more than the 1,500 hours worked in France and the 1,400 hours worked in Germany (though not as much as the 2,200+ in Hong Kong, Singapore, and South Korea). In general, working longer means producing more, which means higher real incomes.

A supply of energy that makes North America energy independent. Natural gas fracking in particular has provided U.S. businesses with plentiful and relatively inexpensive energy.

A favorable regulatory environment. Although U.S. regulations are far from perfect, they are less burdensome on businesses than the regulations imposed by European countries and the European Union.

A smaller size of government than in other industrial countries. According to the OECD, outlays of the U.S. government at the federal, state, and local levels totaled 38% of GDP, while the corresponding figure was 44% in Germany, 51% in Italy, and 57% in France. The higher level of government spending in other countries implies not only a higher share of income taken in taxes but also higher transfer

Source: *Harvard Business Review,* April 20, 2017.

payments that reduce incentives to work. It's no surprise that Americans work a lot; they have extra incentive to do so.

A decentralized political system in which states compete. Competition among states encourages entrepreneurship and work, and states compete for businesses and for individual residents with their legal rules and tax regimes. Some states have no income taxes and have labor laws that limit unionization. States provide high-quality universities with low tuition for in-state students. They compete in their legal liability rules, too. The legal systems attract both new entrepreneurs and large corporations. The United States is perhaps unique among high-income nations in its degree of political decentralization.

Will America maintain these advantages? In his 1942 book, *Socialism, Capitalism, and Democracy,* Joseph Schumpeter warned that capitalism would decline and fail because the political and intellectual environment needed for capitalism to flourish would be undermined by the success of capitalism and by the critique of intellectuals. He argued that popularly elected social democratic parties would create a welfare state that would restrict entrepreneurship.

Although Schumpeter's book was published more than 20 years after he had moved from Europe to the United States, his warning seems more appropriate to Europe today than to the United States. The welfare state has grown in the United States, but much less than it has grown in Europe. And the intellectual climate in the United States is much more supportive of capitalism.

If Schumpeter were with us today, he might point to the growth of the social democratic parties in Europe and the resulting expansion of the welfare state as reasons why the industrial countries of Europe have not enjoyed the same robust economic growth that has prevailed in the United States. ■

Questions to Discuss

1. Which attributes of the United States listed in this article do you think best explain U.S. prosperity? Why?

2. Which of the attributes listed in this article do you think are most at risk of being undermined by poor policy choices? Why?

Mr. Feldstein is a professor of economics at Harvard University.

CHAPTER IN A NUTSHELL

- Economic prosperity, as measured by GDP per person, varies substantially around the world. The average income in the world's richest countries is more than 10 times that in the world's poorest countries. Because growth rates of real GDP also vary substantially, the relative positions of countries can change dramatically over time.
- The standard of living in an economy depends on the economy's ability to produce goods and services. Productivity, in turn, depends on the physical capital, human capital, natural resources, and technological knowledge available to workers.
- Government policies can try to influence the economy's growth rate in many ways: by encouraging saving and investment, facilitating investment from

abroad, fostering education, promoting good health, maintaining property rights and political stability, allowing free trade, and supporting the research and development of new technologies.
- The accumulation of capital is subject to diminishing returns: The more capital an economy has, the less additional output the economy gets from an extra unit of capital. As a result, although higher saving leads to higher growth for a period of time, growth eventually slows down as capital, productivity, and income rise. Also because of diminishing returns, the return to capital is especially high in poor countries. Other things being equal, these countries can grow faster because of the catch-up effect.

- Population growth has a variety of effects on economic growth. On the one hand, more rapid population growth may lower productivity by stretching the supply of natural resources and by reducing the amount of capital available to each worker. On the other hand, a larger population may enhance the rate of technological progress because there are more scientists and engineers.

KEY CONCEPTS

productivity, *p. 129*
physical capital, *p. 129*
human capital, *p. 130*

natural resources, *p. 130*
technological knowledge, *p. 130*
diminishing returns, *p. 133*

catch-up effect, *p. 134*

QUESTIONS FOR REVIEW

1. What does the level of a nation's GDP measure? What does the growth rate of GDP measure? Would you rather live in a nation with a high level of GDP and a low growth rate or in a nation with a low level of GDP and a high growth rate?

2. List and describe four determinants of productivity.

3. In what way is a college degree a form of capital?

4. Explain how higher saving leads to a higher standard of living. What might deter a policymaker from trying to raise the rate of saving?

5. Does a higher rate of saving lead to higher growth temporarily or indefinitely?

6. Why would removing a trade restriction, such as a tariff, lead to more rapid economic growth?

7. How does the rate of population growth influence the level of GDP per person?

8. Describe two ways the U.S. government tries to encourage advances in technological knowledge.

PROBLEMS AND APPLICATIONS

1. Most countries, including the United States, import substantial amounts of goods and services from other countries. Yet the chapter says that a nation can enjoy a high standard of living only if it can produce a large quantity of goods and services itself. Can you reconcile these two facts?

2. Suppose that society decided to reduce consumption and increase investment.
   a. How would this change affect economic growth?
   b. What groups in society would benefit from this change? What groups might be hurt?

3. Societies choose what share of their resources to devote to consumption and what share to devote to investment. Some of these decisions involve private spending; others involve government spending.
   a. Describe some forms of private spending that represent consumption and some forms that represent investment. The national income accounts include tuition as a part of consumer spending. In your opinion, are the resources you devote to your education a form of consumption or a form of investment?
   b. Describe some forms of government spending that represent consumption and some forms that represent investment. In your opinion, should we view government spending on health programs as a form of consumption or investment? Would you distinguish between health programs for the young and health programs for the elderly?

4. What is the opportunity cost of investing in capital? Do you think a country can overinvest in capital? What is the opportunity cost of investing in human capital? Do you think a country can overinvest in human capital? Explain.

5. In the 1990s and the two decades of the 2000s, investors from the Asian economies of Japan and China made significant direct and portfolio investments in the United States. At the time, many

Americans were unhappy that this investment was occurring.

  a. In what way was it better for the United States to receive this foreign investment than not to receive it?

  b. In what way would it have been even better for Americans to have made this investment themselves?

6. In many developing nations, young women have lower enrollment rates in secondary school than do young men. Describe several ways in which greater educational opportunities for young women could lead to faster economic growth in these countries.

7. The International Property Right Index scores countries based on their legal and political environments and the extent to which they protect property rights. Go online and find a recent ranking. Choose three countries with high scores and three countries with low scores. Then find estimates of GDP per person in each of these six countries. What pattern do you find? Give two possible interpretations of the pattern.

8. International data show a positive correlation between income per person and the health of the population.

  a. Explain how higher income might cause better health outcomes.

  b. Explain how better health outcomes might cause higher income.

  c. How might the relative importance of your two hypotheses be relevant for public policy?

9. The great 18th-century economist Adam Smith wrote, "Little else is requisite to carry a state to the highest degree of opulence from the lowest barbarism but peace, easy taxes, and a tolerable administration of justice: all the rest being brought about by the natural course of things." Explain how each of the three conditions Smith describes promotes economic growth.

Quick**Quiz Answers**

1. b   2. c   3. a   4. b   5. d   6. c   7. c   8. a

I magine that you have just graduated from college (with a degree in economics, of course) and you decide to start your own business—an economic forecasting firm. Before you make any money selling your forecasts, you have to incur substantial costs to set up your business. You have to buy computers with which to make your forecasts, as well as desks, chairs, and filing cabinets to furnish your new office. Each of these items is a capital good that your firm will use to produce and sell its services.

How do you obtain the funds to invest in this capital? Perhaps you are able to pay for them out of your past savings. More likely, however, like most entrepreneurs, you do not have enough money of your own to finance the start of your business. As a result, you have to get the money you need from other sources.

There are various ways to finance these capital investments. You could borrow the money from a bank, friend, or relative, promising to return the money at a later date and pay interest for the use of the money. Alternatively, you could convince someone to provide the money you need for your business in exchange for a share of your future profits. In either case, your investment in computers and office equipment would be financed by someone else's saving.

CHAPTER

8

Saving, Investment, and the Financial System

financial system
the group of institutions in the economy that help to match one person's saving with another person's investment

The **financial system** consists of the institutions that help match one person's saving with another person's investment. As we discussed in the previous chapter, saving and investment are key ingredients to long-run economic growth: When a country saves a large portion of its GDP, more resources are available for investment in capital, and higher capital raises a country's productivity and living standard. The previous chapter, however, did not explain how the economy coordinates saving and investment. At any time, some people want to save some of their income for the future and others want to borrow to finance investments in new and growing businesses. What brings these two groups of people together? What ensures that the supply of funds from those who want to save balances the demand for funds from those who want to invest?

This chapter examines how the financial system works. First, we discuss the large variety of institutions that make up the financial system in our economy. Second, we examine the relationship between the financial system and some key macroeconomic variables—notably saving and investment. Third, we develop a model of the supply and demand for funds in financial markets. In the model, the interest rate is the price that adjusts to balance supply and demand. The model shows how various government policies affect the interest rate and, in turn, society's allocation of scarce resources.

8-1 Financial Institutions in the U.S. Economy

At the broadest level, the financial system moves the economy's scarce resources from savers (people who spend less than they earn) to borrowers (people who spend more than they earn). Savers save for various reasons—to put a child through college in several years or to retire comfortably in several decades. Similarly, borrowers borrow for various reasons—to buy a house to live in or to start a business to make a living. Savers supply their money to the financial system with the expectation that they will get it back with interest at a later date. Borrowers demand money from the financial system with the knowledge that they will be required to pay it back with interest at a later date.

The financial system is made up of various financial institutions that help coordinate the actions of savers and borrowers. As a prelude to analyzing the economic forces that drive the financial system, let's discuss the most important of these institutions. Financial institutions can be grouped into two categories: financial markets and financial intermediaries.

8-1a Financial Markets

financial markets
financial institutions through which savers can directly provide funds to borrowers

Financial markets are the institutions through which a person who wants to save can directly supply funds to a person who wants to borrow. The two most important financial markets in our economy are the bond market and the stock market.

bond
a certificate of indebtedness

The Bond Market   When Intel, the giant maker of computer chips, wants to borrow to finance construction of a new factory, it can borrow directly from the public. It does so by selling bonds. A **bond** is a certificate of indebtedness that specifies the obligations of the borrower to the buyer of the bond. Put simply, a bond buyer is a lender, and a bond is an IOU. The bond identifies the time at which the loan will be repaid, called the *date of maturity*, and the rate of interest that the borrower will pay periodically until the loan matures. The buyer of a bond gives his money to Intel in exchange for this promise of interest and eventual repayment of the amount borrowed (called the *principal*). The buyer can hold the bond until maturity, or he can sell the bond at an earlier date to someone else.

There are millions of different bonds in the U.S. economy. When large corporations, the federal government, or state and local governments need to borrow to finance the purchase of a new factory, a new jet fighter, or a new school, they usually do so by issuing bonds. If you look at *The Wall Street Journal* or the business section of your news service, you will find a listing of the prices and interest rates on some of the most important bond issues. These bonds differ according to four significant characteristics.

The first characteristic is a bond's *term*—the length of time until the bond matures. Some bonds have short terms, such as a few months, while others have terms as long as thirty years. (The British government has even issued a bond that never matures, called a *perpetuity*. This bond pays interest forever, but the principal is never repaid.) The interest rate on a bond depends, in part, on its term. Long-term bonds are riskier than short-term bonds because holders of long-term bonds have to wait longer for repayment of principal. If a holder of a long-term bond needs his money earlier than the distant date of maturity, he has no choice but to sell the bond to someone else, perhaps at a reduced price. To compensate for this risk, long-term bonds usually pay higher interest rates than short-term bonds.

The second important characteristic of a bond is its *credit risk*—the probability that the borrower will fail to pay some of the interest or principal. Such a failure to pay is called a *default*. Borrowers can (and sometimes do) default on their loans by declaring bankruptcy. When bond buyers perceive that the probability of default is high, they demand a higher interest rate as compensation for this risk. Because the U.S. government is considered to have low credit risk, U.S. government bonds tend to pay low interest rates. By contrast, financially shaky corporations raise money by issuing *junk bonds*, which pay very high interest rates. Buyers of bonds can judge credit risk by checking with various private agencies that evaluate the credit risk of different bonds. For example, Standard & Poor's rates bonds from AAA (the safest) to D (those already in default).

The third important characteristic of a bond is its *tax treatment*—the way the tax laws treat the interest earned on the bond. The interest on most bonds is taxable income; that is, the bond owner has to pay a portion of the interest he earns in income taxes. By contrast, when state and local governments issue bonds, called *municipal bonds*, the bond owners are not required to pay federal income tax on the interest income. Because of this tax advantage, bonds issued by state and local governments typically pay a lower interest rate than bonds issued by corporations or the federal government.

The fourth important characteristic of a bond is whether it offers *inflation protection*. Most bonds are written in nominal terms—that is, they promise to pay interest and principal in a specific number of dollars (or perhaps another currency). If prices rise and dollars have less purchasing power, the bondholder is worse off. Some bonds, however, index the payments of interest and principal to a measure of inflation so that when prices rise, the payments rise proportionately. Beginning in 1997, the U.S. government started issuing such bonds, called Treasury Inflation-Protected Securities (TIPS). Because TIPS offer inflation protection, they pay a lower interest rate than similar bonds without this feature.

The Stock Market Another way for Intel to raise funds to build a new semiconductor factory is to sell stock in the company. A share of **stock** represents ownership in a firm and is, therefore, a claim to some of the profits that the firm makes. For example, if Intel sells a total of 1,000,000 shares of stock, then each share represents ownership of 1/1,000,000 of the business.

stock
a claim to partial ownership in a firm

The sale of stock to raise money is called *equity finance*, whereas the sale of bonds is called *debt finance*. Although corporations use both equity and debt finance to raise money for new investments, stocks and bonds are very different. The owner of shares of Intel stock is a part owner of Intel, while the owner of an Intel bond is a creditor of the corporation. If Intel is very profitable, the stockholders enjoy the benefits of these profits, whereas the bondholders get only the stated interest on their bonds. And if Intel runs into financial difficulty, the bondholders are paid what they are due before stockholders receive anything at all. Compared to bonds, stocks carry greater risk but offer potentially higher returns.

After a corporation issues stock by selling shares to the public, these shares trade among stockholders on organized stock exchanges. In these transactions, the corporation itself receives no money when its stock changes hands. The most important stock exchanges in the U.S. economy are the New York Stock Exchange and the Nasdaq (National Association of Securities Dealers Automated Quotations). Most of the world's countries have their own stock exchanges on which the shares of local companies trade, the most important being those in Tokyo, Shanghai, Hong Kong, and London.

The prices at which shares trade on stock exchanges are determined by the supply of and demand for the stock in these companies. Because stock represents ownership in a corporation, the demand for a stock (and thus its price) reflects people's perception of the corporation's future profitability. When people become optimistic about a company's future, they raise their demand for its stock and thereby bid up the price of a share of stock. Conversely, when people's expectations of a company's prospects decline, the price of a share falls.

Various stock indexes are available to monitor the overall level of stock prices. A *stock index* is computed as an average of a group of stock prices. The most famous stock index is the Dow Jones Industrial Average, which has been computed regularly since 1896. It is now based on the prices of the stocks of thirty major U.S. companies, such as Disney, Microsoft, Coca-Cola, Boeing, Apple, and Walmart. Another well-known stock index is the Standard & Poor's 500 Index, which is based on the prices of the stocks of 500 major companies. Because stock prices reflect expected profitability, these stock indexes are watched closely as possible indicators of future economic conditions.

8-1b Financial Intermediaries

financial intermediaries
financial institutions through which savers can indirectly provide funds to borrowers

Financial intermediaries are financial institutions through which savers can indirectly provide funds to borrowers. The term *intermediary* reflects the role of these institutions in standing between savers and borrowers. Here we consider two of the most important financial intermediaries: banks and mutual funds.

Banks   If the owner of a small grocery store wants to finance an expansion of his business, he probably proceeds differently than Intel. Unlike Intel, a small grocer would find it difficult to raise funds in the stock and bond markets. Most buyers of stocks and bonds prefer to buy those issued by larger, more familiar companies. The small grocer, therefore, most likely finances his business expansion with a loan from a local bank.

Banks are the financial intermediaries with which people are most familiar. A primary job of banks is to take in deposits from people who want to save and use these deposits to make loans to people who want to borrow. Banks pay depositors interest on their deposits and charge borrowers slightly higher interest on their loans. The difference between these rates of interest covers the banks' costs and returns some profit to the owners of the banks.

Besides being financial intermediaries, banks play another important role in the economy: They facilitate purchases of goods and services by allowing people to write checks against their deposits and to access those deposits with debit cards. In other words, banks help create a special asset that people can use as a *medium of exchange*. A medium of exchange is an item that people can easily use to engage in transactions. A bank's role in providing a medium of exchange distinguishes it from many other financial institutions. While stocks and bonds, like bank deposits, offer a possible *store of value* for the wealth that people have accumulated in past saving, they do not offer the easy, cheap, and immediate access to wealth that writing a check or swiping a debit card allows. For now, we ignore this second role of banks, but we will return to it when we discuss the monetary system later in the book.

Mutual Funds A financial intermediary of increasing importance in the U.S. economy is the mutual fund. A **mutual fund** is an institution that sells shares to the public and uses the proceeds to buy a selection, or *portfolio*, of various types of stocks, bonds, or both stocks and bonds. The shareholder of the mutual fund accepts all the risk and return associated with the portfolio. If the value of the portfolio rises, the shareholder benefits; if the value of the portfolio falls, the shareholder suffers the loss.

mutual fund
an institution that sells shares to the public and uses the proceeds to buy a portfolio of stocks and bonds

The primary advantage of mutual funds is that they allow people with small amounts of money to diversify their holdings. Because the value of any single stock or bond is tied to the fortunes of one company, holding a single kind of stock or bond is very risky. By contrast, people who hold a diverse portfolio of stocks and bonds face less risk because they have only a small stake in each company. Mutual funds make this diversification easy. With only a few hundred dollars, a person can buy shares in a mutual fund and, indirectly, become the part owner or creditor of hundreds of major companies. For this service, the company operating the mutual fund charges shareholders a fee, usually between 0.1 and 1.5 percent of assets each year.

A second advantage claimed by mutual fund companies is that mutual funds give ordinary people access to the skills of professional money managers. The managers of most mutual funds pay close attention to the developments and prospects of the companies in which they buy stock. These managers buy the stock of companies they view as having a profitable future and sell the stock of companies with less promising prospects. This professional management, it is argued, should increase the return that mutual fund depositors earn on their savings.

Financial economists, however, are often skeptical of this argument. Because thousands of money managers are paying close attention to each company's prospects, a company's stock usually trades at a price that reflects the company's true value. As a result, it is hard to "beat the market" by buying good stocks and selling

ARLO AND JANIS by Jimmy Johnson

ARLO AND JANIS REPRINTED BY PERMISSION OF ANDREWS MCMEEL SYNDICATION.

bad ones. In fact, mutual funds called *index funds*, which buy all the stocks in a given stock index, perform somewhat better on average than mutual funds that take advantage of active trading by professional money managers. The explanation for the superior performance of index funds is that they keep costs low by buying and selling very rarely and by not having to pay the salaries of professional money managers.

8-1c Summing Up

The U.S. economy contains a large variety of financial institutions. In addition to the bond market, the stock market, banks, and mutual funds, there are also pension funds, credit unions, insurance companies, and even the local loan shark. These institutions differ in many ways. When analyzing the macroeconomic role of the financial system, however, it is more important to keep in mind that, despite their differences, these financial institutions all serve the same goal: directing the resources of savers into the hands of borrowers.

Quick**Quiz**

1. Carly wants to buy and operate an ice-cream truck but doesn't have the financial resources to start the business. She borrows $20,000 from her friend Freddie, to whom she promises an interest rate of 7 percent, and gets another $30,000 from her friend Sam, to whom she promises a third of her profits. What best describes this situation?
    a. Freddie is a stockholder, and Carly is a bondholder.
    b. Freddie is a stockholder, and Sam is a bondholder.
    c. Sam is a stockholder, and Carly is a bondholder.
    d. Sam is a stockholder, and Freddie is a bondholder.

2. A bond tends to pay a high interest rate if it is
    a. a short-term bond rather than a long-term bond.
    b. a municipal bond exempt from federal taxation.
    c. issued by the federal government rather than a corporation.
    d. issued by a corporation of dubious credit quality.

3. The main advantage of mutual funds is that they provide
    a. a return insured by the government.
    b. an easy way to hold a diversified portfolio.
    c. an asset that is widely used as the medium of exchange.
    d. a way to avoid fluctuations in stock and bond prices.

Answers at end of chapter.

8-2 Saving and Investment in the National Income Accounts

Events that occur within the financial system are central to developments in the overall economy. As we have just seen, the institutions that make up this system—the bond market, the stock market, banks, and mutual funds—serve the role of coordinating the economy's saving and investment. And as we saw in the previous chapter, saving and investment are important determinants of long-run growth in GDP and living standards. As a result, macroeconomists need to understand how financial markets work and how various events and policies affect them.

As a starting point for analyzing financial markets, we discuss the key macroeconomic variables that measure activity in these markets. Our emphasis here is not on behavior but on accounting. *Accounting* refers to the way in which various numbers are defined and added up. A personal accountant might help an individual add up his income and expenses. A national income accountant does the same thing for the economy as a whole. The national income accounts include, in particular, GDP and the many related statistics.

The rules of national income accounting include several important identities. Recall that an *identity* is an equation that must be true because of the way the variables in the equation are defined. Identities are useful to keep in mind because they clarify how different variables are related to one another. Here we consider some accounting identities that shed light on the macroeconomic role of financial markets.

8-2a Some Important Identities

Recall that gross domestic product (GDP) is both total income in an economy and the total expenditure on the economy's output of goods and services. GDP (denoted as Y) is divided into four components of expenditure: consumption (C), investment (I), government purchases (G), and net exports (NX):

$$Y = C + I + G + NX.$$

This equation is an identity because every dollar of expenditure that shows up on the left side also shows up in one of the four components on the right side. Because of the way each of the variables is defined and measured, this equation must always hold.

In this chapter, we simplify our analysis by assuming that the economy we are examining is closed. A *closed economy* is one that does not interact with other economies. In particular, a closed economy does not engage in international trade in goods and services, and it does not engage in international borrowing and lending. Actual economies are *open economies*—that is, they interact with other economies around the world. Nonetheless, assuming a closed economy is a useful simplification with which we can learn some lessons that apply to all economies. Moreover, this assumption applies perfectly to the world economy (interplanetary trade is not yet common!).

Because a closed economy does not engage in international trade, there are no imports and exports, making net exports (NX) exactly zero. We can simplify the identity as

$$Y = C + I + G.$$

This equation states that GDP is the sum of consumption, investment, and government purchases. Each unit of output sold in a closed economy is consumed, invested, or bought by the government.

To see what this identity can tell us about financial markets, we subtract C and G from both sides of this equation to obtain

$$Y - C - G = I.$$

The left side of this equation ($Y - C - G$) is the total income in the economy that remains after paying for consumption and government purchases: This amount is called **national saving**, or just **saving**, and is denoted S. Substituting S for $Y - C - G$, we can write the last equation as

$$S = I.$$

This equation states that saving equals investment.

To understand the meaning of national saving, it is helpful to manipulate the definition a bit more. Let T denote the amount that the government collects from

national saving (saving)
the total income in the economy that remains after paying for consumption and government purchases

households in taxes minus the amount it pays back to households in the form of transfer payments (such as Social Security and welfare). We can then write national saving in either of two ways:

$$S = Y - C - G$$

or

$$S = (Y - T - C) + (T - G).$$

These equations are the same because the two T's in the second equation cancel each other, but each reveals a different way of thinking about national saving. In particular, the second equation separates national saving into two pieces: private saving $(Y - T - C)$ and public saving $(T - G)$.

Consider each of these two pieces. **Private saving** is the amount of income that households have left after paying their taxes and paying for their consumption. In particular, because households receive income of Y, pay taxes of T, and spend C on consumption, private saving is $Y - T - C$. **Public saving** is the amount of tax revenue that the government has left after paying for its spending. The government receives T in tax revenue and spends G on goods and services. If T exceeds G, the government receives more money than it spends. In this case, public saving $(T - G)$ is positive, and the government is said to run a **budget surplus**. If G exceeds T, the government spends more than it receives in tax revenue. In this case, public saving $(T - G)$ is negative, and the government is said to run a **budget deficit**.

Now consider how these accounting identities are related to financial markets. The equation $S = I$ reveals an important fact: *For the economy as a whole, saving must equal investment.* Yet this fact raises some important questions: What mechanisms lie behind this identity? What coordinates those people who are deciding how much to save and those people who are deciding how much to invest? The answer is the financial system. The bond market, the stock market, banks, mutual funds, and other financial markets and intermediaries stand between the two sides of the $S = I$ equation. They take in the nation's saving and direct it to the nation's investment.

private saving
the income that households have left after paying for taxes and consumption

public saving
the tax revenue that the government has left after paying for its spending

budget surplus
an excess of tax revenue over government spending

budget deficit
a shortfall of tax revenue from government spending

8-2b The Meaning of Saving and Investment

The terms *saving* and *investment* can sometimes be confusing. Most people use these terms casually and sometimes interchangeably. By contrast, the macroeconomists who put together the national income accounts use these terms carefully and distinctly.

Consider an example. Suppose that Larry earns more than he spends and deposits his unspent income in a bank or uses it to buy some stock or a bond from a corporation. Because Larry's income exceeds his consumption, he adds to the nation's saving. Larry might think of himself as "investing" his money, but a macroeconomist would call Larry's act saving rather than investment.

In the language of macroeconomics, investment refers to the purchase of new capital, such as equipment or buildings. When Moe borrows from the bank to build himself a new house, he adds to the nation's investment. (Remember, the purchase of a new house is the one form of household spending that is investment rather than consumption.) Similarly, when the Curly Corporation sells some stock and uses the proceeds to build a new factory, it also adds to the nation's investment.

Although the accounting identity $S = I$ shows that saving and investment are equal for the economy as a whole, it does not mean that saving and investment are equal for every individual household or firm. Larry's saving can be greater than his investment, and he can deposit the excess in a bank. Moe's saving can be less than his investment, and he can borrow the shortfall from a bank. Banks and other financial institutions make these individual differences between saving and investment possible by allowing one person's saving to finance another person's investment.

Quick Quiz

4. If the government collects more in tax revenue than it spends, and households consume more than they get in after-tax income, then
   a. private saving and public saving are both positive.
   b. private saving and public saving are both negative.
   c. private saving is positive, but public saving is negative.
   d. private saving is negative, but public saving is positive.

5. A closed economy has income of $1,000, government spending of $200, taxes of $150, and investment of $250. What is private saving?
   a. $100
   b. $200
   c. $300
   d. $400

Answers at end of chapter.

8-3 The Market for Loanable Funds

Having discussed some of the important financial institutions in our economy and the macroeconomic role of these institutions, we are ready to build a model of financial markets. Our purpose in building this model is to explain how financial markets coordinate an economy's saving and investment. The model also gives us a tool with which we can analyze various government policies that influence saving and investment.

To keep things simple, we assume that the economy has only one financial market, called the **market for loanable funds**. All savers go to this market to deposit their saving, and all borrowers go to this market to take out their loans. Thus, the term *loanable funds* refers to all income that people have chosen to save and lend out, rather than use for their own consumption, and to the amount that investors have chosen to borrow to fund new investment projects. In the market for loanable funds, there is one interest rate, which is both the return to saving and the cost of borrowing.

The assumption of a single financial market, of course, is not realistic. As we have seen, the economy has many types of financial institutions. But as we discussed in Chapter 2, the art in building an economic model is simplifying the world in order to explain it. For our purposes here, we can ignore the diversity of financial institutions and assume that the economy has a single financial market.

market for loanable funds
the market in which those who want to save supply funds and those who want to borrow to invest demand funds

8-3a Supply and Demand for Loanable Funds

The economy's market for loanable funds, like other markets in the economy, is governed by supply and demand. To understand how the market for loanable funds operates, therefore, we first look at the sources of supply and demand in that market.

The supply of loanable funds comes from people who have some extra income they want to save and lend out. This lending can occur directly, such as when a household buys a bond from a firm, or it can occur indirectly, such as when a household makes a deposit in a bank, which then uses the funds to make loans. In both cases, *saving is the source of the supply of loanable funds*.

The demand for loanable funds comes from households and firms who wish to borrow to make investments. This demand includes families taking out mortgages to buy new homes. It also includes firms borrowing to buy new equipment or build factories. In both cases, *investment is the source of the demand for loanable funds*.

The interest rate is the price of a loan. It represents the amount that borrowers pay for loans and the amount that lenders receive on their saving. Because a high interest rate makes borrowing more expensive, the quantity of loanable funds demanded falls as the interest rate rises. Similarly, because a high interest rate makes saving more attractive, the quantity of loanable funds supplied rises as the interest rate rises. In other words, the demand curve for loanable funds slopes downward, and the supply curve for loanable funds slopes upward.

Figure 1 shows the interest rate that balances the supply and demand for loanable funds. In the equilibrium shown, the interest rate is 5 percent, and the quantity of loanable funds demanded and the quantity of loanable funds supplied both equal $1,200 billion.

The adjustment of the interest rate to the equilibrium level occurs for the usual reasons. If the interest rate were lower than the equilibrium level, the quantity of loanable funds supplied would be less than the quantity of loanable funds demanded. The resulting shortage of loanable funds would encourage lenders to raise the interest rate they charge. A higher interest rate would encourage saving (thereby increasing the quantity of loanable funds supplied) and discourage borrowing for investment (thereby decreasing the quantity of loanable funds demanded). Conversely, if the interest rate were higher than the equilibrium level, the quantity of loanable funds supplied would exceed the quantity of loanable funds demanded. As lenders compete for the scarce borrowers, interest rates would be driven down. In this way, the interest rate approaches the equilibrium level at which the supply and demand for loanable funds exactly balance.

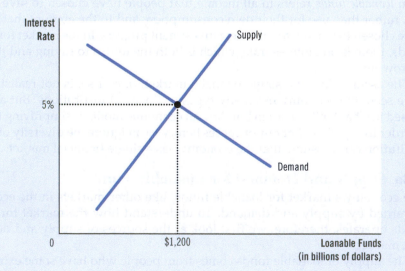

FIGURE 1

The Market for Loanable Funds
The interest rate in the economy adjusts to balance the supply and demand for loanable funds. The supply of loanable funds comes from national saving, including both private saving and public saving. The demand for loanable funds comes from firms and households that want to borrow for purposes of investment. Here the equilibrium interest rate is 5 percent, and $1,200 billion of loanable funds are supplied and demanded.

Recall that economists distinguish between the real interest rate and the nominal interest rate. The nominal interest rate is the monetary return to saving and the monetary cost of borrowing. It is the interest rate as usually reported. The real interest rate is the nominal interest rate corrected for inflation; it equals the nominal interest rate minus the inflation rate. Because inflation erodes the value of money over time, the real interest rate more accurately reflects the real return to saving and the real cost of borrowing. Therefore, the supply and demand for loanable funds depend on the real (rather than nominal) interest rate, and the equilibrium in Figure 1 should be interpreted as determining the real interest rate in the economy. For the rest of this chapter, when you see the term *interest rate*, you should remember that we are talking about the real interest rate.

This model of the supply and demand for loanable funds shows that financial markets work much like other markets in the economy. In the market for milk, for instance, the price of milk adjusts so that the quantity of milk supplied balances the quantity of milk demanded. In this way, the invisible hand coordinates the behavior of dairy farmers and the behavior of milk drinkers. Once we realize that saving represents the supply of loanable funds and investment represents the demand, we can see how the invisible hand coordinates saving and investment. When the interest rate adjusts to balance supply and demand in the market for loanable funds, it coordinates the behavior of people who want to save (the suppliers of loanable funds) and the behavior of people who want to invest (the demanders of loanable funds).

We can now use this model of the market for loanable funds to examine various government policies that affect the economy's saving and investment. Because the model is just supply and demand in a particular market, we analyze the effects of a policy using the three steps discussed in Chapter 4. First, we decide whether the policy shifts the supply curve or the demand curve. Second, we determine the direction of the shift. Third, we use the supply-and-demand diagram to see how the equilibrium changes.

8-3b Policy 1: Saving Incentives

Many economists and policymakers have advocated increases in saving. Their argument is simple. One of the *Ten Principles of Economics* in Chapter 1 is that a country's standard of living depends on its ability to produce goods and services. And as we discussed in the preceding chapter, saving is an important long-run determinant of a nation's productivity. If the United States could somehow raise its saving rate, more resources would be available for capital accumulation, GDP would grow more rapidly, and over time, U.S. citizens would enjoy a higher standard of living.

Another of the *Ten Principles of Economics* is that people respond to incentives. Many economists have used this principle to suggest that the low rate of saving is at least partly attributable to tax laws that discourage saving. The U.S. federal government, as well as many state governments, collects revenue by taxing income, including interest and dividend income. To see the effects of this policy, consider a 25-year-old who saves $1,000 and buys a 30-year bond that pays an interest rate of 9 percent. In the absence of taxes, the $1,000 grows to $13,268 when the individual reaches age 55. But if the interest income is taxed at a rate of, say, 33 percent, the after-tax interest rate is only 6 percent. In this case, the $1,000 grows to only $5,743 over the 30 years. The tax on interest income substantially reduces the future payoff from current saving and, as a result, reduces the incentive for people to save.

In response to this problem, some economists and lawmakers have proposed reforming the tax code to encourage greater saving. For example, one proposal is to expand eligibility for special accounts, such as Individual Retirement Accounts, that allow people to shelter some of their saving from taxation. Let's consider the effect of such a saving incentive on the market for loanable funds, as illustrated in Figure 2. We analyze this policy following our three steps.

First, which curve would this policy affect? Because the tax change would alter the incentive for households to save *at any given interest rate*, it would affect the quantity of loanable funds supplied at each interest rate. Thus, the supply of loanable funds would shift. The demand for loanable funds would remain the same because the tax change would not directly affect the amount that borrowers want to borrow at any given interest rate.

Second, which way would the supply curve shift? Because saving would be taxed less heavily than under current law, households would increase their saving by consuming a smaller fraction of their income. Households would use this additional saving to increase their deposits in banks or to buy more bonds. The supply of loanable funds would increase, and the supply curve would shift to the right from S_1 to S_2, as shown in Figure 2.

Finally, we can compare the old and new equilibria. In the figure, the increased supply of loanable funds reduces the interest rate from 5 percent to 4 percent. The lower interest rate raises the quantity of loanable funds demanded from $1,200 billion to $1,600 billion. That is, the shift in the supply curve moves the market equilibrium along the demand curve. With a lower cost of borrowing, households and firms are motivated to borrow more to finance greater investment. Thus, *if a reform of the tax laws encouraged greater saving, the result would be lower interest rates and greater investment.*

This analysis of the effects of increased saving is widely accepted among economists, but there is less consensus about what kinds of tax changes should be enacted. Many economists endorse tax reform aimed at increasing saving to

FIGURE 2

Saving Incentives Increase the Supply of Loanable Funds

A change in the tax laws to encourage Americans to save more would shift the supply of loanable funds to the right from S_1 to S_2. As a result, the equilibrium interest rate would fall, and the lower interest rate would stimulate investment. Here the equilibrium interest rate falls from 5 percent to 4 percent, and the equilibrium quantity of loanable funds saved and invested rises from $1,200 billion to $1,600 billion.

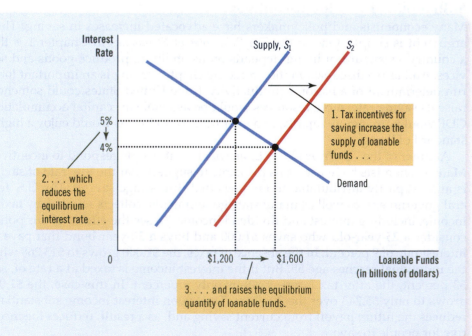

stimulate investment and growth. Yet others are skeptical that these tax changes would have much effect on national saving. These skeptics also doubt the equity of the proposed reforms. They argue that, in many cases, the benefits of the tax changes would accrue primarily to the wealthy, who are least in need of tax relief.

8-3c Policy 2: Investment Incentives

Suppose that Congress passed a tax reform aimed at making investment more attractive—for instance, by instituting an *investment tax credit*, as Congress has done from time to time. An investment tax credit gives a tax advantage to any firm building a new factory or buying a new piece of equipment. Let's consider the effect of such a tax reform on the market for loanable funds, as illustrated in Figure 3.

First, would the tax credit affect supply or demand? Because it would reward firms that borrow and invest in new capital, it would alter investment at any given interest rate and, thereby, change the demand for loanable funds. By contrast, because the tax credit would not affect the amount that households save at any given interest rate, it would not affect the supply of loanable funds.

Second, which way would the demand curve shift? Because firms would have an incentive to increase investment at any interest rate, the quantity of loanable funds demanded would be higher at any given interest rate. Thus, the demand curve for loanable funds would move to the right, as shown by the shift from D_1 to D_2 in the figure.

Third, consider how the equilibrium would change. In Figure 3, the increased demand for loanable funds raises the interest rate from 5 percent to 6 percent, and the higher interest rate in turn increases the quantity of loanable funds supplied from $1,200 billion to $1,400 billion, as households respond by increasing the amount they save. This change in household behavior is represented here as a movement along the supply curve. Thus, *if a reform of the tax laws encouraged greater investment, the result would be higher interest rates and greater saving.*

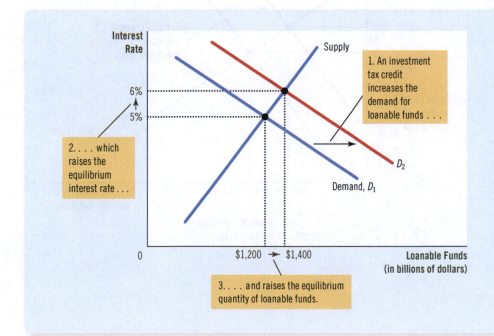

FIGURE 3

Investment Incentives Increase the Demand for Loanable Funds

If the passage of an investment tax credit encouraged firms to invest more, the demand for loanable funds would increase. As a result, the equilibrium interest rate would rise, and the higher interest rate would stimulate saving. Here, when the demand curve shifts from D_1 to D_2, the equilibrium interest rate rises from 5 percent to 6 percent, and the equilibrium quantity of loanable funds saved and invested rises from $1,200 billion to $1,400 billion.

Figure labels:
- Interest Rate
- Supply
- 1. An investment tax credit increases the demand for loanable funds . . .
- 6%
- 5%
- 2. . . . which raises the equilibrium interest rate . . .
- D_2
- Demand, D_1
- 0
- $1,200 → $1,400
- Loanable Funds (in billions of dollars)
- 3. . . . and raises the equilibrium quantity of loanable funds.

8-3d Policy 3: Government Budget Deficits and Surpluses

A perpetual topic of political debate is the status of the government budget. Recall that a *budget deficit* is an excess of government spending over tax revenue. Governments finance budget deficits by borrowing in the bond market, and the accumulation of past government borrowing is called the *government debt*. A *budget surplus*, an excess of tax revenue over government spending, can be used to repay some of the government debt. If government spending exactly equals tax revenue, the government is said to have a *balanced budget*.

Imagine that the government starts with a balanced budget and then, because of an increase in government spending, starts running a budget deficit. We can analyze the effects of the budget deficit by following our three steps in the market for loanable funds, as illustrated in Figure 4.

First, which curve shifts when the government starts running a budget deficit? Recall that national saving—the source of the supply of loanable funds—is composed of private saving and public saving. A change in the government budget balance represents a change in public saving and, therefore, in the supply of loanable funds. Because the budget deficit does not influence the amount that households and firms want to borrow to finance investment at any given interest rate, it does not alter the demand for loanable funds.

Second, which way does the supply curve shift? When the government runs a budget deficit, public saving is negative, so national saving declines. In other words, when the government borrows to finance its budget deficit, it reduces the supply of loanable funds available to finance investment by households and firms. Thus, a budget deficit shifts the supply curve for loanable funds to the left from S_1 to S_2, as shown in Figure 4.

FIGURE 4

The Effect of a Government Budget Deficit

When the government spends more than it receives in tax revenue, the resulting budget deficit lowers national saving. The supply of loanable funds decreases, and the equilibrium interest rate rises. Thus, when the government borrows to finance its budget deficit, it crowds out households and firms that otherwise would borrow to finance investment. Here, when the supply curve shifts from S_1 to S_2, the equilibrium interest rate rises from 5 percent to 6 percent, and the equilibrium quantity of loanable funds saved and invested falls from $1,200 billion to $800 billion.

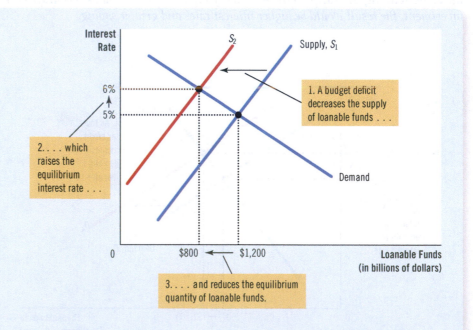

1. A budget deficit decreases the supply of loanable funds . . .

2. . . . which raises the equilibrium interest rate . . .

3. . . . and reduces the equilibrium quantity of loanable funds.

Third, we can compare the old and new equilibria. In the figure, when the budget deficit reduces the supply of loanable funds, the interest rate rises from 5 percent to 6 percent. The quantity of loanable funds demanded then decreases from $1,200 billion to $800 billion as the higher interest rate discourages many demanders of loanable funds. Fewer families buy new homes, and fewer firms choose to build new factories. The fall in investment due to government borrowing is represented by the movement along the demand curve and is called **crowding out**. That is, when the government borrows to finance its budget deficit, it crowds out private borrowers who are trying to finance investment.

crowding out
a decrease in investment that results from government borrowing

Thus, the most basic lesson about budget deficits follows directly from their effects on the supply and demand for loanable funds: *When the government reduces national saving by running a budget deficit, the interest rate rises and investment falls.* Because investment is important for long-run economic growth, government budget deficits reduce the economy's growth rate.

Why, you might ask, does a budget deficit affect the supply of loanable funds, rather than the demand for them? After all, the government finances a budget deficit by selling bonds, thereby borrowing from the private sector. Why does increased borrowing by the government shift the supply curve, whereas increased borrowing by private investors shifts the demand curve? To answer this question, we need to examine more precisely the meaning of "loanable funds." The model as presented here takes this term to mean the *flow of resources available to fund private investment;* thus, a government budget deficit reduces the supply of loanable funds. If, instead, we had defined the term "loanable funds" to mean the *flow of resources available from private saving,* then the government budget deficit would increase demand rather than reduce supply. Changing the interpretation of the term would cause a semantic change in how we described the model, but the upshot of the analysis would be the same: In either case, a budget deficit increases the interest rate, thereby crowding out private borrowers who are relying on financial markets to fund private investment projects.

So far, we have examined a budget deficit that results from an increase in government spending, but a budget deficit that results from a tax cut has similar effects. A tax cut reduces tax revenue T and thus public saving, $T - G$. Private saving, $Y - T - C$, might increase because of lower T, but as long as households respond to the lower taxes by consuming more, C increases, so private saving rises by less than public saving declines. Thus, national saving ($S = Y - C - G$), the sum of public saving and private saving, declines. Once again, the budget deficit reduces the supply of loanable funds, drives up the interest rate, and crowds out borrowers trying to finance capital investments.

Now that we understand the impact of budget deficits, we can turn the analysis around and see that government budget surpluses have the opposite effects. When the government collects more in tax revenue than it spends, it saves the difference by retiring some of the outstanding government debt. This budget surplus, or public saving, contributes to national saving. Thus, *a budget surplus increases the supply of loanable funds, reduces the interest rate, and stimulates investment.* Higher investment, in turn, means greater capital accumulation and more rapid economic growth.

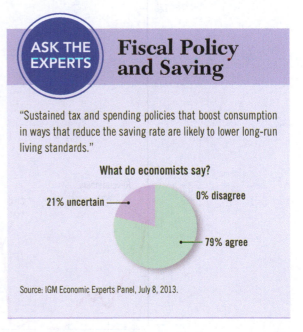

ASK THE EXPERTS

Fiscal Policy and Saving

"Sustained tax and spending policies that boost consumption in ways that reduce the saving rate are likely to lower long-run living standards."

What do economists say?

21% uncertain
0% disagree
79% agree

Source: IGM Economic Experts Panel, July 8, 2013.

THE HISTORY OF U.S. GOVERNMENT DEBT

How indebted is the U.S. government? The answer to this question varies substantially over time. Figure 5 shows the debt of the U.S. federal government expressed as a percentage of U.S. GDP. It shows that the government debt has fluctuated from zero in 1836 to 107 percent of GDP in 1945.

The debt-to-GDP ratio is one gauge of the government's finances. Because GDP is a rough measure of the government's tax base, a declining debt-to-GDP ratio indicates that the government indebtedness is shrinking relative to its ability to raise tax revenue. This suggests that the government is, in some sense, living within its means. By contrast, a rising debt-to-GDP ratio means that the government indebtedness is increasing relative to its ability to raise tax revenue. It is often interpreted as meaning that fiscal policy—government spending and taxes—cannot be sustained forever at current levels.

Throughout history, the primary cause of fluctuations in government debt has been war. When wars occur, government spending on national defense rises substantially to pay for soldiers and military equipment. Taxes sometimes rise as well but typically by much less than the increase in spending. The result is a budget

FIGURE 5

The U.S. Government Debt

The debt of the U.S. federal government, expressed here as a percentage of GDP, has varied throughout history. Wartime spending is typically associated with substantial increases in government debt.

Source: U.S. Department of Treasury; U.S. Department of Commerce; and T. S. Berry, "Production and Population since 1789," Bostwick Paper No. 6, Richmond, 1988.

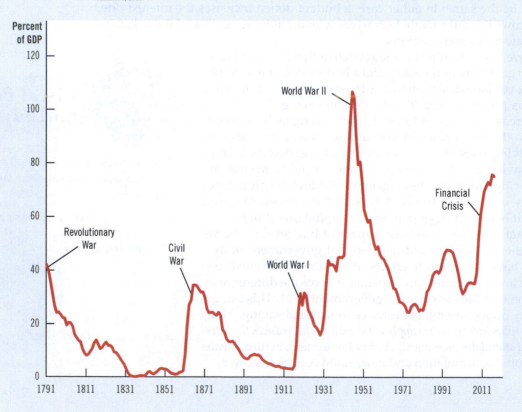

deficit and increasing government debt. When the war is over, government spending declines and the debt-to-GDP ratio starts declining as well.

There are two reasons to believe that debt financing of war is an appropriate policy. First, it allows the government to keep tax rates smooth over time. Without debt financing, wars would require sharp increases in tax rates, which would cause a substantial decline in economic efficiency. Second, debt financing of wars shifts part of the cost of wars to future generations, who will have to pay off the government debt. Putting some of the tax burden on future generations is arguably fair given that they get some of the benefit when a previous generation fights a war to defend the nation from foreign aggressors.

One large increase in government debt that cannot be explained by war is the increase that occurred beginning around 1980. When President Ronald Reagan took office in 1981, he was committed to smaller government and lower taxes. Yet he found cutting government spending to be more difficult politically than cutting taxes. The result was the beginning of a period of large budget deficits that continued not only through Reagan's time in office but also for many years thereafter. As a result, government debt rose from 26 percent of GDP in 1980 to 48 percent of GDP in 1993.

Because government budget deficits reduce national saving, investment, and long-run economic growth, the rise in government debt during the 1980s troubled many economists and policymakers. When Bill Clinton moved into the Oval Office in 1993, deficit reduction was his first major goal. Similarly, when the Republicans took control of Congress in 1995, deficit reduction was high on their legislative agenda. Both of these efforts substantially reduced the size of the government budget deficit. In addition, a booming economy in the late 1990s brought in even more tax revenue. Eventually, the federal budget turned from deficit to surplus, and the debt-to-GDP ratio declined significantly for several years.

This fall in the debt-to-GDP ratio, however, stopped during the presidency of George W. Bush, as the budget surplus turned back into a budget deficit. There were three main reasons for this change. First, President Bush signed into law several major tax cuts, which he had promised during the 2000 presidential campaign. Second, in 2001, the economy experienced a *recession* (a reduction in economic activity), which automatically decreased tax revenue and increased government spending. Third, there were increases in government spending on homeland security following the September 11, 2001 attacks and on the subsequent wars in Iraq and Afghanistan.

Truly dramatic increases in the debt-to-GDP ratio started occurring in 2008, as the economy experienced a financial crisis and a deep recession. (The accompanying FYI box addresses this topic briefly, but we will study it more fully in coming chapters.) The recession automatically increased the budget deficit, and several policy measures enacted during the Bush and Obama administrations aimed at combating the recession reduced tax revenue and increased government spending even more. From 2009 to 2012, the federal government's budget deficit averaged about 9 percent of GDP, levels not seen since World War II. The borrowing to finance these deficits led to an increase in the debt-to-GDP ratio from 39 percent in 2008 to 70 percent in 2012.

After 2012, as the economy recovered, the budget deficits shrank, and the debt-to-GDP ratio stabilized. But many budget analysts are concerned about increases in the debt-to-GDP ratio going forward. One reason is that President Trump enacted a significant tax cut beginning in 2018. More important, as members of the large baby-boom generation reach retirement age, they will become eligible for Social Security and Medicare benefits, putting upward pressure on government spending. Without sizable increases in tax revenue or cuts in government spending, the U.S. federal government will likely experience a rising debt-to-GDP ratio over the next few decades. ●

FYI

Financial Crises

In 2008 and 2009, the U.S. economy and many other major economies around the world experienced a financial crisis, which in turn led to a deep downturn in economic activity. We will examine these events in detail later in this book. But because this chapter introduces the financial system, let's discuss briefly the key elements of financial crises.

The first element of a financial crisis is a large decline in the prices of some assets. In 2008 and 2009, that asset was real estate. House prices, after experiencing a boom earlier in the decade, fell by about 30 percent over just a few years. Such a large decline in real estate prices had not been seen in the United States since the 1930s.

The second element of a financial crisis is widespread insolvencies at financial institutions. (A company is *insolvent* when its liabilities exceed the value of its assets.) In 2008 and 2009, many banks and other financial firms had in effect placed bets on house prices by holding mortgages backed by that real estate. When house prices fell, large numbers of homeowners stopped repaying their loans. These defaults pushed several major financial institutions toward bankruptcy.

The third element of a financial crisis is a decline in confidence in financial institutions. Although some deposits in banks are insured by government policies, not all are. As insolvencies mounted in 2008 and 2009, every financial institution became a candidate for the next bankruptcy. Individuals and firms with uninsured deposits in those institutions pulled out their money. Needing cash to pay back those depositors, banks started selling off assets (sometimes at reduced "fire-sale" prices) and cut back on new lending.

The fourth element of a financial crisis is a credit crunch. With many financial institutions facing difficulties, prospective borrowers had trouble getting loans, even if they had profitable investment projects. In essence, the financial system had trouble performing its normal function of directing the resources of savers into the hands of borrowers with the best investment opportunities.

The fifth element of a financial crisis is an economic downturn. With people unable to obtain financing for new investment projects, the overall demand for goods and services declined. As a result, for reasons we discuss more fully later in the book, national income fell and unemployment rose.

The sixth and final element of a financial crisis is a vicious circle. The economic downturn reduced the profitability of many companies and the value of many assets. Thus, we started over again at step one, and the problems in the financial system and the economic downturn reinforced each other.

Financial crises, such as the one of 2008 and 2009, can have severe consequences. Fortunately, they do end. Financial institutions eventually get back on their feet, perhaps with some help from government policy, and they return to their normal function of financial intermediation. ■

Quick**Quiz**

6. If a popular TV show on personal finance convinces Americans to save more for retirement, the _____ curve for loanable funds would shift, driving the equilibrium interest rate _____.
   a. supply; up
   b. supply; down
   c. demand; up
   d. demand; down

7. If the business community becomes more optimistic about the profitability of capital, the _____ curve for loanable funds would shift, driving the equilibrium interest rate _____.
   a. supply; up
   b. supply; down
   c. demand; up
   d. demand; down

8. Which of the following policy actions would unambiguously reduce the supply of loanable funds and crowd out investment?
   a. an increase in taxes and a decrease in government spending
   b. a decrease in taxes together with an increase in government spending
   c. an increase in both taxes and government spending
   d. a decrease in both taxes and government spending

9. From 2008 to 2012, in the aftermath of the financial crisis, the ratio of government debt to GDP in the United States
   a. increased markedly.
   b. decreased markedly.
   c. was stable at a historically high level.
   d. was stable at a historically low level.

Answers at end of chapter.

8-4 Conclusion

"Neither a borrower nor a lender be," Polonius advises his son in Shakespeare's *Hamlet*. If everyone followed Polonius's advice, this chapter would be unnecessary.

But few do. In our economy, people borrow and lend often, and usually for good reason. You may borrow one day to start your own business or to buy a home. And people may lend to you in the hope that the interest you pay will allow them to enjoy a more prosperous retirement. The financial system's job is to coordinate all this borrowing and lending activity.

In many ways, financial markets are like other markets in the economy. The price of loanable funds—the interest rate—is governed by the forces of supply and demand, just as other prices in the economy are. And we can analyze shifts in supply or demand in financial markets as we do in other markets. One of the *Ten Principles of Economics* in Chapter 1 is that markets are usually a good way to organize economic activity. This principle applies to financial markets as well. When financial markets bring the supply and demand for loanable funds into balance, they help allocate the economy's scarce resources to their most efficient uses.

In one way, however, financial markets are special. Financial markets, unlike most other markets, serve the important role of linking the present and the future. Those who supply loanable funds—savers—do so because they want to convert some of their current income into future purchasing power. Those who demand loanable funds—borrowers—do so because they want to invest today and use the capital to produce goods and services in the future. Thus, well-functioning financial markets are important not only for current generations but also for future generations who will inherit many of the resulting benefits.

CHAPTER IN A NUTSHELL

- The U.S. financial system is made up of many types of financial institutions, such as the bond market, the stock market, banks, and mutual funds. All these institutions direct the resources of households that want to save some of their income into the hands of households and firms that want to borrow.
- National income accounting identities reveal some important relationships among macroeconomic variables. In particular, for a closed economy, national saving must equal investment. Financial institutions are the mechanism through which the economy matches one person's saving with another person's investment.
- The interest rate is determined by the supply and demand for loanable funds. The supply of loanable funds comes from households that want to save some of their income and lend it out. The demand for loanable funds comes from households and firms that want to borrow for investment. To analyze how any policy or event affects the interest rate, one must consider how it affects the supply and demand for loanable funds.
- National saving equals private saving plus public saving. A government budget deficit represents negative public saving and, therefore, reduces national saving and the supply of loanable funds available to finance investment. When a government budget deficit crowds out investment, it reduces the growth of productivity and GDP.

KEY CONCEPTS

financial system, *p. 150*
financial markets, *p. 150*
bond, *p. 150*
stock, *p. 151*
financial intermediaries, *p. 152*

mutual fund, *p. 153*
national saving (saving), *p. 155*
private saving, *p. 156*
public saving, *p. 156*
budget surplus, *p. 156*

budget deficit, *p. 156*
market for loanable funds, *p. 157*
crowding out, *p. 163*

QUESTIONS FOR REVIEW

1. What is the role of the financial system? Name and describe two markets that are part of the financial system in the U.S. economy. Name and describe two financial intermediaries.

2. Why is it important for people who own stocks and bonds to diversify their holdings? What type of financial institution makes diversification easier?

3. What is national saving? What is private saving? What is public saving? How are these three variables related?

4. What is investment? How is it related to national saving in a closed economy?

5. Describe a change in the tax code that might increase private saving. If this policy were implemented, how would it affect the market for loanable funds?

6. What is a government budget deficit? How does it affect interest rates, investment, and economic growth?

PROBLEMS AND APPLICATIONS

1. For each of the following pairs, which bond would you expect to pay a higher interest rate? Explain.
   a. a bond of the U.S. government or a bond of an Eastern European government
   b. a bond that repays the principal in year 2020 or a bond that repays the principal in year 2040
   c. a bond from Coca-Cola or a bond from a software company you run in your garage
   d. a bond issued by the federal government or a bond issued by New York State

2. Many workers hold large amounts of stock issued by the firms at which they work. Why do you suppose companies encourage this behavior? Why might a person *not* want to hold stock in the company where he works?

3. Explain the difference between saving and investment as defined by a macroeconomist. Which of the following situations represent investment and which represent saving? Explain.
   a. Your family takes out a mortgage and buys a new house.
   b. You use your $200 paycheck to buy stock in AT&T.
   c. Your roommate earns $100 and deposits it in his account at a bank.
   d. You borrow $1,000 from a bank to buy a car to use in your pizza delivery business.

4. Suppose GDP is $8 trillion, taxes are $1.5 trillion, private saving is $0.5 trillion, and public saving is $0.2 trillion. Assuming this economy is closed, calculate consumption, government purchases, national saving, and investment.

5. Economists in Funlandia, a closed economy, have collected the following information about the economy for a particular year:

   $Y = 10,000$
   $C = 6,000$
   $T = 1,500$
   $G = 1,700$

The economists also estimate that the investment function is:

$$I = 3,300 - 100r,$$

where r is the country's real interest rate, expressed as a percentage. Calculate private saving, public saving, national saving, investment, and the equilibrium real interest rate.

6. Suppose that Intel is considering building a new chip-making factory.
   a. Assuming that Intel needs to borrow money in the bond market, why would an increase in interest rates affect Intel's decision about whether to build the factory?
   b. If Intel has enough of its own funds to finance the new factory without borrowing, would an increase in interest rates still affect Intel's decision about whether to build the factory? Explain.

7. Three students have each saved $1,000. Each has an investment opportunity in which he or she can invest up to $2,000. Here are the rates of return on the students' investment projects:

Harry	5 percent
Ron	8 percent
Hermione	20 percent

   a. If borrowing and lending are prohibited, so each student can use only personal saving to finance his or her own investment project, how much will each student have a year later when the project pays its return?
   b. Now suppose their school opens up a market for loanable funds in which students can borrow and lend among themselves at an interest rate r. What would determine whether a student would choose to be a borrower or lender in this market?

c. Among these three students, what would be the quantity of loanable funds supplied and quantity demanded at an interest rate of 7 percent? At 10 percent?

d. At what interest rate would the loanable funds market among these three students be in equilibrium? At this interest rate, which student(s) would borrow and which student(s) would lend?

e. At the equilibrium interest rate, how much does each student have a year later after the investment projects pay their return and loans have been repaid? Compare your answers to those you gave in part (a). Who benefits from the existence of the loanable funds market—the borrowers or the lenders? Is anyone worse off?

8. Suppose the government borrows $20 billion more next year than this year.

a. Use a supply-and-demand diagram to analyze this policy. Does the interest rate rise or fall?

b. What happens to investment? To private saving? To public saving? To national saving? Compare the size of the changes to the $20 billion of extra government borrowing.

c. How does the elasticity of supply of loanable funds affect the size of these changes?

d. How does the elasticity of demand for loanable funds affect the size of these changes?

e. Suppose households believe that greater government borrowing today implies higher taxes to pay off the government debt in the future. What does this belief do to private saving and the supply of loanable funds today? Does it increase or decrease the effects you discussed in parts (a) and (b)?

9. This chapter explains that investment can be increased both by reducing taxes on private saving and by reducing the government budget deficit.

a. Why is it difficult to implement both of these policies at the same time?

b. What would you need to know about private saving to determine which of these two policies would be the more effective way to raise investment?

QuickQuiz Answers

1. d   2. d   3. b   4. d   5. c   6. b   7. c   8. b   9. a

At some point in your life, you will interact with the economy's financial system. You will deposit your savings in a bank account, or you will take out a loan to cover tuition or buy a house. After you have a job, your employer will start a retirement account for you, and you will decide whether to invest the funds in stocks, bonds, or other financial instruments. If you try to put together your own portfolio, you will have to decide between investing in established companies such as Coca-Cola or newer ones such as Twitter. And in the media, you will hear reports about whether the stock market is up or down, along with the often feeble attempts to explain why the market behaves as it does.

In almost all of the financial decisions you will make during your life, you will encounter two related elements: time and risk. As we saw in the preceding two chapters, the financial system coordinates the economy's saving and investment, which are crucial determinants of economic growth. Most fundamentally, the financial system concerns decisions and actions we undertake today that will affect our lives in the future. But the future is unknown. When a person decides to allocate some saving, or a firm decides to undertake an investment, the decision is based on a guess about the likely result. The actual result, however, could end up being very different from what was expected.

The Basic Tools of Finance

finance

the field that studies how people make decisions regarding the allocation of resources over time and the handling of risk

This chapter introduces some tools that help us understand the decisions that people make as they participate in financial markets. The field of **finance** develops these tools in great detail, and you may choose to take courses that focus on this topic. But because the financial system is so important to the functioning of the economy, many of the basic insights of finance are central to understanding how the economy works. The tools of finance can also help you think through some of the decisions that you will make in your own life.

This chapter takes up three topics. First, we discuss how to compare sums of money at different points in time. Second, we discuss how to manage risk. Third, we build on our analysis of time and risk to examine what determines the value of an asset, such as a share of stock.

9-1 Present Value: Measuring the Time Value of Money

Imagine that someone offers to give you $100 today or $100 in 10 years. Which would you choose? This is an easy question. Getting $100 today is better because you can deposit the money in a bank, still have it in 10 years, and earn interest on the $100 along the way. The lesson: Money today is more valuable than the same amount of money in the future.

Now consider a harder question: Imagine that someone offers you $100 today or $200 in 10 years. Which would you choose? To answer this question, you need some way to compare sums of money from different points in time. Economists do this with a concept called present value. The **present value** of any future sum of money is the amount of money that, given current interest rates, would be needed today to produce that future sum.

To learn how to use the concept of present value, let's work through a couple of simple examples:

Question: If you put $100 in a bank account today, how much will it be worth in N years? That is, what will be the **future value** of this $100?

Answer: Let's use r to denote the interest rate expressed in decimal form (so an interest rate of 5 percent means $r = 0.05$). Suppose that interest is paid annually and that it remains in the bank account to earn more interest—a process called **compounding**. Then the $100 will become

$(1 + r) \times \$100$	after 1 year,
$(1 + r) \times (1 + r) \times \$100 = (1 + r)^2 \times \$100$	after 2 years,
$(1 + r) \times (1 + r) \times (1 + r) \times \$100 = (1 + r)^3 \times \$100$	after 3 years, ...
$(1 + r)^N \times \$100$	after N years.

For example, if we invest at an interest rate of 5 percent for 10 years, then the future value of the $100 will be $(1.05)^{10} \times \$100$, or $163.

Question: Now suppose you are going to be paid $200 in N years. What is the *present value* of this future payment? That is, how much would you have to deposit in a bank right now to yield $200 in N years?

Answer: To answer this question, just turn the previous answer on its head. In the last question, we computed a future value from a present value by *multiplying* by the factor $(1 + r)^N$. To compute a present value from a future value, we *divide*

present value

the amount of money today needed to produce a future amount of money, given prevailing interest rates

future value

the amount of money in the future that an amount of money today will yield, given prevailing interest rates

compounding

the accumulation of a sum of money in, say, a bank account, where the interest earned remains in the account to earn additional interest in the future by the factor $(1 + r)^N$. Thus, the present value of $200 to be paid in N years is $200/(1 + r)^N$. If that amount is deposited in a bank today, after N years it will become $(1 + r)^N \times [\$200/(1 + r)^N]$, which equals $200. For instance, if the interest rate is 5 percent, the present value of $200 to be paid in 10 years is $200/(1.05)^{10}$, or $123. This means that $123 deposited today in a bank account earning 5 percent interest would be worth $200 after 10 years.

This illustrates the general formula:

- If r is the interest rate, then an amount X to be received in N years has a present value of $X/(1 + r)^N$.

Because the possibility of earning interest reduces the present value below the amount X, the process of finding a present value of a future sum of money is called *discounting*. This formula shows precisely how much future sums should be discounted.

Let's now return to our earlier question: Should you choose $100 today or $200 in 10 years? Based on our calculation of present value using an interest rate of 5 percent, you should prefer the $200 in 10 years. The future $200 has a present value of $123, which is greater than $100. You are better off waiting for the future sum.

Notice that the answer to our question depends on the interest rate. If the interest rate were 8 percent, then the $200 in 10 years would have a present value of $200/(1.08)^{10}$, which is only $93. In this case, you should take the $100 today. Why should the interest rate matter for your choice? The answer is that the higher the interest rate, the more you can earn by depositing your money in a bank, so the more attractive getting $100 today becomes.

The concept of present value is useful in many applications, including the decisions that companies face when evaluating investment projects. For instance, imagine that General Motors is thinking about building a new factory. Suppose that the factory will cost $100 million today and will yield the company $200 million in 10 years. Should General Motors undertake the project? You can see that this decision is exactly like the one we have been studying. To make its decision, the company should compare the present value of the $200 million return to the $100 million cost.

The company's decision, therefore, will depend on the interest rate. If the interest rate is 5 percent, then the present value of the $200 million return from the factory is $123 million, and the company will choose to pay the $100 million cost. By contrast, if the interest rate is 8 percent, then the present value of the return is only $93 million, and the company will decide to forgo the project. Thus, the concept of present value helps explain why investment—and thus the quantity of loanable funds demanded—declines when the interest rate rises.

Here is another application of present value: Suppose you win a million-dollar lottery and are given a choice between $20,000 a year for 50 years (totaling $1,000,000) or an immediate payment of $400,000. Which would you choose? To make the right choice, you need to calculate the present value of the stream of payments. Let's suppose the interest rate is 7 percent. After performing 50 calculations similar to those above (one calculation for each payment) and adding up the results, you would learn that the present value of this million-dollar prize at a 7 percent interest rate is only $276,000. You are better off picking the immediate payment of $400,000. The million dollars may seem like more money, but the future cash flows, once discounted to the present, are worth far less.

FYI

The Magic of Compounding and the Rule of 70

Suppose you observe that one country has an average growth rate of 1 percent per year, while another has an average growth rate of 3 percent per year. At first, this gap might not seem like a big deal. What difference can 2 percent make?

The answer is: a big difference. Growth rates that seem small when written in percentage terms are large after they are compounded for many years.

Consider an example. Suppose that two college graduates—Elliot and Darlene—both take their first jobs at the age of 22 earning $30,000 a year. Elliot lives in an economy where all incomes grow at 1 percent per year, while Darlene lives in one where incomes grow at 3 percent per year. Straightforward calculations show what happens. Forty years later, when both are 62 years old, Elliot earns $45,000 a year, while Darlene earns $98,000. Because of that difference of 2 percentage points in the growth rate, Darlene's salary is more than twice Elliot's.

An old rule of thumb, called the *rule of 70*, is helpful in understanding growth rates and the effects of compounding. According to the rule of 70, if some amount grows at a rate of *x* percent per year, then that amount doubles in approximately 70/*x* years. In Elliot's economy, incomes grow at 1 percent per year, so it takes about 70 years for incomes to double. In Darlene's economy, incomes grow at 3 percent per year, so it takes about 70/3, or 23, years for incomes to double.

The rule of 70 applies not only to a growing economy but also to a growing savings account. Here is an example: In 1791, Ben Franklin died and left $5,000 to be invested for a period of 200 years to benefit medical students and scientific research. If this money had earned 7 percent per year (which would, in fact, have been possible), the investment would have doubled in value every 10 years. Over 200 years, it would have doubled 20 times. At the end of 200 years of compounding, the investment would have been worth $2^{20} \times \$5,000$, which is about $5 billion. (In fact, Franklin's $5,000 grew to only $2 million over 200 years because some of the money was spent along the way.)

As these examples show, growth rates and interest rates compounded over many years can lead to some spectacular results. That is probably why Albert Einstein once called compounding "the greatest mathematical discovery of all time." ∎

Quick**Quiz**

1. If the interest rate is zero, then $100 to be paid in 10 years has a present value that is
   a. less than $100.
   b. exactly $100.
   c. more than $100.
   d. indeterminate.

2. If the interest rate is 10 percent, then the future value in 2 years of $100 today is
   a. $80.
   b. $83.
   c. $120.
   d. $121.

3. If the interest rate is 10 percent, then the present value of $100 to be paid in 2 years is
   a. $80.
   b. $83.
   c. $120.
   d. $121.

Answers at end of chapter.

9-2 Managing Risk

Life is full of gambles. When you go skiing, you risk breaking your leg in a fall. When you drive to work, you risk getting into a car accident. When you put some of your savings in the stock market, you risk losing your money from a fall in stock prices. The rational response to risk is not to avoid it at any cost but to take it into account in your decision making. Let's consider how you might do that as you make financial decisions.

9-2a Risk Aversion

Most people are **risk averse**. This means more than that people dislike bad things happening to them. It means that they dislike bad things more than they like comparable good things.

risk aversion
a dislike of uncertainty

For example, suppose a friend offers you the following deal. She will toss a coin. If it comes up heads, she will pay you $1,000. But if it comes up tails, you will have to pay her $1,000. Would you accept the bargain? You wouldn't if you were risk averse. For a risk-averse person, the pain of losing the $1,000 would exceed the pleasure from winning $1,000.

Economists have developed models of risk aversion using the concept of *utility*, which is a person's subjective measure of well-being or satisfaction. As the utility function in Figure 1 shows, every level of wealth provides a certain amount of utility. But the utility function gets flatter as wealth increases, meaning it exhibits the property of diminishing marginal utility: The more wealth a person has, the less utility she gets from an additional dollar. Because of diminishing marginal utility, the utility forfeited from losing the $1,000 bet exceeds the utility gained from winning it. In other words, diminishing marginal utility is the reason most people are risk averse.

Risk aversion provides the starting point for explaining various things we observe in the economy. Let's consider three of them: insurance, diversification, and the risk-return trade-off.

9-2b The Markets for Insurance

One way to deal with risk is to buy insurance. The general feature of insurance contracts is that a person facing a risk pays a fee to an insurance company, which in return agrees to accept all or part of the risk. There are many types of insurance. Car insurance covers the risk of you getting into an auto accident, fire insurance covers the risk of your house burning down, health insurance covers the risk of you needing expensive medical treatment, and life insurance covers the risk of you dying and leaving your family without your income. There is also insurance against the risk of living too long: For a fee paid today, an insurance company will pay you an *annuity*—a regular income every year until you die.

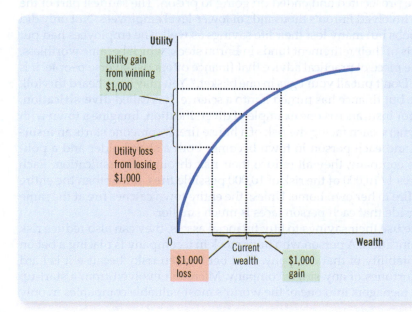

FIGURE 1

The Utility Function
This utility function shows how utility, a subjective measure of satisfaction, depends on wealth. As wealth rises, the utility function becomes flatter, reflecting the property of diminishing marginal utility. Because of diminishing marginal utility, a $1,000 loss decreases utility by more than a $1,000 gain increases it.

In a sense, every insurance contract is a gamble. It is possible that you will not be in an auto accident, that your house will not burn down, and that you will not need expensive medical treatment. In most years, you will pay the insurance company the premium and get nothing in return except peace of mind. Indeed, the insurance company is counting on the fact that most people will not make claims on their policies; otherwise, it couldn't pay out large claims to the unlucky few and still stay in business.

From the standpoint of the economy as a whole, the role of insurance is not to eliminate the risks inherent in life but to spread them around more efficiently. Consider fire insurance, for instance. Owning fire insurance does not reduce the risk of losing your home in a fire. But if that unlucky event occurs, the insurance company compensates you. The risk, rather than being borne by you alone, is shared among the thousands of insurance-company shareholders. Because people are risk averse, it is easier for 10,000 people to bear 1/10,000 of the risk than for one person to bear the entire risk herself.

The markets for insurance suffer from two types of problems that impede their ability to spread risk. One problem is *adverse selection*: A high-risk person is more likely to apply for insurance than a low-risk person because a high-risk person would benefit more from insurance protection. A second problem is *moral hazard*: After people buy insurance, they have less incentive to be careful about their risky behavior because the insurance company will cover much of the resulting losses. Insurance companies are aware of these problems, but they cannot fully guard against them. An insurance company cannot perfectly distinguish between high-risk and low-risk customers, and it cannot monitor all of its customers' risky behavior. The price of insurance reflects the actual risks that the insurance company will face after the insurance is bought. The high price of insurance is why some people, especially those who know themselves to be low-risk, decide against buying it and, instead, endure some of life's uncertainty on their own.

9-2c Diversification of Firm-Specific Risk

In 2001, Enron, a large and once widely respected company, went bankrupt amid accusations of fraud and accounting irregularities. Several of the company's top executives were prosecuted and ended up going to prison. The saddest part of the story, however, involved Enron's thousands of lower-level employees. Not only did they lose their jobs but many lost their life savings as well. The employees had put about two-thirds of their retirement funds in Enron stock, which became worthless.

If there is one piece of practical advice that finance offers risk-averse people, it is the following: "Don't put all your eggs in one basket." You may have heard this folk wisdom before, but finance has turned it into a science. It is called **diversification**.

The market for insurance is one example of diversification. Imagine a town with 10,000 homeowners, each facing the risk of a house fire. If someone starts an insurance company and each person in town becomes both a shareholder and a policyholder of the company, they all reduce their risk through diversification. Each person now faces 1/10,000 of the risk of 10,000 possible fires, rather than the entire risk of a single fire in her own home. Unless the entire town catches fire at the same time, the downside that each person faces is much smaller.

When people use their savings to buy financial assets, they can also reduce risk through diversification. A person who buys stock in a company is placing a bet on the future profitability of that company. That bet is often risky because it is hard to predict the fortunes of any single company. Microsoft evolved from a start-up by some geeky teenagers into one of the world's most valuable companies in only

diversification
the reduction of risk achieved by replacing a single risk with a large number of smaller, unrelated risks

a few years; Enron went from one of the world's most respected companies to an almost worthless one in only a few months. Fortunately, a shareholder need not tie her own fortune to that of any single company. Risk can be reduced by placing a large number of small bets, rather than a small number of large ones.

Figure 2 shows how the risk of a portfolio of stocks depends on the number of stocks in the portfolio. Risk is measured here by a statistic called the *standard deviation*, which may be familiar to you from a math or statistics class. The standard deviation measures the volatility of a variable—that is, how much the variable is likely to fluctuate. The higher the standard deviation of a portfolio's return, the more volatile its return is likely to be, and the riskier it is that someone holding the portfolio will fail to get the return that she expected.

The figure shows that the risk of a stock portfolio falls substantially as the number of stocks increases. For a portfolio with a single stock, the standard deviation is 49 percent. Going from 1 stock to 10 stocks eliminates about half the risk. Going from 10 stocks to 20 stocks reduces the risk by another 10 percent. As the number of stocks continues to increase, risk continues to fall, although the reductions in risk beyond 20 to 30 stocks are small.

Notice that it is impossible to eliminate all risk by increasing the number of stocks in the portfolio. Diversification can eliminate **firm-specific risk**—the uncertainty associated with a specific company. But diversification cannot eliminate **market risk**—the uncertainty associated with the entire economy, which affects all companies traded on the stock market. For example, when the economy goes into a recession, most companies experience falling sales, reduced profit, and lower stock returns. Diversification reduces the risk of holding stocks, but it does not eliminate it.

firm-specific risk
risk that affects only a single company

market risk
risk that affects all companies in the stock market

9-2d The Trade-Off between Risk and Return

One of the *Ten Principles of Economics* in Chapter 1 is that people face trade-offs. The trade-off that is most relevant for understanding financial decisions is the trade-off between risk and return.

As we have seen, there are risks inherent in holding stocks, even in a diversified portfolio. But risk-averse people are willing to accept this uncertainty because they

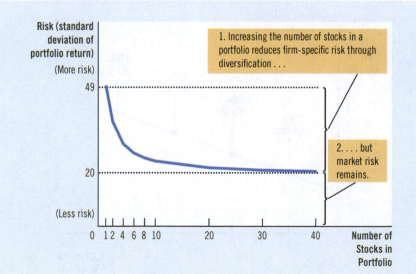

FIGURE 2

Diversification Reduces Risk
This figure shows how the risk of a portfolio, measured here by a statistic called the *standard deviation*, depends on the number of stocks in the portfolio. The investor is assumed to put an equal percentage of her portfolio in each of the stocks. Increasing the number of stocks reduces but does not eliminate the risk in a stock portfolio.

Source: Adapted from Meir Statman, "How Many Stocks Make a Diversified Portfolio?" *Journal of Financial and Quantitative Analysis* 22 (September 1987): 353–364.

are compensated for doing so. Historically, stocks have offered much higher rates of return than alternative financial assets, such as bonds and bank savings accounts. Over the past two centuries, stocks have generated an average real return of about 8 percent per year, while short-term government bonds have paid a real return of only 3 percent per year.

When deciding how to allocate their savings, people have to decide how much risk they are willing to undertake to earn a higher return. For example, consider a person choosing how to allocate her portfolio between two asset classes:

- The first asset class is a diversified group of risky stocks offering an average return of 8 percent and a standard deviation of 20 percent. You may recall from a math or statistics class that a normal random variable stays within 2 standard deviations of its average about 95 percent of the time. Here, 2 standard deviations mean fluctuations of ±40 percent. Thus, while returns are centered around 8 percent, they vary between a 48 percent gain to a 32 percent loss 95 percent of the time.
- The second asset class is a safe alternative, with a return of 3 percent and a standard deviation of zero. That is, this asset always pays exactly 3 percent. The safe alternative can be either a bank savings account or a government bond.

Figure 3 illustrates the trade-off between risk and return. Each point in this figure represents a particular allocation of a portfolio between risky stocks and the safe asset. The figure shows that the more the individual puts into stocks, the greater both the risk and the return are.

Acknowledging the risk-return trade-off does not, by itself, tell us what a person should do. The choice of a particular combination of risk and return depends on a person's risk aversion, which reflects her own preferences. But it is important for stockholders to recognize that the higher average return that they enjoy comes at the price of higher risk.

FIGURE 3

The Trade-Off between Risk and Return
When people increase the percentage of their savings that they have invested in stocks, they increase the average return they can expect to earn, but they also increase the risks they face.

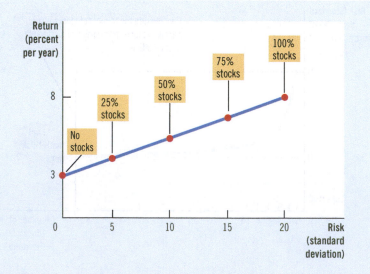

4. The ability of insurance to spread risk is limited by
   a. risk aversion and moral hazard.
   b. risk aversion and adverse selection.
   c. moral hazard and adverse selection.
   d. risk aversion only.

5. The benefit of diversification when constructing a portfolio is that it can eliminate
   a. adverse selection.
   b. risk aversion.
   c. firm-specific risk.
   d. market risk.

6. The extra return that stocks earn over bonds (on average) compensates stockholders for
   a. the greater market risk that stockholding entails.
   b. the greater firm-specific risk that stockholding entails.
   c. the higher taxes levied on stockholders.
   d. the higher brokerage costs incurred buying stocks.

Answers at end of chapter.

9-3 Asset Valuation

Now that we have developed a basic understanding of the two building blocks of finance—time and risk—let's apply this knowledge. This section considers a simple question: What determines the price of a share of stock? As for most prices, the answer is supply and demand. But that is not the end of the story. To understand stock prices, we need to think more deeply about what determines a person's willingness to pay for a share of stock.

9-3a Fundamental Analysis

Let's imagine that you have decided to put 60 percent of your savings into stock and that, to achieve diversification, you have decided to buy 20 different stocks. If you open up the newspaper, you will find thousands of stocks listed. How should you pick the 20 for your portfolio?

When you buy stock, you are buying shares in a business. To decide which businesses you want to own, it is natural to consider two things: the value of that share of the business and the price at which the shares are being sold. If the price is more than the value, the stock is said to be *overvalued*. If the price and the value are equal, the stock is said to be *fairly valued*. And if the price is less than the value, the stock is said to be *undervalued*. Undervalued stocks are a bargain because you pay less than the business is worth. When choosing 20 stocks for your portfolio, you should look for undervalued stocks.

But that is easier said than done. Learning the price of the company's stock is easy: You can just look it up. Determining the value of the company is the hard part. The term **fundamental analysis** refers to the detailed analysis of a company in order to estimate its value. Many Wall Street firms hire stock analysts to conduct such fundamental analysis and offer advice about which stocks to buy.

The value of a stock to a stockholder is what she gets out of owning it, which includes the present value of the stream of dividend payments and the final sale price. Recall that *dividends* are the cash payments that a company makes to its shareholders. A company's ability to pay dividends, as well as the value of the stock when the stockholder sells her shares, depends on the company's ability to earn profits. Its profitability, in turn, depends on a large number of factors: the demand for its product, the amount and kinds of capital it has in place, the degree of competition it confronts, the extent of unionization of its workers, the loyalty of

fundamental analysis
the study of a company's accounting statements and future prospects to determine its value

FYI

Key Numbers for Stock Watchers

When following the stock of a company, you should keep an eye on three key numbers. These numbers are reported on the financial pages of some newspapers, and you can easily obtain them online as well (such as at Yahoo! Finance):

- **Price.** The single most important piece of information about a stock is the price of a share. News services usually present several prices. The "last" price is the price at which the stock more recently traded. The "previous close" is the price of the last transaction that occurred before the stock exchange closed on its previous day of trading. A news service may also give the "high" and "low" prices over the past day of trading and, sometimes, over the past year as well. It may also report the change from the previous day's closing price.

- **Dividend.** Corporations pay out some of their profits to their stockholders; this amount is called the *dividend*. (Profits not paid out are called *retained earnings* and are used by the corporation for additional investment.) News services often report the dividend paid over the previous year for each share of stock. They sometimes report the *dividend yield*, which is the dividend expressed as a percentage of the stock's price.

- **Price-earnings ratio.** A corporation's earnings, or accounting profit, is the amount of revenue it receives for the sale of its products minus its costs of production as measured by its accountants. *Earnings per share* is the company's total earnings divided by the number of shares of stock outstanding. The *price-earnings ratio*, often called the *P/E*, is the price of one share of a corporation's stock divided by the corporation's earnings per share over the past year. Historically, the typical price-earnings ratio has been about 15. A high P/E indicates that a corporation's stock is expensive relative to its recent earnings, suggesting either that people expect earnings to rise in the future or that the stock is overvalued. Conversely, a low P/E indicates that a corporation's stock is cheap relative to its recent earnings, suggesting either that people expect earnings to fall or that the stock is undervalued.

Why do news services report all these data? Many people who invest their savings in stock follow these numbers closely when deciding which stocks to buy and sell. By contrast, other stockholders follow a buy-and-hold strategy: They buy the stock of well-run companies, hold it for long periods of time, and do not respond to daily fluctuations. ■

its customers, the government regulations and taxes it faces, and so on. The goal of fundamental analysis is to take all these factors into account to determine how much a share of stock in the company is worth.

If you want to rely on fundamental analysis to pick a stock portfolio, there are three ways to do it. One way is to do all the necessary research yourself by, for instance, reading through companies' annual reports. A second way is to rely on the advice of Wall Street analysts. A third way is to buy shares in a mutual fund, which has a manager who conducts fundamental analysis and makes decisions for you.

9-3b The Efficient Markets Hypothesis

There is another way to choose 20 stocks for your portfolio: Pick them randomly by, for instance, putting the stock pages on your bulletin board and throwing darts at them. This approach may sound crazy, but there is reason to believe that it won't lead you too far astray. That reason is called the **efficient markets hypothesis**.

To understand this theory, the starting point is to realize that each company listed on a major stock exchange is followed closely by many money managers, such as the individuals who run mutual funds. Every day, these managers monitor news stories and conduct fundamental analysis to try to determine a stock's value. Their job is to buy a stock when its price falls below its fundamental value and to sell it when its price rises above its fundamental value.

The second piece to the efficient markets hypothesis is that the equilibrium of supply and demand sets the market price. This means that, at the market price, the number of shares being offered for sale exactly equals the number of shares that people want to buy. In other words, at the market price, the number of people who

efficient markets hypothesis
the theory that asset prices reflect all publicly available information about the value of an asset

think the stock is overvalued exactly balances the number of people who think it's undervalued. As judged by the typical person in the market, all stocks are fairly valued all the time.

According to this theory, the stock market exhibits **informational efficiency**: It reflects all available information about the value of an asset. Stock prices change when information changes. When good news about a company's prospects becomes public, the company's value and stock price both rise. When a company's prospects deteriorate, its value and price both fall. But at any moment in time, the market price is the best guess of the company's value based on available information.

One implication of the efficient markets hypothesis is that stock prices should follow a **random walk**, meaning that changes in stock prices should be impossible to predict from available information. If, based on publicly available information, a person could predict that a stock price would rise by 10 percent tomorrow, the stock market must be failing to incorporate that information today. According to the theory, the only thing that can move a company's stock price is news that changes the market's perception of the company's value. But news is inherently unpredictable—otherwise, it wouldn't really be news. As a result, changes in stock prices should be unpredictable as well.

If the efficient markets hypothesis is correct, then there is little point in spending many hours studying the business page to decide which 20 stocks to add to your portfolio. If prices reflect all available information, no stock is a better buy than any other. The best you can do is to buy a diversified portfolio.

informational efficiency
the description of asset prices that rationally reflect all available information

random walk
the path of a variable whose changes are impossible to predict

CASE STUDY

RANDOM WALKS AND INDEX FUNDS

The efficient markets hypothesis is a theory about how financial markets work. The theory may not be completely true: As we discuss in the next section, there is reason to doubt that stockholders are always rational and that stock prices are informationally efficient at every moment. Nonetheless, the efficient markets hypothesis describes the world much better than you might expect.

There is much evidence that stock prices follow, even if not exactly a random walk, something very close to it. For example, you might be tempted to buy stocks that have recently risen and avoid stocks that have recently fallen (or perhaps just the opposite). But statistical studies have shown that following such trends (or bucking them) fails to outperform the market. The correlation between how well a stock does one year and how well it does the following year is about zero.

Some of the best evidence in favor of the efficient markets hypothesis comes from the performance of index funds. An index fund is a mutual fund that buys all the stocks in a given stock index. The performance of these funds can be compared

Source: IGM Economic Experts Panel, January 28, 2019.

with that of actively managed mutual funds, where a professional portfolio manager picks stocks based on extensive research and alleged expertise. In essence, index funds buy all stocks and thus offer investors the return on the average stock, whereas actively managed funds seek to buy only the best stocks and thereby outperform the market averages.

In practice, however, active managers usually fail to beat index funds. For example, in the 15-year period ending January 31, 2019, 86 percent of stock mutual funds performed worse than a broadly based index fund holding all stocks traded on U.S. stock exchanges. Over this period, the average annual return on stock funds fell short of the return on the index fund by 0.94 percentage points. Most active portfolio managers failed to beat the market because they trade more frequently, incurring more trading costs, and because they charge greater fees as compensation for their alleged expertise.

What about the 14 percent of managers who did beat the market? Perhaps they are smarter than average, or perhaps they were luckier. If you have 5,000 people flipping coins 10 times, on average about 5 will flip 10 heads; these 5 might claim an exceptional coin-flipping skill, but they would have trouble replicating the feat. Similarly, studies have shown that mutual fund managers with a history of superior performance usually fail to maintain it in subsequent periods.

The efficient markets hypothesis says that it is impossible to beat the market. The accumulation of many studies of financial markets confirms that beating the market is, at best, extremely difficult. Even if the efficient markets hypothesis is not a perfect description of the world, it contains a large element of truth. ●

9-3c Market Irrationality

The efficient markets hypothesis assumes that people buying and selling stock rationally process the information they have about the stock's underlying value. But are participants in the stock market really that rational? Or do stock prices sometimes deviate from reasonable expectations of their true value?

There is a long tradition suggesting that fluctuations in stock prices are partly psychological. In the 1930s, economist John Maynard Keynes suggested that asset markets are driven by the "animal spirits" of investors—irrational waves of optimism and pessimism. In the 1990s, as the stock market soared to new heights, Fed Chair Alan Greenspan questioned whether the boom reflected "irrational exuberance." Stock prices did subsequently fall, but whether the exuberance of the 1990s was irrational given the information available at the time remains debatable. Whenever the price of an asset rises above what appears to be its fundamental value, the market is said to be experiencing a *speculative bubble*.

The possibility of speculative bubbles in the stock market arises in part because the value of the stock to a stockholder depends not only on the stream of dividend payments but also on the final sale price. Thus, a person might be willing to pay more than a stock is worth today if she expects another person to pay even more for it tomorrow. When evaluating a stock, you have to estimate not only the value of the business but also what other people will think the business is worth in the future.

There is much debate among economists about the frequency and importance of departures from rational pricing. Believers in market irrationality point out (correctly) that the stock market often moves in ways that are hard to explain on the basis of news that might alter a rational valuation. Believers in the efficient markets hypothesis point out (correctly) that it is impossible to know the correct, rational valuation of a company, so one should not quickly jump to the conclusion that any particular valuation is irrational. Moreover, if the market were irrational, a rational person should be able to take advantage of this fact and beat the market; yet as the previous case study discussed, beating the market is nearly impossible.

QuickQuiz

7. The goal of fundamental analysis is to
   a. determine the true value of a company.
   b. put together a diversified portfolio.
   c. predict changes in investor irrationality.
   d. eliminate investor risk aversion.

8. According to the efficient markets hypothesis,
   a. excessive diversification can reduce an investor's expected portfolio returns.
   b. changes in stock prices are impossible to predict from public information.
   c. actively managed mutual funds should generate higher returns than index funds.
   d. the stock market moves based on the changing animal spirits of investors.

9. Historically, index funds have had _____ than most actively managed mutual funds.
   a. higher fees
   b. less diversification
   c. larger tax burdens
   d. better returns

Answers at end of chapter.

9-4 Conclusion

This chapter has developed some of the basic tools that people should (and often do) use as they make financial decisions. The concept of present value tells us that a dollar tomorrow is less valuable than a dollar today, and it gives us a way to compare sums of money at different points in time. The theory of risk management tells us that the future is uncertain and that risk-averse people can take precautions to guard against this uncertainty. The study of asset valuation tells us that the stock price of any company should reflect its expected future profitability.

Although most of the tools of finance are well established, there is more controversy about the validity of the efficient markets hypothesis and whether stock prices are, in reality, rational estimates of a company's true worth. Rational or not, the large movements in stock prices that we observe have important macroeconomic implications. Stock market fluctuations often go hand in hand with fluctuations in the economy more broadly. We revisit the stock market when we study economic fluctuations later in the book.

CHAPTER IN A NUTSHELL

- Because savings can earn interest, a sum of money today is more valuable than the same sum of money in the future. A person can compare sums from different times using the concept of present value. The present value of any future sum is the amount that would be needed today, given prevailing interest rates, to produce that future sum.
- Because of diminishing marginal utility, most people are risk averse. Risk-averse people can reduce risk by buying insurance, diversifying their holdings, and choosing a portfolio with lower risk and lower return.

- The value of an asset equals the present value of the cash flows the owner will receive. For a share of stock, these cash flows include the stream of dividends and the final sale price. According to the efficient markets hypothesis, financial markets process available information rationally, so a stock price always equals the best estimate of the value of the underlying business. Some economists question the efficient markets hypothesis, however, and believe that irrational psychological factors also influence asset prices.

KEY CONCEPTS

finance, *p. 172*
present value, *p. 172*
future value, *p. 172*
compounding, *p. 172*

risk aversion, *p. 175*
diversification, *p. 176*
firm-specific risk, *p. 177*
market risk, *p. 177*

fundamental analysis, *p. 179*
efficient markets hypothesis, *p. 180*
informational efficiency, *p. 181*
random walk, *p. 181*

QUESTIONS FOR REVIEW

1. The interest rate is 7 percent. Use the concept of present value to compare $200 to be received in 10 years and $300 to be received in 20 years.

2. What benefit do people get from the market for insurance? What two problems impede the insurance market from working perfectly?

3. What is diversification? Does a stockholder get a greater benefit from diversification when going from 1 stock to 10 stocks or when going from 100 stocks to 120 stocks?

4. Between stocks and government bonds, which type of asset has more risk? Which pays a higher average return?

5. What factors should a stock analyst think about in determining the value of a share of stock?

6. Describe the efficient markets hypothesis, and give a piece of evidence consistent with this hypothesis.

7. Explain the view of those economists who are skeptical of the efficient markets hypothesis.

PROBLEMS AND APPLICATIONS

1. According to an old myth, Native Americans sold the island of Manhattan about 400 years ago for $24. If they had invested this amount at an interest rate of 7 percent per year, how much, approximately, would they have today?

2. A company has an investment project that would cost $10 million today and yield a payoff of $15 million in 4 years.
   a. Should the firm undertake the project if the interest rate is 11 percent? 10 percent? 9 percent? 8 percent?
   b. Can you figure out the exact interest rate at which the firm would be indifferent between undertaking and forgoing the project? (This interest rate is called the project's *internal rate of return*.)

3. Bond A pays $8,000 in 20 years. Bond B pays $8,000 in 40 years. (To keep things simple, assume that these are zero-coupon bonds, meaning the $8,000 is the only payment the bondholder receives.)
   a. If the interest rate is 3.5 percent, what is the value of each bond today? Which bond is worth more? Why? (*Hint*: You can use a calculator, but the rule of 70 should make the calculation easy.)
   b. If the interest rate increases to 7 percent, what is the value of each bond? Which bond has a larger *percentage* change in value?

c. Based on the example above, complete the two blanks in this sentence: "The value of a bond [rises/falls] when the interest rate increases, and bonds with a longer time to maturity are [more/less] sensitive to changes in the interest rate."

4. Your bank account pays an interest rate of 8 percent. You are considering buying a share of stock in XYZ Corporation for $110. After 1, 2, and 3 years, it will pay a dividend of $5. You expect to sell the stock after 3 years for $120. Is XYZ a good investment? Support your answer with calculations.

5. For each of the following kinds of insurance, give an example of behavior that reflects *moral hazard* and another example of behavior that reflects *adverse selection*.
   a. health insurance
   b. car insurance
   c. life insurance

6. Which kind of stock would you expect to pay the higher average return: stock in an industry that is very sensitive to economic conditions (such as an automaker) or stock in an industry that is relatively insensitive to economic conditions (such as a water company)? Why?

7. A company faces two kinds of risk. A firm-specific risk is that a competitor might enter its market and take some of its customers. A market risk is that the economy might enter a recession, reducing sales. Which of these two risks would more likely cause the company's shareholders to demand a higher return? Why?

8. When company executives buy and sell stock based on private information that they obtain as part of their jobs, they are engaging in *insider trading*.
   a. Give an example of inside information that might be useful for buying or selling stock.
   b. Those who trade stocks based on inside information usually earn very high rates of return. Does this fact violate the efficient markets hypothesis?
   c. Insider trading is illegal. Why do you suppose that is?

9. Jamal has a utility function $U = W^{1/2}$, where W is his wealth in millions of dollars and U is the utility he obtains from that wealth. In the final stage of a game show, the host offers Jamal a choice between (A) $4 million for sure and (B) a gamble that pays $1 million with probability 0.6 and $9 million with probability 0.4.
   a. Graph Jamal's utility function. Is he risk averse? Explain.
   b. Does A or B offer Jamal the higher expected prize? Explain your reasoning with appropriate calculations. (*Hint*: The expected value of a random variable is the weighted average of the possible outcomes, where the probabilities are the weights.)
   c. Does A or B offer Jamal the higher expected utility? Again, show your calculations.
   d. Should Jamal pick A or B? Why?

QuickQuiz Answers

1. **b**   2. **d**   3. **b**   4. **c**   5. **c**   6. **a**   7. **a**   8. **b**   9. **d**

Losing a job can be the most distressing economic event in a person's life. Most people rely on their labor earnings to maintain their standard of living, and many people also get a sense of personal accomplishment from working. A job loss means a lower living standard in the present, anxiety about the future, and reduced self-esteem. It is not surprising, therefore, that politicians campaigning for office often speak about how their proposed policies will help create jobs.

In previous chapters, we have seen some of the forces that determine the level and growth of a country's standard of living. A country that saves and invests a high fraction of its income, for instance, enjoys more rapid growth in its capital stock and GDP than a similar country that saves and invests less. An even more obvious determinant of a country's standard of living is the amount of unemployment it typically experiences. People who would like to work but cannot find a job are not contributing to the economy's production of goods and services. Although some degree of unemployment is inevitable in a complex economy with thousands of firms and millions of workers, the amount of unemployment varies substantially over time and across

CHAPTER

10

Unemployment

countries. When a country keeps its workers as fully employed as possible, it achieves a higher level of GDP than it would if it left many of its workers idle.

This chapter begins our study of unemployment. The problem of unemployment can be divided into two categories: the long-run problem and the short-run problem. The economy's *natural rate of unemployment* refers to the amount of unemployment that the economy normally experiences. *Cyclical unemployment* refers to the year-to-year fluctuations in unemployment around its natural rate and is closely associated with the short-run fluctuations in economic activity. We examine the determinants of cyclical unemployment when we study short-run economic fluctuations later in this book. In this chapter, we focus on the determinants of an economy's natural rate of unemployment. As we will see, the designation *natural* does not mean that this rate of unemployment is desirable. Nor does it mean that it is constant over time or impervious to economic policy. It just means that this unemployment does not go away on its own even in the long run.

We begin the chapter by looking at some of the relevant facts that describe unemployment. In particular, we examine three questions: How does the government measure the economy's rate of unemployment? What problems arise in interpreting the unemployment data? How long are the unemployed typically without work?

We then turn to the reasons economies always experience some unemployment and the ways in which policymakers can help the unemployed. We discuss four explanations for the economy's natural rate of unemployment: job search, minimum-wage laws, unions, and efficiency wages. As we will see, long-run unemployment does not arise from a single problem that has a single solution. Instead, it reflects a variety of related problems. As a result, there is no easy way for policymakers to reduce the economy's natural rate of unemployment and, at the same time, to alleviate the hardships experienced by the unemployed.

10-1 Identifying Unemployment

Let's start by examining more precisely what the term *unemployment* means.

10-1a How Is Unemployment Measured?

Measuring unemployment is the job of the Bureau of Labor Statistics (BLS), which is part of the Department of Labor. Every month, the BLS produces data on unemployment and on other aspects of the labor market, including types of employment, length of the average workweek, and the duration of unemployment. These data come from a regular survey of about 60,000 households, called the Current Population Survey.

Based on the answers to survey questions, the BLS places each adult (age 16 and older) in each surveyed household into one of three categories:

- *Employed:* This category includes those who worked as paid employees, worked in their own business, or worked as unpaid workers in a family member's business. Both full-time and part-time workers are counted. This category also includes those who were not working but who had jobs from which they were temporarily absent because of, for example, vacation, illness, or bad weather.
- *Unemployed:* This category includes those who were not employed, were available for work, and had tried to find employment during the previous four weeks. It also includes those waiting to be recalled to a job from which they had been laid off.

- *Not in the labor force:* This category includes those who fit neither of the first two categories, such as full-time students, homemakers, and retirees.

Figure 1 shows the breakdown into these categories for January 2019.

Once the BLS has placed all the individuals covered by the survey in a category, it computes various statistics to summarize the state of the labor market. The BLS defines the **labor force** as the sum of the employed and the unemployed:

$$\text{Labor force} = \text{Number of employed} + \text{Number of unemployed}.$$

The BLS defines the **unemployment rate** as the percentage of the labor force that is unemployed:

$$\text{Unemployment rate} = \frac{\text{Number of unemployed}}{\text{Labor force}} \times 100.$$

The BLS computes unemployment rates for the entire adult population and for specific demographic groups defined by race, gender, and so on.

The BLS uses the same survey to produce data on labor-force participation. The **labor-force participation rate** measures the percentage of the total adult population of the United States that is in the labor force:

$$\text{Labor-force participation rate} = \frac{\text{Labor force}}{\text{Adult population}} \times 100.$$

This statistic tells us the fraction of the population that has chosen to participate in the labor market. The labor-force participation rate, like the unemployment rate, is computed for both the entire adult population and more specific groups.

labor force
the total number of workers, including both the employed and the unemployed

unemployment rate
the percentage of the labor force that is unemployed

labor-force participation rate
the percentage of the adult population that is in the labor force

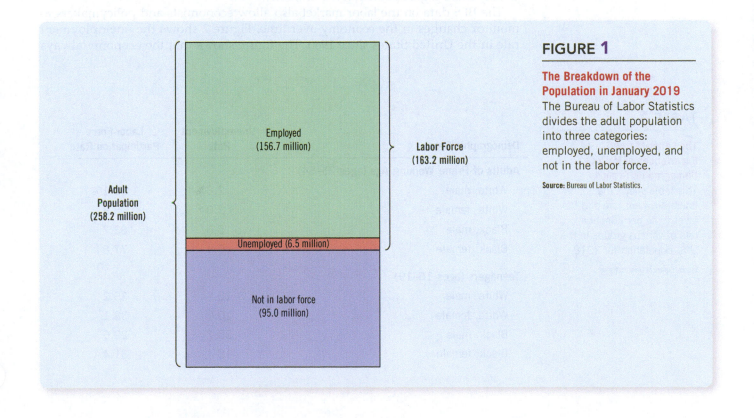

FIGURE 1

The Breakdown of the Population in January 2019
The Bureau of Labor Statistics divides the adult population into three categories: employed, unemployed, and not in the labor force.

Source: Bureau of Labor Statistics.

To see how these data are computed, consider the figures for January 2019. At that time, 156.7 million people were employed, and 6.5 million people were unemployed. The labor force was

$$\text{Labor force} = 156.7 + 6.5 = 163.2 \text{ million.}$$

The unemployment rate was

$$\text{Unemployment rate} = (6.5/163.2) \times 100 = 4.0 \text{ percent.}$$

Because the adult population was 258.2 million, the labor-force participation rate was

$$\text{Labor-force participation rate} = (163.2/258.2) \times 100 = 63.2 \text{ percent.}$$

Hence, in January 2019, almost two-thirds of the U.S. adult population were participating in the labor market, and 4.0 percent of those labor-market participants were without work.

Table 1 shows the statistics on unemployment and labor-force participation for various groups within the U.S. population. Three comparisons are particularly striking. First, women of prime working age (25 to 54 years old) have lower rates of labor-force participation than men, but once in the labor force, men and women have similar rates of unemployment. Second, prime-age blacks have similar rates of labor-force participation as prime-age whites, but they have much higher rates of unemployment. Third, teenagers have much lower rates of labor-force participation and much higher rates of unemployment than older workers. More generally, these data show that labor-market experiences vary widely among groups within the economy.

The BLS data on the labor market also allow economists and policymakers to monitor changes in the economy over time. Figure 2 shows the unemployment rate in the United States since 1960. The figure shows that the economy always

TABLE 1

The Labor-Market Experiences of Various Demographic Groups
This table shows the unemployment rate and the labor-force participation rate of various groups in the U.S. population for 2018.

Source: Bureau of Labor Statistics.

Demographic Group	Unemployment Rate	Labor-Force Participation Rate
Adults of Prime Working Age (ages 25–54)		
White, male	2.8%	90.1%
White, female	3.0	75.3
Black, male	5.6	82.7
Black, female	5.4	77.8
Teenagers (ages 16–19)		
White, male	12.6	36.2
White, female	10.0	38.1
Black, male	25.7	29.6
Black, female	18.4	31.4

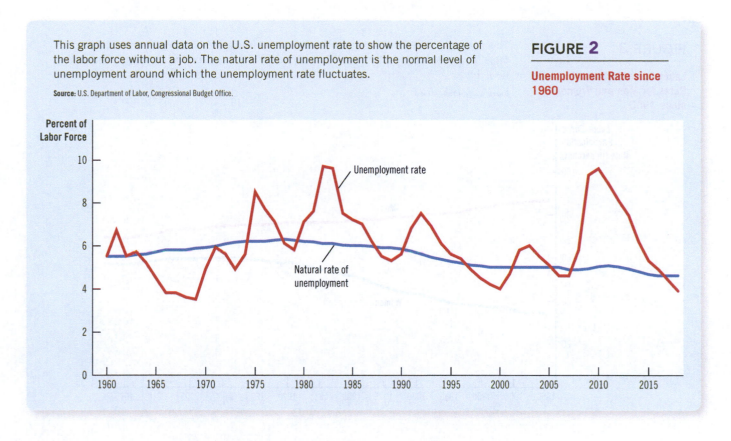

This graph uses annual data on the U.S. unemployment rate to show the percentage of the labor force without a job. The natural rate of unemployment is the normal level of unemployment around which the unemployment rate fluctuates.

Source: U.S. Department of Labor, Congressional Budget Office.

FIGURE 2

Unemployment Rate since 1960

has some unemployment and that the amount changes from year to year. As noted earlier, the normal rate of unemployment around which the unemployment rate fluctuates is called the **natural rate of unemployment**, and the deviation of unemployment from its natural rate is called **cyclical unemployment**. The natural rate of unemployment shown in the figure is a series estimated by economists at the Congressional Budget Office. For 2018, they estimated a natural rate of 4.6 percent, slightly above the actual unemployment rate of 3.9 percent. In the rest of this chapter, we ignore short-run fluctuations in unemployment around its natural rate and examine why there is always some unemployment.

natural rate of unemployment
the normal rate of unemployment around which the unemployment rate fluctuates

cyclical unemployment
the deviation of unemployment from its natural rate

 CASE STUDY

LABOR-FORCE PARTICIPATION OF MEN AND WOMEN IN THE U.S. ECONOMY

Women's role in American society has changed dramatically over the past century. Social commentators have pointed to many causes for this change. In part, it is attributable to new technologies, such as the washing machine, clothes dryer, refrigerator, freezer, and dishwasher, which have reduced the amount of time required to complete routine household tasks. In part, it is attributable to improved birth control, which has reduced the number of children born to the typical family. And in part, it is attributable to changing political and social attitudes, which in turn may have been facilitated by the advances in technology and birth control. Together these developments have had a profound impact on society in general and on the economy in particular.

Nowhere is that impact more obvious than in data on labor-force participation. Figure 3 shows the labor-force participation rates of men and women in the United States since 1950. Just after World War II, men and women had very different roles

FIGURE 3

Labor-Force Participation Rates for Men and Women since 1950

This figure shows the percentage of adult men and women who are members of the labor force. It shows that, over the past 60 years, women have entered the labor force and men have left it.

Source: U.S. Department of Labor.

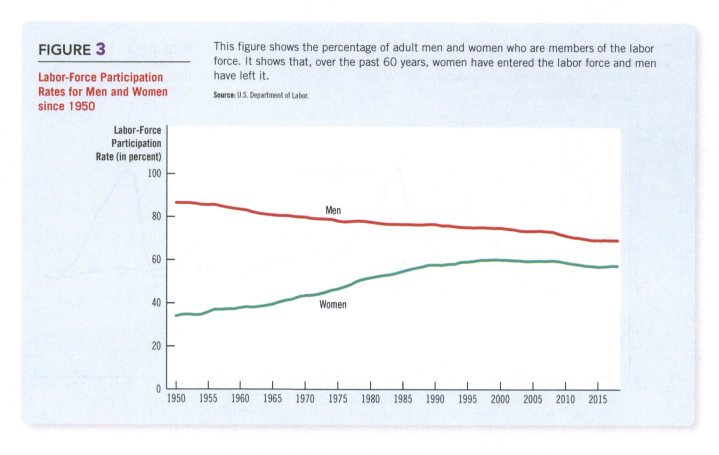

in society. Only 33 percent of women were working or looking for work, in contrast to 87 percent of men. Since then, this difference in participation rates has gradually diminished, as growing numbers of women have entered the labor force and some men have left it. Data for 2018 show that 57 percent of women were in the labor force, in contrast to 69 percent of men. As measured by labor-force participation, men and women are now playing a more equal role in the economy.

The increase in women's labor-force participation is easy to understand, but the fall in men's may seem puzzling. There are several reasons for this decline. First, young men now stay in school longer than their fathers and grandfathers did. Second, older men now retire earlier and live longer. Third, with more women employed, more fathers now stay at home to raise their children. Full-time students, retirees, and stay-at-home dads are all counted as being out of the labor force. ●

10-1b Does the Unemployment Rate Measure What We Want It to Measure?

Measuring the amount of unemployment in the economy might seem a straightforward task, but it is not. While it is easy to distinguish between a person with a full-time job and a person who is not working at all, it is much harder to distinguish between a person who is unemployed and a person who is not in the labor force.

Movements into and out of the labor force are, in fact, common. More than one-third of the unemployed are recent entrants into the labor force. These entrants include young workers looking for their first jobs. They also include, in greater numbers, older workers who had previously left the labor force but have now returned to look for work. Moreover, not all unemployment ends with the job seeker finding a job. Almost half of all spells of unemployment end when the unemployed person leaves the labor force.

Because people move into and out of the labor force so often, statistics on unemployment are difficult to interpret. On the one hand, some of those who report being unemployed may not, in fact, be trying hard to find a job. They may be calling themselves unemployed because they want to qualify for a government program that gives financial assistance to the unemployed or because they are working but paid "under the table" to avoid taxes on their earnings. It may be more accurate to view these individuals as out of the labor force or, in some cases, employed. On the other hand, some of those who report being out of the labor force may want to work. These individuals may have tried to find a job and may have given up after an unsuccessful search. Such individuals, called **discouraged workers**, do not show up in unemployment statistics, even though they are truly prospective workers who cannot find jobs.

Because of these and other problems, the BLS calculates several other measures of labor underutilization, in addition to the official unemployment rate. These alternative measures are presented in Table 2. In the end, it is best to view the official unemployment rate as a useful but imperfect measure of joblessness.

discouraged workers
individuals who would like to work but have given up looking for a job

Measure and Description		Rate
U-1	Persons unemployed 15 weeks or longer, as a percent of the civilian labor force (includes only very long-term unemployed)	1.3%
U-2	Job losers and persons who have completed temporary jobs, as a percent of the civilian labor force (excludes job leavers)	1.9
U-3	Total unemployed, as a percent of the civilian labor force (official unemployment rate)	4.0
U-4	Total unemployed, plus discouraged workers, as a percent of the civilian labor force plus discouraged workers	4.3
U-5	Total unemployed plus all marginally attached workers, as a percent of the civilian labor force plus all marginally attached workers	4.9
U-6	Total unemployed, plus all marginally attached workers, plus total employed part-time for economic reasons, as a percent of the civilian labor force plus all marginally attached workers	8.1

Note: The Bureau of Labor Statistics defines terms as follows.
• *Marginally attached workers* are persons who currently are neither working nor looking for work but indicate that they want and are available for a job and have looked for work sometime in the recent past.
• *Discouraged workers* are marginally attached workers who have given a job-market-related reason for not currently looking for a job.
• *Persons employed part-time for economic reasons* are those who want and are available for full-time work but have had to settle for a part-time schedule.

TABLE 2

Measures of Labor Underutilization
The table shows various measures of joblessness for the U.S. economy. The data are for January 2019.

Source: U.S. Department of Labor.

10-1c How Long Are the Unemployed without Work?

In judging how serious the problem of unemployment is, one question to consider is whether unemployment is typically a short-term or long-term condition. If unemployment is short-term, one might conclude that it is not a big problem. Workers may require a few weeks between jobs to find the openings that best suit their tastes and skills. Yet if unemployment is long-term, one might conclude that it is a serious problem. Workers unemployed for many months are more likely to suffer economic and psychological hardship.

Because the duration of unemployment can affect our view about how big a problem unemployment is, economists have devoted much energy to studying data on the duration of unemployment spells. In this work, they have uncovered a result that is important, subtle, and seemingly contradictory: *Most spells of unemployment are short, but most unemployment observed at any given time is long-term.*

To see how this statement can be true, consider an example. Suppose that you visited the government's unemployment office every week for a year to survey the unemployed. Each week you find that there are four unemployed workers. Three of these workers are the same individuals for the whole year, while the fourth person changes every week. Based on this experience, would you say that unemployment is typically short-term or long-term?

Some simple calculations help answer this question. In this example, you meet a total of 55 unemployed people over the course of a year, 52 who are unemployed for one week and 3 who are unemployed for the full year. This means that 52/55, or 95 percent, of unemployment spells end in one week. Yet whenever you walk into the unemployment office, three of the four people you meet will be unemployed for the entire year. So, even though 95 percent of unemployment spells end in one week, 75 percent of the unemployment observed at any moment is attributable to those individuals who are unemployed for a full year. In this example, as in the world, most spells of unemployment are short, but most unemployment observed at any given time is long-term.

This subtle conclusion implies that economists and policymakers must be careful when interpreting data on unemployment and when designing policies to help the unemployed. Most people who become unemployed will soon find jobs. Yet most of the economy's unemployment problem is attributable to the relatively few workers who are jobless for long periods of time.

10-1d Why Are There Always Some People Unemployed?

We have discussed how the government measures unemployment, the problems that arise in interpreting unemployment statistics, and the findings of labor economists on the duration of unemployment. You should now have a good idea about what unemployment is.

This discussion, however, has not explained why economies experience unemployment. In most markets in the economy, prices adjust to bring quantity supplied and quantity demanded into balance. In an ideal labor market, wages would adjust to balance the quantity of labor supplied and the quantity of labor demanded. This adjustment of wages would ensure that all workers are always fully employed.

Of course, reality does not resemble this ideal. There are always some workers without jobs, even when the overall economy is doing well. In other words, the unemployment rate never falls to zero; instead, it fluctuates around the natural rate of unemployment. To understand this natural rate, the remaining sections of this chapter examine the reasons actual labor markets depart from the ideal of full employment.

To preview our conclusions, we will find that there are four ways to explain unemployment in the long run. The first explanation is that it takes time for workers to search for the jobs that are best suited for them. The unemployment that results from the process of matching workers and jobs is sometimes called **frictional unemployment**, and it is often thought to explain relatively short spells of unemployment.

The next three explanations for unemployment suggest that the number of jobs available in some labor markets may be insufficient to give a job to everyone who wants one. This occurs when the quantity of labor supplied exceeds the quantity demanded. Unemployment of this sort is sometimes called **structural unemployment**, and it is often thought to explain longer spells of unemployment. As we will see, this kind of unemployment results when wages are set above the level that brings supply and demand into equilibrium. We will examine three possible reasons for an above-equilibrium wage: minimum-wage laws, unions, and efficiency wages.

frictional unemployment
unemployment that results because it takes time for workers to search for the jobs that best suit their tastes and skills

structural unemployment
unemployment that results because the number of jobs available in some labor markets is insufficient to provide a job for everyone who wants one

FYI · The Jobs Number

When the Bureau of Labor Statistics announces the unemployment rate at the beginning of every month, it also announces the number of jobs that the economy gained or lost in the previous month. As an indicator of short-run economic trends, the jobs number gets as much attention as the unemployment rate.

Where does the jobs number come from? You might guess that it comes from the same survey of 60,000 households that yields the unemployment rate. And indeed the household survey does produce data on total employment. The jobs number that gets the most attention, however, comes from a separate survey of 160,000 business establishments, which have over 40 million workers on their payrolls. The results from the establishment survey are announced at the same time as the results from the household survey.

Both surveys yield information about total employment, but the results are not always the same. One reason is that the establishment survey has a larger sample, which makes it more reliable. Another reason is that the surveys are not measuring exactly the same thing. For example, a person who has two part-time jobs at different companies would be counted as one employed person in the household survey but as two jobs in the establishment survey. As another example, a person running his own small business would be counted as employed in the household survey but would not show up at all in the establishment survey, because the establishment survey counts only employees on business payrolls.

The establishment survey is closely watched for its data on jobs, but it says nothing about unemployment. To measure the number of unemployed, we need to know how many people without jobs are trying to find them. The household survey is the only source of that information. ■

Quick**Quiz**

1. The population of Ectenia is 100 people: 40 work full-time, 20 work half-time but would prefer to work full-time, 10 are looking for a job, 10 would like to work but are so discouraged that they have given up looking, 10 are not interested in working because they are full-time students, and 10 are retired. What is the number of unemployed?
    a. 10
    b. 20
    c. 30
    d. 40

2. Using the numbers in the preceding question, what is the size of Ectenia's labor force?
    a. 50
    b. 60
    c. 70
    d. 80

Answers at end of chapter.

10-2 Job Search

job search

the process by which workers find appropriate jobs given their tastes and skills

One reason economies always experience some unemployment is job search. **Job search** is the process of matching workers with appropriate jobs. If all workers and all jobs were the same, so that all workers were equally well suited for all jobs, job search would not be a problem. Laid-off workers would quickly find new jobs that were well suited for them. But in fact, workers differ in their tastes and skills, jobs differ in their attributes, and information about job candidates and job vacancies is disseminated slowly among the many firms and households in the economy.

10-2a Why Some Frictional Unemployment Is Inevitable

Frictional unemployment is often the result of changes in the demand for labor among different firms. When consumers decide that they prefer Ford cars to General Motors cars, Ford increases employment and General Motors lays off workers. The former General Motors workers must now search for new jobs, and Ford must decide which new workers to hire for the various jobs that have opened up. The result of this transition is a period of unemployment.

Similarly, because different regions of the country produce different goods, employment can rise in one region while it falls in another. Consider, for instance, what happens when the world price of oil falls. Oil-producing firms in Texas and North Dakota respond to the lower price by cutting back on production and employment. At the same time, cheaper gasoline stimulates car sales, so auto-producing firms in Michigan and Ohio raise production and employment. The opposite happens when the world price of oil rises. Changes in the composition of demand among industries or regions are called *sectoral shifts*. Because it takes time for workers to search for jobs in the new sectors, sectoral shifts temporarily cause unemployment.

Changing patterns of international trade are also a source of frictional unemployment. In Chapter 3, we learned that nations export goods for which they have a comparative advantage and import goods for which other nations have a comparative advantage. Comparative advantage, however, need not be stable over time. As the world economy evolves, nations may find themselves importing and exporting different goods than they have in the past. Workers will therefore need to move among industries. As they make this transition, they may find themselves unemployed for a period of time.

Frictional unemployment is inevitable simply because the economy is always changing. For example, in the U.S. economy from 2006 to 2016, employment fell by 980,000 in construction and 1.8 million in manufacturing. During the same period, employment rose by 706,000 in computer systems design, 2.1 million in food services, and 3.8 million in healthcare. This churning of the labor force is normal in a well-functioning and dynamic economy. Because workers tend to move toward those industries in which they are most valuable, the long-run result of the process is higher productivity and higher living standards. But along the way, workers in declining industries find themselves out of work and searching for new jobs. The result is some amount of frictional unemployment.

10-2b Public Policy and Job Search

Even if some frictional unemployment is inevitable, the precise amount is not. The faster information spreads about job openings and worker availability, the more rapidly the economy can match workers and firms. The Internet, for instance, may help facilitate job search and reduce frictional unemployment. In addition, public policy may play a role. If policy can reduce the time it takes unemployed workers to find new jobs, it can reduce the economy's natural rate of unemployment.

Government programs try to facilitate job search in various ways. One way is through government-run employment agencies, which give out information about job vacancies. Another way is through public training programs, which aim to ease workers' transition from declining to growing industries and to help disadvantaged groups escape poverty. Advocates of these programs believe that they make the economy operate more efficiently by keeping the labor force more fully employed and that they reduce the inequities inherent in a constantly changing market economy.

Critics of these programs question whether the government should get involved with the process of job search. They argue that it is better to let the private market match workers and jobs and that the government is no better—and most likely worse—at disseminating the right information to the right workers and deciding what kinds of worker training would be most valuable. They claim that these decisions are best made privately by workers and employers. In fact, most job search in our economy takes place without government intervention. Newspaper ads, online job sites, college career offices, headhunters, and word of mouth all help spread information about job openings and job candidates. Similarly, much worker education is done privately, through either schools or on-the-job training.

10-2c Unemployment Insurance

One government program that increases the amount of frictional unemployment, without intending to do so, is **unemployment insurance**. This program is designed to offer workers partial protection against job loss. The unemployed who quit their jobs, were fired for cause, or just entered the labor force are not eligible. Benefits are paid only to the unemployed who were laid off because their previous employers no longer needed their skills. The terms of the program vary over time and across states, but a typical worker covered by unemployment insurance in the United States receives 50 percent of his former wages for 26 weeks.

unemployment insurance
a government program that partially protects the incomes of workers who become unemployed

While unemployment insurance reduces the hardship of unemployment, it also increases the amount of unemployment. The explanation is based on one of the *Ten Principles of Economics* in Chapter 1: People respond to incentives. Because unemployment benefits stop when a worker takes a new job, the unemployed devote less effort to job search and are more likely to turn down unattractive job offers. In addition, because unemployment insurance makes unemployment less onerous, workers are less likely to seek guarantees of job security when they negotiate with employers over the terms of their employment.

Many studies by labor economists have analyzed the incentive effects of unemployment insurance. One study examined an experiment run by the state of Illinois in 1985. When unemployed workers applied to collect unemployment insurance benefits, the state randomly selected some of them and offered each a $500 bonus if they found new jobs within 11 weeks. This group was then compared to a control group not offered the incentive. The average spell of unemployment for the group offered the bonus was 7 percent shorter than the average spell for the control group. This experiment shows that the design of the unemployment insurance system influences the effort that the unemployed devote to job search.

Several other studies examined search effort by following a group of workers over time. Unemployment insurance benefits, rather than lasting forever, usually run out after 6 months or 1 year. These studies found that when the unemployed become ineligible for benefits, the probability of their finding a new job rises markedly. Thus, receiving unemployment insurance benefits does reduce the search effort of the unemployed.

Even though unemployment insurance reduces search effort and raises unemployment, we should not necessarily conclude that the policy is bad. The program does achieve its primary goal of reducing the income uncertainty that workers face. In addition, when workers turn down unattractive job offers, they have the opportunity to look for jobs that better suit their tastes and skills. Some economists argue that unemployment insurance improves the ability of the economy to match each worker with the most appropriate job.

The study of unemployment insurance shows that the unemployment rate is an imperfect measure of a nation's overall level of economic well-being. Most economists agree that eliminating unemployment insurance would reduce frictional unemployment. Yet even so, such a change in policy could well diminish economic well-being.

Quick**Quiz**

3. The main policy goal of unemployment insurance is to reduce the
    a. search effort of the unemployed.
    b. income uncertainty that workers face.
    c. role of unions in wage setting.
    d. amount of frictional unemployment.

4. One unintended consequence of unemployment insurance is that it reduces the
    a. search effort of the unemployed.
    b. income uncertainty that workers face.
    c. role of unions in wage setting.
    d. amount of frictional unemployment.

Answers at end of chapter.

10-3 Minimum-Wage Laws

Having seen how frictional unemployment results from the process of matching workers and jobs, let's now examine how structural unemployment results when the number of jobs is insufficient for the number of workers.

To understand structural unemployment, we begin by reviewing how minimum-wage laws can cause unemployment. Minimum wages are not the predominant reason for unemployment in our economy, but they have an important effect on certain groups with particularly high unemployment rates. Moreover, the analysis of minimum wages is a natural place to start because, as we will see, it can be used to understand some of the other reasons for structural unemployment.

Figure 4 reviews the basic economics of a minimum wage. When a minimum-wage law forces the wage to remain above the level that balances supply and demand, it raises the quantity of labor supplied and reduces the quantity of labor demanded compared to the equilibrium level. There is a surplus of labor. Because there are more workers willing to work than there are jobs, some workers are unemployed.

While minimum-wage laws are one reason unemployment exists in the U.S. economy, they do not affect everyone. The vast majority of workers have wages well above the legal minimum, so the law does not prevent most wages

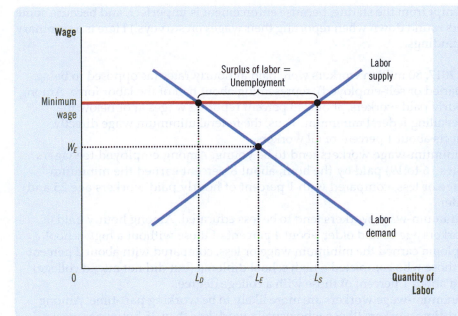

FIGURE 4

Unemployment from a Wage above the Equilibrium Level

In this labor market, supply and demand are balanced at the wage W_E. At this equilibrium wage, the quantity of labor supplied and the quantity of labor demanded both equal L_E. By contrast, if the wage is forced to remain above the equilibrium level, perhaps because of a minimum-wage law, the quantity of labor supplied rises to L_S and the quantity of labor demanded falls to L_D. The resulting surplus of labor, $L_s - L_D$, represents unemployment.

from adjusting to balance supply and demand. Minimum-wage laws matter most for the least skilled and least experienced members of the labor force, such as teenagers. Their equilibrium wages tend to be low and, therefore, are more likely to fall below the legal minimum. It is only among these workers that minimum-wage laws explain the existence of unemployment.

Figure 4 is drawn to show the effects of a minimum-wage law, but it also illustrates a more general lesson: *If the wage is kept above the equilibrium level for any reason, the result is unemployment.* Minimum-wage laws are just one reason wages may be "too high." In the remaining two sections of this chapter, we consider two other reasons wages may be kept above the equilibrium level: unions and efficiency wages. The basic economics of unemployment in these cases is the same as that shown in Figure 4, but these explanations of unemployment can apply to many more of the economy's workers.

At this point, however, we should stop and notice that the structural unemployment that arises from an above-equilibrium wage is, in an important sense, different from the frictional unemployment that arises from the process of job search. The need for job search is not due to the failure of wages to balance labor supply and labor demand. When job search is the explanation for unemployment, workers are *searching* for the jobs that best suit their tastes and skills. By contrast, when the wage is above the equilibrium level, the quantity of labor supplied exceeds the quantity of labor demanded, and workers are unemployed because they are *waiting* for jobs to open up.

WHO EARNS THE MINIMUM WAGE?

In 2018, the Department of Labor released a study showing what kinds of workers reported earnings at or below the minimum wage in 2017, when the minimum wage was $7.25 per hour. (A reported wage below the minimum wage is possible because some workers are exempt from the statute, because enforcement is imperfect, and because some workers round down when reporting their wages on surveys.) Here is a summary of the findings:

- In 2017, 80 million workers were paid at hourly rates (as opposed to being salaried or self-employed), representing about half of the labor force. Among hourly paid workers, about 2.3 percent reported wages at or below the prevailing federal minimum. Thus, the federal minimum wage directly affects about 1 percent of all workers.
- Minimum-wage workers tend to be young. Among employed teenagers (ages 16 to 19) paid by the hour, about 8 percent earned the minimum wage or less, compared with 1 percent of hourly paid workers age 25 and older.
- Minimum-wage workers tend to be less educated. Among hourly paid workers age 16 and older, about 4 percent of those without a high school diploma earned the minimum wage or less, compared with about 2 percent of those who completed a high school diploma (but did not attend college) and about 1 percent of those with a college degree.
- Minimum-wage workers are more likely to be working part-time. Among part-time workers (those who usually work less than 35 hours per week), 6 percent were paid the minimum wage or less, compared with 1 percent of full-time workers.
- The industry with the highest proportion of workers with reported hourly wages at or below the minimum wage was leisure and hospitality (11 percent). About three-fifths of all workers paid at or below the minimum wage were employed in this industry, primarily in restaurants and other food services. For many of these workers, tips supplement their hourly wages.
- The percentage of hourly paid workers earning the prevailing federal minimum wage or less has changed substantially over time. It has declined from 13.4 percent in 1979, when data collection first began on a regular basis, to 2.3 percent in 2017. One reason for this change is that the federal minimum wage has not kept up with inflation. If it had, the minimum wage in 2017 would have been about $10 rather than $7.25 per hour. At a higher level, the minimum wage becomes a binding price floor for more workers. ●

Quick**Quiz**

5. In a competitive labor market, an increase in the minimum wage results in a(n) _____ in the quantity of labor supplied and a(n) _____ in the quantity of labor demanded.
   a. increase; increase
   b. increase; decrease
   c. decrease; increase
   d. decrease; decrease

6. Approximately what percent of U.S. workers are directly affected by the minimum wage?
   a. 1
   b. 6
   c. 12
   d. 25

Answers at end of chapter.

10-4 Unions and Collective Bargaining

A **union** is a worker association that bargains with employers over wages, benefits, and working conditions. In the 1940s and 1950s, when union membership in the United States was at its peak, about 33 percent of the U.S. labor force was unionized. Today less than 11 percent of U.S. workers belong to unions. In many European countries, however, unions continue to play a large role. In Belgium, Norway, and Sweden, more than 50 percent of workers belong to unions. In France, Italy, and Germany, a majority of workers have wages set by collective bargaining by law, even though only some of these workers are themselves union members. In these cases, wages are not determined by the equilibrium of supply and demand in competitive labor markets.

union
a worker association that bargains with employers over wages, benefits, and working conditions

10-4a The Economics of Unions

A union is a type of cartel. Like any cartel, a union is a group of sellers acting together in the hope of exerting their joint market power. Most workers in the U.S. economy discuss their wages, benefits, and working conditions with their employers as individuals. By contrast, workers in a union do so as a group. The process by which unions and firms agree on the terms of employment is called **collective bargaining**.

When a union bargains with a firm, it asks for higher wages, better benefits, and better working conditions than the firm would offer in the absence of a union. If the union and the firm do not reach agreement, the union can organize a withdrawal of labor from the firm, called a **strike**. Because a strike reduces production, sales, and profit, a firm facing a strike threat is likely to agree to pay higher wages than it otherwise would. Economists who study the effects of unions typically find that union workers earn about 10 to 20 percent more than similar workers who do not belong to unions.

collective bargaining
the process by which unions and firms agree on the terms of employment

strike
the organized withdrawal of labor from a firm by a union

When a union raises the wage above the equilibrium level, it raises the quantity of labor supplied and reduces the quantity of labor demanded, resulting in unemployment. Workers who remain employed at the higher wage are better off, but those who were previously employed and are now unemployed are worse off. Indeed, unions are often thought to cause conflict between different groups of workers—between the *insiders* who benefit from high union wages and the *outsiders* who do not get the union jobs.

The outsiders can respond to their status in one of two ways. Some of them remain unemployed and wait for the chance to become insiders and earn the high union wage. Others take jobs in firms that are not unionized. Thus, when unions raise wages in one part of the economy, the supply of labor increases in other parts of the economy. This increase in labor supply, in turn, reduces wages in industries that are not unionized. In other words, workers in unions reap the benefit of collective bargaining, while workers not in unions bear some of the cost.

The role of unions in the economy depends in part on the laws that govern union organization and collective bargaining. Normally, explicit agreements among members of a cartel are illegal. When firms selling similar products agree to set high prices, the agreement is considered a "conspiracy in restraint of trade," and the government prosecutes the firms in civil and criminal court for violating the antitrust laws. Unions, however, are exempt from these laws. The policymakers who wrote the antitrust and labor laws believed that workers needed greater market power as

"Gentlemen, nothing stands in the way of a final accord except that management wants profit maximization and the union wants more moola."

they bargained with employers. Indeed, various laws are designed to encourage the formation of unions. In particular, the National Labor Relations Act (enacted in 1935 and subsequently amended) prohibits employers from interfering in certain ways with workers trying to organize unions, and in unionized companies, it requires employers and unions to bargain in good faith when negotiating the terms of employment.

Legislation affecting the market power of unions is a perennial topic of political debate. For instance, state lawmakers sometimes debate *right-to-work laws*, which bar a union and employer from requiring workers to financially support the union. Absent such laws, a union can seek an agreement during collective bargaining that requires all employees to pay either union dues (for union members) or an agency fee (for nonmembers) as a condition of employment. As of 2018, about half of the U.S. states have right-to-work laws, and some in Congress have proposed enacting national right-to-work legislation. Lawmakers in Washington have also considered laws that would either make strikes more possible or prohibit them in some situations. For example, one proposal would prevent firms from hiring permanent replacements (as opposed to temporary replacements) for workers on strike. If such a law were enacted, striking workers would no longer face the threat of losing their jobs to permanent replacements, making strikes more viable and thereby increasing unions' market power. Another proposal would bar strikes in the airline and railroad industries by requiring unions and employers at the end of collective bargaining to resolve their remaining disagreements through arbitration. How these policy debates are resolved will help determine the future of the union movement.

10-4b Are Unions Good or Bad for the Economy?

Economists disagree about whether unions are good or bad for the economy as a whole. Let's consider both sides of the debate.

Critics argue that unions are merely a type of cartel. When unions raise wages above the level that would prevail in competitive markets, they reduce the quantity of labor demanded, cause some workers to be unemployed, and reduce the wages in the rest of the economy. The resulting allocation of labor, critics argue, is both inefficient and inequitable. It is inefficient because high union wages reduce employment in unionized firms below the efficient, competitive level. It is inequitable because some workers benefit at the expense of other workers.

Advocates contend that unions are a necessary antidote to the market power of the firms that hire workers. The extreme case of this market power is the "company town," where a single firm does most of the hiring in a geographical region. In a company town, if workers do not accept the wages and working conditions that the firm offers, they have little choice but to move or stop working. In the absence of a union, therefore, the firm could use its market power to pay lower wages and offer worse working conditions than it would if it had to compete with other firms for the same workers. In this case, a union may be necessary to check the firm's market power and protect the workers from being at the mercy of the firm's owners.

Advocates of unions also claim that unions are important for helping firms respond efficiently to workers' concerns. Whenever a worker takes a job, the worker and the firm must agree on many attributes of the job in addition to the wage: hours of work, overtime, vacations, sick leave, health benefits, promotion schedules, job security, and so on. By representing workers' views on these issues, unions help firms provide the right mix of job attributes. Even if unions have the adverse effect of pushing wages above the equilibrium level and causing unemployment, they have the benefit of helping firms keep a happy and productive workforce.

In the end, there is no consensus among economists about whether unions are good or bad for the economy. Like many institutions, their influence is probably beneficial in some circumstances and adverse in others.

10-5 The Theory of Efficiency Wages

In addition to job search, minimum-wage laws, and unions, the theory of **efficiency wages** suggests a fourth reason that economies always experience some unemployment. According to this theory, firms operate more efficiently if wages are above the equilibrium level. Therefore, it may be profitable for firms to keep wages high even in the presence of a surplus of labor.

efficiency wages
above-equilibrium wages paid by firms to increase worker productivity

In some ways, the unemployment that arises from efficiency wages is similar to the unemployment that arises from minimum-wage laws and unions. In all three cases, unemployment is the result of wages above the level that balances the quantity of labor supplied and the quantity of labor demanded. Yet there is also an important difference. Minimum-wage laws and unions prevent firms from lowering wages in the presence of a surplus of workers. Efficiency-wage theory states that such a constraint on firms is unnecessary because, in some cases, firms may be better off keeping wages above the equilibrium level.

Why should firms want to keep wages high? Normally, we expect profit-maximizing firms to want to keep costs—and therefore wages—as low as possible. The novel insight of efficiency-wage theory is that paying higher wages might increase profitability by increasing the efficiency of a firm's workers.

There are several types of efficiency-wage theory. Each type suggests a different explanation for why firms may want to pay high wages.

10-5a Worker Health

The first and simplest type of efficiency-wage theory emphasizes the link between wages and worker health. Better-paid workers eat a more nutritious diet, and workers who eat a better diet are healthier and more productive. A firm may find it more profitable to pay high wages and have healthy, productive workers than to pay lower wages and have less healthy, less productive workers.

This type of efficiency-wage theory can be relevant for explaining unemployment in less developed countries where inadequate nutrition can be a problem. In these countries, firms may fear that cutting wages would adversely influence their workers' health and productivity. In other words, nutrition concerns may explain why firms maintain above-equilibrium wages despite a surplus of labor. Worker health concerns are far less relevant for firms in rich countries such as the United States, where the equilibrium wages for most workers are well above the level needed for an adequate diet.

10-5b Worker Turnover

A second type of efficiency-wage theory emphasizes the link between wages and worker turnover. Workers quit jobs for many reasons: to take jobs at other firms, to move to other parts of the country, to leave the labor force, and so on. The frequency with which they quit depends on the entire set of incentives they face, including the benefits of leaving and the benefits of staying. The more a firm pays its workers, the less often its workers will choose to leave. Thus, a firm can reduce turnover among its workers by paying them high wages.

Why do firms care about turnover? The reason is that it is costly for firms to hire and train new workers. Moreover, even after they are trained, newly hired workers are not as productive as experienced ones. Firms with higher turnover, therefore, will tend to have higher production costs. Firms may find it profitable to pay wages above the equilibrium level to reduce worker turnover.

10-5c Worker Quality

A third type of efficiency-wage theory emphasizes the link between wages and worker quality. All firms want workers who are talented, and they strive to pick the best applicants to fill job openings. But because firms cannot perfectly gauge the quality of applicants, hiring has a degree of randomness to it. When a firm pays high wages, it attracts a better pool of workers to apply for its jobs and thereby increases the quality of its workforce. If the firm responded to a surplus of labor by reducing the wage, the most competent applicants—who are more likely to have better alternative opportunities than less competent applicants—may choose not to apply. If this influence of the wage on worker quality is strong enough, it may be profitable for the firm to pay a wage above the level that balances supply and demand.

10-5d Worker Effort

A fourth and final type of efficiency-wage theory emphasizes the link between wages and worker effort. In many jobs, workers have some discretion over how hard to work. As a result, firms monitor the efforts of their workers, and workers caught shirking their responsibilities are fired. But because monitoring is costly and imperfect, firms cannot quickly catch all shirkers. A firm in such a circumstance is always looking for ways to deter shirking.

One solution is paying wages above the equilibrium level. High wages make workers more eager to keep their jobs and thus motivate them to put forward their best effort. If the wage were at the level that balanced supply and demand, workers would have less reason to work hard because if they were fired, they could quickly find new jobs at the same wage. Therefore, firms may raise wages above the equilibrium level to provide an incentive for workers not to shirk their responsibilities.

CASE STUDY

HENRY FORD AND THE VERY GENEROUS $5-A-DAY WAGE

Henry Ford was an industrial visionary. As founder of the Ford Motor Company, he was responsible for introducing modern techniques of production. Rather than building cars with small teams of skilled craftsmen, Ford built cars on assembly lines in which unskilled workers were taught to perform the same simple tasks over and over again. The output of this assembly process was the Model T Ford, one of the most famous early automobiles.

In 1914, Ford introduced another innovation: the $5 workday. This might not seem like much today, but back then $5 was about twice the going wage. It was also far above the wage that balanced supply and demand. When the new $5-a-day wage was announced, long lines of job seekers formed outside the Ford factories. The number of workers willing to work at this wage far exceeded the number of workers Ford needed.

Ford's high-wage policy had many of the effects predicted by efficiency-wage theory. Turnover fell, absenteeism fell, and productivity rose. Workers were so much more efficient that Ford's production costs declined despite higher wages. Thus, paying a wage above the equilibrium level was profitable for the firm. An historian of the early Ford Motor Company wrote, "Ford and his associates freely declared on many occasions that the high-wage policy turned out to be good business. By this they meant that it had improved the discipline of the workers, given them a more loyal interest in the institution, and raised their personal efficiency." Henry Ford himself called the $5-a-day wage "one of the finest cost-cutting moves we ever made."

Why did it take a Henry Ford to introduce this efficiency wage? Why were other firms not already taking advantage of this seemingly profitable business strategy? According to some analysts, Ford's decision was closely linked to his use of the assembly line. Workers organized in an assembly line are highly interdependent. If one worker is absent or works slowly, other workers are less able to complete their own tasks. Thus, while assembly lines made production more efficient, they also raised the importance of low worker turnover, high worker effort, and high worker quality. As a result, paying efficiency wages may have been a better strategy for the Ford Motor Company than for other businesses at the time.

Paying above-equilibrium wages, however, is not unique to Ford. According to a 2018 article in *The California Sun*, the fast-food chain In-N-Out Burger pays its store managers on average more than $160,000 a year, about triple the industry average. Why? Denny Warnick, vice president of operations, said that the policy dates back to the company's founders, who wanted to make quality service a central focus. "Paying their associates well was just one way to help maintain that focus, and those beliefs remain firmly in place with us today," he said. Like Henry Ford, the owners of In-N-Out Burger seem to pay high wages to promote worker efficiency. ●

Quick**Quiz**

9. According to the theory of efficiency wages,
   a. firms may find it profitable to pay above-equilibrium wages.
   b. an excess supply of labor puts downward pressure on wages.
   c. sectoral shifts are the main source of frictional unemployment.
   d. right-to-work laws reduce the bargaining power of unions.

10. When a firm pays an efficiency wage, it may
    a. have trouble attracting enough workers.
    b. have to monitor its workers more closely.
    c. experience declines in worker quality.
    d. find that its workers quit less frequently.

Answers at end of chapter.

10-6 Conclusion

In this chapter, we discussed how unemployment is measured and why economies always experience some degree of unemployment. We have seen how job search, minimum-wage laws, unions, and efficiency wages can all help explain why some workers do not have jobs. Which of these four explanations for the natural rate of unemployment are the most relevant for the U.S. economy and other economies around the world? Unfortunately, there is no easy way to tell. Economists differ in which of these explanations of unemployment they emphasize.

The analysis in this chapter yields an important lesson: Although the economy will always have some unemployment, its natural rate does change over time. Many events and policies can alter the amount of unemployment the economy typically experiences. As the information revolution changes the process of job search, as Congress and state legislatures adjust the minimum wage, as workers form or quit unions, and as firms change their reliance on efficiency wages, the natural rate of unemployment evolves. Unemployment is not a simple problem with a simple solution. But how we choose to organize our society can profoundly influence how prevalent a problem it is.

CHAPTER IN A NUTSHELL

- The unemployment rate is the percentage of those who would like to work who do not have jobs. The Bureau of Labor Statistics calculates this statistic monthly based on a survey of thousands of households.
- The unemployment rate is an imperfect measure of joblessness. Some people who call themselves unemployed may actually not want to work, and some people who would like to work are not counted as unemployed because they have left the labor force after an unsuccessful search.
- In the U.S. economy, most people who become unemployed find work within a short period of time. Nonetheless, most unemployment observed at any given time is attributable to the few people who are unemployed for long periods of time.

- One reason for unemployment is the time it takes workers to search for jobs that best suit their tastes and skills. This frictional unemployment is increased by unemployment insurance, a government policy designed to protect the incomes of workers who lose their jobs.
- A second reason our economy always has some unemployment is minimum-wage laws. By raising the wage of unskilled and inexperienced workers above the equilibrium level, minimum-wage laws raise the quantity of labor supplied and reduce the quantity demanded. The resulting surplus of labor represents unemployment.
- A third reason for unemployment is the market power of unions. When unions push the wages in unionized industries above the equilibrium level, they create a surplus of labor.

- A fourth reason for unemployment is suggested by the theory of efficiency wages. According to this theory, firms find it profitable to pay wages above the equilibrium level. High wages can improve worker health, lower worker turnover, raise worker quality, and increase worker effort.

KEY CONCEPTS

labor force, *p. 189*
unemployment rate, *p. 189*
labor-force participation rate, *p. 189*
natural rate of unemployment, *p. 191*
cyclical unemployment, *p. 191*

discouraged workers, *p. 193*
frictional unemployment, *p. 195*
structural unemployment, *p. 195*
job search, *p. 196*
unemployment insurance, *p. 197*

union, *p. 201*
collective bargaining, *p. 201*
strike, *p. 201*
efficiency wages, *p. 203*

QUESTIONS FOR REVIEW

1. What are the three categories into which the Bureau of Labor Statistics divides everyone? How does the BLS compute the labor force, the unemployment rate, and the labor-force participation rate?

2. Is unemployment typically short-term or long-term? Explain.

3. Why is frictional unemployment inevitable? How might the government reduce the amount of frictional unemployment?

4. Are minimum-wage laws a better explanation for structural unemployment among teenagers or among college graduates? Why?

5. How do unions affect the natural rate of unemployment?

6. What claims do advocates of unions make to argue that unions are good for the economy?

7. Explain four ways in which a firm might increase its profits by raising the wages it pays.

PROBLEMS AND APPLICATIONS

1. In June 2009, at the trough of the Great Recession, the Bureau of Labor Statistics announced that of all adult Americans, 140,196,000 were employed, 14,729,000 were unemployed, and 80,729,000 were not in the labor force. Use this information to calculate:
   a. the adult population.
   b. the labor force.
   c. the labor-force participation rate.
   d. the unemployment rate.

2. Explain whether each of the following events increases, decreases, or has no effect on the unemployment rate and the labor-force participation rate.
   a. After a long search, Jon finds a job.
   b. Tyrion, a full-time college student, graduates and is immediately employed.
   c. After an unsuccessful job search, Arya gives up looking and retires.
   d. Daenerys quits her job to become a stay-at-home mom.
   e. Sansa has a birthday, becomes an adult, but has no interest in working.
   f. Jaime has a birthday, becomes an adult, and starts looking for a job.

   g. Cersei dies while enjoying retirement.
   h. Jorah dies working long hours at the office.

3. Go to the website of the Bureau of Labor Statistics (http://www.bls.gov). What is the national unemployment rate right now? Find the unemployment rate for the demographic group that best fits a description of you (for example, based on age, sex, and race). Is it higher or lower than the national average? Why do you think this is so?

4. Between January 2012 and January 2019, U.S. employment increased by 17.3 million workers, but the number of unemployed workers declined by only 6.3 million. How are these numbers consistent with each other? Why might one expect a reduction in the number of people counted as unemployed to be smaller than the increase in the number of people employed?

5. Economists use labor-market data to evaluate how well an economy is using its most valuable resource—its people. Two closely watched statistics are the unemployment rate and the employment–population ratio (calculated as the percentage of the

adult population that is employed). Explain what happens to each of these statistics in the following scenarios. In your opinion, which statistic is the more meaningful gauge of how well the economy is doing?

a. An auto company goes bankrupt and lays off its workers, who immediately start looking for new jobs.

b. After an unsuccessful search, some of the laid-off workers quit looking for new jobs.

c. Numerous students graduate from college but cannot find work.

d. Numerous students graduate from college and immediately begin new jobs.

e. A stock market boom induces newly enriched 60-year-old workers to take early retirement.

f. Advances in healthcare prolong the life of many retirees.

6. Are the following workers more likely to experience short-term unemployment or long-term unemployment? Explain.

a. a construction worker who is laid off because of bad weather

b. a manufacturing worker who loses his job at a plant in an isolated area

c. a stagecoach-industry worker who is laid off because of competition from railroads

d. a short-order cook who loses his job when a new restaurant opens across the street

e. an expert welder with little formal education who loses his job when the company installs automatic welding machinery

7. Using a diagram of the labor market, show the effect of an increase in the minimum wage on the wage paid to workers, the number of workers supplied, the number of workers demanded, and the amount of unemployment.

8. Consider an economy with two labor markets—one for manufacturing workers and one for service workers. Suppose initially that neither is unionized.

a. If manufacturing workers formed a union, what would you expect to happen to the wages and employment in manufacturing?

b. How would these changes in the manufacturing labor market affect the supply of labor in the market for service workers? What would happen to the equilibrium wage and employment in this labor market?

9. Structural unemployment is sometimes said to result from a mismatch between the job skills that employers want and the job skills that workers have. To explore this idea, consider an economy with two industries: auto manufacturing and aircraft manufacturing.

a. If workers in these two industries require similar amounts of training, and if workers at the beginning of their careers can choose which industry to train for, what would you expect to happen to the wages in these two industries? How long would this process take? Explain.

b. Suppose that one day the economy opens itself to international trade and, as a result, starts importing autos and exporting aircraft. What would happen to the demand for labor in these two industries?

c. Suppose that workers in one industry cannot be quickly retrained for the other. How would these shifts in demand affect equilibrium wages both in the short run and in the long run?

d. If for some reason wages fail to adjust to the new equilibrium levels, what would occur?

10. Suppose that Congress passes a law requiring employers to provide employees some benefit (such as healthcare) that raises the cost of an employee by $4 per hour.

a. What effect does this employer mandate have on the demand for labor? (In answering this and the following questions, be quantitative when you can.)

b. If employees place a value on this benefit exactly equal to its cost, what effect does this employer mandate have on the supply of labor?

c. If the wage can freely adjust to balance supply and demand, how does this law affect the wage and the level of employment? Are employers better or worse off? Are employees better or worse off?

d. Suppose that, before the mandate, the wage in this market was $3 above the minimum wage. In this case, how does the employer mandate affect the wage, the level of employment, and the level of unemployment?

e. Now suppose that workers do not value the mandated benefit at all. How does this alternative assumption change your answers to parts (b) and (c)?

QuickQuiz Answers

1. a   2. c   3. b   4. a   5. b   6. a   7. c   8. d   9. a   10. d

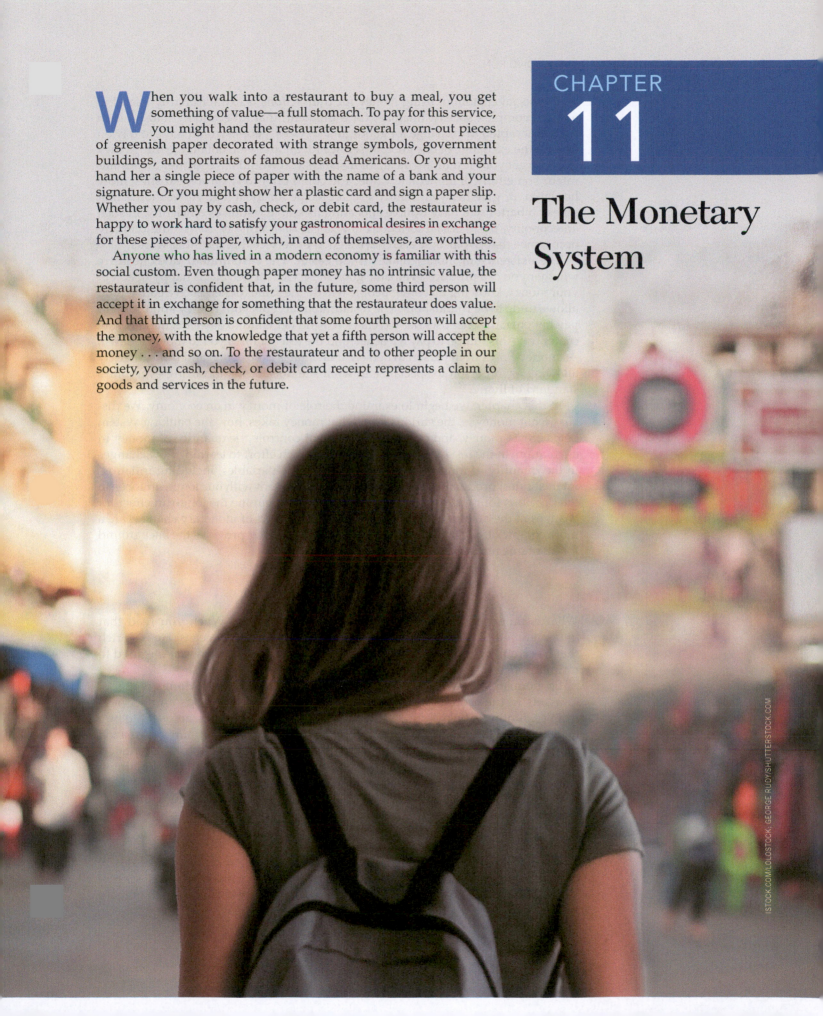

The Monetary System

When you walk into a restaurant to buy a meal, you get something of value—a full stomach. To pay for this service, you might hand the restaurateur several worn-out pieces of greenish paper decorated with strange symbols, government buildings, and portraits of famous dead Americans. Or you might hand her a single piece of paper with the name of a bank and your signature. Or you might show her a plastic card and sign a paper slip. Whether you pay by cash, check, or debit card, the restaurateur is happy to work hard to satisfy your gastronomical desires in exchange for these pieces of paper, which, in and of themselves, are worthless.

Anyone who has lived in a modern economy is familiar with this social custom. Even though paper money has no intrinsic value, the restaurateur is confident that, in the future, some third person will accept it in exchange for something that the restaurateur does value. And that third person is confident that some fourth person will accept the money, with the knowledge that yet a fifth person will accept the money . . . and so on. To the restaurateur and to other people in our society, your cash, check, or debit card receipt represents a claim to goods and services in the future.

The social custom of using money for transactions is extraordinarily useful in a large, complex society. Imagine, for a moment, that an economy had no item widely accepted in exchange for goods and services. People would have to rely on *barter*—the exchange of one good or service for another—to obtain the things they need. To get your restaurant meal, for instance, you would have to offer the restaurateur something of immediate value. You could offer to wash some dishes, mow her lawn, or give her your family's secret recipe for meat loaf. An economy that relies on barter will have trouble allocating its scarce resources efficiently. In such an economy, trade is said to require the *double coincidence of wants*—the unlikely occurrence that two people each have a good or service that the other wants.

The existence of money makes trade easier. The restaurateur does not care whether you can produce a valuable good or service for her. She is happy to accept your money, knowing that other people will do the same for her. Such a convention allows trade to be roundabout. The restaurateur accepts your money and uses it to pay her chef; the chef uses her paycheck to send her child to day care; the day care center uses this tuition to pay a teacher; and the teacher hires you to mow her lawn. As money flows from person to person, it facilitates production and trade, thereby allowing each person to specialize in what she does best and raising everyone's standard of living.

In this chapter, we begin to examine the role of money in an economy. We discuss what money is, the various forms that money takes, how the banking system helps create money, and how the government controls the quantity of money in circulation. In the rest of this book, we devote much effort to learning how changes in the quantity of money affect various economic variables, including inflation, interest rates, production, and employment. Consistent with our long-run focus in the previous four chapters, in the next chapter we examine the long-run effects of changes in the quantity of money. The short-run effects of monetary changes are a more complex topic, which we take up later. This chapter provides the background for all of this further analysis.

11-1   The Meaning of Money

What is money? This might seem like an odd question. When you read that billionaire Jeff Bezos has a lot of money, you know what that means: He is so rich that he can buy almost anything he wants. In this sense, the term *money* is used to mean *wealth*.

money
the set of assets in an economy that people regularly use to buy goods and services from other people

Economists, however, use the word in a more specific sense: **Money** is the set of assets in the economy that people regularly use to buy goods and services from each other. The cash in your wallet is money because you can use it to buy a meal at a restaurant or a shirt at a store. By contrast, the large share of Amazon that makes up much of Jeff Bezos's wealth is not considered a form of money. Mr. Bezos could not buy a meal or a shirt with this wealth without first obtaining some cash. According to the economist's definition, money includes only those few types of wealth that are regularly accepted by sellers in exchange for goods and services.

11-1a   The Functions of Money

Money has three functions: It is a *medium of exchange*, a *unit of account*, and a *store of value*. These three functions together distinguish money from other assets, such as stocks, bonds, real estate, art, and even baseball cards. Let's examine each of these functions of money.

A **medium of exchange** is an item that buyers give to sellers when they purchase goods and services. When you go to a store to buy a shirt, the store gives you the shirt and you give the store your money. This transfer of money from buyer to seller allows the transaction to take place. When you walk into a store, you are confident that the store will accept your money for the items it is selling because money is the commonly accepted medium of exchange.

A **unit of account** is the yardstick people use to post prices and record debts. When you go shopping, you might observe that a shirt costs $50 and a hamburger costs $5. Even though it would be accurate to say that a shirt costs 10 hamburgers and a hamburger costs $\frac{1}{10}$ of a shirt, prices are never quoted in this way. Similarly, if you take out a loan from a bank, the size of your future loan repayments will be measured in dollars, not in a quantity of goods and services. When we want to measure and record economic value, we use money as the unit of account.

A **store of value** is an item that people can use to transfer purchasing power from the present to the future. When a seller accepts money today in exchange for a good or service, that seller can hold the money and become a buyer of another good or service at another time. Money is not the only store of value in the economy: A person can also transfer purchasing power from the present to the future by holding nonmonetary assets such as stocks and bonds. The term *wealth* is used to refer to the total of all stores of value, including both money and nonmonetary assets.

Economists use the term **liquidity** to describe the ease with which an asset can be converted into the economy's medium of exchange. Because money is the economy's medium of exchange, it is the most liquid asset available. Other assets vary widely in their liquidity. Most stocks and bonds can be sold easily with low cost, so they are relatively liquid assets. By contrast, selling a house, a Rembrandt painting, or a 1948 Joe DiMaggio baseball card requires more time and effort, so these assets are less liquid.

When people decide how to allocate their wealth, they have to balance the liquidity of each possible asset against the asset's usefulness as a store of value. Money is the most liquid asset, but it is far from perfect as a store of value. When prices rise, the value of money falls. In other words, when goods and services become more expensive, each dollar in your wallet can buy less. This link between the price level and the value of money is key to understanding how money affects the economy, a topic we start to explore in the next chapter.

11-1b The Kinds of Money

When money takes the form of a commodity with intrinsic value, it is called **commodity money**. The term *intrinsic value* means that the item would have value even if it were not used as money. One example of commodity money is gold. Gold has intrinsic value because it is used in industry and in the making of jewelry. Although today we no longer use gold as money, historically gold was a common form of money because it is relatively easy to carry, measure, and verify for impurities. When an economy uses gold as money (or uses paper money that is convertible into gold on demand), it is said to be operating under a *gold standard*.

Another example of commodity money is cigarettes. In prisoner-of-war camps during World War II, prisoners traded goods and services with one another using cigarettes as the store of value, unit of account, and medium of exchange. Similarly, as the Soviet Union was breaking up in the late 1980s, cigarettes started replacing

medium of exchange
an item that buyers give to sellers when they want to purchase goods and services

unit of account
the yardstick people use to post prices and record debts

store of value
an item that people can use to transfer purchasing power from the present to the future

liquidity
the ease with which an asset can be converted into the economy's medium of exchange

commodity money
money that takes the form of a commodity with intrinsic value

fiat money

money without intrinsic value that is used as money by government decree

the ruble as the preferred currency in Moscow. In both cases, even nonsmokers were happy to accept cigarettes in an exchange, knowing that they could use the cigarettes to buy other goods and services.

Money without intrinsic value is called **fiat money**. A *fiat* is an order or decree, and fiat money is established as money by government decree. For example, compare the paper dollars in your wallet (printed by the U.S. government) with the paper dollars from a game of Monopoly (printed by the Parker Brothers game company). Why can you use the first to pay your bill at a restaurant but not the second? The answer is that the U.S. government has decreed its dollars to be valid money. Each paper dollar in your wallet reads: "This note is legal tender for all debts, public and private."

Although the government is central to establishing and regulating a system of fiat money (by prosecuting counterfeiters, for example), other factors are also required for the success of such a monetary system. To a large extent, the acceptance of fiat money depends as much on expectations and social convention as on government decree. The Soviet government in the 1980s never abandoned the ruble as the official currency. Yet the people of Moscow preferred to accept cigarettes (or even American dollars) in exchange for goods and services because they were more confident that these alternative monies would be accepted by others in the future.

FYI

Cryptocurrencies: A Fad or the Future?

In recent years, the world has seen a proliferation of a new kind of money, called *cryptocurrencies*. These currencies use the tools of cryptography to create a medium of exchange that exists only in electronic form. They rely on a technology called *blockchain* to maintain a decentralized, public ledger that records transactions.

The first of these cryptocurrencies, introduced in 2009, was *bitcoin*. It was conceived by a computer expert called Satoshi Nakamoto. Nakamoto authored and circulated a white paper establishing the bitcoin protocol, but Nakamoto's identity is otherwise unknown. According to the protocol, people create bitcoins by using computers to solve complex mathematical problems. The number of bitcoins that can be "mined" in this way is supposedly limited to 21 million units. Once created, bitcoins can be used in exchange. They can be bought and sold for U.S. dollars on organized bitcoin exchanges, where supply and demand determine the dollar price of a bitcoin. People can hold bitcoins as a store of value, and they can use bitcoins to buy things from any vendor who is willing to accept them.

Bitcoins are neither commodity money nor fiat money. Unlike commodity money, they have no intrinsic value. You can't use bitcoins for anything other than exchange. Unlike fiat money, they are not created by government decree. Fans of bitcoin embrace this new form of money because it exists apart from government. Some bitcoin users are engaged in illicit transactions such as the drug trade and benefit from the anonymity that bitcoin transactions offer.

During bitcoin's brief history, its dollar value has fluctuated wildly. In 2010, the price of a bitcoin ranged between 5 cents to 39 cents. The price rose above $1 in 2011 and above $1,000 in 2013 before falling below $500 in 2014. Over the following few years, the dollar value of a bitcoin skyrocketed, reaching more than $19,000 in 2017. But by early 2019, it had fallen back to $3,500. Meanwhile, a variety of other cryptocurrencies were introduced, such as Ethereum, Litecoin, Ripple, and Zcash, providing competition for bitcoin. These other cryptocurrencies differ from bitcoin in the details of their protocols, but like bitcoin, they have all exhibited large price swings.

The long-term success of cryptocurrencies depends on whether they succeed in performing the functions of money: a store of value, a unit of account, and a medium of exchange. Many economists are skeptical. The great volatility of the dollar prices of cryptocurrencies makes them a risky way to hold wealth and an inconvenient measure in which to post prices. Few retailers accept them in exchange, at least so far. As a result, cryptocurrencies are excluded from standard measures of the quantity of money.

Cryptocurrencies may be the money of the future, or they may be a passing fad. ∎

11-1c Money in the U.S. Economy

As we will see, the quantity of money circulating in the economy, called the *money stock*, has a powerful influence on many economic variables. But before we consider why that is true, we need to ask a preliminary question: What is the quantity of money? In particular, suppose you were given the task of measuring how much money there is in the U.S. economy. What would you include in your measure?

The most obvious asset to include is **currency**—the paper bills and coins in the hands of the public. Currency is clearly the most widely accepted medium of exchange in our economy. There is no doubt that it is part of the money stock.

Yet currency is not the only asset that you can use to buy goods and services. Many stores also accept personal checks. Wealth held in your checking account is almost as convenient for buying things as wealth held in your wallet. To measure the money stock, therefore, you might want to include **demand deposits**—balances in bank accounts that depositors can access on demand simply by writing a check or swiping a debit card at a store.

Once you start to consider balances in checking accounts as part of the money stock, you are led to consider the large variety of other accounts that people hold at banks and other financial institutions. Bank depositors usually cannot write checks against the balances in their savings accounts, but they can easily transfer funds from savings into checking accounts. In addition, depositors in money market mutual funds can often write checks against their balances. Thus, these other accounts should plausibly be counted as part of the U.S. money stock.

In a complex economy such as ours, it is not easy to draw a line between assets that can be called "money" and assets that cannot. The coins in your pocket clearly are part of the money stock, and the Empire State Building clearly is not. But there are many assets in between these extremes for which the choice is less clear. Because different analysts can reasonably disagree about where to draw the dividing line between monetary and nonmonetary assets, various measures of the money stock are available for the U.S. economy. Figure 1 shows the two most commonly used, designated M1 and M2. M2 includes more assets in its measure of money than does M1.

currency
the paper bills and coins in the hands of the public

demand deposits
balances in bank accounts that depositors can access on demand by writing a check

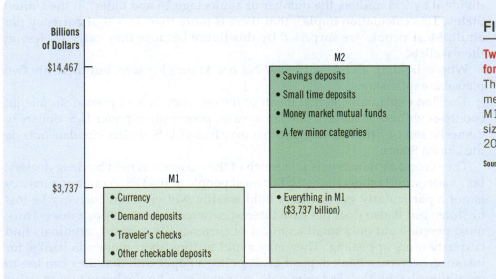

FIGURE 1

Two Measures of the Money Stock for the U.S. Economy
The two most widely followed measures of the money stock are M1 and M2. This figure shows the size of each measure in January 2019.

Source: Federal Reserve.

FYI

Why Credit Cards Aren't Money

It might seem natural to include credit cards as part of the economy's stock of money. After all, people use credit cards to make many of their purchases. Aren't credit cards, therefore, a medium of exchange?

At first this argument may seem persuasive, but credit cards are excluded from all measures of the quantity of money. The reason is that credit cards are not really a method of payment but rather a method of *deferring* payment. When you buy a meal with a credit card, the bank that issued the card pays the restaurant what it is due. At a later date, you will have to repay the bank (perhaps with interest). When the time comes to pay your credit card bill, you will probably do so by writing a check against your checking account. The balance in this checking account is part of the economy's stock of money.

Notice that credit cards are different from debit cards, which automatically withdraw funds from a bank account to pay for items bought. Rather than allowing the user to postpone payment for a purchase, a debit card gives the user immediate access to deposits in a bank account. In this sense, a debit card is more similar to a check than to a credit card. The account balances that lie behind debit cards are included in measures of the quantity of money.

Even though credit cards are not considered a form of money, they are nonetheless important for analyzing the monetary system. People who have credit cards can pay many of their bills together at the end of the month, rather than sporadically as they make purchases. As a result, people with credit cards probably hold less money on average than people without credit cards. Thus, the wide availability of credit cards may reduce the amount of money that people choose to hold. ■

For our purposes in this book, we need not dwell on the differences between the various measures of money. None of our discussions will hinge on the distinction between M1 and M2. The important point is that the money stock for the U.S. economy includes not only currency but also deposits in banks and other financial institutions that can be readily accessed and used to buy goods and services.

CASE STUDY

WHERE IS ALL THE CURRENCY?

One puzzle about the money stock of the U.S. economy concerns the amount of currency. In January 2019, there was $1.7 trillion of currency outstanding. To put this number in perspective, we can divide it by 258 million, the number of adults (age 16 and older) in the United States. This calculation implies that there is more than $6,500 of currency per adult. Most people are surprised by this figure because they carry far less in their wallets.

Who is holding all this currency? No one knows for sure, but there are two plausible explanations.

The first explanation is that much of the currency is held abroad. In foreign countries without a stable monetary system, people often prefer U.S. dollars to domestic assets. Estimates suggest that over half of U.S. dollars circulate outside the United States.

The second explanation is that much of the currency is held by drug dealers, tax evaders, and other criminals. For most people in the U.S. economy, currency is not a particularly good way to hold wealth: Not only can currency be lost or stolen but it also does not earn interest, whereas a bank deposit does. Thus, most people hold only small amounts of currency. By contrast, criminals find currency more appealing. They may avoid putting their money in banks, for instance, because a bank deposit gives police a paper trail that they can use to trace illegal activities. For criminals, currency may be the best store of value available. ●

11-2 The Federal Reserve System

Whenever an economy uses a system of fiat money, as the U.S. economy does, some agency must be responsible for regulating the system. In the United States, that agency is the **Federal Reserve**, often simply called the **Fed**. If you look at the top of a dollar bill, you will see that it is called a "Federal Reserve Note." The Fed is an example of a **central bank**—an institution designed to oversee the banking system and regulate the quantity of money. Other major central banks around the world include the Bank of England, the Bank of Japan, and the European Central Bank.

11-2a The Fed's Organization

The Federal Reserve was created in 1913 after a series of bank failures in 1907 convinced Congress that the United States needed a central bank to ensure the health of the nation's banking system. Today, the Fed is run by its Board of Governors, which has up to seven members appointed by the president and confirmed by the Senate. The governors have 14-year terms. Just as federal judges are given lifetime appointments to insulate them from politics, Fed governors are given long terms to give them independence from short-term political pressures when they formulate monetary policy.

Among the members of the Board of Governors, the most important is the chair. The chair directs the Fed staff, presides over board meetings, and testifies regularly about Fed policy in front of congressional committees. The president appoints the chair to a 4-year term. As this book was going to press, the chair of the Fed was Jerome Powell, who was nominated to the job by President Donald Trump in 2017.

The Federal Reserve System consists of the Federal Reserve Board in Washington, D.C., and 12 regional Federal Reserve Banks located in major cities around the country. The presidents of the regional banks are chosen by each bank's board of directors, whose members are typically drawn from the region's banking and business community.

The Fed has two related jobs. The first is to regulate banks and ensure the health of the banking system. In particular, the Fed monitors each bank's financial condition and facilitates bank transactions by clearing checks. It also acts as a bank's bank. That is, the Fed makes loans to banks when banks themselves want to borrow. When financially troubled banks find themselves short of cash, the Fed acts as a *lender of last resort*—a lender to those who cannot borrow anywhere else—to maintain stability in the overall banking system.

The Fed's second job is to control the quantity of money that is made available in the economy, called the **money supply**. Decisions by policymakers concerning the money supply constitute **monetary policy**. At the Federal Reserve, monetary

Federal Reserve (Fed) the central bank of the United States

central bank an institution designed to oversee the banking system and regulate the quantity of money in the economy

money supply the quantity of money available in the economy

monetary policy the setting of the money supply by policymakers in the central bank

policy is made by the Federal Open Market Committee (FOMC). The FOMC meets about every six weeks in Washington, D.C., to discuss the condition of the economy and consider changes in monetary policy.

11-2b The Federal Open Market Committee

The Federal Open Market Committee consists of the members of the Board of Governors and 5 of the 12 regional bank presidents. All 12 regional presidents attend each FOMC meeting, but only five get to vote. Voting rights rotate among the 12 regional presidents over time. The president of the New York Fed always gets a vote, however, because New York is the traditional financial center of the U.S. economy and because all Fed purchases and sales of government bonds are conducted at the New York Fed's trading desk.

Through the decisions of the FOMC, the Fed has the power to increase or decrease the number of dollars in the economy. In simple metaphorical terms, you can imagine the Fed printing dollar bills and dropping them around the country by helicopter. Similarly, you can imagine the Fed using a giant vacuum cleaner to suck dollar bills out of people's wallets. In reality, the Fed's methods for changing the money supply are more complex and subtle than this, but the helicopter-vacuum metaphor is a good first step to understanding the meaning of monetary policy.

Later in this chapter, we discuss how the Fed actually changes the money supply, but it is worth noting here that the Fed's primary tool is the *open-market operation*—the purchase and sale of U.S. government bonds. (Recall that a U.S. government bond is a certificate of indebtedness of the federal government.) If the FOMC decides to increase the money supply, the Fed creates dollars and uses them to buy government bonds from the public in the nation's bond markets. After the purchase, these dollars are in the hands of the public. Thus, an open-market purchase of bonds by the Fed increases the money supply. Conversely, if the FOMC decides to decrease the money supply, the Fed sells government bonds from its portfolio to the public in the nation's bond markets. After the sale, the dollars the Fed receives for the bonds are out of the hands of the public. Thus, an open-market sale of bonds by the Fed decreases the money supply.

Central banks are important institutions because changes in the money supply can profoundly affect the economy. One of the *Ten Principles of Economics* in Chapter 1 is that prices rise when the government prints too much money. Another of the *Ten Principles of Economics* is that society faces a short-run trade-off between inflation and unemployment. The power of the Fed rests on these principles. For reasons we discuss more fully in the coming chapters, the Fed's policy decisions are key determinants of inflation in the long run and employment and production in the short run. Indeed, the Fed chair has been called the second most powerful person in the United States.

Quick**Quiz**

3. Which of the following is NOT true about the Federal Reserve?
   a. It was established by the U.S. Constitution.
   b. It regulates the banking system.
   c. It lends to banks.
   d. It conducts open-market operations.

4. If the Fed wants to increase the money supply, it can
   a. raise income tax rates.
   b. reduce income tax rates.
   c. buy bonds in open-market operations.
   d. sell bonds in open-market operations.

Answers at end of chapter.

11-3 Banks and the Money Supply

So far, we have introduced the concept of "money" and discussed how the Fed controls the supply of money by buying and selling government bonds in open-market operations. This explanation of the money supply is correct, but it is not complete. In particular, it omits the key role that banks play in the monetary system.

Recall that the amount of money you hold includes both currency (the bills in your wallet and coins in your pocket) and demand deposits (the balance in your checking account). Because demand deposits are held in banks, the behavior of banks can influence the quantity of demand deposits and, therefore, the money supply. This section examines how banks affect the money supply and, in doing so, how they complicate the Fed's job of controlling the money supply.

"I've heard a lot about money, and now I'd like to try some."

11-3a The Simple Case of 100-Percent-Reserve Banking

To see how banks influence the money supply, let's first imagine a world without any banks at all. In this simple world, currency is the only form of money. To be concrete, let's suppose that the total quantity of currency is $100. The supply of money is, therefore, $100.

Now suppose that someone opens a bank, appropriately called First National Bank. First National Bank is only a depository institution—that is, it accepts deposits but does not make loans. The purpose of the bank is to give depositors a safe place to keep their money. Whenever a person deposits some money, the bank keeps the money in its vault until the depositor withdraws it, writes a check, or uses a debit card to access her balance. Deposits that banks have received but have not loaned out are called **reserves**. In this imaginary economy, all deposits are held as reserves, so this system is called *100-percent-reserve banking*.

reserves

deposits that banks have received but have not loaned out

We can express the financial position of First National Bank with a *T-account*, which is a simplified accounting statement that shows changes in a bank's assets and liabilities. Here is the T-account for First National Bank if the economy's entire $100 of money is deposited in the bank:

First National Bank

Assets		Liabilities	
Reserves	$100.00	Deposits	$100.00

On the left side of the T-account are the bank's assets of $100 (the reserves it holds in its vaults). On the right side are the bank's liabilities of $100 (the amount it owes to its depositors). Because the assets and liabilities exactly balance, this accounting statement is called a *balance sheet*.

Now consider the money supply in this imaginary economy. Before First National Bank opens, the money supply is the $100 of currency that people are holding. After the bank opens and people deposit their currency, the money supply is the $100 of demand deposits. (There is no longer any currency outstanding, since it is all in the bank vault.) Each deposit in the bank reduces currency and raises demand deposits by exactly the same amount, leaving the money supply unchanged. Thus, *if banks hold all deposits in reserve, banks do not influence the supply of money.*

11-3b Money Creation with Fractional-Reserve Banking

Eventually, the bankers at First National Bank may start to reconsider their policy of 100-percent-reserve banking. Leaving all that money idle in their vaults seems unnecessary. Why not lend some of it out and earn a profit by charging interest on the loans? Families buying houses, firms building new factories, and students paying for college would all be happy to pay interest to borrow some of that money for a while. First National Bank has to keep some reserves so that currency is available if depositors want to make withdrawals. But if the flow of new deposits is roughly the same as the flow of withdrawals, First National needs to keep only a fraction of its deposits in reserve. Thus, First National adopts a system called **fractional-reserve banking**.

fractional-reserve banking
a banking system in which banks hold only a fraction of deposits as reserves

reserve ratio
the fraction of deposits that banks hold as reserves

The fraction of total deposits that a bank holds as reserves is called the **reserve ratio**. This ratio is influenced by both government regulation and bank policy. As we discuss more fully later in the chapter, the Fed sets a minimum amount of reserves that banks must hold, called a *reserve requirement*. In addition, banks may hold reserves above the legal minimum, called *excess reserves*, so they can be more confident that they will not run short of cash. For our purpose here, we take the reserve ratio as given to examine how fractional-reserve banking influences the money supply.

Let's suppose that First National has a reserve ratio of 1/10, or 10 percent. This means that it keeps 10 percent of its deposits in reserve and loans out the rest. Now let's look again at the bank's T-account:

First National Bank

Assets		Liabilities	
Reserves	$10.00	Deposits	$100.00
Loans	90.00		

First National still has $100 in liabilities because making the loans did not alter the bank's obligation to its depositors. But now the bank has two kinds of assets: It has $10 of reserves in its vault, and it has loans of $90. (These loans are liabilities of the people borrowing from First National, but they are assets of the bank because the borrowers will later repay the loans.) In total, First National's assets still equal its liabilities.

Once again consider the economy's supply of money. Before First National makes any loans, the money supply is the $100 of deposits. Yet when First National lends out some of these deposits, the money supply increases. The depositors still have demand deposits totaling $100, but now the borrowers hold $90 in currency. The money supply (which equals currency plus demand deposits) equals $190. Thus, *when banks hold only a fraction of deposits in reserve, the banking system creates money.*

At first, this creation of money by fractional-reserve banking may seem too good to be true: It appears that the bank has created money out of thin air. To make this feat seem less miraculous, note that when First National Bank loans out some of its reserves and creates money, it does not create any wealth. Loans from First National give the borrowers some currency and thus the ability to buy goods and services. Yet the borrowers are also taking on debts, so the loans do not make them any richer. In other words, as a bank creates the asset of money, it also creates a corresponding liability for those who borrowed the created money. At the end of this process of money creation, the economy is more liquid in the sense that there is more of the medium of exchange, but the economy is no wealthier than before.

11-3c The Money Multiplier

The creation of money does not stop with First National Bank. Suppose the borrower from First National uses the $90 to buy something from someone who then deposits the currency in Second National Bank. Here is the T-account for Second National Bank:

Second National Bank		
Assets		**Liabilities**
Reserves	$ 9.00	Deposits $90.00
Loans	81.00	

After the deposit, Second National has liabilities of $90. If Second National also has a reserve ratio of 10 percent, it keeps assets of $9 in reserve and makes $81 in loans. In this way, Second National creates an additional $81 of money. If this $81 is eventually deposited in Third National Bank, which also has a reserve ratio of 10 percent, Third National keeps $8.10 in reserve and makes $72.90 in loans. Here is the T-account for Third National Bank:

Third National Bank		
Assets		**Liabilities**
Reserves	$ 8.10	Deposits $81.00
Loans	72.90	

The process goes on and on. Each time that money is deposited and a bank loan is made, more money is created.

How much money is eventually created in this economy? Let's add it up:

Original deposit	= $100.00
First National lending	= $ 90.00 (= .9 × $100.00)
Second National lending	= $ 81.00 (= .9 × $90.00)
Third National lending	= $ 72.90 (= .9 × $81.00)
•	•
•	•
•	•
Total money supply	= $1,000.00

It turns out that even though this process of money creation can continue forever, it does not create an infinite amount of money. If you laboriously add the infinite sequence of numbers in the preceding example, you find that the $100 of reserves generates $1,000 of money. The amount of money the banking system generates with each dollar of reserves is called the **money multiplier**. In this imaginary economy, where the $100 of reserves generates $1,000 of money, the money multiplier is 10.

What determines the size of the money multiplier? It turns out that the answer is simple: *The money multiplier is the reciprocal of the reserve ratio.* If R is the reserve ratio for all banks in the economy, then each dollar of reserves generates $1/R$ dollars of money. In our example, $R = 1/10$, so the money multiplier is 10.

This reciprocal formula for the money multiplier makes sense. If a bank holds $1,000 in deposits, then a reserve ratio of 1/10 (10 percent) means that the bank

money multiplier
the amount of money the banking system generates with each dollar of reserves

must hold $100 in reserves. The money multiplier just turns this idea around: If the banking system as a whole holds a total of $100 in reserves, it can have only $1,000 in deposits. In other words, if R is the ratio of reserves to deposits at each bank (that is, the reserve ratio), then the ratio of deposits to reserves in the banking system (that is, the money multiplier) must be $1/R$.

This formula shows how the amount of money banks create depends on the reserve ratio. If the reserve ratio were only $1/20$ (5 percent), then the banking system would have 20 times as much in deposits as in reserves, implying a money multiplier of 20. Each dollar of reserves would generate $20 of money. Similarly, if the reserve ratio were $1/4$ (25 percent), deposits would be 4 times reserves, the money multiplier would be 4, and each dollar of reserves would generate $4 of money. Thus, *the higher the reserve ratio, the less of each deposit banks loan out, and the smaller the money multiplier*. In the special case of 100-percent-reserve banking, the reserve ratio is 1, the money multiplier is 1, and banks do not make loans or create money.

11-3d Bank Capital, Leverage, and the Financial Crisis of 2008–2009

In the previous sections, we have seen a simplified explanation of how banks work. But the reality of modern banking is a bit more complex, and this complexity played a key role in the financial crisis of 2008 and 2009. Before looking at that crisis, we need to learn a bit more about how banks actually function.

In each of the bank balance sheets we have seen so far, a bank accepts deposits and either uses those deposits to make loans or holds them as reserves. More realistically, a bank gets financial resources not only from accepting deposits but also, like other companies, from issuing equity and debt. The resources that a bank obtains from issuing equity to its owners are called **bank capital**. A bank uses these financial resources in various ways to generate profit for its owners. It not only makes loans and holds reserves but also buys financial securities, such as stocks and bonds.

bank capital
the resources a bank's owners have put into the institution

Here is a more realistic example of a bank's balance sheet:

More Realistic National Bank

Assets		Liabilities and Owners' Equity	
Reserves	$200	Deposits	$800
Loans	700	Debt	150
Securities	100	Capital (owners' equity)	50

On the right side of this balance sheet are the bank's liabilities and capital (also called *owners' equity*). This bank obtained $50 of resources from its owners. It also took in $800 of deposits and issued $150 of debt. The total of $1,000 was put to use in three ways, listed on the left side of the balance sheet, which shows the bank's assets. This bank held $200 in reserves, made $700 in bank loans, and used $100 to buy financial securities, such as government or corporate bonds. The bank decides how to allocate its resources among asset classes based on their risk and return, as well as on any regulations (such as reserve requirements) that restrict the bank's choices.

By the rules of accounting, the reserves, loans, and securities on the left side of the balance sheet must always equal, in total, the deposits, debt, and capital on the right side of the balance sheet. There is no magic in this equality. It occurs because the value of the owners' equity is, by definition, the value of the bank's assets (reserves, loans, and securities) minus the value of its liabilities (deposits and debt). Therefore, the left and right sides of the balance sheet always sum to the same total.

Many businesses rely on **leverage**, the use of borrowed money to supplement existing funds for investment purposes. Indeed, whenever a business uses debt to finance an investment project, it is applying leverage. Leverage is particularly important for banks, however, because borrowing and lending are at the heart of what they do. To fully understand banking, therefore, it is crucial to understand how leverage works.

leverage
the use of borrowed money to supplement existing funds for purposes of investment

The **leverage ratio** is the ratio of the bank's total assets to bank capital. In this example, the leverage ratio is \$1,000/\$50, or 20. A leverage ratio of 20 means that for every dollar of capital that the bank owners have contributed, the bank has \$20 of assets. Of the \$20 of assets, \$19 are financed with borrowed money—either by taking in deposits or issuing debt.

leverage ratio
the ratio of assets to bank capital

You may have learned in a science class that a lever can amplify a force: A boulder that you cannot move with your arms alone will move more easily if you use a lever. A similar result occurs with bank leverage. To see how this amplification works, let's continue with this numerical example. Suppose that the bank's assets were to rise in value by 5 percent because, say, some of the securities the bank was holding rose in price. Then the \$1,000 of assets would now be worth \$1,050. Because the depositors and debt holders are still owed \$950, the bank capital rises from \$50 to \$100 (\$1050 − \$950). Thus, when the leverage rate is 20, a 5-percent increase in the value of assets increases the owners' equity by 100 percent.

The same principle works on the downside, but with troubling consequences. Suppose that some people who borrowed from the bank default on their loans, reducing the value of the bank's assets by 5 percent, to \$950. Once again, the depositors and debt holders are still owed \$950, so the value of the owners' equity falls to zero (\$950 − \$950). Thus, when the leverage ratio is 20, a 5-percent fall in the value of the bank's assets leads to a 100-percent fall in bank capital. If the value of assets were to fall by more than 5 percent, the bank's assets would fall below its liabilities. In this case, the bank would be *insolvent*, and it would be unable to pay off its debt holders and depositors in full.

Bank regulators require banks to hold a certain amount of capital. The goal of such a **capital requirement** is to ensure that banks will be able to pay off their depositors (without having to resort to government-provided deposit insurance funds). The amount of capital required depends on the kind of assets a bank holds. A bank holding risky assets such as loans to borrowers whose credit is of dubious quality would be, all other things equal, required to hold more capital than a bank holding safe assets such as government bonds.

capital requirement
a government regulation specifying a minimum amount of bank capital

Economic turmoil can result when banks find themselves with too little capital to satisfy capital requirements. An example of this phenomenon arose in 2007 and 2008, when many banks incurred sizable losses on some of their assets—specifically, mortgage loans and securities backed by mortgage loans. The shortage of capital induced the banks to reduce lending, a phenomenon called a *credit crunch*, which in turn contributed to a severe downturn in economic activity. (This event is discussed more fully in Chapter 15.) To address this problem, the U.S. Treasury, working together with the Fed, put many billions of dollars of public funds into the banking system to increase the amount of bank capital. As a result, it temporarily made the U.S. taxpayer a part owner of many banks. The goal of this unusual policy was to recapitalize the banking system so that bank lending could return to a more normal level. And, in fact, by late 2009, it did.

5. Isabella takes $100 of currency from her wallet and deposits it into her checking account. If the bank adds the entire $100 to reserves, the money supply _____, but if the bank lends out some of the $100, the money supply _____.
    a. increases; increases even more
    b. increases; increases by less
    c. is unchanged; increases
    d. decreases; decreases by less

6. If the reserve ratio is $\frac{1}{4}$ and the central bank increases the quantity of reserves in the banking system by $120, the money supply increases by
    a. $90.
    b. $150.
    c. $160.
    d. $480.

7. A bank has capital of $200 and a leverage ratio of 5. If the value of the bank's assets declines by 10 percent, then its capital will be reduced to
    a. $100.
    b. $150.
    c. $180.
    d. $185.

Answers at end of chapter.

11-4   The Fed's Tools of Monetary Control

As we have discussed, the Federal Reserve is responsible for controlling the supply of money. Now that we understand how banking works, we are in a better position to understand how the Fed carries out this job. Because banks create money in a system of fractional-reserve banking, the Fed's control of the money supply is indirect. When the Fed decides to change the money supply, it must consider how its actions will work through the banking system.

The Fed has various tools in its monetary toolbox. We can group the tools into two groups: those that influence the quantity of reserves and those that influence the reserve ratio and in turn the money multiplier.

11-4a   How the Fed Influences the Quantity of Reserves

The first way the Fed can change the money supply is by changing the quantity of reserves. The Fed alters the quantity of reserves either by buying or selling bonds in open-market operations or by making loans to banks (or by some combination of the two). Let's consider each of these methods in turn.

open-market operations
the purchase and sale of U.S. government bonds by the Fed

Open-Market Operations   As we noted earlier, the Fed conducts **open-market operations** when it buys or sells government bonds. To increase the money supply, the Fed instructs its bond traders at the New York Fed to buy bonds from the public in the nation's bond markets. By paying for the bonds with newly created dollars, the Fed increases the number of dollars in the economy. Some of these new dollars are held as currency, and some are deposited in banks. Each new dollar held as currency increases the money supply by exactly $1. Each new dollar deposited in a bank increases the money supply by more than a dollar because it increases reserves and, thereby, increases the amount of money that the banking system can create.

To reduce the money supply, the Fed does just the opposite: It sells government bonds to the public in the nation's bond markets. The public pays for these bonds with its holdings of currency and bank deposits, directly reducing the amount of money in circulation. In addition, as people make withdrawals from banks to buy these bonds from the Fed, banks find themselves with a smaller quantity of reserves. In response, banks reduce the amount of lending, and the process of money creation reverses itself.

Open-market operations are easy to conduct. In fact, the Fed's purchases and sales of government bonds in the nation's bond markets are similar to the transactions that any individual might undertake for her own portfolio. (Of course, when two individuals engage in a purchase or sale with each other, money changes hands, but the amount of money in circulation remains the same.) In addition, the Fed can use open-market operations to change the money supply by a small or large amount on any day without major changes in laws or bank regulations. Therefore, open-market operations are the tool of monetary policy that the Fed uses most often.

Fed Lending to Banks The Fed can also increase the quantity of reserves by lending reserves to banks. Banks borrow from the Fed when they feel they do not have enough reserves on hand, either to satisfy bank regulators, meet depositor withdrawals, make new loans, or for some other business reason.

There are various ways banks can borrow from the Fed. Traditionally, banks borrow from the Fed's *discount window* and pay an interest rate on that loan called the **discount rate**. When the Fed makes such a loan to a bank, the banking system has more reserves than it otherwise would, and these additional reserves allow the banking system to create more money.

discount rate
the interest rate on the loans that the Fed makes to banks

The Fed can alter the money supply by changing the discount rate. A higher discount rate discourages banks from borrowing from the Fed, decreasing the quantity of reserves in the banking system and in turn the money supply. Conversely, a lower discount rate encourages banks to borrow from the Fed, increasing the quantity of reserves and the money supply.

At times, the Fed has set up other mechanisms for banks to borrow from it. For example, from 2007 to 2010, under the *Term Auction Facility*, the Fed set a quantity of funds it wanted to lend to banks, and eligible banks then bid to borrow those funds. The loans went to the highest eligible bidders—that is, to the banks that had acceptable collateral and offered to pay the highest interest rate. Unlike at the discount window, where the Fed sets the price of a loan and the banks determine the quantity of borrowing, at the Term Auction Facility the Fed set the quantity of borrowing and competitive bidding among banks determined the price. The more funds the Fed made available, the greater the quantity of reserves and the larger the money supply.

The Fed lends to banks not only to control the money supply but also to help financial institutions when they are in trouble. For example, when the stock market crashed by 22 percent on October 19, 1987, many Wall Street brokerage firms found themselves temporarily in need of funds to finance the high volume of stock trading. The next morning, before the stock market opened, Fed Chair Alan Greenspan announced the Fed's "readiness to serve as a source of liquidity to support the economic and financial system." Many economists believe that Greenspan's reaction to the stock crash was an important reason it had few repercussions.

Similarly, in 2008 and 2009, a fall in housing prices throughout the United States led to a sharp rise in the number of homeowners defaulting on their mortgage loans, and many financial institutions holding those mortgages ran into trouble. In an attempt to prevent these events from having broader economic ramifications, the Fed provided many billions of dollars in loans to financial institutions in distress.

11-4b How the Fed Influences the Reserve Ratio

In addition to influencing the quantity of reserves, the Fed changes the money supply by influencing the reserve ratio and thus the money multiplier. The Fed can influence the reserve ratio either through regulating the quantity of reserves banks must hold or through the interest rate that the Fed pays banks on their reserves. Again, let's consider each of these policy tools in turn.

Reserve Requirements   One way the Fed can influence the reserve ratio is by altering **reserve requirements**, the regulations that set the minimum amount of reserves that banks must hold against their deposits. Reserve requirements influence how much money the banking system can create with each dollar of reserves. An increase in reserve requirements means that banks must hold more reserves and, therefore, can loan out less of each dollar that is deposited. As a result, an increase in reserve requirements raises the reserve ratio, lowers the money multiplier, and decreases the money supply. Conversely, a decrease in reserve requirements lowers the reserve ratio, raises the money multiplier, and increases the money supply.

The Fed changes reserve requirements only rarely because such changes disrupt the business of banking. When the Fed increases reserve requirements, for instance, some banks find themselves short of reserves, even though they have seen no change in deposits. As a result, they have to curtail lending until they build their reserves to the new required level. Moreover, this particular tool has become less effective in recent years as banks have increasingly decided to hold excess reserves (that is, reserves above the required level).

Paying Interest on Reserves   Traditionally, banks did not earn any interest on the reserves they held on deposit at the Fed. In October 2008, however, the Fed began paying *interest on reserves*. That is, when a bank holds reserves at the Fed, the Fed now pays the bank interest on those deposits. As a result, the Fed has another tool with which to influence the economy. The higher the interest rate on reserves, the more reserves banks will choose to hold. Thus, an increase in the interest rate on reserves will tend to increase the reserve ratio, lower the money multiplier, and lower the money supply.

11-4c Problems in Controlling the Money Supply

The Fed's various tools—open-market operations, bank lending, reserve requirements, and interest on reserves—have powerful effects on the money supply. Yet the Fed's control of the money supply is not precise. The Fed must wrestle with two problems, each of which arises because much of the money supply is created by our system of fractional-reserve banking.

The first problem is that the Fed does not control the amount of money that households choose to hold as deposits in banks. The more money households deposit, the more reserves banks have, and the more money the banking system can create. The less money households deposit, the less reserves banks have, and the less money the banking system can create. To see why this is a problem, suppose that one day people lose confidence in the banking system and withdraw some of their deposits to hold more currency. When this happens, the banking system loses reserves and creates less money. The money supply falls, even without any Fed action.

The second problem of monetary control is that the Fed does not control the amount that bankers choose to lend. When money is deposited in a bank, it creates more money only when the bank loans it out. Because banks can choose to hold

reserve requirements
regulations on the minimum amount of reserves that banks must hold against deposits

excess reserves instead, the Fed cannot be sure how much money the banking system will create. For instance, suppose that one day bankers become more cautious about economic conditions and decide to make fewer loans and hold greater reserves. In this case, the banking system creates less money than it otherwise would. Because of the bankers' decision, the money supply falls.

Hence, in a system of fractional-reserve banking, the amount of money in the economy depends in part on the behavior of depositors and bankers. Because the Fed cannot control or perfectly predict this behavior, it cannot perfectly control the money supply. Yet if the Fed is vigilant, these problems need not be large. The Fed collects data on deposits and reserves from banks every week, so it quickly becomes aware of any changes in depositor or banker behavior. It can, therefore, respond to these changes and keep the money supply close to whatever level it chooses.

BANK RUNS AND THE MONEY SUPPLY

You have probably never witnessed a bank run in real life, but you may have seen one depicted in movies such as *Mary Poppins* or *It's a Wonderful Life*. A bank run occurs when depositors fear that a bank may be having financial troubles and "run" to the bank to withdraw their deposits. The United States has not seen a major bank run in recent history, but in the United Kingdom, a bank called Northern Rock experienced a run in 2007 and, as a result, was eventually taken over by the government.

Bank runs are a problem for banks under fractional-reserve banking. Because a bank holds only a fraction of its deposits in reserve, it cannot satisfy withdrawal requests from all depositors. Even if the bank is *solvent* (meaning that its assets exceed its liabilities), it will not have enough cash on hand to allow all depositors immediate access to all of their money. When a run occurs, the bank is forced to close its doors until some bank loans are repaid or until some lender of last resort (such as the Fed) provides it with the currency it needs to satisfy depositors.

Bank runs complicate the control of the money supply. An important example of this problem occurred during the Great Depression in the early 1930s. After a wave of bank runs and bank closings, households and bankers became more cautious. Households withdrew their deposits from banks, preferring to hold their money in the form of currency. This decision reversed the process of money creation, as bankers responded to falling reserves by reducing bank loans. At the same time, bankers increased their reserve ratios so that they would have enough cash on hand to meet their depositors' demands in any future bank runs. The higher reserve ratio reduced the money multiplier and thereby further reduced the money supply. From 1929 to 1933, the money supply fell by 28 percent, without the Fed taking any deliberate contractionary action. Many economists point to this massive fall in the money supply to explain the high unemployment and falling prices that prevailed during this period. (In future chapters, we examine the mechanisms by which changes in the money supply affect unemployment and prices.)

Today, bank runs are not a major problem for the U.S. banking system or the Fed. The federal government now guarantees the safety of deposits at most banks, primarily through the Federal Deposit Insurance Corporation (FDIC). Depositors do not make runs on their banks because they are confident that, even if their bank goes bankrupt, the FDIC will make good on the deposits. The policy of government deposit insurance has costs: Bankers whose deposits are guaranteed may have too little incentive to avoid bad risks when making loans. But one benefit of deposit insurance is a more stable banking system. As a result, most people see bank runs only in the movies. ●

A not-so-wonderful bank run

IN THE NEWS

A Trip to Jekyll Island

Here's the story of how the Federal Reserve came into being.

The stranger-than-fiction story of how the Fed was created

By Roger Lowenstein

According to opinion surveys, no institution save the Internal Revenue Service is held in lower regard than the Federal Reserve. It's also a font of conspiracy theories stoked by radical libertarians, who insist the Fed is debauching the currency and will ultimately bankrupt the country.

The Fed's unpopularity would make sense if it had, say, failed to intervene and save the system during the 2008 financial crisis. But, in fact, the Fed did rescue the economy....

Nonetheless, dissatisfaction is alive in Congress, where various bills would strip the Fed's autonomy and subject sensitive monetary decisions to the scrutiny of elected politicians. Some bills would go even further and explore a return to the gold standard.

For central bank watchers, this dynamic—effective policy rewarded with populist scorn—is nothing new. In America, it has always been thus.

At Alexander Hamilton's urging, Congress first chartered a national bank—the ur-Fed—in 1791. However, Thomas Jefferson, who famously mistrusted banks (he thought agriculture more virtuous), and who was fearful of a strong central government, opposed this development. After 20 years, the Jeffersonians won and Congress let the charter expire.

This decision led to disaster: ruinous inflation. So Congress chartered a Second Bank of the United States, which began in 1817, providing the growing country with a better, more uniform currency and improved its public finances. But success couldn't save it. Andrew Jackson despised the Second Bank as a tool of East Coast elites, and it too was abolished.

For most of the 19th century, the U.S., unlike most nations in Europe, did not have a lender of last resort. Frequent panics and credit shortages were the result. Yet some of the very people who could have benefited most from a central bank, such as farmers who were starved for credit, preferred the status quo. Like Jackson and Jefferson before them, they were fearful that a government bank would tyrannize the people, perhaps in cahoots with Wall Street.

After a financial panic in 1907 virtually shut down the banking system, reformers began to press once more for a central bank. But popular mistrust remained so pronounced that they were afraid to go public.

This is the point—105 years ago—when the story seems to have been hijacked by a future Hollywood scriptwriter.

On a November evening in 1910, a powerful senator, Rhode Island Republican Nelson W. Aldrich, boarded his private rail car near New York. A light snow was falling, muting the hushed, conspiratorial tones of his guests, which is exactly how Aldrich wanted it.

The reform-minded banker Paul Warburg, one of his guests, was toting a hunting rifle, but he had no interest in hunting. The party also included a member of the powerful Morgan bank, as well as an assistant U.S.

11-4d The Federal Funds Rate

If you read about U.S. monetary policy in the news, you will find much discussion of the federal funds rate. This raises several questions:

Q: What is the federal funds rate?

A: The **federal funds rate** is the short-term interest rate that banks charge one another for loans. If one bank finds itself short of reserves while another bank has excess reserves, the second bank can lend some reserves to the first. The loans are temporary—typically overnight. The price of the loan is the federal funds rate.

Q: How is the federal funds rate different from the discount rate?

A: The discount rate is the interest rate banks pay to borrow directly from the Federal Reserve through the discount window. Borrowing reserves from another bank in the federal funds market is an alternative to borrowing reserves from the Fed, and a bank short of reserves will typically do whichever is cheaper. In practice, the discount rate and the federal funds rate move closely together.

federal funds rate
the interest rate at which banks make overnight loans to one another

Treasury secretary, and Frank Vanderlip, head of the country's largest bank, National City.

"On what sort of errand are we going?" Vanderlip inquired.

"It may be a wild-goose chase; it may the biggest thing you and I ever did," Warburg replied.

Masquerading as duck hunters, they disembarked in Brunswick, Ga., and traveled by launch to Jekyll Island, home of an exclusive club surrounded by pine and palmetto groves. Over the course of a week, Aldrich and his bankers mapped out a draft of what was to become the Federal Reserve Act, changing the U.S. economy forever.

Congress was never told that Aldrich's bill had been drafted by Wall Street moguls. His bill did not pass, but it was the basis of a successor bill, the Federal Reserve Act, which Woodrow Wilson signed in 1913. Years later, when the Jekyll trip was revealed to the public, extremists seized on this stranger-than-fiction episode to bolster their claim that the Fed was a bankers' plot against the American people. For conspiracy theorists, the bankers' conclave on Jekyll became a metaphor for the Fed itself. The obvious irony is that, fearing Americans' irrational suspicion of central

banking, Aldrich and his crew resorted to a plot that, ultimately, deepened the country's paranoia.

Despite their clandestine tactics, the financiers' motives were actually patriotic. Aldrich had visited Europe and studied its central banks. He wanted expert help to draft an American equivalent. And in between sumptuous meals featuring wild turkey and freshly scalloped oysters, his group of wealthy

Senator Nelson Aldrich

LIBRARY OF CONGRESS, PRINTS & PHOTOGRAPHS DIVISION, REPRODUCTION NUMBER LC-USZ62-30740 (B&W FILM COPY NEG.)

bankers earnestly wrestled with issues that still provoke us today: How should power over the economy be apportioned between Washington and localities? How should the central bank set interest rates and the money supply?

The Federal Reserve today is not perfect. But it is more transparent than ever, thanks to reforms instituted by the previous chairman, Ben S. Bernanke, and it is no less necessary than was a central bank in 1791. Americans' paranoia is unjustified, just as it has always been. ■

Questions to Discuss

1. Why do you think Senator Aldrich wanted to keep the meeting on Jekyll Island a secret? In your view, was this secrecy justified?

2. Most people do not understand what the Federal Reserve does. How do you suppose this lack of understanding affects the job of central bankers?

Roger Lowenstein is the author of America's Bank: The Epic Struggle to Create the Federal Reserve.

Source: *Los Angeles Times*, November 2, 2015.

Q: Does the federal funds rate matter only for banks?

A: Not at all. Only banks borrow directly in the federal funds market, but the economic impact of this market is much broader. Because different parts of the financial system are highly interconnected, interest rates on different kinds of loans are strongly correlated with one another. So when the federal funds rate rises or falls, other interest rates often move in the same direction.

Q: What does the Fed have to do with the federal funds rate?

A: In recent years, the Fed has set a target goal for the federal funds rate. When the Federal Open Market Committee meets approximately every six weeks, it decides whether to raise or lower that target.

Q: How can the Fed make the federal funds rate hit the target it sets?

A: Although the actual federal funds rate is set by supply and demand in the market for loans among banks, the Fed can use open-market operations to influence that market. For example, when the Fed buys bonds in open-market operations, it injects reserves into the banking system. With more reserves in the system, fewer banks find themselves needing to borrow reserves to meet reserve requirements. The fall in demand for borrowing reserves decreases the price of such borrowing, which is the federal funds rate. Conversely, when the Fed sells bonds and withdraws reserves from the banking system, more banks find themselves short of reserves, and they bid up the price of borrowing reserves. Thus, open-market purchases lower the federal funds rate, and open-market sales raise the federal funds rate.

Q: But don't these open-market operations affect the money supply?

A: Yes, absolutely. When the Fed announces a change in the federal funds rate, it is committing itself to the open-market operations necessary to make that change happen, and these open-market operations will alter the supply of money. Decisions by the FOMC to change the target for the federal funds rate are also decisions to change the money supply. They are two sides of the same coin. Other things being equal, a decrease in the target for the federal funds rate means an expansion in the money supply, and an increase in the target for the federal funds rate means a contraction in the money supply.

Quick**Quiz**

8. Which of the following actions by the Fed would tend to increase the money supply?
   a. an open-market sale of government bonds
   b. a decrease in reserve requirements
   c. an increase in the interest rate paid on reserves
   d. an increase in the discount rate on Fed lending

9. If the Fed raises the interest rate it pays on reserves, it will _____ the money supply by increasing _____.

   a. decrease; the money multiplier
   b. decrease; excess reserves
   c. increase; the money multiplier
   d. increase; excess reserves

10. In a system of fractional-reserve banking, even without any action by the central bank, the money supply declines if households choose to hold _____ currency or if banks choose to hold _____ excess reserves.
    a. more; more
    b. more; less
    c. less; more
    d. less; less

Answers at end of chapter.

11-5 Conclusion

Some years ago, a book made the best-seller list with the title *Secrets of the Temple: How the Federal Reserve Runs the Country*. Though no doubt an exaggeration, this title highlighted the important role of the monetary system in our daily lives. Whenever we buy or sell anything, we are relying on the extraordinarily useful social convention called "money." Now that we know what money is and what determines its supply, we can discuss how changes in the quantity of money affect the economy. We begin to address that topic in the next chapter.

CHAPTER IN A NUTSHELL

- The term *money* refers to assets that people regularly use to buy goods and services.
- Money serves three functions. As a medium of exchange, it is the item used to make transactions. As a unit of account, it provides the way to record prices and other economic values. As a store of value, it offers a way to transfer purchasing power from the present to the future.
- Commodity money, such as gold, is money that has intrinsic value: It would be valued even if it were not used as money. Fiat money, such as paper dollars, is money without intrinsic value: It would be worthless if it were not used as money.
- In the U.S. economy, money takes the form of currency and various types of bank deposits, such as checking accounts.
- The Federal Reserve, the central bank of the United States, is responsible for regulating the U.S. monetary system. The Fed chair is appointed by the president and confirmed by the Senate every four years. The chair is the head of the Federal Open Market Committee, which meets about every six weeks to consider changes in monetary policy.
- Bank depositors provide resources to banks by depositing their funds into bank accounts. These deposits are part of a bank's liabilities. Bank owners also provide resources (called bank capital) for the bank. Because of leverage (the use of borrowed funds for investment), a small change in the value of a bank's assets can lead to a large change in the value of the bank's capital. To protect depositors, bank regulators require banks to hold a certain minimum amount of capital.
- The Fed controls the money supply primarily through open-market operations: The purchase of government bonds increases the money supply, and the sale of government bonds decreases the money supply. The Fed also has other tools to control the money supply. It can expand the money supply by decreasing the discount rate, increasing its lending to banks, lowering reserve requirements, or decreasing the interest rate on reserves. It can contract the money supply by increasing the discount rate, decreasing its lending to banks, raising reserve requirements, or increasing the interest rate on reserves.
- When individuals deposit money in banks and banks loan out some of these deposits, the quantity of money in the economy increases. Because the banking system influences the money supply in this way, the Fed's control of the money supply is imperfect.
- The Fed has in recent years set monetary policy by choosing a target for the federal funds rate, a short-term interest rate at which banks make loans to one another. As the Fed pursues its target, it adjusts the money supply.

KEY CONCEPTS

money, *p. 210*
medium of exchange, *p. 211*
unit of account, *p. 211*
store of value, *p. 211*
liquidity, *p. 211*
commodity money, *p. 211*
fiat money, *p. 212*
currency, *p. 213*
demand deposits, *p. 213*

Federal Reserve (Fed), *p. 215*
central bank, *p. 215*
money supply, *p. 215*
monetary policy, *p. 215*
reserves, *p. 217*
fractional-reserve banking, *p. 218*
reserve ratio, *p. 218*
money multiplier, *p. 219*
bank capital, *p. 220*

leverage, *p. 221*
leverage ratio, *p. 221*
capital requirement, *p. 221*
open-market operations, *p. 222*
discount rate, *p. 223*
reserve requirements, *p. 224*
federal funds rate, *p. 226*

QUESTIONS FOR REVIEW

1. What distinguishes money from other assets in the economy?

2. What is commodity money? What is fiat money? Which kind do we use?

3. What are demand deposits and why should they be included in the stock of money?

4. Who is responsible for setting monetary policy in the United States? How is this group chosen?

5. If the Fed wants to increase the money supply with open-market operations, what does it do?

6. Why don't banks hold 100-percent reserves? How is the amount of reserves banks hold related to the amount of money the banking system creates?

7. Bank A has a leverage ratio of 10, while Bank B has a leverage ratio of 20. Similar losses on bank loans at the two banks cause the value of their assets to fall by 7 percent. Which bank shows a larger change in bank capital? Does either bank remain solvent? Explain.

8. What is the discount rate? What happens to the money supply when the Fed raises the discount rate?

9. What are reserve requirements? What happens to the money supply when the Fed raises reserve requirements?

10. Why can't the Fed control the money supply perfectly?

PROBLEMS AND APPLICATIONS

1. Which of the following are considered money in the U.S. economy? Which are not? Explain your answers by discussing each of the three functions of money.
    a. a U.S. penny
    b. a Mexican peso
    c. a Picasso painting
    d. a plastic credit card

2. Explain whether each of the following events increases or decreases the money supply.
    a. The Fed buys bonds in open-market operations.
    b. The Fed reduces the reserve requirement.
    c. The Fed increases the interest rate it pays on reserves.
    d. Citibank repays a loan it had previously taken from the Fed.
    e. After a rash of pickpocketing, people decide to hold less currency.
    f. Fearful of bank runs, bankers decide to hold more excess reserves.
    g. The FOMC increases its target for the federal funds rate.

3. Your uncle repays a $100 loan from Tenth National Bank (TNB) by writing a $100 check from his TNB checking account. Use T-accounts to show the effect of this transaction on your uncle and on TNB. Has your uncle's wealth changed? Explain.

4. Beleaguered State Bank (BSB) holds $250 million in deposits and maintains a reserve ratio of 10 percent.
    a. Show a T-account for BSB.
    b. Now suppose that BSB's largest depositor withdraws $10 million in cash from her account and that BSB decides to restore its reserve ratio by reducing the amount of loans outstanding. Show its new T-account.

    c. Explain what effect BSB's action will have on other banks.
    d. Why might it be difficult for BSB to take the action described in part (b)? Discuss another way for BSB to return to its original reserve ratio.

5. You take $100 you had kept under your mattress and deposit it in your bank account. If this $100 stays in the banking system as reserves and if banks hold reserves equal to 10 percent of deposits, by how much does the total amount of deposits in the banking system increase? By how much does the money supply increase?

6. Happy Bank starts with $200 in bank capital. It then accepts $800 in deposits. It keeps 12.5 percent (1/8th) of deposits in reserve. It uses the rest of its assets to make bank loans.
    a. Show the balance sheet of Happy Bank.
    b. What is Happy Bank's leverage ratio?
    c. Suppose that 10 percent of the borrowers from Happy Bank default and that these bank loans become worthless. Show the bank's new balance sheet.
    d. By what percentage do the bank's total assets decline? By what percentage does the bank's capital decline? Which change is larger? Why?

7. The Fed conducts a $10 million open-market purchase of government bonds. If the required reserve ratio is 10 percent, what are the largest and smallest possible increases in the money supply that could result? Explain.

8. Assume that the reserve requirement is 5 percent. All other things being equal, will the money supply expand more if the Fed buys $2,000 worth of bonds or if someone deposits in a bank $2,000 that she had

been hiding in her cookie jar? If one of these actions creates more money than the other, how much more does it create? Support your thinking.

9. Suppose that the reserve requirement for checking deposits is 10 percent and that banks do not hold any excess reserves.
   a. If the Fed sells $1 million of government bonds, what is the effect on the economy's reserves and money supply?
   b. Now suppose that the Fed lowers the reserve requirement to 5 percent but that banks choose to hold another 5 percent of deposits as excess reserves. Why might banks do so? What is the overall change in the money multiplier and the money supply as a result of these actions?

10. Assume that the banking system has total reserves of $100 billion. Assume also that required reserves are 10 percent of checking deposits and that banks hold no excess reserves and households hold no currency.
    a. What is the money multiplier? What is the money supply?
    b. If the Fed now raises required reserves to 20 percent of deposits, what are the change in reserves and the change in the money supply?

11. Assume that the reserve requirement is 20 percent. Also assume that banks do not hold excess reserves and that the public does not hold any cash. The Fed decides that it wants to expand the money supply by $40 million.
    a. If the Fed is using open-market operations, will it buy or sell bonds?
    b. What quantity of bonds does the Fed need to buy or sell to accomplish the goal? Explain your reasoning.

12. The economy of Elmendyn contains 2,000 $1 bills.
    a. If people hold all money as currency, what is the quantity of money?
    b. If people hold all money as demand deposits and banks maintain 100 percent reserves, what is the quantity of money?
    c. If people hold equal amounts of currency and demand deposits and banks maintain 100 percent reserves, what is the quantity of money?
    d. If people hold all money as demand deposits and banks maintain a reserve ratio of 10 percent, what is the quantity of money?
    e. If people hold equal amounts of currency and demand deposits and banks maintain a reserve ratio of 10 percent, what is the quantity of money?

Quick**Quiz** Answers

1. b   2. c   3. a   4. c   5. c   6. d   7. a   8. b   9. b   10. a

Today, if you want to buy an ice-cream cone, you need at least a couple of dollars. But that has not always been the case. In the 1930s, my grandmother ran a sweet shop in Trenton, New Jersey, where she sold ice-cream cones in two sizes. A cone with a small scoop of ice cream cost 3 cents. Hungry customers could buy a large scoop for a nickel.

You may not be surprised at the increase in the price of ice cream. In most modern economies, most prices tend to rise over time. This increase in the overall level of prices is called *inflation*. Earlier in the book, we discussed how economists measure the inflation rate as the percentage change in the consumer price index (CPI), the GDP deflator, or some other index of the overall price level. These price indexes show that, in the United States over the past 80 years, prices have risen on average 3.7 percent per year. Accumulated over so many years, a 3.7 percent annual inflation rate amounts to an eighteenfold increase in the price level.

Money Growth and Inflation

Inflation may seem natural to a person who grew up in the United States during recent decades, but in fact, it is not inevitable. There were long periods in the 19th century during which most prices fell—a phenomenon called *deflation*. The average level of prices in the U.S. economy was 23 percent lower in 1896 than in 1880, and this deflation was a major issue in the presidential election of 1896. Farmers, who had accumulated large debts, suffered when declines in crop prices reduced their incomes and thus their ability to pay off their debts. They advocated government policies to reverse the deflation.

Although inflation has been the norm in more recent U.S. history, there has been substantial variation in the rate at which prices rise. From 2008 to 2018, prices rose at an average rate of 1.5 percent per year. By contrast, in the 1970s, prices rose by 7.8 percent per year. As a result, the price level more than doubled over the decade.

International data show an even broader range of inflation experiences. In 2018, while the inflation rate in the United States was 2.4 percent, it was 1.2 percent in Japan, 4.8 percent in Mexico, 12 percent in Nigeria, 15 percent in Turkey, and 32 percent in Argentina. And even the high inflation rates in Nigeria, Turkey, and Argentina are moderate by some standards. According to the International Monetary Fund, inflation in Venezuela in 2018 reached 1.4 million percent per year, equivalent to an increase in prices of about 2.6 percent *per day*. Such an extraordinarily high rate of inflation is called *hyperinflation*.

What determines whether an economy experiences inflation and, if so, how much? This chapter answers this question by developing the *quantity theory of money*. Chapter 1 summarized this theory as one of the *Ten Principles of Economics*: Prices rise when the government prints too much money. This insight has a long and venerable tradition among economists. The quantity theory was discussed by the famous 18th-century philosopher and economist David Hume and was advocated more recently by the prominent economist Milton Friedman. This theory can explain moderate inflations, such as those we have experienced in the United States, as well as hyperinflations.

After developing a theory of inflation, we turn to a related question: Why is inflation a problem? At first glance, the answer to this question may seem obvious: Inflation is a problem because people don't like it. In the 1970s, when the United States experienced relatively high inflation, opinion polls placed inflation as the most important issue facing the nation. President Ford echoed this sentiment in 1974 when he called inflation "public enemy number one." Ford wore a "WIN" button on his lapel—for Whip Inflation Now. And when President Jimmy Carter ran for reelection in 1980, challenger Ronald Reagan pointed to high inflation as one of the failures of Carter's economic policy.

But what, exactly, are the costs that inflation imposes on a society? The answer may surprise you. Identifying the various costs of inflation is not as straightforward as it first appears. All economists decry hyperinflation, but some argue that the costs of moderate inflation are not nearly as large as the public believes.

12-1 The Classical Theory of Inflation

We begin our study of inflation by developing the quantity theory of money. This theory is often called "classical" because it was developed by some of the earliest economic thinkers. Most economists today rely on this theory to explain the long-run determinants of the price level and the inflation rate.

12-1a The Level of Prices and the Value of Money

Suppose we observe that over some period of time the price of an ice-cream cone rises from a nickel to a dollar. What conclusion should we draw from the fact that people are willing to give up so much more money in exchange for a cone? It is possible that people have come to enjoy ice cream more (perhaps because some chemist has developed a miraculous new flavor). But it is more likely that people's enjoyment of ice cream has stayed roughly the same and that, over time, the money used to buy ice cream has become less valuable. Indeed, the first insight about inflation is that it is more about the value of money than about the value of goods.

This insight helps point the way toward a theory of inflation. When the consumer price index and other measures of the price level rise, commentators are often tempted to look at the many individual prices that make up these price indexes: "The CPI rose by 3 percent last month, led by a 20 percent rise in the price of coffee and a 30 percent rise in the price of heating oil." This approach contains some interesting information about what's happening in the economy, but it misses a key point: Inflation is an economy-wide phenomenon that concerns, first and foremost, the value of the economy's medium of exchange.

The economy's overall price level can be viewed in two ways. So far, we have viewed the price level as the price of a basket of goods and services. When the price level rises, people have to pay more for the goods and services they buy. Alternatively, we can view the price level as a measure of the value of money. A rise in the price level means a lower value of money because each dollar in your wallet now buys a smaller quantity of goods and services.

It may help to express these ideas mathematically. Suppose P is the price level as measured by the consumer price index or the GDP deflator. Then P measures the number of dollars needed to buy a basket of goods and services. Now turn this idea around: The quantity of goods and services that can be bought with \$1 equals $1/P$. In other words, if P is the price of goods and services measured in terms of money, $1/P$ is the value of money measured in terms of goods and services.

"So what's it going to be? The same size as last year or the same price as last year?"

This math is simplest to understand in an economy that produces only a single good—say, ice-cream cones. In that case, P would be the price of a cone. When the price of a cone (P) is \$2, then the value of a dollar ($1/P$) is half a cone. When the price (P) rises to \$3, the value of a dollar ($1/P$) falls to a third of a cone. The actual economy produces thousands of goods and services, so in practice we use a price index rather than the price of a single good. But the logic remains the same: When the overall price level rises, the value of money falls.

12-1b Money Supply, Money Demand, and Monetary Equilibrium

What determines the value of money? The answer to this question, like the answer to many questions in economics, is supply and demand. Just as the supply and demand for bananas determines the price of bananas, the supply and demand for money determines the value of money. Thus, our next step in developing the quantity theory of money is to consider the determinants of money supply and money demand.

First consider money supply. In the preceding chapter, we discussed how the Federal Reserve, together with the banking system, determines the supply of money. When the Fed sells bonds in open-market operations, it receives dollars in exchange and contracts the money supply. When the Fed buys government bonds, it pays out dollars and expands the money supply. In addition, if any of these dollars are deposited in banks, which hold some as reserves and loan out the rest, the money multiplier swings into action, and these open-market operations can have an even greater effect on the money supply. For our purposes in this chapter, we ignore the complications introduced by the banking system and simply take the quantity of money supplied as a policy variable that the Fed controls.

Now consider money demand. Most fundamentally, the demand for money reflects how much wealth people want to hold in liquid form. Many factors influence the quantity of money demanded. The amount of currency that people hold in their wallets, for instance, depends on how much they rely on credit cards and how easily they can find an automatic teller machine. And as we will emphasize in Chapter 16, the quantity of money demanded depends on the interest rate that a person could earn by using the money to buy an interest-bearing bond rather than leaving it in his wallet or low-interest checking account.

Although many variables affect the demand for money, one variable is particularly important: the average level of prices in the economy. People hold money because it is the medium of exchange. Unlike other assets, such as bonds or stocks, people can use money to buy the goods and services on their shopping lists. How much money they choose to hold for this purpose depends on the prices of those goods and services. The higher prices are, the more money the typical transaction requires, and the more money people will choose to hold in their wallets and checking accounts. That is, a higher price level (a lower value of money) increases the quantity of money demanded.

What ensures that the quantity of money the Fed supplies balances the quantity of money people demand? The answer depends on the time horizon being considered. Later in this book, we examine the short-run answer and learn that interest rates play a key role. The long-run answer, however, is much simpler. *In the long run, money supply and money demand are brought into equilibrium by the overall level of prices.* If the price level is above the equilibrium level, people will want to hold more money than the Fed has created, so the price level must fall to balance supply and demand. If the price level is below the equilibrium level, people will want to hold less money than the Fed has created, and the price level must rise to balance supply and demand. At the equilibrium price level, the quantity of money that people want to hold exactly balances the quantity of money supplied by the Fed.

Figure 1 illustrates these ideas. The horizontal axis of this graph shows the quantity of money. The left vertical axis shows the value of money $1/P$, and the right vertical axis shows the price level P. Notice that the price-level axis on the right is inverted: A low price level is shown near the top of this axis, and a high price level is shown near the bottom. This inverted axis illustrates that when the value of money is high (as shown near the top of the left axis), the price level is low (as shown near the top of the right axis).

The two curves in this figure are the supply and demand curves for money. The supply curve is vertical because the Fed has fixed the quantity of money available. The demand curve for money slopes downward, indicating that when the value

The horizontal axis shows the quantity of money. The left vertical axis shows the value of money, and the right vertical axis shows the price level. The supply curve for money is vertical because the quantity of money supplied is fixed by the Fed. The demand curve for money slopes downward because people want to hold a larger quantity of money when each dollar buys less. At the equilibrium, point A, the value of money (on the left axis) and the price level (on the right axis) have adjusted to bring the quantity of money supplied and the quantity of money demanded into balance.

FIGURE 1

How the Supply and Demand for Money Determine the Equilibrium Price Level

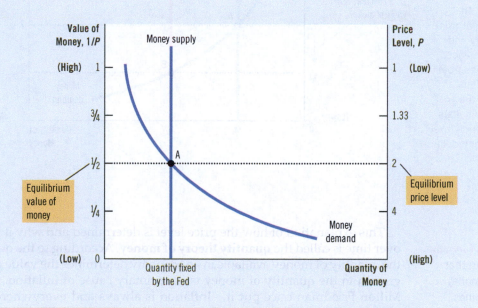

of money is low (and the price level is high), people demand a larger quantity of money to buy goods and services. At the equilibrium, shown in the figure as point A, the quantity of money demanded balances the quantity of money supplied. This equilibrium of money supply and money demand determines the value of money and the price level.

12-1c The Effects of a Monetary Injection

Let's now consider the effects of a change in monetary policy. To do so, imagine that the economy is in equilibrium and then, suddenly, the Fed doubles the supply of money by printing some dollar bills and dropping them around the country from helicopters. (Or, less dramatically and more realistically, the Fed could inject money into the economy by buying some government bonds from the public in open-market operations.) What happens after such a monetary injection? How does the new equilibrium compare with the old one?

Figure 2 shows what happens. The monetary injection shifts the supply curve to the right from MS_1 to MS_2, and the equilibrium moves from point A to point B. As a result, the value of money (shown on the left axis) decreases from ½ to ¼, and the equilibrium price level (shown on the right axis) increases from 2 to 4. In other words, when an increase in the money supply makes dollars more plentiful, the result is an increase in the price level that makes each dollar less valuable.

FIGURE 2

An Increase in the Money Supply

When the Fed increases the supply of money, the money supply curve shifts from MS_1 to MS_2. The value of money (on the left axis) and the price level (on the right axis) adjust to bring supply and demand back into balance. The equilibrium moves from point A to point B. Thus, when an increase in the money supply makes dollars more plentiful, the price level increases, making each dollar less valuable.

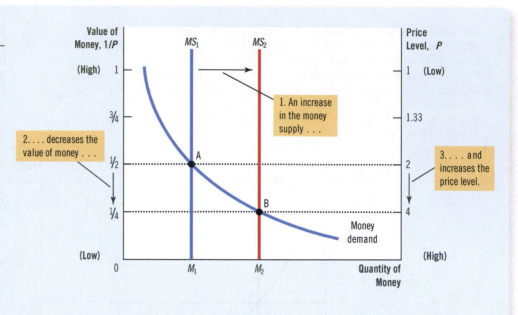

quantity theory of money
a theory asserting that the quantity of money available determines the price level and that the growth rate in the quantity of money available determines the inflation rate

This explanation of how the price level is determined and why it might change over time is called the **quantity theory of money**. According to the quantity theory, the quantity of money available in an economy determines the value of money, and growth in the quantity of money is the primary cause of inflation. As economist Milton Friedman once put it, "Inflation is always and everywhere a monetary phenomenon."

12-1d A Brief Look at the Adjustment Process

So far, we have compared the old equilibrium and the new equilibrium after an injection of money. How does the economy move from the old to the new equilibrium? A complete answer to this question requires an understanding of short-run economic fluctuations, which we examine later in this book. Here, we briefly consider the adjustment process that occurs after a change in the money supply.

The immediate effect of a monetary injection is to create an excess supply of money. Before the injection, the economy was in equilibrium (point A in Figure 2). At the prevailing price level, people had exactly as much money as they wanted. But after the helicopters drop the new money and people pick it up off the streets, people have more dollars in their wallets than they want. At the prevailing price level, the quantity of money supplied now exceeds the quantity demanded.

People try to get rid of this excess supply of money in various ways. They might use it to buy goods and services. Or they might use this excess money to make loans to others by buying bonds or by depositing the money in a bank savings account. These loans allow other people to buy goods and services. In either case, the injection of money increases the demand for goods and services.

The economy's ability to supply goods and services, however, has not changed. As we saw in the chapter on production and growth, the economy's output of goods and services is determined by the available labor, physical capital, human capital, natural resources, and technological knowledge. None of these is altered by the injection of money.

Thus, the greater demand for goods and services causes the prices of goods and services to increase. The increase in the price level, in turn, increases the quantity of money demanded because people are using more dollars for every transaction. Eventually, the economy reaches a new equilibrium (point B in Figure 2) at which the quantity of money demanded again equals the quantity of money supplied. In this way, the overall price level for goods and services adjusts to bring money supply and money demand into balance.

12-1e The Classical Dichotomy and Monetary Neutrality

We have seen how changes in the money supply lead to changes in the average level of prices of goods and services. How do monetary changes affect other variables, such as production, employment, real wages, and real interest rates? This question has long intrigued economists, including David Hume in the 18th century.

Hume and his contemporaries suggested that economic variables should be divided into two groups. The first group consists of **nominal variables**—variables measured in monetary units. The second group consists of **real variables**—variables measured in physical units. For example, the income of corn farmers is a nominal variable because it is measured in dollars, whereas the quantity of corn they produce is a real variable because it is measured in bushels. Nominal GDP is a nominal variable because it measures the dollar value of the economy's output of goods and services; real GDP is a real variable because it measures the total quantity of goods and services produced and is not influenced by the current prices of those goods and services. The separation of real and nominal variables is now called the **classical dichotomy**. (A *dichotomy* is a division into two groups, and *classical* refers to the earlier economic thinkers.)

Applying the classical dichotomy is tricky when we turn to prices. Most prices are quoted in units of money and, therefore, are nominal variables. When we say that the price of corn is $2 a bushel or that the price of wheat is $1 a bushel, both prices are nominal variables. But what about a *relative* price—the price of one thing in terms of another? In our example, we could say that the price of a bushel of corn is 2 bushels of wheat. This relative price is not measured in terms of money. When comparing the prices of any two goods, the dollar signs cancel, and the resulting number is measured in physical units. Thus, while dollar prices are nominal variables, relative prices are real variables.

This lesson has many applications. For instance, the real wage (the dollar wage adjusted for inflation) is a real variable because it measures the rate at which people exchange goods and services for a unit of labor. Similarly, the real interest rate (the nominal interest rate adjusted for inflation) is a real variable because it measures the rate at which people exchange goods and services today for goods and services in the future.

Why separate variables into these groups? The classical dichotomy is useful because different forces influence real and nominal variables. According to classical analysis, nominal variables are influenced by developments in the economy's monetary system, whereas real variables are not.

This idea was implicit in our discussion of the real economy in the long run. In previous chapters, we examined the determinants of real GDP, saving, investment, real interest rates, and unemployment without mentioning the existence of money. In that analysis, the economy's production of goods and services depends on technology and factor supplies, the real interest rate balances the supply and demand for loanable funds, the real wage balances the supply and demand for

nominal variables
variables measured in monetary units

real variables
variables measured in physical units

classical dichotomy
the theoretical separation of nominal variables and real variables

labor, and unemployment results when the real wage is above the equilibrium level. These conclusions have nothing to do with the quantity of money supplied.

Changes in the supply of money, according to classical analysis, affect nominal variables but not real ones. When the central bank doubles the money supply, the price level doubles, the dollar wage doubles, and all other dollar values double. Real variables, such as production, employment, real wages, and real interest rates, are unchanged. The irrelevance of monetary changes to real variables is called **monetary neutrality**.

monetary neutrality
the proposition that changes in the money supply do not affect real variables

An analogy helps explain monetary neutrality. As the unit of account, money is the yardstick we use to measure economic transactions. When a central bank doubles the money supply, all prices double, and the value of the unit of account falls by half. A similar change would occur if the government were to reduce the length of the yard from 36 to 18 inches: With the new, shorter yardstick, all *measured* distances (nominal variables) would double, but the *actual* distances (real variables) would remain the same. The dollar, like the yard, is merely a unit of measurement, so a change in its value should not have real effects.

Is monetary neutrality realistic? Not completely. A change in the length of the yard from 36 to 18 inches would not matter in the long run, but in the short run, it would lead to confusion and mistakes. Similarly, most economists today believe that over short periods of time—within the span of a year or two—monetary changes affect real variables. Hume himself also doubted that monetary neutrality would apply in the short run. (We will study short-run non-neutrality later in the book, and this topic will help explain why the Fed changes the money supply over time.)

Yet classical analysis is right about the economy in the long run. Over the course of a decade, monetary changes have significant effects on nominal variables (such as the price level) but only negligible effects on real variables (such as real GDP). When studying long-run changes in the economy, the neutrality of money offers a good description of how the world works.

12-1f Velocity and the Quantity Equation

We can obtain another perspective on the quantity theory of money by considering the following question: How many times per year is the typical dollar bill used to pay for a newly produced good or service? The answer to this question is given by a variable called the **velocity of money**. In physics, the term *velocity* refers to the speed at which an object travels. In economics, the velocity of money refers to the speed at which the typical dollar bill travels around the economy from wallet to wallet.

velocity of money
the rate at which money changes hands

To calculate the velocity of money, we divide the nominal value of output (nominal GDP) by the quantity of money. If P is the price level (the GDP deflator), Y the quantity of output (real GDP), and M the quantity of money, then velocity is

$$V = (P \times Y)/M.$$

To see why this makes sense, imagine a simple economy that produces only pizza. Suppose that the economy produces 100 pizzas in a year, that a pizza sells for $10, and that the quantity of money in the economy is $50. Then the velocity of money is

$$V = (\$10 \times 100)/\$50$$
$$= 20.$$

In this economy, people spend a total of $1,000 per year on pizza. For this $1,000 of spending to take place with only $50 of money, each dollar bill must change hands on average 20 times per year.

With slight algebraic rearrangement, this equation can be rewritten as

$$M \times V = P \times Y.$$

This equation states that the quantity of money (M) times the velocity of money (V) equals the price of output (P) times the amount of output (Y). It is called the **quantity equation** because it relates the quantity of money (M) to the nominal value of output ($P \times Y$). The quantity equation shows that an increase in the quantity of money in an economy must be reflected in one of the other three variables: The price level must rise, the quantity of output must rise, or the velocity of money must fall.

In many cases, it turns out that the velocity of money is relatively stable. For example, Figure 3 shows nominal GDP, the quantity of money (as measured by M2), and the velocity of money for the U.S. economy since 1960. During this period, the money supply and nominal GDP both increased about fortyfold. By contrast, the velocity of money, although not exactly constant, has not changed dramatically. Thus, for some purposes, the assumption of constant velocity is a good approximation.

quantity equation
the equation $M \times V = P \times Y$, which relates the quantity of money, the velocity of money, and the dollar value of the economy's output of goods and services

---

This figure shows the nominal value of output as measured by nominal GDP, the quantity of money as measured by M2, and the velocity of money as measured by their ratio. For comparability, all three series have been scaled to equal 100 in 1960. Notice that nominal GDP and the quantity of money have grown dramatically over this period, while velocity has been relatively stable.

Source: U.S. Department of Commerce; Federal Reserve Board.

FIGURE 3

Nominal GDP, the Quantity of Money, and the Velocity of Money

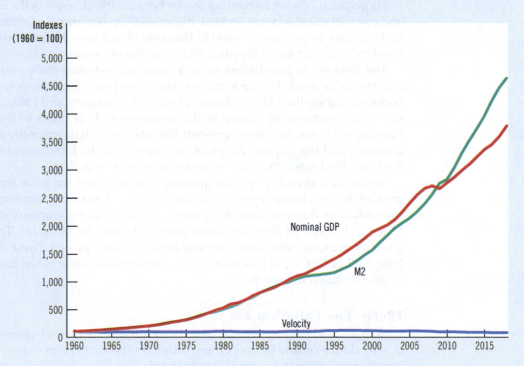

We now have all the elements necessary to explain the equilibrium price level and inflation rate. They are as follows:

1. The velocity of money is relatively stable over time.
2. Because velocity is stable, when the central bank changes the quantity of money (M), it causes proportionate changes in the nominal value of output ($P \times Y$).
3. The economy's output of goods and services (Y) is determined by factor supplies (labor, physical capital, human capital, and natural resources) and the available production technology. In particular, since money is neutral, money does not affect output.
4. Because output (Y) is fixed by factor supplies and technology, when the central bank alters the money supply (M) and induces a proportional change in the nominal value of output ($P \times Y$), this change is reflected in a change in the price level (P).
5. Therefore, when the central bank increases the money supply rapidly, the result is a high rate of inflation.

These five points are the essence of the quantity theory of money.

MONEY AND PRICES DURING FOUR HYPERINFLATIONS

Although earthquakes can wreak havoc on a society, they have the beneficial by-product of providing much useful data for seismologists. These data can shed light on alternative theories and, thereby, help society predict and deal with future threats. Similarly, hyperinflations offer monetary economists a natural experiment they can use to study the effects of money on the economy.

Hyperinflations are interesting in part because the changes in the money supply and price level are so large. Indeed, hyperinflation is generally defined as inflation that exceeds 50 percent *per month*. This rate of inflation amounts to more than a hundredfold increase in the price level over the course of a year.

The data on hyperinflation show a clear link between the quantity of money and the price level. Figure 4 graphs data from four classic hyperinflations that occurred during the 1920s in Austria, Hungary, Germany, and Poland. Each graph shows the quantity of money in the economy and an index of the price level. The slope of the money line represents the rate at which the quantity of money was growing, and the slope of the price line represents the inflation rate. The steeper the lines, the higher the rates of money growth or inflation.

Notice that in each graph the quantity of money and the price level are almost parallel. In each instance, growth in the quantity of money is moderate at first and so is inflation. But over time, the quantity of money in the economy starts growing faster and faster. At about the same time, inflation also takes off. Then when the quantity of money stabilizes, the price level stabilizes as well. These episodes illustrate well one of the *Ten Principles of Economics*: Prices rise when the government prints too much money. ●

12-1g The Inflation Tax

If inflation is so easy to explain, why do countries experience hyperinflation? That is, why do the central banks of these countries choose to print so much money that its value is certain to fall rapidly over time?

This figure shows the quantity of money and the price level during four hyperinflations. (Note that because these variables are graphed on *logarithmic* scales, equal vertical distances on the graph represent equal *percentage* changes in the variable.) In each case, the quantity of money and the price level move closely together. The strong association between these two variables is consistent with the quantity theory of money, which states that growth in the money supply is the primary cause of inflation.

Source: Adapted from Thomas J. Sargent, "The End of Four Big Inflations," in Robert Hall, ed., *Inflation* (Chicago: University of Chicago Press, 1983), pp. 41–93.

FIGURE 4

Money and Prices during Four Hyperinflations

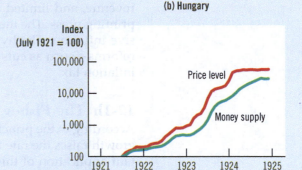

The answer is that the governments of these countries are using money creation as a way to pay for their spending. When the government wants to build roads, pay salaries to its soldiers, or give transfer payments to the poor or elderly, it first has to raise the necessary funds. Normally, the government does this by levying taxes, such as income and sales taxes, and by borrowing from the public by selling government bonds. Yet the government can also pay for spending simply by printing the money it needs.

When the government raises revenue by printing money, it is said to levy an **inflation tax**. The inflation tax is not exactly like other taxes, however, because no one receives a bill from the government for this tax. Instead, the inflation tax is subtler. When the government prints money, the price level rises, and the dollars in your wallet become less valuable. Thus, *the inflation tax is like a tax on everyone who holds money.*

The importance of the inflation tax varies from country to country and over time. In the United States in recent years, the inflation tax has been a trivial source of revenue: It has accounted for less than 3 percent of government

inflation tax
the revenue the government raises by creating money

revenue. During the 1770s, however, the Continental Congress of the fledgling United States relied heavily on the inflation tax to pay for military spending. Because the new government had a limited ability to raise funds through regular taxes or borrowing, printing dollars was the easiest way to pay the American soldiers. As the quantity theory predicts, the result was a high rate of inflation: Prices measured in terms of the continental dollar rose more than a hundredfold over a few years.

Almost all hyperinflations follow the same pattern as the hyperinflation during the American Revolution. The government has high spending, inadequate tax revenue, and limited ability to borrow. To pay for its spending, it turns to the printing press. The massive increases in the quantity of money then lead to massive inflation. The hyperinflation ends when the government institutes fiscal reforms—such as cuts in government spending—that eliminate the need for the inflation tax.

12-1h The Fisher Effect

According to the principle of monetary neutrality, an increase in the rate of money growth raises the rate of inflation but does not affect any real variable. An important application of this principle concerns the effect of money on interest rates. Interest rates are important variables for macroeconomists to understand because they link the economy of the present and the economy of the future through their effects on saving and investment.

To understand the relationship among money, inflation, and interest rates, recall the distinction between the nominal interest rate and the real interest rate. The *nominal interest rate* is the interest rate you hear about at your bank. If you have a savings account, for instance, the nominal interest rate tells you how fast the number of dollars in your account will rise over time. The *real interest rate* corrects the nominal interest rate for the effect of inflation to tell you how fast the purchasing power of your savings account will rise over time. The real interest rate is the nominal interest rate minus the inflation rate:

$$\text{Real interest rate} = \text{Nominal interest rate} - \text{Inflation rate.}$$

For example, if the bank posts a nominal interest rate of 7 percent per year and the inflation rate is 3 percent per year, then the real value of the deposits grows by 4 percent per year.

We can rewrite this equation to show that the nominal interest rate is the sum of the real interest rate and the inflation rate:

$$\text{Nominal interest rate} = \text{Real interest rate} + \text{Inflation rate.}$$

This way of looking at the nominal interest rate is useful because different forces determine each of the two terms on the right side of this equation. As we discussed earlier in the book, the supply and demand for loanable funds determine the real interest rate. And according to the quantity theory of money, growth in the money supply determines the inflation rate.

Let's now consider how growth in the money supply affects interest rates. In the long run over which money is neutral, a change in money growth should not affect the real interest rate. The real interest rate is, after all, a real variable. For the real interest rate to remain unchanged, a change in the inflation rate must result in a one-for-one change in the nominal interest rate. Thus, *when the Fed increases the rate of money growth, the long-run result is both a higher inflation rate and a higher nominal interest rate.* This adjustment of the nominal interest rate to the inflation rate is called the **Fisher effect**, after Irving Fisher (1867–1947), the economist who first studied it.

Keep in mind that our analysis of the Fisher effect has maintained a long-run perspective. The Fisher effect need not hold in the short run because inflation may be unanticipated. A nominal interest rate is a payment on a loan, and it is typically set when the loan is first made. If a jump in inflation catches the borrower and lender by surprise, the nominal interest rate they agreed on will fail to reflect the higher inflation. But if inflation remains high, people will eventually come to expect it, and the nominal interest rates set in loan agreements will reflect this expectation. To be precise, therefore, the Fisher effect states that the nominal interest rate adjusts to expected inflation. Expected inflation moves with actual inflation in the long run but not necessarily in the short run.

The Fisher effect is crucial for understanding changes over time in the nominal interest rate. Figure 5 shows the nominal interest rate and the inflation rate in the U.S. economy since 1960. The close association between these two variables is clear. The nominal interest rate rose from the early 1960s through the 1970s because inflation was also rising during this time. Similarly, the nominal interest rate fell from the early 1980s through the 1990s because the Fed got inflation under control. In recent years, both the nominal interest rate and the inflation rate have been low by historical standards.

Fisher effect
the one-for-one adjustment of the nominal interest rate to the inflation rate

This figure uses annual data since 1960 to show the nominal interest rate on three-month Treasury bills and the inflation rate as measured by the consumer price index. The close association between these two variables provides evidence for the Fisher effect: When the inflation rate rises, so does the nominal interest rate.

Source: U.S. Department of Treasury; U.S. Department of Labor.

FIGURE 5

The Nominal Interest Rate and the Inflation Rate

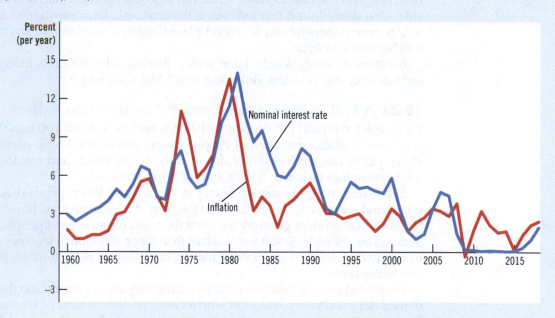

1. The classical principle of monetary neutrality states that changes in the money supply do not influence _____ variables, and it is thought most applicable in the _____ run.
   a. nominal; short
   b. nominal; long
   c. real; short
   d. real; long

2. If nominal GDP is $400, real GDP is $200, and the money supply is $100, then
   a. the price level is ½, and velocity is 2.
   b. the price level is ½, and velocity is 4.
   c. the price level is 2, and velocity is 2.
   d. the price level is 2, and velocity is 4.

3. According to the quantity theory of money, which variable in the quantity equation is most stable over long periods of time?
   a. money
   b. velocity
   c. price level
   d. output

4. Hyperinflation occurs when the government runs a large budget _____, which the central bank finances with a substantial monetary _____.
   a. deficit; contraction
   b. deficit; expansion
   c. surplus; contraction
   d. surplus; expansion

5. According to the quantity theory of money and the Fisher effect, if the central bank increases the rate of money growth, then
   a. inflation and the nominal interest rate both increase.
   b. inflation and the real interest rate both increase.
   c. the nominal interest rate and the real interest rate both increase.
   d. inflation, the real interest rate, and the nominal interest rate all increase.

Answers at end of chapter.

12-2 The Costs of Inflation

In the late 1970s, when the U.S. inflation rate reached about 10 percent per year, inflation dominated debates over economic policy. And even though inflation has been low over the past 20 years, it remains a closely watched macroeconomic variable. One study found that *inflation* is the economic term mentioned most often in U.S. newspapers (ahead of second-place finisher *unemployment* and third-place finisher *productivity*).

Inflation is closely watched and widely discussed because it is thought to be a serious economic problem. But is that true? And if so, why?

12-2a A Fall in Purchasing Power? The Inflation Fallacy

If you ask the typical person why inflation is bad, he will tell you that the answer is obvious: Inflation robs him of the purchasing power of his hard-earned dollars. When prices rise, each dollar of income buys fewer goods and services. Thus, it might seem that inflation directly lowers living standards.

Yet further thought reveals a fallacy in this answer. When prices rise, buyers of goods and services pay more for what they buy. At the same time, however, sellers of goods and services get more for what they sell. Because most people earn their incomes by selling their services, such as their labor, inflation in incomes goes hand in hand with inflation in prices. Thus, *inflation does not in itself reduce people's real purchasing power.*

People believe the inflation fallacy because they do not appreciate the principle of monetary neutrality. A worker who receives an annual raise of 10 percent tends to view that raise as a reward for his own talent and effort. When an inflation rate of 6 percent reduces the real value of that raise to only 4 percent, the worker might feel that he has been cheated of what is rightfully his due. In fact, as we discussed in the chapter on production and growth, real incomes are determined by real variables, such as physical capital, human capital, natural resources, and the available production technology. Nominal incomes are determined by a combination of those factors and the overall price level. If the Fed lowered the inflation rate from 6 percent to zero, our worker's annual raise would fall from 10 percent to 4 percent. He might feel less robbed by inflation, but his real income would not rise more quickly.

If nominal incomes tend to keep pace with rising prices, why then is inflation a problem? It turns out that there is no single answer to this question. Instead, economists have identified several costs of inflation. Each of these costs shows some way in which persistent growth in the money supply does, in fact, have some adverse effect on real variables.

12-2b Shoeleather Costs

As we have discussed, inflation is like a tax on the holders of money. The tax itself is not a cost to society: It is only a transfer of resources from households to the government. Yet most taxes give people an incentive to alter their behavior to avoid paying the tax, and this distortion of incentives causes deadweight losses for society as a whole. Like other taxes, the inflation tax also causes deadweight losses because people waste scarce resources trying to avoid it.

How can a person avoid paying the inflation tax? Because inflation erodes the real value of the money in your wallet, you can avoid the inflation tax by holding less money. One way to do this is to go to the bank more often. For example, rather than withdrawing $200 every four weeks, you might withdraw $50 once a week. By making more frequent trips to the bank, you can keep more of your wealth in your interest-bearing savings account and less in your wallet, where inflation erodes its value.

The cost of reducing your money holdings is called the **shoeleather cost** of inflation because making more frequent trips to the bank causes your shoes to wear out more quickly. Of course, this term is not to be taken literally: The actual cost of reducing your money holdings is not the wear and tear on your shoes but the time and convenience you must sacrifice to keep less money on hand than you would if there were no inflation.

shoeleather costs
the resources wasted when inflation encourages people to reduce their money holdings

The shoeleather costs of inflation may seem trivial. Indeed, they are in the U.S. economy, which has had only moderate inflation in recent years. But this cost is magnified in countries experiencing hyperinflation. Here is a description of one person's experience in Bolivia during its hyperinflation (as reported in the August 13, 1985, issue of *The Wall Street Journal*):

> When Edgar Miranda gets his monthly teacher's pay of 25 million pesos, he hasn't a moment to lose. Every hour, pesos drop in value. So, while his wife rushes to market to lay in a month's supply of rice and noodles, he is off with the rest of the pesos to change them into black-market dollars.
>
> Mr. Miranda is practicing the First Rule of Survival amid the most out-of-control inflation in the world today. Bolivia is a case study of how runaway inflation undermines a society. Price increases are so huge that the figures build up almost beyond comprehension. In one six-month period, for example, prices soared at an annual rate of 38,000 percent. By official count, however, last year's inflation reached 2,000 percent, and this year's is expected to hit 8,000 percent—though other estimates range many times higher. In any event,

Bolivia's rate dwarfs Israel's 370 percent and Argentina's 1,100 percent—two other cases of severe inflation.

It is easier to comprehend what happens to the thirty-eight-year-old Mr. Miranda's pay if he doesn't quickly change it into dollars. The day he was paid 25 million pesos, a dollar cost 500,000 pesos. So he received $50. Just days later, with the rate at 900,000 pesos, he would have received $27.

As this story shows, the shoeleather costs of inflation can be large. With the high inflation rate, Mr. Miranda does not have the luxury of holding the local money as a store of value. Instead, he is forced to convert his pesos quickly into goods or into U.S. dollars, which offer a more stable store of value. The time and effort that Mr. Miranda expends to reduce his money holdings are wasted resources. If the monetary authority pursued a low-inflation policy, Mr. Miranda would be happy to hold pesos, and he could put his time and effort to more productive use. In fact, shortly after this article was written, the inflation rate in Bolivia fell substantially as a result of more restrictive monetary policy.

12-2c Menu Costs

Most firms do not change the prices of their products every day. Instead, firms often announce prices and leave them unchanged for weeks, months, or even years. One survey found that the typical U.S. firm changes its prices about once a year.

menu costs
the costs of changing prices

Firms change prices infrequently because there are costs to changing prices. Costs of price adjustment are called **menu costs**, a term derived from a restaurant's cost of printing a new menu. Menu costs include the costs of deciding on new prices, printing new price lists and catalogs, sending these new price lists and catalogs to dealers and customers, advertising the new prices, and even dealing with customer annoyance over price changes.

Inflation increases the menu costs that firms must bear. In the low-inflation environment of the current U.S. economy, annual price adjustment is an appropriate business strategy for many firms. But when high inflation makes firms' costs rise rapidly, annual price adjustment is impractical. During hyperinflations, for example, firms must change their prices daily or even more often just to keep up with all the other prices in the economy.

12-2d Relative-Price Variability and the Misallocation of Resources

Suppose that the Eatabit Eatery prints a new menu with new prices every January and then leaves its prices unchanged for the rest of the year. If there is no inflation, Eatabit's relative prices—the prices of its meals compared with other prices in the economy—would be constant over the course of the year. By contrast, if the inflation rate is 12 percent per year, Eatabit's relative prices will automatically fall by 1 percent each month. The restaurant's relative prices will be highest in the early months of the year, just after it has printed a new menu, and lowest in the later months. And the higher the inflation rate, the greater this swing in relative prices will be. Thus, because prices change only once in a while, inflation causes relative prices to vary more than they otherwise would.

Why does this matter? The reason is that market economies rely on relative prices to allocate scarce resources. Consumers decide what to buy by comparing the quality and prices of various goods and services. Through these decisions, they determine how the scarce factors of production are allocated among industries and firms. When inflation distorts relative prices, consumer decisions are distorted and markets are less able to allocate resources to their best use.

12-2e Inflation-Induced Tax Distortions

Almost all taxes distort incentives, cause people to alter their behavior, and lead to a less efficient allocation of the economy's resources. Many taxes, however, become even more problematic in the presence of inflation. The reason is that lawmakers often fail to take inflation into account when writing the tax laws. Economists who have studied the tax code conclude that inflation tends to raise the tax burden on income earned from savings.

One example of how inflation discourages saving is the tax treatment of *capital gains*—the profits made by selling an asset for more than its purchase price. Suppose that in 1974 you used some of your savings to buy stock in IBM for $10 and that in 2019 you sold the stock for $140. According to the tax law, you have earned a capital gain of $130, which you must include in your income when computing how much income tax you owe. But because the overall price level increased fivefold from 1974 to 2019, the $10 you invested in 1974 is equivalent (in terms of purchasing power) to $50 in 2019. So when you sell your stock for $140, you have a real gain (an increase in purchasing power) of only $90 ($140 − $50). The tax code, however, ignores inflation and taxes you on a gain of $130. Thus, inflation exaggerates the size of capital gains and inadvertently increases the tax burden on this type of income.

Another example is the tax treatment of interest income. The income tax treats the *nominal* interest earned on savings as income, even though part of the nominal interest rate merely compensates for inflation. To see the effects of this policy, consider the numerical example in Table 1. The table compares two economies, both of which tax interest income at a rate of 25 percent. In Economy A, inflation is zero and the nominal and real interest rates are both 4 percent. In this case, the 25 percent tax on interest income reduces the real interest rate from 4 percent to 3 percent. In Economy B, the real interest rate is again 4 percent but the inflation rate is 8 percent. As a result of the Fisher effect, the nominal interest rate is 12 percent. Because the income tax treats this entire 12 percent interest as income, the 25 percent tax leaves an after-tax nominal interest rate of only 9 percent and, after correcting for 8 percent inflation, an after-tax real interest rate of only 1 percent. In this case, the 25 percent tax on interest income reduces the real interest rate from

	Economy A (zero inflation)	Economy B (high inflation)
Real interest rate	4%	4%
Inflation rate	0	8
Nominal interest rate (real interest rate + inflation rate)	4	12
Reduced interest due to 25 percent tax (0.25 × nominal interest rate)	1	3
After-tax nominal interest rate (0.75 × nominal interest rate)	3	9
After-tax real interest rate (after-tax nominal interest rate − inflation rate)	3	1

TABLE 1

How Inflation Raises the Tax Burden on Saving

In the presence of zero inflation, a 25 percent tax on interest income reduces the real interest rate from 4 percent to 3 percent. In the presence of 8 percent inflation, the same tax reduces the real interest rate from 4 percent to 1 percent.

4 percent to 1 percent. Because the after-tax real interest rate provides the incentive to save, saving is much less attractive in the economy with inflation (Economy B) than in the economy with stable prices (Economy A).

The taxes on nominal capital gains and on nominal interest income are two examples of how the tax code interacts with inflation. There are many others. Because of these inflation-induced tax changes, higher inflation tends to discourage people from saving. Recall that the economy's saving provides the resources for investment, which in turn is a key ingredient to long-run economic growth. Thus, when inflation raises the tax burden on saving, it tends to depress the economy's long-run growth rate. There is, however, no consensus among economists about the size of this effect.

One solution to this problem, other than eliminating inflation, is to index the tax system. That is, the tax laws could be revised to account for the effects of inflation. In the case of capital gains, for example, the tax code could adjust the purchase price using a price index and assess the tax only on the real gain. In the case of interest income, the government could tax only real interest income by excluding that portion of the interest income that merely compensates for inflation. To some extent, the tax laws have moved in the direction of indexation. For example, the income levels at which income tax rates change are adjusted automatically each year based on changes in the consumer price index. Yet many other aspects of the tax laws—such as the tax treatment of capital gains and interest income—are not indexed.

In an ideal world, the tax laws would be written so that inflation would not alter anyone's real tax liability. In the real world, however, tax laws are far from perfect. More complete indexation would probably be desirable, but it would further complicate a tax code that many people already consider onerous.

12-2f Confusion and Inconvenience

Imagine that we took a poll and asked people the following question: "This year the yard is 36 inches. How long do you think it should be next year?" Assuming we could get people to take us seriously, they would tell us that the yard should stay the same length—36 inches. Anything else would just complicate life needlessly.

What does this finding have to do with inflation? Recall that money, as the economy's unit of account, is what we use to quote prices and record debts. In other words, money is the yardstick with which we measure economic transactions. The job of the Federal Reserve is a bit like the job of the Bureau of Standards—to ensure the reliability of a commonly used unit of measurement. When the Fed increases the money supply and creates inflation, it erodes the real value of the unit of account.

It is difficult to judge the costs of the confusion and inconvenience that arise from inflation. Earlier, we discussed how the tax code incorrectly measures real incomes in the presence of inflation. Similarly, accountants incorrectly measure firms' earnings when prices are rising over time. Because inflation causes dollars at different times to have different real values, computing a firm's profit—the difference between its revenue and costs—is more complicated in an economy with inflation. Therefore, to some extent, inflation makes investors less able to sort successful firms from unsuccessful firms, impeding financial markets in their role of allocating the economy's saving among alternative types of investment.

12-2g A Special Cost of Unexpected Inflation: Arbitrary Redistributions of Wealth

So far, the costs of inflation we have discussed occur even if inflation is steady and predictable. Inflation has another cost, however, when it comes as a surprise. Unexpected inflation redistributes wealth among the population in a way that has nothing to do with either merit or need. These redistributions occur because many loans in the economy are specified in terms of the unit of account—money.

Consider an example. Suppose that Sophie Student takes out a $20,000 loan at a 7 percent interest rate from Bigbank to attend college. In 10 years, the loan will come due. After her debt has compounded for 10 years at 7 percent, Sophie will owe Bigbank $40,000. The real value of this debt will depend on inflation over the decade. If Sophie is lucky, the economy will have a hyperinflation. In this case, wages and prices will rise so high that Sophie will be able to pay the $40,000 debt out of pocket change. By contrast, if the economy goes through a major deflation, then wages and prices will fall, and Sophie will find the $40,000 debt a greater burden than she anticipated.

This example shows that unexpected changes in prices redistribute wealth among debtors and creditors. A hyperinflation enriches Sophie at the expense of Bigbank because it diminishes the real value of the debt; Sophie can repay the loan in dollars that are less valuable than she anticipated. Deflation enriches Bigbank at Sophie's expense because it increases the real value of the debt; in this case, Sophie has to repay the loan in dollars that are more valuable than she anticipated. If inflation were predictable, then Bigbank and Sophie could take inflation into account when setting the nominal interest rate. (Recall the Fisher effect.) But if inflation is hard to predict, it imposes risk on Sophie and Bigbank that both would prefer to avoid.

This cost of unexpected inflation is important to consider together with another fact: Inflation is especially volatile and uncertain when the average rate of inflation is high. This fact is seen most simply by examining the experience of different countries. Countries with low average inflation, such as Germany in the late 20th century, tend to have stable inflation. Countries with high average inflation, such as many countries in Latin America, tend to have unstable inflation. There are no known examples of economies with high, stable inflation. This relationship between the level and volatility of inflation points to another cost of inflation. If a country pursues a high-inflation monetary policy, it will have to bear not only the costs of high expected inflation but also the arbitrary redistributions of wealth associated with unexpected inflation.

12-2h Inflation Is Bad, but Deflation May Be Worse

In recent U.S. history, inflation has been the norm. But the level of prices has fallen at times, such as during the late 19th century and early 1930s. From 1998 to 2012, Japan experienced a 4-percent decline in its overall price level. So as we conclude our discussion of the costs of inflation, we should briefly consider the costs of deflation as well.

Some economists have suggested that a small and predictable amount of deflation may be desirable. Milton Friedman pointed out that deflation would lower the nominal interest rate (via the Fisher effect) and that a lower nominal interest rate would reduce the cost of holding money. The shoeleather costs of holding money would, he argued, be minimized by a nominal interest rate close to zero, which in turn would require deflation equal to the real interest rate. This prescription for moderate deflation is called the *Friedman rule*.

Yet there are also costs of deflation. Some of these mirror the costs of inflation. For example, just as a rising price level induces menu costs and relative-price variability, so does a falling price level. Moreover, in practice, deflation is rarely as steady and predictable as Friedman recommended. More often, it comes as a surprise, resulting in the redistribution of wealth toward creditors and away from debtors. Because debtors are often poorer, these redistributions in wealth are particularly painful.

Perhaps most important, deflation often arises from broader macroeconomic difficulties. As we will see in future chapters, falling prices result when some event, such as a monetary contraction, reduces the overall demand for goods and services in the economy. This fall in aggregate demand can lead to falling incomes and rising unemployment. In other words, deflation is often a symptom of deeper economic problems.

CASE STUDY

THE WIZARD OF OZ AND THE FREE-SILVER DEBATE

As a child, you probably saw the movie *The Wizard of Oz*, based on a children's book written in 1900. The movie and book tell the story of a young girl, Dorothy, who finds herself lost in a strange land far from home. You probably did not know, however, that some scholars believe that the story is actually an allegory about U.S. monetary policy in the late 19th century.

From 1880 to 1896, the price level in the U.S. economy fell by 23 percent. Because this event was unanticipated, it led to a major redistribution of wealth. Most farmers in the western part of the country were debtors. Their creditors were the bankers in the east. When the price level fell, the real value of these debts rose, enriching the bankers at the expense of the farmers.

According to Populist politicians of the time, the solution to the farmers' problem was the free coinage of silver. During this period, the United States was operating with a gold standard. The quantity of gold determined the money supply and, thereby, the price level. The free-silver advocates wanted silver, in addition to gold, to be used as money. If adopted, this proposal would have increased the money supply, pushed up the price level, and reduced the real burden of the farmers' debts.

The debate over silver was heated, and it was central to the politics of the 1890s. A common election slogan of the Populists was "We Are Mortgaged. All but Our Votes." One prominent advocate of free silver was William Jennings Bryan, the Democratic nominee for president in 1896. He is remembered in part for a speech at the Democratic Party's nominating convention in which he said, "You shall not press down upon the brow of labor this crown of thorns. You shall not crucify mankind upon a cross of gold." Rarely since then have politicians waxed so poetic about alternative approaches to monetary policy. Nonetheless, Bryan lost the election to Republican William McKinley, and the United States remained on the gold standard.

L. Frank Baum, author of the book *The Wonderful Wizard of Oz*, was a Midwestern journalist. When he sat down to write a story for children, he made the characters represent protagonists in the major political battle of his time. Here is how economic historian Hugh Rockoff, writing in the *Journal of Political Economy* in 1990, interprets the story:

DOROTHY:	Traditional American values
TOTO:	Prohibitionist party, also called the Teetotalers
SCARECROW:	Farmers
TIN WOODSMAN:	Industrial workers
COWARDLY LION:	William Jennings Bryan
MUNCHKINS:	Citizens of the East
WICKED WITCH OF THE EAST:	Grover Cleveland
WICKED WITCH OF THE WEST:	William McKinley
WIZARD:	Marcus Alonzo Hanna, chairman of the Republican Party
OZ:	Abbreviation for ounce of gold
YELLOW BRICK ROAD:	Gold standard

At the end of Baum's story, Dorothy does find her way home, but it is not by just following the yellow brick road. After a long and perilous journey, she learns that the wizard is incapable of helping her or her friends. Instead, Dorothy finally discovers the magical power of her *silver* slippers. (When the book was made into a movie in 1939, Dorothy's slippers were changed from silver to ruby. The Hollywood filmmakers were more interested in showing off the new technology of Technicolor than in telling a story about 19th-century monetary policy.)

An early debate over monetary policy

The Populists lost the debate over the free coinage of silver, but they eventually got the monetary expansion and inflation that they wanted. In 1898, prospectors discovered gold near the Klondike River in the Canadian Yukon. Increased supplies of gold also arrived from the mines of South Africa. As a result, the money supply and the price level started to rise in the United States and in other countries operating on the gold standard. Within 15 years, prices in the United States returned to the levels that had prevailed in the 1880s, and farmers were better able to handle their debts. ●

QuickQuiz

6. Ongoing inflation does not automatically reduce most people's incomes because
   a. the tax code is fully indexed for inflation.
   b. people respond to inflation by holding less money.
   c. wage inflation goes together with price inflation.
   d. higher inflation lowers real interest rates.

7. If an economy always has inflation of 10 percent per year, which of the following costs of inflation will it NOT suffer?
   a. shoeleather costs from reduced holdings of money
   b. menu costs from more frequent price adjustment

   c. distortions from the taxation of nominal capital gains
   d. arbitrary redistributions between debtors and creditors

8. Because most loans are written in _____ terms, an unexpected increase in inflation hurts _____.
   a. real; creditors
   b. real; debtors
   c. nominal; creditors
   d. nominal; debtors

Answers at end of chapter.

Life During Hyperinflation

The costs of inflation are most apparent when inflation becomes extreme.

What 52,000 Percent Inflation Can Do to a Country

By Brook Larmer

I walked into the empty restaurant in Managua carrying a backpack stuffed with cash, thick stacks of Nicaraguan córdobas bound by rubber bands. The waiter, as expected, asked me to hand over the entire stash. It may have looked like an illicit transaction. But this was Nicaragua, in 1990, at the end of its war with the American-trained contra rebels, and I was only trying to buy a meal before my money lost its value. A decade of guerrilla war and deficit spending had whipped up a maelstrom of hyperinflation and shortages. Only two items on the menu were available, and prices had doubled in a matter of weeks. With inflation surging past 13,000 percent annually, the restaurant now demanded payment upfront—to ensure that the staff had enough time to tally it. As I ate my rice and beans, two waiters at another table counted every bill. I finished before they did, even though the meal—and all those millions of córdobas—added up to less than $10.

Hyperinflation is a mercurial phenomenon, a rupture that occurs when a government persistently spends (or prints) money that it doesn't have, and the public loses confidence in the process. The distortions that emerge—like the backpack full of soon-to-be-worthless cash—can seem absurd, even laughable. Yet there is nothing amusing about the damage that hyperinflation can inflict on the lives of people and nations. "If you can't trust the money the government issues, then you can't trust anything," says Steve Hanke, a professor of applied economics at Johns Hopkins University and a leading expert on hyperinflation (which he has defined as 50 percent monthly inflation sustained for at least 30 days). Hanke has studied the 58 cases of hyperinflation that have been recorded, from Germany's Weimar Republic to the episode I witnessed in Nicaragua, each one an earthquake that caused people to lose faith in the very foundation—the value of money—on which their lives depended.

The newest addition to the ignominious list, and a cause for alarm in Washington, is the crisis in Venezuela. Even with the world's most-abundant oil fields, Venezuela has mismanaged its way to economic disaster. Hyperinflation and its common companion, chronic shortages of food and medicine, have impoverished almost all of the country's 31 million people. Nine out of 10 Venezuelans

do not earn enough money to buy sufficient food, according to a recent survey. Over all, Venezuelans have lost an average of 24 pounds each. Malaria is on the rise, as is crime. Those who can are getting out: More than 2.3 million Venezuelans have fled the country, including more than half of the nation's doctors.

The situation is still out of control. Venezuela's economy shrank by 35 percent between 2013 and 2017, and economists forecast another 18 percent drop in 2018. Oil production, crippled by the lack of maintenance and investment, fell in July to its lowest point in nearly seven decades. According to Hanke, the rate of inflation over the last 12 months was 52,000 percent. The chaos poses a risk for the entire region. "Venezuela has sparked the most serious economic, humanitarian and political crisis in the Americas in decades," says the Brazilian economist Monica de Bolle, the director of Latin American studies at the Johns Hopkins University School for Advanced International Studies. "There has never been a crisis quite like this in the region, and we've had plenty."

Nearly a century ago, Vladimir Lenin was quoted in *The New York Times* saying that hyperinflation was "the simplest way to exterminate the very spirit of capitalism." If a country were flooded with high face-value notes untethered to anything of real value, he reasoned, "men will cease to covet and hoard

12-3 Conclusion

This chapter discussed the causes and costs of inflation. The primary cause of inflation is growth in the quantity of money. When the central bank creates money in large quantities, the value of money falls quickly. To maintain stable prices, the central bank must maintain strict control over the money supply.

The costs of inflation are more subtle. They include shoeleather costs, menu costs, increased variability of relative prices, unintended changes in tax liabilities, confusion and inconvenience, and arbitrary redistributions of wealth. Are these costs, in total, large or small? All economists agree that they become huge during

[money] so soon as they discover it will not buy anything, and the great illusion of the value and power of money, on which the capitalist state is based, will have been definitely destroyed."

Lenin's dark musings seemed almost prophetic in the jittery aftermath of World War I. Weimar Germany had gambled, badly, in financing its losing war effort with borrowed funds. Buried in debt and forced, in 1921, to pay reparations to the victorious Allies, Germany printed bank notes and ignited the most infamous bout of hyperinflation. By late 1923, prices were doubling roughly every three and a half days, and at one point a single American dollar was worth 6.7 trillion German marks. An even more severe hyperinflation followed the end of World War II, when Hungary printed notes of ever-higher value to finance its recovery. The fastest-ever recorded hyperinflation resulted: At its peak in July 1946, prices doubled every 15 hours.

War has often played a catalytic role in hyperinflation, but it rarely acts alone. In the early 1990s, the phenomenon stalked countries in Eastern Europe (Yugoslavia, Bosnia-Herzegovina, Armenia) that were confronting wars and the fall of the Soviet Union. A decade later in Zimbabwe, despite a long slide in agricultural output, Robert Mugabe's regime printed money to pay the bloated bureaucracy and to line its own pockets. By the time Mugabe declared inflation illegal in 2007, people had lost belief in their currency.

Source: *The New York Times*, November 4, 2018.

Within a year, inflation shot up to 79.6 billion percent, so high that even the government's $100 trillion bills became useless souvenirs soon after they were printed.

Hyperinflation is not, as some might assume, just inflation gone bad. It's a different beast altogether, driven by politics and psychology as much as economics. A government's decision to continue spending (or printing money) far beyond its means is political, whether done to finance war, win an election or assuage its populace. Such monetary incontinence, unchecked, leads to a spiral of food shortages, price hikes and currency devaluations. Those hit hardest are not the rich (whose wealth is in property, stocks and commodities) but the middle class, which depends on local-currency salaries, savings and pensions whose value is siphoned off by hyperinflation.

No conflict or natural calamity can be blamed for Venezuela's descent into chaos. Its leaders did this on their own. With proven oil reserves of 300 billion barrels—surpassing even Saudi Arabia's—Venezuela should be rich. But the country's early oil boom, led largely by foreign companies, yielded only spotty development. When Hugo Chávez won the presidency in 1998, he vowed to give power and wealth to the people. Buoyed by a sustained rise in oil prices, he nationalized companies and funneled oil revenues into welfare programs and food imports. Poverty and unemployment rates fell by half. When oil prices cratered in 2008, Chávez kept spending

as if nothing had changed. Since his death in 2013, his successor, Nicolás Maduro, has doubled down on Chávez's policies, even as he has violently repressed the opposition. . . .

A new era isn't likely to begin as long as Maduro remains in power. He has shown no interest in taking steps that might restore economic balance, like cutting spending and tying the bolívar to a solid foreign currency. Washington murmurs about regime change. But the biggest threat to Maduro now may be a series of civil cases in American courts against Citgo. The Venezuela-owned company is the regime's biggest generator of hard currency, the only asset creditors can go after. If these cases succeed in claiming damages for being nationalized by the Chávez regime, Maduro's main lifeline could be cut off. "If the money disappears," de Bolle says, "so does his support, and the regime crumbles." Only then, it seems, will Venezuelans be able to escape a nightmare in which they can't trust the money in their hands. ■

Questions to Discuss

1. The article mentions that Venezuela's hyperinflation coincided with a shrinking economy. How does declining output contribute to hyperinflation? How does hyperinflation contribute to declining output?

2. Why do you think politicians pursue policies that lead to hyperinflation?

hyperinflation. But during periods of moderate inflation—when prices rise by less than 10 percent per year—the size of these costs is more open to debate.

This chapter presented many of the most important lessons about inflation, but the analysis is incomplete. When the central bank reduces the rate of money growth, prices rise less rapidly, as the quantity theory suggests. Yet as the economy makes the transition to the lower inflation rate, the change in monetary policy will likely disrupt production and employment. That is, even though monetary policy is neutral in the long run, it has profound effects on real variables in the short run. Later in this book we will examine the reasons for short-run monetary non-neutrality to enhance our understanding of the causes and effects of inflation.

CHAPTER IN A NUTSHELL

- The overall level of prices in an economy adjusts to bring money supply and money demand into balance. When the central bank increases the supply of money, it causes the price level to rise. Persistent growth in the quantity of money supplied leads to continuing inflation.

- The principle of monetary neutrality asserts that changes in the quantity of money influence nominal variables but not real variables. Most economists believe that monetary neutrality approximately describes the behavior of the economy in the long run.

- A government can pay for some of its spending simply by printing money. When countries rely heavily on this "inflation tax," the result is hyperinflation.

- One application of the principle of monetary neutrality is the Fisher effect. According to the Fisher effect, when the inflation rate rises, the nominal interest rate

rises by the same amount so that the real interest rate remains the same.

- Many people think that inflation makes them poorer because it raises the cost of what they buy. This view is a fallacy, however, because inflation also raises nominal incomes.

- Economists have identified six costs of inflation: shoeleather costs associated with reduced money holdings, menu costs associated with more frequent adjustment of prices, increased variability of relative prices, unintended changes in tax liabilities due to nonindexation of the tax code, confusion and inconvenience resulting from a changing unit of account, and arbitrary redistributions of wealth between debtors and creditors. Many of these costs are large during hyperinflation, but the size of these costs for moderate inflation is less clear.

KEY CONCEPTS

quantity theory of money, *p. 238*
nominal variables, *p. 239*
real variables, *p. 239*
classical dichotomy, *p. 239*

monetary neutrality, *p. 240*
velocity of money, *p. 240*
quantity equation, *p. 241*
inflation tax, *p. 243*

Fisher effect, *p. 245*
shoeleather costs, *p. 247*
menu costs, *p. 248*

QUESTIONS FOR REVIEW

1. Explain how an increase in the price level affects the real value of money.

2. According to the quantity theory of money, what is the effect of an increase in the quantity of money?

3. Explain the difference between nominal variables and real variables and give two examples of each. According to the principle of monetary neutrality, which variables are affected by changes in the quantity of money?

4. In what sense is inflation like a tax? How does thinking about inflation as a tax help explain hyperinflation?

5. According to the Fisher effect, how does an increase in the inflation rate affect the real interest rate and the nominal interest rate?

6. What are the costs of inflation? Which of these costs do you think are most important for the U.S. economy?

7. If inflation is less than expected, who benefits— debtors or creditors? Explain.

PROBLEMS AND APPLICATIONS

1. Suppose that this year's money supply is $500 billion, nominal GDP is $10 trillion, and real GDP is $5 trillion.
   a. What is the price level? What is the velocity of money?
   b. Suppose that velocity is constant and the economy's output of goods and services rises by 5 percent each year. What will happen to nominal GDP and the price level next year if the Fed keeps the money supply constant?
   c. What money supply should the Fed set next year if it wants to keep the price level stable?
   d. What money supply should the Fed set next year if it wants inflation of 10 percent?

2. Suppose that changes in bank regulations expand the availability of credit cards so that people can hold less cash.
   a. How does this event affect the demand for money?
   b. If the Fed does not respond to this event, what will happen to the price level?
   c. If the Fed wants to keep the price level stable, what should it do?

3. It is sometimes suggested that the Fed should try to achieve zero inflation. If we assume that velocity is constant, does this zero-inflation goal require that the rate of money growth equal zero? If yes, explain why. If no, explain what the rate of money growth should equal.

4. Suppose that a country's inflation rate increases sharply. What happens to the inflation tax on the holders of money? Why is wealth held in savings accounts *not* subject to a change in the inflation tax? Can you think of any way in which holders of savings accounts are hurt by the increase in inflation?

5. Let's consider the effects of inflation in an economy composed of only two people: Bob, a bean farmer, and Rita, a rice farmer. Bob and Rita both always consume equal amounts of rice and beans. In 2019, the price of beans was $1 and the price of rice was $3.
   a. Suppose that in 2020 the price of beans was $2 and the price of rice was $6. What was inflation? Did the price changes leave Bob better off, worse off, or unaffected? What about Rita?
   b. Now suppose that in 2020 the price of beans was $2 and the price of rice was $4. What was inflation? Did the price changes leave Bob better off, worse off, or unaffected? What about Rita?
   c. Finally, suppose that in 2020 the price of beans was $2 and the price of rice was $1.50. What was inflation? Did the price changes leave Bob better off, worse off, or unaffected? What about Rita?
   d. What matters more to Bob and Rita—the overall inflation rate or the relative price of rice and beans?

6. Assuming a tax rate of 40 percent, compute the before-tax real interest rate and the after-tax real interest rate for each of the following cases.
   a. The nominal interest rate is 10 percent, and the inflation rate is 5 percent.
   b. The nominal interest rate is 6 percent, and the inflation rate is 2 percent.
   c. The nominal interest rate is 4 percent, and the inflation rate is 1 percent.

7. Recall that money serves three functions in the economy. What are those functions? How does inflation affect the ability of money to serve each of these functions?

8. Suppose that people expect inflation to be 3 percent but that, in fact, prices rise by 5 percent. Describe how this unexpectedly high inflation would help or hurt the following:
   a. the government
   b. a homeowner with a fixed-rate mortgage
   c. a union worker in the second year of a labor contract
   d. a college that has invested some of its endowment in government bonds

9. Explain whether the following statements are true, false, or uncertain.
   a. "Inflation hurts borrowers and helps lenders, because borrowers must pay a higher rate of interest."
   b. "If prices change in a way that leaves the overall price level unchanged, then no one is made better or worse off."
   c. "Inflation does not reduce the purchasing power of most workers."

Quick Quiz Answers

1. **d**   2. **d**   3. **b**   4. **b**   5. **a**   6. **c**   7. **d**   8. **c**

Open-Economy
Macroeconomics:
Basic Concepts

When you decide to buy a car, you may compare the latest models offered by Ford and Toyota. When you take your next vacation, you may consider spending it on a beach in Florida or in Mexico. When you start saving for your retirement, you may choose between a mutual fund that buys stock in U.S. companies and one that buys stock in foreign companies. In all these cases, you are participating not just in the U.S. economy but also in economies around the world.

International trade yields clear benefits: Trade allows people to produce what they produce best and to consume the great variety of goods and services produced around the world. Indeed, one of the *Ten Principles of Economics* in Chapter 1 is that trade can make everyone better off. International trade can raise living standards in all countries by allowing each country to specialize in producing those goods and services in which it has a comparative advantage.

So far, our development of macroeconomics has largely ignored the domestic economy's interaction with other economies around the world. For most questions in macroeconomics, international issues are peripheral. For instance, when we discuss the natural rate of unemployment and the causes of inflation, the effects of international trade can safely be ignored. Indeed, to

closed economy

an economy that does not interact with other economies in the world

open economy

an economy that interacts freely with other economies around the world

keep their models simple, macroeconomists often assume a **closed economy**—an economy that does not interact with other economies.

Yet when macroeconomists study an **open economy**—an economy that interacts freely with other economies around the world—they encounter a whole set of new issues. This chapter and the next provide an introduction to open-economy macroeconomics. We begin in this chapter by discussing the key macroeconomic variables that describe an open economy's interactions in world markets. You may have heard of these variables—exports, imports, the trade balance, and exchange rates—from the news. Our first job is to understand what these data mean. In the next chapter, we develop a model to explain how these variables are determined and how they are affected by various government policies.

13-1   The International Flows of Goods and Capital

An open economy interacts with other economies in two ways: It buys and sells goods and services in world product markets, and it buys and sells capital assets such as stocks and bonds in world financial markets. Here we discuss these two activities and the close relationship between them.

exports

goods and services produced domestically and sold abroad

imports

goods and services produced abroad and sold domestically

net exports

the value of a nation's exports minus the value of its imports; also called the trade balance

trade balance

the value of a nation's exports minus the value of its imports; also called net exports

trade surplus

an excess of exports over imports

trade deficit

an excess of imports over exports

balanced trade

a situation in which exports equal imports

13-1a   The Flow of Goods: Exports, Imports, and Net Exports

Exports are goods and services that are produced domestically and sold abroad, and **imports** are goods and services that are produced abroad and sold domestically. When Boeing, the U.S. aircraft manufacturer, builds a plane and sells it to Air France, the sale is an export for the United States and an import for France. When Volvo, the Swedish car manufacturer, makes a car and sells it to a U.S. resident, the sale is an import for the United States and an export for Sweden.

The **net exports** of any country are the difference between the value of its exports and the value of its imports:

$$\text{Net exports} = \text{Value of country's exports} - \text{Value of country's imports.}$$

The Boeing sale raises U.S. net exports, and the Volvo sale reduces U.S. net exports. Because net exports tell us whether a country is, in sum, a seller or a buyer in world markets for goods and services, net exports are also called the **trade balance**. If a country's net exports are positive, its exports are greater than its imports, indicating that the country sells more goods and services abroad than it buys from other countries. In this case, the country is said to run a **trade surplus**. If a country's net exports are negative, its exports are less than its imports, indicating that the country sells fewer goods and services abroad than it buys from other countries. In this case, the country is said to run a **trade deficit**. If a country's net exports are zero, its exports and imports are exactly equal, and the country is said to have **balanced trade**.

In the next chapter, we develop a theory that explains an economy's trade balance, but even at this early stage, it is easy to think of many factors that might influence a country's exports, imports, and net exports. Those factors include the following:

- Consumer tastes for domestic and foreign goods
- The prices of goods at home and abroad
- The exchange rates at which people can use domestic currency to buy foreign currencies

- The incomes of consumers at home and abroad
- The cost of transporting goods from country to country
- Government policies toward international trade

As these factors change, so does the amount of international trade.

CASE STUDY

THE INCREASING OPENNESS OF THE U.S. ECONOMY

One dramatic change in the U.S. economy over the past six decades has been the increasing importance of international trade and finance. This change is illustrated in Figure 1, which shows the total value of goods and services exported to other countries and imported from other countries expressed as a percentage of gross domestic product. In the 1950s, imports and exports were typically between 4 and 5 percent of GDP. In recent years, they have been about three times that level. The trading partners of the United States include a diverse group of countries. As of 2018, the largest trading partner, as measured by the sum of imports and exports, was China, followed by Canada, Mexico, Japan, Germany, South Korea, and the United Kingdom.

The increase in international trade over the past several decades is partly due to improvements in transportation. In 1950, the average merchant ship carried less than 10,000 tons of cargo; today, many ships carry more than 100,000 tons. The long-distance jet was introduced in 1958 and the wide-body jet in 1967, making air transport far cheaper than it had been previously. These developments

"But we're not just talking about buying a car—we're talking about confronting this country's trade deficit with Japan."

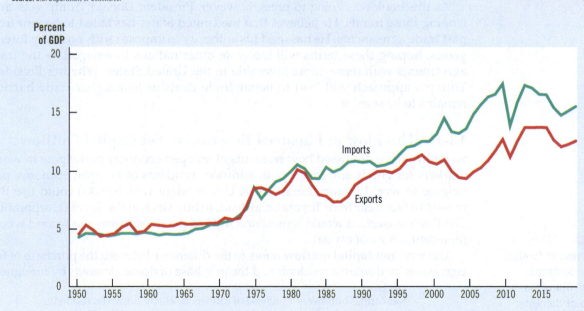

This figure shows exports and imports of the U.S. economy as a percentage of U.S. GDP since 1950. The substantial increases over time show the increasing importance of international trade and finance.

Source: U.S. Department of Commerce.

FIGURE 1

The Internationalization of the U.S. Economy

allow goods that once had to be produced locally to be traded around the world. Cut flowers grown in Israel are flown to the United States to be sold. Fresh fruits and vegetables that can grow in the United States only in summer can now be consumed in winter as well because they can be shipped from countries in the Southern Hemisphere.

The increase in international trade has also been facilitated by advances in telecommunications, which have allowed businesses to reach overseas customers more easily. For example, the first transatlantic telephone cable was not laid until 1956. As recently as 1966, the technology allowed only 138 simultaneous conversations between North America and Europe. Today, because e-mail is such a common form of business communication, it is almost as easy to communicate with a customer across the world as it is to communicate with one across town.

Technological progress has also fostered international trade by changing the kinds of goods that economies produce. When bulky raw materials (such as steel) and perishable goods (such as foodstuffs) were a large part of the world's output, transporting goods was often costly and sometimes impossible. By contrast, goods produced with modern technology are often light and easy to transport. Consumer electronics, for instance, have low weight for every dollar of value, making them easy to produce in one country and sell in another. An even more extreme example is the film industry. Once a studio in Hollywood makes a movie, it can send copies of the film around the world at almost zero cost. And indeed, movies are a major export of the United States.

Governments' trade policies have also been a factor in increasing international trade. As we discussed earlier in this book, economists have long believed that free trade between countries is mutually beneficial. Over time, most policymakers around the world have come to accept these conclusions. International agreements, such as the North American Free Trade Agreement (NAFTA) and the General Agreement on Tariffs and Trade (GATT), have gradually lowered tariffs, import quotas, and other trade barriers. Thus, the pattern of increasing trade illustrated in Figure 1 is a phenomenon that most economists and policymakers have endorsed and encouraged.

As this book was going to press, however, President Donald Trump was challenging these trends. He believes that the United States has failed to benefit from past trade agreements. He has used his authority to impose tariffs on many foreign goods, hoping these tariffs will motivate other nations to renegotiate the trade agreements with terms more favorable to the United States. Whether President Trump's approach will lead to better trade deals or just higher trade barriers remains to be seen. ●

13-1b The Flow of Financial Resources: Net Capital Outflow

So far, we have discussed how residents of an open economy participate in world markets for goods and services. In addition, residents of an open economy participate in world financial markets. A U.S. resident with $25,000 could use that money to buy a car from Toyota or, instead, to buy stock in the Toyota Corporation. The first transaction would represent a flow of goods, whereas the second would represent a flow of capital.

net capital outflow
the purchase of foreign assets by domestic residents minus the purchase of domestic assets by foreigners

The term **net capital outflow** refers to the difference between the purchase of foreign assets by domestic residents and the purchase of domestic assets by foreigners:

Net capital outflow = Purchase of foreign assets by domestic residents
− Purchase of domestic assets by foreigners.

When a U.S. resident buys stock in Petrobras, the Brazilian energy company, the purchase increases the first term on the right side of this equation and, therefore, increases U.S. net capital outflow. When a Japanese resident buys a bond issued by the U.S. government, the purchase increases the second term on the right side of this equation and, therefore, decreases U.S. net capital outflow.

The flow of capital between the U.S. economy and the rest of the world takes two forms: *foreign direct investment* and *foreign portfolio investment*. An example of foreign direct investment is McDonald's opening up a fast-food outlet in Russia. An example of foreign portfolio investment is an American buying stock in a Russian corporation. In the first case, the American owner (McDonald's Corporation) actively manages the investment, whereas in the second case, the American owner (the stockholder) has a more passive role. In both cases, U.S. residents are buying assets located in another country, so both purchases increase U.S. net capital outflow.

The net capital outflow (sometimes called *net foreign investment*) can be either positive or negative. When it is positive, domestic residents are buying more foreign assets than foreigners are buying domestic assets, and capital is said to be flowing out of the country. When the net capital outflow is negative, domestic residents are buying fewer foreign assets than foreigners are buying domestic assets, and capital is said to be flowing into the country. That is, when net capital outflow is negative, a country is experiencing a capital inflow.

We develop a theory to explain net capital outflow in the next chapter. Here let's consider briefly some of the more important variables that influence net capital outflow:

- The real interest rates paid on foreign assets
- The real interest rates paid on domestic assets
- The perceived economic and political risks of holding assets abroad
- The government policies that affect foreign ownership of domestic assets

For example, consider U.S. investors deciding whether to buy Mexican government bonds or U.S. government bonds. (Recall that a bond is, in essence, an IOU of the issuer.) To make this decision, U.S. investors compare the real interest rates offered on the two bonds. The higher a bond's real interest rate, the more attractive it is. While making this comparison, however, U.S. investors must also take into account the risk that one of these governments might default on its debt (that is, not pay interest or principal when it is due), as well as any restrictions that the Mexican government has imposed, or might impose in the future, on foreign investors in Mexico.

13-1c The Equality of Net Exports and Net Capital Outflow

We have seen that an open economy interacts with the rest of the world in two ways—in world markets for goods and services and in world financial markets. Net exports and net capital outflow each measure a type of imbalance in these markets. Net exports measure an imbalance between a country's exports and its imports. Net capital outflow measures an imbalance between the amount of foreign assets bought by domestic residents and the amount of domestic assets bought by foreigners.

An important but subtle fact of accounting states that, for an economy as a whole, net capital outflow (*NCO*) must always equal net exports (*NX*):

$$NCO = NX.$$

This equation holds because every transaction that affects one side of this equation affects the other side by exactly the same amount. This equation is an *identity*—an equation that must hold because of how the variables in the equation are defined and measured.

To see why this accounting identity is true, let's consider an example. Imagine that you are a computer programmer residing in the United States. One day, you write some software and sell it to a Japanese consumer for 10,000 yen. The sale of software is an export of the United States, so it increases U.S. net exports. What else happens to ensure that this identity holds? The answer depends on what you do with the 10,000 yen you are paid.

First, let's suppose that you simply stuff the yen in your mattress. (We might say you have a yen for yen.) In this case, you are using some of your income to invest in the Japanese economy. That is, a domestic resident (you) has acquired a foreign asset (the Japanese currency). The increase in U.S. net exports is matched by an increase in the U.S. net capital outflow.

But if you want to invest in the Japanese economy, you probably won't do so by holding on to Japanese currency. More likely, you will use the 10,000 yen to buy stock in a Japanese corporation, or you might buy a Japanese government bond. Yet the result of your decision is much the same: A domestic resident ends up acquiring a foreign asset. The increase in U.S. net capital outflow (the purchase of the Japanese stock or bond) exactly equals the increase in U.S. net exports (the sale of software).

Let's now change the example. Suppose that instead of using the 10,000 yen to buy a Japanese asset, you use it to buy a good made in Japan, such as a Sony TV. As a result of the TV purchase, U.S. imports increase. Together, the software export and the TV import represent balanced trade. Because exports and imports increase by the same amount, net exports are unchanged. In this case, no American ends up acquiring a foreign asset and no foreigner ends up acquiring a U.S. asset, so there is also no impact on U.S. net capital outflow.

A final possibility is that you go to a local bank to exchange your 10,000 yen for U.S. dollars. But this decision doesn't change the situation because the bank now has to do something with the 10,000 yen. It can buy Japanese assets (a U.S. net capital outflow); it can buy a Japanese good (a U.S. import); or it can sell the yen to another American who wants to make such a transaction. In the end, U.S. net exports must equal U.S. net capital outflow.

This example started with a U.S. programmer selling some software abroad, but the story is much the same when Americans buy goods and services from other countries. For example, if Walmart buys $50 million of clothing from China and sells it to American consumers, something must happen to that $50 million. China could use the $50 million to invest in the U.S. economy. This capital inflow from China might take the form of Chinese purchases of U.S. government bonds. In this case, the purchase of the clothing reduces U.S. net exports, and the sale of bonds reduces U.S. net capital outflow. Alternatively, China could use the $50 million to buy a plane from Boeing, the U.S. aircraft manufacturer. In this case, the U.S. import of clothing balances the U.S. export of aircraft, so net exports and net capital outflow are both unchanged. In all cases, the transactions have the same effect on net exports and net capital outflow.

We can summarize these conclusions for the economy as a whole.

- When a nation is running a trade surplus ($NX > 0$), it is selling more goods and services to foreigners than it is buying from them. What is it doing with the foreign currency it receives from the net sale of goods and services abroad? It must be using it to buy foreign assets. Capital is flowing out of the country ($NCO > 0$).

- When a nation is running a trade deficit ($NX < 0$), it is buying more goods and services from foreigners than it is selling to them. How is it financing the net purchase of these goods and services in world markets? It must be selling assets abroad. Capital is flowing into the country ($NCO < 0$).

The international flow of goods and services and the international flow of capital are two sides of the same coin.

13-1d Saving, Investment, and Their Relationship to the International Flows

A nation's saving and investment are crucial to its long-run economic growth. As we saw in an earlier chapter, saving and investment are equal in a closed economy. But matters are not as simple in an open economy. Let's now consider how saving and investment are related to the international flows of goods and capital as measured by net exports and net capital outflow.

As you may recall, the term *net exports* appeared earlier in the book when we discussed the components of gross domestic product. The economy's GDP (denoted Y) is divided among four components: consumption (C), investment (I), government purchases (G), and net exports (NX). We write this as

$$Y = C + I + G + NX.$$

Total expenditure on the economy's output of goods and services is the sum of expenditure on consumption, investment, government purchases, and net exports. Because each dollar of expenditure is placed into one of these four components, this equation is an accounting identity: It must be true because of the way the variables are defined and measured.

Recall that national saving is the income of the nation that is left after paying for current consumption and government purchases. National saving (S) equals $Y - C - G$. If we rearrange the equation to reflect this fact, we obtain

$$Y - C - G = I + NX$$
$$S = I + NX.$$

Because net exports (NX) also equal net capital outflow (NCO), we can write this equation as

$$S = I + NCO$$

$$\text{Saving} = \frac{\text{Domestic}}{\text{investment}} + \frac{\text{Net capital}}{\text{outflow}}.$$

This equation shows that a nation's saving must equal its domestic investment plus its net capital outflow. In other words, when a U.S. citizen saves a dollar of her income for the future, that dollar can be used to finance the accumulation of domestic capital or it can be used to finance the purchase of foreign capital.

This equation should look somewhat familiar. Earlier in the book, when we analyzed the role of the financial system, we considered this identity for the special case of a closed economy. In a closed economy, net capital outflow is zero ($NCO = 0$), so saving equals investment ($S = I$). By contrast, an open economy has two uses for its saving: domestic investment and net capital outflow.

As before, we can view the financial system as standing between the two sides of this identity. For example, suppose the Garcia family decides to save some of its income for retirement. This decision contributes to national saving, the left side of our equation. If the Garcias deposit their saving in a mutual fund, the mutual fund may use some of the deposit to buy stock issued by General Motors, which uses the proceeds to build a factory in Ohio. In addition, the mutual fund may use some of the Garcias' deposit to buy stock issued by Toyota, which uses the proceeds to build a factory in Osaka. These transactions show up on the right side of the equation. From the standpoint of U.S. accounting, the General Motors expenditure on a new factory is domestic investment, and the purchase of Toyota stock by a U.S. resident is net capital outflow. Thus, all saving in the U.S. economy shows up as investment in the U.S. economy or as U.S. net capital outflow.

The bottom line is that saving, investment, and international capital flows are inextricably linked. When a nation's saving exceeds its domestic investment, its net capital outflow is positive, indicating that the nation is using some of its saving to buy assets abroad. When a nation's domestic investment exceeds its saving, its net capital outflow is negative, indicating that foreigners are financing some of this investment by purchasing domestic assets.

13-1e Summing Up

Table 1 summarizes many of the ideas presented so far in this chapter. It describes the three possibilities for an open economy: a country with a trade deficit, a country with balanced trade, and a country with a trade surplus.

Consider first a country with a trade surplus. By definition, a trade surplus means that the value of exports exceeds the value of imports. Because net exports are exports minus imports, net exports, NX, are positive. As a result, income, $Y = C + I + G + NX$, must be greater than domestic spending, $C + I + G$. But if income, Y, is more than spending, $C + I + G$, then saving, $S = Y - C - G$, must be more than investment, I. Because the country is saving more than it is investing, it must be sending some of its saving abroad. That is, the net capital outflow must be positive.

Similar logic applies to a country with a trade deficit (such as the U.S. economy in recent years). By definition, a trade deficit means that the value of exports is less than the value of imports. Because net exports are exports minus imports, net exports, NX, are negative. Thus, income, $Y = C + I + G + NX$, must be less than domestic spending, $C + I + G$. But if income, Y, is less than spending, $C + I + G$, then saving, $S = Y - C - G$, must be less than investment, I. Because the country is investing more than it is saving, it must be financing some domestic investment by selling assets abroad. That is, the net capital outflow must be negative.

A country with balanced trade falls between these cases. Exports equal imports, so net exports are zero. Income equals domestic spending, and saving equals investment. The net capital outflow equals zero.

TABLE 1

International Flows of Goods and Capital: Summary
This table shows the three possible outcomes for an open economy.

Trade Deficit	Balanced Trade	Trade Surplus
Exports < Imports	Exports = Imports	Exports > Imports
Net Exports < 0	Net Exports = 0	Net Exports > 0
$Y < C + I + G$	$Y = C + I + G$	$Y > C + I + G$
Saving < Investment	Saving = Investment	Saving > Investment
Net Capital Outflow < 0	Net Capital Outflow = 0	Net Capital Outflow > 0

CASE STUDY

IS THE U.S. TRADE DEFICIT A NATIONAL PROBLEM?

You may have heard the press call the United States "the world's largest debtor." The nation earned that description by borrowing heavily in world financial markets during the past four decades to finance large trade deficits. Why did the United States do this, and should this practice give Americans reason to worry?

To answer these questions, let's see what the macroeconomic accounting identities tell us about the U.S. economy. Panel (a) of Figure 2 shows national saving and domestic investment as a percentage of GDP since 1960. Panel (b) shows net

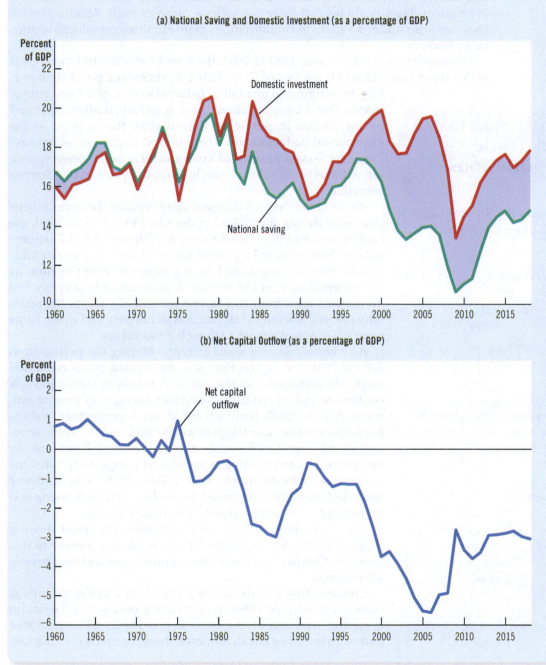

(a) National Saving and Domestic Investment (as a percentage of GDP)

Domestic investment

National saving

(b) Net Capital Outflow (as a percentage of GDP)

Net capital outflow

FIGURE 2

National Saving, Domestic Investment, and Net Capital Outflow

Panel (a) shows national saving and domestic investment as a percentage of GDP. Panel (b) shows net capital outflow as a percentage of GDP. You can see from the figure that national saving has been lower since 1980 than it was before 1980. This fall in national saving has been reflected primarily in reduced net capital outflow rather than in reduced domestic investment.

Source: U.S. Department of Commerce.

capital outflow (that is, the trade balance) as a percentage of GDP. Notice that, as the identities require, net capital outflow always equals national saving minus domestic investment. The figure shows that both national saving and domestic investment, as a percentage of GDP, fluctuate substantially over time. Before 1980, they tended to fluctuate together, so the net capital outflow was typically small—between −1 and 1 percent of GDP. Since 1980, national saving has often fallen well below domestic investment, leading to sizable trade deficits and substantial inflows of capital. That is, in recent decades, the net capital outflow has often been a large negative number.

To understand the fluctuations in Figure 2, we need to go beyond these data and discuss the policies and events that influence national saving and domestic investment. History shows that there is no single cause of trade deficits. Rather, they can arise under a variety of circumstances. Here are three prominent historical episodes.

Unbalanced fiscal policy: From 1980 to 1987, the flow of capital into the United States went from 0.5 to 3.0 percent of GDP. This 2.5 percentage point change is largely attributable to a fall in national saving of 2.7 percentage points. This decline in national saving, in turn, is often explained by the decline in public saving—that is, the increase in the government budget deficit. These budget deficits arose because President Ronald Reagan cut taxes and increased defense spending without being able to enact his proposed cuts in nondefense spending.

An investment boom: A different story explains the trade deficits that arose during the following decade. From 1991 to 2000, the capital flow into the United States went from 0.5 to 3.7 percent of GDP. None of this 3.2 percentage point change is attributable to a decline in saving; in fact, saving increased over this time, as the government's budget switched from deficit to surplus. But investment went from 15.3 to 19.8 percent of GDP, as the economy enjoyed a boom in information technology and many firms were eager to make these high-tech investments.

An economic downturn and recovery: During the period from 2000 to 2018, the capital flow into the United States remained large. The consistency of this variable, however, stands in stark contrast to the remarkable changes in saving and investment. From 2000 to 2009, both fell by about 6 percentage points. Investment fell because tough economic times made capital accumulation less profitable, while national saving fell because the government began running extraordinarily large budget deficits in response to the downturn. From 2009 to 2018, as the economy recovered, these forces reversed themselves, and both saving and investment increased by about 4 percentage points.

Are these trade deficits and international capital flows a problem for the U.S. economy? There is no easy answer to this question. One has to evaluate the circumstances and the possible alternatives.

Consider first a trade deficit induced by a fall in saving, as occurred during the 1980s. Lower saving means that the nation is putting away less of its income to provide for its future. Once national saving has fallen, however, there is no reason to deplore

ASK THE EXPERTS | **Trade Balances and Trade Negotiations**

"A typical country can increase its citizens' welfare by enacting policies that would increase its trade surplus (or decrease its trade deficit)."

What do economists say?

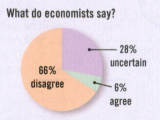

66% disagree
28% uncertain
6% agree

"An important reason why many workers in Michigan and Ohio have lost jobs in recent years is because U.S. presidential administrations over the past 30 years have not been tough enough in trade negotiations."

What do economists say?

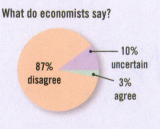

87% disagree
10% uncertain
3% agree

Source: IGM Economic Experts Panel, December 9, 2014 and March 22, 2016.

the resulting trade deficits. If national saving fell without inducing a trade deficit, investment in the United States would have to fall. This fall in investment, in turn, would adversely affect the growth in the capital stock, labor productivity, and real wages. In other words, once U.S. saving has declined, it is better to have foreigners invest in the U.S. economy than no one at all.

Now consider a trade deficit induced by an investment boom, like the trade deficits of the 1990s. In this case, the economy is borrowing from abroad to finance the purchase of new capital goods. If this additional capital provides a good return in the form of higher production of goods and services, then the economy should be able to handle the debts it has accumulated. On the other hand, if the investment projects fail to yield the expected returns, the debts will look less desirable, at least with the benefit of hindsight.

Just as an individual can go into debt in either a prudent or a profligate manner, so can a nation. A trade deficit is not a problem in itself, but it can sometimes be a symptom of a problem. ●

Quick**Quiz**

1. As a percentage of U.S. GDP, today exports are _____ and imports are _____ than they were in 1950.
   a. higher; higher
   b. lower; lower
   c. higher; lower
   d. lower; higher

2. In an open economy, national saving equals domestic investment
   a. plus the government's budget deficit.
   b. minus the net exports of goods and services.

   c. plus the net outflow of capital.
   d. minus foreign portfolio investment.

3. If the value of a nation's imports exceeds the value of its exports, which of the following is NOT true?
   a. Net exports are negative.
   b. GDP is less than the sum of consumption, investment, and government purchases.
   c. Domestic investment is greater than national saving.
   d. The nation is experiencing a net outflow of capital.

Answers at end of chapter.

13-2 The Prices for International Transactions: Real and Nominal Exchange Rates

So far, we have discussed measures of the flow of goods and services and the flow of capital across a nation's border. In addition to these quantity variables, macroeconomists also study variables that measure the prices at which these international transactions take place. Just as the price in any market serves the important role of coordinating buyers and sellers in that market, international prices help coordinate the decisions of consumers and producers as they interact in world markets. Here we discuss the two most important international prices: the nominal and real exchange rates.

13-2a Nominal Exchange Rates

The **nominal exchange rate** is the rate at which a person can trade the currency of one country for the currency of another. For example, when you go to a bank, you might see a posted exchange rate of 80 yen per dollar. If you give the bank

nominal exchange rate
the rate at which a person can trade the currency of one country for the currency of another

1 U.S. dollar, you will receive 80 Japanese yen in return; and if you give the bank 80 Japanese yen, you will receive 1 U.S. dollar. (In actuality, the bank will post slightly different prices for buying and selling yen. The difference gives the bank some profit for offering this service. For our purposes here, we can ignore these differences.)

An exchange rate can always be expressed in two ways. If the exchange rate is 80 yen per dollar, it is also 1/80 (= 0.0125) dollar per yen. Throughout this book, we always express the nominal exchange rate as units of foreign currency per U.S. dollar, such as 80 yen per dollar.

appreciation

an increase in the value of a currency as measured by the amount of foreign currency it can buy

If the exchange rate changes so that a dollar buys more foreign currency, that change is called an **appreciation** of the dollar. If the exchange rate changes so that a dollar buys less foreign currency, that change is called a **depreciation** of the dollar. For example, when the exchange rate rises from 80 to 90 yen per dollar, the dollar is said to appreciate. At the same time, because a Japanese yen now buys less of the U.S. currency, the yen is said to depreciate. When the exchange rate falls from 80 to 70 yen per dollar, the dollar is said to depreciate, and the yen is said to appreciate.

depreciation

a decrease in the value of a currency as measured by the amount of foreign currency it can buy

At times, you may have heard the media report that the dollar is either "strong" or "weak." These descriptions usually refer to recent changes in the nominal exchange rate. When a currency appreciates, it is said to *strengthen* because it can then buy more foreign currency. Similarly, when a currency depreciates, it is said to *weaken*.

For any country, there are many nominal exchange rates. The U.S. dollar can be used to buy Japanese yen, British pounds, Mexican pesos, and so on. When economists study changes in the exchange rate, they often use indexes that average these many exchange rates. Just as the consumer price index turns the many prices in the economy into a single measure of the price level, an exchange-rate index turns these many exchange rates into a single measure of the international value of a currency. So when economists talk about the dollar appreciating or depreciating, they often are referring to an exchange-rate index that includes many individual exchange rates.

13-2b Real Exchange Rates

real exchange rate

the rate at which a person can trade the goods and services of one country for the goods and services of another

The **real exchange rate** is the rate at which a person can trade the goods and services of one country for the goods and services of another. For example, if you go shopping and find that a pound of Swiss cheese is twice as expensive as a pound of American cheese, the real exchange rate is ½ pound of Swiss cheese per pound of American cheese. Notice that, like the nominal exchange rate, we express the real exchange rate as units of the foreign item per unit of the domestic item. But in this instance, the item is a good rather than a currency.

Real and nominal exchange rates are closely related. For example, suppose that a bushel of American rice sells for $100 and a bushel of Japanese rice sells for 16,000 yen. What is the real exchange rate between American and Japanese rice? To answer this question, we must first use the nominal exchange rate to convert the prices into a common currency. If the nominal exchange rate is 80 yen per dollar, then a price for American rice of $100 per bushel is equivalent to 8,000 yen per bushel. American rice is half as expensive as Japanese rice. The real exchange rate is ½ bushel of Japanese rice per bushel of American rice.

We can summarize this calculation for the real exchange rate with the following formula:

$$\text{Real exchange rate} = \frac{\text{Nominal exchange rate} \times \text{Domestic price}}{\text{Foreign price}}.$$

FYI

The Euro

You may have once heard of, or perhaps even seen, currencies such as the French franc, the German mark, or the Italian lira. These types of money no longer exist. During the 1990s, many European nations decided to give up their national currencies and instead use a common currency called the *euro*. The euro started circulating on January 1, 2002, when 12 nations began using it as their official money. As of 2019, there were 23 nations using the euro. Several European countries, such as the United Kingdom, Sweden, and Denmark, have declined to join these nations and have kept their own currencies.

Monetary policy for the euro area is set by the European Central Bank (ECB), which brings together representatives from all of the participating countries. The ECB issues the euro and controls the supply of this money, much as the Federal Reserve controls the supply of dollars in the U.S. economy.

Why did these countries adopt a common currency? One benefit of a common currency is that it makes trade easier. Imagine if each of the 50 U.S. states had a different currency. Every time you crossed a state border, you would need to change your money and perform the kind of exchange-rate calculations discussed in the text. This exercise would be inconvenient, and it might deter you from buying goods and services outside your own state. The countries of Europe decided that as their economies became more integrated, it would be better to avoid this inconvenience.

PETER STONE/ALAMY STOCK PHOTO

To some extent, the adoption of a common currency in Europe was a political decision based on concerns beyond the scope of standard economics. Some advocates of the euro wanted to reduce nationalistic feelings and to make Europeans appreciate more fully their shared history and destiny. A single money for most of the continent, they argued, would help achieve this goal.

There are, however, costs of choosing a common currency. If the nations of Europe have only one money, they can have only one monetary policy. If they disagree about what monetary policy is best, they will have to reach some kind of agreement, rather than each country going its own way. Because adopting a single money has both benefits and costs, there is debate among economists about whether Europe's adoption of the euro was a good decision.

From 2010 to 2015, the euro question heated up as several European nations dealt with various economic difficulties. Greece, in particular, had run up a large government debt and found itself facing possible default. As a result, it had to raise taxes and cut back government spending substantially. Some observers suggested that dealing with these problems would have been easier if the Greek government had had an additional tool—a national monetary policy. The possibility of Greece leaving the euro area and reintroducing its own currency was discussed, but in the end that outcome did not occur. ■

Using the numbers in our example, the formula applies as follows:

$$\text{Real exchange rate} = \frac{(80 \text{ yen/dollar}) \times (\$100/\text{bushel of American rice})}{16{,}000 \text{ yen/bushel of Japanese rice}}$$

$$= \frac{8{,}000 \text{ yen/bushel of American rice}}{16{,}000 \text{ yen/bushel of Japanese rice}}$$

$$= \tfrac{1}{2} \text{ bushel of Japanese rice/bushel of American rice.}$$

Thus, the real exchange rate depends on the nominal exchange rate and on the prices of goods in the two countries measured in the local currencies.

Why does the real exchange rate matter? As you might guess, the real exchange rate is a key determinant of how much a country exports and imports. When Uncle Ben's, Inc., is deciding whether to buy U.S. rice or Japanese rice to put into its boxes, it will ask which rice is cheaper. The real exchange rate gives the answer. As another example, imagine that you are deciding whether to take a seaside vacation in Miami, Florida, or in Cancún, Mexico. You might ask your travel agent the price of a hotel room in Miami (measured in dollars), the price of a hotel room in

Cancún (measured in pesos), and the exchange rate between pesos and dollars. If you decide where to vacation by comparing costs, you are basing your decision on the real exchange rate.

When studying an economy as a whole, macroeconomists focus on overall prices rather than the prices of individual items. That is, to measure the real exchange rate, they use price indexes, such as the consumer price index, which measure the price of a basket of goods and services. By using a price index for a U.S. basket (P), a price index for a foreign basket (P^*), and the nominal exchange rate between the U.S. dollar and foreign currencies (e), we can compute the overall real exchange rate between the United States and other countries as follows:

$$\text{Real exchange rate} = (e \times P)/P^*.$$

This real exchange rate measures the price of a basket of goods and services available domestically relative to a basket of goods and services available abroad.

As we examine more fully in the next chapter, a country's real exchange rate is a key determinant of its net exports of goods and services. A depreciation (fall) in the U.S. real exchange rate means that U.S. goods have become cheaper relative to foreign goods. This change encourages consumers both at home and abroad to buy more U.S. goods and fewer goods from other countries. As a result, U.S. exports rise and U.S. imports fall; both of these changes raise U.S. net exports. Conversely, an appreciation (rise) in the U.S. real exchange rate means that U.S. goods have become more expensive compared to foreign goods, so U.S. net exports fall.

Quick**Quiz**

4. If a nation's currency doubles in value on foreign exchange markets, the currency is said to _____, reflecting a change in the _____ exchange rate.
   a. appreciate; nominal
   b. appreciate; real
   c. depreciate; nominal
   d. depreciate; real

5. If the U.S. dollar appreciates and prices remain the same at home and abroad, foreign goods become _____ expensive relative to American goods, pushing the U.S. trade balance toward _____.
   a. more; surplus
   b. more; deficit

   c. less; surplus
   d. less; deficit

6. The dollar–yen exchange rate falls from 100 to 80 yen per dollar. At the same time, the price level in the United States rises from 180 to 200, and the price level in Japan remains the same. As a result,
   a. American goods have become more expensive relative to Japanese goods.
   b. American goods have become less expensive relative to Japanese goods.
   c. the relative price of American and Japanese goods has not changed.
   d. both American and Japanese goods have become relatively less expensive.

Answers at end of chapter.

13-3 A First Theory of Exchange-Rate Determination: Purchasing-Power Parity

Exchange rates vary substantially over time. In 1970, a U.S. dollar could buy 3.65 German marks or 627 Italian lira. In 1998, as both Germany and Italy were getting ready to adopt the euro as their common currency, a U.S. dollar could buy 1.76 German marks or 1,737 Italian lira. In other words, over this period, the value of the dollar fell by more than half compared to the mark, while it more than doubled compared to the lira.

What explains these large and opposite changes? Economists have developed many models to explain how exchange rates are determined, each emphasizing just some of the many forces at work. Here we develop the simplest theory of exchange rates, called **purchasing-power parity**. This theory states that a unit of any given currency should be able to buy the same quantity of goods in all countries. Many economists believe that purchasing-power parity describes the forces that determine exchange rates in the long run. We now consider the logic on which this long-run theory of exchange rates is based, as well as the theory's implications and limitations.

purchasing-power parity
a theory of exchange rates whereby a unit of any given currency should be able to buy the same quantity of goods in all countries

13-3a The Basic Logic of Purchasing-Power Parity

The theory of purchasing-power parity is based on a principle called the *law of one price*. This law asserts that a good must sell for the same price in all locations. Otherwise, there would be opportunities for profit left unexploited. For example, suppose that coffee beans sold for less in Seattle than in Dallas. A person could buy coffee in Seattle for, say, $4 a pound and then sell it in Dallas for $5 a pound, making a profit of $1 per pound from the difference in price. The process of taking advantage of price differences for the same item in different markets is called *arbitrage*. In our example, as people took advantage of this arbitrage opportunity, they would increase the demand for coffee in Seattle and increase the supply in Dallas. The price of coffee would rise in Seattle (in response to greater demand) and fall in Dallas (in response to greater supply). This process would continue until, eventually, the prices were the same in the two markets.

Now consider how the law of one price applies to the international marketplace. If a dollar (or any other currency) could buy more coffee in the United States than in Japan, international traders could profit by buying coffee in the United States and selling it in Japan. This export of coffee from the United States to Japan would drive up the U.S. price of coffee and drive down the Japanese price. Conversely, if a dollar could buy more coffee in Japan than in the United States, traders could buy coffee in Japan and sell it in the United States. This import of coffee into the United States from Japan would drive down the U.S. price of coffee and drive up the Japanese price. In the end, the law of one price tells us that a dollar must buy the same amount of coffee in all countries.

This logic leads us to the theory of purchasing-power parity. According to this theory, a currency must have the same purchasing power in all countries. That is, a U.S. dollar must buy the same quantity of goods in the United States and Japan, and a Japanese yen must buy the same quantity of goods in Japan and the United States. Indeed, the name of this theory describes it well. *Parity* means equality, and *purchasing power* refers to the value of money in terms of the quantity of goods it can buy. *Purchasing-power parity* states that a unit of a currency must have the same real value in every country.

13-3b Implications of Purchasing-Power Parity

What does the theory of purchasing-power parity say about exchange rates? It tells us that the nominal exchange rate between the currencies of two countries depends on the price levels in those countries. If a dollar buys the same quantity of goods in the United States (where prices are measured in dollars) as in Japan (where prices are measured in yen), then the number of yen per dollar must reflect the prices of goods in the United States and Japan. For example, if a pound of coffee costs 500 yen in Japan and $5 in the United States, then the nominal exchange rate must be 100 yen per dollar (500 yen/$5 = 100 yen per dollar). Otherwise, the purchasing power of the dollar would not be the same in the two countries.

To see more fully how this works, it is helpful to use just a bit of mathematics. Suppose that P is the price of a basket of goods in the United States (measured in dollars), P^* is the price of a basket of goods in Japan (measured in yen), and e is the nominal exchange rate (the number of yen a dollar can buy). Now consider the quantity of goods a dollar can buy at home and abroad. At home, the price level is P, so the purchasing power of $1 at home is $1/P$. That is, a dollar can buy $1/P$ units of goods. Abroad, a dollar can be exchanged into e units of foreign currency, which in turn have purchasing power e/P^*. For the purchasing power of a dollar to be the same in the two countries, it must be the case that

$$1/P = e/P^*.$$

With rearrangement, this equation becomes

$$1 = eP/P^*.$$

Notice that the left side of this equation is a constant and the right side is the real exchange rate. Thus, *if the purchasing power of the dollar is always the same at home and abroad, then the real exchange rate—the relative price of domestic and foreign goods—cannot change.*

To see the implication of this analysis for the nominal exchange rate, we can rearrange the last equation to solve for the nominal exchange rate:

$$e = P^*/P.$$

That is, the nominal exchange rate equals the ratio of the foreign price level (measured in units of the foreign currency) to the domestic price level (measured in units of the domestic currency). *According to the theory of purchasing-power parity, the nominal exchange rate between the currencies of two countries must reflect the price levels in those countries.*

A key implication of this theory is that nominal exchange rates change when price levels change. As we saw in the preceding chapter, the price level in any country adjusts to bring the quantity of money supplied and the quantity of money demanded into balance. Because the nominal exchange rate depends on the price levels, it also depends on the money supply and demand in each country. When a central bank in any country increases the money supply and causes the price level to rise, it also causes that country's currency to depreciate relative to other currencies in the world. In other words, *when the central bank prints large quantities of money, that money loses value both in terms of the goods and services it can buy and in terms of the amount of other currencies it can buy.*

We can now answer the question that began this section: Why did the U.S. dollar lose value compared to the German mark and gain value compared to the Italian lira? The answer is that Germany pursued a less inflationary monetary policy than the United States, and Italy pursued a more inflationary monetary policy. From 1970 to 1998, inflation in the United States was 5.3 percent per year. By contrast, inflation was 3.5 percent in Germany and 9.6 percent in Italy. As U.S. prices rose relative to German prices, the value of the dollar fell relative to the mark. Similarly, as U.S. prices fell relative to Italian prices, the value of the dollar rose relative to the lira.

Germany and Italy now have a common currency—the euro. Sharing a currency means that the two countries share a single monetary policy and, as a result, have similar inflation rates. But the historical lessons of the lira and the mark will apply to the euro as well. Whether the U.S. dollar buys more or fewer euros 20 years from now than it does today depends on whether the European Central Bank generates more or less inflation in Europe than the Federal Reserve does in the United States.

CASE STUDY

THE NOMINAL EXCHANGE RATE DURING A HYPERINFLATION

Macroeconomists can only rarely conduct controlled experiments. Most often, they must glean what they can from the natural experiments that history gives them. One natural experiment is hyperinflation—the high inflation that arises when a government turns to the printing press to pay for large amounts of government spending. Because hyperinflations are so extreme, they illustrate some basic economic principles with clarity.

Consider the German hyperinflation of the early 1920s. Figure 3 shows the German money supply, the German price level, and the nominal exchange rate (measured as U.S. cents per German mark) for that period. Notice that these series move closely together. When the supply of money starts growing quickly, the price level also takes off, and the German mark depreciates. When the money supply stabilizes, so do the price level and the exchange rate.

The pattern shown in this figure appears during every hyperinflation. It leaves no doubt that there is a fundamental link among money, prices, and the nominal exchange rate. The quantity theory of money discussed in the previous chapter explains how the money supply affects the price level. The theory of purchasing-power parity discussed here explains how the price level affects the nominal exchange rate. ●

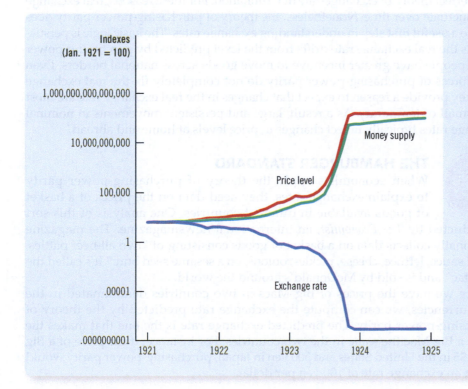

FIGURE 3

Money, Prices, and the Nominal Exchange Rate during the German Hyperinflation

This figure shows the money supply, the price level, and the nominal exchange rate (measured as U.S. cents per mark) for the German hyperinflation from January 1921 to December 1924. Notice how similarly these three variables move. When the quantity of money started growing quickly, the price level followed and the mark depreciated relative to the dollar. When the German central bank stabilized the money supply, the price level and exchange rate stabilized as well.

Source: Adapted from Thomas J. Sargent, "The End of Four Big Inflations," in Robert Hall, ed., *Inflation* (Chicago: University of Chicago Press, 1983), pp. 41–93.

13-3c Limitations of Purchasing-Power Parity

Purchasing-power parity provides a simple model of how exchange rates are determined. For understanding many economic phenomena, the theory works well. In particular, it can explain many long-term trends, such as the depreciation of the U.S. dollar against the German mark and the appreciation of the U.S. dollar against the Italian lira. It can also explain the major changes in exchange rates that occur during hyperinflations.

Yet the theory of purchasing-power parity is not completely accurate. That is, exchange rates do not always move to ensure that a dollar has the same real value in all countries all the time. There are two reasons the theory of purchasing-power parity does not always hold in practice.

The first reason is that many goods are not easily traded. Imagine, for instance, that haircuts are more expensive in Paris than in New York. International travelers might avoid getting their haircuts in Paris, and some haircutters might move from New York to Paris. Yet such arbitrage would be too limited to eliminate the differences in prices. Thus, the deviation from purchasing-power parity might persist, and a dollar (or euro) would continue to buy less of a haircut in Paris than in New York.

The second reason that purchasing-power parity does not always hold is that even tradable goods are not always perfect substitutes when they are produced in different countries. For example, some consumers prefer German cars, and others prefer American cars. Moreover, consumer tastes can change over time. If German cars suddenly become more popular, the increase in demand will drive up the price of German cars relative to American cars. Despite this difference in prices in the two markets, there might be no opportunity for profitable arbitrage because consumers do not view the two cars as equivalent.

Thus, both because some goods are not tradable and because some tradable goods are not perfect substitutes for their foreign counterparts, purchasing-power parity is not a perfect theory of exchange-rate determination. For these reasons, real exchange rates fluctuate over time. Nonetheless, the theory of purchasing-power parity does provide a useful first step in understanding exchange rates. The basic logic is persuasive: As the real exchange rate drifts from the level predicted by purchasing-power parity, people have greater incentive to move goods across national borders. Even if the forces of purchasing-power parity do not completely fix the real exchange rate, they provide a reason to expect that changes in the real exchange rate are most often small or temporary. As a result, large and persistent movements in nominal exchange rates typically reflect changes in price levels at home and abroad.

THE HAMBURGER STANDARD

CASE STUDY

When economists apply the theory of purchasing-power parity to explain exchange rates, they need data on the prices of a basket of goods available in different countries. One analysis of this sort is conducted by *The Economist*, an international newsmagazine. The magazine occasionally collects data on a basket of goods consisting of "two all-beef patties, special sauce, lettuce, cheese, pickles, onions, on a sesame seed bun." It's called the "Big Mac" and is sold by McDonald's around the world.

Once we have the prices of Big Macs in two countries denominated in the local currencies, we can compute the exchange rate predicted by the theory of purchasing-power parity. The predicted exchange rate is the one that makes the cost of a Big Mac the same in the two countries. For instance, if the price of a Big Mac is $5 in the United States and 500 yen in Japan, purchasing-power parity would predict an exchange rate of 100 yen per dollar.

You can find a Big Mac almost anywhere you look.

How well does purchasing-power parity work when applied using Big Mac prices? Here are some examples from January 2019, when the price of a Big Mac was $5.58 in the United States:

Country	Price of a Big Mac	Predicted Exchange Rate	Actual Exchange Rate
Indonesia	33,000 rupiah	5,914 rupiah/$	14,090 rupiah/$
South Korea	4,500 won	806 won/$	1,119 won/$
Japan	390 yen	70 yen/$	108 yen/$
Sweden	52 krona	9.3 krona/$	8.9 krona/$
Mexico	49 pesos	8.8 pesos/$	19.3 pesos/$
China	20.9 renminbi	3.7 renminbi/$	6.8 renminbi/$
Euro area	4.05 euros	0.73 euros/$	0.87 euros/$
Britain	3.19 pounds	0.57 pounds/$	0.78 pounds/$

You can see that the predicted and actual exchange rates are not exactly the same. After all, international arbitrage in Big Macs is not easy. Yet the two exchange rates are often in the same ballpark. Purchasing-power parity is not a precise theory of exchange rates, but it can provide a reasonable first approximation. ●

13-4 Conclusion

The purpose of this chapter has been to develop some basic concepts that macroeconomists use to study open economies. You should now understand how a nation's trade balance is related to the international flow of capital and how national saving can differ from domestic investment in an open economy. You should understand that when a nation is running a trade surplus, it must be sending capital abroad, and that when it is running a trade deficit, it must be experiencing a capital inflow. You should also understand the meaning of the nominal and real exchange rates, as well as the implications and limitations of purchasing-power parity as a theory of how exchange rates are determined.

The macroeconomic variables defined here offer a starting point for analyzing an open economy's interactions with the rest of the world. In the next chapter, we develop a model that can explain what determines these variables. We can then discuss how various events and policies affect a country's trade balance and the rate at which nations make exchanges in world markets.

CHAPTER IN A NUTSHELL

- Net exports are the value of domestic goods and services sold abroad (exports) minus the value of foreign goods and services sold domestically (imports). Net capital outflow is the acquisition of foreign assets by domestic residents (capital outflow) minus the acquisition of domestic assets by foreigners (capital inflow). Because every international transaction involves an exchange of an asset for a good or service, an economy's net capital outflow always equals its net exports.

- An economy's saving can be used either to finance investment at home or to buy assets abroad. Thus, national saving equals domestic investment plus net capital outflow.

- The nominal exchange rate is the relative price of the currency of two countries, and the real exchange rate is the relative price of the goods and services of two countries. When the nominal exchange rate changes so that each dollar buys more foreign currency, the dollar is said to *appreciate* or *strengthen*. When the nominal exchange rate changes so that each dollar buys less foreign currency, the dollar is said to *depreciate* or *weaken*.

- According to the theory of purchasing-power parity, a dollar (or a unit of any other currency) should be able to buy the same quantity of goods in all countries. This theory implies that the nominal exchange rate between the currencies of two countries should reflect the price levels in those countries. As a result, countries with relatively high inflation should have depreciating currencies, and countries with relatively low inflation should have appreciating currencies.

KEY CONCEPTS

closed economy, *p. 260*
open economy, *p. 260*
exports, *p. 260*
imports, *p. 260*
net exports, *p. 260*

trade balance, *p. 260*
trade surplus, *p. 260*
trade deficit, *p. 260*
balanced trade, *p. 260*
net capital outflow, *p. 262*

nominal exchange rate, *p. 269*
appreciation, *p. 270*
depreciation, *p. 270*
real exchange rate, *p. 270*
purchasing-power parity, *p. 273*

QUESTIONS FOR REVIEW

1. Define *net exports* and *net capital outflow*. Explain how and why they are related.

2. Explain the relationship among saving, investment, and net capital outflow.

3. If a Japanese car costs 1,500,000 yen, a similar American car costs $30,000, and a dollar can buy 100 yen, what are the nominal and real exchange rates?

4. Describe the economic logic behind the theory of purchasing-power parity.

5. If the Fed started printing large quantities of U.S. dollars, what would happen to the number of Japanese yen a dollar could buy? Why?

PROBLEMS AND APPLICATIONS

1. How would the following transactions affect U.S. exports, imports, and net exports?
   a. An American art professor spends the summer touring museums in Europe.
   b. Students in Paris flock to see the latest movie from Hollywood.
   c. Your uncle buys a new Volvo.
   d. The student bookstore at Oxford University in England sells a copy of this textbook.
   e. A Canadian citizen shops at a store in northern Vermont to avoid Canadian sales taxes.

2. Would each of the following transactions be included in U.S. net exports or in U.S. net capital outflow? Indicate whether it would represent an increase or a decrease in that variable.
   a. An American buys a Sony TV.
   b. An American buys a share of Sony stock.
   c. The Sony pension fund buys a bond from the U.S. Treasury.
   d. A worker at a Sony plant in Japan buys some Georgia peaches from an American farmer.

3. Describe the difference between foreign direct investment and foreign portfolio investment. Who is more likely to engage in foreign direct investment—a corporation or an individual investor? Who is more likely to engage in foreign portfolio investment?

4. Explain how the following transactions would affect U.S. net capital outflow. For each transaction, state whether it represents direct investment or portfolio investment.
   a. An American cellular phone company establishes an office in the Czech Republic.
   b. Harrods of London sells stock to the General Motors pension fund.
   c. Honda expands its factory in Marysville, Ohio.
   d. A Fidelity mutual fund sells its Volkswagen stock to a French investor.

5. Would each of the following groups be happy or unhappy if the U.S. dollar appreciated? Explain.
   a. Dutch pension funds holding U.S. government bonds
   b. U.S. manufacturing industries
   c. Australian tourists planning a trip to the United States
   d. an American firm trying to purchase property overseas

6. What is happening to the U.S. real exchange rate in each of the following situations? Explain.
   a. The U.S. nominal exchange rate is unchanged, but prices rise faster in the United States than abroad.
   b. The U.S. nominal exchange rate is unchanged, but prices rise faster abroad than in the United States.
   c. The U.S. nominal exchange rate declines, and prices are unchanged in the United States and abroad.
   d. The U.S. nominal exchange rate declines, and prices rise faster abroad than in the United States.

7. A can of soda costs $1.25 in the United States and 25 pesos in Mexico. What is the peso–dollar exchange rate (measured in pesos per dollar) if purchasing-power parity holds? If a monetary expansion causes all prices in Mexico to double, so that a soda now costs 50 pesos, what happens to the peso–dollar exchange rate?

8. A case study in the chapter analyzed purchasing-power parity using the prices of Big Macs in several countries. Here are data for a few more countries:

Country	Price of a Big Mac	Predicted Exchange Rate	Actual Exchange Rate
Chile	2,640 pesos	____ pesos/$	679 pesos/$
Hungary	850 forints	____ forints/$	280 forints/$
Czech Republic	85 korunas	____ korunas/$	22.3 korunas/$
Brazil	16.9 real	____ real/$	3.72 real/$
Canada	6.77 C$	____ C$/$	1.33 C$/$

   a. For each country, compute the predicted exchange rate in terms of the local currency per U.S. dollar. (Recall that the U.S. price of a Big Mac was $5.58.)
   b. According to purchasing-power parity, what is the predicted exchange rate between the Chilean peso and the Canadian dollar? What is the actual exchange rate?
   c. How well does the theory of purchasing-power parity explain exchange rates?

9. Purchasing-power parity holds between the nations of Ectenia and Wiknam, where the only commodity is Spam.
   a. In 2020, a can of Spam costs 4 dollars in Ectenia and 24 pesos in Wiknam. What is the exchange rate between Ectenian dollars and Wiknamian pesos?
   b. Over the next 20 years, inflation is expected to be 3.5 percent per year in Ectenia and 7 percent per year in Wiknam. If this inflation comes to pass, what will the price of Spam and the exchange rate be in 2040? (*Hint*: Recall the rule of 70 from Chapter 9.)
   c. Which of these two nations will likely have a higher nominal interest rate? Why?
   d. A friend of yours suggests a get-rich-quick scheme: Borrow from the nation with the lower nominal interest rate, invest in the nation with the higher nominal interest rate, and profit from the interest-rate differential. Do you see any potential problems with this idea? Explain.

Quick**Quiz Answers**

1. **a**   2. **c**   3. **d**   4. **a**   5. **d**   6. **b**   7. **b**   8. **d**

A Macroeconomic Theory of the Open Economy

Over the past three decades, the United States has consistently imported more goods and services than it has exported. That is, U.S. net exports have been negative. While economists debate whether these trade deficits are a problem for the U.S. economy, the nation's business community often has a strong opinion. Many business leaders claim that the trade deficits reflect unfair competition: Foreign firms are allowed to sell their products in U.S. markets, they contend, while foreign governments impede U.S. firms from selling U.S. products abroad.

Imagine that you are the president and you want to end these trade deficits. What should you do? Should you try to limit imports, perhaps by imposing a tariff on textiles from China or a quota on cars from Japan? Or should you try to address the nation's trade deficit in some other way?

To understand the factors that determine a country's trade balance and how government policies can affect it, we need a macroeconomic theory that explains how an open economy works. The preceding chapter introduced some of the key macroeconomic variables that describe an economy's relationship with other economies, including net exports, net capital outflow, and the real and nominal exchange rates. This chapter develops a model that identifies the forces that determine these variables and explains how these variables are related to one another.

To develop this macroeconomic model of an open economy, we build on our previous analysis in two ways. First, the model takes the economy's GDP as given. We assume that the economy's output of goods and services, as measured by real GDP, is determined by the quantities of the factors of production and by the available production technology that turns these inputs into output. Second, the model takes the economy's price level as given. We assume that the price level adjusts to bring the supply and demand for money into balance. In other words, this chapter takes as a starting point the lessons learned in previous chapters about the determination of the economy's output and price level.

The goal of the model in this chapter is to highlight the forces that determine the economy's trade balance and exchange rate. In one sense, the model is simple: It applies the tools of supply and demand to an open economy. Yet the model is also more complex than others we have seen because it involves looking simultaneously at two related markets: the market for loanable funds and the market for foreign-currency exchange. After we develop this model of the open economy, we use it to examine how various events and policies affect the economy's trade balance and exchange rate. We will then be able to determine the government policies that are most likely to reverse the trade deficits that the U.S. economy has experienced over the past three decades.

14-1 Supply and Demand for Loanable Funds and for Foreign-Currency Exchange

To understand the forces at work in an open economy, we focus on supply and demand in two markets. The first is the market for loanable funds, which coordinates the economy's saving, investment, and flow of loanable funds abroad (called the net capital outflow). The second is the market for foreign-currency exchange, which coordinates people who want to exchange the domestic currency for the currency of other countries. In this section, we discuss supply and demand in each of these markets separately. In the next section, we put these markets together to explain the overall equilibrium for an open economy.

14-1a The Market for Loanable Funds

When we first analyzed the role of the financial system in Chapter 8, we made the simplifying assumption that the financial system consists of only one market, called the *market for loanable funds*. All savers go to this market to deposit their saving, and all borrowers go to this market to get their loans. In this market, there is one interest rate, which is both the return to saving and the cost of borrowing.

To understand the market for loanable funds in an open economy, the place to start is the identity discussed in the preceding chapter:

$$S \quad = \quad I \quad + \quad NCO$$

$$\text{Saving} = \frac{\text{Domestic}}{\text{investment}} + \frac{\text{Net capital}}{\text{outflow}}.$$

Whenever a nation saves a dollar of its income, it can use that dollar to finance the purchase of domestic capital or to finance the purchase of an asset abroad. The two sides of this identity represent the two sides of the market for loanable funds. The supply of loanable funds comes from national saving (S), and the demand for loanable funds comes from domestic investment (I) and net capital outflow (NCO).

Loanable funds should be interpreted as the domestically generated flow of resources available for capital accumulation. The purchase of a capital asset adds to the demand for loanable funds, regardless of whether that asset is located at home (I) or abroad (NCO). Because net capital outflow can be either positive or negative, it can either add to or subtract from the demand for loanable funds that arises from domestic investment. When $NCO > 0$, the country is experiencing a net outflow of capital; the net purchase of capital overseas adds to the demand for domestically generated loanable funds. When $NCO < 0$, the country is experiencing a net inflow of capital; the capital resources coming from abroad reduce the demand for domestically generated loanable funds.

As we learned in our earlier discussion of the market for loanable funds, the quantity of loanable funds supplied and the quantity of loanable funds demanded depend on the real interest rate. A higher real interest rate means a higher return to saving, which encourages people to save and therefore raises the quantity of loanable funds supplied. A higher interest rate also means a higher cost of borrowing to finance capital projects, which discourages investment and reduces the quantity of loanable funds demanded.

In addition to influencing national saving and domestic investment, a country's real interest rate affects its net capital outflow. To see why, consider two mutual funds—one in the United States and one in Germany—deciding whether to buy a U.S. government bond or a German government bond. Each mutual fund manager would make this decision in part by comparing the real interest rates in the United States and Germany. When the U.S. real interest rate rises, the U.S. bond becomes more attractive to both mutual funds. Thus, an increase in the U.S. real interest rate discourages Americans from buying foreign assets and encourages foreigners to buy U.S. assets. For both reasons, a rise in the U.S. real interest rate reduces U.S. net capital outflow.

We illustrate the market for loanable funds using the familiar supply-and-demand diagram in Figure 1. As in our earlier analysis of the financial system, the supply curve slopes upward because a higher interest rate increases the quantity of loanable funds supplied, and the demand curve slopes downward because a higher interest rate decreases the quantity of loanable funds demanded. Unlike the situation in our previous discussion, however, the demand side of the market now represents both domestic investment and net capital outflow. That is, in an open economy, the demand for loanable funds comes not only from those who want loanable funds to buy domestic capital goods but also from those who want loanable funds to buy foreign assets.

The interest rate adjusts to bring the supply and demand for loanable funds into balance. If the interest rate were below the equilibrium level, the quantity of loanable funds supplied would be less than the quantity demanded. The resulting shortage of loanable funds would push the interest rate upward. Conversely, if the interest rate were above the equilibrium level, the quantity of loanable funds supplied would exceed the quantity demanded. The surplus of loanable funds would drive the interest rate downward. At the equilibrium interest rate, the supply of

FIGURE 1

The Market for Loanable Funds
The interest rate in an open economy, as in a closed economy, is determined by the supply and demand for loanable funds. National saving is the source of the supply of loanable funds. Domestic investment and net capital outflow are the sources of the demand for loanable funds. At the equilibrium interest rate, the amount that people want to save exactly balances the amount that people want to borrow for the purpose of buying domestic capital and foreign assets.

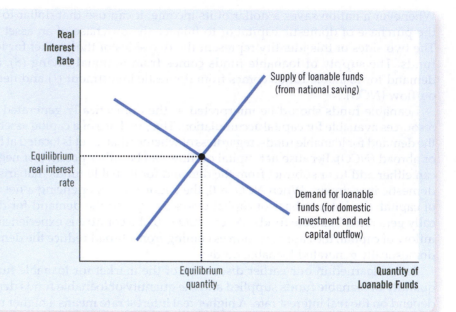

loanable funds exactly balances the demand. In other words, *at the equilibrium interest rate, the amount that people want to save exactly balances the desired quantities of domestic investment and net capital outflow.*

14-1b The Market for Foreign-Currency Exchange

The second market in our model of the open economy is the market for foreign-currency exchange. Participants in this market trade U.S. dollars in exchange for foreign currencies. To understand the market for foreign-currency exchange, we begin with another identity from the last chapter:

$$NCO = NX$$

Net capital outflow = Net exports.

This identity states that the imbalance between the purchase and sale of capital assets abroad (NCO) equals the imbalance between exports and imports of goods and services (NX). For example, when the U.S. economy is running a trade surplus ($NX > 0$), foreigners are buying more U.S. goods and services than Americans are buying foreign goods and services. What are Americans doing with the foreign currency they are getting from this net sale of goods and services abroad? They must be buying foreign assets, so U.S. capital is flowing abroad ($NCO > 0$). Conversely, if the United States is running a trade deficit ($NX < 0$), Americans are spending more on foreign goods and services than they are earning from selling goods and services abroad. Some of this spending must be financed by selling American assets abroad, so foreign capital is flowing into the United States ($NCO < 0$).

Our model of the open economy treats the two sides of this identity as representing the two sides of the market for foreign-currency exchange. Net capital outflow represents the quantity of dollars supplied for the purpose of buying foreign assets. For example, when a U.S. mutual fund wants to buy a Japanese government bond, it needs to change dollars into yen, so it supplies dollars in the market for foreign-currency exchange. Net exports represent the quantity of dollars demanded for the purpose of buying U.S. net exports of goods and services. For example, when a Japanese airline wants to buy a plane made by Boeing, it needs to change its yen into dollars, so it demands dollars in the market for foreign-currency exchange.

What price balances the supply and demand in the market for foreign-currency exchange? The answer is the real exchange rate. As we saw in the preceding chapter, the real exchange rate is the relative price of domestic and foreign goods and, therefore, is a key determinant of net exports. When the U.S. real exchange rate appreciates, U.S. goods become more expensive relative to foreign goods, making U.S. goods less attractive to consumers both at home and abroad. As a result, exports from the United States fall, and imports into the United States rise. For both reasons, net exports fall. Hence, an appreciation of the real exchange rate reduces the quantity of dollars demanded in the market for foreign-currency exchange.

Figure 2 shows supply and demand in the market for foreign-currency exchange. The demand curve slopes downward for the reason we just discussed: A higher real exchange rate makes U.S. goods more expensive and reduces the quantity of dollars demanded to buy those goods. The supply curve is vertical because the quantity of dollars supplied for net capital outflow does not depend on the real exchange rate. (As discussed earlier, net capital outflow depends on the real interest rate. When discussing the market for foreign-currency exchange, we take the real interest rate and net capital outflow as given.)

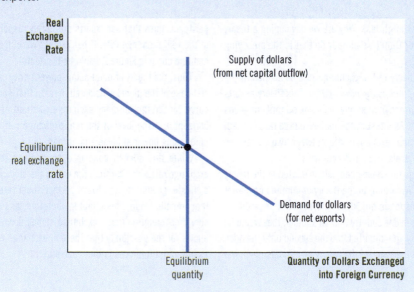

The real exchange rate is determined by the supply and demand for foreign-currency exchange. The supply of dollars to be exchanged into foreign currency comes from net capital outflow. Because net capital outflow does not depend on the real exchange rate, the supply curve is vertical. The demand for dollars comes from net exports. Because a lower real exchange rate stimulates net exports (and thus increases the quantity of dollars demanded to pay for these net exports), the demand curve slopes downward. At the equilibrium real exchange rate, the number of dollars people supply to buy foreign assets exactly balances the number of dollars people demand to buy net exports.

FIGURE 2

The Market for Foreign-Currency Exchange

It might seem strange at first that net capital outflow does not depend on the exchange rate. After all, a higher exchange value of the U.S. dollar not only makes foreign goods less expensive for American buyers but also makes foreign assets less expensive. One might guess that a stronger dollar would therefore make foreign assets more attractive. But remember that an American investor will eventually want to turn the foreign asset, as well as any profits earned on it, back into dollars. For example, an increase in the value of the dollar makes it less expensive for an American to buy stock in a Japanese company. But any dividends that the stock pays will be in yen. As these yen are exchanged for dollars, the higher value of the dollar means that the dividends will buy fewer dollars than before. Thus, changes in the exchange rate influence both the cost of buying foreign assets and the benefit of owning them, and these two effects offset each other. For these reasons, our model of the open economy posits that net capital outflow does not depend on the real exchange rate, as represented by the vertical supply curve in Figure 2.

The real exchange rate moves to ensure equilibrium in this market. It adjusts to balance the supply and demand for dollars just as the price of any good adjusts to balance supply and demand for that good. If the real exchange rate were below the equilibrium level, the quantity of dollars supplied would be less than the quantity demanded. The resulting shortage of dollars would push the value of the dollar upward. Conversely, if the real exchange rate were above the equilibrium level, the quantity of dollars supplied would exceed the quantity demanded. The surplus of dollars would drive the value of the dollar downward. *At the equilibrium real exchange rate, the demand for dollars by foreigners arising from the U.S. net exports of goods and services exactly balances the supply of dollars from Americans arising from U.S. net capital outflow.*

FYI   Purchasing-Power Parity as a Special Case

An alert reader of this book might ask: Why are we developing a theory of the exchange rate here? Didn't we already do that in the preceding chapter?

As you may recall, the theory of the exchange rate developed in the preceding chapter is called *purchasing-power parity*. This theory asserts that a dollar (or any other currency) must buy the same quantity of goods and services in every country. As a result, the real exchange rate is fixed, and all changes in the nominal exchange rate between two currencies reflect changes in the price levels in the two countries.

The model of the exchange rate developed here is related to the theory of purchasing-power parity. According to the theory of purchasing-power parity, international trade responds quickly to international price differences. If goods were cheaper in one country than in another, they would be exported from the first country and imported into the second until the price difference disappeared. In other words, the theory of purchasing-power

parity assumes that net exports are highly responsive to small changes in the real exchange rate. If net exports were in fact so responsive, the demand curve in Figure 2 would be horizontal.

Thus, the theory of purchasing-power parity can be viewed as a special case of the model considered here. In that special case, the demand curve for foreign-currency exchange, instead of sloping downward, is horizontal at the level of the real exchange rate that ensures parity of purchasing power at home and abroad.

While this special case is a good place to start when studying exchange rates, it is far from the end of the story. In practice, foreign and domestic goods are not always perfect substitutes, and there are costs that impede trade. This chapter, therefore, assumes that the demand curve for foreign-currency exchange slopes downward. This assumption allows for the possibility that the real exchange rate changes over time, as in fact it often does in the real world. ■

14-2 Equilibrium in the Open Economy

So far, we have discussed supply and demand in two markets: the market for loanable funds and the market for foreign-currency exchange. Let's now consider how these markets are related to each other.

14-2a Net Capital Outflow: The Link between the Two Markets

We begin by recapping what we've learned so far in this chapter. We have been discussing how the economy coordinates four important macroeconomic variables: national saving (S), domestic investment (I), net capital outflow (NCO), and net exports (NX). Keep in mind the following identities:

$$S = I + NCO$$

and

$$NCO = NX.$$

In the market for loanable funds, supply comes from national saving (S), demand comes from domestic investment (I) and net capital outflow (NCO), and the real interest rate balances supply and demand. In the market for foreign-currency exchange, supply comes from net capital outflow (NCO), demand comes from net exports (NX), and the real exchange rate balances supply and demand.

Net capital outflow is the variable that links these two markets. In the market for loanable funds, net capital outflow is a component of demand. An American who wants to buy an asset abroad must finance this purchase by obtaining resources in the U.S. market for loanable funds. In the market for foreign-currency exchange, net capital outflow is the source of supply. An American who wants to buy an asset in another country must supply dollars to exchange them for the currency of that country.

The key determinant of net capital outflow, as we have discussed, is the real interest rate. When the U.S. interest rate is high, owning U.S. assets is attractive, and U.S. net capital outflow is low. Figure 3 shows this negative relationship between the interest rate and net capital outflow. This net-capital-outflow curve is the link between the market for loanable funds and the market for foreign-currency exchange.

FIGURE 3

How Net Capital Outflow Depends on the Interest Rate
Because a higher domestic real interest rate makes domestic assets more attractive, it reduces net capital outflow. Note the position of zero on the horizontal axis: Net capital outflow can be positive or negative. A negative value of net capital outflow means that the economy is experiencing a net inflow of capital.

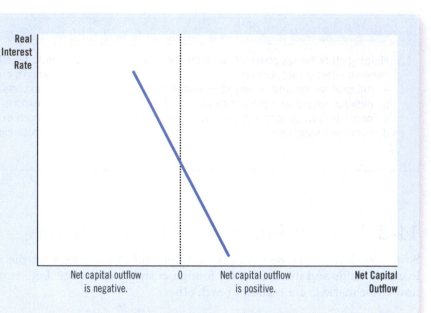

Real Interest Rate

Net capital outflow is negative.   0   Net capital outflow is positive.   **Net Capital Outflow**

14-2b Simultaneous Equilibrium in Two Markets

We can now put all the pieces of our model together in Figure 4. This figure shows how the market for loanable funds and the market for foreign-currency exchange jointly determine the important macroeconomic variables of an open economy.

Panel (a) of the figure shows the market for loanable funds (taken from Figure 1). As before, national saving is the source of the supply of loanable funds. Domestic investment and net capital outflow are the source of the demand for loanable funds. The equilibrium real interest rate (r_1) brings the quantity of loanable funds supplied and the quantity of loanable funds demanded into balance.

Panel (b) of the figure shows net capital outflow (taken from Figure 3). The interest rate comes from panel (a) and then determines net capital outflow. A higher interest rate at home makes domestic assets more attractive, reducing net capital outflow. Therefore, the net-capital-outflow curve in panel (b) slopes downward.

Panel (c) of the figure shows the market for foreign-currency exchange (taken from Figure 2). Because foreign assets must be purchased with foreign currency, the quantity of net capital outflow from panel (b) determines the supply of dollars to be exchanged into foreign currencies. The real exchange rate does not affect net capital outflow, so the supply curve is vertical. The demand for dollars comes from net exports. Because a depreciation of the real exchange rate increases net exports, the demand curve for foreign-currency exchange slopes downward. The equilibrium real exchange rate (E_1) brings into balance the quantity of dollars supplied and the quantity of dollars demanded in the market for foreign-currency exchange.

The two markets shown in Figure 4 determine two relative prices: the real interest rate and the real exchange rate. The real interest rate determined in panel (a) is

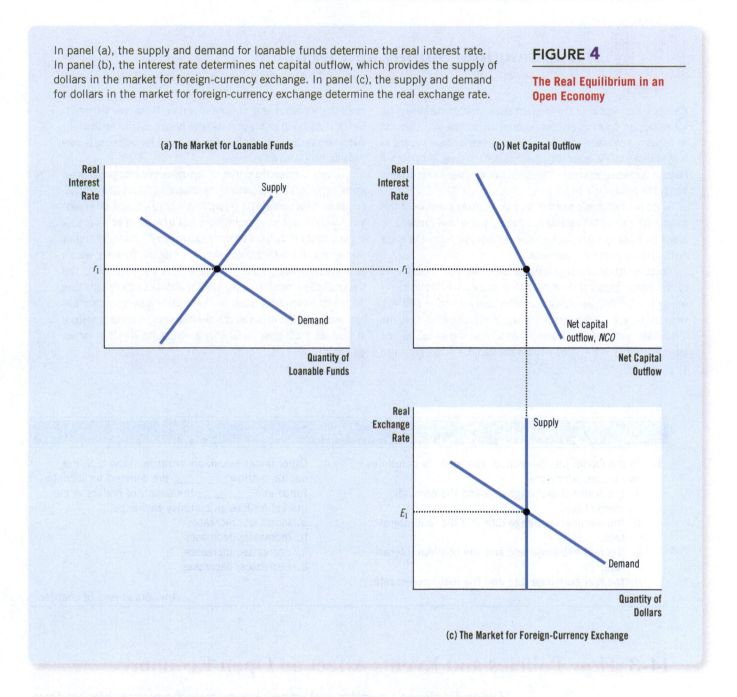

In panel (a), the supply and demand for loanable funds determine the real interest rate. In panel (b), the interest rate determines net capital outflow, which provides the supply of dollars in the market for foreign-currency exchange. In panel (c), the supply and demand for dollars in the market for foreign-currency exchange determine the real exchange rate.

FIGURE 4

The Real Equilibrium in an Open Economy

(a) The Market for Loanable Funds

Real Interest Rate

Supply

r_1

Demand

Quantity of Loanable Funds

(b) Net Capital Outflow

Real Interest Rate

r_1

Net capital outflow, NCO

Net Capital Outflow

Real Exchange Rate

Supply

E_1

Demand

Quantity of Dollars

(c) The Market for Foreign-Currency Exchange

the price of goods and services in the present relative to goods and services in the future. The real exchange rate determined in panel (c) is the price of domestic goods and services relative to foreign goods and services. These two relative prices adjust simultaneously to balance supply and demand in these two markets. As they do so, they determine national saving, domestic investment, net capital outflow, and net exports. We can use this model to see how all these variables change when some policy or event causes one of these curves to shift.

FYI

Disentangling Supply and Demand

Suppose the owner of an apple orchard decides to consume some of his own apples. Does this decision represent an increase in the demand for apples or a decrease in the supply? Either answer is defensible, and as long as we are careful in our subsequent analysis, nothing important will hinge on the answer we choose. Sometimes how we divide things between supply and demand is a bit arbitrary.

In the macroeconomic model of the open economy developed in this chapter, the division of transactions between "supply" and "demand" is also a bit arbitrary—both in the market for loanable funds and in the market for foreign-currency exchange.

Consider first the market for loanable funds. The model treats the net capital outflow as part of the demand for loanable funds. Yet instead of writing $S = I + NCO$, we could just as easily have written $S - NCO = I$. When the equation is rewritten in this way, a capital outflow looks like a reduction in the supply of loanable funds. Either way works. The first interpretation ($S = I + NCO$) emphasizes loanable funds generated

domestically whether used at home or abroad. The second interpretation ($S - NCO = I$) emphasizes loanable funds available for domestic investment whether generated at home or abroad. The difference is more semantic than substantive.

Similarly, consider the market for foreign-currency exchange. In our model, net exports are the source of the demand for dollars, and net capital outflow is the source of the supply. Thus, when a U.S. resident imports a car made in Japan, our model treats that transaction as a decrease in the quantity of dollars demanded (because net exports fall) rather than an increase in the quantity of dollars supplied. Similarly, when a Japanese citizen buys a U.S. government bond, our model treats that transaction as a decrease in the quantity of dollars supplied (because net capital outflow falls) rather than an increase in the quantity of dollars demanded. This definition of terms may seem somewhat unnatural at first, but it will prove useful when analyzing the effects of various policies. ■

Quick Quiz

3. In the model just developed, two markets determine two prices, which are
   a. the nominal exchange rate and the nominal interest rate.
   b. the nominal exchange rate and the real interest rate.
   c. the real exchange rate and the nominal interest rate.
   d. the real exchange rate and the real interest rate.

4. Other things equal, an increase in the U.S. net capital outflow _____ the demand for loanable funds and _____ the supply of dollars in the market for foreign currency exchange.
   a. increases; increases
   b. increases; decreases
   c. decreases; increases
   d. decreases; decreases

Answers at end of chapter.

14-3 How Policies and Events Affect an Open Economy

Having developed a model to explain how key macroeconomic variables are determined in an open economy, we can now use the model to analyze how changes in policy and other events alter the economy's equilibrium. As we proceed, keep in mind that our model is just supply and demand in two markets: the market for loanable funds and the market for foreign-currency exchange. When using the model to analyze any event, we can apply the three steps outlined in Chapter 4. First, we determine which of the supply and demand curves the event affects. Second, we determine the direction in which the curves shift. Third, we use the supply-and-demand diagrams to examine how these shifts alter the economy's equilibrium.

14-3a Government Budget Deficits

When we first discussed the supply and demand for loanable funds earlier in the book, we examined the effects of government budget deficits, which occur when government spending exceeds government revenue. Because a government budget deficit represents *negative* public saving, it reduces national saving (the sum of public and private saving). Thus, a government budget deficit reduces the supply of loanable funds, drives up the interest rate, and crowds out investment.

Now let's consider the effects of a budget deficit in an open economy. First, which curve in our model shifts? As in a closed economy, the initial impact of the budget deficit is on national saving and, therefore, on the supply curve for loanable funds. Second, in which direction does this supply curve shift? Again as in a closed economy, a budget deficit represents *negative* public saving, so it reduces national saving and shifts the supply curve for loanable funds to the left. This result is shown as the shift from S_1 to S_2 in panel (a) of Figure 5.

Our third and final step is to compare the old and new equilibria. Panel (a) shows the impact of a U.S. budget deficit on the U.S. market for loanable funds. Because fewer funds are available for borrowers in U.S. financial markets, the interest rate rises from r_1 to r_2 to balance supply and demand. Faced with a higher interest rate, borrowers in the market for loanable funds choose to borrow less. This change is represented in the figure as the movement from point A to point B along the demand curve for loanable funds. In particular, households and firms reduce their purchases of capital goods. As in a closed economy, budget deficits crowd out domestic investment.

In an open economy, however, the reduced supply of loanable funds has additional effects. Panel (b) shows that the increase in the interest rate from r_1 to r_2 reduces net capital outflow. [This fall in net capital outflow is also part of the decrease in the quantity of loanable funds demanded in the movement from point A to point B in panel (a).] Because saving kept at home now earns higher rates of return, investing abroad is less attractive, and domestic residents buy fewer foreign assets. Higher interest rates also attract foreign investors, who want to earn the higher returns on U.S. assets. Thus, when budget deficits raise interest rates, both domestic and foreign behavior cause U.S. net capital outflow to fall.

Panel (c) shows how budget deficits affect the market for foreign-currency exchange. Because net capital outflow is reduced, Americans need less foreign currency to buy foreign assets and, therefore, supply fewer dollars in the market for foreign-currency exchange. The supply curve for dollars shifts leftward from S_1 to S_2. The reduced supply of dollars causes the real exchange rate to appreciate from E_1 to E_2. That is, the dollar becomes more valuable relative to foreign currencies. This appreciation, in turn, makes U.S. goods more expensive relative to foreign goods. Because people both in the United States and abroad switch their purchases away from the more expensive U.S. goods, exports from the United States fall and imports into the United States rise. For both reasons, U.S. net exports fall. Hence, *in an open economy, government budget deficits raise real interest rates, crowd out domestic investment, cause the currency to appreciate, and push the trade balance toward deficit.*

An important example of this lesson occurred in the United States in the 1980s. Shortly after Ronald Reagan was elected president in 1980, the fiscal policy of the U.S. federal government changed dramatically. The president and Congress enacted large tax cuts, but they did not reduce government spending by nearly as much. The result was a large budget deficit. Our model of the open economy

FIGURE 5

The Effects of a Government Budget Deficit

When the government runs a budget deficit, it reduces the supply of loanable funds from S_1 to S_2 in panel (a). The interest rate rises from r_1 to r_2 to balance the supply and demand for loanable funds. In panel (b), the higher interest rate reduces net capital outflow. Reduced net capital outflow, in turn, reduces the supply of dollars in the market for foreign-currency exchange from S_1 to S_2 in panel (c). This fall in the supply of dollars causes the real exchange rate to appreciate from E_1 to E_2. The appreciation of the exchange rate pushes the trade balance toward deficit.

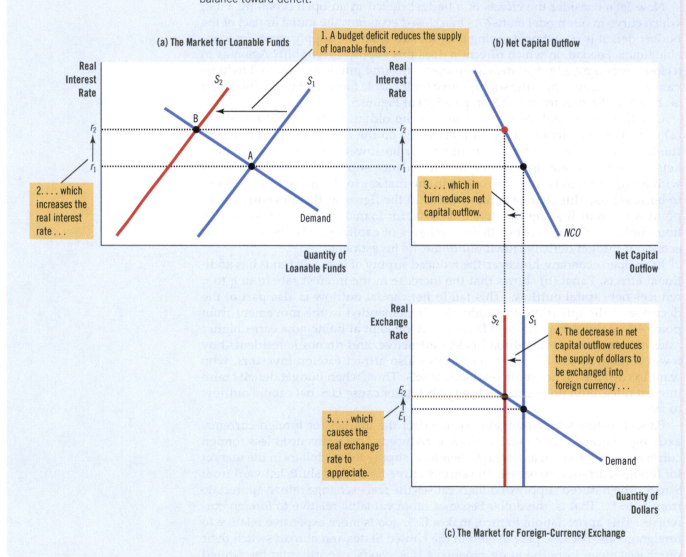

(a) The Market for Loanable Funds

1. A budget deficit reduces the supply of loanable funds . . .

(b) Net Capital Outflow

2. . . . which increases the real interest rate . . .

3. . . . which in turn reduces net capital outflow.

4. The decrease in net capital outflow reduces the supply of dollars to be exchanged into foreign currency . . .

5. . . . which causes the real exchange rate to appreciate.

(c) The Market for Foreign-Currency Exchange

predicts that such a policy should have led to a trade deficit, and in fact it did, as we saw in a case study in the preceding chapter. Because the budget deficit and trade deficit during this period were so closely related in both theory and practice, they were nicknamed the *twin deficits*. We should not, however, view these twins as identical, for many factors beyond fiscal policy can influence the trade deficit.

14-3b Trade Policy

Trade policy is government policy that directly influences the quantity of goods and services that a country imports or exports. Trade policy takes various forms, usually with the purpose of supporting a particular domestic industry. One common trade policy is a *tariff*, a tax on imported goods. Another is an *import quota*, a limit on the quantity of a good produced abroad that can be sold domestically.

Let's consider the macroeconomic impact of trade policy. Suppose that the U.S. auto industry, concerned about competition from Japanese automakers, convinces the U.S. government to impose a quota on the number of cars that can be imported from Japan. In making their case, lobbyists for the auto industry assert that the trade restriction would shrink the size of the U.S. trade deficit. Are they right? Our model, illustrated in Figure 6, offers an answer.

The first step in analyzing the trade policy is to determine which curve shifts. The initial impact of the import restriction is, not surprisingly, on imports. Because net exports equal exports minus imports, the policy also affects net exports. And because net exports are the source of demand for dollars in the market for foreign-currency exchange, the policy affects the demand curve in this market.

The second step is to determine the direction in which this demand curve shifts. Because the quota restricts the number of Japanese cars sold in the United States, it reduces imports at any given real exchange rate. Net exports, which equal exports minus imports, will therefore *rise* for any given real exchange rate. Because foreigners need dollars to buy U.S. net exports, the rise in net exports increases the demand for dollars in the market for foreign-currency exchange. This increase in the demand for dollars is shown in panel (c) of Figure 6 as the shift from D_1 to D_2.

The third step is to compare the old and new equilibria. As we can see in panel (c), the increase in the demand for dollars causes the real exchange rate to appreciate from E_1 to E_2. Because nothing has happened in the market for loanable funds in panel (a), there is no change in the real interest rate. Because there is no change in the real interest rate, there is also no change in net capital outflow, shown in panel (b). And because there is no change in net capital outflow, there can be no change in net exports, even though the import quota has reduced imports.

It might seem puzzling that net exports stay the same while imports fall. This puzzle is resolved by noting the change in the real exchange rate: When the dollar appreciates in the market for foreign-currency exchange, domestic goods become more expensive relative to foreign goods. This appreciation encourages imports and discourages exports, and both of these changes offset the direct increase in net exports due to the import quota. In the end, an import quota reduces both imports and exports, but net exports (exports minus imports) are unchanged.

We have thus arrived at a surprising result: *Trade policies do not affect the trade balance.* That is, policies that directly influence exports or imports do not alter net exports. This conclusion seems less surprising if one recalls the accounting identity:

$$NX = NCO = S - I.$$

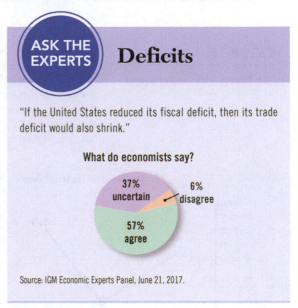

ASK THE EXPERTS

Deficits

"If the United States reduced its fiscal deficit, then its trade deficit would also shrink."

What do economists say?

37% uncertain
6% disagree
57% agree

Source: IGM Economic Experts Panel, June 21, 2017.

trade policy
government policy that directly influences the quantity of goods and services that a country imports or exports

FIGURE 6

The Effects of an Import Quota

When the U.S. government imposes a quota on the import of Japanese cars, nothing happens in the market for loanable funds in panel (a) or to net capital outflow in panel (b). The only effect is a rise in net exports (exports minus imports) for any given real exchange rate. As a result, the demand for dollars in the market for foreign-currency exchange rises, as shown by the shift from D_1 to D_2 in panel (c). This increase in the demand for dollars causes the value of the dollar to appreciate from E_1 to E_2. This appreciation of the dollar tends to reduce net exports, offsetting the direct effect of the import quota on the trade balance.

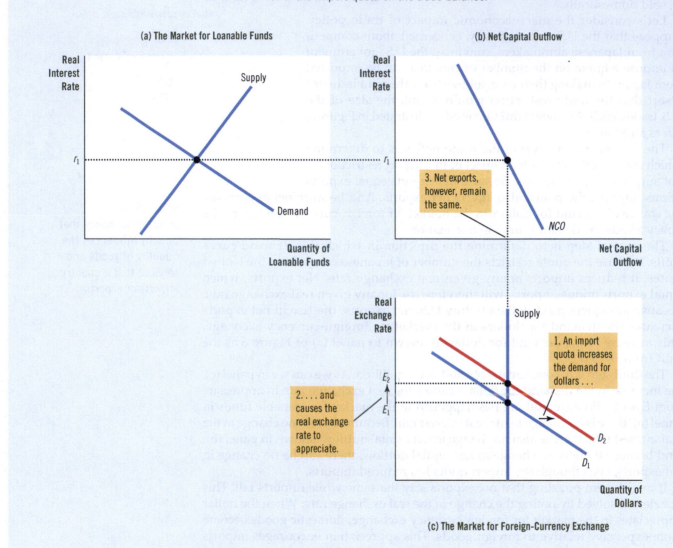

(a) The Market for Loanable Funds

(b) Net Capital Outflow

3. Net exports, however, remain the same.

1. An import quota increases the demand for dollars . . .

2. . . . and causes the real exchange rate to appreciate.

(c) The Market for Foreign-Currency Exchange

Net exports equal net capital outflow, which equals national saving minus domestic investment. Trade policies do not alter the trade balance because they do not alter national saving or domestic investment. For given levels of national saving and domestic investment, the real exchange rate adjusts to keep the trade balance the same, regardless of the trade policies the government puts in place.

Although trade policies do not affect a country's overall trade balance, these policies do affect specific firms, industries, and countries. When the U.S. government imposes an import quota on Japanese cars, General Motors has less competition from abroad and sells more cars. At the same time, because the dollar has appreciated, Boeing, the U.S. aircraft maker, finds it harder to compete with Airbus, the European aircraft maker. U.S. exports of aircraft fall, and U.S. imports of aircraft rise. In this case, the import quota on Japanese cars increases net exports of cars and decreases net exports of planes. In addition, it increases net exports from the United States to Japan and decreases net exports from the United States to Europe. The overall trade balance of the U.S. economy, however, stays the same.

The effects of trade policies are, therefore, more microeconomic than macroeconomic. Although advocates of trade policies sometimes suggest (contrary to what our model predicts) that these policies can alter a country's trade balance, they are usually more motivated by concerns about particular firms or industries. One should not be surprised, for instance, to hear an executive from General Motors advocating import quotas on Japanese cars. Economists usually oppose such trade policies. Free trade allows economies to specialize in doing what they do best, making residents of all countries better off. Trade restrictions interfere with these gains from trade and, therefore, reduce overall economic well-being.

14-3c Political Instability and Capital Flight

In 1994, political instability in Mexico, including the assassination of a prominent political leader, made world financial markets nervous. People began to view Mexico as a much less stable country than they had previously thought. They decided to pull some of their assets out of Mexico and move these funds to the United States and other "safe havens." Such a large and sudden movement of funds out of a country is called **capital flight**. To see the implications of capital flight for the Mexican economy, we again follow our three steps for analyzing a change in equilibrium. But this time, we apply our model of the open economy from the perspective of Mexico rather than the United States.

capital flight
a large and sudden reduction in the demand for assets located in a country

Consider first which curves in our model capital flight affects. When investors around the world observe political problems in Mexico, they decide to sell some of their Mexican assets and use the proceeds to buy U.S. assets. This act increases Mexican net capital outflow and, therefore, affects both markets in our model. Most obviously, it affects the net-capital-outflow curve, and this change in net capital outflow in turn influences the supply of pesos in the market for foreign-currency exchange. In addition, because the demand for loanable funds comes from both domestic investment and net capital outflow, capital flight affects the demand curve in the market for loanable funds.

Now consider the direction in which these curves shift. When net capital outflow increases, there is greater demand for loanable funds to finance these purchases of capital assets abroad. Thus, as panel (a) of Figure 7 shows, the demand curve for loanable funds shifts to the right from D_1 to D_2. In addition, because net capital outflow is higher for any interest rate, the net-capital-outflow curve also shifts to the right from NCO_1 to NCO_2, as in panel (b).

To see the effects of capital flight on the Mexican economy, we compare the old and new equilibria. Panel (a) of Figure 7 shows that the increased demand for loanable funds causes the interest rate in Mexico to rise from r_1 to r_2. Panel (b) shows that Mexican net capital outflow increases. (Although the rise in the interest rate makes Mexican assets more attractive, this change only partly offsets the impact of capital flight on net capital outflow.) Panel (c) shows that the increase in net capital outflow raises the supply of pesos in the market for foreign-currency exchange from S_1 to S_2. That is, as people try to get out of Mexican assets, there is a large supply

FIGURE 7

The Effects of Capital Flight

If people decide that Mexico is a risky place to keep their savings, they will move their funds to safe havens such as the United States, resulting in an increase in Mexican net capital outflow. Consequently, the demand for loanable funds in Mexico rises from D_1 to D_2, as shown in panel (a), driving up the Mexican real interest rate from r_1 to r_2. Because net capital outflow is higher for any interest rate, that curve also shifts to the right from NCO_1 to NCO_2 in panel (b). At the same time, in the market for foreign-currency exchange, the supply of pesos rises from S_1 to S_2, as shown in panel (c). This increase in the supply of pesos causes the peso to depreciate from E_1 to E_2, so the peso becomes less valuable relative to other currencies.

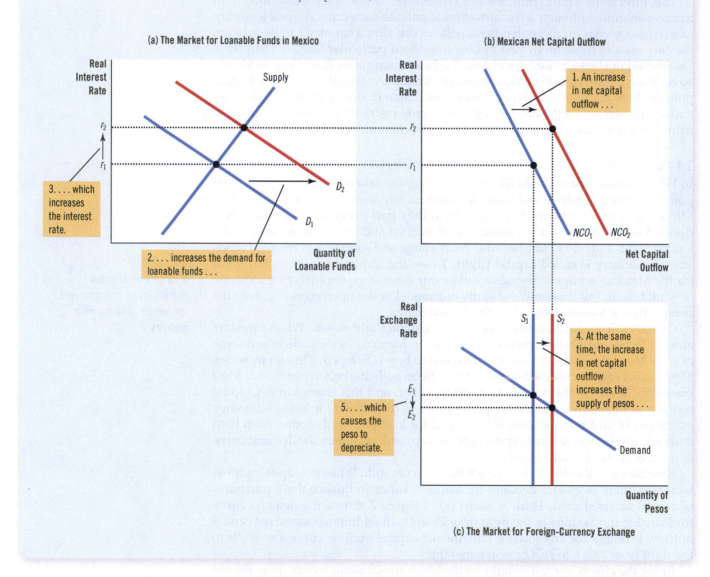

(a) The Market for Loanable Funds in Mexico

(b) Mexican Net Capital Outflow

(c) The Market for Foreign-Currency Exchange

of pesos to be converted into dollars. This increase in supply causes the peso to depreciate from E_1 to E_2. Thus, *capital flight from Mexico increases Mexican interest rates and decreases the value of the Mexican peso in the market for foreign-currency exchange.* This is exactly what was observed in 1994. From November 1994 to March 1995, the interest rate on short-term Mexican government bonds rose from 14 percent to 70 percent, and the peso depreciated from 29 to 15 U.S. cents per peso.

These price changes that result from capital flight influence some key macroeconomic quantities. The depreciation of the currency makes exports cheaper and imports more expensive, pushing the trade balance toward surplus. At the same time, the increase in the interest rate reduces domestic investment, slowing capital accumulation and economic growth.

Capital flight has its largest impact on the country from which capital is fleeing, but it also affects other countries. When capital flows out of Mexico into the United States, for instance, it has the opposite effect on the U.S. economy as it has on the Mexican economy. In particular, the rise in Mexican net capital outflow coincides with a fall in U.S. net capital outflow. As the peso depreciates and Mexican interest rates rise, the dollar appreciates and U.S. interest rates fall. The size of this impact on the U.S. economy is small, however, because the economy of the United States is much larger than that of Mexico.

The events that we have been describing in Mexico could happen to any economy in the world, and, in fact, they do from time to time. In 1997, the world learned that the banking systems of several Asian economies, including Thailand, South Korea, and Indonesia, were at or near the point of bankruptcy, and this news induced capital to flee from these nations. In 1998, the Russian government defaulted on its debt, prompting international investors to take whatever money they could and run. A similar (but more complicated) set of events unfolded in Argentina in 2002. In each of these cases of capital flight, the results were much as our model predicts: rising interest rates and a falling currency.

CAPITAL FLOWS FROM CHINA

According to our analysis of capital flight, a nation that experiences an outflow of capital sees its currency weaken in foreign exchange markets, and this depreciation in turn increases the nation's net exports. The country into which the capital is flowing sees its currency strengthen, and this appreciation pushes its trade balance toward deficit.

With these lessons in mind, consider this question: Suppose a nation's government, as a matter of policy, encourages capital to flow to another country, perhaps by making foreign investments itself. What effects would this policy have? The answer is much the same: Other things equal, it leads to a weaker currency and a trade surplus for the nation encouraging the capital outflows and a stronger currency and a trade deficit for the recipient of those capital flows.

This analysis sheds light on a recent policy dispute between the United States and China. The Chinese government has at times tried to depress the value of its currency, the renminbi, in foreign exchange markets to promote its export industries. It did this by accumulating foreign assets, including substantial amounts of U.S. government bonds. From 2000 to 2014, China's total reserves of foreign assets rose from $160 billion to about $4 trillion.

The U.S. government at times objected to China's interventions in foreign exchange markets. By holding down the value of the renminbi, the policy made Chinese goods less expensive relative to American goods, pushing the U.S. trade balance toward deficit and hurting American producers who made products that competed with imports from China. Because of these effects, the U.S. government encouraged China to stop influencing the exchange value of its currency using government-sponsored capital flows. Some members of Congress even went so far as to advocate tariffs on Chinese imports unless China ceased its "currency manipulation."

Yet the impact of the Chinese policy on the U.S. economy was not all bad. American consumers of Chinese imports benefited from lower prices. In addition,

IN THE NEWS

Separating Fact from Fiction

Politicians on both the right and left often hold mistaken views about the role of international trade in a nation's economic well-being.

Five Big Truths About Trade

By Alan S. Blinder

International trade is, once again, a hot-button political issue, making this an unpropitious time for rational discourse about the subject. Nonetheless, here are five issues on which the overwhelming majority of economists, liberal and conservative, agree.

1. Most job losses are not due to international trade. Every month roughly five million new jobs are created in the U.S. and almost that many are destroyed, leaving a small net increment. International trade accounts for only a minor share of that staggering job churn. Vastly more derives from the hurly-burly

of competition and from technological change, which literally creates and destroys entire industries. Competition and technology are widely and correctly applauded—international trade is not so fortunate.

2. Trade is more about efficiency—and hence wages—than about the number of jobs. You probably don't sew your own clothes or grow your own food. Instead, you buy these things from others, using the wages you earn doing something you do better. Imagine how much lower your standard of living would be if you had to sew your own clothes, grow your own food . . . and a thousand other things.

The case for international trade is no different. It's not mainly about creating or destroying jobs. It's about using labor more efficiently, which is one key to higher wages.

But there is a catch: Whenever trade patterns change, some people will gain (either jobs or wages) but others will lose. The federal government could and should help them more, but it doesn't. So Americans who do lose their

jobs due to international trade have a legitimate gripe.

3. Bilateral trade imbalances are inevitable and mostly uninteresting. Each month I run a trade deficit with Public Service Electric & Gas. They sell me gas and electricity; I sell them nothing. But I run a bilateral trade surplus with Princeton University, to which I sell teaching services but from which I buy little. Should I seek balanced trade with PSE&G or Princeton? Of course not. Neither should countries.

4. Running an overall trade deficit does not make us "losers." The U.S. multilateral trade balance—its balance with all of its trading partners—has been in deficit for decades. Does that mean that our country is in some sort of trouble? Probably not. For example, people who claim that our trade deficit kills jobs need to explain how the U.S. managed to achieve 4% unemployment in 2000, when our trade deficit was larger, as a share of GDP, than it is today.

ASK THE EXPERTS

Currency Manipulation

"Economic analysis can identify whether countries are using their exchange rates to benefit their own people at the expense of their trading partners' welfare."

What do economists say?

- 34% disagree
- 36% uncertain
- 30% agree

Source: IGM Economic Experts Panel, June 16, 2015.

the inflow of capital from China reduced U.S. interest rates, increasing investment in the U.S. economy. To some extent, the Chinese government was financing U.S. economic growth. The Chinese policy of investing in the U.S. economy created winners and losers among Americans. All things considered, the net impact on the U.S. economy was probably small.

The harder question concerns the motives behind the policy: Why were the Chinese leaders interested in producing for export and investing abroad rather than producing for domestic consumption and investment? One possibility is that China wanted to accumulate a reserve of foreign assets on which it could draw in emergencies—a kind of national "rainy-day fund." In any case, after 2014, as growth in the Chinese economy slowed, the Chinese government started to spend some of the fund. From 2014 to 2018, its reserves of foreign assets fell by almost $1 trillion. ●

A trade deficit means that foreigners send us more goods and services than we send them. To balance the books, they get our IOUs, which means they wind up holding paper—U.S. Treasury bills, corporate bonds or other private debt instruments. That doesn't sound so terrible for us, does it?

One exceptional country—the U.S.—is the source of the world's major international reserve currency, the U.S. dollar. Since ever-expanding world commerce requires ever more dollars, the U.S. must run trade deficits regularly. That's sometimes called our "exorbitant privilege," since we get to import more than we export.

5. Trade agreements barely affect a nation's trade balance. Much of the political angst is directed not at trade in general, but at specific international trade agreements. The North American Free Trade Agreement allegedly shipped U.S. jobs to Mexico. . . .

There is a grain of truth here. Some U.S. jobs were indeed destroyed when NAFTA liberalized trade with Mexico—and those people deserved better treatment from the government than they got. But NAFTA also created a number of new jobs in the U.S. (See No. 2.)

Source: *The Wall Street Journal,* April 22, 2016.

But there's more. "Trade" and "trade agreements" are not synonyms. We traded with Mexico long before NAFTA, and that trade was growing. Our trade with China has burgeoned in recent decades without a succession of trade agreements.

Most fundamentally, but least understood, a nation's overall trade balance is determined by its domestic decisions, not by trade deals. Think about the accounting involved here.

As noted above, borrowing from abroad is the bookkeeping counterpart of running a trade deficit. One implies the other. The amount we borrow from abroad must equal the gap between our total spending as a nation (including government spending) and our total income (including the government's income from taxation). Spendthrift nations like the U.S. have trade deficits because we don't save much. But these saving decisions are domestic; they do not derive from trade agreements.

America's chronic trade deficits stem from the dollar's international role and from Americans' decisions not to save much, not from trade deals. Trade deficits are not a major cause of either job losses or job gains. But some people do lose their jobs from shifting

trade patterns; and the government should do more to help them. Importantly, trade makes American workers more productive and, presumably, better paid.

Now, would someone please tell this to Bernie Sanders and Donald Trump? ■

Questions to Discuss

1. Do you think running a trade deficit necessarily puts a nation at a disadvantage? Why or why not? According to the dictionary, the word *deficit* means "an excess of expenditure over revenue," but another definition is "deficiency or disadvantage." Might this dual meaning mislead pundits and policymakers into being more worried about trade deficits than Professor Blinder is?

2. How do you think the government should help workers who lose their jobs because of changing patterns of trade? Should these workers receive government assistance different from that given to workers who lose jobs for other reasons, such as changing technology?

Mr. Blinder is a professor of economics at Princeton University.

QuickQuiz

5. The government in an open economy cuts spending to reduce the budget deficit. As a result, the interest rate _____, leading to a capital _____ and a currency _____.
   a. falls; outflow; appreciation
   b. falls; outflow; depreciation
   c. falls; inflow; appreciation
   d. rises; inflow; appreciation

6. The nation of Elbonia has long banned the export of its highly prized puka shells. A newly elected president, however, removes the export ban. This change in policy causes the nation's currency to _____, making the goods Elbonia imports _____ expensive.
   a. depreciate; less
   b. depreciate; more
   c. appreciate; less
   d. appreciate; more

7. A civil war abroad causes foreign investors to move their funds to the safe haven of the United States, leading to _____ U.S. interest rates and a _____ U.S. dollar.
   a. higher; weaker
   b. higher; stronger
   c. lower; weaker
   d. lower; stronger

8. If business leaders in Great Britain become more confident in their economy, they will increase investment, causing the British pound to _____ and pushing the British trade balance toward _____.
   a. appreciate; deficit
   b. appreciate; surplus
   c. depreciate; deficit
   d. depreciate; surplus

Answers at end of chapter.

14-4   Conclusion

International economics is a topic of increasing importance. More and more, American citizens are buying goods produced abroad and producing goods to be sold overseas. Through mutual funds and other financial institutions, they borrow and lend in world financial markets. As a result, a full analysis of the U.S. economy requires an understanding of how the U.S. economy interacts with other economies in the world. This chapter has provided a basic model for thinking about the macroeconomics of open economies.

The study of international economics is valuable, but we should be careful not to exaggerate its importance. Policymakers and commentators are often quick to blame foreigners for problems facing the U.S. economy. By contrast, economists more often view these problems as homegrown. For example, politicians often discuss foreign competition as a threat to American living standards, while economists are more likely to lament the low level of national saving. Low saving impedes growth in capital, productivity, and living standards, regardless of whether the economy is open or closed. Foreigners are a convenient target for politicians because blaming foreigners provides a way to avoid responsibility without insulting any domestic constituency. Whenever you hear popular discussions of international trade and finance, therefore, it is especially important to separate myth from reality. The tools you have learned in this chapter and the preceding one should help in that endeavor.

CHAPTER IN A NUTSHELL

- Two markets are central to the macroeconomics of open economies: the market for loanable funds and the market for foreign-currency exchange. In the market for loanable funds, the real interest rate adjusts to balance the supply of loanable funds (from national saving) and the demand for loanable funds (for domestic investment and net capital outflow). In the market for foreign-currency exchange, the real exchange rate adjusts to balance the supply of dollars (from net capital outflow) and the demand for dollars (for net exports). Because net capital outflow contributes to the demand for loanable funds and also provides the supply of dollars for foreign-currency exchange, it is the variable that connects these two markets.

- A policy that reduces national saving, such as a government budget deficit, reduces the supply of loanable funds and drives up the interest rate. The higher interest rate causes the net capital outflow to decline, reducing the supply of dollars in the market for foreign-currency exchange. The dollar appreciates, and net exports fall.

- Although restrictive trade policies, such as tariffs or quotas on imports, are sometimes advocated as a way to alter the trade balance, they do not necessarily have that effect. A trade restriction increases net exports for any given exchange rate and, therefore, increases the demand for dollars in the market for foreign-currency exchange. As a result, the dollar appreciates, making domestic goods more expensive relative to foreign goods. This appreciation offsets the initial impact of the trade restriction on net exports.

- When investors change their attitudes about holding assets of a country, the ramifications for the country's economy can be profound. In particular, political instability can lead to capital flight, which tends to increase interest rates and cause the currency to depreciate.

KEY CONCEPTS

trade policy, *p. 293*   capital flight, *p. 295*

QUESTIONS FOR REVIEW

1. Describe supply and demand in the market for loanable funds and in the market for foreign-currency exchange. How are these markets linked?

2. Why are budget deficits and trade deficits sometimes called the twin deficits?

3. Suppose that a textile workers' union encourages people to buy only American-made clothes.

What would this policy do to the trade balance and the real exchange rate? What is the impact on the textile industry? What is the impact on the auto industry?

4. What is capital flight? When a country experiences capital flight, what is the effect on its interest rate and exchange rate?

PROBLEMS AND APPLICATIONS

1. Japan generally runs a significant trade surplus. Do you think this surplus is most related to high foreign demand for Japanese goods, low Japanese demand for foreign goods, a high Japanese saving rate relative to Japanese investment, or structural barriers against imports into Japan? Explain your answer.

2. Suppose that Congress is considering an investment tax credit, which subsidizes domestic investment.
   a. How does this policy affect national saving, domestic investment, net capital outflow, the interest rate, the exchange rate, and the trade balance?
   b. Representatives of several large exporters oppose the policy. Why might that be the case?

3. The chapter notes that the rise in the U.S. trade deficit during the 1980s was largely due to the rise in the U.S. budget deficit. On the other hand, the popular press sometimes claims that the increased trade deficit resulted from a decline in the quality of U.S. products relative to foreign products.
   a. Assume that U.S. products did decline in relative quality during the 1980s. How did this decline affect net exports *at any given exchange rate*?
   b. Draw a three-panel diagram to show the effect of this shift in net exports on the U.S. real exchange rate and trade balance.

   c. Is the claim in the popular press consistent with the model in this chapter? Does a decline in the quality of U.S. products have any effect on our standard of living? (*Hint*: When we sell our goods to foreigners, what do we receive in return?)

4. An economist discussing trade policy in *The New Republic* wrote, "One of the benefits of the United States removing its trade restrictions [is] the gain to U.S. industries that produce goods for export. Export industries would find it easier to sell their goods abroad—even if other countries didn't follow our example and reduce their trade barriers." Explain in words why U.S. *export* industries would benefit from a reduction in restrictions on *imports* to the United States.

5. Suppose the French suddenly develop a strong taste for California wines. Answer the following questions in words and with a diagram.
   a. What happens to the demand for dollars in the market for foreign-currency exchange?
   b. What happens to the value of the dollar in the market for foreign-currency exchange?
   c. What happens to U.S. net exports?

6. A senator renounces his past support for protectionism: "The U.S. trade deficit must be reduced, but import quotas only annoy our trading partners. If we subsidize U.S. exports instead, we can

reduce the deficit by increasing our competitiveness." Using a three-panel diagram, show the effect of an export subsidy on net exports and the real exchange rate. Do you agree with the senator?

7. Suppose the United States decides to subsidize the export of U.S. agricultural products, but it does not increase taxes or decrease any other government spending to offset this expenditure. Using a three-panel diagram, show what happens to national saving, domestic investment, net capital outflow, the interest rate, the exchange rate, and the trade balance. Also explain in words how this U.S. policy affects the amount of imports, exports, and net exports.

8. Suppose that real interest rates increase across Europe. Explain how this development affects U.S. net capital outflow. Then explain how it affects U.S. net exports by using a formula from the chapter and by drawing a diagram. What happens to the U.S. real interest rate and real exchange rate?

9. Suppose that Americans decide to increase their saving.
   a. If the elasticity of U.S. net capital outflow with respect to the real interest rate is very high, will this increase in private saving have a large or small effect on U.S. domestic investment?
   b. If the elasticity of U.S. exports with respect to the real exchange rate is very low, will this increase in private saving have a large or small effect on the U.S. real exchange rate?

Quick**Quiz Answers**

1. **c**   2. **b**   3. **d**   4. **a**   5. **b**   6. **c**   7. **d**   8. **a**

Aggregate Demand and Aggregate Supply

Economic activity fluctuates from year to year. In most years, the production of goods and services rises. Because of increases in the labor force, increases in the capital stock, and advances in technological knowledge, the economy can produce more and more over time. This growth allows everyone to enjoy a higher standard of living. On average, over the past half century, the production of the U.S. economy as measured by real GDP has grown by about 3 percent per year.

In some years, however, instead of expanding, the economy contracts. Firms find themselves unable to sell all the goods and services they have to offer, so they reduce production. Workers are laid off, unemployment becomes widespread, and factories are left idle. With the economy producing fewer goods and services, real GDP and other measures of income decline. Such a period of falling

recession
a period of declining
real incomes and rising
unemployment

depression
a severe recession

incomes and rising unemployment is called a **recession** if it is relatively mild and a **depression** if it is more severe.

An example of such a downturn occurred in 2008 and 2009 in what is now referred to as "The Great Recession." From the fourth quarter of 2007 to the second quarter of 2009, real GDP for the U.S. economy fell by 4.0 percent. The unemployment rate rose from 4.4 percent in May 2007 to 10.0 percent in October 2009—the highest level in more than a quarter century. Not surprisingly, for students graduating during this time, good jobs were hard to find.

What causes short-run fluctuations in economic activity? What, if anything, can public policy do to prevent periods of falling incomes and rising unemployment? When recessions and depressions occur, how can policymakers reduce their length and severity? We now take up these questions.

The variables at the center of our analysis are familiar from previous chapters. They include GDP, unemployment, interest rates, and the price level. Also familiar are the policy instruments of government spending, taxes, and the money supply. What differs from our earlier discussions is the time horizon. So far, our goal has been to explain the behavior of these variables in the long run. Our goal now is to explain their short-run deviations from long-run trends. In other words, instead of focusing on the forces that explain economic growth from generation to generation, we are now interested in the forces that explain economic fluctuations from year to year.

Economists still debate how best to explain short-run fluctuations, but most use the *model of aggregate demand and aggregate supply*. Learning how to use this model to analyze the short-run effects of various events and policies is the main task ahead. This chapter introduces the model's two pieces: the aggregate-demand curve and the aggregate-supply curve. Before turning to the model, however, let's look at some of the key facts that describe the ups and downs of the economy.

15-1 Three Key Facts about Economic Fluctuations

Short-run fluctuations in economic activity have occurred in all countries throughout history. As a starting point for understanding these year-to-year fluctuations, let's discuss some of their most important properties.

15-1a Fact 1: Economic Fluctuations Are Irregular and Unpredictable

Fluctuations in the economy are often called *the business cycle*. As this term suggests, economic fluctuations correspond to changes in business conditions. When real GDP grows rapidly, business is good. During such periods of economic expansion, most firms find that customers are plentiful and that profits are growing. When real GDP falls during recessions, businesses have trouble. During such periods of economic contraction, most firms experience declining sales and dwindling profits.

The term *business cycle* is somewhat misleading because it suggests that economic fluctuations follow a regular, predictable pattern. In fact, economic fluctuations are not at all regular, and they are almost impossible to predict with much accuracy. Panel (a) of Figure 1 shows the real GDP of the U.S. economy since 1972. The shaded areas represent times of recession. As the figure shows, recessions do not come at regular intervals. Sometimes recessions are close together, such as the recessions of 1980 and 1982. Sometimes the economy goes many years without a

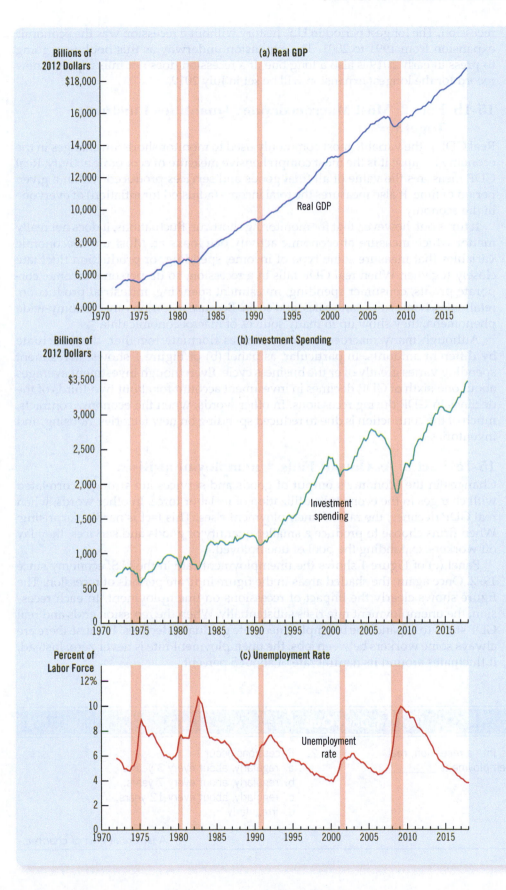

(a) Real GDP

Billions of 2012 Dollars

(b) Investment Spending

Billions of 2012 Dollars

Investment spending

(c) Unemployment Rate

Percent of Labor Force

Unemployment rate

FIGURE 1

A Look at Short-Run Economic Fluctuations

This figure shows real GDP in panel (a), investment spending in panel (b), and unemployment in panel (c) for the U.S. economy. Recessions are shown as the shaded areas. Notice that real GDP and investment spending decline during recessions, while unemployment rises.

Source: U.S. Department of Commerce; U.S. Department of Labor.

recession. The longest period in U.S. history without a recession was the economic expansion from 1991 to 2001. The expansion underway as this book was going to press in early 2019 is also a long one. If a recession does not interrupt it, a new record for the longest expansion will be set in July 2019.

15-1b   Fact 2: Most Macroeconomic Quantities Fluctuate Together

Real GDP is the variable most commonly used to monitor short-run changes in the economy because it is the most comprehensive measure of economic activity. Real GDP measures the value of all final goods and services produced within a given period of time. It also measures the total income (adjusted for inflation) of everyone in the economy.

It turns out, however, that for monitoring short-run fluctuations, it does not really matter which measure of economic activity one looks at. Most macroeconomic variables that measure some type of income, spending, or production fluctuate closely together. When real GDP falls in a recession, so do personal income, corporate profits, consumer spending, investment spending, industrial production, retail sales, home sales, auto sales, and so on. Because recessions are economy-wide phenomena, they show up in many sources of macroeconomic data.

Although many macroeconomic variables fluctuate together, they fluctuate by different amounts. In particular, as panel (b) of Figure 1 shows, investment spending varies greatly over the business cycle. Even though investment averages about one-sixth of GDP, declines in investment account for about two-thirds of the declines in GDP during recessions. In other words, when the economy contracts, much of the contraction is due to reduced spending on new factories, housing, and inventories.

"You're fired. Pass it on."

15-1c   Fact 3: As Output Falls, Unemployment Rises

Changes in the economy's output of goods and services are strongly correlated with changes in the economy's utilization of its labor force. In other words, when real GDP declines, the rate of unemployment rises. This fact is hardly surprising: When firms choose to produce a smaller quantity of goods and services, they lay off workers, expanding the pool of unemployed.

Panel (c) of Figure 1 shows the unemployment rate in the U.S. economy since 1972. Once again, the shaded areas in the figure indicate periods of recession. The figure shows clearly the impact of recessions on unemployment. In each recession, the unemployment rate rises substantially. When the recession ends and real GDP starts to expand, the unemployment rate gradually declines. Because there are always some workers between jobs, the unemployment rate is never zero. Instead, it fluctuates around its natural rate of about 5 percent.

Quick**Quiz**

1. When the economy goes into a recession, real GDP _____ and unemployment _____.
   a. rises; rises
   b. rises; falls
   c. falls; rises
   d. falls; falls

2. Recessions occur
   a. regularly, about every 3 years.
   b. regularly, about every 7 years.
   c. regularly, about every 12 years.
   d. irregularly.

Answers at end of chapter.

15-2 Explaining Short-Run Economic Fluctuations

Describing what happens to economies as they fluctuate over time is easy. Explaining what causes these fluctuations is more difficult. Indeed, compared to the topics we have studied in previous chapters, the theory of economic fluctuations remains controversial. In this chapter, we begin to develop the model that most economists use to explain short-run fluctuations in economic activity.

15-2a The Assumptions of Classical Economics

In previous chapters, we developed theories to explain what determines most important macroeconomic variables in the long run. Chapter 7 explained the level and growth of productivity and real GDP. Chapters 8 and 9 explained how the financial system works and how the real interest rate adjusts to balance saving and investment. Chapter 10 explained why there is always some unemployment in the economy. Chapters 11 and 12 explained the monetary system and how changes in the money supply affect the price level, the inflation rate, and the nominal interest rate. Chapters 13 and 14 extended this analysis to open economies to explain the trade balance and the exchange rate.

All of this previous analysis was based on two related ideas: the classical dichotomy and monetary neutrality. Recall that the classical dichotomy is the separation of variables into real variables (those that measure quantities or relative prices) and nominal variables (those measured in terms of money). According to classical macroeconomic theory, changes in the money supply affect nominal variables but not real variables. As a result of this monetary neutrality, Chapters 7 through 10 were able to examine the determinants of real variables (real GDP, the real interest rate, and unemployment) without introducing nominal variables (the money supply and the price level).

In a sense, money does not matter in a classical world. If the quantity of money in the economy were to double, everything would cost twice as much, and everyone's income would be twice as high. But so what? The change would be *nominal* (by the standard meaning of "nearly insignificant"). The things that people *really* care about—whether they have a job, how many goods and services they can afford, and so on—would be exactly the same.

This classical view is sometimes described by the saying, "Money is a veil." That is, nominal variables may be the first things we see when we observe an economy because economic variables are often expressed in units of money. But more important are the real variables and the forces that determine them. According to classical theory, to understand these real variables, we need to look behind the veil.

15-2b The Reality of Short-Run Fluctuations

Do these assumptions of classical macroeconomic theory apply to the world in which we live? The answer to this question is central to understanding how the economy works. *Most economists believe that classical theory describes the world in the long run but not in the short run.*

Consider again the impact of money on the economy. Most economists believe that, beyond a period of several years, changes in the money supply affect prices and other nominal variables but do not affect real GDP, unemployment, and other real variables—just as classical theory says. When studying year-to-year changes in the economy, however, the assumption of monetary neutrality is no longer appropriate. In the short run, real and nominal variables are highly intertwined, and changes in the money supply can temporarily push real GDP away from its long-run trend.

Even the classical economists themselves, such as David Hume, realized that classical economic theory did not hold in the short run. From his vantage point in 18th-century England, Hume observed that when the money supply expanded after gold discoveries, it took some time for prices to rise and that, in the meantime, the economy enjoyed higher employment and production.

To understand how the economy works in the short run, we need a new model. This new model can be built using many of the tools we developed in previous chapters, but it must abandon the classical dichotomy and the neutrality of money. We can no longer separate our analysis of real variables such as output and employment from our analysis of nominal variables such as money and the price level. Our new model focuses on how real and nominal variables interact.

15-2c The Model of Aggregate Demand and Aggregate Supply

Our model of short-run economic fluctuations focuses on the behavior of two variables. The first variable is the economy's output of goods and services, as measured by real GDP. The second is the average level of prices, as measured by the CPI or the GDP deflator. Notice that output is a real variable, whereas the price level is a nominal variable. By focusing on the relationship between these two variables, we are departing from the classical assumption that real and nominal variables can be studied separately.

We analyze fluctuations in the economy as a whole using the **model of aggregate demand and aggregate supply**, which is illustrated in Figure 2. On the vertical axis is the overall price level in the economy. On the horizontal axis is the overall quantity of goods and services produced in the economy. The **aggregate-demand curve** shows the quantity of goods and services that households, firms, the government, and customers abroad want to buy at each price level. The **aggregate-supply curve** shows the quantity of goods and services that firms produce and sell at each price level. According to this model, the price level and the quantity of output adjust to bring aggregate demand and aggregate supply into balance.

model of aggregate demand and aggregate supply
the model that most economists use to explain short-run fluctuations in economic activity around its long-run trend

aggregate-demand curve
a curve that shows the quantity of goods and services that households, firms, the government, and customers abroad want to buy at each price level

aggregate-supply curve
a curve that shows the quantity of goods and services that firms choose to produce and sell at each price level

FIGURE 2

Aggregate Demand and Aggregate Supply
Economists use the model of aggregate demand and aggregate supply to analyze economic fluctuations. On the vertical axis is the overall level of prices. On the horizontal axis is the economy's total output of goods and services. Output and the price level adjust to the point at which the aggregate-supply and aggregate-demand curves intersect.

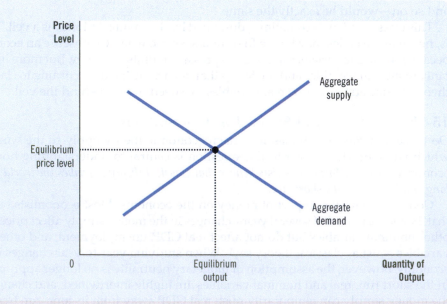

It is tempting to view the model of aggregate demand and aggregate supply as nothing more than a large version of the model of market demand and market supply introduced in Chapter 4. But in fact, this model is quite different. When we consider demand and supply in the market for a specific good—ice cream, for instance—the behavior of buyers and sellers depends on the ability of resources to move from one market to another. When the price of ice cream rises, the quantity demanded falls because buyers will use their incomes to buy products other than ice cream. Similarly, a higher price of ice cream raises the quantity supplied because firms that produce ice cream can increase production by hiring workers away from other parts of the economy. This *microeconomic* substitution from one market to another is impossible for the economy as a whole. After all, the quantity that our model is trying to explain—real GDP—measures the *total* quantity of goods and services produced by *all* firms in *all* markets. To understand why the aggregate-demand curve slopes downward and why the aggregate-supply curve slopes upward, we need a *macroeconomic* theory that explains the total quantity of goods and services demanded and the total quantity of goods and services supplied. Developing such a theory is our next task.

QuickQuiz

3. According to classical macroeconomic theory and monetary neutrality, changes in the money supply affect
   a. the unemployment rate.
   b. real GDP.
   c. the GDP deflator.
   d. none of the above.

4. Most economists believe that classical macroeconomic theory
   a. is valid only in the long run.
   b. is valid only in the short run.
   c. is always valid.
   d. is never valid.

5. In the model of aggregate demand and aggregate supply, the quantity of _____ is on the horizontal axis, and the _____ is on the vertical axis.
   a. output; interest rate
   b. output; price level
   c. money; interest rate
   d. money; price level

Answers at end of chapter.

15-3 The Aggregate-Demand Curve

The aggregate-demand curve tells us the quantity of all goods and services demanded in the economy at any given price level. As Figure 3 illustrates, the aggregate-demand curve slopes downward. Other things being equal, a decrease in the economy's overall level of prices (from, say, P_1 to P_2) raises the quantity of goods and services demanded (from Y_1 to Y_2). Conversely, an increase in the price level reduces the quantity of goods and services demanded.

15-3a Why the Aggregate-Demand Curve Slopes Downward

Why does a change in the price level move the quantity of goods and services demanded in the opposite direction? To answer this question, it is useful to recall that an economy's GDP (which we denote as Y) is the sum of its consumption (C), investment (I), government purchases (G), and net exports (NX):

$$Y = C + I + G + NX.$$

FIGURE 3

The Aggregate-Demand Curve

A fall in the price level from P_1 to P_2 increases the quantity of goods and services demanded from Y_1 to Y_2. There are three reasons for this negative relationship. As the price level falls, real wealth rises, interest rates fall, and the exchange rate depreciates. These effects stimulate spending on consumption, investment, and net exports. Increased spending on any or all of these components of output means a larger quantity of goods and services demanded.

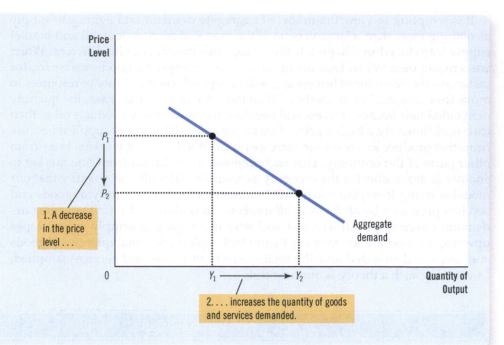

1. A decrease in the price level . . .

Aggregate demand

2. . . . increases the quantity of goods and services demanded.

Each of these four components contributes to the aggregate demand for goods and services. For now, we assume that government spending is fixed by policy. The other three components of spending—consumption, investment, and net exports—depend on economic conditions and, in particular, on the price level. Therefore, to understand the downward slope of the aggregate-demand curve, we must examine how the price level affects the quantity of goods and services demanded for consumption, investment, and net exports.

The Price Level and Consumption: The Wealth Effect Consider the money that you hold in your wallet and your bank account. The nominal value of this money is fixed: One dollar is always worth one dollar. Yet the *real* value of a dollar is not fixed. If a candy bar costs one dollar, then a dollar is worth one candy bar. If the price of a candy bar falls to 50 cents, then one dollar is worth two candy bars. Thus, when the price level falls, the dollars you hold rise in value, increasing your real wealth and your ability to buy goods and services.

This logic gives us the first reason the aggregate-demand curve slopes downward. *A decrease in the price level raises the real value of money and makes consumers wealthier, thereby encouraging them to spend more. The increase in consumer spending means a larger quantity of goods and services demanded. Conversely, an increase in the price level reduces the real value of money and makes consumers poorer, thereby reducing consumer spending and the quantity of goods and services demanded.*

The Price Level and Investment: The Interest-Rate Effect The price level is one determinant of the quantity of money demanded. When the price level is lower, households do not need to hold as much money to buy the goods and services they want. Therefore, when the price level falls, households try to reduce their holdings of money by lending some of it out. For instance, a household might use its excess money to buy interest-bearing bonds. Or it might deposit its excess money in an interest-bearing savings account, and the bank would use these funds to make more loans. In either case, as households try to convert some of their money into interest-bearing assets, they drive down interest rates. (The next chapter analyzes this process in more detail.)

Interest rates, in turn, affect spending on goods and services. Because a lower interest rate makes borrowing less expensive, it encourages firms to borrow more to invest in new plants and equipment, and it encourages households to borrow more to invest in new housing. (A lower interest rate might also stimulate consumer spending, especially spending on large durable purchases such as cars, which are often bought on credit.) Thus, a lower interest rate increases the quantity of goods and services demanded.

This logic gives us the second reason the aggregate-demand curve slopes downward. *A lower price level reduces the interest rate, encourages greater spending on investment goods, and thereby increases the quantity of goods and services demanded. Conversely, a higher price level raises the interest rate, discourages investment spending, and decreases the quantity of goods and services demanded.*

The Price Level and Net Exports: The Exchange-Rate Effect As we have just discussed, a lower price level in the United States lowers the U.S. interest rate. In response to the lower interest rate, some U.S. investors will seek higher returns by investing abroad. For instance, as the interest rate on U.S. government bonds falls, a mutual fund might sell U.S. government bonds to buy German government bonds. As the mutual fund tries to convert its dollars into euros to buy the German bonds, it increases the supply of dollars in the market for foreign-currency exchange.

The increased supply of dollars to be exchanged for euros causes the dollar to depreciate relative to the euro. This alters the real exchange rate—the relative price of domestic and foreign goods. Because each dollar buys fewer units of foreign currencies, foreign goods become more expensive relative to domestic goods.

The change in relative prices affects spending, both at home and abroad. Because foreign goods are now more expensive, Americans buy less from other countries, causing U.S. imports of goods and services to decrease. At the same time, because U.S. goods are now cheaper, foreigners buy more from the United States, so U.S. exports increase. Net exports equal exports minus imports, so both of these changes cause U.S. net exports to increase. Thus, the depreciation of the dollar leads to an increase in the quantity of goods and services demanded.

This logic yields the third reason the aggregate-demand curve slopes downward. *When a fall in the U.S. price level causes U.S. interest rates to fall, the real value of the dollar declines in foreign exchange markets. This depreciation stimulates U.S. net exports and thereby increases the quantity of goods and services demanded. Conversely, when the U.S. price level rises and causes U.S. interest rates to rise, the real value of the dollar increases, and this appreciation reduces U.S. net exports and the quantity of goods and services demanded.*

Summing Up There are three distinct but related reasons a fall in the price level increases the quantity of goods and services demanded:

1. Consumers become wealthier, stimulating the demand for consumption goods.
2. Interest rates fall, stimulating the demand for investment goods.
3. The currency depreciates, stimulating the demand for net exports.

The same three effects work in reverse: When the price level rises, decreased wealth depresses consumer spending, higher interest rates depress investment spending, and a currency appreciation depresses net exports.

Here is a thought experiment to hone your intuition about these effects. Imagine that one day you wake up and notice that, for some mysterious reason, the prices of all goods and services have fallen by half, so the dollars you are holding are worth twice as much. In real terms, you now have twice as much money as you had when you went to bed the night before. What would you do with the extra money? You could spend it at your favorite restaurant, increasing consumer spending. You could lend it out (by buying a bond or depositing it in a bank), reducing interest rates and increasing investment spending. Or you could invest it overseas (by buying shares in an international mutual fund), reducing the real exchange value of the dollar and increasing net exports. Whichever of these three responses you choose, the fall in the price level leads to an increase in the quantity of goods and services demanded. This relationship is what the downward slope of the aggregate-demand curve represents.

It is important to keep in mind that the aggregate-demand curve (like all demand curves) is drawn holding "other things equal." In particular, our three explanations of the downward-sloping aggregate-demand curve assume that the money supply is fixed. That is, we have been considering how a change in the price level affects the demand for goods and services, holding the amount of money in the economy constant. As we will see, a change in the quantity of money shifts the aggregate-demand curve. At this point, just keep in mind that the aggregate-demand curve is drawn for a given quantity of the money supply.

15-3b Why the Aggregate-Demand Curve Might Shift

The downward slope of the aggregate-demand curve shows that a fall in the price level raises the overall quantity of goods and services demanded. Many other factors, however, affect the quantity of goods and services demanded at a given price level. When one of these other factors changes, the quantity of goods and services demanded at every price level changes and the aggregate-demand curve shifts.

Let's consider some examples of events that shift aggregate demand. We can categorize them according to the component of spending that is most directly affected.

Shifts Arising from Changes in Consumption   Suppose Americans suddenly become more concerned about saving for retirement and, as a result, reduce their current consumption. Because the quantity of goods and services demanded at any price level is now lower, the aggregate-demand curve shifts to the left. Conversely, imagine that a stock market boom makes people wealthier and less concerned about saving. The resulting increase in consumer spending means a greater quantity of goods and services demanded at any given price level, so the aggregate-demand curve shifts to the right.

Thus, any event that changes how much people want to consume at a given price level shifts the aggregate-demand curve. One policy variable that has this effect is the level of taxation. When the government cuts taxes, it encourages people to spend more, so the aggregate-demand curve shifts to the right. When the government raises taxes, people cut back on their spending and the aggregate-demand curve shifts to the left.

Shifts Arising from Changes in Investment   Any event that changes how much firms want to invest at a given price level also shifts the aggregate-demand curve. For instance, imagine that the computer industry introduces a faster line of computers and many firms decide to invest in new computer systems. Because the quantity of goods and services demanded at any price level is now higher, the aggregate-demand curve shifts to the right. Conversely, if firms become pessimistic about future business conditions, they may cut back on investment spending, shifting the aggregate-demand curve to the left.

Tax policy can also influence aggregate demand through investment. For example, an investment tax credit (a tax rebate tied to a firm's investment spending) increases the quantity of investment goods that firms demand at any given interest rate and therefore shifts the aggregate-demand curve to the right. The repeal of an investment tax credit reduces investment and shifts the aggregate-demand curve to the left.

Another policy variable that can influence investment and aggregate demand is the money supply. As we discuss more fully in the next chapter, an increase in the money supply lowers the interest rate in the short run. This decrease in the interest rate makes borrowing less costly, stimulating investment spending and thereby shifting the aggregate-demand curve to the right. Conversely, a decrease in the money supply raises the interest rate, discourages investment spending, and thereby shifts the aggregate-demand curve to the left. Many economists believe that throughout U.S. history, changes in monetary policy have been an important source of shifts in aggregate demand.

Shifts Arising from Changes in Government Purchases   The most direct way that policymakers shift the aggregate-demand curve is through government purchases. For example, suppose Congress decides to reduce purchases of new weapons systems. Because the quantity of goods and services demanded at any price level is now lower, the aggregate-demand curve shifts to the left. Conversely, if state governments start building more highways, the result is a greater quantity of goods and services demanded at any price level, so the aggregate-demand curve shifts to the right.

Shifts Arising from Changes in Net Exports   Any event that changes net exports for a given price level also shifts aggregate demand. For instance, when Europe experiences a recession, it buys fewer goods from the United States. U.S. net exports decline at every price level, shifting the aggregate-demand curve for the U.S. economy to the left. When Europe recovers from its recession, it buys more U.S. goods and the aggregate-demand curve shifts to the right.

Net exports can also change because international speculators cause movements in the exchange rate. Suppose, for instance, that these speculators lose confidence in foreign economies and want to move some of their wealth into the U.S. economy. In doing so, they bid up the value of the U.S. dollar in the foreign exchange market. This appreciation of the dollar makes U.S. goods more expensive relative to foreign goods, depressing net exports and shifting the aggregate-demand curve to the left. Conversely, speculation that causes a depreciation of the dollar stimulates net exports and shifts the aggregate-demand curve to the right.

Summing Up   In the next chapter, we analyze the aggregate-demand curve in more detail. There we examine more precisely how the tools of monetary and fiscal policy can shift aggregate demand and whether policymakers should use these tools for that purpose. At this point, however, you should have some idea about why the aggregate-demand curve slopes downward and what kinds of events and policies can shift this curve. Table 1 summarizes what we have learned so far.

TABLE 1

The Aggregate-Demand Curve: Summary

Why Does the Aggregate-Demand Curve Slope Downward?

1. *The Wealth Effect:* A lower price level increases real wealth, stimulating spending on consumption.
2. *The Interest-Rate Effect:* A lower price level reduces the interest rate, stimulating spending on investment.
3. *The Exchange-Rate Effect:* A lower price level causes the real exchange rate to depreciate, stimulating spending on net exports.

Why Might the Aggregate-Demand Curve Shift?

1. *Shifts Arising from Changes in Consumption:* An event that causes consumers to spend more at a given price level (a tax cut, a stock market boom) shifts the aggregate-demand curve to the right. An event that causes consumers to spend less at a given price level (a tax hike, a stock market decline) shifts the aggregate-demand curve to the left.
2. *Shifts Arising from Changes in Investment:* An event that causes firms to invest more at a given price level (optimism about the future, a fall in interest rates due to an increase in the money supply) shifts the aggregate-demand curve to the right. An event that causes firms to invest less at a given price level (pessimism about the future, a rise in interest rates due to a decrease in the money supply) shifts the aggregate-demand curve to the left.
3. *Shifts Arising from Changes in Government Purchases:* An increase in government purchases of goods and services (greater spending on defense or highway construction) shifts the aggregate-demand curve to the right. A decrease in government purchases on goods and services (a cutback in defense or highway spending) shifts the aggregate-demand curve to the left.
4. *Shifts Arising from Changes in Net Exports:* An event that raises spending on net exports at a given price level (a boom overseas, speculation that causes a currency depreciation) shifts the aggregate-demand curve to the right. An event that reduces spending on net exports at a given price level (a recession overseas, speculation that causes a currency appreciation) shifts the aggregate-demand curve to the left.

Quick**Quiz**

6. The aggregate-demand curve slopes downward because a fall in the price level causes
   a. real wealth to decrease.
   b. the interest rate to decline.
   c. the currency to appreciate.
   d. all of the above.

7. Which of the following would shift the aggregate-demand curve to the left?
   a. A decline in the stock market.
   b. An increase in taxes.
   c. A decrease in government spending.
   d. All of the above.

Answers at end of chapter.

15-4 The Aggregate-Supply Curve

The aggregate-supply curve tells us the total quantity of goods and services that firms produce and sell at any given price level. Unlike the aggregate-demand curve, which always slopes downward, the aggregate-supply curve shows a relationship that depends crucially on the time horizon examined. *In the long run, the aggregate-supply curve is vertical, whereas in the short run, the aggregate-supply curve slopes upward.* To understand short-run economic fluctuations, and how the short-run behavior of the economy deviates from its long-run behavior, we need to examine both the long-run aggregate-supply curve and the short-run aggregate-supply curve.

15-4a Why the Aggregate-Supply Curve Is Vertical in the Long Run

What determines the quantity of goods and services supplied in the long run? We implicitly answered this question earlier in the book when we analyzed the process of economic growth. *In the long run, an economy's production of goods and services (its real GDP) depends on its supplies of labor, capital, and natural resources and on the available technology used to turn these factors of production into goods and services.*

When we analyzed these forces that govern long-run growth, we did not need to make any reference to the overall level of prices. We examined the price level in a separate chapter, where we saw that it was determined by the quantity of money. We learned that if two economies were identical in every way except that one had twice as much money in circulation as the other, the price level would be twice as high in the economy with more money. But since the amount of money does not affect technology or the supplies of labor, capital, and natural resources, the output of goods and services in the two economies would be the same.

Because the price level does not affect the long-run determinants of real GDP, the long-run aggregate-supply curve is vertical, as in Figure 4. In other words, in the long run, the economy's labor, capital, natural resources, and technology determine the

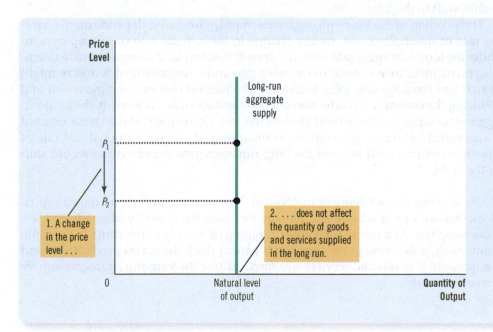

FIGURE 4

The Long-Run Aggregate-Supply Curve

In the long run, the quantity of output supplied depends on the economy's quantities of labor, capital, and natural resources and on the technology for turning these inputs into output. Because the quantity supplied does not depend on the overall price level, the long-run aggregate-supply curve is vertical at the natural level of output.

total quantity of goods and services supplied, and this quantity supplied is the same regardless of the price level.

The vertical long-run aggregate-supply curve is a graphical representation of the classical dichotomy and monetary neutrality. As we have already discussed, classical macroeconomic theory is based on the assumption that real variables do not depend on nominal variables. The long-run aggregate-supply curve is consistent with this idea because it implies that the quantity of output (a real variable) does not depend on the level of prices (a nominal variable). As noted earlier, most economists believe this principle works well when studying the economy over a period of many years but not when studying year-to-year changes. Thus, *the aggregate-supply curve is vertical only in the long run.*

15-4b Why the Long-Run Aggregate-Supply Curve Might Shift

Because classical macroeconomic theory predicts the quantity of goods and services produced by an economy in the long run, it also explains the position of the long-run aggregate-supply curve. The long-run level of production is sometimes called *potential output* or *full-employment output*. To be more precise, we call it the **natural level of output** because it shows what the economy produces when unemployment is at its natural, or normal, rate. The natural level of output is the rate of production toward which the economy gravitates in the long run.

Any change in the economy that alters the natural level of output shifts the long-run aggregate-supply curve. Because output in the classical model depends on labor, capital, natural resources, and technological knowledge, we can categorize shifts in the long-run aggregate-supply curve as arising from these four sources.

Shifts Arising from Changes in Labor   Imagine that an economy experiences an increase in immigration. Because increased immigration results in a greater number of workers, the quantity of goods and services supplied would increase. As a result, the long-run aggregate-supply curve would shift to the right. Conversely, if many workers left the economy to go abroad, the long-run aggregate-supply curve would shift to the left.

The position of the long-run aggregate-supply curve also depends on the natural rate of unemployment, so any change in the natural rate of unemployment shifts the long-run aggregate-supply curve. For example, if Congress made unemployment insurance substantially more generous, unemployed workers might search less hard for new jobs, increasing the natural rate of unemployment and reducing the economy's production of goods and services. As a result, the long-run aggregate-supply curve would shift to the left. Conversely, if Congress enacted a successful job training program for unemployed workers, the natural rate of unemployment would fall and the long-run aggregate-supply curve would shift to the right.

Shifts Arising from Changes in Capital   An increase in the economy's capital stock increases productivity and thereby increases the quantity of goods and services supplied. As a result, the long-run aggregate-supply curve shifts to the right. Conversely, a decrease in the economy's capital stock decreases productivity and the quantity of goods and services supplied, shifting the long-run aggregate-supply curve to the left.

natural level of output
the production of goods and services that an economy achieves in the long run when unemployment is at its normal rate

Notice that the same logic applies regardless of whether we are discussing physical capital such as machines and factories or human capital such as college degrees. An increase in either type of capital will raise the economy's ability to produce goods and services and, thus, shift the long-run aggregate-supply curve to the right.

Shifts Arising from Changes in Natural Resources An economy's production depends on its natural resources, including its land, minerals, and weather. The discovery of a new mineral deposit shifts the long-run aggregate-supply curve to the right. A change in weather patterns that makes farming more difficult shifts the long-run aggregate-supply curve to the left.

In many countries, crucial natural resources are imported. A change in the availability of these resources can also shift the aggregate-supply curve. For example, as we discuss later in this chapter, developments in the world oil market have historically been an important source of shifts in aggregate supply for the United States and other oil-importing nations.

Shifts Arising from Changes in Technological Knowledge Perhaps the most important reason that the economy today produces more than it did a generation ago is that our technological knowledge has advanced. The invention of the computer, for instance, has allowed us to produce more goods and services from any given amounts of labor, capital, and natural resources. As computer use has spread throughout the economy, it has shifted the long-run aggregate-supply curve to the right.

Although not literally technological, many other events act like changes in technology. For instance, opening up international trade has effects similar to inventing new production processes because it allows a country to specialize in higher-productivity industries; therefore, it also shifts the long-run aggregate-supply curve to the right. Conversely, if the government passes new regulations preventing firms from using some production methods, perhaps to address worker safety or environmental concerns, the result is a leftward shift in the long-run aggregate-supply curve.

Summing Up Because the long-run aggregate-supply curve reflects the classical model of the economy we developed in previous chapters, it provides a new way to describe our earlier analysis. Any policy or event that raised real GDP in previous chapters can now be described as increasing the quantity of goods and services supplied and shifting the long-run aggregate-supply curve to the right. Any policy or event that lowered real GDP in previous chapters can now be described as decreasing the quantity of goods and services supplied and shifting the long-run aggregate-supply curve to the left.

15-4c Using Aggregate Demand and Aggregate Supply to Depict Long-Run Growth and Inflation

Having introduced the economy's aggregate-demand curve and the long-run aggregate-supply curve, we now have a new way to describe the economy's long-run trends. Figure 5 illustrates the changes that occur in an economy from decade to decade. Notice that both curves are shifting. Although many forces influence the economy in the long run and can in theory cause such shifts, the two most important forces in practice are technology and monetary policy. Technological progress enhances an economy's ability to produce goods and services, and the resulting

FIGURE 5

Long-Run Growth and Inflation in the Model of Aggregate Demand and Aggregate Supply

As the economy becomes better able to produce goods and services over time, primarily because of technological progress, the long-run aggregate-supply curve shifts to the right. At the same time, as the Fed increases the money supply, the aggregate-demand curve also shifts to the right. In this figure, output grows from Y_{2000} to Y_{2010} and then to Y_{2020}, and the price level rises from P_{2000} to P_{2010} and then to P_{2020}. Thus, the model of aggregate demand and aggregate supply offers a new way to describe the classical analysis of growth and inflation.

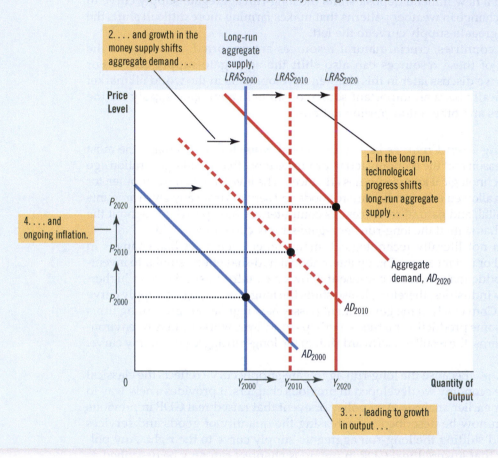

increases in output are reflected in continual shifts of the long-run aggregate-supply curve to the right. At the same time, because the Fed increases the money supply over time, the aggregate-demand curve also shifts to the right. As the figure illustrates, the result is continuing growth in output (as shown by increasing Y) and continuing inflation (as shown by increasing P). This is just another way of representing the classical analysis of growth and inflation we conducted in earlier chapters.

The purpose of developing the model of aggregate demand and aggregate supply, however, is not to dress our previous long-run conclusions in new clothing. Instead, it is to provide a framework for short-run analysis, as we will see in a moment. As we develop the short-run model, we keep the analysis simple by omitting the continuing growth and inflation shown by the shifts in Figure 5. But always remember that long-run trends are the background on which short-run fluctuations are superimposed. *The short-run fluctuations in output and the price level that we will be studying should be viewed as deviations from the long-run trends of output growth and inflation.*

15-4d Why the Aggregate-Supply Curve Slopes Upward in the Short Run

The key difference between the economy in the short run and in the long run is the behavior of aggregate supply. The long-run aggregate-supply curve is vertical because, in the long run, the overall level of prices does not affect the economy's ability to produce goods and services. By contrast, in the short run, the price level *does* affect the economy's output. That is, over a period of a year or two, an increase in the overall level of prices in the economy tends to raise the quantity of goods and services supplied, and a decrease in the level of prices tends to reduce the quantity of goods and services supplied. As a result, the short-run aggregate-supply curve slopes upward, as shown in Figure 6.

Why do changes in the price level affect output in the short run? Macroeconomists have proposed three theories for the upward slope of the short-run aggregate-supply curve. In each theory, a specific market imperfection causes the supply side of the economy to behave differently in the short run than it does in the long run. The following theories differ in their details, but they share a common theme: *The quantity of output supplied deviates from its long-run, or natural, level when the actual price level in the economy deviates from the price level that people expected to prevail.* When the price level rises above the level that people expected, output rises above its natural level, and when the price level falls below the expected level, output falls below its natural level.

The Sticky-Wage Theory   The first explanation of the upward slope of the short-run aggregate-supply curve is the sticky-wage theory. This theory is the simplest of the three approaches to aggregate supply, and some economists believe it highlights the most important reason why the economy in the short run differs from the economy in the long run. Therefore, it is the theory of short-run aggregate supply that we emphasize in this book.

According to this theory, the short-run aggregate-supply curve slopes upward because nominal wages are slow to adjust to changing economic conditions.

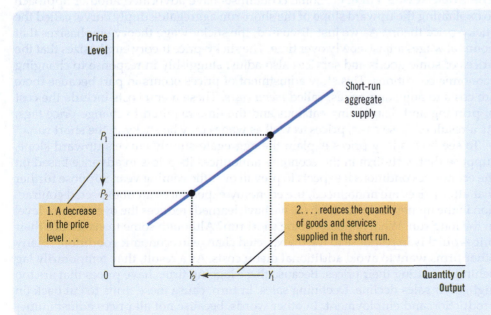

FIGURE 6

The Short-Run Aggregate-Supply Curve

In the short run, a fall in the price level from P_1 to P_2 reduces the quantity of output supplied from Y_1 to Y_2. This positive relationship could be due to sticky wages, sticky prices, or misperceptions. Over time, wages, prices, and perceptions adjust, so this positive relationship is only temporary.

In other words, wages are "sticky" in the short run. To some extent, the slow adjustment of nominal wages is attributable to long-term contracts between workers and firms that fix nominal wages, sometimes for as long as three years. In addition, this prolonged adjustment may be attributable to slowly changing social norms and notions of fairness that influence wage setting.

An example can help explain how sticky nominal wages can result in a short-run aggregate-supply curve that slopes upward. Imagine that a year ago a firm expected the price level today to be 100, and based on this expectation, it signed a contract with its workers agreeing to pay them, say, $20 an hour. In fact, the price level turns out to be only 95. Because prices have fallen below expectations, the firm gets 5 percent less than expected for each unit of its product that it sells. The cost of labor used to make the output, however, is stuck at $20 per hour. Production is now less profitable, so the firm hires fewer workers and reduces the quantity of output supplied. Over time, the labor contract will expire, and the firm can renegotiate with its workers for a lower wage (which they may accept because prices are lower), but in the meantime, employment and production will remain below their long-run levels.

The same logic works in reverse. Suppose the price level turns out to be 105 and the wage remains stuck at $20. The firm sees that the amount it is paid for each unit sold is up by 5 percent, while its labor costs are not. In response, it hires more workers and increases the quantity of output supplied. Eventually, the workers will demand higher nominal wages to compensate for the higher price level. But for a while, the firm can take advantage of the profit opportunity by increasing employment and production above their long-run levels.

In short, according to the sticky-wage theory, the short-run aggregate-supply curve slopes upward because nominal wages are based on expected prices and do not respond immediately when the actual price level turns out to be different from what was expected. This stickiness of wages gives firms an incentive to produce less output when the price level turns out lower than expected and to produce more when the price level turns out higher than expected.

The Sticky-Price Theory   Some economists have advocated another approach to explaining the upward slope of the short-run aggregate-supply curve, called the sticky-price theory. As we just discussed, the sticky-wage theory emphasizes that nominal wages adjust slowly over time. The sticky-price theory emphasizes that the prices of some goods and services also adjust sluggishly in response to changing economic conditions. This slow adjustment of prices occurs in part because there are costs to adjusting prices, called *menu costs*. These menu costs include the cost of printing and distributing catalogs and the time required to change price tags. As a result of these costs, prices as well as wages may be sticky in the short run.

To see how sticky prices explain the aggregate-supply curve's upward slope, suppose that each firm in the economy announces its prices in advance based on the economic conditions it expects to prevail over the coming year. Suppose further that after prices are announced, the economy experiences an unexpected contraction in the money supply, which (as we have learned) reduces the overall price level in the long run. What happens in the short run? Although some firms reduce their prices quickly in response to the unexpected change in economic conditions, many other firms want to avoid additional menu costs. As a result, they temporarily lag behind in cutting their prices. Because these lagging firms have prices that are too high, their sales decline. Declining sales, in turn, cause these firms to cut back on production and employment. In other words, because not all prices adjust immediately to changing conditions, an unexpected fall in the price level leaves some firms with higher-than-desired prices, and these higher-than-desired prices depress sales and induce firms to reduce the quantity of goods and services they produce.

Similar reasoning applies when the money supply and price level turn out to be above what firms expected when they originally set their prices. While some firms raise their prices quickly in response to the new economic environment, other firms lag behind, keeping their prices at the lower-than-desired levels. These low prices attract customers, inducing these firms to increase employment and production. Thus, during the time these lagging firms are operating with outdated prices, there is a positive association between the overall price level and the quantity of output. This positive association is represented by the upward slope of the short-run aggregate-supply curve.

The Misperceptions Theory A third approach to explaining the upward slope of the short-run aggregate-supply curve is the misperceptions theory. According to this theory, changes in the overall price level can temporarily mislead suppliers about what is happening in the individual markets in which they sell their output. As a result of these short-run misperceptions, suppliers respond to changes in the level of prices, and this response leads to an upward-sloping aggregate-supply curve.

To see how this might work, suppose the overall price level falls below the level that suppliers expected. When suppliers see the prices of their products fall, they may mistakenly believe that their *relative* prices have fallen; that is, they may believe that their prices have fallen compared to other prices in the economy. For example, wheat farmers may notice a fall in the price of wheat before they notice a fall in the prices of the many items they buy as consumers. They may infer from this observation that the reward for producing wheat is temporarily low, and they may respond by reducing the quantity of wheat they supply. Similarly, workers may notice a fall in their nominal wages before they notice that the prices of the goods they buy are also falling. They may infer that the reward for working is temporarily low and respond by reducing the quantity of labor they supply. In both cases, a lower price level causes misperceptions about relative prices, and these misperceptions induce suppliers to respond to the lower price level by decreasing the quantity of goods and services supplied.

Similar misperceptions arise when the price level is above what was expected. Suppliers of goods and services may notice the price of their output rising and infer, mistakenly, that their relative prices are rising. They would conclude that it is a good time to produce. Until their misperceptions are corrected, they respond to the higher price level by increasing the quantity of goods and services supplied. This behavior results in a short-run aggregate-supply curve that slopes upward.

Summing Up There are three alternative explanations for the upward slope of the short-run aggregate-supply curve: (1) sticky wages, (2) sticky prices, and (3) misperceptions about relative prices. Economists debate which of these theories is correct, and it is possible that each contains an element of truth. For our purposes in this book, the similarities of the theories are more important than the differences. All three theories suggest that output deviates in the short run from its natural level when the actual price level deviates from the price level that people had expected to prevail. We can express this mathematically as follows:

$$
\begin{pmatrix} \text{Quantity} \\ \text{of output} \\ \text{supplied} \end{pmatrix} = \begin{pmatrix} \text{Natural} \\ \text{level of} \\ \text{output} \end{pmatrix} + a \begin{pmatrix} \text{Actual} \\ \text{price} \\ \text{level} \end{pmatrix} - \begin{pmatrix} \text{Expected} \\ \text{price} \\ \text{level} \end{pmatrix} ,
$$

where a is a number that determines how much output responds to unexpected changes in the price level.

Notice that each of the three theories of short-run aggregate supply emphasizes a problem that is likely to be temporary. Whether the upward slope of the aggregate-supply curve is attributable to sticky wages, sticky prices, or misperceptions, these conditions will not persist forever. Over time, nominal wages will become unstuck, prices will become unstuck, and misperceptions about relative prices will be corrected. In the long run, it is reasonable to assume that wages and prices are flexible rather than sticky and that people are not confused about relative prices. Thus, while we have several good theories to explain why the short-run aggregate-supply curve slopes upward, they are all consistent with a long-run aggregate-supply curve that is vertical.

15-4e Why the Short-Run Aggregate-Supply Curve Might Shift

The short-run aggregate-supply curve tells us the quantity of goods and services supplied in the short run for any given level of prices. This curve is similar to the long-run aggregate-supply curve, but it is upward-sloping rather than vertical because of sticky wages, sticky prices, and misperceptions. Thus, when thinking about what shifts the short-run aggregate-supply curve, we have to consider all those variables that shift the long-run aggregate-supply curve. In addition, we have to consider a new variable—the expected price level—that influences the wages that are stuck, the prices that are stuck, and the perceptions about relative prices that may be flawed.

Let's start with what we know about the long-run aggregate-supply curve. As we discussed earlier, shifts in the long-run aggregate-supply curve normally arise from changes in labor, capital, natural resources, or technological knowledge. These same variables shift the short-run aggregate-supply curve. For example, when an increase in the economy's capital stock increases productivity, the economy is able to produce more output, so both the long-run and short-run aggregate-supply curves shift to the right. When an increase in the minimum wage raises the natural rate of unemployment, the economy has fewer employed workers and thus produces less output, so both the long-run and short-run aggregate-supply curves shift to the left.

The important new variable that affects the position of the short-run aggregate-supply curve is the price level that people expected to prevail. As we have discussed, the quantity of goods and services supplied depends, in the short run, on sticky wages, sticky prices, and misperceptions. Yet wages, prices, and perceptions are set based on the expected price level. So when people change their expectations of the price level, the short-run aggregate-supply curve shifts.

To make this idea more concrete, let's consider a specific theory of aggregate supply—the sticky-wage theory. According to this theory, when workers and firms expect the price level to be high, they are likely to reach a bargain with a higher level of nominal wages. Higher wages raise firms' costs, and for any given actual price level, higher costs reduce the quantity of goods and services supplied. Thus, when the expected price level rises, wages are higher, costs increase, and firms produce a smaller quantity of goods and services at any given actual price level. Thus, the short-run aggregate-supply curve shifts to the left. Conversely, when the expected price level falls, wages are lower, costs decline, firms increase output at any given price level, and the short-run aggregate-supply curve shifts to the right.

A similar logic applies in each theory of aggregate supply. The general lesson is the following: *An increase in the expected price level reduces the quantity of goods and services supplied and shifts the short-run aggregate-supply curve to the left.*

A decrease in the expected price level raises the quantity of goods and services supplied and shifts the short-run aggregate-supply curve to the right. As we will see in the next section, the influence of expectations on the position of the short-run aggregate-supply curve plays a key role in explaining how the economy makes the transition from the short run to the long run. In the short run, expectations are fixed and the economy finds itself at the intersection of the aggregate-demand curve and the short-run aggregate-supply curve. In the long run, if people observe that the price level is different from what they expected, their expectations adjust and the short-run aggregate-supply curve shifts. This shift ensures that the economy eventually finds itself at the intersection of the aggregate-demand curve and the long-run aggregate-supply curve.

You should now have some understanding about why the short-run aggregate-supply curve slopes upward and what events and policies can cause this curve to shift. Table 2 summarizes our discussion.

TABLE 2

The Short-Run Aggregate-Supply Curve: Summary

Why Does the Short-Run Aggregate-Supply Curve Slope Upward?
1. *The Sticky-Wage Theory:* An unexpectedly low price level raises the real wage, causing firms to hire fewer workers and produce a smaller quantity of goods and services.
2. *The Sticky-Price Theory:* An unexpectedly low price level leaves some firms with higher-than-desired prices, depressing their sales and leading them to cut back production.
3. *The Misperceptions Theory:* An unexpectedly low price level leads some suppliers to think their relative prices have fallen, inducing a fall in production.

Why Might the Short-Run Aggregate-Supply Curve Shift?
1. *Shifts Arising from Changes in Labor:* An increase in the quantity of labor available (perhaps due to a fall in the natural rate of unemployment) shifts the aggregate-supply curve to the right. A decrease in the quantity of labor available (perhaps due to a rise in the natural rate of unemployment) shifts the aggregate-supply curve to the left.
2. *Shifts Arising from Changes in Capital:* An increase in physical or human capital shifts the aggregate-supply curve to the right. A decrease in physical or human capital shifts the aggregate-supply curve to the left.
3. *Shifts Arising from Changes in Natural Resources:* An increase in the availability of natural resources shifts the aggregate-supply curve to the right. A decrease in the availability of natural resources shifts the aggregate-supply curve to the left.
4. *Shifts Arising from Changes in Technology:* An advance in technological knowledge shifts the aggregate-supply curve to the right. A decrease in the available technology (perhaps due to government regulation) shifts the aggregate-supply curve to the left.
5. *Shifts Arising from Changes in the Expected Price Level:* A decrease in the expected price level shifts the short-run aggregate-supply curve to the right. An increase in the expected price level shifts the short-run aggregate-supply curve to the left.

Quick**Quiz**

8. One reason the short-run aggregate-supply curve slopes upward is that a higher price level
   a. raises nominal wages if real wages are sticky.
   b. reduces nominal wages if real wages are sticky.
   c. raises real wages if nominal wages are sticky.
   d. reduces real wages if nominal wages are sticky.

9. A change in which of the following would shift the short-run aggregate-supply curve but not the long-run aggregate-supply curve?
   a. the labor force
   b. the capital stock
   c. the state of technology
   d. the expected price level

Answers at end of chapter.

15-5 Two Causes of Economic Fluctuations

Now that we have introduced the model of aggregate demand and aggregate supply, we have the basic tools we need to analyze fluctuations in economic activity. In particular, we can use what we have learned about aggregate demand and aggregate supply to examine the two basic causes of short-run fluctuations: shifts in aggregate demand and shifts in aggregate supply.

To keep things simple, we assume the economy begins in long-run equilibrium, as shown in Figure 7. Output and the price level are determined in the long run by the intersection of the aggregate-demand curve and the long-run aggregate-supply curve, shown as point A in the figure. At this point, output is at its natural level. Because the economy is always in a short-run equilibrium, the short-run aggregate-supply curve passes through this point as well, indicating that the expected price level has adjusted to this long-run equilibrium. That is, when an economy is in its long-run equilibrium, the expected price level must equal the actual price level so that the intersection of aggregate demand with short-run aggregate supply is the same as the intersection of aggregate demand with long-run aggregate supply.

FIGURE 7

The Long-Run Equilibrium
The long-run equilibrium of the economy is found where the aggregate-demand curve crosses the long-run aggregate-supply curve (point A). When the economy reaches this long-run equilibrium, the expected price level will have adjusted to equal the actual price level. As a result, the short-run aggregate-supply curve crosses this point as well.

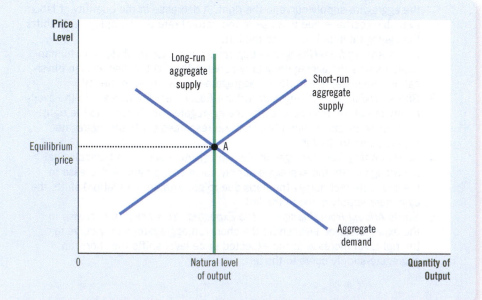

15-5a The Effects of a Shift in Aggregate Demand

Suppose that a wave of pessimism suddenly overtakes the economy. The cause might be a scandal in the White House, a crash in the stock market, or the outbreak of war overseas. Because of this event, many people lose confidence in the future and alter their plans. Households cut back on their spending and delay major purchases, and firms put off buying new equipment.

What is the macroeconomic impact of such a wave of pessimism? In answering this question, we can follow the three steps we used in Chapter 4 when analyzing supply and demand in specific markets. First, we determine whether the event affects aggregate demand or aggregate supply. Second, we determine the direction that the curve shifts. Third, we use the diagram of aggregate demand and aggregate supply to compare the initial and new equilibria. The new wrinkle is that we need to add a fourth step: We have to keep track of a new short-run equilibrium, a new long-run equilibrium, and the transition between them. Table 3 summarizes the four steps to analyzing economic fluctuations.

The first two steps are straightforward. First, because the wave of pessimism affects spending plans, it affects the aggregate-demand curve. Second, because households and firms now want to buy a smaller quantity of goods and services for any given price level, the event reduces aggregate demand. As Figure 8 shows, the aggregate-demand curve shifts to the left from AD_1 to AD_2.

Using this figure, we can perform step three: By comparing the initial and new equilibria, we can see the effects of the fall in aggregate demand. In the short run, the economy moves along the initial short-run aggregate-supply curve, AS_1, going from point A to point B. As the economy moves between these two points, output falls from Y_1 to Y_2 and the price level falls from P_1 to P_2. The falling level of output indicates that the economy is in a recession. Although not shown in the figure, firms respond to lower sales and production by reducing employment. Thus, the pessimism that caused the shift in aggregate demand is, to some extent, self-fulfilling: Pessimism about the future leads to falling incomes and rising unemployment.

Now comes step four—the transition from the short-run equilibrium to the new long-run equilibrium. Because of the reduction in aggregate demand, the price level initially falls from P_1 to P_2. The price level is thus below the level that people were expecting (P_1) before the sudden fall in aggregate demand. People can be surprised in the short run, but they will not remain surprised. Over time, their expectations catch up with this new reality, and the expected price level falls as well. The fall in

TABLE 3

Four Steps for Analyzing Macroeconomic Fluctuations

1. Decide whether the event shifts the aggregate-demand curve or the aggregate-supply curve (or perhaps both).
2. Decide the direction in which the curve shifts.
3. Use the diagram of aggregate demand and aggregate supply to determine the impact on output and the price level in the short run.
4. Use the diagram of aggregate demand and aggregate supply to analyze how the economy moves from its new short-run equilibrium to its new long-run equilibrium.

FIGURE 8

A Contraction in Aggregate Demand
A fall in aggregate demand is represented by a leftward shift in the aggregate-demand curve from AD_1 to AD_2. In the short run, the economy moves from point A to point B. Output falls from Y_1 to Y_2, and the price level falls from P_1 to P_2. Over time, as the expected price level adjusts, the short-run aggregate-supply curve shifts to the right from AS_1 to AS_2, and the economy reaches point C, where the new aggregate-demand curve crosses the long-run aggregate-supply curve. In the long run, the price level falls to P_3, and output returns to its natural level, Y_1.

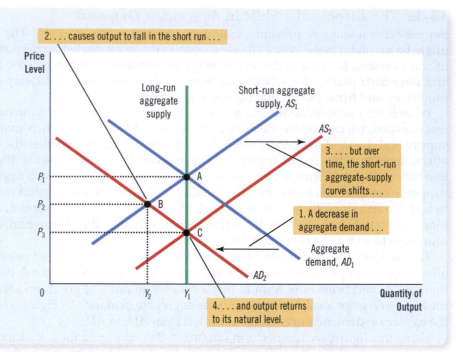

2. . . . causes output to fall in the short run . . .

Price Level

Long-run aggregate supply

Short-run aggregate supply, AS_1

AS_2

3. . . . but over time, the short-run aggregate-supply curve shifts . . .

P_1 · · · · · · · · · · · · · · · A

P_2 · · · · · · · B

1. A decrease in aggregate demand . . .

P_3 · · · · · · · · · · · · · C

Aggregate demand, AD_1

AD_2

0   Y_2 Y_1 Quantity of Output

4. . . . and output returns to its natural level.

the expected price level alters wages, prices, and perceptions, and these changes in turn affect the position of the short-run aggregate-supply curve. For example, according to the sticky-wage theory, once workers and firms come to expect a lower level of prices, they start to strike bargains for lower nominal wages; the reduction in labor costs encourages firms to hire more workers and expand production at any given level of prices. Thus, the fall in the expected price level shifts the short-run aggregate-supply curve to the right from AS_1 to AS_2 in Figure 8. This shift allows the economy to approach point C, where the new aggregate-demand curve (AD_2) crosses the long-run aggregate-supply curve.

In the new long-run equilibrium, point C, output is back to its natural level. The economy has corrected itself: The decline in output is reversed in the long run, even without action by policymakers. Although the wave of pessimism has reduced aggregate demand, the price level has fallen sufficiently (to P_3) to offset the shift in the aggregate-demand curve, and people have come to expect this new lower price level as well. Thus, in the long run, the shift in aggregate demand is reflected fully in the price level and not at all in the level of output. In other words, the long-run effect of a shift in aggregate demand is a nominal change (the price level is lower) but not a real change (output is the same).

What should policymakers do when faced with a sudden fall in aggregate demand? In this analysis, we assumed they did nothing. But another possibility is that, as soon as the economy heads into recession (moving from point A to point B), policymakers take action to increase aggregate demand. As we noted earlier, an increase in government spending or an increase in the money supply would increase the quantity of goods and services demanded at any price and thereby shift the aggregate-demand curve to the right. If policymakers act with sufficient speed and precision, they can offset the initial shift in aggregate demand, return the aggregate-demand curve to AD_1, and bring the economy back to point A. If the

FYI

Monetary Neutrality Revisited

According to classical economic theory, money is neutral. That is, changes in the quantity of money affect nominal variables such as the price level but not real variables such as output. Earlier in this chapter, we noted that most economists accept this conclusion as a description of how the economy works in the long run but not in the short run. Using the model of aggregate demand and aggregate supply, we can illustrate this conclusion and explain it more fully.

Suppose that the Fed reduces the quantity of money in the economy. What effect does this change have? As we discussed, the money supply is one determinant of aggregate demand. The reduction in the money supply shifts the aggregate-demand curve to the left.

The analysis looks just like Figure 8. Even though the cause of the shift in aggregate demand is different, we would observe the same effects on output and the price level. In the short run, both output and the price level fall. The economy experiences a recession. But over time, the expected price level falls as well. Firms and workers respond to their new expectations by, for instance, agreeing to lower nominal wages. As they do so, the short-run aggregate-supply curve shifts to the right. Eventually, the economy finds itself back on the long-run aggregate-supply curve.

Figure 8 shows when money matters for real variables and when it does not. In the long run, money is neutral, as represented by the movement of the economy from point A to point C. But in the short run, a change in the money supply has real effects, as represented by the movement of the economy from point A to point B. An old saying summarizes the analysis: "Money is a veil, but when the veil flutters, real output sputters." ■

---

policy is successful, the painful period of depressed output and employment can be reduced in length and severity. The next chapter discusses in more detail the ways in which monetary and fiscal policy influence aggregate demand, as well as some of the practical difficulties in using these policy instruments.

To sum up, this story about shifts in aggregate demand has three important lessons:

- In the short run, shifts in aggregate demand cause fluctuations in the economy's output of goods and services.
- In the long run, shifts in aggregate demand affect the overall price level but do not affect output.
- Because policymakers influence aggregate demand, they can potentially mitigate the severity of economic fluctuations.

TWO BIG SHIFTS IN AGGREGATE DEMAND: THE GREAT DEPRESSION AND WORLD WAR II

At the beginning of this chapter, we established three key facts about economic fluctuations by looking at data since 1972. Let's now take a longer look at U.S. economic history. Figure 9 shows data since 1900 on the percentage change in real GDP over the previous three years. In an average three-year period, real GDP grows about 10 percent—a bit more than 3 percent per year. The business cycle, however, causes fluctuations around this average. Two episodes jump out as being particularly significant: the large drop in real GDP in the early 1930s and the large increase in real GDP in the early 1940s. Both of these events are attributable to shifts in aggregate demand.

The economic calamity of the early 1930s is called the *Great Depression*, and it is by far the largest economic downturn in U.S. history. Real GDP fell by 26 percent from 1929 to 1933, and unemployment rose from 3 percent to

FIGURE 9

U.S. Real GDP Growth since 1900

Over the course of U.S. economic history, two fluctuations stand out as especially large. During the early 1930s, the economy went through the Great Depression, when the production of goods and services plummeted. During the early 1940s, the United States entered World War II and the economy experienced rapidly rising production. Both of these events are usually explained by large shifts in aggregate demand.

Source: Louis D. Johnston and Samuel H. Williamson, "What Was GDP Then?" http://www.measuringworth.com/usgdp/; Department of Commerce.

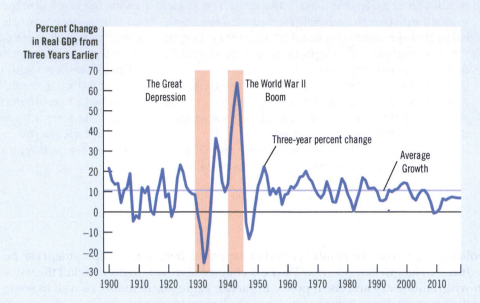

25 percent. At the same time, the price level fell by 22 percent over these four years. Many other countries experienced similar declines in output and prices during this period.

Economic historians continue to debate the causes of the Great Depression, but most explanations center on a large decline in aggregate demand. What caused aggregate demand to contract? Here is where the disagreement arises.

Many economists place primary blame on the decline in the money supply: From 1929 to 1933, the money supply fell by 28 percent. As you may recall from our discussion of the monetary system, this decline in the money supply was due to problems in the banking system. As households withdrew their money from financially shaky banks and bankers became more cautious and started holding greater reserves, the process of money creation under fractional-reserve banking went into reverse. The Fed, meanwhile, failed to offset this fall in the money multiplier with expansionary open-market operations. As a result, the money supply declined. Many economists blame the Fed's failure to act for the Great Depression's severity.

Other economists have suggested alternative reasons for the collapse in aggregate demand. For example, stock prices fell about 90 percent during this period, depressing household wealth and consumer spending. In addition, the banking problems may have prevented some firms from obtaining the financing they wanted for new projects and business expansions, reducing investment spending. It is possible that all these forces may have acted together to contract aggregate demand during the Great Depression.

The second significant episode in Figure 9—the economic boom of the early 1940s—is easier to explain. The cause of this event was World War II. As the United States entered the war overseas, the federal government had to devote more resources to the military. Government purchases of goods and services increased almost fivefold from 1939 to 1944. This huge expansion in aggregate demand almost doubled the economy's production of goods and services and led to a 20 percent increase in the price level (although widespread government price controls limited the rise in prices). Unemployment fell from 17 percent in 1939 to about 1 percent in 1944—the lowest level in U.S. history. ●

The outcome of a massive decrease in aggregate demand

THE GREAT RECESSION OF 2008–2009

CASE STUDY

In 2008 and 2009, the U.S. economy experienced a financial crisis and a severe downturn in economic activity. In many ways, it was the worst macroeconomic event in more than half a century.

The story of this downturn begins a few years earlier with a substantial boom in the housing market. The boom was, in part, fueled by low interest rates. In the aftermath of the recession of 2001, the Fed lowered interest rates to historically low levels. Low interest rates helped the economy recover, but by making it less expensive to get a mortgage and buy a home, they also contributed to a rise in house prices.

In addition to low interest rates, various developments in the mortgage market made it easier for *subprime borrowers*—borrowers with a higher risk of default based on their income and credit history—to get loans to buy homes. One development was *securitization*, the process by which a financial institution (specifically, a mortgage originator) makes loans and then (with the help of an investment bank) bundles them together into financial instruments called *mortgage-backed securities*. These mortgage-backed securities were then sold to other institutions (such as banks and insurance companies), which may not have fully appreciated the risks in these securities. Some economists blame inadequate regulation for these high-risk loans. Others blame misguided government policy: Certain policies encouraged this high-risk lending to make the goal of homeownership more attainable for low-income families. Together, these many forces drove up housing demand and house prices. From 1995 to 2006, average house prices in the United States more than doubled.

The high price of housing, however, proved unsustainable. From 2006 to 2009, house prices nationwide fell about 30 percent. Such price fluctuations should not necessarily be a problem in a market economy. After all, price movements are how markets equilibrate supply and demand. In this case, however, the price decline had two repercussions that led to a large fall in aggregate demand.

The first repercussion was a rise in mortgage defaults and home foreclosures. During the housing boom, many homeowners had bought their homes with mostly borrowed money and minimal down payments. When house prices declined, these homeowners were *underwater* (they owed more on their mortgages than their homes were worth). Many of these homeowners stopped repaying their loans. The banks servicing the mortgages responded to these defaults by taking the houses away in foreclosure procedures and then selling them off. The banks' goal was to recoup whatever they could from the bad loans. But the increase in the supply of houses for sale exacerbated the downward spiral of house prices. As house prices fell, spending on residential construction collapsed.

A second repercussion was that the various financial institutions that owned mortgage-backed securities suffered large losses. In essence, by borrowing large sums to buy high-risk mortgages, these companies had bet that house prices would keep rising; when this bet turned bad, they found themselves at or near the point of bankruptcy. Because of these losses, many financial institutions did not have funds to loan out, and the ability of the financial system to channel resources to those who could best use them was impaired. Even creditworthy customers found themselves unable to borrow to finance investment spending. Such an event is called a *credit crunch*.

As a result of the residential investment collapse and credit crunch, the economy experienced a contractionary shift in aggregate demand. Real GDP and employment both fell sharply. The figures cited in this chapter's introduction are worth repeating: Real GDP declined by 4.0 percent between the fourth quarter of 2007 and the second quarter of 2009, and the rate of unemployment rose from 4.4 percent in May 2007 to 10.0 percent in October 2009. This experience served as a vivid reminder that deep economic downturns and the personal hardship they cause are not a relic of history but a constant risk in the modern economy.

As the crisis unfolded, the U.S. government responded in various ways. Three policy actions—all aimed in part at returning aggregate demand to its previous level—are most noteworthy.

First, the Fed cut its target for the federal funds rate from 5.25 percent in September 2007 to about zero in December 2008. In addition, in a policy called *quantitative easing*, the Fed started buying mortgage-backed securities and other long-term debt in open-market operations. The goals of quantitative easing were to lower long-term interest rates and to provide the financial system with additional funds so that banks would make loans more readily available.

Second, in an even more unusual move in October 2008, Congress appropriated $700 billion for the Treasury to use to rescue the financial system. Much of this money was used to inject capital into banks. That is, the Treasury put funds into the banking system, which the banks could use to make loans and otherwise continue their normal operations; in exchange for these funds, the U.S. government became a part owner of these banks, at least temporarily. The goal of this policy was to stem the crisis on Wall Street and make it easier for businesses and individuals to borrow.

Finally, when Barack Obama became president in January 2009, his first major initiative was a large increase in government spending. After brief congressional debate, he signed a $787 billion stimulus bill on February 17, 2009. This policy move is discussed more fully in the next chapter when we consider the impact of fiscal policy on aggregate demand.

The recovery from this recession began in June 2009, but it was meager by historical standards. Over the next seven years, real GDP growth averaged only 2.2 percent per year, well below the average rate of growth over the past half century of about 3 percent. The unemployment rate did not fall below 5.0 percent until 2016.

Which, if any, of the many policy moves were most important for ending the recession? And what other policies might have promoted a more robust recovery? These are questions that macroeconomic historians continue to debate. ●

15-5b The Effects of a Shift in Aggregate Supply

Imagine once again an economy in its long-run equilibrium. Now suppose that suddenly some firms experience an increase in their costs of production. For example, bad weather in farm states might destroy some crops, driving up the cost of producing food products. Or a war in the Middle East might interrupt the shipping of crude oil, driving up the cost of producing oil products.

To analyze the macroeconomic impact of such an increase in production costs, we follow the same four steps as always. First, which curve is affected? Because production costs affect the firms that supply goods and services, changes in production costs alter the position of the aggregate-supply curve. Second, in which direction does the curve shift? Because higher production costs make selling goods and services less profitable, firms now supply a smaller quantity of output for any given price level. Thus, as Figure 10 shows, the short-run aggregate-supply curve shifts to the left, from AS_1 to AS_2. (Depending on the event, the long-run aggregate-supply curve might also shift. To keep things simple, however, we will assume that it does not.)

The figure allows us to perform step three of comparing the initial and new equilibria. In the short run, the economy goes from point A to point B, moving along the existing aggregate-demand curve. The output of the economy falls from Y_1 to Y_2, and the price level rises from P_1 to P_2. Because the economy is experiencing both *stagnation* (falling output) and *inflation* (rising prices), such an event is sometimes called **stagflation**.

Now consider step four—the transition from the short-run equilibrium to the long-run equilibrium. According to the sticky-wage theory, the key issue is how stagflation affects nominal wages. Firms and workers may at first respond to

stagflation
a period of falling output and rising prices

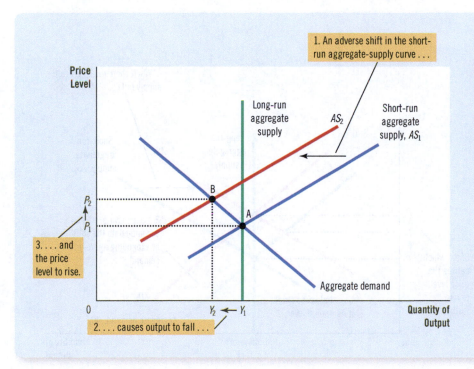

FIGURE 10

An Adverse Shift in Aggregate Supply

When some event increases firms' costs, the short-run aggregate-supply curve shifts to the left from AS_1 to AS_2. The economy moves from point A to point B. The result is stagflation: Output falls from Y_1 to Y_2, and the price level rises from P_1 to P_2.

the higher level of prices by raising their expectations of the price level and setting higher nominal wages. In this case, firms' costs will rise yet again, and the short-run aggregate-supply curve will shift farther to the left, making the problem of stagflation even worse. This phenomenon of higher prices leading to higher wages, in turn leading to even higher prices, is sometimes called a *wage-price spiral*.

At some point, this spiral of ever-rising wages and prices will slow. The low level of output and employment will put downward pressure on workers' wages because workers have less bargaining power when unemployment is high. As nominal wages fall, producing goods and services becomes more profitable and the short-run aggregate-supply curve shifts to the right. As it shifts back toward AS_1, the price level falls and the quantity of output approaches its natural level. In the long run, the economy returns to point A, where the aggregate-demand curve crosses the long-run aggregate-supply curve.

This transition back to the initial equilibrium assumes, however, that aggregate demand is held constant throughout the process. In the real world, that may not be the case. Policymakers who control monetary and fiscal policy might attempt to offset some of the effects of the shift in the short-run aggregate-supply curve by shifting the aggregate-demand curve. This possibility is shown in Figure 11. In this case, changes in policy shift the aggregate-demand curve to the right, from AD_1 to AD_2—exactly enough to prevent the shift in aggregate supply from affecting output. The economy moves directly from point A to point C. Output remains at its natural level, and the price level rises from P_1 to P_3. In this case, policymakers are said to *accommodate* the shift in aggregate supply. An accommodative policy accepts a permanently higher level of prices to maintain a higher level of output and employment.

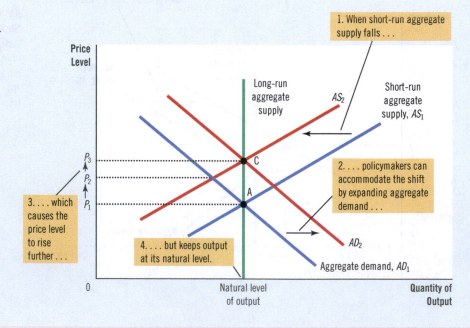

FIGURE 11

Accommodating an Adverse Shift in Aggregate Supply

Faced with an adverse shift in aggregate supply from AS_1 to AS_2, policymakers who can influence aggregate demand might try to shift the aggregate-demand curve to the right from AD_1 to AD_2. The economy would move from point A to point C. This policy would prevent the supply shift from reducing output in the short run, but the price level would permanently rise from P_1 to P_3.

Price Level

1. When short-run aggregate supply falls . . .

Long-run aggregate supply

AS_2

Short-run aggregate supply, AS_1

C

2. . . . policymakers can accommodate the shift by expanding aggregate demand . . .

P_3
P_2
P_1

A

3. . . . which causes the price level to rise further . . .

4. . . . but keeps output at its natural level.

AD_2

Aggregate demand, AD_1

0

Natural level of output

Quantity of Output

To sum up, this story about shifts in aggregate supply has two important lessons:

- Shifts in aggregate supply can cause stagflation—a combination of recession (falling output) and inflation (rising prices).
- Policymakers who can influence aggregate demand can mitigate the adverse impact on output but only at the cost of exacerbating the problem of inflation.

OIL AND THE ECONOMY

CASE STUDY

Some of the largest economic fluctuations in the U.S. economy since 1970 have originated in the oil fields of the Middle East. Crude oil is a key input into the production of many goods and services, and much of the world's oil comes from Saudi Arabia, Kuwait, and other Middle Eastern countries. When some event (usually political in origin) reduces the supply of crude oil flowing from this region, the price of oil rises around the world. Firms in the United States that produce gasoline, tires, and many other products experience rising costs, and they find it less profitable to supply their output of goods and services at any given price level. The result is a leftward shift in the aggregate-supply curve, which in turn leads to stagflation.

The first episode of this sort occurred in the mid-1970s. The countries with large oil reserves started to exert their influence on the world economy as members of OPEC, the Organization of the Petroleum Exporting Countries. OPEC is a *cartel*—a group of sellers that attempts to thwart competition and reduce production to raise prices. And indeed, oil prices rose substantially. From 1973 to 1975, oil approximately doubled in price. Oil-importing countries around the world experienced simultaneous inflation and recession. The U.S. inflation rate as measured by the CPI exceeded 10 percent for the first time in decades. Unemployment rose from 4.9 percent in 1973 to 8.5 percent in 1975.

Almost the same thing happened a few years later. In the late 1970s, the OPEC countries again restricted the supply of oil to raise the price. From 1978 to 1981, the price of oil more than doubled. Once again, the result was stagflation. Inflation, which had subsided somewhat after the first OPEC event, again rose above 10 percent per year. But because the Fed was not willing to accommodate such a large rise in inflation, a recession soon followed. Unemployment rose from about 6 percent in 1978 and 1979 to about 10 percent a few years later.

Developments in the world market for oil can also be a source of favorable shifts in aggregate supply. In 1986, squabbling broke out among members of OPEC. Member countries reneged on their agreements to restrict oil production. In the world market for crude oil, prices fell by about half. This fall in oil prices reduced costs to U.S. firms, which now found it more profitable to supply goods and services at any given price level. As a result, the aggregate-supply curve shifted to the right. The U.S. economy experienced the opposite of stagflation: Output grew rapidly, unemployment fell, and the inflation rate reached its lowest level in many years.

In recent years, developments in the world oil market have not been as important a source of fluctuations for the U.S. economy. One reason is that conservation efforts, changes in technology, and the availability of alternative energy sources have reduced the economy's dependence on oil. The amount of oil used to produce a unit of real GDP has declined by more than 50 percent since the OPEC shocks of the 1970s. As a result, the impact of any change in oil prices on the U.S. economy is smaller today than it was in the past. ●

Changes in Middle East oil production are one source of U.S. economic fluctuations.

YASSER AL-ZAYYAT/AFP/GETTY IMAGES

FYI

The Origins of the Model of Aggregate Demand and Aggregate Supply

KEYSTONE/GETTY IMAGES

John Maynard Keynes

Now that we have a basic understanding of the model of aggregate demand and aggregate supply, it is worthwhile to step back and consider its history. How did this model of short-run fluctuations develop? The answer is that this model, to a large extent, is a by-product of the Great Depression of the 1930s. Economists and policymakers at the time were puzzled about what had caused this calamity and were uncertain about how to deal with it.

In 1936, economist John Maynard Keynes published a book titled *The General Theory of Employment, Interest, and Money*, which attempted to explain short-run economic fluctuations in general and the Great Depression in particular. Keynes's main message was that recessions and depressions can occur because of inadequate aggregate demand for goods and services.

Keynes had long been a critic of classical economic theory—the theory we examined earlier in the book—because it could explain only the long-run effects of policies. A few years before offering *The General Theory*, Keynes had written the following about classical economics:

The long run is a misleading guide to current affairs. In the long run we are all dead. Economists set themselves too easy, too useless a task if in tempestuous seasons they can only tell us when the storm is long past, the ocean will be flat.

Keynes's message was aimed at policymakers as well as economists. As the world's economies suffered with high unemployment, Keynes advocated policies to increase aggregate demand, including government spending on public works.

In the next chapter, we examine in detail how policymakers can use the tools of monetary and fiscal policy to influence aggregate demand. The analysis in the next chapter, as well as in this one, owes much to the legacy of John Maynard Keynes. ■

QuickQuiz

10. A sudden increase in business pessimism shifts the aggregate-_____ curve, leading to _____ output.
    a. supply; lower
    b. supply; higher
    c. demand; lower
    d. demand; higher

11. An increase in the aggregate demand for goods and services has a larger impact on output _____ and a larger impact on the price level _____.
    a. in the short run; in the long run
    b. in the long run; in the short run

    c. in the short run; also in the short run
    d. in the long run; also in the long run

12. Stagflation is caused by a
    a. leftward shift in the aggregate-demand curve.
    b. rightward shift in the aggregate-demand curve.
    c. leftward shift in the aggregate-supply curve.
    d. rightward shift in the aggregate-supply curve.

Answers at end of chapter.

15-6 Conclusion

This chapter has achieved two goals. First, we have discussed some of the important facts about short-run fluctuations in economic activity. Second, we have introduced a basic model to explain those fluctuations, called the model of aggregate demand and aggregate supply. We continue our study of this model in the next chapter to understand more fully what causes fluctuations in the economy and how policymakers might respond to these fluctuations.

CHAPTER IN A NUTSHELL

- All societies experience short-run economic fluctuations around long-run trends. These fluctuations are irregular and largely unpredictable. When recessions occur, real GDP and other measures of income, spending, and production fall, while unemployment rises.

- Classical economic theory is based on the assumption that nominal variables such as the money supply and the price level do not influence real variables such as output and employment. Most economists believe that this assumption is accurate in the long run but not in the short run. Economists analyze short-run economic fluctuations using the model of aggregate demand and aggregate supply. According to this model, the output of goods and services and the overall level of prices adjust to balance aggregate demand and aggregate supply.

- The aggregate-demand curve slopes downward for three reasons. The first is the wealth effect: A lower price level raises the real value of households' money holdings, stimulating consumer spending. The second is the interest-rate effect: A lower price level reduces the quantity of money households demand; as households try to convert money into interest-bearing assets, interest rates fall, stimulating investment spending. The third is the exchange-rate effect: As a lower price level reduces interest rates, the dollar depreciates in the market for foreign-currency exchange, stimulating net exports.

- Any event or policy that raises consumption, investment, government purchases, or net exports at any given price level increases aggregate demand. Any event or policy that reduces consumption, investment, government purchases, or net exports at any given price level decreases aggregate demand.

- The long-run aggregate-supply curve is vertical. In the long run, the quantity of goods and services supplied depends on the economy's labor, capital, natural resources, and technology but not on the overall level of prices.

- Three theories have been proposed to explain the upward slope of the short-run aggregate-supply curve. According to the sticky-wage theory, an unexpected fall in the price level temporarily raises real wages, inducing firms to reduce employment and production. According to the sticky-price theory, an unexpected fall in the price level leaves some firms with prices that are temporarily too high, reducing their sales and causing them to cut back production. According to the misperceptions theory, an unexpected fall in the price level leads suppliers to mistakenly believe that their relative prices have fallen, inducing them to reduce production. All three theories imply that output deviates from its natural level when the actual price level deviates from the price level that people expected.

- Events that alter the economy's ability to produce output, such as changes in labor, capital, natural resources, or technology, shift the short-run aggregate-supply curve (and may shift the long-run aggregate-supply curve as well). In addition, the position of the short-run aggregate-supply curve depends on the expected price level.

- One possible cause of economic fluctuations is a shift in aggregate demand. When the aggregate-demand curve shifts to the left, for instance, output and prices fall in the short run. Over time, as a change in the expected price level causes wages, prices, and perceptions to adjust, the short-run aggregate-supply curve shifts to the right. This shift returns the economy to its natural level of output at a new, lower price level.

- A second possible cause of economic fluctuations is a shift in aggregate supply. When the short-run aggregate-supply curve shifts to the left, the effect is falling output and rising prices—a combination called stagflation. Over time, as wages, prices, and perceptions adjust, the short-run aggregate-supply curve shifts back to the right, returning the price level and output to their original levels.

KEY CONCEPTS

recession, p. 304
depression, p. 304
model of aggregate demand and
  aggregate supply, p. 308

aggregate-demand curve, p. 308
aggregate-supply curve, p. 308

natural level of output, p. 316
stagflation, p. 331

QUESTIONS FOR REVIEW

1. Name two macroeconomic variables that decline when the economy goes into a recession. Name one macroeconomic variable that rises during a recession.

2. Draw a diagram showing aggregate demand, short-run aggregate supply, and long-run aggregate supply. Be careful to label the axes correctly.

3. List and explain the three reasons the aggregate-demand curve slopes downward.

4. Explain why the long-run aggregate-supply curve is vertical.

5. List and explain the three theories for why the short-run aggregate-supply curve slopes upward.

6. What might shift the aggregate-demand curve to the left? Use the model of aggregate demand and aggregate supply to trace the short-run and long-run effects of such a shift on output and the price level.

7. What might shift the aggregate-supply curve to the left? Use the model of aggregate demand and aggregate supply to trace the short-run and long-run effects of such a shift on output and the price level.

PROBLEMS AND APPLICATIONS

1. Suppose the economy is in a long-run equilibrium.
   a. Draw a diagram to illustrate the state of the economy. Be sure to show aggregate demand, short-run aggregate supply, and long-run aggregate supply.
   b. Now suppose that a stock market crash causes aggregate demand to fall. Use your diagram to show what happens to output and the price level in the short run. What happens to the unemployment rate?
   c. Use the sticky-wage theory of aggregate supply to explain what happens to output and the price level in the long run (assuming no change in policy). What role does the expected price level play in this adjustment? Be sure to illustrate your analysis in a graph.

2. Explain whether each of the following events increases, decreases, or has no effect on long-run aggregate supply.
   a. The United States experiences a wave of immigration.
   b. Congress raises the minimum wage to $15 per hour.
   c. Intel invents a new and more powerful computer chip.
   d. A severe hurricane damages factories along the East Coast.

3. Suppose an economy is in long-run equilibrium.
   a. Use the model of aggregate demand and aggregate supply to illustrate the initial equilibrium (call it point A). Be sure to include both short-run aggregate supply and long-run aggregate supply.
   b. The central bank raises the money supply by 5 percent. Use your diagram to show what

happens to output and the price level as the economy moves from the initial equilibrium to the new short-run equilibrium (call it point B).
   c. Now show the new long-run equilibrium (call it point C). What causes the economy to move from point B to point C?
   d. According to the sticky-wage theory of aggregate supply, how do nominal wages at point A compare with nominal wages at point B? How do nominal wages at point A compare with nominal wages at point C?
   e. According to the sticky-wage theory of aggregate supply, how do real wages at point A compare with real wages at point B? How do real wages at point A compare with real wages at point C?
   f. Judging by the impact of the money supply on nominal and real wages, is this analysis consistent with the proposition that money has real effects in the short run but is neutral in the long run?

4. In 1939, with the U.S. economy not yet fully recovered from the Great Depression, President Franklin Roosevelt proclaimed that Thanksgiving would fall a week earlier than usual so that the shopping period before Christmas would be longer. (The policy was dubbed "Franksgiving.") Explain what President Roosevelt might have been trying to achieve, using the model of aggregate demand and aggregate supply.

5. Explain why the following statements are false.
   a. "The aggregate-demand curve slopes downward because it is the horizontal sum of the demand curves for individual goods."
   b. "The long-run aggregate-supply curve is vertical because economic forces do not affect long-run aggregate supply."

c. "If firms adjusted their prices every day, then the short-run aggregate-supply curve would be horizontal."

d. "Whenever the economy enters a recession, its long-run aggregate-supply curve shifts to the left."

6. For each of the three theories for the upward slope of the short-run aggregate-supply curve, carefully explain the following:

a. how the economy recovers from a recession and returns to its long-run equilibrium without any policy intervention

b. what determines the speed of that recovery

7. The economy begins in long-run equilibrium. Then one day, the president appoints a new Fed chair. This new chair is well known for her view that inflation is not a major problem for an economy.

a. How would this news affect the price level that people expect to prevail?

b. How would this change in the expected price level affect the nominal wage that workers and firms agree to in their new labor contracts?

c. How would this change in the nominal wage affect the profitability of producing goods and services at any given price level?

d. How would this change in profitability affect the short-run aggregate-supply curve?

e. If aggregate demand is held constant, how would this shift in the aggregate-supply curve affect the price level and the quantity of output produced?

f. Do you think appointing this Fed chair was a good decision?

8. Explain whether each of the following events shifts the short-run aggregate-supply curve, the aggregate-demand curve, both, or neither. For each event that

does shift a curve, draw a diagram to illustrate the effect on the economy.

a. Households decide to save a larger share of their income.

b. Florida orange groves suffer a prolonged period of below-freezing temperatures.

c. Increased job opportunities overseas cause many people to leave the country.

9. For each of the following events, explain the short-run and long-run effects on output and the price level, assuming policymakers take no action.

a. The stock market declines sharply, reducing consumers' wealth.

b. The federal government increases spending on national defense.

c. A technological improvement raises productivity.

d. A recession overseas causes foreigners to buy fewer U.S. goods.

10. Suppose firms become optimistic about future business conditions and invest heavily in new capital equipment.

a. Draw an aggregate-demand/aggregate-supply diagram to show the short-run effect of this optimism on the economy. Label the new levels of prices and real output. Explain in words why the aggregate quantity of output *supplied* changes.

b. Now use the diagram from part (a) to show the new long-run equilibrium of the economy. (For now, assume there is no change in the long-run aggregate-supply curve.) Explain in words why the aggregate quantity of output *demanded* changes between the short run and the long run.

c. How might the investment boom affect the long-run aggregate-supply curve? Explain.

Quick**Quiz Answers**

1. c   2. d   3. c   4. a   5. b   6. b   7. d   8. d   9. d   10. c   11. a   12. c

magine that you are a member of the Federal Open Market Committee, the group at the Federal Reserve that sets monetary policy. You observe that the president and Congress have agreed to raise taxes. How should the Fed respond to this change in fiscal policy? Should it expand the money supply, contract the money supply, or leave it unchanged?

To answer this question, you need to consider the impact of monetary and fiscal policy on the economy. In the preceding chapter, we used the model of aggregate demand and aggregate supply to explain short-run economic fluctuations. We saw that shifts in the aggregate-demand curve or the aggregate-supply curve cause fluctuations in the economy's overall output of goods and services and its overall level of prices. As we noted in the previous chapter, both monetary and fiscal policy influence aggregate demand. Thus, a change in one of these policies can lead to short-run fluctuations in output and prices. Policymakers will want to anticipate this effect and, perhaps, adjust the other policy in response.

In this chapter, we examine in more detail how the government's policy tools influence the position of the

The Influence of Monetary and Fiscal Policy on Aggregate Demand

ISTOCK.COM/LOLOSTOCK; GEORGE RUDY/SHUTTERSTOCK.COM

aggregate-demand curve. These tools include monetary policy (the supply of money set by the central bank) and fiscal policy (the levels of government spending and taxation set by the president and Congress). We have previously discussed the long-run effects of these policies. In Chapters 7 and 8, we saw how fiscal policy affects saving, investment, and long-run economic growth. In Chapters 11 and 12, we saw how monetary policy influences the price level in the long run. We now look at how these policy tools can shift the aggregate-demand curve and thereby affect macroeconomic variables in the short run.

As we have already learned, many factors influence aggregate demand besides monetary and fiscal policy. In particular, desired spending by households and firms determines the overall demand for goods and services. When desired spending changes, aggregate demand shifts. If policymakers do not respond, such shifts in aggregate demand cause short-run fluctuations in output and employment. As a result, monetary and fiscal policymakers sometimes use the policy levers at their disposal to try to offset these shifts in aggregate demand and stabilize the economy. Here we discuss the theory behind these policy actions and some of the difficulties that arise in using this theory in practice.

16-1 How Monetary Policy Influences Aggregate Demand

The aggregate-demand curve shows the total quantity of goods and services demanded in the economy for any price level. The preceding chapter discussed three reasons why the aggregate-demand curve slopes downward:

- *The wealth effect:* A lower price level raises the real value of households' money holdings, which are part of their wealth. Higher real wealth stimulates consumer spending and thus increases the quantity of goods and services demanded.
- *The interest-rate effect:* A lower price level reduces the amount of money people want to hold. As people try to lend out their excess money holdings, the interest rate falls. The lower interest rate stimulates investment spending and thus increases the quantity of goods and services demanded.
- *The exchange-rate effect:* When a lower price level reduces the interest rate, investors move some of their funds overseas in search of higher returns. This movement of funds causes the real value of the domestic currency to fall in the market for foreign-currency exchange. Domestic goods become less expensive relative to foreign goods. This change in the real exchange rate stimulates spending on net exports and thus increases the quantity of goods and services demanded.

These three effects occur simultaneously to increase the quantity of goods and services demanded when the price level falls and to decrease it when the price level rises.

Although all three effects work together to explain the downward slope of the aggregate-demand curve, they are not of equal importance. Because money holdings are a small part of household wealth, the wealth effect is the least important of the three. In addition, because exports and imports represent only a small fraction of U.S. GDP, the exchange-rate effect is not large for the U.S. economy. (This effect is more important for smaller countries, which typically export and import a higher fraction of their GDP.) *For the U.S. economy, the most important reason for the downward slope of the aggregate-demand curve is the interest-rate effect.*

To better understand aggregate demand, we now examine the short-run determination of interest rates in more detail. Here we develop the **theory of liquidity preference**. This theory of interest rates helps explain the downward slope of the aggregate-demand curve, as well as how monetary and fiscal policy can shift this curve. By shedding new light on aggregate demand, the theory of liquidity preference expands our understanding of what causes short-run economic fluctuations and what policymakers can potentially do about them.

theory of liquidity preference
Keynes's theory that the interest rate adjusts to bring money supply and money demand into balance

16-1a The Theory of Liquidity Preference

In his classic book *The General Theory of Employment, Interest, and Money*, John Maynard Keynes proposed the theory of liquidity preference to explain the factors that determine an economy's interest rate. The theory is, in essence, an application of supply and demand. According to Keynes, the interest rate adjusts to balance the supply of and demand for money.

You may recall that economists distinguish between two interest rates: The *nominal interest rate* is the interest rate as usually reported, and the *real interest rate* is the interest rate corrected for the effects of inflation. When there is no inflation, the two rates are the same. But when borrowers and lenders expect prices to rise over the term of the loan, they agree to a nominal interest rate that exceeds the real interest rate by the expected rate of inflation. The higher nominal interest rate compensates for the fact that they expect the loan to be repaid in less valuable dollars.

Which interest rate are we now trying to explain with the theory of liquidity preference? The answer is both. In the analysis that follows, we hold constant the expected rate of inflation. This assumption is reasonable for studying the economy in the short run, because expected inflation is typically stable over short periods of time. In this case, nominal and real interest rates differ by a constant: When the nominal interest rate rises or falls, the real interest rate that people expect to earn rises or falls by the same amount. For the rest of this chapter, when we discuss changes in the interest rate, these changes refer to both the real interest rate and the nominal interest rate.

Let's now develop the theory of liquidity preference by considering the supply and demand for money and how each depends on the interest rate.

Money Supply The first piece of the theory of liquidity preference is the supply of money. As we first discussed in Chapter 11, the money supply in the U.S. economy is controlled by the Federal Reserve. The Fed alters the money supply primarily by changing the quantity of reserves in the banking system through the purchase and sale of government bonds in open-market operations. When the Fed buys government bonds, the dollars it pays for the bonds are typically deposited in banks, and these dollars are added to bank reserves. When the Fed sells government bonds, the dollars it receives for the bonds are withdrawn from the banking system, and bank reserves fall. These changes in bank reserves, in turn, lead to changes in banks' ability to make loans and create money. Thus, by buying and selling bonds in open-market operations, the Fed alters the supply of money in the economy.

In addition to open-market operations, the Fed can influence the money supply using various other tools. One option is for the Fed to change how much it lends to banks. For example, a decrease in the discount rate (the interest rate at which banks can borrow reserves from the Fed) encourages banks to borrow, increasing bank reserves and in turn the money supply. Conversely, an increase in the discount rate discourages banks from borrowing, decreasing bank reserves and the money supply. The Fed also alters the money supply by changing reserve requirements (the amount of reserves banks must hold against deposits) and by changing the interest rate it pays banks on the reserves they hold.

These details of monetary control are important for the implementation of Fed policy, but they are not crucial for the analysis in this chapter. Our goal here is to examine how changes in the money supply affect the aggregate demand for goods and services. For this purpose, we can ignore the details of how Fed policy is implemented and assume that the Fed controls the money supply directly. In other words, the quantity of money supplied in the economy is fixed at whatever level the Fed decides to set it.

Because the quantity of money supplied is fixed by Fed policy, it does not depend on other economic variables. In particular, it does not depend on the interest rate. Once the Fed has made its policy decision, the quantity of money supplied is the same, regardless of the prevailing interest rate. We represent a fixed money supply with a vertical supply curve, as in Figure 1.

Money Demand   The second piece of the theory of liquidity preference is the demand for money. To understand money demand, recall that an asset's *liquidity* refers to the ease with which that asset can be converted into the economy's

FIGURE 1

Equilibrium in the Money Market

According to the theory of liquidity preference, the interest rate adjusts to bring the quantity of money supplied and the quantity of money demanded into balance. If the interest rate is above the equilibrium level (such as at r_1), the quantity of money people want to hold (M_1^d) is less than the quantity the Fed has created, and this surplus of money puts downward pressure on the interest rate. Conversely, if the interest rate is below the equilibrium level (such as at r_2), the quantity of money people want to hold (M_2^d) exceeds the quantity the Fed has created, and this shortage of money puts upward pressure on the interest rate. Thus, the forces of supply and demand in the market for money push the interest rate toward the equilibrium interest rate, at which people are content holding the quantity of money the Fed has created.

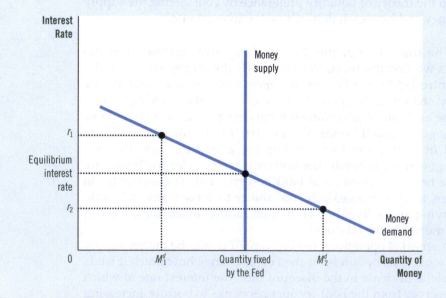

medium of exchange. Because money is the economy's medium of exchange, it is by definition the most liquid asset available. The liquidity of money explains the demand for it: People choose to hold money instead of other assets that offer higher rates of return so they can use the money to buy goods and services.

Although many factors determine the quantity of money demanded, the theory of liquidity preference emphasizes the interest rate because it is the opportunity cost of holding money. That is, when you hold wealth as cash in your wallet, rather than as an interest-bearing bond or in an interest-bearing bank account, you lose the interest you could have earned. An increase in the interest rate raises the cost of holding money and, as a result, reduces the quantity of money demanded. A decrease in the interest rate reduces the cost of holding money and raises the quantity demanded. Thus, as shown in Figure 1, the money demand curve slopes downward.

Equilibrium in the Money Market According to the theory of liquidity preference, the interest rate adjusts to balance the supply and demand for money. There is one interest rate, called the *equilibrium interest rate*, at which the quantity of money demanded exactly balances the quantity of money supplied. If the interest rate is at any other level, people will try to adjust their portfolios of money and nonmonetary assets and, as a result, drive the interest rate toward the equilibrium.

For example, suppose that the interest rate is above the equilibrium level, such as r_1 in Figure 1. In this case, the quantity of money that people want to hold, M_1^d, is less than the quantity of money that the Fed has supplied. Those people who are holding the surplus of money will try to get rid of it by buying interest-bearing bonds or by depositing it in interest-bearing bank accounts. Because bond issuers and banks prefer to pay lower interest rates, they respond to this surplus of money by lowering the interest rates they offer. As the interest rate falls, people become more willing to hold money until, at the equilibrium interest rate, people are happy to hold exactly the amount of money the Fed has supplied.

Conversely, at interest rates below the equilibrium level, such as r_2 in Figure 1, the quantity of money that people want to hold, M_2^d, exceeds the quantity of money that the Fed has supplied. As a result, people try to increase their holdings of money by reducing their holdings of bonds and other interest-bearing assets. As people cut back on their holdings of bonds, bond issuers find that they have to offer higher interest rates to attract buyers. Thus, the interest rate rises until it reaches the equilibrium level.

16-1b The Downward Slope of the Aggregate-Demand Curve

Having seen how the theory of liquidity preference explains the economy's equilibrium interest rate, we now consider the theory's implications for the aggregate demand for goods and services. As a warm-up exercise, let's begin by using the theory to reexamine a topic we already understand—the interest-rate effect and the downward slope of the aggregate-demand curve. In particular, suppose that the overall level of prices in the economy rises. What happens to the interest rate that balances the supply and demand for money, and how does that change affect the quantity of goods and services demanded?

As we discussed in Chapter 12, the price level is one determinant of the quantity of money demanded. At higher prices, more money is exchanged every time a good or service is sold. As a result, people will choose to hold a larger quantity of money.

FYI

Interest Rates in the Long Run and the Short Run

In an earlier chapter, we said that the interest rate adjusts to balance the supply of loanable funds (national saving) and the demand for loanable funds (desired investment). Here we just said that the interest rate adjusts to balance the supply of and demand for money. Can we reconcile these two theories?

To answer this question, we need to focus on three macroeconomic variables: the economy's output of goods and services, the interest rate, and the price level. According to the classical macroeconomic theory we developed earlier in the book, these variables are determined as follows:

1. *Output* is determined by the supplies of capital and labor and the available production technology for turning capital and labor into output. (We call this the natural level of output.)
2. For any given level of output, the *interest rate* adjusts to balance the supply and demand for loanable funds.
3. Given output and the interest rate, the *price level* adjusts to balance the supply and demand for money. Changes in the supply of money lead to proportionate changes in the price level.

These are three of the essential propositions of classical economic theory. Most economists believe that these propositions do a good job of describing how the economy works *in the long run*.

Yet these propositions do not hold in the short run. As we discussed in the preceding chapter, many prices are slow to adjust to changes in the money supply; this fact is reflected in a short-run aggregate-supply curve that is upward-sloping rather than vertical. As a result, *in the short run*, the overall price level cannot, by itself, move to balance the supply of and demand for money. This stickiness of the price level requires the interest

rate to move to bring the money market into equilibrium. These changes in the interest rate, in turn, affect the aggregate demand for goods and services. As aggregate demand fluctuates, the economy's output of goods and services moves away from the level determined by factor supplies and technology.

To think about the operation of the economy in the short run (day to day, week to week, month to month, or quarter to quarter), it is best to keep in mind the following logic:

1. The *price level* is stuck at some level (based on previously formed expectations) and, in the short run, is relatively unresponsive to changing economic conditions.
2. For any given (stuck) price level, the *interest rate* adjusts to balance the supply of and demand for money.
3. The interest rate that balances the money market influences the quantity of goods and services demanded and thus the level of *output*.

Notice that this logic precisely reverses the order of analysis used to study the economy in the long run.

The two different theories of the interest rate are useful for different purposes. When thinking about the long-run determinants of the interest rate, it is best to keep in mind the loanable-funds theory, which highlights the importance of an economy's saving propensities and investment opportunities. By contrast, when thinking about the short-run determinants of the interest rate, it is best to keep in mind the liquidity-preference theory, which highlights the importance of monetary policy. ∎

That is, a higher price level increases the quantity of money demanded for any given interest rate. Thus, an increase in the price level from P_1 to P_2 shifts the money demand curve to the right from MD_1 to MD_2, as shown in panel (a) of Figure 2.

Notice how this shift in money demand affects the equilibrium in the money market. For a fixed money supply, the interest rate must rise to balance money supply and money demand. Because the higher price level has increased the amount of money people want to hold, it has shifted the money demand curve to the right. Yet the quantity of money supplied is unchanged, so the interest rate must rise from r_1 to r_2 to discourage the additional demand.

This increase in the interest rate has ramifications not only for the money market but also for the quantity of goods and services demanded, as shown in panel (b). At a higher interest rate, the cost of borrowing and the return to saving are greater. Fewer households choose to borrow to buy a new house, and those who do buy smaller houses, so the demand for residential investment falls. Fewer firms choose to borrow to build new factories and buy new equipment, so business investment falls. Thus, when the price level rises from P_1 to P_2, increasing money demand from

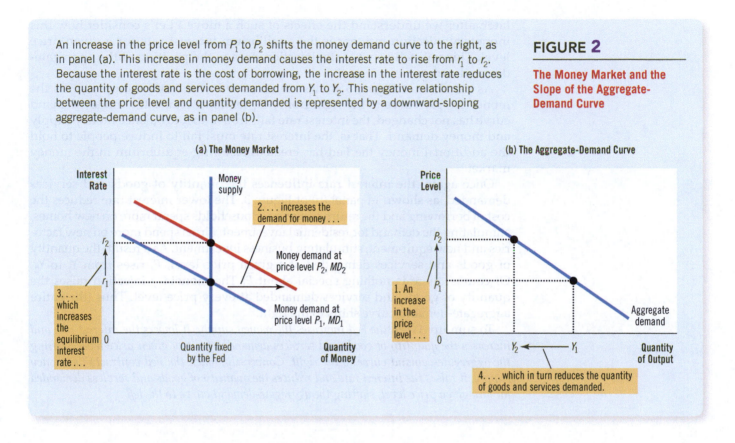

An increase in the price level from P_1 to P_2 shifts the money demand curve to the right, as in panel (a). This increase in money demand causes the interest rate to rise from r_1 to r_2. Because the interest rate is the cost of borrowing, the increase in the interest rate reduces the quantity of goods and services demanded from Y_1 to Y_2. This negative relationship between the price level and quantity demanded is represented by a downward-sloping aggregate-demand curve, as in panel (b).

FIGURE 2

The Money Market and the Slope of the Aggregate-Demand Curve

(a) The Money Market

Interest Rate

Money supply

2. . . . increases the demand for money . . .

Money demand at price level P_2, MD_2

r_2

r_1

3. . . . which increases the equilibrium interest rate . . .

Money demand at price level P_1, MD_1

0   Quantity fixed by the Fed   Quantity of Money

(b) The Aggregate-Demand Curve

Price Level

P_2

P_1

1. An increase in the price level . . .

Aggregate demand

0   Y_2 ← Y_1 Quantity of Output

4. . . . which in turn reduces the quantity of goods and services demanded.

MD_1 to MD_2 and raising the interest rate from r_1 to r_2, the quantity of goods and services demanded falls from Y_1 to Y_2.

This analysis of the interest-rate effect can be summarized in three steps: (1) A higher price level raises money demand. (2) Higher money demand leads to a higher interest rate. (3) A higher interest rate reduces the quantity of goods and services demanded. The same logic works for a decline in the price level: A lower price level reduces money demand, leading to a lower interest rate and a larger quantity of goods and services demanded. The result of this analysis is a negative relationship between the price level and the quantity of goods and services demanded, as illustrated by a downward-sloping aggregate-demand curve.

16-1c Changes in the Money Supply

So far, we have used the theory of liquidity preference to explain more fully how the total quantity of goods and services demanded in the economy changes as the price level changes. That is, we have examined movements along a downward-sloping aggregate-demand curve. The theory also sheds light, however, on some of the other events that alter the quantity of goods and services demanded. Whenever the quantity of goods and services demanded changes *for any given price level*, the aggregate-demand curve shifts.

One important variable that shifts the aggregate-demand curve is monetary policy. To see how monetary policy affects the economy in the short run, suppose that the Fed increases the money supply by buying government bonds in open-market operations. (Why the Fed might do this will become clear later, after we understand the effects of such a move.) Let's consider how this monetary injection influences the equilibrium interest rate for a given price level. This will tell us what the injection does to the position of the aggregate-demand curve.

As panel (a) of Figure 3 shows, an increase in the money supply shifts the money supply curve to the right from MS_1 to MS_2. Because the money demand curve has not changed, the interest rate falls from r_1 to r_2 to balance money supply and money demand. That is, the interest rate must fall to induce people to hold the additional money the Fed has created, restoring equilibrium in the money market.

Once again, the interest rate influences the quantity of goods and services demanded, as shown in panel (b) of Figure 3. The lower interest rate reduces the cost of borrowing and the return to saving. Households spend more on new homes, stimulating the demand for residential investment. Firms spend more on new factories and new equipment, stimulating business investment. As a result, the quantity of goods and services demanded at a given price level, $\overline{P}$, rises from Y_1 to Y_2. Of course, there is nothing special about $\overline{P}$: The monetary injection raises the quantity of goods and services demanded at every price level. Thus, the entire aggregate-demand curve shifts to the right.

To sum up: *When the Fed increases the money supply, it lowers the interest rate and increases the quantity of goods and services demanded for any given price level, shifting the aggregate-demand curve to the right. Conversely, when the Fed contracts the money supply, it raises the interest rate and reduces the quantity of goods and services demanded for any given price level, shifting the aggregate-demand curve to the left.*

FIGURE 3

A Monetary Injection

In panel (a), an increase in the money supply from MS_1 to MS_2 reduces the equilibrium interest rate from r_1 to r_2. Because the interest rate is the cost of borrowing, the fall in the interest rate raises the quantity of goods and services demanded at a given price level from Y_1 to Y_2. Thus, in panel (b), the aggregate-demand curve shifts to the right from AD_1 to AD_2.

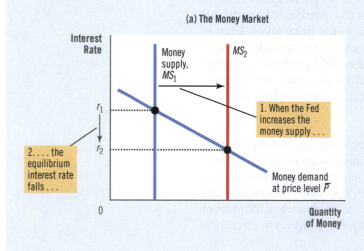

(a) The Money Market

1. When the Fed increases the money supply . . .

2. . . . the equilibrium interest rate falls . . .

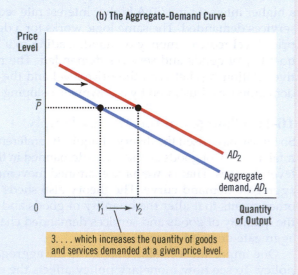

(b) The Aggregate-Demand Curve

3. . . . which increases the quantity of goods and services demanded at a given price level.

16-1d The Role of Interest-Rate Targets in Fed Policy

How does the Federal Reserve affect the economy? Our discussion here and earlier in the book has treated the money supply as the Fed's policy instrument. When the Fed buys government bonds in open-market operations, it increases the money supply and expands aggregate demand. When the Fed sells government bonds in open-market operations, it decreases the money supply and contracts aggregate demand.

Focusing on the money supply is a good starting point, but another perspective is useful when thinking about recent policy. In the past, the Fed has at times set a target for the money supply, but that is no longer the case. The Fed now conducts policy by setting a target for the *federal funds rate*—the interest rate that banks charge one another for short-term loans. This target is reevaluated every six weeks at meetings of the Federal Open Market Committee (FOMC).

There are several related reasons for the Fed's decision to use the federal funds rate as its target. One is that the money supply is hard to measure with sufficient precision. Another is that money demand fluctuates over time. For any given money supply, fluctuations in money demand lead to fluctuations in interest rates, aggregate demand, and output. By contrast, when the Fed announces a target for the federal funds rate, it essentially accommodates the day-to-day shifts in money demand by adjusting the money supply accordingly.

The Fed's decision to target an interest rate does not fundamentally alter our analysis of monetary policy. The theory of liquidity preference illustrates an important principle: *Monetary policy can be described either in terms of the money supply or in terms of the interest rate.* When the FOMC sets a target for the federal funds rate of, say, 4 percent, the Fed's bond traders are told: "Conduct whatever open-market operations are necessary to ensure that the equilibrium interest rate is 4 percent." In other words, when the Fed sets a target for the interest rate, it commits itself to adjusting the money supply to make the equilibrium in the money market hit that target.

As a result, changes in monetary policy can be viewed either in terms of changing the interest rate target or in terms of changing the money supply. When you read in the news that "the Fed has lowered the federal funds rate from 4 to 3 percent," you should understand that this occurs only because the Fed's bond traders are doing what it takes to make sure that the interest rate changes. To lower the federal funds rate, the Fed's bond traders buy government bonds, and this purchase increases the money supply and lowers the equilibrium interest rate (just as in Figure 3). Conversely, when the FOMC raises the target for the federal funds rate, the bond traders sell government bonds, and this sale decreases the money supply and raises the equilibrium interest rate.

The lessons from this analysis are simple: *Changes in monetary policy aimed at expanding aggregate demand can be described either as increasing the money supply or as lowering the interest rate. Changes in monetary policy aimed at contracting aggregate demand can be described either as decreasing the money supply or as raising the interest rate.*

CASE STUDY

WHY THE FED WATCHES THE STOCK MARKET (AND VICE VERSA)

"The stock market has predicted nine out of the past five recessions."

So quipped Paul Samuelson, the famed economist (and textbook author). Samuelson was right that the stock market is highly volatile and can give wrong signals about the economy. But fluctuations in stock prices are often a sign of broader economic developments. The economic boom of the 1990s, for example, appeared not only in rapid GDP growth and falling unemployment but also in rising stock prices, which increased about fourfold during this decade. Similarly, the Great Recession of 2008 and 2009 was reflected in falling stock prices: From November 2007 to March 2009, the stock market lost about half its value.

How should the Fed respond to stock market fluctuations? The Fed has no reason to care about stock prices in themselves, but it does have the job of monitoring and responding to developments in the overall economy, and the stock market is a piece of that puzzle. When the stock market booms, households become wealthier, and this increased wealth stimulates consumer spending. In addition, a rise in stock prices makes it more attractive for firms to sell new shares of stock and thereby stimulates investment spending. For both reasons, a booming stock market expands the aggregate demand for goods and services.

As we discuss more fully later in the chapter, one of the Fed's goals is to stabilize aggregate demand, because greater stability in aggregate demand means greater stability in output and the price level. To promote stability, the Fed might respond to a stock market boom by keeping the money supply lower and interest rates higher than it otherwise would. The contractionary effects of higher interest rates would offset the expansionary effects of higher stock prices. In fact, this analysis does describe Fed behavior: Real interest rates were kept high by historical standards during the stock market boom of the late 1990s.

The opposite occurs when the stock market falls. Spending on consumption and investment tends to decline, depressing aggregate demand and pushing the economy toward recession. To stabilize aggregate demand, the Fed would increase the money supply and lower interest rates. And indeed, that is what it typically does. For example, on October 19, 1987, the stock market fell by 22.6 percent—one of the biggest one-day drops in history. The Fed responded to the market crash by increasing the money supply and lowering interest rates. The federal funds rate fell from 7.7 percent at the beginning of October to 6.6 percent at the end of the month. In part because of the Fed's quick action, the economy avoided a recession. Similarly, as we discussed in a case study in the preceding chapter, the Fed also reduced interest rates during the economic downturn and stock market decline of 2008 and 2009, but this time monetary policy was not sufficient to avert a deep recession.

While the Fed keeps an eye on the stock market, stock market participants also keep an eye on the Fed. Because the Fed can influence interest rates and economic activity, it can alter the value of stocks. For example, when the Fed raises interest rates by reducing the money supply, it makes owning stocks less attractive for two reasons. First, a higher interest rate means that bonds, an alternative to stocks, earn a higher return. Second, a tightening of monetary policy reduces the demand for goods and services and thereby reduces profits. As a result, stock prices often fall when the Fed raises interest rates. ●

16-1e The Zero Lower Bound

As we have just seen, monetary policy works through interest rates. This conclusion raises a question: What if the Fed's target interest rate has fallen as far as it can? In the Great Recession of 2008 and 2009, the federal funds rate fell to about zero. In this situation, what, if anything, can monetary policy do to stimulate the economy?

Some economists describe this situation as a *liquidity trap*. According to the theory of liquidity preference, expansionary monetary policy works by reducing interest rates and stimulating investment spending. But if interest rates have already fallen to around zero, monetary policy may no longer be effective. Nominal interest rates cannot fall much below zero: Rather than making a loan at a negative nominal interest rate, a person would just hold cash. In this environment, expansionary monetary policy raises the supply of money, making the public's asset portfolio more liquid, but because interest rates can't fall any further, the extra liquidity might not have any effect. Aggregate demand, production, and employment may be "trapped" at low levels.

Other economists are skeptical about the relevance of liquidity traps and believe that a central bank continues to have tools to expand the economy, even after its interest rate target hits its lower bound of zero. One option is to have the central bank commit itself to keeping interest rates low for an extended period of time. Such a policy is sometimes called *forward guidance*. Even if the central bank's current target for the interest rate cannot fall any further, the promise that interest rates will remain low may help stimulate investment spending.

A second option is to have the central bank conduct expansionary open-market operations using a larger variety of financial instruments. Normally, the Fed conducts expansionary open-market operations by buying short-term government bonds. But it could also buy mortgage-backed securities and longer-term government bonds to lower the interest rates on these kinds of loans. This type of unconventional monetary policy is sometimes called *quantitative easing* because it increases the quantity of bank reserves. During the Great Recession, the Fed engaged in both forward guidance and quantitative easing.

Some economists have suggested that the possibility of hitting the zero lower bound for interest rates justifies setting the target rate of inflation well above zero. Under zero inflation, the real interest rate, like the nominal interest rate, can never fall below zero. But if the normal rate of inflation is, say, 4 percent, then the central bank can easily push the real interest rate to negative 4 percent by lowering the nominal interest rate to zero. Thus, a higher inflation target gives monetary policymakers more room to stimulate the economy when needed, reducing the risk of hitting the zero lower bound and having the economy fall into a liquidity trap.

QuickQuiz

1. According to the theory of liquidity preference, an economy's interest rate adjusts
   a. to balance the supply and demand for loanable funds.
   b. to balance the supply and demand for money.
   c. one-for-one to changes in expected inflation.
   d. to equal the interest rate prevailing in world financial markets.

2. If the central bank wants to contract aggregate demand, it can _____ the money supply and thereby _____ the interest rate.
   a. increase; increase
   b. increase; decrease

   c. decrease; increase
   d. decrease; decrease

3. The Fed's target for the federal funds rate
   a. is an extra policy tool for the central bank, in addition to and independent of the money supply.
   b. commits the Fed to set a particular money supply so that it hits the announced target.
   c. is a goal that is rarely achieved because the Fed can determine only the money supply.
   d. matters to banks that borrow and lend federal funds but does not influence aggregate demand.

Answers at end of chapter.

16-2 How Fiscal Policy Influences Aggregate Demand

The government can influence the behavior of the economy not only with monetary policy but also with fiscal policy. **Fiscal policy** refers to the government's choices regarding the overall levels of government purchases and taxes. Earlier in the book, we examined how fiscal policy influences saving, investment, and growth in the long run. In the short run, however, the primary effect of fiscal policy is on the aggregate demand for goods and services.

16-2a Changes in Government Purchases

When policymakers change the money supply or the level of taxes, they shift the aggregate-demand curve indirectly by influencing the spending decisions of firms or households. By contrast, when the government alters its own purchases of goods and services, it shifts the aggregate-demand curve directly.

Suppose, for instance, that the U.S. Department of Defense places a $20 billion order for new fighter planes with Boeing, the large aircraft manufacturer. This order raises the demand for the output produced by Boeing, inducing the company to hire more workers and increase production. Because Boeing is part of the economy, the increase in the demand for Boeing planes means an increase in the total quantity of goods and services demanded at each price level. As a result, the aggregate-demand curve shifts to the right.

By how much does this $20 billion order from the government shift the aggregate-demand curve? At first, one might guess that the aggregate-demand curve shifts to the right by exactly $20 billion. It turns out, however, that this is not the case. There are two macroeconomic effects that cause the size of the shift in aggregate demand to differ from the change in government purchases. The first—the multiplier effect—suggests the shift in aggregate demand could be *larger* than $20 billion. The second—the crowding-out effect—suggests the shift in aggregate demand could be *smaller* than $20 billion. We discuss these two effects in turn.

16-2b The Multiplier Effect

When the government buys $20 billion of goods from Boeing, that purchase has repercussions. The immediate impact of the higher demand from the government is to raise employment and profits at Boeing. Then, as the workers see higher earnings and the firm's owners see higher profits, they respond to this increase in income by raising their own spending on consumer goods. As a result, the government purchase from Boeing raises the demand for the products of many other firms in the economy. Because each dollar spent by the government can raise the aggregate demand for goods and services by more than a dollar, government purchases are said to have a **multiplier effect** on aggregate demand.

This multiplier effect continues even after this first round. When consumer spending rises, the firms that produce these consumer goods hire more people and experience higher profits. Higher earnings and profits stimulate consumer spending once again and so on. Thus, there is positive feedback as higher demand leads to higher income, which in turn leads to even higher demand. Once all these effects are added together, the total impact on the quantity of goods and services demanded can be much larger than the initial boost from higher government spending.

Figure 4 illustrates the multiplier effect. The increase in government purchases of $20 billion initially shifts the aggregate-demand curve to the right from AD_1 to AD_2 by exactly $20 billion. But once consumers respond by increasing their spending, the aggregate-demand curve shifts still further to AD_3.

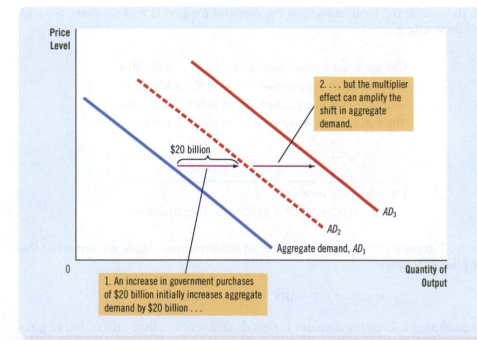

FIGURE 4

The Multiplier Effect

An increase in government purchases of $20 billion can shift the aggregate-demand curve to the right by more than $20 billion. This multiplier effect arises because increases in aggregate income stimulate additional spending by consumers.

This multiplier effect arising from the response of consumer spending can be strengthened by the response of investment to higher levels of demand. For instance, Boeing might respond to the higher demand for planes by deciding to buy more equipment or build another plant. In this case, higher government demand spurs higher demand for investment goods. This positive feedback from demand to investment is sometimes called the *investment accelerator*.

16-2c A Formula for the Spending Multiplier

Some simple algebra allows us to derive a formula for the size of the multiplier effect that arises when an increase in government purchases induces increases in consumer spending. An important number in this formula is the *marginal propensity to consume (MPC)*—the fraction of extra income that a household consumes rather than saves. For example, suppose that the marginal propensity to consume is ¾. This means that for every extra dollar that a household earns, the household spends $0.75 (¾ of the dollar) and saves $0.25. With an *MPC* of ¾, when the workers and owners of Boeing earn $20 billion from the government contract, they increase their consumer spending by ¾ × $20 billion, or $15 billion.

To gauge the impact of a change in government purchases on aggregate demand, we follow the effects step-by-step. The process begins when the government spends $20 billion and, as a result, increases national income (earnings and profits) by the same amount. With an extra $20 billion of income, consumers increase spending by *MPC* × $20 billion. This additional consumer spending raises the income for the workers and owners of the firms that produce the consumption goods by the same amount. With this second increase in income, consumers increase spending again, this time by *MPC* × (*MPC* × $20 billion). These feedback effects go on and on.

To determine the total impact on the demand for goods and services, we add up all these effects:

Change in government purchases =	$20 billion
First change in consumption	= MPC × $20 billion
Second change in consumption	= MPC^2 × $20 billion
Third change in consumption	= MPC^3 × $20 billion
⋮	⋮

Total change in demand

$$= (1 + MPC + MPC^2 + MPC^3 + \ldots) \times \$20 \text{ billion.}$$

Here "..." represents an infinite number of similar terms. Thus, we can write the multiplier as follows:

$$\text{Multiplier} = 1 + MPC + MPC^2 + MPC^3 + \ldots.$$

This multiplier tells us the demand for goods and services that each dollar of government purchases generates.

To simplify this equation for the multiplier, recall from math class that this expression is an infinite geometric series. For x between −1 and +1,

$$1 + x + x^2 + x^3 + \ldots = 1/(1 - x).$$

In our case, $x = MPC$. Thus,

$$\text{Multiplier} = 1/(1 - MPC).$$

For example, if MPC is ¾, the multiplier is $1/(1 - ¾)$, which is 4. In this case, the $20 billion of government spending generates $80 billion of demand for goods and services.

This formula for the multiplier shows that the size of the multiplier depends on the marginal propensity to consume. While an MPC of ¾ leads to a multiplier of 4, an MPC of ½ leads to a multiplier of only 2. Thus, a higher MPC means a larger multiplier. To see why, remember that the multiplier arises because higher income induces greater consumer spending. The higher the MPC, the more consumption responds to a change in income, and the larger the multiplier.

16-2d Other Applications of the Multiplier Effect

Because of the multiplier effect, a dollar of government purchases can generate more than a dollar of aggregate demand. The logic of the multiplier effect, however, is not restricted to changes in government purchases. Instead, it applies to any event that alters spending on any component of GDP—consumption, investment, government purchases, or net exports.

For example, suppose that a recession overseas reduces the demand for U.S. net exports by $10 billion. This reduced spending on U.S. goods and services depresses U.S. national income and in turn reduces spending by U.S. consumers.

If the marginal propensity to consume is ¾ and the multiplier is 4, then the $10 billion fall in net exports leads to a $40 billion contraction in aggregate demand.

As another example, suppose that a stock market boom increases households' wealth and stimulates their spending on goods and services by $20 billion. This extra consumer spending increases national income and in turn generates even more consumer spending. If the marginal propensity to consume is ¾ and the multiplier is 4, then the initial increase of $20 billion in consumer spending translates into an $80 billion increase in aggregate demand.

The multiplier is an important concept in macroeconomics because it shows how the economy can amplify the impact of changes in spending. A small initial change in consumption, investment, government purchases, or net exports can end up having a large effect on aggregate demand and, therefore, the economy's production of goods and services.

16-2e The Crowding-Out Effect

The multiplier effect seems to suggest that when the government buys $20 billion of planes from Boeing, the resulting expansion in aggregate demand is necessarily larger than $20 billion. Yet another effect works in the opposite direction. While an increase in government purchases stimulates the aggregate demand for goods and services, it also causes the interest rate to rise, reducing investment spending and putting downward pressure on aggregate demand. The reduction in aggregate demand that results when a fiscal expansion raises the interest rate is called the **crowding-out effect**.

To see why crowding out occurs, let's consider what happens in the money market when the government buys planes from Boeing. As we have discussed, this increase in demand raises the incomes of the workers and owners of this firm (and, because of the multiplier effect, of other firms as well). As incomes rise, households plan to buy more goods and services and, as a result, choose to hold more of their wealth in liquid form. That is, the increase in income caused by the fiscal expansion raises the demand for money.

The effect of the increase in money demand is shown in panel (a) of Figure 5. Because the Fed has not changed the money supply, the vertical supply curve remains the same. When the higher level of income shifts the money demand curve to the right from MD_1 to MD_2, the interest rate must rise from r_1 to r_2 to keep supply and demand in balance.

The increase in the interest rate, in turn, reduces the quantity of goods and services demanded. In particular, because borrowing is more expensive, the demand for residential and business investment goods declines. In other words, as the increase in government purchases increases the demand for goods and services, it may also crowd out investment. This crowding-out effect partially offsets the impact of government purchases on aggregate demand, as illustrated in panel (b) of Figure 5. The increase in government purchases initially shifts the aggregate-demand curve from AD_1 to AD_2, but once crowding out takes place, the aggregate-demand curve drops back to AD_3.

To sum up: *When the government increases its purchases by $20 billion, the aggregate demand for goods and services could rise by more or less than $20 billion depending on the sizes of the multiplier and crowding-out effects.* The multiplier effect makes the shift in aggregate demand greater than $20 billion. The crowding-out effect pushes the aggregate-demand curve in the opposite direction and can, if large enough, result in an aggregate-demand shift of less than $20 billion.

crowding-out effect
the offset in aggregate demand that results when expansionary fiscal policy raises the interest rate and thereby reduces investment spending

FIGURE 5

The Crowding-Out Effect

Panel (a) shows the money market. When the government increases its purchases of goods and services, income increases, raising the demand for money from MD_1 to MD_2 and thereby increasing the equilibrium interest rate from r_1 to r_2. Panel (b) shows the effects on aggregate demand. The initial impact of the increase in government purchases shifts the aggregate-demand curve from AD_1 to AD_2. Yet because the interest rate is the cost of borrowing, the increase in the interest rate tends to reduce the quantity of goods and services demanded, particularly for investment goods. This crowding out of investment partially offsets the impact of the fiscal expansion on aggregate demand. In the end, the aggregate-demand curve shifts only to AD_3.

(a) The Money Market

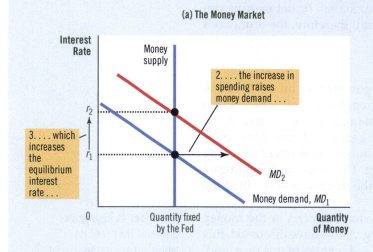

(b) The Shift in Aggregate Demand

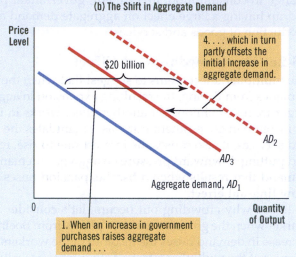

16-2f Changes in Taxes

The other important instrument of fiscal policy, besides the level of government purchases, is the level of taxation. When the government cuts personal income taxes, for instance, it increases households' take-home pay. Households will save some of this additional income, but they will also spend some of it on consumer goods. Because it increases consumer spending, the tax cut shifts the aggregate-demand curve to the right. Similarly, a tax increase depresses consumer spending and shifts the aggregate-demand curve to the left.

The size of the shift in aggregate demand resulting from a tax change is also affected by the multiplier and crowding-out effects. When the government cuts taxes and stimulates consumer spending, earnings and profits rise, further stimulating consumer spending. This is the multiplier effect. At the same time, the increase in income raises money demand, increasing interest rates. Higher interest rates mean a higher cost of borrowing, which reduces investment spending. This is the crowding-out effect. Depending on the sizes of the multiplier and crowding-out effects, the shift in aggregate demand could be larger or smaller than the tax change that causes it.

In addition to the multiplier and crowding-out effects, there is another important determinant of the size of the shift in aggregate demand that results from a tax change: households' perceptions about whether the tax change is permanent or temporary. For example, suppose that the government announces a tax cut of $1,000 per household. In deciding how much of this $1,000 to spend, households must ask themselves how long this extra income will last. If they expect the tax cut to be permanent, they will view it as adding substantially to their financial resources and, therefore, increase their spending by a large amount. In this case, the tax cut will have a large impact on aggregate demand. By contrast, if households expect the tax change to be temporary, they will view it as adding only slightly to their financial resources and, therefore, increase their spending by only a small amount. In this case, the tax cut will have a small impact on aggregate demand.

An extreme example of a temporary tax cut was the one announced in 1992. In that year, President George H. W. Bush faced a lingering recession and an upcoming reelection campaign. He responded to these circumstances by announcing a reduction in the amount of income tax that the federal government would withhold from workers' paychecks. Because legislated income tax rates did not change, however, every dollar of reduced withholding in 1992 meant an extra dollar of taxes due on April 15, 1993, when income tax returns for 1992 were to be filed. Thus, this "tax cut" actually represented only a short-term loan from the government. Not surprisingly, the impact of the policy on consumer spending and aggregate demand was relatively small.

FYI

How Fiscal Policy Might Affect Aggregate Supply

So far, our discussion of fiscal policy has stressed how changes in government purchases and changes in taxes influence the quantity of goods and services demanded. Most economists believe that the short-run macroeconomic effects of fiscal policy work primarily through aggregate demand. Yet fiscal policy can potentially influence the quantity of goods and services supplied as well.

For instance, consider the effects of tax changes on aggregate supply. One of the *Ten Principles of Economics* in Chapter 1 is that people respond to incentives. When government policymakers cut tax rates, workers get to keep more of each dollar they earn, so they have a greater incentive to work and produce goods and services. If they respond to this incentive, the quantity of goods and services supplied will be greater at each price level, and the aggregate-supply curve will shift to the right.

Economists who stress the importance of tax policy for aggregate supply rather than aggregate demand are sometimes called *supply siders*. Supply-side economists have been particularly prominent as advisers to President Donald Trump, and they were instrumental in helping design the tax cut he signed into law at the end of 2017. The large cut in corporate tax rates aimed to promote capital accumulation and long-run growth.

At times, some supply siders have argued that the influence of taxes on aggregate supply is so large that a cut in tax rates will stimulate enough additional production and income to increase tax revenue. This outcome is a theoretical possibility, but most economists do not consider it the normal case. While the supply-side effects of taxes are important to consider, they are rarely large enough to cause tax revenue to rise when tax rates fall.

Like changes in taxes, changes in government purchases can also affect aggregate supply. Suppose, for instance, that the government increases expenditure on a form of government-provided capital, such as roads. Roads are used by private businesses to make deliveries to their customers, so an increase in the quantity or quality of roads increases these businesses' productivity. Hence, when the government spends more on roads, it increases the quantity of goods and services supplied at any given price level and thereby shifts the aggregate-supply curve to the right. This effect on aggregate supply is probably more important in the long run than in the short run, however, because it takes time for the government to build new roads and put them into use. ■

4. If the government wants to expand aggregate demand, it can _____ government purchases or _____ taxes.
   a. increase; increase
   b. increase; decrease
   c. decrease; increase
   d. decrease; decrease

5. With the economy in a recession due to inadequate aggregate demand, the government increases its purchases by $1,200. Suppose the central bank adjusts the money supply to hold the interest rate constant, investment spending remains unchanged, and the marginal propensity to consume is 2/3. How large is the increase in aggregate demand?
   a. $400
   b. $800
   c. $1,800
   d. $3,600

6. If the central bank in the preceding question had instead held the money supply constant and allowed the interest rate to adjust, the change in aggregate demand resulting from the increase in government purchases would have been
   a. larger.
   b. the same.
   c. smaller but still positive.
   d. negative.

Answers at end of chapter.

16-3 Using Policy to Stabilize the Economy

We have seen how monetary and fiscal policy can affect the economy's aggregate demand for goods and services. These theoretical insights raise some important policy questions: Should policymakers use these instruments to control aggregate demand and stabilize the economy? If so, when? If not, why not?

16-3a The Case for Active Stabilization Policy

Let's return to the question that began this chapter: When the president and Congress raise taxes, how should the Federal Reserve respond? As we have seen, the level of taxation is one determinant of the position of the aggregate-demand curve. When the government raises taxes, aggregate demand falls, depressing production and employment in the short run. If the Fed wants to prevent this adverse effect of the fiscal policy, it can expand aggregate demand by increasing the money supply. A monetary expansion would reduce interest rates, stimulate investment spending, and expand aggregate demand. If monetary policy is set appropriately, the combined changes in monetary and fiscal policy could leave the aggregate demand for goods and services unaffected.

This analysis is exactly the sort followed by members of the Federal Open Market Committee. They know that monetary policy is an important determinant of aggregate demand. They also know that there are other important determinants as well, including fiscal policy set by the president and Congress. As a result, the FOMC watches the debates over fiscal policy with a keen eye.

This response of monetary policy to the change in fiscal policy is an example of a more general phenomenon: the use of policy instruments to stabilize aggregate demand and, in turn, production and employment. Economic stabilization has been an explicit goal of U.S. policy since the Employment Act of 1946. This act states that "it is the continuing policy and responsibility of the federal government to

. . . promote full employment and production." In essence, the government has chosen to hold itself accountable for short-run macroeconomic performance.

The Employment Act has two implications. The first, more modest, implication is that the government should avoid being a cause of economic fluctuations. Thus, most economists advise against large and sudden changes in monetary and fiscal policy, for such changes are likely to cause fluctuations in aggregate demand. Moreover, when large changes do occur, it is important that monetary and fiscal policymakers be aware of and respond to each others' actions.

The second, more ambitious, implication of the Employment Act is that the government should respond to changes in the private economy to stabilize aggregate demand. The act was passed not long after the publication of Keynes's *The General Theory of Employment, Interest, and Money*, which has been one of the most influential books ever written about economics. In it, Keynes emphasized the key role of aggregate demand in explaining short-run economic fluctuations. Keynes claimed that the government should actively stimulate aggregate demand when aggregate demand appears insufficient to maintain production at its full-employment level.

Keynes (and his many followers) argued that aggregate demand fluctuates because of largely irrational waves of pessimism and optimism. He used the term "animal spirits" to refer to these arbitrary changes in attitude. When pessimism reigns, households reduce consumption spending and firms reduce investment spending. The result is reduced aggregate demand, lower production, and higher unemployment. Conversely, when optimism reigns, households and firms increase spending. The result is higher aggregate demand, higher production, and inflationary pressure. Notice that these changes in attitude are, to some extent, self-fulfilling.

In principle, the government can adjust its monetary and fiscal policy in response to these waves of optimism and pessimism and, thereby, stabilize the economy. For example, when people are excessively pessimistic, the Fed can expand the money supply to lower interest rates and expand aggregate demand. When they are excessively optimistic, it can contract the money supply to raise interest rates and dampen aggregate demand. Former Fed Chairman William McChesney Martin described this view of monetary policy very simply: "The Federal Reserve's job is to take away the punch bowl just as the party gets going."

KEYNESIANS IN THE WHITE HOUSE

CASE STUDY

When a reporter in 1961 asked President John F. Kennedy why he advocated a tax cut, Kennedy replied, "To stimulate the economy. Don't you remember your Economics 101?" Kennedy's policy was, in fact, based on the analysis of fiscal policy we have developed in this chapter. His goal was to enact a tax cut, which would raise consumer spending, expand aggregate demand, and increase the economy's production and employment.

In choosing this policy, Kennedy was relying on his team of economic advisers. This team included such prominent

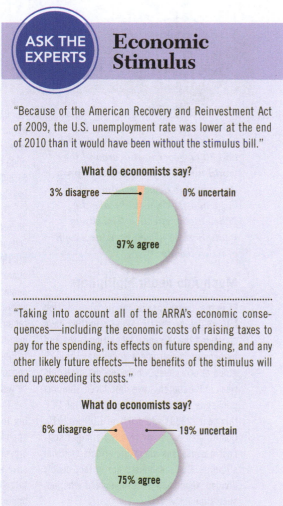

ASK THE EXPERTS

Economic Stimulus

"Because of the American Recovery and Reinvestment Act of 2009, the U.S. unemployment rate was lower at the end of 2010 than it would have been without the stimulus bill."

What do economists say?

3% disagree — 0% uncertain

97% agree

"Taking into account all of the ARRA's economic consequences—including the economic costs of raising taxes to pay for the spending, its effects on future spending, and any other likely future effects—the benefits of the stimulus will end up exceeding its costs."

What do economists say?

6% disagree — 19% uncertain

75% agree

Source: IGM Economic Experts Panel, July 29, 2014.

economists as James Tobin and Robert Solow, both of whom would later win Nobel Prizes for their contributions to the field. As students in the 1940s, these economists had closely studied John Maynard Keynes's *General Theory*, which was then only a few years old. When the Kennedy advisers proposed tax cuts, they were putting Keynes's ideas into action.

Although tax changes have a potent influence on aggregate demand, they can also alter the aggregate supply of goods and services, as discussed earlier in an FYI box. Part of the Kennedy proposal was an investment tax credit that gave a tax break to firms that invested in new capital. Higher investment would not only stimulate aggregate demand immediately but also increase the economy's productive capacity over time. Thus, the short-run goal of increasing production through higher aggregate demand was coupled with a long-run goal of increasing production through higher aggregate supply. And indeed, when the tax cut Kennedy proposed was finally enacted in 1964, it helped usher in a period of robust economic growth.

Since the 1964 tax cut, policymakers have from time to time used fiscal policy as a tool for controlling aggregate demand. For example, when President

IN THE NEWS

How Large Is the Fiscal Policy Multiplier?

During the Great Recession of 2008 and 2009, governments around the world turned to fiscal policy to prop up aggregate demand, hoping that large multipliers would make the policy highly effective. The size of multipliers, however, remains a topic of much debate.

Much Ado about Multipliers

It is the biggest peacetime fiscal expansion in history. Across the globe countries have countered the recession by cutting taxes and by boosting government spending. The G20 group of economies, whose leaders meet this week in Pittsburgh, have introduced stimulus packages worth an average of 2% of GDP this year [2009] and 1.6% of GDP in 2010. Coordinated action on this scale might suggest a consensus about the effects of fiscal stimulus. But economists are in fact deeply divided about how well, or indeed whether, such stimulus works.

The debate hinges on the scale of the "fiscal multiplier." This measure, first formalized in 1931 by Richard Kahn, a student of John Maynard Keynes, captures how effectively tax cuts or increases in government spending stimulate output. A multiplier of one means that a $1 billion increase in government spending will increase a country's GDP by $1 billion.

The size of the multiplier is bound to vary according to economic conditions. For an economy operating at full capacity, the fiscal multiplier should be zero. Since there are no spare resources, any increase in government demand would just replace spending elsewhere. But in a recession, when workers and factories lie idle, a fiscal boost can increase overall demand. And if the initial stimulus triggers a cascade of expenditure among consumers and businesses, the multiplier can be well above one.

The multiplier is also likely to vary according to the type of fiscal action. Government spending on building a bridge may have a bigger multiplier than a tax cut if consumers save a portion of their tax windfall. A tax cut targeted at poorer people may have a bigger impact on spending than one for the affluent, since poorer folk tend to spend a higher share of their income.

Crucially, the overall size of the fiscal multiplier also depends on how people react to higher government borrowing. If the government's actions bolster confidence and revive animal spirits, the multiplier could rise as demand goes up and private investment is "crowded in." But if interest rates climb in response to government borrowing then some private investment that would otherwise have occurred could get "crowded out." And if consumers expect higher future taxes in order to finance new government borrowing, they could spend less today. All that would reduce the fiscal multiplier, potentially to below zero.

Different assumptions about the impact of higher government borrowing on interest rates and private spending explain wild variations in the estimates of multipliers from today's stimulus spending. Economists in the Obama administration, who assume that the federal funds rate stays constant for a four-year period, expect a multiplier of 1.6 for government purchases and 1.0 for tax cuts from America's fiscal stimulus. An alternative assessment by John Cogan, Tobias Cwik, John Taylor and Volker Wieland uses models

Barack Obama moved into the Oval Office in 2009, he faced an economy in the midst of a recession. One of his first policy initiatives was a stimulus bill, called the American Recovery and Reinvestment Act (ARRA), which included substantial increases in government spending. The accompanying In the News box discusses some of the debate over this policy initiative. ●

16-3b The Case against Active Stabilization Policy

Some economists argue that the government should avoid active use of monetary and fiscal policy to try to stabilize the economy. They claim that these policy instruments should be set to achieve long-run goals, such as rapid economic growth and low inflation, and that the economy should be left to deal with short-run fluctuations on its own. These economists may admit that monetary and fiscal policy can stabilize the economy in theory, but they doubt whether it can do so in practice.

The main argument against active monetary and fiscal policy is that these policies affect the economy with a long lag. As we have seen, monetary policy works

in which interest rates and taxes rise more quickly in response to higher public borrowing. Their multipliers are much smaller. They think America's stimulus will boost GDP by only one-sixth as much as the Obama team expects.

When forward-looking models disagree so dramatically, careful analysis of previous fiscal stimuli ought to help settle the debate. Unfortunately, it is extremely tricky to isolate the impact of changes in fiscal policy. One approach is to use microeconomic case studies to examine consumer behavior in response to specific tax rebates and cuts. These studies, largely based on tax changes in America, find that permanent cuts have a bigger impact on consumer spending than temporary ones and that consumers who find it hard to borrow, such as those close to their credit-card limit, tend to spend more of their tax windfall. But case studies do not measure the overall impact of tax cuts or spending increases on output.

An alternative approach is to try to tease out the statistical impact of changes in government spending or tax cuts on GDP. The difficulty here is to isolate the effects of fiscal-stimulus measures from the rises

in social-security spending and falls in tax revenues that naturally accompany recessions. This empirical approach has narrowed the range of estimates in some areas. It has also yielded interesting cross-country comparisons. Multipliers are bigger in closed economies than open ones (because less of the stimulus leaks abroad via imports). They have traditionally been bigger in rich countries than emerging ones (where investors tend to take fright more quickly, pushing interest rates up). But overall economists find as big a range of multipliers from empirical estimates as they do from theoretical models.

To add to the confusion, the post-war experiences from which statistical analyses are drawn differ in vital respects from the current situation. Most of the evidence on multipliers for government spending is based on military outlays, but today's stimulus packages are heavily focused on infrastructure. Interest rates in many rich countries are now close to zero, which may increase the potency of, as well as the need for, fiscal stimulus. Because of the financial crisis relatively more people face borrowing constraints, which would increase the effectiveness of a tax cut. At the

same time, highly indebted consumers may now be keen to cut their borrowing, leading to a lower multiplier. And investors today have more reason to be worried about rich countries' fiscal positions than those of emerging markets.

Add all this together and the truth is that economists are flying blind. They can make relative judgments with some confidence. Temporary tax cuts pack less punch than permanent ones, for instance. Fiscal multipliers will probably be lower in heavily indebted economies than in prudent ones. But policymakers looking for precise estimates are deluding themselves. ■

Questions to Discuss

1. How should uncertainty about the size of fiscal multipliers affect the reliance on monetary and fiscal policy as tools for stabilizing the economy?

2. Do you think it is easier for governments to change taxes or spending plans? Why? What does your answer imply for policy?

Source: *The Economist*, September 24, 2009.

by changing interest rates, which in turn influence investment spending. But many firms make investment plans far in advance. Thus, most economists believe that it takes at least six months for changes in monetary policy to have much effect on output and employment. Moreover, once these effects occur, they can last for several years. Critics of stabilization policy argue that because of this lag, the Fed should not try to fine-tune the economy. They claim that the Fed often reacts too late to changing economic conditions and, as a result, ends up causing rather than curing economic fluctuations. These critics advocate a passive monetary policy, such as slow and steady growth in the money supply.

Fiscal policy also works with a lag, but unlike the lag in monetary policy, the lag in fiscal policy is largely attributable to the political process. In the United States, most changes in government spending and taxes must go through congressional committees in both the House and the Senate, be passed by both legislative bodies, and then be signed by the president. Completing this process can take months or, in some cases, years. By the time the change in fiscal policy is passed and ready to implement, the condition of the economy may have changed.

These lags in monetary and fiscal policy are a problem in part because economic forecasting is so imprecise. If forecasters could accurately predict the condition of the economy a year in advance, then monetary and fiscal policymakers could look ahead when making policy decisions. In this case, policymakers could stabilize the economy despite the lags they face. In practice, however, major recessions and depressions arrive without much advance warning. The best that policymakers can do is to respond to economic changes as they occur.

16-3c Automatic Stabilizers

All economists—both advocates and critics of stabilization policy—agree that the lags in implementation reduce the efficacy of policy as a tool for short-run stabilization. The economy would be more stable, therefore, if policymakers could find a way to avoid some of these lags. In fact, they have. **Automatic stabilizers** are changes in fiscal policy that stimulate aggregate demand when the economy goes into a recession but that occur without policymakers having to take any deliberate action.

The most important automatic stabilizer is the tax system. When the economy goes into a recession, the amount of taxes collected by the government falls automatically because almost all taxes are closely tied to economic activity. The personal income tax depends on households' incomes, the payroll tax depends on workers' earnings, and the corporate income tax depends on firms' profits. Because incomes, earnings, and profits all fall in a recession, the government's tax revenue falls as well. This automatic tax cut stimulates aggregate demand and, thereby, reduces the magnitude of economic fluctuations.

Some government spending also acts as an automatic stabilizer. In particular, when the economy goes into a recession and workers are laid off, more people become eligible for unemployment insurance benefits, welfare benefits, and other forms of income support. This automatic increase in government spending stimulates aggregate demand at exactly the time when aggregate demand is insufficient to maintain full employment. Indeed, when the unemployment insurance system was first enacted in the 1930s, economists who advocated this policy did so in part because they recognized its power as an automatic stabilizer.

The automatic stabilizers in the U.S. economy are not sufficiently strong to prevent recessions completely. Nonetheless, without these automatic stabilizers, output and employment would probably be more volatile than they are. For this reason, many economists oppose a constitutional amendment that would require the federal government to always run a balanced budget, as some politicians have proposed. When the economy goes into a recession, taxes fall, government spending rises, and the government's budget moves toward deficit. If the government faced a strict balanced-budget rule, it would be forced to look for ways to raise taxes or cut spending in a recession. In other words, a strict balanced-budget rule would eliminate the automatic stabilizers inherent in our current system of taxes and government spending.

automatic stabilizers changes in fiscal policy that stimulate aggregate demand when the economy goes into a recession but that occur without policymakers having to take any deliberate action

---

QuickQuiz

7. Suppose a wave of negative "animal spirits" overruns the economy, and people become pessimistic about the future. To stabilize aggregate demand, the Fed could _____ its target for the federal funds rate or Congress could _____ taxes.
   a. increase; increase
   b. increase; decrease
   c. decrease; increase
   d. decrease; decrease

8. Monetary policy affects the economy with a lag mainly because it takes a long time
   a. for central banks to make policy changes.
   b. to change the money supply after a policy decision has been made.

   c. for a change in the money supply to affect interest rates.
   d. for a change in interest rates to affect investment spending.

9. Which of the following is an example of an automatic stabilizer? When the economy goes into a recession,
   a. more people become eligible for unemployment insurance benefits.
   b. stock prices decline, particularly for firms in cyclical industries.
   c. Congress begins hearings about a possible stimulus package.
   d. the Fed changes its target for the federal funds rate.

Answers at end of chapter.

16-4 Conclusion

Before policymakers make any change in policy, they need to consider all the effects of their decisions. Earlier in the book, we examined classical models of the economy, which describe the long-run effects of monetary and fiscal policy. There we saw how fiscal policy influences saving, investment, and long-run growth and how monetary policy influences the price level and the inflation rate.

In this chapter, we examined the short-run effects of monetary and fiscal policy. We saw how these policy instruments can change the aggregate demand for goods and services and alter the economy's production and employment in the short run. When Congress reduces government spending to balance the budget, it needs to consider both the long-run effects on saving and growth and the short-run effects on aggregate demand and employment. When the Fed reduces the growth rate of the money supply, it must take into account the long-run effect on inflation as well as the short-run effect on production. In all parts of government, policymakers must keep in mind both long-run and short-run goals.

CHAPTER IN A NUTSHELL

- In developing a theory of short-run economic fluctuations, Keynes proposed the theory of liquidity preference to explain the determinants of the interest rate. According to this theory, the interest rate adjusts to balance the supply and demand for money.

- An increase in the price level raises money demand and increases the interest rate that brings the money market into equilibrium. Because the interest rate represents the cost of borrowing, a higher interest rate reduces investment spending and, thereby, reduces the quantity of goods and services demanded. The downward-sloping aggregate-demand curve expresses this negative relationship between the price level and the quantity demanded.

- Policymakers can influence aggregate demand using monetary policy. An increase in the money supply reduces the equilibrium interest rate for any given price level. Because a lower interest rate stimulates investment spending, the aggregate-demand curve shifts to the right. Conversely, a decrease in the money supply raises the equilibrium interest rate for any given price level and shifts the aggregate-demand curve to the left.

- Policymakers can also influence aggregate demand using fiscal policy. An increase in government purchases or a cut in taxes shifts the aggregate-demand curve to the right. A decrease in government purchases or an increase in taxes shifts the aggregate-demand curve to the left.

- When the government alters spending or taxes, the resulting shift in aggregate demand can be larger or smaller than the fiscal change. The multiplier effect tends to amplify the effects of fiscal policy on aggregate demand. The crowding-out effect tends to dampen the effects of fiscal policy on aggregate demand.

- Because monetary and fiscal policy can influence aggregate demand, the government sometimes uses these policy instruments in an attempt to stabilize the economy. Economists disagree about how active the government should be in this effort. According to advocates of active stabilization policy, changes in attitudes by households and firms shift aggregate demand; if the government does not respond, the result is undesirable and unnecessary fluctuations in output and employment. According to critics of active stabilization policy, monetary and fiscal policy work with such long lags that attempts at stabilizing the economy often end up being destabilizing.

KEY CONCEPTS

theory of liquidity preference, *p. 341*
fiscal policy, *p. 350*

multiplier effect, *p. 350*
crowding-out effect, *p. 353*

automatic stabilizers, *p. 361*

QUESTIONS FOR REVIEW

1. What is the theory of liquidity preference? How does it help explain the downward slope of the aggregate-demand curve?

2. Use the theory of liquidity preference to explain how a decrease in the money supply affects the aggregate-demand curve.

3. The government spends $3 billion to buy police cars. Explain why aggregate demand might increase by more or less than $3 billion.

4. Suppose that survey measures of consumer confidence indicate a wave of pessimism is sweeping the country. If policymakers do nothing, what will happen to aggregate demand? What should the Fed do if it wants to stabilize aggregate demand? If the Fed does nothing, what might Congress do to stabilize aggregate demand? Explain your reasoning.

5. Give an example of a government policy that acts as an automatic stabilizer. Explain why the policy has this effect.

PROBLEMS AND APPLICATIONS

1. Explain how each of the following developments would affect the supply of money, the demand for money, and the interest rate. Use diagrams to illustrate your answers.
   a. The Fed's bond traders buy bonds in open-market operations.
   b. An increase in credit-card availability reduces the amount of cash people want to hold.
   c. The Fed reduces reserve requirements.
   d. Households decide to hold more money to use for holiday shopping.
   e. A wave of optimism boosts business investment and expands aggregate demand.

2. The Fed expands the money supply by 5 percent.
   a. Use the theory of liquidity preference to illustrate in a graph the impact of this policy on the interest rate.
   b. Use the model of aggregate demand and aggregate supply to illustrate the impact of this change in the interest rate on output and the price level in the short run.
   c. When the economy makes the transition from its short-run equilibrium to its new long-run equilibrium, what happens to the price level?

   d. How does this change in the price level affect the demand for money and the equilibrium interest rate?
   e. Is this analysis consistent with the proposition that money has real effects in the short run but is neutral in the long run?

3. Suppose a computer virus disables the nation's automatic teller machines, making withdrawals from bank accounts less convenient. As a result, people want to keep more cash on hand, increasing the demand for money.
   a. Assume the Fed does not change the money supply. According to the theory of liquidity preference, what happens to the interest rate? What happens to aggregate demand?
   b. If instead the Fed wants to stabilize aggregate demand, how should it change the money supply?
   c. If it wants to accomplish this change in the money supply using open-market operations, what should it do?

4. Consider two policies—a tax cut that lasts for only one year and a tax cut that is expected to be permanent. Which policy will stimulate greater

spending by consumers? Which policy will have the greater impact on aggregate demand? Explain.

5. The economy is in a recession with high unemployment and low output.
   a. Draw a graph of aggregate demand and aggregate supply to illustrate the current situation. Be sure to include the aggregate-demand curve, the short-run aggregate-supply curve, and the long-run aggregate-supply curve.
   b. Identify an open-market operation that would restore the economy to its natural rate.
   c. Draw a graph of the money market to illustrate the effect of this open-market operation. Show the resulting change in the interest rate.
   d. Draw a graph similar to the one in part a to show the effect of the open-market operation on output and the price level. Explain in words why the policy has the effect that you have shown in the graph.

6. In the early 1980s, new legislation allowed banks to pay interest on checking deposits, which they could not do previously.
   a. If we define money to include checking deposits, what effect did this legislation have on money demand? Explain.
   b. If the Fed had maintained a constant money supply in the face of this change, what would have happened to the interest rate? What would have happened to aggregate demand and aggregate output?
   c. If the Fed had maintained a constant market interest rate (the interest rate on nonmonetary assets) in the face of this change, what change in the money supply would have been necessary? What would have happened to aggregate demand and aggregate output?

7. Suppose economists observe that an increase in government spending of $10 billion raises the total demand for goods and services by $30 billion.
   a. If these economists ignore the possibility of crowding out, what would they estimate the marginal propensity to consume (MPC) to be?
   b. Now suppose the economists allow for crowding out. Would their new estimate of the MPC be larger or smaller than their initial one?

8. An economy is producing output $400 billion less than the natural level of output, and fiscal policymakers want to close this recessionary gap. The central bank agrees to adjust the money supply to hold the interest rate constant, so there is no crowding out. The marginal propensity to consume is ⅘, and the price level is completely fixed in the short run. In what direction and by how much must government spending change to close the recessionary gap? Explain your thinking.

9. Suppose government spending increases. Would the effect on aggregate demand be larger if the Fed held the money supply constant in response or if the Fed committed to maintaining a fixed interest rate? Explain.

10. Is expansionary fiscal policy more likely to lead to a short-run increase in investment
    a. when the investment accelerator is large or when it is small? Explain.
    b. when the interest sensitivity of investment is large or when it is small? Explain.

11. Consider an economy described by the following equations:

$$Y = C + I + G$$
$$C = 100 + 0.75(Y - T)$$
$$I = 500 - 50r$$
$$G = 125$$
$$T = 100$$

where Y is GDP, C is consumption, I is investment, G is government purchases, T is taxes, and r is the interest rate. If the economy were at full employment (that is, at its natural level of output), GDP would be 2,000.
    a. Explain the meaning of each of these equations.
    b. What is the marginal propensity to consume in this economy?
    c. Suppose the central bank adjusts the money supply to maintain the interest rate at 4 percent, so r = 4. Solve for GDP. How does it compare to the full-employment level?
    d. Assuming no change in monetary policy, what change in government purchases would restore full employment?
    e. Assuming no change in fiscal policy, what change in the interest rate would restore full employment?

Quick Quiz Answers

1. b   2. c   3. b   4. b   5. d   6. c   7. d   8. d   9. a

nflation and unemployment are two of the most closely watched indicators of economic performance. When the Bureau of Labor Statistics releases data on these variables each month, policymakers are eager to hear the news. Some commentators have added together the inflation rate and the unemployment rate to produce a *misery index*, which they use to gauge the health of the economy.

How are these two measures of economic performance related to each other? Earlier in the book, we discussed the long-run determinants of unemployment and the long-run determinants of inflation. We saw that the natural rate of unemployment depends on various features of the labor market, such as minimum-wage laws, the market power of unions, the role of efficiency wages, and the effectiveness of job search. By contrast, the inflation rate depends primarily on growth in the money supply, which a nation's central bank controls. In the long run, therefore, inflation and unemployment are largely unrelated problems.

The Short-Run Trade-Off between Inflation and Unemployment

In the short run, just the opposite is true. One of the *Ten Principles of Economics* in Chapter 1 is that society faces a short-run trade-off between inflation and unemployment. If monetary and fiscal policymakers expand aggregate demand and move the economy up along the short-run aggregate-supply curve, they can expand output and reduce unemployment for a while, but only at the cost of a more rapidly rising price level. If policymakers contract aggregate demand and move the economy down the short-run aggregate-supply curve, they can reduce inflation, but only at the cost of temporarily lower output and higher unemployment.

In this chapter, we examine the inflation–unemployment trade-off more closely. The relationship between inflation and unemployment has attracted the attention of some of the most brilliant economists of the last half century. The best way to understand this relationship is to see how economists' thinking about it has evolved. As we will see, the history of thought regarding inflation and unemployment since the 1950s is inextricably connected to the history of the U.S. economy. These two histories will show why the trade-off between inflation and unemployment holds in the short run, why it does not hold in the long run, and what issues the trade-off raises for policymakers.

17-1 The Phillips Curve

Phillips curve

a curve that shows the short-run trade-off between inflation and unemployment

"Probably the single most important macroeconomic relationship is the Phillips curve." These are the words of economist George Akerlof from the lecture he gave when he received the Nobel Prize in 2001. The **Phillips curve** is the short-run relationship between inflation and unemployment. We begin our story with the discovery of the Phillips curve and its migration to America.

17-1a Origins of the Phillips Curve

In 1958, economist A. W. Phillips published an article in the British journal *Economica* that would make him famous. The article was titled "The Relationship between Unemployment and the Rate of Change of Money Wages in the United Kingdom, 1861–1957." In it, Phillips showed a negative correlation between the rate of unemployment and the rate of inflation. That is, Phillips showed that years with low unemployment tend to have high inflation, and years with high unemployment tend to have low inflation. (Phillips examined inflation in nominal wages rather than inflation in prices. For our purposes, the distinction is not important because these two measures of inflation usually move together.) Phillips concluded that two important macroeconomic variables—inflation and unemployment—were linked in a way that economists had not previously appreciated.

Although Phillips's discovery was based on data for the United Kingdom, researchers quickly extended his finding to other countries. Two years after Phillips published his article, economists Paul Samuelson and Robert Solow published an article in the *American Economic Review* called "Analytics of Anti-Inflation Policy" in which they showed a similar negative correlation between inflation and unemployment in data for the United States. They reasoned that this correlation arose because low unemployment was associated with high aggregate demand, which in turn put upward pressure on wages and prices throughout the economy. Samuelson and Solow dubbed the negative association between inflation and unemployment the *Phillips curve*. Figure 1 shows an example of a Phillips curve like the one found by Samuelson and Solow.

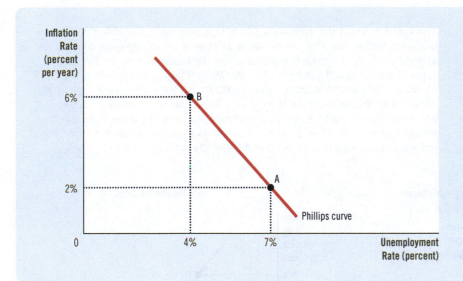

FIGURE 1

The Phillips Curve
The Phillips curve illustrates a negative association between the inflation rate and the unemployment rate. At point A, inflation is low and unemployment is high. At point B, inflation is high and unemployment is low.

As the title of their paper suggests, Samuelson and Solow were interested in the Phillips curve because they believed it held important lessons for policymakers. In particular, they suggested that the Phillips curve offers policymakers a menu of possible economic outcomes. By altering monetary and fiscal policy to influence aggregate demand, policymakers could choose any point on this curve. Point A offers high unemployment and low inflation. Point B offers low unemployment and high inflation. Policymakers might prefer both low inflation and low unemployment, but the historical data as summarized by the Phillips curve indicate that this combination is impossible. According to Samuelson and Solow, policymakers face a trade-off between inflation and unemployment, and the Phillips curve illustrates that trade-off.

17-1b Aggregate Demand, Aggregate Supply, and the Phillips Curve

The model of aggregate demand and aggregate supply provides an easy explanation for the menu of possible outcomes described by the Phillips curve. *The Phillips curve shows the combinations of inflation and unemployment that arise in the short run as shifts in the aggregate-demand curve move the economy along the short-run aggregate-supply curve.* As we saw in the preceding two chapters, an increase in the aggregate demand for goods and services leads, in the short run, to a larger output of goods and services and a higher price level. Larger output means greater employment and, thus, a lower rate of unemployment. In addition, a higher price level translates into a higher rate of inflation. Thus, shifts in aggregate demand push inflation and unemployment in opposite directions in the short run—a relationship illustrated by the Phillips curve.

To see more fully how this works, let's consider an example. To keep the numbers simple, imagine that the price level (as measured, for instance, by the consumer price index) equals 100 in the year 2020. Figure 2 shows two possible outcomes that might occur in the year 2021 depending on the strength of aggregate demand. One outcome occurs if aggregate demand is high, and the other occurs if aggregate

FIGURE 2

How the Phillips Curve Is Related to the Model of Aggregate Demand and Aggregate Supply

This figure assumes a price level of 100 for the year 2020 and charts possible outcomes for the year 2021. Panel (a) shows the model of aggregate demand and aggregate supply. If aggregate demand is low, the economy is at point A; output is low (15,000), and the price level is low (102). If aggregate demand is high, the economy is at point B; output is high (16,000), and the price level is high (106). Panel (b) shows the implications for the Phillips curve. Point A, which arises when aggregate demand is low, has high unemployment (7 percent) and low inflation (2 percent). Point B, which arises when aggregate demand is high, has low unemployment (4 percent) and high inflation (6 percent).

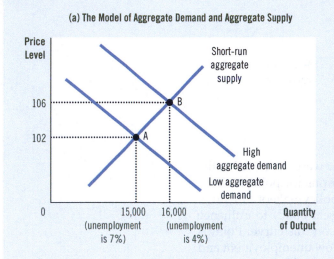

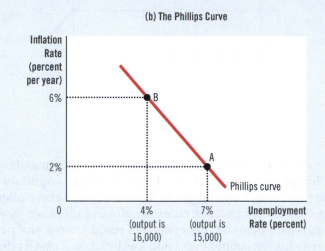

demand is low. Panel (a) shows these two outcomes using the model of aggregate demand and aggregate supply. Panel (b) illustrates the same two outcomes using the Phillips curve.

Panel (a) of the figure shows what happens to output and the price level in the year 2021. If the aggregate demand for goods and services is low, the economy experiences outcome A. The economy produces output of 15,000, and the price level is 102. By contrast, if aggregate demand is high, the economy experiences outcome B. Output is 16,000, and the price level is 106. This is an example of a familiar conclusion: Higher aggregate demand moves the economy to an equilibrium with higher output and a higher price level.

Panel (b) shows what these two possible outcomes mean for unemployment and inflation. Because firms need more workers when they produce a greater output of goods and services, unemployment is lower in outcome B than in outcome A. In this example, when output rises from 15,000 to 16,000, unemployment falls from 7 percent to 4 percent. Moreover, because the price level is higher at outcome B than at outcome A, the inflation rate (the percentage change in the price level from the previous year) is also higher. In particular, since the price level was 100 in the year 2020, outcome A has an inflation rate of 2 percent and outcome B has an inflation rate of 6 percent. The two possible outcomes for the economy can be compared either in terms of output and the price level (using the model of aggregate demand and aggregate supply) or in terms of unemployment and inflation (using the Phillips curve).

Because monetary and fiscal policy can shift the aggregate-demand curve, they can move an economy along the Phillips curve. Increases in the money supply, increases in government spending, or cuts in taxes expand aggregate demand and move the economy to a point on the Phillips curve with higher inflation and lower unemployment. Decreases in the money supply, cuts in government spending, or increases in taxes contract aggregate demand and move the economy to a point on the Phillips curve with lower inflation and higher unemployment. In this sense, the Phillips curve offers policymakers a menu of combinations of inflation and unemployment.

QuickQuiz

1. The Phillips curve started as an observed _____ correlation between the inflation rate and the

   _____.

   a. positive; nominal interest rate
   b. positive; unemployment rate
   c. negative; nominal interest rate
   d. negative; unemployment rate

2. When the Federal Reserve increases the money supply and expands aggregate demand, it moves the economy along the Phillips curve to a point with _____ inflation and _____ unemployment.

   a. higher; higher
   b. higher; lower
   c. lower; higher
   d. lower; lower

Answers at end of chapter.

17-2 Shifts in the Phillips Curve: The Role of Expectations

Although the Phillips curve seems to offer policymakers a menu of inflation–unemployment outcomes, it raises a crucial question: Does this set of possible choices remain the same over time? In other words, is the downward-sloping Phillips curve a stable relationship on which policymakers can rely? Economists took up this issue in the late 1960s, shortly after Samuelson and Solow had introduced the Phillips curve into the macroeconomic policy debate.

17-2a The Long-Run Phillips Curve

In 1968, economist Milton Friedman published a paper in the *American Economic Review* based on an address he had recently given as president of the American Economic Association. The paper, titled "The Role of Monetary Policy," contained sections on "What Monetary Policy Can Do" and "What Monetary Policy Cannot Do." Friedman argued that one thing monetary policy cannot do, other than for a short time, is lower unemployment by raising inflation. At about the same time, another economist, Edmund Phelps, reached the same conclusion. Like Friedman, Phelps published a paper denying the existence of a long-run trade-off between inflation and unemployment.

Both Friedman and Phelps based their conclusions on classical principles of macroeconomics. Classical theory points to growth in the money supply as the primary determinant of inflation. But classical theory also states that monetary growth does not affect real variables such as output and employment; it merely alters all prices and nominal incomes proportionately. In particular, monetary growth does not influence those factors that determine the economy's unemployment rate, such as the market power of unions, the role of efficiency wages, and the process of job search. As a result, Friedman and Phelps concluded that, in the long run, the rate of inflation and the rate of unemployment would not be related.

Here, in his own words, is Friedman's view about what the Federal Reserve can hope to accomplish for the economy in the long run:

> The monetary authority controls nominal quantities—directly, the quantity of its own liabilities [currency plus bank reserves]. In principle, it can use this control to peg a nominal quantity—an exchange rate, the price level, the nominal level of national income, the quantity of money by one definition or another—or to peg the change in a nominal quantity—the rate of inflation or deflation, the rate of growth or decline in nominal national income, the rate of growth of the quantity of money. It cannot use its control over nominal quantities to peg a real quantity—the real rate of interest, the rate of unemployment, the level of real national income, the real quantity of money, the rate of growth of real national income, or the rate of growth of the real quantity of money.

According to Friedman, monetary policymakers face a long-run Phillips curve that is vertical, as in Figure 3. If the Fed increases the money supply slowly, the inflation rate is low and the economy finds itself at point A. If the Fed increases the money supply quickly, the inflation rate is high and the economy finds itself at point B. In either case, the unemployment rate tends toward its normal level, called the *natural rate of unemployment*. The vertical long-run Phillips curve illustrates the conclusion that unemployment does not depend on money growth and inflation in the long run.

The vertical long-run Phillips curve is, in essence, one expression of the classical idea of monetary neutrality. Previously, we expressed monetary neutrality with a vertical long-run aggregate-supply curve. Figure 4 shows that the vertical long-run Phillips curve and the vertical long-run aggregate-supply curve are two sides of the same coin. In panel (a) of this figure, an increase in the money supply shifts the aggregate-demand curve to the right from AD_1 to AD_2. As a result of this shift, the long-run equilibrium moves from point A to point B. The price level rises from P_1 to P_2, but because the aggregate-supply curve is vertical, output remains the same. In panel (b), more rapid growth in the money supply raises the

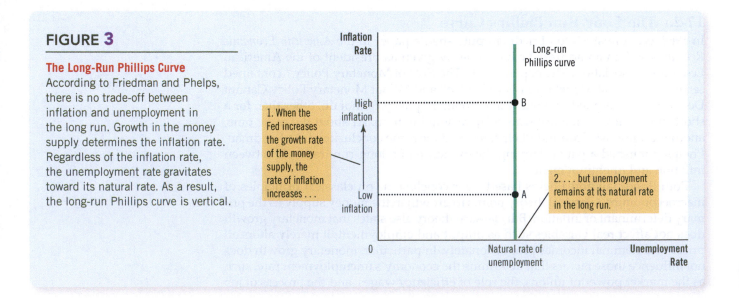

FIGURE 3

The Long-Run Phillips Curve
According to Friedman and Phelps, there is no trade-off between inflation and unemployment in the long run. Growth in the money supply determines the inflation rate. Regardless of the inflation rate, the unemployment rate gravitates toward its natural rate. As a result, the long-run Phillips curve is vertical.

1. When the Fed increases the growth rate of the money supply, the rate of inflation increases . . .

2. . . . but unemployment remains at its natural rate in the long run.

Panel (a) shows the model of aggregate demand and aggregate supply with a vertical aggregate-supply curve. When expansionary monetary policy shifts the aggregate-demand curve to the right from AD_1 to AD_2, the equilibrium moves from point A to point B. The price level rises from P_1 to P_2, while output remains the same. Panel (b) shows the long-run Phillips curve, which is vertical at the natural rate of unemployment. In the long run, expansionary monetary policy moves the economy from lower inflation (point A) to higher inflation (point B) without changing the rate of unemployment.

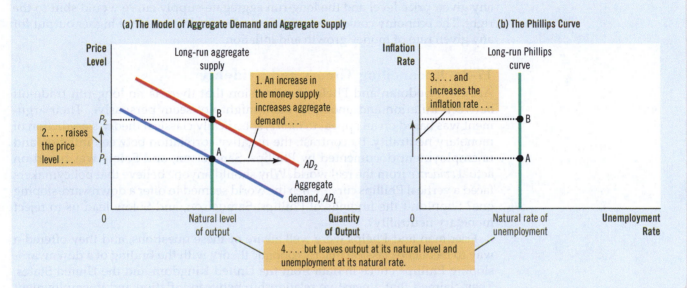

inflation rate by moving the economy from point A to point B. But because the Phillips curve is vertical, the rate of unemployment is the same at these two points. Thus, the vertical long-run aggregate-supply curve and the vertical long-run Phillips curve both imply that monetary policy influences nominal variables (the price level and the inflation rate) but not real variables (output and unemployment). In the long run, regardless of the monetary policy pursued by the Fed, output is at its natural level and unemployment is at its natural rate.

17-2b The Meaning of "Natural"

What is so "natural" about the natural rate of unemployment? Friedman and Phelps used this adjective to describe the unemployment rate toward which the economy gravitates in the long run. Yet the natural rate of unemployment is not necessarily the socially desirable rate of unemployment. Nor is the natural rate of unemployment constant over time.

For example, suppose that a newly formed union uses its market power to raise the real wages of some workers above the equilibrium level. The result is an excess supply of workers and, therefore, a higher natural rate of unemployment. This unemployment is natural not because it is good but because it is beyond the influence of monetary policy. More rapid money growth would reduce neither the market power of the union nor the level of unemployment; it would lead only to more inflation.

Although monetary policy cannot influence the natural rate of unemployment, other types of policy can. To reduce the natural rate of unemployment, policymakers should look to policies that improve the functioning of the labor market. Earlier in the book, we discussed how various labor-market policies, such as minimum-wage laws, collective-bargaining laws, unemployment insurance, and job-training programs, affect the natural rate of unemployment. A policy change that reduced the natural rate of unemployment would shift the long-run Phillips curve to the left. In addition, because lower unemployment means more workers are producing goods and services, the quantity of goods and services supplied would be larger at any given price level and the long-run aggregate-supply curve would shift to the right. The economy could then enjoy lower unemployment and higher output for any given rate of money growth and inflation.

17-2c   Reconciling Theory and Evidence

At first, Friedman and Phelps's conclusion that there is no long-run trade-off between inflation and unemployment might not seem persuasive. Their argument was based on an appeal to *theory*, specifically classical theory's prediction of monetary neutrality. By contrast, the negative correlation between inflation and unemployment documented by Phillips, Samuelson, and Solow was based on actual *evidence* from the real world. Why should anyone believe that policymakers faced a vertical Phillips curve when the world seemed to offer a downward-sloping one? Shouldn't the findings of Phillips, Samuelson, and Solow lead us to reject monetary neutrality?

Friedman and Phelps were well aware of these questions, and they offered a way to reconcile classical macroeconomic theory with the finding of a downward-sloping Phillips curve in data from the United Kingdom and the United States. They claimed that a negative relationship between inflation and unemployment exists in the short run but that it cannot be used by policymakers as a menu of outcomes in the long run. Policymakers can pursue expansionary monetary policy to achieve lower unemployment for a while, but eventually, unemployment will return to its natural rate. In the long run, more expansionary monetary policy leads only to higher inflation.

Friedman and Phelps's work was the basis of our discussion of the difference between the short-run and long-run aggregate-supply curves in Chapter 15. As you may recall, the long-run aggregate-supply curve is vertical, indicating that the price level does not influence quantity supplied in the long run. But the short-run aggregate-supply curve slopes upward, indicating that an increase in the price level raises the quantity of goods and services that firms supply. According to the sticky-wage theory of aggregate supply, for instance, nominal wages are set in advance based on the price level that workers and firms expect to prevail. When prices turn out to be higher than expected, firms have an incentive to increase production and employment; when prices are lower than expected, firms reduce production and employment. Yet because the expected price level and nominal wages will eventually adjust, the positive relationship between the actual price level and quantity supplied exists only in the short run.

Friedman and Phelps applied this same logic to the Phillips curve. Just as the aggregate-supply curve slopes upward only in the short run, the trade-off between inflation and unemployment holds only in the short run. And just as the long-run aggregate-supply curve is vertical, the long-run Phillips curve is also vertical. Once again, expectations are the key to understanding how the short run and the long run are related.

Friedman and Phelps introduced a new variable into the analysis of the inflation–unemployment trade-off: *expected inflation*. Expected inflation measures how much people expect the overall price level to change. Because the expected price level affects nominal wages, expected inflation is one factor that determines the position of the short-run aggregate-supply curve. In the short run, the Fed can take expected inflation (and, thus, the short-run aggregate-supply curve) as already determined. When the money supply changes, the aggregate-demand curve shifts and the economy moves along a given short-run aggregate-supply curve. In the short run, therefore, monetary changes lead to unexpected fluctuations in output, prices, unemployment, and inflation. In this way, Friedman and Phelps explained the downward-sloping Phillips curve that Phillips, Samuelson, and Solow had documented.

The Fed's ability to create unexpected inflation by increasing the money supply exists only in the short run. In the long run, people come to expect whatever inflation rate the Fed chooses to produce and nominal wages will adjust to keep pace with inflation. As a result, the long-run aggregate-supply curve is vertical. Changes in aggregate demand, such as those due to changes in the money supply, affect neither the economy's output of goods and services nor the number of workers that firms need to hire to produce those goods and services. Friedman and Phelps concluded that unemployment returns to its natural rate in the long run.

17-2d The Short-Run Phillips Curve

The analysis of Friedman and Phelps can be summarized by the following equation:

$$\text{Unemployment rate} = \text{Natural rate of unemployment} - a \left(\text{Actual inflation} - \text{Expected inflation} \right).$$

This equation (which is, in essence, another expression of the aggregate-supply equation we have seen previously) relates the unemployment rate to the natural rate of unemployment, actual inflation, and expected inflation. In the short run, expected inflation is given, so higher actual inflation is associated with lower unemployment. (The variable a is a parameter that measures how much unemployment responds to unexpected inflation.) In the long run, people come to expect whatever inflation the Fed produces, so actual inflation equals expected inflation, and unemployment is at its natural rate.

This equation implies there can be no stable short-run Phillips curve. Each short-run Phillips curve reflects a particular expected rate of inflation. (To be precise, if you graph the equation, you'll find that the downward-sloping short-run Phillips curve intersects the vertical long-run Phillips curve at the expected rate of inflation.) When expected inflation changes, the short-run Phillips curve shifts.

According to Friedman and Phelps, it is dangerous to view the Phillips curve as a menu of options available to policymakers. To see why, imagine an economy that starts with low inflation, with an equally low rate of expected inflation, and with unemployment at its natural rate. In Figure 5, the economy is at point A. Now suppose that policymakers try to take advantage of the trade-off between inflation and unemployment by using monetary or fiscal policy to expand aggregate demand. In the short run, when expected inflation is given, the economy goes from point A to point B. Unemployment falls below its natural rate, and the actual inflation rate rises above expected inflation. As the economy moves from point A to point B, policymakers might think they have achieved permanently lower unemployment at the cost of higher inflation—a bargain that, if possible, might be worth making.

FIGURE 5

How Expected Inflation Shifts the Short-Run Phillips Curve

The higher the expected rate of inflation, the higher the curve representing the short-run trade-off between inflation and unemployment. At point A, expected inflation and actual inflation are equal at a low rate and unemployment is at its natural rate. If the Fed pursues an expansionary monetary policy, the economy moves from point A to point B in the short run. At point B, expected inflation is still low, but actual inflation is high. Unemployment is below its natural rate. In the long run, expected inflation rises, and the economy moves to point C. At point C, expected inflation and actual inflation are both high, and unemployment is back to its natural rate.

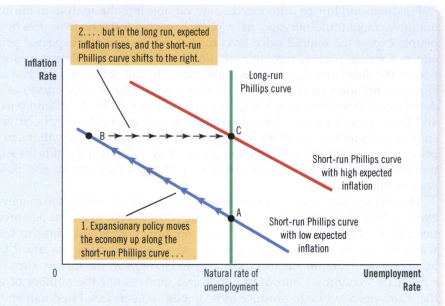

This situation, however, will not persist. Over time, people get used to this higher inflation rate, and they raise their expectations of inflation. When expected inflation rises, firms and workers start taking higher inflation into account when setting wages and prices. The short-run Phillips curve then shifts to the right, as shown in the figure. The economy ends up at point C, with higher inflation than at point A but with the same level of unemployment. Thus, Friedman and Phelps concluded that policymakers face only a temporary trade-off between inflation and unemployment. In the long run, expanding aggregate demand more rapidly will yield higher inflation without any reduction in unemployment.

17-2e The Natural Experiment for the Natural-Rate Hypothesis

Friedman and Phelps had made a bold prediction in 1968: If policymakers try to take advantage of the Phillips curve by choosing higher inflation to reduce unemployment, they will succeed at reducing unemployment only temporarily. This view—that unemployment eventually returns to its natural rate, regardless of the rate of inflation—is called the **natural-rate hypothesis**. A few years after Friedman and Phelps proposed this hypothesis, monetary and fiscal policymakers inadvertently created a natural experiment to test it. Their laboratory was the U.S. economy.

Before we examine the outcome of this test, however, let's look at the data that Friedman and Phelps had when they made their prediction in 1968. Figure 6 shows the unemployment and inflation rates for the period from 1961 to 1968. These data trace out an almost perfect Phillips curve. As inflation rose over these eight years, unemployment fell. The economic data from this era seemed to confirm that policymakers faced a trade-off between inflation and unemployment.

natural-rate hypothesis
the claim that unemployment eventually returns to its normal, or natural, rate, regardless of the rate of inflation

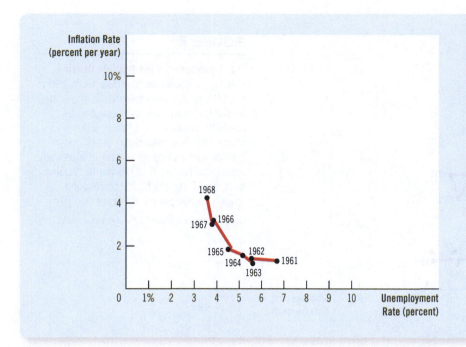

FIGURE 6

The Phillips Curve in the 1960s
This figure uses annual data from 1961 to 1968 on the unemployment rate and on the inflation rate (as measured by the GDP deflator) to show the negative relationship between inflation and unemployment.

Source: U.S. Department of Labor; U.S. Department of Commerce.

The apparent success of the Phillips curve in the 1960s made the prediction of Friedman and Phelps all the bolder. In 1958, Phillips had suggested a negative association between inflation and unemployment. In 1960, Samuelson and Solow had shown that it existed in U.S. data. Another decade of data had confirmed the relationship. To some economists at the time, it seemed ridiculous to claim that the historically reliable Phillips curve would start shifting once policymakers tried to take advantage of it.

In fact, that is exactly what happened. Beginning in the late 1960s, the government followed policies that expanded the aggregate demand for goods and services. In part, this expansion was due to fiscal policy: Government spending rose as the Vietnam War heated up. In part, it was due to monetary policy: Because the Fed was trying to hold down interest rates in the face of expansionary fiscal policy, the money supply (as measured by M2) rose about 13 percent per year during the period from 1970 to 1972, compared with 7 percent per year in the early 1960s. As a result, inflation stayed high (about 5 to 6 percent per year in the late 1960s and early 1970s, compared with about 1 to 2 percent per year in the early 1960s). But as Friedman and Phelps had predicted, unemployment did not stay low.

Figure 7 displays the history of inflation and unemployment from 1961 to 1973. It shows that the simple negative relationship between these two variables started to break down around 1970. In particular, as inflation remained high in the early 1970s, people's expectations of inflation caught up with reality, and the unemployment rate reverted to the 5 percent to 6 percent range that had prevailed in the early 1960s. Notice that the history illustrated in Figure 7 resembles the theory of a shifting short-run Phillips curve shown in Figure 5. By 1973, policymakers had learned that Friedman and Phelps were right: There is no trade-off between inflation and unemployment in the long run.

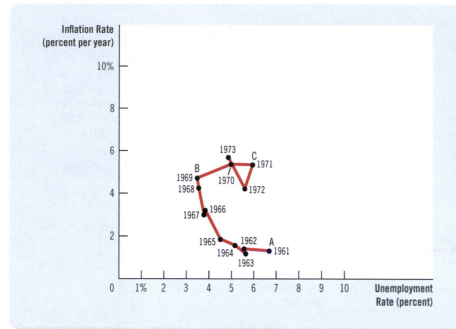

FIGURE 7

The Breakdown of the Phillips Curve
This figure shows annual data from 1961 to 1973 on the unemployment rate and on the inflation rate (as measured by the GDP deflator). The Phillips curve of the 1960s breaks down in the early 1970s, just as Friedman and Phelps had predicted. Notice that the points labeled A, B, and C in this figure correspond roughly to the points in Figure 5.

Source: U.S. Department of Labor; U.S. Department of Commerce.

QuickQuiz

3. The natural rate of unemployment is
    a. the socially optimal level of joblessness.
    b. the level of joblessness the economy reaches in the short run.
    c. the amount of joblessness that cannot be reduced by public policies.
    d. the normal level of joblessness, regardless of inflation.

4. If the Federal Reserve reduces the rate of money growth and maintains it at the new lower rate, eventually expected inflation will _____ and the short-run Phillips curve will shift _____.
    a. decrease; downward
    b. decrease; upward
    c. increase; downward
    d. increase; upward

Answers at end of chapter.

17-3 Shifts in the Phillips Curve: The Role of Supply Shocks

Friedman and Phelps had suggested in 1968 that changes in expected inflation shift the short-run Phillips curve, and the experience of the early 1970s convinced most economists that Friedman and Phelps were right. Within a few years, however, the economics profession would turn its attention to a different source of shifts in the short-run Phillips curve: shocks to aggregate supply.

This time, the change in focus came not from two American economics professors but from a group of Arab sheiks. In 1974, the Organization of Petroleum Exporting Countries (OPEC) began to exert its market power as a cartel in the world oil market to increase its members' profits. The countries of OPEC, including Saudi Arabia, Kuwait, and Iraq, restricted the amount of crude oil they pumped and sold on world markets. Within a few years, this reduction in supply caused the world price of oil to almost double.

A large increase in the world price of oil is an example of a supply shock. A **supply shock** is an event that directly affects firms' costs of production and thus the prices they charge; it shifts the economy's aggregate-supply curve and, as a result, the Phillips curve. For example, when an oil price increase raises the cost of producing gasoline, heating oil, tires, and many other products, it reduces the quantity of goods and services supplied at any given price level. As panel (a) of Figure 8 shows, this reduction in supply is represented by the leftward shift in the aggregate-supply curve from AS_1 to AS_2. Output falls from Y_1 to Y_2, and the price level rises from P_1 to P_2. The economy experiences *stagflation*—the combination of falling output (stagnation) and rising prices (inflation).

This shift in aggregate supply is associated with a similar shift in the short-run Phillips curve, shown in panel (b). Because firms need fewer workers to produce the smaller output, employment falls and unemployment rises. Because the price level is higher, the inflation rate—the percentage change in the price level from the previous year—is also higher. Thus, the shift in aggregate supply leads to higher unemployment and higher inflation. The short-run trade-off between inflation and unemployment shifts to the right from PC_1 to PC_2.

Confronted with an adverse shift in aggregate supply, policymakers face a difficult choice between fighting inflation and fighting unemployment. If they contract aggregate demand to fight inflation, they will raise unemployment further. If they expand aggregate demand to fight unemployment, they will raise inflation further. In other words, policymakers face a less favorable trade-off between inflation and unemployment than they did before the shift in aggregate supply: They have to live with a higher rate of inflation for a given rate of unemployment, a higher

supply shock
an event that directly alters firms' costs and prices, shifting the economy's aggregate-supply curve and thus the Phillips curve

---

Panel (a) shows the model of aggregate demand and aggregate supply. When the aggregate-supply curve shifts to the left from AS_1 to AS_2, the equilibrium moves from point A to point B. Output falls from Y_1 to Y_2, and the price level rises from P_1 to P_2. Panel (b) shows the short-run trade-off between inflation and unemployment. The adverse shift in aggregate supply moves the economy from a point with lower unemployment and lower inflation (point A) to a point with higher unemployment and higher inflation (point B). The short-run Phillips curve shifts to the right from PC_1 to PC_2. Policymakers now face a worse set of options for inflation and unemployment.

FIGURE 8

An Adverse Shock to Aggregate Supply

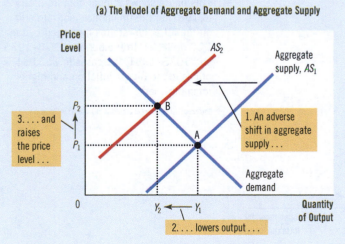

(a) The Model of Aggregate Demand and Aggregate Supply

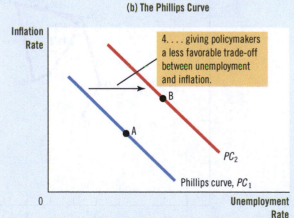

(b) The Phillips Curve

rate of unemployment for a given rate of inflation, or some combination of higher unemployment and higher inflation.

Faced with such an adverse shift in the Phillips curve, policymakers will ask whether the shift is temporary or permanent. The answer depends on how people adjust their expectations of inflation. If people view the rise in inflation due to the supply shock as a temporary aberration, expected inflation will not change and the Phillips curve will soon revert to its former position. But if people believe the shock will lead to a new era of higher inflation, then expected inflation will rise and the Phillips curve will remain at its new, less desirable position.

In the United States during the 1970s, expected inflation did rise substantially. This rise in expected inflation was partly attributable to the Fed's decision to accommodate the supply shock with higher money growth. (Recall that policymakers are said to *accommodate* an adverse supply shock when they respond to it by increasing aggregate demand in an effort to keep output from falling.) Because of this policy decision, the recession that resulted from the supply shock was smaller than it otherwise might have been, but the U.S. economy faced an unfavorable trade-off between inflation and unemployment for many years. The problem was compounded in 1979 when OPEC once again started to exert its market power, more than doubling the price of oil. Figure 9 shows inflation and unemployment in the U.S. economy during this period.

In 1980, after two OPEC supply shocks, the U.S. economy had an inflation rate of more than 9 percent and an unemployment rate of about 7 percent. This combination of inflation and unemployment was not at all near the trade-off that seemed possible in the 1960s. (In the 1960s, the Phillips curve suggested that an unemployment rate of 7 percent would be associated with an inflation rate of only 1 percent. Inflation of more than 9 percent was unthinkable.) With the misery index in 1980 near a historic high, the public was widely dissatisfied with the performance of the economy. Largely because of this dissatisfaction, President Jimmy Carter lost his bid for reelection in November 1980 and was replaced by Ronald Reagan. Something had to be done, and soon it would be.

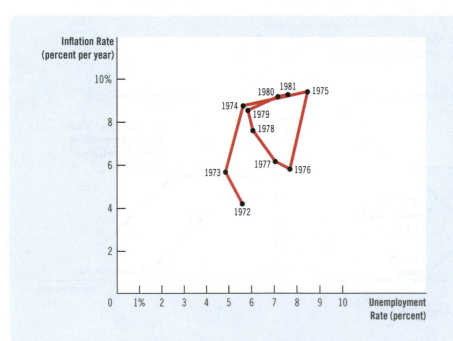

FIGURE 9

The Supply Shocks of the 1970s
This figure shows annual data from 1972 to 1981 on the unemployment rate and on the inflation rate (as measured by the GDP deflator). In the periods 1973–1975 and 1978–1981, increases in world oil prices led to higher inflation and higher unemployment.

Source: U.S. Department of Labor; U.S. Department of Commerce.

5. When an adverse supply shock shifts the short-run aggregate-supply curve to the left, it also
   a. moves the economy along the short-run Phillips curve to a point with higher inflation and lower unemployment.
   b. moves the economy along the short-run Phillips curve to a point with lower inflation and higher unemployment.
   c. shifts the short-run Phillips curve to the right.
   d. shifts the short-run Phillips curve to the left.

6. From one year to the next, inflation falls from 5 to 4 percent, while unemployment rises from 6 to 7 percent. Which of the following events could be responsible for this change?
   a. The central bank increases the growth rate of the money supply.
   b. The government cuts spending and raises taxes to reduce the budget deficit.

   c. Newly discovered oil reserves cause world oil prices to plummet.
   d. The appointment of a new Fed chair increases expected inflation.

7. From one year to the next, inflation falls from 5 to 4 percent, while unemployment falls from 7 to 6 percent. Which of the following events could be responsible for this change?
   a. The central bank increases the growth rate of the money supply.
   b. The government cuts spending and raises taxes to reduce the budget deficit.
   c. Newly discovered oil reserves cause world oil prices to plummet.
   d. The appointment of a new Fed chair increases expected inflation.

Answers at end of chapter.

17-4 The Cost of Reducing Inflation

In October 1979, as OPEC was imposing adverse supply shocks on the world's economies for the second time in a decade, Fed Chairman Paul Volcker decided that the time for action had come. Volcker had been appointed chairman by President Carter only two months earlier, and he had taken the job knowing that inflation had reached unacceptable levels. As guardian of the nation's monetary system, he felt he had little choice but to pursue a policy of disinflation. *Disinflation* is a reduction in the rate of inflation, and it should not be confused with *deflation*, a reduction in the price level. To draw an analogy to a car's motion, disinflation is like slowing down, whereas deflation is like going in reverse. Chairman Volcker, along with many other Americans, wanted the economy's rising level of prices to slow down.

Volcker had no doubt that the Fed could reduce inflation through its ability to control the quantity of money. But what would be the short-run cost of disinflation? The answer to this question was much less certain.

17-4a The Sacrifice Ratio

To reduce the inflation rate, the Fed has to pursue contractionary monetary policy. Figure 10 shows some of the effects of such a decision. When the Fed slows growth in the money supply, it contracts aggregate demand. The fall in aggregate demand, in turn, reduces the quantity of goods and services that firms produce, and this fall in production leads to a rise in unemployment. The economy begins at point A in the figure and moves along the short-run Phillips curve to point B, which has lower inflation and higher unemployment. Over time, as people come to understand that prices are rising more slowly, expected inflation falls, and the short-run Phillips curve shifts downward. The economy moves from point B to point C. Inflation is lower than it was initially at point A, and unemployment is back at its natural rate.

FIGURE 10

Disinflationary Monetary Policy in the Short Run and Long Run

When the Fed pursues contractionary monetary policy to reduce inflation, the economy moves along a short-run Phillips curve from point A to point B. Over time, expected inflation falls, and the short-run Phillips curve shifts downward. When the economy reaches point C, unemployment is back at its natural rate.

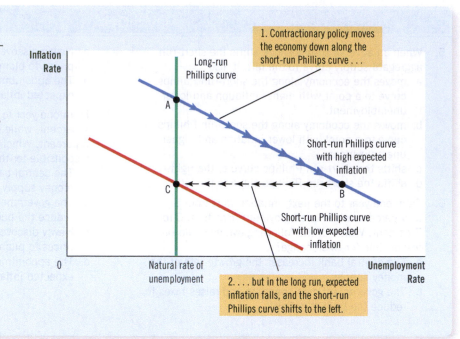

1. Contractionary policy moves the economy down along the short-run Phillips curve . . .

2. . . . but in the long run, expected inflation falls, and the short-run Phillips curve shifts to the left.

sacrifice ratio

the number of percentage points of annual output lost in the process of reducing inflation by 1 percentage point

Thus, if a nation wants to reduce inflation, it must endure a period of high unemployment and low output. In Figure 10, this cost is represented by the movement of the economy through point B as it travels from point A to point C. The size of this cost depends on the slope of the Phillips curve and how quickly expectations of inflation adjust to the new monetary policy.

Many studies have examined the data on inflation and unemployment to estimate the cost of reducing inflation. The findings of these studies are often summarized in a statistic called the **sacrifice ratio**. The sacrifice ratio is the number of percentage points of annual output lost in the process of reducing inflation by 1 percentage point. A typical estimate of the sacrifice ratio is 5. That is, for each percentage point that inflation is reduced, 5 percent of annual output must be sacrificed in the transition.

Such estimates surely must have made Paul Volcker apprehensive as he confronted the task of reducing inflation. Inflation was running at almost 10 percent per year. To reach moderate inflation of, say, 4 percent per year would mean reducing inflation by 6 percentage points. If each percentage point costs 5 percent of the economy's annual output, then reducing inflation by 6 percentage points would require sacrificing 30 percent of annual output.

According to studies of the Phillips curve and the cost of disinflation, this sacrifice could be paid in various ways. An immediate reduction in inflation would depress output by 30 percent for a single year, but that outcome was surely too harsh even for an inflation hawk like Paul Volcker. It would be better, many argued, to spread out the cost over several years. If the reduction in inflation took place over five years, for instance, then output would have to average only 6 percent below trend during that period to add up to a sacrifice of 30 percent. An even more gradual approach would be to reduce inflation slowly over a decade so that output would have to be only 3 percent below trend. Whatever path was chosen, however, it seemed that reducing inflation would not be easy.

17-4b Rational Expectations and the Possibility of Costless Disinflation

Just as Paul Volcker was pondering how costly reducing inflation might be, a group of economics professors was leading an intellectual revolution that would challenge the conventional wisdom on the sacrifice ratio. This group included such prominent economists as Robert Lucas, Thomas Sargent, and Robert Barro. Their revolution was based on a new approach to economic theory and policy called **rational expectations**. According to the theory of rational expectations, people optimally use all the information they have, including information about government policies, when forecasting the future.

This new approach has had profound implications for many areas of macroeconomics, but none is more important than its application to the trade-off between inflation and unemployment. As Friedman and Phelps had first emphasized, expected inflation is an important variable that explains why there is a trade-off between inflation and unemployment in the short run but not in the long run. How quickly the short-run trade-off disappears depends on how quickly people adjust their expectations of inflation. Proponents of rational expectations expanded upon the Friedman–Phelps analysis to argue that when economic policies change, people adjust their expectations of inflation accordingly. The studies of inflation and unemployment that had tried to estimate the sacrifice ratio had failed to take account of the direct effect of the policy regime on expectations. As a result, estimates of the sacrifice ratio were, according to the rational-expectations theorists, unreliable guides for policy.

In a 1981 paper titled "The End of Four Big Inflations," Thomas Sargent described this new view as follows:

> An alternative "rational expectations" view denies that there is any inherent momentum to the present process of inflation. This view maintains that firms and workers have now come to expect high rates of inflation in the future and that they strike inflationary bargains in light of these expectations. However, it is held that people expect high rates of inflation in the future precisely because the government's current and prospective monetary and fiscal policies warrant those expectations. . . . An implication of this view is that inflation can be stopped much more quickly than advocates of the "momentum" view have indicated and that their estimates of the length of time and the costs of stopping inflation in terms of forgone output are erroneous. . . . This is not to say that it would be easy to eradicate inflation. On the contrary, it would require more than a few temporary restrictive fiscal and monetary actions. It would require a change in the policy regime. . . . How costly such a move would be in terms of forgone output and how long it would be in taking effect would depend partly on how resolute and evident the government's commitment was.

According to Sargent, the sacrifice ratio could be much smaller than suggested by previous estimates. Indeed, in the most extreme case, it could be zero: If the government made a credible commitment to a policy of low inflation, people would be rational enough to lower their expectations of inflation immediately. The short-run Phillips curve would shift downward, and the economy would reach low inflation quickly without the cost of temporarily high unemployment and low output.

rational expectations
the theory that people optimally use all the information they have, including information about government policies, when forecasting the future

17-4c The Volcker Disinflation

As we have seen, when Paul Volcker faced the prospect of reducing inflation from its peak of about 10 percent, the economics profession offered two conflicting predictions. One group of economists offered estimates of the sacrifice ratio and concluded that reducing inflation would have great cost in terms of lost output and high unemployment. Another group offered the theory of rational expectations and concluded that reducing inflation could be much less costly and, perhaps, could even have no cost at all. Who was right?

Figure 11 shows inflation and unemployment from 1979 to 1987. As you can see, Volcker did succeed at reducing inflation. Inflation came down from almost 10 percent in 1980 and 1981 to about 4 percent in 1983 and 1984. Credit for this reduction in inflation goes completely to monetary policy. Fiscal policy at this time was acting in the opposite direction: The increases in the budget deficit during the Reagan administration were expanding aggregate demand, which tends to raise inflation. The fall in inflation from 1981 to 1984 is attributable to the tough anti-inflation policies of Fed Chairman Paul Volcker.

The figure shows that the Volcker disinflation did come at the cost of high unemployment. In 1982 and 1983, the unemployment rate was about 10 percent—about 4 percentage points above its level when Paul Volcker was appointed Fed chairman. At the same time, the production of goods and services as measured by real GDP was well below its trend level. The Volcker disinflation produced a recession that was, at the time, the deepest the United States had experienced since the Great Depression of the 1930s.

Does this episode refute the possibility of costless disinflation as suggested by the rational-expectations theorists? Some economists have argued that the answer to this question is a resounding yes. Indeed, the pattern of disinflation shown in Figure 11 is similar to the pattern predicted in Figure 10. To make the transition from high inflation (point A in both figures) to low inflation (point C), the economy had to experience a painful period of high unemployment (point B).

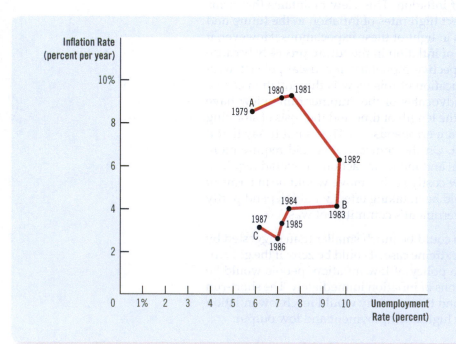

FIGURE 11

The Volcker Disinflation

This figure shows annual data from 1979 to 1987 on the unemployment rate and on the inflation rate (as measured by the GDP deflator). The reduction in inflation during this period came at the cost of very high unemployment in 1982 and 1983. Note that the points labeled A, B, and C in this figure correspond roughly to the points in Figure 10.

Source: U.S. Department of Labor; U.S. Department of Commerce.

Yet there are two reasons not to reject the conclusions of the rational-expectations theorists so quickly. First, even though the Volcker disinflation did impose a cost of temporarily high unemployment, the cost was not as large as many economists had predicted. Most estimates of the sacrifice ratio based on the Volcker disinflation are smaller than estimates that had been obtained from previous data. Perhaps Volcker's tough stand on inflation did have some direct effect on expectations, as the rational-expectations theorists claimed.

Second, and more important, even though Volcker announced that he would aim monetary policy to lower inflation, much of the public did not believe him. Because few people thought Volcker would reduce inflation as quickly as he did, expected inflation did not fall immediately; as a result, the short-run Phillips curve did not shift down as quickly as it might have. Some evidence for this hypothesis comes from the forecasts made by commercial forecasting firms: Their forecasts of inflation fell more slowly in the 1980s than did actual inflation. Thus, the Volcker disinflation does not necessarily refute the rational-expectations view that credible disinflation can be costless. It does show, however, that policymakers cannot count on people to immediately believe them when they announce a policy of disinflation.

17-4d The Greenspan Era

After the OPEC inflation of the 1970s and the Volcker disinflation of the 1980s, the U.S. economy experienced relatively mild fluctuations in inflation and unemployment. Figure 12 shows inflation and unemployment from 1984 to 2005. This period is called the Greenspan era, after Alan Greenspan who in 1987 followed Paul Volcker as chairman of the Federal Reserve.

This period began with a favorable supply shock. In 1986, OPEC members started arguing over production levels, and their long-standing agreement to restrict supply broke down. Oil prices fell by about half. As the figure shows, this favorable supply shock led to falling inflation and falling unemployment from 1984 to 1986.

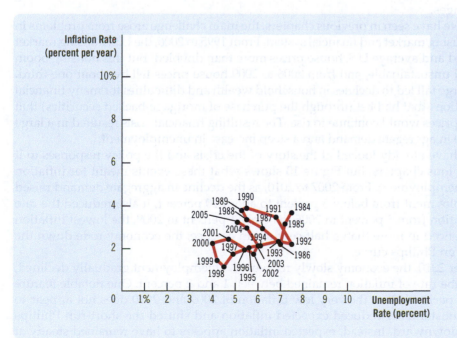

FIGURE 12

The Greenspan Era

This figure shows annual data from 1984 to 2005 on the unemployment rate and on the inflation rate (as measured by the GDP deflator). During most of this period, Alan Greenspan was chairman of the Federal Reserve. Fluctuations in inflation and unemployment were relatively small.

Source: U.S. Department of Labor; U.S. Department of Commerce.

Throughout the Greenspan era, the Fed was careful to avoid repeating the policy mistakes of the 1960s, when excessive aggregate demand pushed unemployment below the natural rate and raised inflation. When unemployment fell and inflation rose in 1989 and 1990, the Fed raised interest rates and contracted aggregate demand, leading to a small recession in 1991 and 1992. Unemployment then rose above most estimates of the natural rate, and inflation fell once again.

The rest of the 1990s witnessed technological boom and a period of economic prosperity. Inflation gradually drifted downward, approaching zero by the end of the decade. Unemployment also drifted downward, leading many observers to believe that the natural rate of unemployment had fallen. Part of the credit for this good economic performance goes to Greenspan and his colleagues at the Fed, for low inflation can be achieved only with prudent monetary policy. But good luck in the form of favorable supply shocks is also part of the story.

In 2001, however, the economy ran into problems. The end of the dot-com stock market bubble, the 9/11 terrorist attacks, and corporate accounting scandals all depressed aggregate demand. Unemployment rose as the economy experienced its first recession in a decade. But a combination of expansionary monetary and fiscal policies helped end the downturn, and by early 2005, unemployment was close to most estimates of the natural rate.

In 2005, President Bush nominated Ben Bernanke to succeed Alan Greenspan as Fed chair. Bernanke was sworn in on February 1, 2006. In 2009, Bernanke was reappointed by President Obama. At the time of his initial nomination, Bernanke said, "My first priority will be to maintain continuity with the policies and policy strategies established during the Greenspan years."

17-4e A Financial Crisis Takes Us for a Ride along the Phillips Curve

Ben Bernanke may have hoped to continue the policies of the Greenspan era and to enjoy the relative calm of those years, but his wishes would not be fulfilled. During his first few years on the job, the new Fed chairman faced some daunting challenges.

As we have seen in previous chapters, the main challenge arose from problems in the housing market and financial system. From 1995 to 2006, the U.S. housing market boomed and average U.S. house prices more than doubled. But this housing boom proved unsustainable, and from 2006 to 2009 house prices fell by about one-third. This large fall led to declines in household wealth and difficulties for many financial institutions that had bet (through the purchase of mortgage-backed securities) that house prices would continue to rise. The resulting financial crisis resulted in a large decline in aggregate demand and a steep increase in unemployment.

We have already looked at the story of the crisis and the policy responses to it in previous chapters, but Figure 13 shows what these events meant for inflation and unemployment. From 2007 to 2010, as the decline in aggregate demand raised unemployment from below 5 percent to about 10 percent, it also reduced the rate of inflation from 3 percent in 2006 to below 1 percent in 2009, the lowest inflation experienced in more than a half-century. In essence, the economy rode down the short-run Phillips curve.

After 2010, the economy slowly recovered. Unemployment gradually declined, while the rate of inflation remained between 1 and 2 percent. One notable feature of this period is that the very low inflation of 2009 and 2010 does not appear to have substantially reduced expected inflation and shifted the short-run Phillips curve downward. Instead, expected inflation appears to have remained steady at

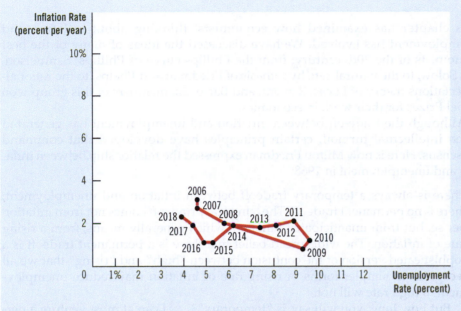

FIGURE 13

The Phillips Curve during and after the Recession of 2008–2009
This figure shows annual data from 2006 to 2018 on the unemployment rate and on the inflation rate (as measured by the GDP deflator). A financial crisis caused aggregate demand to plummet, leading to much higher unemployment and pushing inflation down to a very low level.

Source: U.S. Department of Labor; U.S. Department of Commerce.

about 2 percent, keeping the short-run Phillips curve relatively stable. A common explanation for this phenomenon is that the Federal Reserve had, over the previous 20 years, established a lot of credibility in its commitment to keep inflation at about 2 percent. This credibility kept expected inflation well-anchored. As a result, the position of the short-run Phillips curve reacted less to the dramatic short-run events.

By 2018, the unemployment rate fell below 4 percent, and inflation reached 2.3 percent, its highest level since 2007. With unemployment below most estimates of the natural rate and inflation slightly above the Fed's target of 2 percent, the Fed pursued a more contractionary monetary policy, raising the federal funds rate from the roughly zero rates that prevailed from December 2008 to December 2015 to 2.4 percent in early 2019. How much more monetary tightening would be needed, if any, to keep unemployment near its natural rate and inflation near its target was a hotly debated topic.

8. Reducing inflation will tend to be costly if
   a. policymakers are credibly committed to low inflation.
   b. wages and prices are not very sticky.
   c. expectations of inflation are slow to adjust.
   d. central bankers exhibit a strong dislike of inflation.

9. Advocates of the theory of rational expectations believe that
   a. the sacrifice ratio can be much smaller if policymakers make a credible commitment to low inflation.
   b. if disinflation catches people by surprise, it will have minimal impact on unemployment.
   c. wage and price setters never expect the central bank to follow through on its announcements.
   d. expected inflation depends on the rates of inflation that people have recently observed.

Answers at end of chapter.

17-5 Conclusion

This chapter has examined how economists' thinking about inflation and unemployment has evolved. We have discussed the ideas of many of the best economists of the 20th century: from the Phillips curve of Phillips, Samuelson, and Solow, to the natural-rate hypothesis of Friedman and Phelps, to the rational-expectations theory of Lucas, Sargent, and Barro. Six members of this group won Nobel Prizes for their work in economics.

Although the trade-off between inflation and unemployment has generated much intellectual turmoil, certain principles have developed that command consensus. Here is how Milton Friedman expressed the relationship between inflation and unemployment in 1968:

> There is always a temporary tradeoff between inflation and unemployment; there is no permanent tradeoff. The temporary tradeoff comes not from inflation per se, but from unanticipated inflation, which generally means, from a rising rate of inflation. The widespread belief that there is a permanent tradeoff is a sophisticated version of the confusion between "high" and "rising" that we all recognize in simpler forms. A rising rate of inflation may reduce unemployment, a high rate will not.
>
> But how long, you will say, is "temporary"? . . . I can at most venture a personal judgment, based on some examination of the historical evidence, that the initial effects of a higher and unanticipated rate of inflation last for something like two to five years.

Today, more than a half-century later, this statement still reflects the view of most macroeconomists.

CHAPTER IN A NUTSHELL

- The Phillips curve describes a negative relationship between inflation and unemployment. By expanding aggregate demand, policymakers can choose a point on the Phillips curve with higher inflation and lower unemployment. By contracting aggregate demand, policymakers can choose a point on the Phillips curve with lower inflation and higher unemployment.

- The trade-off between inflation and unemployment described by the Phillips curve holds only in the short run. In the long run, expected inflation adjusts to changes in actual inflation, and the short-run Phillips curve shifts. As a result, the long-run Phillips curve is vertical at the natural rate of unemployment.

- The short-run Phillips curve also shifts because of shocks to aggregate supply. An adverse supply shock, such as an increase in world oil prices, gives policymakers a less favorable trade-off between inflation and unemployment. That is, after an adverse supply shock, policymakers have to accept a higher rate of inflation for any given rate of unemployment or a higher rate of unemployment for any given rate of inflation.

- When the Fed contracts growth in the money supply to reduce inflation, it moves the economy along the short-run Phillips curve, resulting in temporarily high unemployment. The cost of disinflation depends on how quickly expectations of inflation fall. Some economists argue that a credible commitment to low inflation can reduce the cost of disinflation by inducing a quick adjustment of expectations.

KEY CONCEPTS

QUESTIONS FOR REVIEW

1. Draw the short-run trade-off between inflation and unemployment. How might the Fed move the economy from one point on this curve to another?

2. Draw the long-run trade-off between inflation and unemployment. Explain how the short-run and long-run trade-offs are related.

3. What is "natural" about the natural rate of unemployment? Why might the natural rate of unemployment differ across countries?

4. Suppose a drought destroys farm crops and drives up the price of food. What is the effect on the short-run trade-off between inflation and unemployment?

5. The Fed decides to reduce inflation. Use the Phillips curve to show the short-run and long-run effects of this policy. How might the short-run costs be reduced?

PROBLEMS AND APPLICATIONS

1. Suppose the natural rate of unemployment is 6 percent. On one graph, draw two Phillips curves that describe the four situations listed here. Label the point that shows the position of the economy in each case.
   a. Actual inflation is 5 percent, and expected inflation is 3 percent.
   b. Actual inflation is 3 percent, and expected inflation is 5 percent.
   c. Actual inflation is 5 percent, and expected inflation is 5 percent.
   d. Actual inflation is 3 percent, and expected inflation is 3 percent.

2. Illustrate the effects of the following developments on both the short-run and long-run Phillips curves. Give the economic reasoning underlying your answers.
   a. a rise in the natural rate of unemployment
   b. a decline in the price of imported oil
   c. a rise in government spending
   d. a decline in expected inflation

3. Suppose that a fall in consumer spending causes a recession.
   a. Illustrate the immediate change in the economy using both an aggregate-supply/aggregate-demand diagram and a Phillips-curve diagram. On both graphs, label the initial long-run equilibrium as point A and the resulting short-run equilibrium as point B. What happens to inflation and unemployment in the short run?
   b. Now suppose that over time expected inflation changes in the same direction that actual inflation changes. What happens to the position of the short-run Phillips curve? After the recession is over, does the economy face a better or worse set of inflation–unemployment combinations? Explain.

4. Suppose the economy is in a long-run equilibrium.
   a. Draw the economy's short-run and long-run Phillips curves.
   b. Suppose a wave of business pessimism reduces aggregate demand. Show the effect of this shock on your diagram from part *a*. If the Fed undertakes expansionary monetary policy, can it return the economy to its original inflation rate and original unemployment rate?
   c. Now suppose the economy is back in long-run equilibrium and then the price of imported oil rises. Show the effect of this shock with a new diagram like that in part *a*. If the Fed undertakes expansionary monetary policy, can it return the economy to its original inflation rate and original unemployment rate? If the Fed undertakes contractionary monetary policy, can it return the economy to its original inflation rate and original unemployment rate? Explain why this situation differs from that in part *b*.

5. The inflation rate is 10 percent, and the central bank is considering slowing the rate of money growth to reduce inflation to 5 percent. Economist Milton believes that expectations of inflation change quickly in response to new policies, whereas economist James believes that expectations are very sluggish. Which economist is more likely to favor the proposed change in monetary policy? Why?

6. Suppose the Federal Reserve's policy is to maintain low and stable inflation by keeping unemployment at its natural rate. However, the Fed believes that the natural rate of unemployment is 4 percent when the actual natural rate is 5 percent. If the Fed based its policy decisions on its belief, what would happen to the economy? How might the Fed come to realize that its belief about the natural rate was mistaken?

7. Suppose the Federal Reserve announced that it would pursue contractionary monetary policy to reduce inflation. For each of the following conditions, explain whether it would make the ensuing recession more or less severe.
    a. Wage contracts have short durations.
    b. There is little confidence in the Fed's determination to reduce inflation.
    c. Expectations of inflation adjust quickly to actual inflation.

8. The Federal Reserve in 2008 faced a decrease in aggregate demand caused by the housing and financial crises and a decrease in short-run aggregate supply caused by rising commodity prices.
    a. Starting from a long-run equilibrium, illustrate the effects of these two changes using both an aggregate-supply/aggregate-demand diagram and a Phillips-curve diagram. On both diagrams, label the initial long-run equilibrium as point A and the resulting short-run equilibrium as point B. For each of the following variables, state whether it rises or falls or whether the impact is ambiguous: output, unemployment, the price level, the inflation rate.
    b. Suppose the Fed responds quickly to these shocks and adjusts monetary policy to keep unemployment and output at their natural rates. What action would it take? On the same set of graphs from part *a*, show the results. Label the new equilibrium as point C.
    c. Why might the Fed choose not to pursue the course of action described in part *b*?

QuickQuiz Answers

1. **d**   2. **b**   3. **d**   4. **a**   5. **c**   6. **b**   7. **c**   8. **c**   9. **a**

It is hard to follow the news without finding some politician or editorial writer advocating a change in economic policy. The president should raise taxes to reduce the budget deficit, or he should stop worrying about the budget deficit. The Federal Reserve should cut interest rates to stimulate a flagging economy, or it should avoid such moves in order not to risk higher inflation. Congress should reform the tax system to promote faster economic growth, or it should reform the tax system to achieve a more equal distribution of income. Such economic issues are central to the ongoing political debate in the United States and other countries around the world.

Previous chapters have developed the tools that economists use to analyze the behavior of the economy as a whole and the impact of policies on the economy. This final chapter considers six classic questions about macroeconomic policy. Economists have long debated these questions, and they will likely continue to do so for years to come. The knowledge you have accumulated in this course provides the foundation upon which we can discuss these important, unsettled issues. It should help you choose a side in these debates or, at least, help you see why choosing a side is so difficult.

Six Debates over Macroeconomic Policy

18-1 Should Monetary and Fiscal Policymakers Try to Stabilize the Economy?

In the preceding three chapters, we saw how changes in aggregate demand and aggregate supply can lead to short-run fluctuations in production and employment. We also saw how monetary and fiscal policy can shift aggregate demand and influence these fluctuations. But even if policymakers *can* influence short-run economic fluctuations, does that mean they *should*? Our first debate concerns whether monetary and fiscal policymakers should use the tools at their disposal in an attempt to smooth the ups and downs of the business cycle.

18-1a Pro: Policymakers Should Try to Stabilize the Economy

Left on their own, economies fluctuate. When households and firms become pessimistic, for instance, they cut back on spending, thereby reducing the aggregate demand for goods and services. The fall in aggregate demand, in turn, reduces the production of goods and services. Firms lay off workers, and the unemployment rate rises. Real GDP and other measures of income fall. Rising unemployment and falling income help confirm the pessimism that initially generated the economic downturn.

Such a recession has no benefit for society—it represents a sheer waste of resources. Workers who lose their jobs because of declining aggregate demand would rather be working. Business owners whose factories are idle during a recession would rather be producing valuable goods and services and selling them at a profit.

There is no reason for society to suffer through the booms and busts of the business cycle. Macroeconomic theory shows policymakers how to reduce the severity of economic fluctuations. By "leaning against the wind" of economic change, monetary and fiscal policy can stabilize aggregate demand and, in turn, production and employment. When aggregate demand is inadequate to ensure full employment, policymakers should boost government spending, cut taxes, and expand the money supply. When aggregate demand is excessive, risking higher inflation, policymakers should cut government spending, raise taxes, and reduce the money supply. Such policy actions put macroeconomic theory to its best use by leading to a more stable economy, which benefits everyone.

18-1b Con: Policymakers Should Not Try to Stabilize the Economy

Monetary and fiscal policy can be used to stabilize the economy in theory, but there are substantial obstacles to the use of such policies in practice.

One problem is that monetary and fiscal policies do not affect the economy immediately but instead work with a long lag. Monetary policy affects aggregate demand primarily by changing interest rates, which in turn affect spending, particularly residential and business investment. But many households and firms set their spending plans in advance. As a result, it takes time for changes in interest rates to alter the aggregate demand for goods and services. Many studies indicate that changes in monetary policy have little effect on aggregate demand until about six months after the change is made.

Fiscal policy works with a lag because of the long political process that governs changes in spending and taxes. To make any change in fiscal policy, a bill must go

FRANK MODELL/THE NEW YORKER COLLECTION/THE CARTOON BANK

through congressional committees, pass both the House and the Senate, and be signed by the president. It can take years to propose, pass, and implement a major change in fiscal policy.

Because of these long lags, policymakers who want to stabilize the economy need to look ahead to economic conditions that are likely to prevail when their actions will take effect. Unfortunately, economic forecasting is highly imprecise, in part because macroeconomics is such a primitive science and in part because the shocks that cause economic fluctuations are intrinsically unpredictable. Thus, when policymakers change monetary or fiscal policy, they must rely on educated guesses about future economic conditions.

Too often, policymakers trying to stabilize the economy end up having the opposite effect. Economic conditions can easily change between the time a policy action begins and the time it takes effect. As a result, policymakers can inadvertently exacerbate rather than mitigate the magnitude of economic fluctuations. Some economists have claimed that many of the major economic fluctuations in history, including the Great Depression of the 1930s, can be traced to destabilizing policy actions.

A rule that all physicians learn early in their training is "first, do no harm." The human body has natural restorative powers. Confronted with a sick patient and an uncertain diagnosis, often a doctor should do nothing but leave the patient's body to its own devices. Intervening in the absence of reliable knowledge merely risks making matters worse.

The same can be said about treating an ailing economy. It might be desirable for policymakers to eliminate all economic fluctuations, but such a goal is not realistic given the limits of macroeconomic knowledge and the inherent unpredictability of world events. Economic policymakers should refrain from intervening often with monetary and fiscal policy and be content if they do no harm.

1. Approximately how long does it take a change in monetary policy to influence aggregate demand?
    a. one month
    b. six months
    c. two years
    d. five years

2. Fiscal policy has a long lag mainly because
    a. policymakers at the Federal Reserve do not meet frequently.

    b. firms making investments are slow to respond to changes in interest rates.
    c. the political process is slow to enact changes in government spending or taxes.
    d. consumers are slow to respond to changes in their after-tax incomes.

Answers at end of chapter.

18-2 Should the Government Fight Recessions with Spending Hikes Rather Than Tax Cuts?

When George W. Bush became president in 2001, the economy was slipping into a recession. He responded by cutting tax rates. When Barack Obama became president in 2009, the economy was in the middle of the Great Recession, the worst economic downturn in many decades. He responded with a stimulus package that offered some tax reductions but also included substantial increases in government spending. The contrast between these two policies illustrates a classic question of macroeconomics: Which instrument of fiscal policy—government spending or taxes—is a better tool for reducing the severity of economic downturns?

18-2a Pro: The Government Should Fight Recessions with Spending Hikes

John Maynard Keynes transformed economics when he wrote *The General Theory of Employment, Interest and Money* in the midst of the Great Depression of the 1930s, the worst economic downturn in U.S. history. Since then, economists have understood that the fundamental problem during recessions is inadequate aggregate demand. When firms are unable to sell a sufficient quantity of goods and services, they reduce production and employment. The key to ending recessions is to restore aggregate demand to a level consistent with full employment of the economy's labor force.

To be sure, monetary policy is the first line of defense against economic downturns. By increasing the money supply, the central bank reduces interest rates. Lower interest rates in turn reduce the cost of borrowing to finance investment projects, such as new factories and new housing. Increased spending on investment adds to aggregate demand and helps to restore normal levels of production and employment.

Fiscal policy provides an additional tool to combat recessions. When the government cuts taxes, it increases households' disposable income, encouraging them to increase spending on consumption. When the government buys goods and services, it adds directly to aggregate demand. Moreover, these fiscal actions can have multiplier effects: Higher aggregate demand leads to higher incomes, higher incomes lead to additional consumer spending, and additional consumer spending leads to further increases in aggregate demand.

Fiscal policy is particularly useful when the tools of monetary policy lose their effectiveness. During the Great Recession of 2008 and 2009, for example, the Federal Reserve cut its target interest rate to about zero. The Fed cannot reduce interest rates below zero, because, at that point, people would hold onto their cash rather than lending it out at a negative interest rate. Thus, once interest rates are at zero, the Fed loses its most powerful tool for stimulating the economy. In this circumstance, it is natural for the government to turn to fiscal policy—taxes and government spending—to prop up aggregate demand.

Traditional Keynesian analysis indicates that increases in government purchases are a more potent tool than decreases in taxes. When households get extra disposable income from a tax cut, they will likely save some of that additional income rather than spend it all (especially if households view the tax reduction as temporary rather than permanent). The fraction of the extra income saved does not contribute to the aggregate demand for goods and services. By contrast, when the government spends a dollar buying a good or service, that dollar immediately and fully adds to aggregate demand.

In 2009, economists in the Obama administration used a conventional macroeconomic model to calculate the magnitude of these effects. According to their computer simulations, each dollar of tax cuts increases GDP by $0.99, whereas each dollar of government purchases increases GDP by $1.59. Thus, increases in government spending offer a bigger "bang for the buck" than decreases in taxes. For this reason, the policy response in 2009 featured fewer federal tax cuts and more increases in federal spending.

Policymakers focused on three kinds of spending. First, there was spending on "shovel-ready" projects. These were public works projects such as repairs to highways and bridges on which construction could begin immediately, putting the unemployed back to work. Second, there was federal aid to state and local governments. Because many of these governments are constitutionally required to run balanced budgets, falling tax revenues during recessions can make it necessary for them to lay off teachers, police, and other public workers; federal aid prevented that outcome or, at least, reduced its severity. Third, there were increased payments to the jobless through the unemployment insurance system. Because the unemployed are often financially stretched, they were thought to be likely to spend rather than save this extra income. Thus, these transfer payments were thought to contribute more to aggregate demand—and in turn to production and employment—than tax cuts would. According to the macroeconomic model used by the Obama administration, the $800 billion stimulus package would create or save more than 3 million jobs by the end of the president's second year in office.

It is impossible to know for sure what effect the stimulus in fact had. Because we get only one run at history, we cannot observe what would have happened without the stimulus package. Yet one thing is clear: While the economic downturn of 2008–2009 was severe, it could have been worse. In the Great Depression of the 1930s, real GDP fell by 27 percent and unemployment reached 25 percent. In the Great Recession, real GDP fell by only 4 percent and unemployment reached only 10 percent. As judged by either GDP or unemployment, the Great Recession did not approach the magnitude of the Great Depression.

18-2b Con: The Government Should Fight Recessions with Tax Cuts

There is a long tradition of using tax policy to stimulate a moribund economy. President Kennedy proposed a tax reduction as one of his major economic initiatives; it eventually passed under President Johnson in 1964. President Reagan also signed into law significant tax cuts when he became president in 1981. Both of these tax reductions were soon followed by robust economic growth.

Tax cuts have a powerful influence on both aggregate demand and aggregate supply. They increase aggregate demand by increasing households' disposable income, as emphasized in traditional Keynesian analysis. But they can also increase aggregate demand by altering incentives. For example, if the tax reductions take the form of an expanded investment tax credit, they can induce increased spending on investment goods. Because investment spending is the most volatile component of GDP over the business cycle, stimulating investment is a key to ending recessions. Policymakers can target investment using well-designed tax policy.

At the same time that tax cuts increase aggregate demand, they can also increase aggregate supply. When the government reduces marginal tax rates, workers keep a higher fraction of any income they earn. As a result, the unemployed have a greater incentive to search for jobs, and the employed have a greater incentive to work longer hours. Increased aggregate supply, along with the increased aggregate demand, means that the production of goods and services can expand without putting upward pressure on the rate of inflation.

There are various problems with increasing government spending during recessions. First of all, consumers understand that higher government spending, together with the government borrowing needed to finance it, will likely lead to higher taxes in the future. The anticipation of those future taxes induces consumers to cut back spending today. Moreover, like most taxes, future taxes are likely to cause a variety of deadweight losses. As businesses look ahead to a more highly distorted future economy, they may reduce their expectations of future profits and reduce investment spending today. Because of these various effects, government-spending multipliers may be smaller than is conventionally believed.

It is also far from clear whether the government can spend money both wisely and quickly. Large government spending projects often require years of planning, as policymakers and voters weigh the costs and benefits of the many alternative courses of action. By contrast, when unemployment soars during recessions, the need for additional aggregate demand is immediate. If the government increases spending quickly, it may end up buying things of little public value. But if it tries to be careful and deliberate in planning its expenditures, it may fail to increase aggregate demand in a timely fashion.

Tax cuts have the advantage of decentralizing spending decisions, rather than relying on a centralized and highly imperfect political process. Households spend their disposable income on things they value. Firms spend their investment dollars on projects they expect to be profitable. By contrast, when the government tries to spend large sums of money fast, subject to various political pressures, it may end up building "bridges to nowhere." Ill-conceived public projects may employ some workers, but they create little lasting value. Moreover, they will leave future generations of taxpayers with significant additional debts. In the end, the short-run benefits of additional aggregate demand from increased government spending may fail to compensate for the long-run costs.

Quick**Quiz**

3. According to traditional Keynesian analysis, which of the following increases aggregate demand the most?
   a. $100 billion increase in taxes
   b. $100 billion decrease in taxes
   c. $100 billion increase in government purchases
   d. $100 billion decrease in government purchases

4. A cut in income tax rates tends to _____ aggregate demand and _____ aggregate supply.
   a. increase; increase
   b. increase; decrease
   c. decrease; increase
   d. decrease; decrease

Answers at end of chapter.

18-3 Should Monetary Policy Be Made by Rule Rather Than by Discretion?

As we learned in the chapter on the monetary system, the Federal Open Market Committee sets monetary policy in the United States. The committee meets about every six weeks to evaluate the state of the economy. Based on this evaluation and forecasts of future economic conditions, it chooses whether to raise, lower, or leave unchanged the level of short-term interest rates. The Fed then adjusts the money supply to reach that interest-rate target, which will normally remain unchanged until the next meeting.

The Federal Open Market Committee operates with almost complete discretion over how to conduct monetary policy. The laws that created the Fed give the institution only vague recommendations about what goals it should pursue. A 1977 amendment to the 1913 Federal Reserve Act said the Fed "shall maintain long run growth of the monetary and credit aggregates commensurate with the economy's long run potential to increase production, so as to promote effectively the goals of maximum employment, stable prices, and moderate long-term interest rates." But the act does not specify how to weight these various goals, nor does it tell the Fed how to pursue whatever objective it might choose.

Some economists are critical of this institutional design. Our next debate over macroeconomic policy, therefore, focuses on whether the Fed should have its discretionary powers reduced and, instead, be committed to following a rule for how it conducts monetary policy.

18-3a Pro: Monetary Policy Should Be Made by Rule

Discretion in the conduct of monetary policy has two problems. The first is that it does not limit incompetence and abuse of power. When the government sends police into a community to maintain civic order, it gives them strict guidelines about how to carry out their job. Because police have great power, allowing them to exercise that power however they wanted would be dangerous. Yet when the government gives central bankers the authority to maintain economic order, it gives them few guidelines. Monetary policymakers are allowed undisciplined discretion.

One example of the abuse of power is that central bankers are sometimes tempted to use monetary policy to affect the outcome of elections. Suppose that the vote for the incumbent president is based on economic conditions at the time he is up for reelection. A central banker sympathetic to the incumbent might be tempted to pursue expansionary policies just before the election to stimulate production and employment, knowing that the resulting inflation will not show up until after the election. Thus, to the extent that central bankers ally themselves with politicians, discretionary policy can lead to economic fluctuations that reflect the electoral calendar. Economists call such fluctuations the *political business cycle*. Prior to the election of 1972, for instance, President Richard Nixon pressured Fed Chair Arthur Burns to pursue a more expansionary monetary policy, presumably to bolster Nixon's reelection chances.

The second and subtler problem with discretionary monetary policy is that it might lead to higher inflation than is desirable. Central bankers, knowing that there is no long-run trade-off between inflation and unemployment, often announce that their goal is zero inflation. Yet they rarely achieve price stability. Why? Perhaps it is because, once the public forms expectations of inflation, policymakers face a short-run trade-off between inflation and unemployment. They are tempted to renege on their announcement of price stability to achieve lower unemployment. This discrepancy between announcements (what policymakers *say* they are going to do) and actions (what they subsequently in fact do) is called the *time inconsistency of policy*. Because policymakers can be time inconsistent, people are skeptical when central bankers announce their intentions to reduce inflation. As a result, people often expect higher inflation than monetary policymakers claim they are trying to achieve. Higher expectations of inflation, in turn, shift the short-run Phillips curve upward, making the short-run trade-off between inflation and unemployment less favorable than it otherwise might be.

One way to avoid these two problems with discretionary policy is to commit the central bank to a policy rule. For example, suppose that Congress passed a law requiring the Fed to increase the money supply by exactly 3 percent per year. (Why 3 percent? Because real GDP grows on average about 3 percent per year, and because money demand grows with real GDP, 3 percent growth in the money supply is roughly the rate necessary to produce long-run price stability.) Such a law would eliminate incompetence and abuse of power on the part of the Fed, and it would make the political business cycle impossible. In addition, policy could no longer be time inconsistent. People would now believe the Fed's announcement of low inflation because the Fed would be legally required to pursue a low-inflation monetary policy. With low expected inflation, the economy would face a more favorable short-run trade-off between inflation and unemployment.

Other rules for monetary policy are also possible. A more active rule might allow some feedback from the state of the economy to changes in monetary policy. For example, a more active rule might require the Fed to increase monetary growth by 1 percentage point for every percentage point that unemployment rises above its natural rate. Regardless of the precise form of the rule, committing the Fed to some rule would yield advantages by limiting incompetence, abuse of power, and time inconsistency in the conduct of monetary policy.

18-3b   Con: Monetary Policy Should Not Be Made by Rule

There may be pitfalls with discretionary monetary policy, but there is also an important advantage to it: flexibility. The Fed has to confront various circumstances, not all of which can be foreseen. In the 1930s, banks failed in record numbers. In the 1970s, the price of oil skyrocketed around the world. In October 1987, the stock market fell by 22 percent in a single day. From 2007 to 2009, house prices dropped, home foreclosures soared, and the financial system experienced significant problems. The Fed must decide how to respond to these shocks to the economy. A designer of a policy rule could not possibly consider all the contingencies and specify in advance the right policy response. It is better to appoint good people to conduct monetary policy and then give them the freedom to do the best they can.

Moreover, the alleged problems with discretion are largely hypothetical. The practical importance of the political business cycle, for instance, is far from clear. While it is true that Nixon tried to pressure Burns in 1972, it is not clear that he succeeded: Interest rates rose significantly during the election year. Moreover, in some cases, just the opposite seems to occur. President Jimmy Carter appointed Paul Volcker to head the Federal Reserve in 1979. Nonetheless, in October of that year, Volcker switched to a contractionary monetary policy to combat the high inflation that he had inherited from his predecessor. The predictable result of Volcker's decision was a recession, and the predictable result of the recession was a decline in Carter's popularity. Rather than using monetary policy to help the president who had appointed him, Volcker took actions he thought were in the national interest, even though they contributed to Carter's defeat by Ronald Reagan in the November 1980 election.

The practical importance of time inconsistency is also far from clear. Although most people are skeptical of central-bank announcements, central bankers can achieve credibility over time by backing up their words with actions. In the 1990s and 2000s, the Fed achieved and maintained a low rate of inflation, despite the ever-present temptation to take advantage of the short-run trade-off between inflation and unemployment. This experience shows that low inflation does not require that the Fed be committed to a policy rule.

Any attempt to replace discretion with a rule must confront the difficult task of specifying a precise rule. Despite much research examining the costs and benefits of alternative rules, economists have not reached consensus about what a good rule would be. Until there is consensus, society has little choice but to give central bankers discretion to conduct monetary policy as they see fit.

FYI   Inflation Targeting

Over the past few decades, many central banks around the world have adopted a policy called *inflation targeting*. Sometimes this policy takes the form of a central bank announcing its intentions regarding the inflation rate over the next few years. At other times it takes the form of a national law that specifies an inflation goal for the central bank.

Inflation targeting is not a commitment to an ironclad rule. In all the countries that have adopted inflation targeting, central banks still have a fair amount of discretion. Inflation targets are often set as a range—an inflation rate of 1 to 3 percent, for example—rather than a single number. Thus, the central bank can choose where in the range it wants to be. Moreover, the central bank is sometimes allowed to adjust its target for inflation, at least temporarily, if some event (such as a shock to world oil prices) pushes inflation outside the target range.

Although inflation targeting leaves the central bank with some discretion, the policy does constrain how that discretion is used. When a central bank is told simply to "do the right thing," it is hard to hold the central bank accountable, because people can argue forever about what is right. By contrast, when a central bank has an inflation target, the public can more easily judge whether the central bank is meeting its goals. Inflation targeting does not tie the hands of the central bank, but it does increase the transparency and accountability of monetary policy. In a sense, inflation targeting is a compromise in the debate over rules versus discretion.

Compared with other central banks around the world, the Federal Reserve was slow to adopt a policy of inflation targeting, although some commentators had long suggested that the Fed had an implicit inflation target of about 2 percent. In January 2012, the Federal Open Market Committee made the policy more explicit. Its press release read as follows:

The inflation rate over the longer run is primarily determined by monetary policy, and hence the Committee has the ability to specify a longer-run goal for inflation. The Committee judges that inflation at the rate of 2 percent, as measured by the annual change in the price index for personal consumption expenditures, is most consistent over the longer run with the Federal Reserve's statutory mandate. Communicating this inflation goal clearly to the public helps keep longer-term inflation expectations firmly anchored, thereby fostering price stability and moderate long-term interest rates and enhancing the Committee's ability to promote maximum employment in the face of significant economic disturbances. ∎

Source: "Policy Makers Rethink a 2% Inflation Target." *Wall Street Journal*, September 24, 2018

5. Advocates for setting monetary policy by rule rather than discretion often argue that
   a. central bankers with discretion are tempted to renege on their announced commitments to low inflation.
   b. central bankers following a rule will be more responsive to the needs of the political process.
   c. fiscal policy is better than monetary policy as a tool for economic stabilization.
   d. it is sometimes useful to give the economy a burst of surprise inflation.

6. A policy of inflation targeting
   a. removes the need for discretionary decision making by central bankers.
   b. frees central bankers from having to respond to shocks to aggregate demand.
   c. makes central bank policy more transparent and accountable.
   d. has been abandoned by most central banks around the world.

Answers at end of chapter.

18-4 Should the Central Bank Aim for Zero Inflation?

One of the *Ten Principles of Economics* introduced in Chapter 1, and developed more fully in the chapter on money growth and inflation, is that prices rise when the government prints too much money. Another of the *Ten Principles of Economics* introduced in Chapter 1, and developed more fully in the preceding chapter, is that society faces a short-run trade-off between inflation and unemployment. Put together, these two principles raise a question for policymakers: How much inflation should the central bank be willing to tolerate? Our next debate is whether zero is the right target for the inflation rate.

18-4a Pro: The Central Bank Should Aim for Zero Inflation

Inflation confers no benefit on society, but it imposes several real costs. As we have discussed, economists have identified six costs of inflation:

- Shoeleather costs associated with reduced money holdings
- Menu costs associated with more frequent adjustment of prices
- Increased variability of relative prices
- Unintended changes in tax liabilities due to non-indexation of the tax code
- Confusion and inconvenience resulting from a changing unit of account
- Arbitrary redistributions of wealth associated with dollar-denominated debts

Some economists argue that these costs are small, at least at moderate rates of inflation, such as the 2 percent inflation experienced in the United States during the first two decades of the 21st century. But other economists claim these costs can be substantial, even during periods of moderate inflation. Moreover, there is no doubt that the public dislikes inflation. When inflation heats up, opinion polls identify inflation as one of the nation's leading problems.

The benefits of zero inflation have to be weighed against the costs of achieving it. Reducing inflation usually requires a period of high unemployment and low output, as illustrated by the short-run Phillips curve. But this disinflationary recession is only temporary. Once people come to understand that policymakers are aiming for zero inflation, expectations of inflation will fall and the short-run trade-off will improve. Because expectations adjust, there is no trade-off between inflation and unemployment in the long run.

Reducing inflation is, therefore, a policy with temporary costs and permanent benefits. Once the disinflationary recession is over, the benefits of zero inflation persist into the future. If policymakers are farsighted, they should be willing to incur the temporary costs for the permanent benefits. This was precisely the calculation made by Paul Volcker in the early 1980s, when he tightened monetary policy and reduced inflation from about 10 percent in 1980 to about 4 percent in 1983. Although in 1982 unemployment reached its highest level since the Great Depression, the economy eventually recovered from the recession, leaving a legacy of low inflation. Today, Volcker is considered a hero among central bankers.

Moreover, the costs of reducing inflation need not be as large as some economists claim. If the Fed announces a credible commitment to zero inflation, it can directly influence expectations of inflation. Such a change in expectations can improve the short-run trade-off between inflation and unemployment, allowing the economy to reach lower inflation at a reduced cost. The key to this strategy is credibility: People must believe that the Fed is actually going to carry through on its announced policy. Congress could help in this regard by passing legislation that makes price stability the Fed's primary goal. Such a law would decrease the cost of achieving zero inflation without reducing any of the resulting benefits.

One advantage of a zero-inflation target is that zero provides a more natural focal point for policymakers than any other number. In recent years, the Fed has pursued an inflation target of 2 percent, and inflation has remained reasonably close to that target. But will the Fed continue to stick to that 2 percent target? If events inadvertently pushed inflation up to 3 or 4 percent, why wouldn't the Fed just raise the target? There is, after all, nothing special about the number 2. By contrast, zero is the only number for the inflation rate at which the Fed can claim that it has achieved price stability and fully eliminated the costs of inflation.

18-4b Con: The Central Bank Should Not Aim for Zero Inflation

Price stability may be desirable, but the additional benefits of having zero inflation rather than having moderate inflation are small, whereas the costs of reaching zero inflation are large. Estimates of the sacrifice ratio suggest that reducing inflation by 1 percentage point requires giving up about 5 percent of one year's output. Reducing inflation from, say, 4 percent to zero requires a loss of 20 percent of a year's output. People might dislike inflation of 4 percent, but it is not at all clear that they would (or should) be willing to pay 20 percent of a year's income to get rid of it.

The social costs of disinflation are even larger than this 20 percent figure suggests, for the lost income is not spread equitably over the population. When the economy goes into recession, all incomes do not fall proportionately. Instead, the fall in aggregate income is concentrated on those workers who lose their jobs. The vulnerable workers are often those with the least skills and experience. Hence, much of the cost of reducing inflation is borne by those who can least afford to pay it.

Economists can list several costs of inflation, but there is no professional consensus that these costs are substantial. The shoeleather costs, menu costs, and others that economists have identified do not seem great, at least for moderate rates of inflation. It is true that the public dislikes inflation, but the public may be misled into believing the inflation fallacy—the view that inflation erodes living standards. Economists understand that living standards depend on productivity, not monetary policy. Because inflation in nominal incomes goes hand in hand with inflation in prices, reducing inflation would not cause real incomes to rise more rapidly.

Moreover, policymakers can reduce many of the costs of inflation without actually reducing inflation. They can eliminate the problems associated with the non-indexed tax system by rewriting the tax laws to account for the effects of inflation. They can also reduce the arbitrary redistributions of wealth between creditors and debtors caused by unexpected inflation by issuing indexed government bonds, as the Clinton administration did in 1997. Such an act insulates holders of government debt from inflation. In addition, by setting an example, the policy might encourage private borrowers and lenders to write debt contracts indexed for inflation.

Reducing inflation might be desirable if it could be done at no cost, as some economists argue is possible. Yet this trick seems hard to carry out in practice. When economies reduce their rate of inflation, they almost always experience a period of high unemployment and low output. It is risky to believe that the central bank could achieve credibility so quickly as to make disinflation painless.

Indeed, a disinflationary recession can potentially leave permanent scars on the economy. Firms in all industries reduce their spending on new plants and equipment substantially during recessions, making investment the most volatile component of GDP. Even after the recession is over, the smaller stock of capital reduces productivity, incomes, and living standards below the levels they otherwise would have achieved. In addition, when workers become unemployed in recessions, they lose job skills, permanently reducing their value as workers.

IN THE NEWS

A Central Bank Assesses Its Policy

Fed policymakers have been rethinking how best to implement their target for inflation.

Fed Officials to Mull Inflation Target Shift

By Nick Timiraos

Top Federal Reserve officials said Friday that the central bank would consider broad changes to its policy framework to encourage periods of modestly higher inflation, a response to the challenges the Fed has faced in driving inflation higher in recent years.

New York Fed President John Williams, speaking at a conference in New York, said central bankers need to guard against consumers and businesses coming to anticipate low inflation, lest their expectations become self-fulfilling.

The Fed set a 2% inflation target in 2012, but inflation has run below that level for much of the recent expansion. A measure of inflation that excludes volatile food and energy categories has averaged 1.6%, though it was running at 1.9% at the end of last year. The Fed seeks to maintain stable prices by influencing households' and businesses' inflation expectations.

Many Fed officials believe the American public has generally come to expect inflation around 2%, helping restrain price pressures, in contrast to the 1970s when people's expectations of rapidly rising prices helped to actually push them higher.

"The persistent undershoot of the Fed's target risks undermining the 2% inflation anchor," said Mr. Williams. Because short-term interest rates aren't likely to rise as high as they have in the past, the Fed will likely have less room to cut rates to stimulate growth in a downturn.

"The risk of the inflation-expectations anchor slipping toward shore calls for a reassessment of the dominant inflation-targeting framework," Mr. Williams said.

With the Fed's current target, the central bank aims for 2% inflation every year, no matter what happened the year before.

Under a forthcoming review of the Fed's strategies, Fed Vice Chairman Richard Clarida said Friday that the central bank would consider a policy, such as one advocated by Mr. Williams, under which it might react to what happened in the past if it undershoots inflation—a so-called "makeup" policy.

Academic models show that "these makeup strategies lead to better average

A little bit of inflation may even be a good thing. Some economists believe that inflation "greases the wheels" of the labor market. Because workers resist cuts in nominal wages, a fall in real wages is more easily accomplished with a rising price level. Inflation thus makes it easier for real wages to adjust to changes in labor-market conditions.

In addition, inflation allows for the possibility of negative real interest rates. Nominal interest rates can never fall below zero, because lenders can always hold on to their money rather than lending it out at a negative return. If inflation is zero, real interest rates can also never be negative. However, if inflation is positive, then a cut in nominal interest rates below the inflation rate produces negative real interest rates. Sometimes the economy may need negative real interest rates to provide sufficient stimulus to aggregate demand—an option ruled out by zero inflation.

In light of all these arguments, why should policymakers put the economy through a costly and inequitable disinflationary recession to achieve zero inflation? Economist Alan Blinder, who was once vice chairman of the Federal Reserve, argued in his book *Hard Heads, Soft Hearts* that policymakers should not make this choice:

> The costs that attend the low and moderate inflation rates experienced in the United States and in other industrial countries appear to be quite modest—more like a bad cold than a cancer on society. . . . As rational individuals, we do not volunteer for a lobotomy to cure a head cold. Yet, as a collectivity, we routinely prescribe the economic equivalent of lobotomy (high unemployment) as a cure for the inflationary cold.

Blinder concludes that it is better to learn to live with moderate inflation.

performance" of meeting the Fed's goals of keeping prices stable while maximizing employment, he said, speaking separately at the same conference.

One critical question, he added, is whether those policies can work as effectively in the real world, where central banks must convince households and businesses that they will indeed follow through in encouraging higher inflation.

The Fed said last fall that it would conduct a review this year of its monetary-policy strategy and communications, to culminate in a research conference sponsored by the central bank in Chicago in early June.

Mr. Williams responded to a paper presented at the conference in New York on Friday by highlighting the prospects for inflation to pick up as unemployment has fallen.

At issue is the framework known as the Phillips curve, which has long animated thinking in mainstream economics and inside the central bank. It holds that inflation rises as

slack—the unused or under-utilized resources across the economy—declines, and that the disappearance of slack can best be measured as unemployment declines below a level estimated to be consistent with stable prices.

Several changes in the structure of the economy have weakened the relationship between inflation and unemployment, said San Francisco Fed President Mary Daly, who also discussed the paper at the New York conference on Friday. Those changes include weaker bargaining power for workers, as well as changes in the composition of the workforce that could create more slack than is measured by the unemployment rate.

Given those changes and the weak response of inflation to tighter labor markets in recent years, "you don't want to react too quickly to the idea inflation could be just around the corner," Ms. Daly said.

While the paper presented Friday warned of so-called nonlinearities in the relationship

between prices and unemployment—that is, the potential for prices to accelerate higher as unemployment drops lower—Ms. Daly played down her concern about the prospect for any acceleration that would catch Fed officials flat-footed.

Price pressures "form in such a way that we can see them in advance," she said. ■

Questions to Discuss

1. Do you think it is a good idea for the Fed, when it undershoots its inflation target, to make up for the past miss by subsequently overshooting its inflation target? Why or why not?

2. If, as the article suggests, the Phillips curve relationship between inflation and unemployment has weakened in recent years, how should that development alter the conduct of monetary policy? As a result of this change, should the Fed focus more on unemployment or more on inflation?

Source: *The Wall Street Journal*, February 23, 2019.

7. Which of the following is NOT an argument for a zero rate of inflation?
   a. It eliminates distortions from a non-indexed tax code.
   b. It encourages people to hold a greater quantity of money.
   c. It reduces the menu costs that firms have to incur.
   d. It stops real wages from falling if nominal wages cannot be cut.

8. Which of the following is NOT an argument for a positive rate of inflation?
   a. It permits real interest rates to be negative.
   b. It increases the variability of relative prices.
   c. It allows real wages to fall without cuts in nominal wages.
   d. It would be costly to reduce inflation to zero.

Answers at end of chapter.

18-5 Should the Government Balance Its Budget?

A persistent macroeconomic debate concerns the government's finances. Whenever the government spends more than it collects in tax revenue, it finances this budget deficit by issuing government debt. In our study of financial markets, we saw how budget deficits affect saving, investment, and interest rates. But how big a problem are budget deficits? Our next debate concerns whether fiscal policymakers should make balancing the government's budget a high priority.

18-5a Pro: The Government Should Balance Its Budget

The U.S. federal government is far more indebted today than it was four decades ago. In 1980, the federal debt was $712 billion; in 2018, it was $15.8 trillion. If we divide today's debt by the size of the population, we learn that each person's share of the government debt is about $48,000.

The most direct effect of the government debt is to place a burden on future generations of taxpayers. When these debts and accumulated interest come due, future taxpayers will face a difficult choice. They can choose some combination of higher taxes and less government spending to make resources available to pay off the debt and accumulated interest. Or, instead, they can delay the day of reckoning and put the government into even deeper debt by borrowing once again to pay off the old debt and interest. In essence, when the government runs a budget deficit and issues government debt, it allows current taxpayers to pass the bill for some of their government spending on to future taxpayers. Inheriting such a large debt will lower the living standard of future generations.

In addition to this direct effect, budget deficits have various macroeconomic effects. Because budget deficits represent *negative* public saving, they lower national saving (the sum of private and public saving). Reduced national saving causes real interest rates to rise and investment to fall. Reduced investment leads over time to a smaller stock of capital. A lower capital stock reduces labor productivity, real wages, and the economy's production of goods and services. Thus, when the government increases its debt, future generations are born into an economy with lower incomes as well as higher taxes.

There are, nevertheless, situations in which running a budget deficit is justifiable. Throughout history, the most common cause of increased government debt has been war. When a military conflict raises government spending temporarily, it is reasonable to finance this extra spending by borrowing. Otherwise, taxes during wartime would have to rise precipitously. Such high tax rates would greatly distort the incentives faced by those who are taxed, leading to large deadweight losses. In addition, such high tax rates would be unfair to current citizens who are making the sacrifice of fighting the war to ensure security and freedom not only for themselves but also for future generations.

Similarly, it is reasonable to allow a budget deficit during a temporary downturn in economic activity. When the economy goes into a recession, tax revenue falls automatically because the income tax and the payroll tax are levied on measures of income. If the government tried to balance its budget during a recession, it would have to raise taxes or cut spending at a time of high unemployment. Such a policy would tend to depress aggregate demand at precisely the time it needed to be stimulated and, therefore, would tend to increase the magnitude of economic fluctuations.

Yet not all budget deficits can be justified as a result of war or recession. In 2019, the Congressional Budget Office (CBO) projected that, if current policies are maintained, U.S. government debt as a percentage of GDP would increase from 78 percent in 2019 to 147 percent in 2049. Yet the CBO made the optimistic assumption the nation will experience neither a major military conflict nor a major economic downturn during this period. The government was projected to run sizable budget deficits simply because presidents and Congresses had committed the federal government to a variety of spending programs without passing the taxes necessary to fund them.

This projected policy is unsustainable. Eventually, the government will need to admit its past mistakes and enact measures to bring spending in line with tax revenue. The open question is whether the fiscal adjustment should take the form of reduced spending, increased taxes, or a combination of the two. Compared with the alternative of ongoing budget deficits, a balanced budget means greater national saving, increased capital accumulation, and faster economic growth. It means that future college graduates will enter a more prosperous economy.

"What?!? My share of the government debt is $48,000?"

18-5b Con: The Government Should Not Balance Its Budget

The problem of government debt is often exaggerated. Although the government debt does represent a tax burden on younger generations, it is not large compared to the average person's lifetime income. The debt of the U.S. federal government is about $48,000 per person. A person who works 40 years for $50,000 a year will earn $2 million over his lifetime. His share of the government debt represents only about 2.4 percent of his lifetime resources.

Moreover, it is misleading to consider the effects of budget deficits in isolation. The budget deficit is just one piece of a larger picture of how the government chooses to raise and spend money. In making these decisions about fiscal policy, policymakers affect different generations of taxpayers in many ways. The government's budget deficit or surplus should be evaluated together with these other policies.

For example, suppose the government reduces the budget deficit by cutting spending on public investments, such as education. Does this policy make younger generations better off? The government debt will be smaller when they enter the labor force, reducing their tax burden. Yet if they are less educated than they otherwise would be, their productivity and incomes will be lower. Many studies find that the return to schooling (the increase in a worker's wage that results from an additional year in school) is quite large. Reducing the budget deficit rather than funding more education spending could, all things considered, make future generations worse off.

Single-minded concern about the budget deficit is also dangerous because it draws attention away from various other policies that redistribute income across generations. For example, in the 1960s and 1970s, the U.S. federal government raised Social Security benefits for the elderly. It financed this higher spending by increasing the payroll tax on the working-age population. This policy redistributed income away from younger generations toward older generations, even though it did not affect the government debt. Thus, the budget deficit is only a small part of the larger issue of how government policy affects the welfare of different generations.

To some extent, forward-looking parents can reverse the adverse effects of government debt. Parents can offset the impact simply by saving and leaving a larger bequest. The bequest would enhance their children's ability to bear the burden of future taxes. Some economists claim that people do in fact behave this way. If this were true, higher private saving by parents would offset the public dissaving of budget deficits; as a result, deficits would not affect the economy. Most economists doubt that parents are so farsighted, but some people probably do act this way, and anyone could. Deficits give people the opportunity to consume at the expense of their children, but deficits do not require them to do so. If the government debt were actually a great problem facing future generations, some parents would help to solve it.

Critics of budget deficits sometimes assert that the government debt cannot continue to rise forever, but in fact, it can. Just as a bank evaluating a loan application would compare a person's debts to his income, we should judge the burden of the government debt relative to the size of the nation's income. Population growth and technological progress cause the total income of the U.S. economy to grow over time. As a result, the nation's ability to pay the interest on the government debt grows over time as well. As long as the government debt grows more slowly than the nation's income, there is nothing to prevent the government debt from growing forever.

Some numbers can put this into perspective. The CBO projects that the real output of the U.S. economy will grow by about 2 percent per year. If the inflation rate is also 2 percent per year, as the Fed is targeting, then nominal income will grow at 4 percent per year. The government debt can therefore rise by 4 percent per year without increasing the ratio of debt to income. In 2018, the federal government debt was $15.8 trillion; 4 percent of this figure is $632 billion. As long as the federal budget deficit is smaller than $632 billion, the policy is sustainable.

To be sure, very large budget deficits cannot persist forever. The $1 trillion budget deficits projected for 2020 and beyond may be too large. But zero is the wrong target for fiscal policymakers. As long as the deficit is only moderate in size, there will never be a day of reckoning that forces government borrowing to end or the economy to collapse.

Quick**Quiz**

9. Throughout U.S. history, what has been the most common cause of substantial increases in government debt?
    a. recessions
    b. wars
    c. financial crises
    d. tax cuts

10. Other things equal, when the government runs a large budget deficit, it _____ national saving and thereby _____ capital formation and productivity growth.
    a. increases; increases
    b. increases; decreases
    c. decreases; increases
    d. decreases; decreases

Answers at end of chapter.

18-6 Should the Tax Laws Be Reformed to Encourage Saving?

A nation's standard of living depends on its ability to produce goods and services. This was one of the *Ten Principles of Economics* in Chapter 1. As we saw in the chapter on production and growth, a nation's productive capability, in turn, is determined largely by how much it saves and invests for the future. Our last debate is whether policymakers should reform the tax laws to encourage greater saving and investment.

18-6a Pro: The Tax Laws Should Be Reformed to Encourage Saving

A nation's saving rate is a key determinant of its long-run prosperity. When the saving rate is higher, more resources are available for investment in new plant and equipment. A larger stock of plant and equipment, in turn, raises labor productivity, wages, and incomes. It is, therefore, no surprise that international data show a positive correlation between national saving rates and measures of economic well-being.

Another of the *Ten Principles of Economics* in Chapter 1 is that people respond to incentives. This lesson should apply to people's decisions about how much to save. If a nation's laws make saving attractive, people will save a higher fraction of their incomes, and this higher saving will lead to a more prosperous future.

Unfortunately, the U.S. tax system discourages saving by taxing the return to saving quite heavily. For example, consider a 25-year-old worker who saves $1,000 of his income to have a more comfortable retirement at the age of 70. If he buys a bond that pays an interest rate of 10 percent, the $1,000 will accumulate at the end of 45 years to $72,900 in the absence of taxes on interest. But suppose he faces a marginal tax rate on interest income of 40 percent, which is typical for many workers once federal and state income taxes are added together. In this case, his after-tax interest rate is only 6 percent, and the $1,000 will accumulate at the end of 45 years to only $13,800. That is, accumulated over this long span of time, the tax rate on interest income reduces the benefit of saving $1,000 from $72,900 to $13,800—or by about 80 percent.

The tax code further discourages saving by taxing some forms of capital income twice. Suppose a person uses some of his saving to buy stock in a corporation. When the corporation earns a profit from its capital investments, it first pays tax on this profit in the form of the corporate income tax. If the corporation pays out the rest of the profit to the stockholder in the form of dividends, the stockholder pays tax on this income a second time in the form of the individual income tax. This double taxation substantially reduces the return to the stockholder, thereby reducing the incentive to save.

The tax laws again discourage saving if a person wants to leave his accumulated wealth to his children (or anyone else) rather than consuming it during his lifetime. Parents can bequeath some money to their children tax-free, but if the bequest becomes large, the estate tax rate can be as high as 40 percent. To a large extent, concern about national saving is motivated by a desire to ensure economic prosperity for future generations. It is odd, therefore, that the tax laws discourage the most direct way in which one generation can help the next.

In addition to the tax code, many other policies and institutions in our society reduce the incentive for households to save. Some government benefits, such as welfare and Medicaid, are means-tested. That is, the benefits are reduced for those who in the past have been prudent enough to save some of their income. Similarly,

ASK THE EXPERTS

Taxing Capital and Labor

"One drawback of taxing capital income at a lower rate than labor income is that it gives people incentives to relabel income that policymakers find hard to categorize as 'capital' rather than 'labor'."

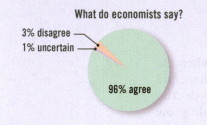

What do economists say?

3% disagree
1% uncertain
96% agree

"Despite relabeling concerns, taxing capital income at a permanently lower rate than labor income would result in higher average long-term prosperity, relative to an alternative that generated the same amount of tax revenue by permanently taxing capital and labor income at equal rates instead."

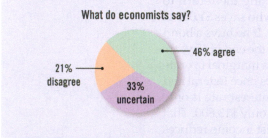

What do economists say?

46% agree
21% disagree
33% uncertain

"Although they do not always agree about the precise likely effects of different tax policies, another reason why economists often give disparate advice on tax policy is because they hold differing views about choices between raising average prosperity and redistributing income."

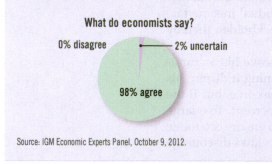

What do economists say?

0% disagree
2% uncertain
98% agree

Source: IGM Economic Experts Panel, October 9, 2012.

colleges and universities grant financial aid as a function of the wealth of the students and their parents. Such a policy is like a tax on wealth and, as such, discourages students and parents from saving.

There are various ways in which the tax code could provide an incentive to save, or at least reduce the disincentive that households now face. Already the tax laws give preferential treatment to some types of retirement saving. When a taxpayer puts income into an Individual Retirement Account (IRA), for instance, that income and the interest it earns are not taxed until the funds are withdrawn at retirement. The tax code gives a similar tax advantage to retirement accounts that go by other names, such as 401(k), 403(b), and profit-sharing plans. There are, however, limits on who is eligible to use these plans and on the amount an eligible person can put into them. Moreover, because there are penalties for withdrawal before retirement age, these retirement plans provide little incentive for other types of saving, such as saving to buy a house or pay for college. A small step to encourage greater saving would be to expand the ability of households to use such tax-advantaged savings accounts.

A more comprehensive approach would be to reconsider the entire basis by which the government collects revenue. The centerpiece of the U.S. tax system is the income tax. A dollar earned is taxed the same whether it is spent or saved. An alternative advocated by many economists is a consumption tax. Under a consumption tax, a household pays taxes only on the basis of what it spends. Income that is saved is exempt from taxation until the saving is later withdrawn and spent on consumption goods. In essence, a consumption tax automatically puts all saving into a tax-advantaged savings account, much like an IRA. A switch from income taxation to consumption taxation would greatly increase the incentive to save.

18-6b Con: The Tax Laws Should Not Be Reformed to Encourage Saving

Increasing saving may be desirable, but it is not the only goal of tax policy. Policymakers also must be sure to distribute the tax burden fairly. The problem with proposals to increase the incentive to save is that they increase the tax burden on those who can least afford it.

It is undeniable that high-income households save a greater fraction of their income than low-income households. As a result, any tax change that favors people who save will also tend to favor people with high income. Policies such as tax-advantaged retirement accounts may seem appealing, but they lead to a less egalitarian society. By reducing the tax burden on the wealthy who can take advantage of these accounts, they force the government to raise the tax burden on the poor.

Moreover, tax policies designed to encourage saving may not be effective at achieving that goal. Economic theory does not give a clear prediction about whether a higher rate of return would increase saving. The outcome depends on the relative size of two conflicting forces, called the *substitution effect* and the *income effect*. On the one hand, a higher rate of return raises the benefit of saving: Each dollar saved today produces more consumption in the future. This substitution effect tends to increase saving. On the other hand, a higher rate of return lowers the need for saving: A household has to save less to achieve any target level of consumption in the future. This income effect tends to reduce saving. If the substitution and income effects approximately cancel each other, as some studies suggest, then saving will not change when lower taxation of capital income raises the rate of return.

There are ways to increase national saving other than by giving tax breaks to the rich. National saving is the sum of private and public saving. Instead of trying to alter the tax code to encourage greater private saving, policymakers can simply raise public saving by reducing the budget deficit, perhaps by raising taxes on the wealthy. This approach offers a direct way of raising national saving and increasing prosperity for future generations.

Indeed, once public saving is taken into account, tax provisions to encourage saving might backfire. Tax changes that reduce the taxation of capital income reduce government revenue and, thereby, lead to a larger budget deficit. To increase national saving, such changes in the tax code must increase private saving by more than they decrease public saving. If they fail to do so, so-called saving incentives can potentially make matters worse.

QuickQuiz

11. Advocates of taxing consumption rather than income argue that
    a. the current tax code discourages people from saving.
    b. the rich consume a higher fraction of income than the poor.
    c. a consumption tax is a better automatic stabilizer.
    d. taxing consumption does not cause any deadweight losses.

12. Critics of taxing consumption rather than income argue that
    a. switching to a consumption tax would benefit the rich.
    b. private saving does not respond much to tax incentives.
    c. reducing the budget deficit is a better way to raise national saving.
    d. All of the above.

Answers at end of chapter.

18-7 Conclusion

This chapter has considered six classic debates over macroeconomic policy. For each, it began with a controversial proposition and then offered the arguments pro and con. If you find it hard to choose a side in these debates, you may find some comfort in the fact that you are not alone. The study of economics does not always make it easy to choose among alternative policies. Indeed, by clarifying the trade-offs that policymakers face, it can make the choice more difficult.

Difficult choices, however, have no right to seem easy. When you hear politicians or commentators proposing something that sounds too good to be true, it probably is. If they appear to be offering you a free lunch, you should look for the hidden price tag. Few policies come with benefits and no costs. By helping you see through the fog of rhetoric so common in political discourse, the study of economics should make you a better participant in our national debates.

CHAPTER IN A NUTSHELL

- Advocates of active monetary and fiscal policy view the economy as inherently unstable and believe that policy can manage aggregate demand to offset the inherent instability. Critics of active monetary and fiscal policy emphasize that policy affects the economy with a lag and that our ability to forecast future economic conditions is poor. As a result, attempts to stabilize the economy can end up being destabilizing.

- Advocates of increased government spending to fight recessions argue that because the extra income from tax cuts may be saved rather than spent, direct government spending provides a greater boost to increase aggregate demand, which is key to promoting production and employment. Critics of spending hikes argue that tax cuts can expand both aggregate demand and aggregate supply and that hasty increases in government spending may lead to wasteful public projects.

- Advocates of rules for monetary policy argue that discretionary policy can suffer from incompetence, the abuse of power, and time inconsistency. Critics of rules for monetary policy argue that discretionary policy is more flexible in responding to changing economic circumstances.

- Advocates of a zero-inflation target emphasize that inflation has many costs and few benefits. Moreover, the cost of eliminating inflation—depressed output and increased unemployment—is only temporary. Even this cost can be reduced if the central bank announces a credible plan to reduce inflation, thereby directly lowering expectations of inflation. Critics of a zero-inflation target claim that moderate inflation imposes only small costs on society and that the recession necessary to reduce inflation to zero is quite costly. The critics also point out several ways in which moderate inflation may be helpful to an economy.

- Advocates of a balanced government budget argue that budget deficits impose an unjustifiable burden on future generations by raising their taxes and lowering their incomes. Critics of a balanced government budget argue that the deficit is only one small piece of fiscal policy. Single-minded concern about the budget deficit can obscure the many ways in which policy, including various spending programs, affects different generations.

- Advocates of tax incentives for saving point out that our society discourages saving in many ways, such as by heavily taxing capital income and by reducing benefits for those who have accumulated wealth. They endorse reforming the tax laws to encourage saving, perhaps by switching from an income tax to a consumption tax. Critics of tax incentives for saving argue that many proposed changes to stimulate saving would primarily benefit the wealthy, who do not need a tax break. They also argue that such changes might have only a small effect on private saving. Raising public saving by reducing the government's budget deficit would provide a more direct and equitable way to increase national saving.

QUESTIONS FOR REVIEW

1. What causes the lags in the effect of monetary and fiscal policy on aggregate demand? What are the implications of these lags for the debate over active versus passive policy?

2. According to traditional Keynesian analysis, why does a tax cut have a smaller effect on GDP than a similarly sized increase in government spending? Why might the opposite be the case?

3. What might motivate a central banker to cause a political business cycle? What does the political business cycle imply for the debate over policy rules?

4. Explain how credibility might affect the cost of reducing inflation.

5. Why are some economists against a target of zero inflation?

6. Explain two ways in which a government budget deficit hurts a future worker.

7. What are two situations in which most economists view a budget deficit as justifiable?

8. Some economists say that the government can continue running a budget deficit forever. How is that possible?

9. Some income from capital is taxed twice. Explain.

10. What adverse effect might be caused by tax incentives to increase saving?

PROBLEMS AND APPLICATIONS

1. The chapter suggests that the economy, like the human body, has "natural restorative powers."
   a. Illustrate the short-run effect of a fall in aggregate demand using an aggregate-demand/aggregate-supply diagram. What happens to total output, income, and employment?
   b. If the government does not use stabilization policy, what happens to the economy over time? Illustrate this adjustment on your diagram. Does it generally occur in a matter of months or a matter of years?
   c. Do you think the "natural restorative powers" of the economy mean that policymakers should be passive in response to the business cycle?

2. Policymakers who want to stabilize the economy must decide how much to change the money supply, government spending, or taxes. Why is it difficult for policymakers to choose the appropriate strength of their actions?

3. The problem of time inconsistency applies to fiscal policy as well as to monetary policy. Suppose the government announced a reduction in taxes on income from capital investments, like new factories.
   a. If investors believed that capital taxes would remain low, how would the government's action affect the level of investment?
   b. After investors have responded to the announced tax reduction, does the government have an incentive to renege on its policy? Explain.
   c. Given your answer to part (b), would investors believe the government's announcement? What can the government do to increase the credibility of announced policy changes?

   d. Explain why this situation is similar to the time-inconsistency problem faced by monetary policymakers.

4. Chapter 2 explains the difference between positive analysis and normative analysis. In the debate about whether the central bank should aim for zero inflation, which areas of disagreement involve positive statements and which involve normative judgments?

5. Why are the benefits of reducing inflation permanent and the costs temporary? Why are the costs of increasing inflation permanent and the benefits temporary? Use Phillips-curve diagrams in your answer.

6. Suppose the federal government cuts taxes and increases spending, raising the budget deficit to 12 percent of GDP. If nominal GDP is rising 5 percent per year, are such budget deficits sustainable forever? Explain. If budget deficits of this size are maintained for 20 years, what is likely to happen to your taxes and your children's taxes in the future? Can you personally do something today to offset this future effect?

7. Explain how each of the following policies redistributes income across generations. Is the redistribution from young to old or from old to young?
   a. an increase in the budget deficit
   b. more generous subsidies for education loans
   c. greater investments in highways and bridges
   d. an increase in Social Security benefits

8. What is the fundamental trade-off that society faces if it chooses to save more? How might the government increase national saving?

QuickQuiz Answers

1. b   2. c   3. c   4. a   5. a   6. c   7. d   8. b   9. b   10. d   11. a   12. d

Glossary

A

absolute advantage the ability to produce a good using fewer inputs than another producer

aggregate-demand curve a curve that shows the quantity of goods and services that households, firms, the government, and customers abroad want to buy at each price level

aggregate-supply curve a curve that shows the quantity of goods and services that firms choose to produce and sell at each price level

appreciation an increase in the value of a currency as measured by the amount of foreign currency it can buy

automatic stabilizers changes in fiscal policy that stimulate aggregate demand when the economy goes into a recession without policymakers having to take any deliberate action

B

balanced trade a situation in which exports equal imports

bank capital the resources a bank's owners have put into the institution

bond a certificate of indebtedness

budget deficit a shortfall of tax revenue from government spending

budget surplus an excess of tax revenue over government spending

business cycle fluctuations in economic activity, such as employment and production

C

capital flight a large and sudden reduction in the demand for assets located in a country

capital requirement a government regulation specifying a minimum amount of bank capital

catch-up effect the property whereby countries that start off poor tend to grow more rapidly than countries that start off rich

central bank an institution designed to oversee the banking system and regulate the quantity of money in the economy

circular-flow diagram a visual model of the economy that shows how dollars flow through markets among households and firms

classical dichotomy the theoretical separation of nominal and real variables

closed economy an economy that does not interact with other economies in the world

collective bargaining the process by which unions and firms agree on the terms of employment

commodity money money that takes the form of a commodity with intrinsic value

comparative advantage the ability to produce a good at a lower opportunity cost than another producer

competitive market a market with many buyers and sellers trading identical products so that each buyer and seller is a price taker

complements two goods for which an increase in the price of one leads to a decrease in the demand for the other

compounding the accumulation of a sum of money in, say, a bank account, where the interest earned remains in the account to earn additional interest in the future

consumer price index (CPI) a measure of the overall cost of the goods and services bought by a typical consumer

consumption spending by households on goods and services, with the exception of purchases of new housing

core CPI a measure of the overall cost of consumer goods and services excluding food and energy

crowding out a decrease in investment that results from government borrowing

crowding-out effect the offset in aggregate demand that results when expansionary fiscal policy raises the interest rate and thereby reduces investment spending

currency the paper bills and coins in the hands of the public

cyclical unemployment the deviation of unemployment from its natural rate

D

demand curve a graph of the relationship between the price of a good and the quantity demanded

demand deposits balances in bank accounts that depositors can access on demand by writing a check

demand schedule a table that shows the relationship between the price of a good and the quantity demanded

depreciation a decrease in the value of a currency as measured by the amount of foreign currency it can buy

depression a severe recession

diminishing returns the property whereby the benefit from an extra unit of an input declines as the quantity of the input increases

discount rate the interest rate on the loans that the Fed makes to banks

discouraged workers individuals who would like to work but have given up looking for a job

diversification the reduction of risk achieved by replacing a single risk with a large number of smaller, unrelated risks

E

economics the study of how society manages its scarce resources

efficiency the property of a resource allocation of maximizing the total surplus received by all members of society

efficiency wages above-equilibrium wages paid by firms to increase worker productivity

efficient markets hypothesis the theory that asset prices reflect all publicly available information about the value of an asset

equality the property of distributing economic prosperity uniformly among the members of society

equilibrium a situation in which the market price has reached the level at which quantity supplied equals quantity demanded

equilibrium price the price that balances quantity supplied and quantity demanded

equilibrium quantity the quantity supplied and the quantity demanded at the equilibrium price

exports goods and services that are produced domestically and sold abroad

externality the uncompensated impact of one person's actions on the well-being of a bystander

F

federal funds rate the interest rate at which banks make overnight loans to one another

Federal Reserve (Fed) the central bank of the United States

fiat money money without intrinsic value that is used as money by government decree

finance the field that studies how people make decisions regarding the allocation of resources over time and the handling of risk

financial intermediaries financial institutions through which savers can indirectly provide funds to borrowers

financial markets financial institutions through which savers can directly provide funds to borrowers

financial system the group of institutions in the economy that help to match one person's saving with another person's investment

firm-specific risk risk that affects only a single company

fiscal policy the setting of the level of government spending and taxation by government policymakers

Fisher effect the one-for-one adjustment of the nominal interest rate to the inflation rate

fractional-reserve banking a banking system in which banks hold only a fraction of deposits as reserves

frictional unemployment unemployment that results because it takes time for workers to search for the jobs that best suit their tastes and skills

fundamental analysis the study of a company's accounting statements and future prospects to determine its value

future value the amount of money in the future that an amount of money today will yield, given prevailing interest rates

G

GDP deflator a measure of the price level calculated as the ratio of nominal GDP to real GDP times 100

government purchases spending on goods and services by local, state, and federal governments

gross domestic product (GDP) the market value of all final goods and services produced within a country in a given period of time

H

human capital the knowledge and skills that workers acquire through education and on-the-job training

I

imports goods and services that are produced abroad and sold domestically

incentive something that induces a person to act

indexation the automatic correction by law or contract of a dollar amount for the effects of inflation

inferior good a good for which an increase in income reduces the quantity demanded

inflation an increase in the overall level of prices in the economy

inflation rate the percentage change in the price index from the preceding period

inflation tax the revenue the government raises by creating money

informational efficiency the description of asset prices that rationally reflect all available information

investment spending on business capital, residential capital, and inventories

J

job search the process by which workers find appropriate jobs given their tastes and skills

L

labor force the total number of workers, including both the employed and the unemployed

labor-force participation rate the percentage of the adult population that is in the labor force

law of demand the claim that, other things being equal, the quantity demanded of a good falls when the price of the good rises

law of supply the claim that, other things being equal, the quantity supplied of a good rises when the price of the good rises

law of supply and demand the claim that the price of any good adjusts to bring the quantity supplied and the quantity demanded for that good into balance

leverage the use of borrowed money to supplement existing funds for purposes of investment

leverage ratio the ratio of assets to bank capital

liquidity the ease with which an asset can be converted into the economy's medium of exchange

M

macroeconomics the study of economy-wide phenomena, including inflation, unemployment, and economic growth

marginal change a small incremental adjustment to a plan of action

market a group of buyers and sellers of a particular good or service

market economy an economy that allocates resources through the decentralized decisions of many firms and households as they interact in markets for goods and services

market failure a situation in which a market left on its own fails to allocate resources efficiently

market for loanable funds the market in which those who want to save supply funds and those who want to borrow to invest demand funds

market power the ability of a single economic actor (or small group of actors) to have a substantial influence on market prices

market risk risk that affects all companies in the stock market

medium of exchange an item that buyers give to sellers when they want to purchase goods and services

menu costs the costs of changing prices

microeconomics the study of how households and firms make decisions and how they interact in markets

model of aggregate demand and aggregate supply the model that most economists use to explain short-run fluctuations in economic activity around its long-run trend

monetary neutrality the proposition that changes in the money supply do not affect real variables

monetary policy the setting of the money supply by policymakers in the central bank

money the set of assets in an economy that people regularly use to buy goods and services from other people

money multiplier the amount of money the banking system generates with each dollar of reserves

money supply the quantity of money available in the economy

multiplier effect the additional shifts in aggregate demand that result when expansionary fiscal policy increases income and thereby increases consumer spending

mutual fund an institution that sells shares to the public and uses the proceeds to buy a portfolio of stocks and bonds

N

national saving (saving) the total income in the economy that remains after paying for consumption and government purchases

natural level of output the production of goods and services that an economy achieves in the long run when unemployment is at its normal rate

natural-rate hypothesis the claim that unemployment eventually returns to its normal, or natural, rate, regardless of the rate of inflation

natural rate of unemployment the normal rate of unemployment around which the unemployment rate fluctuates

natural resources the inputs into the production of goods and services that are provided by nature, such as land, rivers, and mineral deposits

net capital outflow the purchase of foreign assets by domestic residents minus the purchase of domestic assets by foreigners

net exports spending on domestically produced goods by foreigners (exports) minus spending on foreign goods by domestic residents (imports)

nominal exchange rate the rate at which a person can trade the currency of one country for the currency of another

nominal GDP the production of goods and services valued at current prices

nominal interest rate the interest rate as usually reported without a correction for the effects of inflation

nominal variables variables measured in monetary units

normal good a good for which an increase in income raises the quantity demanded

normative statements claims that attempt to prescribe how the world should be

O

open economy an economy that interacts freely with other economies around the world

open-market operations the purchase and sale of U.S. government bonds by the Fed

opportunity cost whatever must be given up to obtain some item

P

Phillips curve a curve that shows the short-run trade-off between inflation and unemployment

physical capital the stock of equipment and structures that are used to produce goods and services

positive statements claims that attempt to describe the world as it is

present value the amount of money today that would be needed to produce a future amount of money, given prevailing interest rates

private saving the income that households have left after paying for taxes and consumption

producer price index (PPI) a measure of the cost of a basket of goods and services bought by firms

production possibilities frontier a graph that shows the combinations of output that the economy can possibly produce given the available factors of production and the available production technology

productivity the quantity of goods and services produced from each unit of labor input

property rights the ability of an individual to own and exercise control over scarce resources

public saving the tax revenue that the government has left after paying for its spending

purchasing-power parity a theory of exchange rates whereby a unit of any given currency should be able to buy the same quantity of goods in all countries

Q

quantity demanded the amount of a good that buyers are willing and able to purchase

quantity equation the equation $M \times V = P \times Y$, which relates the quantity of money, the velocity of money, and the dollar value of the economy's output of goods and services

quantity supplied the amount of a good that sellers are willing and able to sell

quantity theory of money a theory asserting that the quantity of money available determines the price level and that the growth rate in the quantity of money available determines the inflation rate

R

random walk the path of a variable whose changes are impossible to predict

rational expectations the theory that people optimally use all the information they have, including information about government policies, when forecasting the future

rational people people who systematically and purposefully do the best they can to achieve their objectives

real exchange rate the rate at which a person can trade the goods and services of one country for the goods and services of another

real GDP the production of goods and services valued at constant prices

real interest rate the interest rate corrected for the effects of inflation

real variables variables measured in physical units

recession a period of declining real incomes and rising unemployment

reserve ratio the fraction of deposits that banks hold as reserves

reserve requirements regulations on the minimum amount of reserves that banks must hold against deposits

reserves deposits that banks have received but have not loaned out

risk aversion a dislike of uncertainty

S

sacrifice ratio the number of percentage points of annual output lost in the process of reducing inflation by 1 percentage point

scarcity the limited nature of society's resources

shoeleather costs the resources wasted when inflation encourages people to reduce their money holdings

shortage a situation in which quantity demanded is greater than quantity supplied

stagflation a period of falling output and rising prices

stock a claim to partial ownership in a firm

store of value an item that people can use to transfer purchasing power from the present to the future

strike the organized withdrawal of labor from a firm by a union

structural unemployment unemployment that results because the number of jobs available in some labor markets is insufficient to provide a job for everyone who wants one

substitutes two goods for which an increase in the price of one leads to an increase in the demand for the other

supply curve a graph of the relationship between the price of a good and the quantity supplied

supply schedule a table that shows the relationship between the price of a good and the quantity supplied

supply shock an event that directly alters firms' costs and prices, shifting the economy's aggregate-supply curve and thus the Phillips curve

surplus a situation in which quantity supplied is greater than quantity demanded

T

technological knowledge society's understanding of the best ways to produce goods and services

theory of liquidity preference Keynes's theory that the interest rate adjusts to bring money supply and money demand into balance

trade balance the value of a nation's exports minus the value of its imports; also called net exports

trade deficit an excess of imports over exports

trade policy a government policy that directly influences the quantity of goods and services that a country imports or exports

trade surplus an excess of exports over imports

U

unemployment insurance a government program that partially protects workers' incomes when they become unemployed

unemployment rate the percentage of the labor force that is unemployed

union a worker association that bargains with employers over wages and working conditions

unit of account the yardstick people use to post prices and record debts

V

velocity of money the rate at which money changes hands

Index

Page numbers in **boldface** refer to pages where key terms are defined.

SUGGESTIONS FOR
SUMMER READING

If you enjoyed the economics course that you just finished, you might like to read more about economic issues in the following books.

Daron Acemoglu and James A. Robinson

Why Nations Fail: The Origins of Power, Prosperity, and Poverty

(New York: Crown Publishing, 2012)

An economist and political scientist argue that establishing the right institutions is the key to economic success.

Abhijit Banerjee and Esther Duflo

Poor Economics

(New York: Public Affairs, 2011)

Two prominent development economists offer their proposal on how to fight global poverty.

Yoram Bauman and Grady Klein

The Cartoon Introduction to Economics

(New York: Hill and Wang, 2010)

Basic economic principles, with humor.

Bryan Caplan

The Myth of the Rational Voter: Why Democracies Choose Bad Policies

(Princeton, NJ: Princeton University Press, 2008)

An economist asks why elected leaders often fail to follow the policies that economists recommend.

Kimberly Clausing

Open: The Progressive Case for Free Trade, Immigration, and Global Capital

(Cambridge, MA: Harvard University Press, 2019)

An economist explains why Americans benefit from interacting with the rest of the world.

Avinash Dixit and Barry Nalebuff

The Art of Strategy: A Game Theorist's Guide to Success in Business and Life

(New York: Norton, 2008)

This introduction to game theory discusses how all people—from corporate executives to criminals under arrest—should and do make strategic decisions.

William Easterly

The Tyranny of Experts: Economists, Dictators, and the Forgotten Rights of the Poor

(New York: Basic Books, 2013)

A former World Bank economist examines the many attempts to help the world's poorest nations and why these attempts have so often failed.

Milton Friedman

Capitalism and Freedom

(Chicago: University of Chicago Press, 1962)

In this classic book, one of the most important economists of the 20th century argues that society should rely less on the government and more on the free market.

Robert L. Heilbroner

The Worldly Philosophers

(New York: Touchstone, 1953, revised 1999)

A classic introduction to the lives, times, and ideas of the great economic thinkers, including Adam Smith, David Ricardo, and John Maynard Keynes.

Steven E. Landsburg

The Armchair Economist: Economics and Everyday Life

(New York: Free Press, 2012)

Why does popcorn cost so much at movie theaters? Steven Landsburg discusses this and other puzzles of economic life.

Steven D. Levitt and Stephen J. Dubner

Freakonomics: A Rogue Economist Explores the Hidden Side of Everything

(New York: Morrow, 2005)

Economic principles and clever data analysis applied to a wide range of offbeat topics, including drug dealing, online dating, and sumo wrestling.

Michael Lewis

The Big Short: Inside the Doomsday Machine

(New York: Norton, 2010)

How a few savvy investors managed to make money during the financial crisis of 2008 and 2009.

Roger Lowenstein

America's Bank: The Epic Struggle to Create the Federal Reserve

(New York: Penguin Press, 2015)

A history of the founding of one of the most important policymaking institutions in the United States.

Burton G. Malkiel

A Random Walk Down Wall Street

(New York: Norton, 2015)

This introduction to stocks, bonds, and financial economics is not a "get rich quick" book, but it might help you get rich slowly.

John McMillan

Reinventing the Bazaar: A Natural History of Markets

(New York: Norton, 2002)

A deep and nuanced, yet still very readable, analysis of how society can make the best use of market mechanisms.

Branko Milanovic

The Haves and the Have-Nots: A Brief and Idiosyncratic History of Global Inequality

(New York: Basic Books, 2011)

A series of provocative essays about economic inequality around the world.

Sendhil Mullainathan and Eldar Shafir

Scarcity: Why Having Too Little Means So Much

(New York: Times Books, 2013)

An economist and psychologist team up to examine the causes and consequences of our limited cognitive abilities.

Sylvia Nasar

Grand Pursuit: The Story of Economic Genius

(New York: Simon and Schuster, 2011)

A sweeping narrative that tells the story of economic discovery.

Roger W. Spencer and David A. Macpherson

Lives of the Laureates

(Cambridge, MA: MIT Press, 2014)

Twenty-three winners of the Nobel Prize in Economics offer autobiographical essays about their lives and work.

ISBN-13: 978-0-357-13373-6
ISBN-10: 0-357-13373-0

9 780357 133736

90000